The Early Christian-Muslim Dialogue

A Collection of Documents from the
First Three Islamic Centuries
(632 - 900 A.D.)
Translations with Commentary

Edited by
N. A. Newman

Interdisciplinary Biblical Research Institute

Hatfield, Pennsylvania

The Early Christian-Muslim Dialogue:
A Collection of Documents from the
First Three Islamic Centuries (632 - 900 A.D.):
Translations with Commentary

Copyright for new materials 1993, N. A. Newman

Published by
Interdisciplinary Biblical Research Institute
PO Box 423, Hatfield, PA 19440-0423 USA

Library of Congress Catalog Card Number 93-61140

ISBN 0-944788-91-2

IBRI publications serve as a forum to stimulate discussion
of topics relevant to the Bible and its interaction with
various academic disciplines. Opinions expressed are the
author's own. IBRI's doctrinal statement is published in
its annual catalog of publications, free upon request.

CONTENTS

ACKNOWLEDGEMENTS

As with any work of such length, the editor is faced with the almost impossible task of thanking all of those who have in some way contributed to its preparation and publication. Indeed were he to name everyone who has influenced the course of this book, Christian and Muslim alike, the list would exceed several pages. The following, however, deserve special recognition.

The editor would like to express his gratitude to the School of Oriental and African Studies in London for granting permission to publish Anton Tien's translation of al-Kindi's *Apology*, and to the Interdisciplinary Biblical Research Institute for their willingness to distribute the present publication. A special note of thanks is deserved by Eugen Pietras, who translated F. Nau's article on the Patriarch John I, Joseph Stassi, who helped with the indices and some typing and Perikles and Georgios Kalfopoulos, who also worked on the indices. The editor gratefully acknowledges the assistance of his uncle Dr. Robert C. Newman, without whose contributions of time, labor and expertise over the years this present work would have hardly come to fruition and whose proof-reading caught many a mistake the editor had overlooked. The responsibility for any remaining deficiencies lies solely with the editor.

A great part of the editor's appreciation is due his wife, who not only directly aided in the preparation of manuscripts for this book, but who also shares in the joy of finally seeing it published.

The history of the Christian-Muslim dialogue, as long and complex as it is, documents more than just centuries of interaction between two opposing faiths. In the purest sense it records the theological and rhetorical struggle of nations and peoples, of emperors and caliphs, of patriarchs and mullahs, of the intelligentsia and unlearned, in their quest for the truth. In this present collection the first three centuries of Christian-Muslim dialogues and their results will be examined. This work is not meant to contain all of the discussions available to us from this period, but rather to show those major texts which appear to have characterized and influenced the development of these talks in general.

Although most of the literature presented in this collection was preserved by Christians and not Muslims, its spectrum of religious groups, peoples and even geography is quite broad. The meeting between the Patriarch John I and 'Amr al-'As was written and preserved by Jacobite Syrian Christians. The Muslims of Spain appear to have retained the letter of 'Umar II. The correspondence of the Byzantine Emperor Leo III was preserved by the Armenians, and the works of John of Damascus by the Byzantines. The dialogue of the Patriarch Timothy I was written by Nestorians but apparently preserved by the Jacobites also. The fictitious *Religious Dialogue of Jerusalem,* whose present manuscript was obtained in Egypt, appears to have been written by Jacobites but also transmitted by some Nestorians. The manuscripts of al-Kindi's correspondence were found in both Egypt and modern-day Turkey. The book of 'Ali Tabari has been preserved in Arabic apparently by Muslims. The manuscripts for some works of Jahiz were found in Islamic libraries in Egypt.

Of the Christians taking part in the dialogues, one was an emperor, two were patriarchs, one a monk and another alleged to have been one, and one a courtier of a caliph. Of the Muslims two were caliphs,

one was the cousin of a caliph, one was an amir and one alleged to
have been one, and two were scholars in the court of a caliph. The
main speakers or authors for the Christians in this collection were
either Melkite (Greek Orthodox), Jacobite or Nestorian. The main
Muslim speakers or authors were either orthodox, 'Alid-sympathetic,
Mu'tazilite, or converts from Christianity to Islam.

Groups which are not well represented in this collection are the Copts
and Armenians on the side of the Christians and many of the early
splinter groups of the Muslims. The apologetic works of the Copts
which were written in Arabic and have survived appear to have been
composed later than 900 A.D.[1] It is almost certain, though, that the
Copts had such works earlier than this, even if only in Coptic originally,
but very little of this material seems to have survived to the present.
Although the correspondence of the Byzantine Emperor Leo III was
preserved in the *History* of the Armenian Ghevond, the first really
Armenian work addressing Islam does not seem to have been written
before the 14th century.[2] As far as the early rival groups of Islam go,
aside from the Mu'tazilites and Shiites, most of them were short-lived
and probably so occupied with establishing themselves that they had
little opportunity to develop a very organized polemic against Christianity.

Even what we know today as orthodox Islam was still evolving during
the first three centuries, to 900 A.D. The earliest collections of "genuine" or "sound" (*sahih*) hadith were committed to writing about the
middle of the 9th century, and the history of Muhammad's life by Ibn
Ishaq, which does not appear to have survived in its entirety, may have
been composed sometime in the middle of the 8th century.[3] As will be
seen, this gradual development of orthodox Islam, moreover, did not
remain unaffected by the polemic of the various Christian Churches of
the East.

There are a few works which definitely fall into the time period and
coincide with the subject matter of the present investigation, but which
were not included with the other texts of this collection. The reasons

for the omission of some of these should also not escape our mention.

Several manuscripts exist of an alleged Christian-Muslim discussion between Theodore Abu Qurra (d. ca. 830 A.D.), the celebrated student of John of Damascus, and four (or five) Muslim scholars in the court of the Caliph Ma'mun. In defending the authenticity of one manuscript of this work,[4] Guillaume shows that Bacha had supported this favorable view earlier, but that Graf rejected the historicity of this meeting.[5] After disposing of Graf's main objections, Guillaume also finds no possible motive for later generations of scribes to have composed a fictitious work and ascribe it to the well-known Abu Qurra.[6] Neither Graf nor Guillaume seem to have argued their points very convincingly though. If for no other reason the name Abu Qurra would attract a Christian readership initially, as would the name of a caliph for Muslims. An additional benefit for using the name of Abu Qurra could have been to avoid acts of vengeance; if anything went awry, the Syrians, who appear to have had a great interest in preserving and modifying the text, could always say it was the work of some Melkite who had died centuries earlier. It is interesting to note that not a single manuscript of this discussion seems to have been transmitted in Greek.

In his work on the history of Arabic Christian literature, which was published about two decades after Guillaume's articles, Graf showed that there are actually quite a few manuscripts of this alleged meeting of Abu Qurra, some of which definitely betray signs of having been corrupted.[7] According to Graf, the general outline of subjects in the various Arabic manuscripts is as follows: the duty of circumcision, the Deity of Christ, the Trinity of God, whether Christ suffered willingly or not, worship of the cross, the human life of Christ, His permitting the death of His mother, etc.[8] Graf also states that the earliest manuscripts for the discussion appear to date from the 14th century and that some of them seem to have the dialogue between the Patriarch Timothy I and the Caliph Mahdi as their model.[9] According to Graf, the name of Abu Qurra was written in for that of Timothy I "apparently after some delay" in the Arabic MS. 215 (1590 A.D.) of the Bibliothèque Nationale in Paris.[10] Furthermore, the discussion of Abu Qurra also shares some affinity with the *Religious Dialogue of Jerusalem* in that the monk Abraham of Tiberias is surnamed Abu Qurra in MS Sbath 542 (1529 A.D.) and the original name of Abraham is exchanged with that of Abu Qurra in the Arabic MS. Vatican 136.[11] This same sort of tendency can also be seen in the Syriac MSS. Mingana 190a (1874 A.D.) and Mingana 444b (1890 A.D.), where five and four Muslim scholars are opposed, respectively, and the bishop Simon of Tûr 'Abdin is referred to as Abu Qurra in both.[12]

It appears that the story of a meeting of Abu Qurra and the Muslim scholars, much as the *Religious Dialogue of Jerusalem* and its related narrations, actually only served as a "podium" for generations of Syrian polemicists, who seemed to have kept improving its text and its argumentation. Since this collection contains the dialogue of the Patriarch Timothy I with the Caliph Mahdi and the *Religious Dialogue of Jerusalem,* the manuscripts of which appear to be older and more primary than those of Abu Qurra, the text of the latter has been excluded.

Another work which certainly fits into the time period under consideration but which was not included in this collection is *Kitab radd 'ala an-Nasara* written by the Zaydi Shiite al-Qasim b. Ibrahim (d. 860 A.D.).[13] Di Matteo lists five Arabic manuscripts of the text, one as in the Königliche Bibliothek in Berlin[14] and four (which he consulted for his edition) in the Biblioteca Ambrosiana of Milan.[15] As Fritsch has noted, the southern Arabian Zaydis rejected the more extreme Shiite doctrine of the deity of 'Ali[16] and this is of special importance here because Qasim has chosen the deity of Christ as his main topic in *Kitab radd 'ala an-Nasara.* The initial arguments of Qasim against the deity of Christ are essentially Qur'anic, following which he begins a fairly systematic investigation of the book of Matthew. Although Fritsch is of the opinion that Qasim's polemic differs little in content from that of orthodox Muslims,[17] it appears that Qasim did believe in the integrity of the Torah and the Gospel and quotes Qur'an 5:70 in this context.[18] Where Qasim sees some evidence of corruption is not in he transmission of the text, but rather in its interpretation, as both di Matteo and Fritsch have pointed out.[19] An illustration of this idea can be found in Qasim's prolonged discussion of Matt. 1:1 sqq. where he cites Matt. 3:17; 17:5 and 16:16. Applying logic somewhat similar to that found in a certain tradition,[20] Qasim (without even examining Aramaic, Greek, or the history of the period) claims that in the time of Christ the word "son" was used in adoption and as a term of endearment rather than as denoting a son by generation.[21] Qasim's investigation of the book of Matthew ends abruptly at Matt. 8:22,[22] and thus Fritsch seems justified in presuming Qasim's text to have been transmitted to us incompletely.[23]

Aside from being the work of a Shiite and representing an early Muslim attempt to comment on the text of the Gospel somewhat systematically, the *Kitab radd 'ala an-Nasara,* in part owing to its deficient preservation, would have added little new or influential material to this present collection of Christian-Muslim dialogues.

Another composition not included which falls within the period under investigation is Nicetas of Byzantium's ANATPOΠH THΣ ΠAPA TOY APABOΣ MΩAMET ΠΛAΣTOΓPAΦHΘEIΣHΣ BIBΛOY, thought to date from ca. 875-886 A.D.[24] The text is found in *Patrologia Graeca,* ed. Migne, 105, cols. 669-805. Nicetas is said to have been commissioned by the Emperor Basileios to confute the "book of the Arabs, Muhammad and the false belief of the Hagarenes which is found within."[25] Proceeding in a manner somewhat similar yet converse to that of Qasim, Nicetas explains the doctrines of the Muslims from the standpoint of the Bible and gives a short and relatively systematic commentary on the Qur'an. Opinion as to whether or not Nicetas could read Arabic seems to be divided. Both Migne[26] and Eichner[27] appear to regard Nicetas as the translator of the Qur'an text he used, whereas Güterbock justifiably believes that the author probably used a Greek translation.[28] After defending the orthodoxy of Christianity (without quoting a single verse from the Bible), Nicetas gives his arguments against Islam, examines suras 2-18 specifically and the remainder of the Qur'an generally, and in conclusion he recapitulates and refutes certain doctrinal fallacies of Islam.

Many of the inconsistencies Nicetas found in the Qur'an had already been employed by earlier Orthodox polemicists. The vain search for prophetic witness concerning Muhammad's advent[29] and the Qur'anic confusion of Mary the mother of Jesus for Miriam the sister of Aaron and Moses[30] can also be found in Leo III's letter to 'Umar II[31] and John of Damascus' treatise on Islam.[32] The identification of Jesus as God's Word and Spirit in the Qur'an[33] is also mentioned in John of Damascus.[34] The argument of Nicetas for Muhammad's apparent rejection of the Resurrection of Jesus (in that the same would have been expected of him)[35] is remotely similar to a charge which al-Kindi makes regarding Muhammad's death.[36]

But Nicetas also appears to have found some deficient passages in the Qur'an on his own. Among other things, he questions the Qur'an's high opinion of Solomon who later worshipped idols,[37] notices that Muhammad confused the works of Gideon with those of King Saul and placed both (with David) in the time of Joshua,[38] and wonders how Alexander the Great could be mentioned as Monotheistic.[39] Nicetas also seems to have known that the Muslims of his day credited Muhammad with splitting the moon in two.[40] However, in the process of his discussion, the author makes several errors which not only point to his dependence upon a deficient Qur'an translation but also show that he could not have had much contact with Muslims. In reference to Qur'an 112:2, Nicetas says that Muhammad thought of God as a "solid sphere" (ὁλόσφυρος),[41] an apparent mistranslation of *as-Samadu* (=the Eternal, Absolute)[42] as *'samm* (=solid) and *dawa'ir* (=sphere). With respect to Qur'an 96:2, that man was created of "gum" (βδέλλα),[43] where the translator seems to have mistaken *'ilk* (=mastic, gum) for *'alaq* (=blood-clot). Both of these mistakes, however, may indicate that the underlying Arabic manuscript was old enough to lack diacritical marks.

Another peculiar feature of this work is that Nicetas states the Qur'an is composed of only 113 suras.[44] Güterbock was of the opinion that Nicetas presumed the first sura to be an invocation and not part of the text,[45] while Eichner shows that Nicetas very clearly describes sura 2 as

the "first" (sura).[46] Naturally, this omission could be due to the negligence of the original translator, or to a defect in the Arabic text he
used, but it is also well-known that the pre-'Uthmanic codices of the
Qur'an were not in agreement with respect to the number or arrangement of suras and in particular that the codex of Ibn Ma'sud contained
none of the suras 1, 113, or 114.[47] Nicetas seems to have counted the
suras 113 and 114 to arrive at the total of 113 suras, though he does
not appear to cite anything from them in his text.[48] Furthermore, the
sura ordering of Nicetas' text appears to be 'Uthmanic and does not
match any of the somewhat unreliable orderings we have for Ibn
Mas'ud's codex in other Islamic sources.[49] On the other hand, just as
the translation mistakes mentioned above seem to indicate that the
underlying Qur'an manuscript was without diacritical marks, and thus
relatively old, other errors in Nicetas' present work appear to show that
it was probably also pre-'Uthmanic. Nicetas relates how the Qur'an
depicts Alexander the Great as observing the sun set in *warm* water,[50]
and several early Qur'an codices, including Ibn Mas'ud's, also had
hamiya (=hot) instead of the 'Uthmanic reading *hami'* (=muddy).[51]
Moreover, the accusation of Nicetas that Muhammad understood the
sun and the moon (in their orbits) to be *riders*[52] in Qur'an 21:34 seems
to be much more in agreement with the *ya'malu* (thus "*doing* a circuit
[orbit]") of Ibn Mas'ud's codex[53] than the *yasbahu* (=swimming) of
'Uthman's. Unfortunately, Nicetas does not really quote the Qur'an as
often as Eichner would lead us to believe.[54] If he had, perhaps many
other peculiarities would have been evident.

At least one earlier attempt to show that a (Syriac) translation of the
Qur'an was based on a pre-'Uthmanic manuscript was unsuccessful in
the end.[55] Yet based on the evidence mentioned above — that the
underlying text used by Nicetas was missing sura 1, that it lacked
diacritical marks, that some of the words seem to agree with non-'Uthmanic codices, and that such codices are known to have survived until
at least the 10th century[56] — there seems to be good reason for believing that this text may have been both pre-'Uthmanic and somehow
related to the codex of Ibn Mas'ud.

Theologically, the present work of Nicetas — because it was written near the end of the 9th century, probably only existed in Greek, and contained serious mistakes, etc. — does not seem to have had any effect on the overall Christian-Muslim dialogue of its day, and thus was not included in this collection. The significance of Nicetas' composition can be found in its being commissioned by a Byzantine Emperor and being an early Christian attempt to systematically evaluate the Qur'an.

A few of the works in this collection of the Christian-Muslim dialogue are being published for the first time in English. "Un colloque du patriarche Jean avec l'èmir des Agarèens," by F. Nau in *Journal Asiatique,* (1915), pp. 225-279 has been translated by Eugen Pietras from the French. "Das Religionsgespräch von Jerusalem," by K. Vollers in *Zeitschrift für Kirchengeschichte,* 29 (1908), pp. 29-71 and 197-221 has been translated by the present editor from German. Anton Tien's relatively complete translation of the famous *Apology* of al-Kindi,[57] appears in print here for the first time, courtesy of the School of Oriental and African Studies in London.

All the articles and previously published books included in this collection have been re-edited in order to make them more uniform. Some portions of works have been deleted in places as specific material was deemed to be somewhat superfluous to the subject at hand; notices have been made where deletions occur. The bodies of the original texts have been marked alphabetically per paragraph to enable a more accurate system of inter-referencing, and endnotes which have been added by the editor are followed by the abbreviation "-ed." We have attempted to make spellings consistent throughout the collection and in conformity with modern Islamic-English and American usage. Owing to font limitations we apologize that some transliterations of Arabic and Syriac are not as exact as they should be. References to the Qur'an follow the Cairo system of verse division; the traditions of *Sahih Bukhari* follow the edition of Muhammad Muhsin Khan, and those of *Sahih Muslim* the edition of Abdul Hamid Siddiqi. General, topical, Biblical and Qur'anic indices, as well as an annotated bibliography, have been provided at the close of this work.

It is hoped that the present book will not only help illuminate the events and developments of the early stages of the Christian-Muslim dialogue, but that it will also contribute to a genuine spirit of mutual honesty and openness between Christians and Muslims in the quest for the truth.

Notes:

[1] See Graf, *Geschichte der christlichen arabischen Literatur*, vol. 2, pp. 300 ff.

[2] Jeffery, "Gregory of Tathew's 'Contra Mohammedanos'," *Moslem World*, vol. 32 (1942), p. 219.

[3] *Shorter Encyclopedia of Islam*, p. 149.

[4] I.e., Arabic MS. 70 (15th century) of the Bibliothèque Nationale, Paris; see Guillaume, *Journal of the Royal Asiatic Society*, Cent. Supplement (1924) p. 233; or essentially the same article in Guillaume, "Theodore Abu Qurra as Apologist," *Moslem World*, vol. 15 (1925), p. 42.

[5] Ibid., pp. 233, 235.

[6] Ibid., p. 235.

[7] Graf, *Geschichte der christlichen arabischen Literatur*, vol. 2, pp. 21 ff.

[8] Ibid., p. 21.

[9] Ibid.

[10] Ibid., p. 22; see also Religious Dialogue, p. 276.

[11] Ibid., p. 22.

[12] Mingana, *Catalogue of the Mingana Collection of Manuscripts,* vol. 1, Cambridge (England), pp. 414, 788.

[13] Di Matteo, "Confutazione contro i christiani dello Zaydita al-Qasim b. Ibrahim," *Rivista degli Studi Orientali,* 9 (1922), pp. 301-364.

[14] Fritsch appears to have consulted this manuscript in preparing his booklet: *Islam und Christentum im Mittelalter,* see p. 13.

[15] Di Matteo, "Confutazione contro i christiani," *RSO,* p. 303.

[16] Fritsch, *Islam und Christentum im Mittelalter,* p. 13.

[17] Ibid., p. 13.

[18] Di Matteo, "Confutazione contro i christiani," *RSO,* 9 (1922), pp. 320, 351.

[19] Fritsch references di Matteo *Islam und Christentum,* p. 56.

[20] *Sahih Muslim,* Kitab al-Adab, ch. 896, hadith 5351, vol. 3, p. 1175.

[21] Di Matteo, "Confutazione contro i christiani," *RSO,* 9 (1922), pp. 322-3, 354.

[22] Ibid., pp. 331, 364.

[23] Fritsch, *Islam und Christentum im Mittelalter,* p. 13.

[24] Güterbock, *Der Islam im Lichte der byzantinischen Polemik,* p. 26.

[25] Ibid., p. 25.

[26] Migne in *Patrologia Graece,* 105, col. 725, n. 64; col. 765, n. 25; etc.

[27] Eichner, "Die Nachrichten über den Islam bei den Byzantiner," *Der Islam,* 23 (1936), pp. 138, 210.

[28] Güterbock, *Der Islam im Lichte,* p. 27.

[29] Nicetas, 705; Eichner, "Die Nachrichten," *Der Islam,* 23 (1936), p. 152.

[30] Nicetas, 727-728, 789-790. Qur'an 4:169.

[31] Leo III, parags. G and AH; parag. AH.

[32] John of Damascus, parag. C; parag. B.

[33] Nicetas, 735-736; Eichner, "Die Nachrichten," *Der Islam,* 23 (1936), p. 198.

[34] John of Damascus, parag. B.

[35] Nicetas, 733-736; Güterbock, *Der Islam im Lichte,* p. 30.

[36] al-Kindi, parag. CF.

[37] Nicetas, 717-718; Eichner, "Die Nachrichten," *Der Islam,* 23 (1936), p. 206; Qur'an 2:96.

[38] Nicetas, 723-724, Eichner, "Die Nachrichten," *Der Islam,* 23 (1936), p. 207; Qur'an 2:247-252.

[39] Nicetas, 767-768, Eichner, "Die Nachrichten," *Der Islam,* 23 (1936), p. 207; Qur'an 18:85-86.

[40] Nicetas, 769-770; cf. Qur'an 54:1.

[41] Nicetas, 707, 776, 784; Güterbock, *Der Islam im Lichte,* p. 27, n. 2.

[42] According to Yusuf Ali, *The Holy Qur'an,* vol. 2, p. 1806, n. 6298.

[43] Nicetas, 708; Eichner, "Die Nachrichten über den Islam," *Der Islam,* 23 (1936), p. 210.

[44] Nicetas, 708.

[45] Güterbock, *Der Islam im Lichte der byzantinischen Polemik,* p. 27.

[46] Eichner, "Die Nachrichten über den Islam," *Der Islam,* p. 151; Nicetas, 708.

[47] Jeffery, *Materials,* p. 21.

[48] The reference to Qur'an 113 in Nicetas, 775, n. 85, is an error; it should read Qur'an 112.

[49] Jeffery, *Materials,* pp. 22-23.

[50] Nicetas, 767-768; Eichner, "Die Nachricht," *Der Islam,* 23 (1936), pp. 207, 210.

[51] Jeffery, *Materials,* p. 57.

[52] Nicetas, 768; Eichner, "Die Nachricht," *Der Islam,* 23 (1936), p. 210.

[53] Jeffery, *Materials,* p. 62.

[54] "Nicetas appears to have a perfect command of the Qur'an and

with diminishing exceptions quotes it quite correctly." - Eichner, "Die Nachricht," *Der Islam,* 23 (1936), p. 138.

[55] Mingana, "An Ancient Syriac Translation of the Kur'an Exhibiting New Verses and Variants," repr. from *The Bulletin of the John Rylands Library,* vol. 9, no. 1, 1925; see Jeffery, *Materials,* pp. 14-15, n. 1.

[56] an-Nadim, *The Fihrist of al-Nadim,* trans. Dodge, pp. 53-63.

[57] MS. 25190 of the School of Oriental and African Studies, London.

INTRODUCTION

Seen from a certain perspective, the Christian-Muslim dialogue actually began before the institution of many of the Islamic rites, and although the subject of Christian influences on the origins of early Islam is not within the scope of this present work, it would probably be helpful to at least mention the contact Muhammad is reported to have had with Christians in his day. On examination of the Qur'an, hadith, and (to a lesser extent) Islamic histories, it is obvious that Muhammad was far more familiar with Judaism than Christianity. Be that as it may, there is evidence, of varying degrees of credibility, that Muhammad did have significant contact with Christians.

One of the earliest meetings which the youth Muhammad is reported to have had with a Christian was with the monk, whom Muslim historians name Bahira.[1] Several versions of this tradition appear to have been so widespread among Muslims and (as will be seen in several of the works in this collection) Christians, that there probably is some measure of truth to it.[2] Shortly after he received his first revelations, Muhammad is said to have been taken by Khadija to consult with her cousin Waraqa, who is alleged to have become a Christian and read the scriptures. Waraqa is then reported to have encouraged Muhammad and said that the angel who appeared to him was Gabriel.[3] The credibility of this tradition is somewhat blighted by the fact that the name "Gabriel" only appears in the Medinan suras where Muhammad had much more contact with Jews who had read the Old Testament.

Perhaps the most striking evidence of Muhammad's early contact with Christians, which same evidence is said to have later facilitated his alienation from the Jews, can be found in the mention of Zacharias, John, Mary and Jesus in the 19th sura of the Qur'an. On an evaluation of the text of this Meccan sura, it becomes quite obvious that Muhammad's Christian acquaintances were probably illiterate, as Muhammad

1

himself is said to have been, and that they were of heretical background. When some of the Muslims had to flee Mecca because of persecution there, it was the Christians of Abyssinia who granted them asylum. According to several traditions, when the Quraysh sent Abu Rabi'a and 'Amr al-'As to bring back the refugees, the first description of Islam is said to have been given to a Christian ruler, i.e., Negus, who had summoned the Muslims. According to tradition, Ja'far b. Abu Talib enumerates almsgiving and fasting among the rites of Islam, and cites verses from Qur'an 19 in his speech.[4] Since almsgiving and fasting were first made obligatory in Medina though, it is extremely probable that this tradition was modified by later writers.[5] The arrival of a deputation of Christians from Abyssinia (or possibly Najran) in Mecca also seems to have been a later invention.[6] Muhammad is reported to have received a Christian delegation from Najran in Medina, and resultant to this several passages of the Qur'an relevant to Christian beliefs are said to have been revealed.[7] Whether this event really occurred or not can be shown to be of secondary importance here, for the suras of the Qur'an revealed in Medina do demonstrate that Muhammad had a better knowledge of Judaism and Christianity after the Hagira, and thus, that he must have had some sort of contact with Christians there. The hadith concerning the objection that Mary could not have been the "sister of Aaron" (Qur'an 19:29) allegedly made by the Christians of Najran[8] is more probably a later innovation, as this question is only later dealt with in depth.[9] Muhammad is also said to have sent envoys to the leaders of the kingdoms bordering Arabia in order to invite them to the religion of Islam,[10] but the content of these traditions is so naive (e.g., Heraclius accepts Muhammad as the "prophet to come," Negus proclaims his fealty to Muhammad, etc.) as to dismiss any notion of their being credible.

Notwithstanding these doubtful traditions, the most overwhelming evidence against Muhammad having any *lasting* contact with *institutionalized* Christianity is again borne out by the witness of the Qur'an itself. Muhammad not only thought that Mary was the sister of Aaron and that Jesus spoke in the cradle, as is shown in a sura of the Meccan period (Qur'an 19:28 sqq.), he also believed Jesus gave life to clay birds (Qur'an 3:43) and he equated His Incarnation with the creation of Adam (Qur'an 3:52) in an early sura of Medina. Later in this same period Muhammad fancied his advent to have been foretold by Jesus (Qur'an 61:6), and as is shown in one of the last suras to be revealed before his death, Muhammad assumed Mary to be a member of the Trinity (Qur'an 5:116) and the Communion to be a Christian feast which was based on a table being sent down from Heaven (Qur'an 5:112-115).

Further evidence displaying the poor knowledge of the Bible and Christianity among the early Muslims can still be found in Islamic histories and commentaries. According to Ibn 'Abbas, Ibn Mas'ud and some of Muhammad's companions, Nebuchadnezzar invaded Israel after John the Baptist had been killed;[11] later even Ibn Ishaq is reported to have said that the Babylonian king Herod waged war against Israel after John's being killed.[12] It is said that Ibn Mas'ud and some of Muhammad's companions (somewhat similar to the Qur'an) showed Mary, a descendant of Aaron, as giving birth to Jesus in the same area where Zacharias and "her sister" (Elizabeth) lived. Zacharias then fled from the Jews, who were falsely accusing him, was enclosed in a tree by Satan and sawed up (by the Jews); no mention is made of Joseph.[13] According to a tradition preserved in Ibn Hisham, God is alleged to have told Muhammad that after Zacharias, Jurayji, a carpenter, looked after Mary, whose fate had been so decided by casting lots (arrows!).[14]

But it was not just the Muslims who began at a deficit in the Christian-Muslim dialogue which was yet to come. In the following dialogue between the Jacobite Patriarch John I and 'Amr al-'As it is apparent that none of the Eastern Christians had even bothered to translate the Bible into Arabic prior to the advent of Islam. This cardinal failure, which was paramount to making Christians in part guilty for the spiritual condition of the Arabs, not only provided fertile soil for the evolution of Islam, but was also a mistake for which generations of Christians were to pay. As Christian communities were first confronted with the Muslims, it appears they thought them to be members of a sect which had broken off from Christianity.[15] Indeed, the decision to surrender their cities may well have partially been influenced by the view that they were simply trading off one "foreign Christian" oppressor for another more sympathetic one. In time, of course, Islam would prove to be otherwise.

In general, the little knowledge of Christianity which the Muslims did have at the beginning of the Christian-Muslim dialogue, was certainly more than the almost total lack of information which Christians possessed concerning Islam. Unfortunately, practically no discussions appear to have been preserved from the first 100 years of Christian-Muslim interaction, but it is likely that the earliest polemic of the Christians against Islam was just as flawed by inaccuracies as the early polemic of the Muslims was against Christianity. As we will attempt to show in the following works, the manner in which the Christian-Muslim dialogue developed was, perhaps more than any other single factor, affected by the amount and quality of information which each side had acquired of the other.

Notes:

[1] Ibn Ishaq, *Life of Muhammad*, trans. Guillaume, pp. 79 ff; al-Tabari, *History*, vol. 6, pp. 44 ff.

[2] Christians later did much to corrupt this tradition in an effort to malign Muhammad; see Gerard Salinger, "A Christian Muhammad Legend and a Muslim Ibn Tumart Legend in the 13th Century," *ZDMG*, 117 (1967), pp. 318-328.

[3] Ibn Ishaq, *Life of Muhammad*, trans. Guillaume, p. 107; al-Tabari, *History*, vol. 6, p. 72.

[4] Ibn Ishaq, *Life of Muhammad*, trans. Guillaume, pp. 150 ff.

[5] Tabari, for example, (*History*, vol. 6, p. 105) makes no mention of Ja'far's speech on this occasion.

[6] Ibn Ishaq, *Life of Muhammad*, trans. Guillaume, p. 179.

[7] Ibid., pp. 270 ff.

[8] *Sahih Muslim*, Kitab al-Adab, ch. 891, hadith 5326, vol. 3, p. 1169.

[9] al-Tabari, *History*, vol. 4, p. 120; Abdelmajid Charfi, "Christianity in the Qur'an Commentary of Tabari," *Islamochristiana*, 6 (1980), pp. 111-113; Suyuti, *el-Itkan*, vol. 2, pp. 366, 503.

[10] See Tabari's edition of this in *Life of Muhammad*, trans. Guillaume, pp. 652 ff.

[11] al-Tabari, *History*, vol. 4, pp. 103-107.

[12] Ibid., p. 108.

[13] Ibid., pp. 118-120.

[14] Ibn Hisham in *Life of Muhammad*, ed. Guillaume, p. 275.

[15] Sahas, *John of Damascus on Islam*, pp. 129-130.

THE DIALOGUE OF THE PATRIARCH JOHN I WITH 'AMR AL-'AS

The dialogue which follows and a description of a meeting between the bishop Gabriel and the Caliph 'Umar, were first translated into French by F. Nau in *Journal Asiatique*, (1915), pp. 225-279. Nau's discussions of these and other documents show not only the rapid advance of the Muslim Arabs into the predominantly Christian areas west of Arabia, but they also indicate how the religious leaders of the Syrians and the Copts, who had suffered religious persecution under the Byzantines, willingly capitulated to the Muslims, aiding thereby the success of their new overlords.

The general atmosphere of the dialogue, which is very brief in itself, again reflects the situation of its environment. Neither 'Amr al-'As nor the Patriarch John I are very aggressive in their respective charges against and apology for Christianity. In his questions concerning the singularity and universality of the Gospel,[1] the Amir seems to show that the Muslims were slowly realizing the Qur'anic description of the Gospel did not fit the Book which Christians possessed. The Patriarch naturally replies that the Gospel is both unique and universal, and Nau shows Michael the Syrian's report that the Patriarch John had an Arabic translation of the Gospel made at the request of the Amir.[2] Since the Patriarch had already mentioned the unity of the Gospel, there is a good chance that that which he had translated for 'Amr was really the Diatessaron. The Patriarch does not appear to have known what the Qur'an says about the Gospel.

Although the theological element of the discussion appears to have been quite simple, there are some things which should be mentioned. 'Amr's approach is both direct and inquisitive; he centers on the versions of the Gospel, Christ's deity, the faith of Abraham and Moses, and then the rather political question regarding the law of the Christians. In reply to the Amir, the Patriarch does not appear to know of any division among the Muslims of his day and uses an apologetic approach which seems to have been developed for answering the polemic of the Jews. The Patriarch does not appear to have known Qur'an 4:169 in mentioning Christ as God's Word, and even though he makes note of the fact that Muslims also believe that the Torah was given Moses (something which would not require his knowledge of the Qur'an), he seems to have assumed that the Muslims would know that Moses remained on the mount for forty days.[3] For his part, 'Amr somewhat disappointed this apologetic of the Patriarch when he refused to accept the Books of the Prophets[4] (which are not mentioned in the Qur'an) as authoritative. John I's reaction then was to limit his references to passages from the Torah. This early dialogue contains only the bare essentials of what was later to follow; the Muslim centers in on the versions of the Gospel and the deity of Christ, and the Christian reply draws heavily on Old Testament references. The Patriarch never cites verses from the Qur'an, and the Amir never quotes the Bible; it is almost certain that neither had read, or perhaps even seen, the other's Books up until the time of their meeting. As short and as simple as the Patriarch and Amir's discussion may seem, it was a beginning, the beginning of the Christian-Muslim dialogue.

The very brief description of the meeting between the bishop Gabriel and the Caliph 'Umar contains no report of a theological discussion, but rather presents one specific case of the Syrians' general negotiations for religious toleration in exchange for political aid. Portions of Nau's original work have been deleted in this edition, as they were judged as being not directly related to the subjects under investigation. The editor would like to express his appreciation to Eugen Pietras for doing most of the translation work in the following text. Those wishing to read the complete version of Nau's article, may do so by consulting

Journal Asiatique, (1915), pp. 225-279, from which the present text was translated.

Notes:

[1] John I, parag. B.

[2] John I, p. 17.

[3] John I, parag. E.

[4] John I, parag. H.

A DIALOGUE BETWEEN PATRIARCH JOHN AND THE AMIR OF THE HAGARENES... according to the manuscript ADD. 17193 of the British Museum with an appendix... about a document which was said to have been given to the bishop of Tûr 'Abdin by 'Umar.

INTRODUCTION

I. The dialogue: 1. Manuscript, speakers, date; 2-4. The circumstances: the Arab expansion; 'Amr, his dialogues with the Emperor Constantine in 638 and with the Coptic Patriarch Benjamin in 643; 5-6. Analysis of the dialogue of 9 May 639 (18 A.H:); the goal; 7-10. The results: Because of their grievances against the Greek Empire, the power of the Christian dissidents is used by the Muslims. These do not delay either, to vex and persecute their allies and to show that they acted poorly.

II. Summary of the various events. [deleted]

1. A Syriac manuscript of the British Museum,[1] completed on Tuesday 17 August 874, contains a "letter of Mar John the (Jacobite) Patriarch concerning the dialogue which he had with the Amir of the Hagarenes", on Sunday, 9 May. The names which are in this letter, a parallel passage in the *Chronicle* of Michael the Syrian,[2] the general history and the chronology, permit us to say that it concerns a dialogue of "the Jacobite Patriarch John I[3] with the Amir 'Amr[4] in a city of Syria[5] on Sunday, 9 May 639[6] (18 A.H.)." The Patriarch, summoned by the Amir, came to see him in the company of five bishops, prominent Christians and numerous believers. A few days after the dialogue he wrote a report[7] which he sent to the Christians in Mesopotamia to inform them, to reassure them and to request (that) "they should pray for the illustrious Amir, that God give him the wisdom and enlightenment about that which pleases the Lord." This is the report, transcribed and forgotten in the manuscript since 874, which we intend to make known. First we would like to place the report in its setting, in that we will dedicate four pages to the Arab invasion, its causes, its results, as well as the personality of 'Amr, to better understand the feelings and motives of both the famous speakers.

2. Arabia, "land of drought and poverty,"[8] knew prosperity for hundreds of years when the trade between India and Syria and the West went through its ports on the Persian Gulf and the Red Sea; but from the 6th to the 7th centuries the desolation of the Persians from Syria down into Egypt, combined with that of the Vandals and the Goths in the West, stopped these transactions, and the Arabs, in the refuge of their sand dunes, grew in their uncleanliness and their poverty and only waited for a reason to cross the borders to occupy the place of wealthier and less-populated nations.

The pretext had taken the name pan-Islamism.[9] In the beginning this name corresponded to a poorly defined feeling, which was originally economic and political as well as religious. The starving Bedouins served themselves to obtain the fruitful areas of land[10] and the lodgings,[11] but they at first respected the freedom of religion for the "People of the Book" and even the Christian Arabs — irrespective of whether they were the Nestorian Arabs of Oman from Qatar and Hira, or the Jacobite Arabs of Mesopotamia and Syria — it sufficed to construct a more or less loose political tie among them. As the tie quickly became tighter when the Christian Arabs were brought to change religions out of indifference, weariness or force, yet they showed that they followed Islam less than "the great Arab idea": those of the "hegemony of their race, who protected the latter with their triumphant banner."[12] Following the example of the Tamimits, who answered Muhammad himself: "Only the tribes of robbers have recognized you,"[13] the recently converted Syrians did not want to step down to follow the Muslims of the first hour, the "flea-ridden" of the Hijaz, all these Bedouins, the eaters of lizards and desert mice, who on their arrival in Syria (each) wore only one shabby tunic, which did not even reach the knees.[14] Overall their pan-Islamism was only a pan-Arabism, or "Arabia over everything."

3. The war machinery, which unified the wishes and desires of millions of people, would only confront a Greek Empire made weary by long wars, an empire which was so broken that it delivered its provinces and armies into the hands of foreign soldiers, which empire was so divided by intolerant imperialism, which in the name of the dogma of state persecuted millions of renegade Christians and Jews. Its pangs of death were brief; the Arabs, who had come through the desert of Syria, took Busra in 634, Damascus 635, Saroug, Seleucia-Ctesiphon and Jerusalem 637,[15] Antioch and the cities of the coast 638. At this date, before the conclusion of the conquest of Mesopotamia in 639, where the Jacobites were powerful it was (only) natural for 'Amr that he would summon the Patriarch to try to make him into an ally. 'Amr was moreover a man of discussion: "Eloquent, experienced in the management of great matters, skillful at solving the hardest situations,"[16] the conference at Adroh brought him yet the reputation of being "the most cunning and unscrupulous" diplomat "of his time."[17] He had already been commissioned with two missions to Abyssinia to

demand the return of deserters.[18] Aside from this we know of two
other discussions which surround that of ours: the one with the Emper-
or Constantine in the year 638, the other with the Coptic Jacobite
Patriarch Benjamin in the year 643. Before Constantine[19] 'Amr employed the coarse form when the Emperor asked him what supposed
right the Arabs had for possessing Syria: "The right which the Creator
gives," answered 'Amr. "The earth belongs to God; He gives it as an
inheritance to those of His servants, who please Him, and it is the
success of the weapons which reveal His will." This theory, for which
the desire for success is sufficient to justify the invasion of a coveted
land, is very old, as is seen. It is interesting to notice it in the half
brutal half mystical form, which it took in the mouth of a former camel
driver in the year 17 A.H. colored by Islam.

4. Five years later, 'Amr shows himself to be unctuous in his discussion with the Egyptian Jacobite Patriarch Benjamin.[20] The Jacobites in
his army, especially the duke Sanutius, told him of the persecutions of
the Greeks against the Jacobites; in particular, he knows that their
Patriarch Benjamin, driven away from Alexandria, has been wandering
in the monasteries of Upper Egypt for thirteen years and conceives the
plan to make them his allies. He addresses a letter of safe-conduct to
him, then, as he sees him coming, he calls out: "Truly, in all the lands
which we have possessed (up) until now, I have never seen such a man
of God as this one here." "Because Benjamin," says the writer of the
history, "was of good appearance, he was eloquent and he spoke with
calmness and dignity." Afterwards, 'Amr turned to him and said to
him: "Resume your rule of all the churches and of your people again
and manage their affairs, and if you pray for me, since I will be going
to the West and to the Pentapolis to possess them as the rest of Egypt,
and if I return after a quick success, I will give you all that you request
from me."[21] And the writer of the history adds that Benjamin prayed
for the 'Amr and that he held an eloquent speech with which the 'Amr
and all his assistants were astonished. We do not know the contents of
the speech this time, we do not know if Benjamin had praised the
godliness of 'Amr, the new mystic, or if he caused his (men) to open
the gates of the cities for them. But the writer of the history continues: "And all that the holy father said to the Amir 'Amr, the son of

'As, that he did, and he did not leave out a single letter thereof." And Michael the Syrian, a Jacobite writer, gravely records in his chronicle: "Concerning the land of Egypt, we have found in the histories that Benjamin, Patriarch of the Orthodox (Jacobites) delivered Egypt to the Tayyâyê." That is an exaggeration, but it is at least certain that the unctuous diplomacy of 'Amr was not in vain.

5. We now arrive at the intermediary discussion of the year 18 of the Hagira (9 May 639). One will find the text [deleted] and translation further below, it suffices us here to name the main questions which were asked: "The illustrious general 'Amir asked whether this is one and the same Gospel, without any difference(s), which is held by all who are Christians and carry this name throughout the world... Why, since there is only one Gospel, is the faith different (divided)?... Who is Christ, is He God or not?... When Christ, of Whom the Christians say He is God, was in Mary's womb, who carried and ruled Heaven and earth?... Which were the opinion and faith of Abraham and of Moses?... Why did not they write clearly and make known that which concerns Christ?" The discussion is scriptural, and the author continues: "When the Amir heard all that, he only asked that this be proven him by reason and from the Torah alone that Christ is God and that He was born of the virgin and that God has a Son." John quotes and shows the Greek and Syriac texts of the Bible. The Amir assumed the viewpoint of a Jew present in order to learn whether the Hebrew text conformed with them. The Jew answered, "I do not know exactly," and "the illustrious general Amir" knew much less. Therefore the Amir hurried to bring the discussion to the legal casuistry, which he knew better than the Greek and the Syriac: "The Amir gradually came to ask about the laws of the Christians, which ones and how they are; whether they are the Gospel or not? He added: When a man dies and leaves behind boys or girls and a wife and a mother and a sister and a cousin, according to which agreement is the inheritance divided among them?" After the answer of the Patriarch, he ended the discussion with: "I beseech you to make one thing of three: either to show me that your laws are written in the Gospel and that you act according to them,[22] or that you adhere to the law of the Muslims." The Patriarch troubled himself to show that the Christians could have other books

besides the Gospel, but this claim of 'Amr, to bring the Christians back to one single book, the Gospel, prepared us for the dilemma which by virtue of advice from 'Umar, he is to have burned the library of Alexandria, in order to bring everything back again to one single book: the Qur'an.

In order to show the importance of this discussion, let us call to remembrance that the Patriarch was quoted as having come with five bishops and nobles, so that "not only there were they congregated in great numbers, the nobles of the Hagarenes, but rather the leaders and governors of the cities and the faithful peoples and the friends of Christ: the Tanûkâyê, the Tu'âyê and the 'Aqûlâyê." These three last names show the three most important Arabic tribes who were Jacobites.[23] The author also informs us that the Amir had at the same time quoted certain leading adherents of the Council of Chalcedon, and he closes with: "We send your Grace these few words of numerous things, which were moved in this moment, so that you pray for us without ceasing with zeal and care, and that you supplicate the Lord, that according to His mercy He may visit His churches and His people, and so that Christ provide a solution in these matters, which pleases His will, that He help His church and comfort His people. Even those of the Council of Chalcedon, as we have said further above, prayed for the holy Patriarch, because he had spoken for all Christians and because he had brought them no harm. They sent to him continually and requested his Grace to speak for all (the Christians) and not to bring anything against them; because they knew their weakness and the greatness of the danger and the peril which threatened, if God, according to His mercy, would not visit His church."

Moreover this discussion had a next day, of which Michael the Syrian relates: " 'Amr wrote our Patriarch John. When he came to him, 'Amr first said unusual words against the scriptures, and he began to ask him hard questions. The Patriarch solved them all with examples he had taken from the Old and New Testaments and by natural arguments. When he saw his courage and the extent of his knowledge, 'Amr was astonished. Then he gave the following command: 'Translate your Gospel for me into the language of the Saracenes, that means the

Tayyâyê. Only you should not speak of the deity of Christ, nor of baptism, nor of the cross.' The holy one, being strengthened by the Lord answered: 'It would not please God, if I were to cut away a single iota or a single point from the Gospel, even if I were to be pierced with all of the spears and lances which are in your armory.' When he saw that he could not persuade him (otherwise), 'Amr said to him: 'Go and write as you will.'

The Patriarch gathered the bishops and had the Tanûkâyê, 'Aqûlâyê and Tu'âyê come, those who knew the Arabic and Syriac languages, and he commanded them to translate the Gospel into the Arabic language. He ordered that each sentence which they translated must pass before the eyes of all the translators. The Gospel was translated in this manner and presented to the king." (*Chronicle*, II, 431-432)

6. So was the discussion in the year 18. 'Amr, informed of the dissensions which divided the Christians, conceived of a plan to bind them all together in Islam — at least the Jacobite Christians. He accepted only the text of the Torah;[24] which is really the most used book in the Qur'an.[25] He reduced the main difficulties to three: that Christ is God, that God was born of the virgin and that God has a Son. He could indeed quote numerous verses from the Qur'an contrary to these claims.[26] But he had not thought that the discussion concerning the Greek and Syriac texts of the Torah would be continued and had therefore certainly prepared a quick end for it. A few days later, he had at least wished to receive an Arabic Gospel, which was not in contradiction to the Qur'an and which would allow him to bring all the Christian Arabs as a whole over to his side. Certainly that is why he first asked if it was one and the same Gospel, which was held by all Christians, because if there had been many of them, he would have chosen the one most to his advantage, or had at least taken hold of this pretext to demand one more. It had been sufficient for him if it contained no evidence 1. of the deity of Christ, which had already been fought over in the conference; 2. of baptism, which he probably wanted to substitute with the Muslim initiation; 3. of the cross and the crucifixion, which was indeed in contradiction to the Qur'an.[27]

'Amr had to have seen that if he continued to insist that this would only lead to martyrs being crowned and the creation of enemies — 'Umar seems to have intervened in favor of the Christians — so it appears since he had again applied the unctuous politic, which we saw him practice four years later with the Egyptian Patriarch Benjamin: to promise his support, to give back a few churches, to allow the procession[28] and to ask for the aid of prayer and (the) sympathies of the believing Jacobites, up until the danger of later taking back one by one (of all) that which he had conceded as a whole.

We want to use the conclusion of this introduction to develop the results of the conference, in that we make a sketch of the might of the Christian Arabs in the beginning of the Hagira, the services they performed for Islam and what resulted out of this for them. We will conclude that the Christian Patriarchs were wrong in giving their support to pan-Islamism, which had the appearance of being cultivated, moderate and mystical, but was in reality brutal and barbarian.

7. The Christians surrounded Arabia. The Nestorians had bishops in Najran, in Sana, the capital of Yemen, in Socotora, the island of Aloes, in Sohar, the capital of Oman, called Mazoun then, in Khota, in Qatar, in Hagar, on the islands of Deirin, Tharon and Mashmahiq, in Basra, in Hira, in Damascus, in Busra;[29] the Jacobites, who were powerful in Yemen, claimed all of the Arab tribes of the north, from Damascus to the Tigris. Aside from this the wilderness was traversed by monks and pilgrims, who — in groups of 700 or 800 people — went to Jerusalem and to Sinai;[30] the novels and stories praised proselytism among the Arabs, (and) their trade with India mobilized numerous caravans; the life of a hermit was so well loved, that as a manner of speech there were not any deserts or mountains without dwellers, one could also say that the polytheistic Arabs in Arabia only formed a small island, which was traversed by Christians from all directions. These polytheists, who were named Saracenes by the Greek authors of the 6th and 7th centuries, [deleted] (were to them) ignorant barbarians, shepherds and hunters, in general harmless.[31] It also occurs among them to go to war especially when hunger or the hope of plunder drives them to it, but

one guards himself against this misfortune in that he surrounds his monastery with a solid wall, which is only interrupted by a single opening, which was four or five meters above the ground. The visitor who properly identifies himself, would be let in by a basket, the honorable predecessor of our elevator.[32] The Christians began to equip these barbarians with an alphabet and a script (6th to 7th centuries).[33] At the same time they made traditions in that they took Mecca, its springs and tribes of the area and connected it with Hagar and her son Ishmael,[34] just as later they connected the Mongolian rulers of Tangout with the three wise men, and how they showed the mountain in Turkestan on which the ark of Noah rested.[35] The role of the Christian monk Sergius, the proven (Bahira) near to Muhammad, is not only probable but necessary,[36] in that the Muslim authors, here as in other places, took a Syriac epithet for a personal name.[37] The biographies of Muhammad tell of his struggles with the pagans and the Jews, but they do not report that he was at war with the Christian tribes; to the contrary they cite two commendations which he had given to the Christians of Adrok and Aila, he even gave his coat to the latter of these in the city. When we read that Muhammad allowed the people of Najran to remain Christian, we assume that this favor must have been recorded in writing, and the Nestorians indeed produce a credible document in whose preamble one has Muhammad say that the pagan or Jewish Arabs fought with the people of God and argued his doctrine, but that the Christians never had done this.[38]

It is there where one needs to look for the reason first successes of the Muslims from southern Egypt to deep into Persia.[39] We have seen that 'Amr negotiated with the Syrian Christians in 639, and that they performed a service for him in translating the Gospel, the beginning of all the works and all the sciences that the Syrians should later transmit to Islam. In the following year (640) the Arabs crossed the Euphrates; the Edessans came out to negotiate with them and opened their city without resistance, the Jacobite Primates of the Orient handed over Tagrit,[40] the Bishop Gabriel handed over Tûr 'Abdin (see Appendix 3), and "the armies of the Romans," said Michael, "painfully retired from all the cities."[41] One soon saw the conversion of the cities and peoples all together, as the Ghassanids of Syria and the inhabitants of the whole coast of the Persian Gulf. These desertions with weapons and equipment necessitated the introduction of schools and monasteries, the philosophy and the mysticism of the Christians into Islam. "Where is the great people of the Mazonites,"[42] wrote a Nestorian Patriarch in the year 650; "where is the great people of the Mazonites, which has rushed into the abyss of apostasy, just out of love to the half of their goods?[43] Where are the holy places of the Karamani and the whole Fars?"[44]

In Egypt, John of Nikiou teaches us that since the year 641 they helped the Muslims due to the persecution of Heraclius; the inhabitants of Fayoum subjugated themselves to the Arabs, paid them tribute and killed all the Roman soldiers which they met. [45] After this discussion with Benjamin and 'Amr in the year 643, this movement could do nothing else but grow. Makrizi also relates that 70,000 monks left the desert and came to 'Amr b. al-'As to congratulate him.[46]

8. We condemn this contribution which was performed by the Coptic and Syrian Patriarchs for pan-Islamism, but we do not wish to conceal their motives: they were only Greeks by conquest; their government, instead of attempting to let peace reign among all of its citizens, as was its duty, fomented too much civil discord in that it made itself the instrument of partiality; the Jacobites also saw how their monasteries were confiscated and how their communicants were dispersed.[47] They had realized that this government, which was so brutal against beings who were without defence, was undermined by materialism and corruption, in that, in the midst of luxury, which lends us the epithet "Byzantine," and with a budget which had not been raised till then, did not think of preparing either arms or permanent or moveable fortifications, in the absence of which bravery alone is nothing more than carelessness and folly. They had seen how their provinces were invaded, and could still ask themselves if certain materialists were in the position to appreciate the ideas of sacrifice and devotion, and whether they had not limited themselves to exploiting them in time of peril.[48] Because of this one understands how one of them is to have written:

Heraclius did not allow the Orthodox to appear before him

and did not accept their complaint due to the robbing of their churches. For this reason the God of vengeance, who alone is Almighty, who changes the empire of men as He wills, (and) gives to whom He will, and in that manner raises the humble, because He saw the evil of the Romans, who everywhere they ruled plundered our churches and monasteries in a cruel manner and condemned us without grace (and) led the sons of Ishmael out of the region of the south to liberate us out of the hands of the Romans through them.[49]

9. They were freed from the Romans, but they had suffered no less from the pan-Islamists. Limiting ourselves to Egypt, we find that the Muslims took famous personalities as hostage, they mistreated and killed them to sow terror, because John of Nikiou writes: " 'Amr had the Roman magistrates arrested and bound their hands and feet with chains and with pieces of wood, and he performed numberless acts of violence, afterwards there was panic in all the cities of Egypt; the inhabitants fled and left their goods behind."[50]

This departure gave them the desired pretext to clean out the empty houses and to possess the abandoned goods, to demand regular and unjustifiable sums of money and to burn the cities. John of Nikiou writes:[51] "When the Muslims came into a city accompanied by rene-gades, they possessed the goods of the Christians, who had fled..., they forced the Christians, to bring the Muslims fodder for their beasts and to deliver milk, honey, fruit and many other things in addition to the regular rations... 'Amr had the houses of the inhabitants of Alexandria who had fled destroyed, and he ordered the city of the two rivers to be burned. The inhabitants, who were (all) informed of the danger, rescued their goods and left the city, and the Muslims set it afire."

It also occurred that 'Amr had some cathedrals set on fire, as St. Mark's of Alexandria,[52] or some of the libraries, as the one in the same city.[53] One wanted to cleanse his memory of such abominable crimes, which is not unique in the history of Islam,[54] but it is not probable that he took the books out of it before he set it on fire, because this trick supposes a finer culture than his.

21

One part of the inhabitants were taken into captivity; the others were hit with taxes, because John of Nikiou writes:[55] "After he had defeated the inhabitants of the Pentapolis, 'Amr did not let them remain living there, rather he took a great booty from this land and a large number of prisoners... and the Muslims possessed all of Egypt, of the south and of the north, and they tripled the taxes. It came about that the inhabitants offered to trade their children for enormous sums of money, which they had to pay each month." And if one asks how one can harmonize the deeds of 'Amr with his words, John of Nikiou instructs us that he considered treaties as shreds of paper: " 'Amr dealt with the Egyptians without pity, said John, and did not fulfil the agreements which were made with him, because he was from a barbarous race."[56]

It was much worse when the renegades, who were already dreadful enough in the time of John of Nikiou,[57] entered the scene with their characteristic rage; they went so far as to form a plot and simultaneously burn down most of the churches of Egypt. "In this moment," writes Makrisi, "the people left the mosques, who had performed the Friday prayers, and were witnesses of a fearful sight: a thick dust, the smoke of the fire, the tumult of the crowd, which was taking away the booty, made one ponder the horrors of the Last Judgment."[58] The Sultan wanted to punish the guilty, but the Amir showed him that "the true cause of the fire was the perversity of the Christians and their excess of godlessness, for which God (May He be praised!) wanted to punish them."[59] "A great number of Christians were then killed, and — after various events — the Sultan of Egypt commanded, 'to bring all Christians to him, which could be found.' Everyone who would apprehend them, would be master of their goods and lives..., so that the Christians had to avoid appearing on public roads and that a great number of them became Muslims."[60]

10. These are the consequences of the discussion of 'Amr with John in 639 and with Benjamin in 643. The Christian Arabs, numerous and wealthy, were once more able to serve as a rampart for the Greek Empire and to stop the exodus of the Hagarenes, who let the over-population, poverty and greed come out of the sands of the Hijaz.[61]

They were the natural dike against all pan-Arabic movements, which were either to fail or develop under their leadership.

When the two Jacobite Patriarchs pacted with the Hagarenes, they took away this last dike, and the pan-Arabism, which triumphed aside from their leadership, quickly became pan-Islamism. The God of vengeance, whom they called, had certainly confronted them with the results of their compromises: He showed them Christian blood, which had been shed by Arab Muslims from Persia to the Pyrenees and the ruins which had been heaped up by the Muslim Turks, from their homeland Siberia[62] to India and to the Danube. From a Christian viewpoint and a patriotic viewpoint, they could have seen that they had acted badly. They should have left off the care of providence to each that which was fitting for him to receive, to offer their past suffering in the holocaust for their salvation and for the salvation of their people and to give their ruler faithful support, simply because he was their ruler and because the plundering Arabs were unjust aggressors. And if they had failed, if their sacrifice had been in vain, they would have at least had the satisfaction which the fulfillment of duty provides and they would have been able to repeat that which Judas the Maccabee said in an analogous situation: "It is more worthy for us to die in battle, than to see the suffering of our nation. When our day comes, then let us die for our brethren with courage."[63]

The various facts, which are recorded in our manuscript at the end of our discussion, are similar to the colophons and thus have a chance of being the personal work of the one who compiled them. The agreement of days of the week and the dates of the month are moreover exact. The earthquake on 28 February 713, which is related in much detail, is mentioned in three lines in Theophanes, Agapius and Michael the Syrian. The other events appear to belong to the person of our author: the comet on 8 April 712; the plague from 712 to 713; the plague, the locusts, the hurricane (20 May 714); the hail; the death of Walid (February 715), the avarice of Suleyman; the hail on 27 April 715 and on 20 April 716. [The section of the manuscript listing the events of 712-716 A.D. has been deleted in this edition.]

F. Nau

TRANSLATION

(A) Then, the letter of the Mar John, Patriarch, concerning the discussion which he had with the Amir of the Hagarenes (Mahgroyê[64])

(B) Because we know that you are anxious and fearful on our account, due to the matter for which we have been called in this area,[65] (with) our holy father the Patriarch, [66] we inform your Grace that on the ninth of this month of May, the day of the holy Sunday,[67] we went to the famous General Amir, and this holy father of all (the Christians) was questioned by him, whether this is one and the same Gospel, without any differences, which is held by all of those who are Christians and who carry this name throughout the whole world. - The blessed answered him that it is one and the same among the Greeks, the Romans, the Syrians, the Egyptians, the Cushites, the Hindus, the Armenians, the Persians and the rest of all the peoples and (all) languages.[68]

(C) He asked him yet: "Why, since the Gospel is unique, is the faith different (divided)?" and the blessed answered: "Just as the Law (the Pentateuch) is one and the same and it is accepted by us Christians and by you Hagarenes (Mahgroyê), and by the Jews and by the Samaritans, and each people is divided in faith; it is the same with the faith in the Gospel, each heresy understands and interprets it in various manners, and not as we."

(D) He asked yet: "What do you say (concerning) who the Christ is; is He God or not?" - And our father answered: "(We say) that He is God and the Word, which is born from God the Father, who is eternal and without beginning, and at the end of time He (Christ) became flesh and made Himself into a man for the salvation of mankind by the Holy Spirit and of the holy virgin, the mother of God, Mary, and He became human."

(E) The famous Amir asked him yet this: "When Christ was in the womb of Mary, He, of whom you say He is God, who carried and ruled Heaven and earth?"[69] - Our blessed father replied with the same argument: "When God came down to Mount Sinai and spoke with Moses for forty days and nights,[70] who carried and ruled heaven and earth? because you say that you receive Moses and his scriptures."[71] - The Amir said: "It is God, who was and who ruled the Heaven and earth." - And just after this he heard from our father: "It is also so with the Christ-God; when He was in the womb of the virgin, He carried and ruled the Heaven and earth and everything which is in them as Almighty God."

(F) The illustrious Amir said yet: "Which was the form and the opinion of the faith of Abraham and of Moses?" - Our blessed father said: "Abraham, Isaac, Jacob, Moses, Aaron and the rest of the prophets, all the wise and the righteous held to the faith of the Christians." - The Amir said: "Why have they not written clearly since then and not made known concerning Christ?" - Our blessed father answered: "They knew it, because they were trusted and near (God), but — (due to) the childishness and the coarseness of the people then, which were inclined to polytheism and held to it, in such measure that they regarded wood, stones and many other things as God, made idols, honored them and brought them sacrifices. Those in error did not want to give them a reason to distance themselves from the living God and to follow error,[72] rather they proclaimed what the truth is reservedly: 'Hear, Israel, the Lord God is one Lord.'[73] because they knew in truth, that there is only one God and only one deity, that of the Father, the Son and the Holy Spirit; they also wrote and spoke in a mysterious manner concerning God that the same is one in deity and (that He is) three substances and persons, then it is not so, one confesses neither three gods nor three deities, nor in any manner three gods or deities, because it is a single deity of the Father, the Son and the Holy Spirit, as we have said, and the Son and the Holy Spirit proceed from the Father; and, if you want, I am prepared and inclined to confirm this with the aid of the Holy Books."

(G) Then when the Amir heard all of this, he requested only to prove that the Christ is God and that He was born of the virgin and that God

has a Son by demonstrations of reason and from the Law (Pentateuch).
- And the blessed said that not only Moses, but also all of the holy
prophets prophesied beforehand and wrote this concerning Christ. The
one had written concerning His birth from a virgin, another that He
would be born in Bethlehem, another (wrote) concerning His baptism;
all (of them) so to say (wrote) about His Passion, which brought
salvation and about His life-giving death and about His glorious resurrection from the grave after three days; and he began to confirm (this)
according to all of the prophets and according to Moses at the same
time.[74]

(H) And the illustrious Amir did not accept the (words) of the prophets,[75] but rather demanded that it be proven him from Moses that
Christ is God; and the blessed, along with many other things, quoted
this (passage from) Moses: "The Lord let fire and sulfur come down
from the Lord on Sodom and on Gomorrah."[76] The famous Amir
demanded, that one show it himself in the book, and our father let him
see it, without (possible) error, in the complete Greek and Syriac
books. Certain Hagarenes (Mahgroyê) were present with us at this
place, and they saw the passages and the glorious names of the Lords
and Lord[77] with their own eyes. The Amir called a Jew, who was there
and whom they called knowledgeable in the scriptures, and asked him
if it was literally so in the Law. And this one answered: "I do not
know exactly."[78]

(I) The Amir then came from this to ask him concerning the laws of
the Christians; which and how they are; whether they are in the Gospel
or not? He added: "If a man dies and leaves behind boys or girls and
a wife and a mother and a sister and a cousin, how does he determine
how to divide the estate among them?"[79] - Then our father said that
the divine Gospel instructs and imposes heavenly doctrine and the life-
giving regulations, that it curses all sins and wickedness, that it teaches
excellence and righteousness and that many things were quoted concerning these — there were not only the nobles of the Hagarenes
(Maghroyê) assembled in the crowd, but also the leaders and the
rulers of the cities and the believing peoples and friends of Christ, the
Tanûkâyê, the Tu'âyê and the 'Aqûlâyê [80]. - The famous Amir said:

"I ask you to make one thing of three: to show me either that your
laws are written in the Gospel and that you act according to them, or
that you submit to the Muslim law (Mahgra)." And when our father
had answered that we Christians have laws, which are just and straight,
which agree with the doctrine and the commandments of the Gospel
and the canons of the apostles and the laws of the church, the assembly
of the first day was dismissed, and we have not succeeded (in being
able) to appear before him until now.

(J) (The Amir) also had certain persons of the main followers of the
Council of Chalcedon come, and all who were present, Orthodox or
Chalcedonian, pled for the life and the retainment of the holy Patriarch; they praised and exalted God, who had given the word of truth in
his mouth in rich measure, and who had filled him with His power and
grace, according to His true promises, as He said: "They will bring you
before the kings and the governors on account of Me, but do not
become anxious about how or what you will speak, for it will be given
you in that hour what you are to speak, for it is not you who speak, but
the Spirit of your Father speaks in you."[81]

(K) We send your Grace these words of numerous things, which were
brought into motion in these moments, so that you pray for us without
ceasing with zeal and care and so that you entreat the Lord, that He in
His compassion visit His churches and His people and that Christ grant
a way out of these matters, which pleases His will, that He help His
churches and comfort His people. As we have said further above, even
those of the Council of Chalcedon prayed for the holy Patriarch,
because he had spoken for all Christians, and because he had not
caused them any harm. The sent to him continually and they asked his
Grace to speak thus for all (the Christians) and not to bring anything
against them, because they knew their weakness and the dimension of
the danger (κίνδυνος) and the peril which threatened, if the Lord
should not visit His churches according to His compassion.[82]

(L) Pray for the famous Amir, so that God give him wisdom and
enlightenment for that which pleases the Lord and what is advantageous for Him. The holy father of the entirety (of the Christians) and

the holy[83] fathers, who are with him: Abbas Mar Thomas and Mar Severus, and Mar Sergius[84] and Mar Aitilaha[85] and Mar John and all of their holy escort and the leaders and the believers, who are assembled together with us; and foremost our beloved and wise principal[86] protected by Christ, Mar André and we, the Humble in the Lord, we request your salvation and prayers, always.

II

APPENDIX

[The sections 1 and 2 have been deleted in this edition.]

3. Concerning the document which was given the bishop of Tûr 'Abdin by 'Umar.

[The sections on 1° and 2° have been deleted in this edition.]

3° We have summarized the story of Gabriel the bishop of Tûr 'Abdin (593-667 our calendar) in *les Actes du XIV. Congrès international des orientalistes*, vol. II, Paris, 1906. pp. 55-67. We write, p. 68: "We are led to date the ordination of Gabriel in 629. He was 36 years old then. Later he went down to Gozarta to the Caliph 'Umar b. Khattab. This visit with 'Umar, which interested us little in 1906, today deserves to be placed next to the discussion of John with 'Amr. It is regretful that the story of Gabriel displays some anachronisms which make it suspect. It is possible that it was composed from the 9th to the 10th century, after the plundering of the monastery which is reported by Bar Hebraeus, *Chron. syr.*, ed. Bedjan, p. 144, about the year 830, as one would like to reconstruct the history of the monastery. Nevertheless, it is also possible that the author preserves even older traditions. For example it is interesting to see that he is Nestorian (the Catholicos) and that the leader of the wise could bring questions of the crosses and processions. One could believe that the monks from Tûr 'Abdin, after they had opened their land to the Arabs, had raised objection to the measures of 'Amr.[87] It is also interesting to see that the bishop of Tûr 'Abdin pretends to have 'the authority over Tûr 'Abdin to Babylon' from 'Umar, because that was very much the demand of these bishops since the time of the Patriarch Severus bar Mosqa (668-680); they wanted to ordain the bishops of Mesopotamia themselves, cf. Michael, *Chronicle*, II, 456, and caused many schisms. Bar Hebraeus summarizes our history, *Chron. eccl.*, I, 122 (including his anachronism),[88] without contesting them: 'Gabriel, Archimandrite of Qartamin, was consecrated as bishop in the year 965 of the Greeks (654); he went down to 'Umar b. Khattab,[89] the King of the Arabs, as he was in Gezirta of Bayt Zabdê, and he received a document (Sigilion) [with] authority over the people of the Christians.' "

This is the summarization of the events which we will transmit and translate. Since Bar Hebraeus saw this as authentic, it is certain, that it — in truth or supposition — had an influence on the fate of Tûr 'Abdin, and that it deserves to be published. One will compare it to the much harder conditions which were laid upon the inhabitants of Jerusalem by 'Umar. (Lebeau, *Histoire du bas Empire*, LVIII, 47.)

[The Syriac text has been deleted.]

TRANSLATION

(M) In the year 965 (654, read: 629)[90] — in which the Persians left Mesopotamia and Heraclius came to Edessa — the holy Mar Gabriel was consecrated as bishop by the Patriarch Athanasius, in the monastery of Mar Jacob, which is on the mountain of Qoros. And later the holy Mar Gabriel went to the Caliph of the Hanafi,[91] who is 'Umar bar Khattab, in the city of Gezirta, and (this one) received him with great joy. When he was with him for a while, he requested from the Caliph a pergament seal (concerning) the canons with respect to the laws of the Syrians and with respect to the bells and with respect to the processions, which they perform on the feasts of the Lord, and with respect to the crosses,[92] (to know) whether they would be hindered, and with respect to the churches[93] and the monasteries and with respect to the priests and with respect to the deacons, so that they would not be subject to tribute, and with respect to the monks, so that they be free to speak the litany (*ma'nioto*) before the dead, when they come out of the house to accompany them and to read the litany and the hymns before the (chapels of the) martyrs and to speak before the bishop when he visits his flock,[94] and everything which they wanted to have according to their rites, so that no one would harass them and that they would not be robbed of their laws.

(N) And the Caliph rejoiced over the arrival of the Mar Gabriel and gave him his signature, so that he could build churches and monasteries as he wished, and he gave him authority from Tûr 'Abdin to Babylon, and he honored him very much, because Mar Gabriel was on the side of the Arabs,[95] and as they came to this land he let them rule over it, and he made (it so) that the bad Romans disappeared from these regions. And 'Umar knew that the holy Mar Gabriel was an elect of God and that his prayer was heard of God — everything which he requested of God, He gave him — and he accepted his words with favor and came with him into this land, and he subjected it to him and said to the saint: "Demand whatever you will." And he requested mercy from him for all of the Syrians, for the churches and for the monasteries and above all for his monastery. And he gave him a document signed by himself, and behold, it remains to this day, and it was written within that the priests and the deacons did not have to pay any tribute and that the wealthy farmer (each) man had to pay four *zouzes*.[96] He also ordered in his writing, that if one of the *Hanife* (pagan = Arab) would find a Syrian on a mountain or on a road, that he should go with him to his house, he who would sleep on the mountain or in a vineyard or in the field, he should remain with him and protect him up to his house.[97] He issued many other ordinances concerning the orphans, the poor and widows, so that one might have pity on them, and for the occasions of the church and the feasts: if one went out at the time of a funeral and one made a procession,[98] on the feast of Psalms and on Good Friday and at the feast of the Resurrection, if one went out with crosses and the priests and the deacons wore their ornaments, that no one should hinder them. "And everyone who did them harm, should come under a curse: here (below) he would (experience) the judgment and the beatings, and there (above) he would (experience) hell and torment, because he has trampled under foot our commandment and the commandment of the Prophet of God, Muhammad." And then Mar Gabriel took the writing which (contained) these orders, and he received it and returned to his monastery with great joy, in that he prayed for 'Umar, and he thanked God that He let him find grace before him. Honor be to God! who exalts His servants, who honor His name. To Him be glory, honor and praise, now and forever, in the century of centuries! Amen.

Notes:

[1] Add., ms. 17193. - This is a volume of collections titled "Volume de démonstrations, de collections et de lettres". The extracts are, in general, very brief: 125 different subjects on 99 leaves. The only subjects which we show are the historical ones, and the following catalogue "of the kings of the Tayyâyê": Muhammad came to earth (hagira) in the (year) 932 of Alexander the son of Philip the Macedonian (621 A.D.), then he reigned 7 years (d. 7 June 632 ?). After him Abu Bakr reigned two years (d. 22 August 634). After him 'Umar reigned 12 years (d. 3 Nov. 644 ?). After him 'Uthman reigned 12 years (d. 17 June 656) and they were without leader in the war of Safa (Siffin) five and a half years. After this Marwan reigned 20 years (d. April 680). After this Yazid the son of Marwan reigned three and a half years (d. 11 November 683). After Yazid they were without a leader for one year. After him 'Abdulmelek reigned 21 years (d. 8 October 705). After him his son Walid began to reign 1017 in the beginning of the first Tichri (October 705). See the text of Land, "Anecdota Syriaca," II, Leyden, 1868, p. 11, and the dates (according to Weil). Ibid., I, 41-42. One will notice that Jacob of Edessa (ed. Brooks) also ascribes Muhammad seven years, from 621-628.

[2] We are quoting the translation of this passage (p. 16), below.

[3] The Jacobite patriarchs with the name John previous to our manuscript are: John I, 635 - 14 Dec. 648; John II, 744 - Oct. 754; John III, 846-873; the text of Michael, which we have quoted later in the introduction, shows us that it is the first (of these). In addition to this, the catalogue of the "Kings of Tayyâyê" ends with the Walid (705-715). cf. above, note 1; and the historical events which we will show, and those immediately following the letter of John from 712-716. It appears that the compilation was carried out at this period of time (which excludes John II and III). Finally the bishops mentioned at the end are placed around 630 by Michael, especially Aitilaha who has a name which was not used often (cf. above, p. 28), are not found under John II and III. Particularly, see the lists of the Jacobite bishops in the *Chronicle* of Michael or the *Revue de l'Orient chrétien*, IV (1899), pp. 447-451, 495-500. The accord between Chalcedonians and the Jacobites also shows that the dialogue took place at the time of the first defeat of the Chalcedonian Greeks, cf. below, note 82. See note in appendix concerning John I, below, p. 268 [deleted].

[4] This name requires discussion. It is transmitted by Michael the Syrian, II, 431. Michael explains in four lines, in accordance with a first abbreviated source, that " 'Amr the son of Sa'd," the Amir of Tayyâyê forbade that the crosses appear outside of the churches; he adds the report concerning " 'Amr" and the Patriarch John, which we relate further above in the introduction (p. 16). This source of Michael seems to define both 'Amrs as Bar Hebraeus also understood them, *Chron. eccl.*, I, 275, when he transmitted Michael. Another very developed source, written by Michael in the parallel column, mentions the bubonic plague (Ibid., II, 431, col. 1, and 432, col. 1) and then the prohibition of the crosses in Homs and Damascus by " 'Amr" (quoted, below, n. 87). We know that 'Ubayda, the ruler of Syria, died during the plague mentioned above, and he had 'Amr b. al-'As as his successor, and it thus appears to us to be certain that it is this one here to whom one must attribute this discussion, and also possibly, in spite of *one* of the sources of Michael, the prohibition of the crosses, because the first source is only a brief summary (perhaps of the second), and the second, which transmits the (more) developed version, brings no

special accusation against 'Amr. Moreover Michael never mentions 'Amr "b. al-'As,' as he should have, II, 450, on the occasion of an assassination attempt against him in Egypt, he names him Sa'id, a name which was often exchanged for Sa'd, cf. *Patr. or.*, I, 501, which gives us one further reason to suppose that the "son of Sa'd" further above was used in place of "son of 'As."

[5] This is shown by the presence of the three Arab tribes, who lived "west of the Euphrates." Cf. below, p. 261 *, n. 3.

[6] In the time of John I, 9 May 633, 639, 644 fall on Sundays. The date of 644 is improbable, because 'Amr, who entered Alexandria in Dec. 643 (*Patr. or.*, I, 494), had to use the next years to conquer the Pentapolis. The date 9 May 633 appears to be too soon, because the Arabs only invaded Syria, and 'Amr, who laid siege to Gaza with 7000 men, was absolutely not qualified to have summoned the Patriarch, because Abu 'Ubayda was his superior (he commanded 37,000 men, cf. Lebeau, *Histoire du bas Empire*, LVIII, 19). Thus only the 9th of May 639 remains.

[7] Add. 17193, fol. 73-75.

[8] H. Lammens, *Mélanges de la Faculté orientale de Beyrouth*, I. 1906, p. 57, which quotes the *Kitab al-Agâni*, XIV, 156, 16.

[9] For us this word means "the religious duty to go out and compel all nations by force to accept Islam."

[10] In certain instances they would confiscate half of the lands if the inhabitants did not want to accept Islam. Cf. *L'expansion nestorienne en Asie*, pp. 230-234. At other times they would take everything, and would divide it among themselves or impose a pact interest, cf. G. Salmon, *Introduction topographique à l'histoire de Bagdad*, Paris, 1904, pp. 15-19.

[11] About 684 A.D. (65 A.H.), in the region of Homs alone there

were 20,000 Yemeṇites, who together with their relatives formed a group of 100,000 people in lodgings. (H. Lammens, loc. cit., I, 9 ff.) See the interest on lodgings in Noël Desvergers, *L'Arabie*, Paris, 1847, p. 238.

[12] H. Lammens, *Mèlanges*, etc., I, 53.

[13] Ibid., III, 1908, p. 287.

[14] See the references which were quoted by H. Lammens, loc. cit., I, 53, and 56-57. Let us add the following story of Michael, *Chronicle*, II, 421, somewhat abbreviated by Bar Hebraeus, *Chron. syr.*, ed. Bedjan, p. 101, and which shows us which day the Arabian invaders introduced themselves to the Persians. These sent a man from Hirta to spy on the Arabs; "he saw a ma'deen, who [deleted], ate bread and cleaned his shirt (killing the insects). He asked him: 'What are you doing?' The ma'deen answered: 'As you see I am letting new ones come in and driving the old ones out, and I kill the enemies.' And the man from Hirta went to the Persians and said: 'I saw a barefoot people which are poorly clothed but very courageous.' "

[15] We have taken the preceding dates from K. Krumbacher, *Byz. Literatur*, Munich, 1897, p. 950. See the continuation of the events in C. Huart, *Histoire des Arabes*, vol. I, ch. IX-X.

[16] H. Lammens, loc. cit., II, 1907, p. 22.

[17] Idem, ibid., p. 24.

[18] Cf. the Qur'an trans. Savary, Paris, Garnier, pp. 15, 16 and 66. - 'Amr also attacked the Christians in Oman in 629, cf. J. Périer, *Vie d'Al Hadjdjadj*, Paris, 1904, p. 244.

[19] Lebeau, *Histoire de bas Empire*, I, LVIII, ch. 56.

[20] *Patr. Orientalis*, vol. I, pp. 494-498.

[21] The chronology of the *Histoire des patriarches d'Alexandrie* is certainly exact. The Arabs enter Egypt during the year 357 of Diocletian (29 August 640 to 641); they distinguish themselves on 6 June 641; take Cairo in March 642; receive tribute for one year from the Melkite Patriarch of Alexandria; finally take Alexandria in December 643, and then conquer the Pentapolis, cf. *Patr. Orientalis*, I, 492-495. - The conquest of Africa was prosecuted further by the successor of 'Amr until the battle of Iacouba, in which the patrician Gregor was killed by 'Abdullah b. Zubayr. One should note that the latter on that occasion expressed the axiom: "Every hairy man is a coward." Cf. É. Quatremère, in *Journal Asiat.*, vol. IX, April 1832, pp. 297-298, quoted by Noël Desvergers, *L'Arabie*, p. 253.

[22] Cf. the Qur'an, sura 5:50,51; "The Christians are to judge according to the Gospel."

[23] Cf. below, p. 43, n. 80.

[24] Concerning the books which are accepted among the Muslims, we wish to remark, that on the 1st, 6th, 12th, 18th, and 24th of the month of Ramadan they celebrate the sending down from heaven of the books of Abraham, Moses, David, the Gospel and the Qur'an; see our edition of "Des fêtes des Muslumans et de leurs jours remarquables," in the *Review de l'Orient chrétien*, vol. XVII (1912), pp. 98-99.

[25] Qur'an 5:45,48,50,70,72,110; 7:156,168,169; 61:6; etc.

[26] Cf. Qur'an 5:19,76,77,79; 6:100,101; 19:91-93; 43:81; 63:59; etc. "Those who say that God is the Messiah, Son of Mary, are unbelievers... If God had a Son, I would be the first to honor Him... Not much is lacking, and the heavens cleave at these words, the earth opens and the mountains break apart at this, that they attribute a Son to the Merciful..."; cf. Qur'an 23:93 - "God has no Son at all." The Trinity is also expressly denied: "Do not say that there is a Trinity in God. He is one," Qur'an 4:169. It is true that for Muhammad the Trinity appears

to have been composed of the Father, Mary and the Son; cf. Qur'an 4:169; 5:116.

[27] Qur'an 4:156 - "They have not crucified him in any way; a man, who resembled him was set in his place." According to the Islamic gospel, which is claimed to be from Barnabas, it is Judas who was crucified in the place of Jesus. When this gospel was referred to, the learned, for whom imperfection is a proof of antiquity, saw in this the Christianity of the Jewish Christians, (allegedly) older than our Gospels. (This is the same *postulate* of two bad Syriac versions of bad Greek manuscripts which predate the Peshitta.) Since the edition of the gospel of Barnabas of L. Ragg, *The Gospel of Barnabas*, Oxford, 1907, James dates its composition in the 16th century. Cf. *Journal of theolog. studies*, vol. IX, April 1908, pp. 458-459. - It is probably our 'Amr b. al-'As who forbid to carry the crosses outside of the church. (Michael, *Chronicle*, II, 432, col. 1), though (he) is said to have (used) an abbreviation of 'Amr bar Sa'd, Ibid., 431, col. 2. Cf. below p. 45, n. 87.

[28] Cf. Appendices, 3°, pp. 277-278.

[29] We have developed this subject and identified the lesser-known names in "L'expansion nestorienne en Asie," *Bibliothèque de vulgarisation du Musée Guimet*, vol. XL, Chalon-sur-Saône, 1914, pp. 205-212.

[30] Ibid., p. 214, n. 2.

[31] See especially, *Les récrits du moine Anastase sur les Pères du Sinaï*, trans. from the Greek by F. NAU, Paris, 1902.

[32] It is so in Sinai and Scété.

[33] We do not believe that one can prove that the Arabs had written a few works or even pieces of verse, before they had converted the "People of the Book," since pre-Islamic poetry was not even committed to writing, until 100 years after the Hagira; cf. C. Huart, *Journal of*

asiat., Xth. Series, vol. IV (1904), pp. 142-145. We do not fail to recognize what the Arabs *later* did for the arts and sciences.

[34] Cf. Noël Desvergers, *L'Arabie*, Paris, Didot, 1847, pp. 12-13, 98-99. It is in Mecca where the angel let the spring Zamzam bubble to quench the thirst of Hagar and her son Ishmael, who married and became a people group in the area. Abraham built the Ka'ba. The father L. Cheikho published numerous articles in the *Machriq*, (Beirut, 1913-14) about "Christianity and Literature before Islam," which we could not use. Bar Hebraeus writes *Chron. eccl.*, II, 114, that the city Yathrib or Medina, which he punctuates as Median *ytrb dhy mdyn*, took its name from the fourth son whom Abraham received from Keturah, Midian, cf. Gen 25:2. We are far away from the usual etymology of *Medinat al-Nabi*, "The city of the Prophet." Our document only gives the Muslims the name the Agareens (*mahgroyê*, aphel participle, formed from *Hagar* to describe the condition); the counterparts in Greek are Ἀγαρηνοί, *Jean Damascène*, ed. Le Quien, I, 110; and with an initial "m," μαγαρισμόν which is close to "Islam"; ἦλθεν ὁ Μουχαμὲθ κηρύσσων τὸν μαγαρισμόν "Muhammad (Moukameth) came to preach Magarism (to be Hagarene)." Cf. Theodore Abucara (Abu Qurra) in the works of John of Damascus, I, 470. (John of Damascus, parag. AG, - ed.) Most frequently one finds Σαρρακηνοί, which either correctly or incorrectly refers to Sarah, and sometimes "Ishmaelites." All of these names directly connect the Muslims with Judeo-Christian traditions.

[35] Cf. *L'Expansion nestorienne en Asie*, loc. cit., pp. 276-277.

[36] We have highlighted the personality of Sergius the proven (Bahira) at length in *L'Expansion nestorienne en Asie*, loc. cit., pp. 213-223. The German scholars wanted to reconstruct the role of Sergius with the help of the Arabic writers, which are secondary sources, since they saw the epithet as a personal name. These secondary sources and sources of inclination make of the story of "Bahira" a sort of deceptive presentation, cf. C. Huart, in *Journ. asiat.*, 10th series, vol. IV (1904), p. 127. One must look at the works of the Greeks (and

Syrians) to see what Sergius could have been.

[37] The epithet *bhyr'* (Bahira = proven) is commonly used in Syriac, for example, in the lonely life of John the Small, *Revue de l'Orient chrétien*, vol. XVII (1912), p. 351: ... *twb tsh't' d'b' wdsh' wbhyr' wm"'*... *mry ywhnn "wr'. The story of the holy and proven (Bahira) sublime father... Mar John the Small.* - Ibid., p. 357: *hw mn rb' hw' dyry' bqy' wbhyr'. The great (one) was a chosen and proven (Bahira) monk.* - Ibid., p. 366 - *'stqbl sb' hd rb' wbhyr' d'mr tmn. A great and proven (Bahira) old man from there, who remained there,* etc. In the same manner: concerning Abraham who was first a pagan (*hnp'* = Hanfa) — His apocalypse itself relates, that he went to sell the idols which his father had made — one made of this word "pagan" the name of a religion. (see al-Kindi, parags. E and BD - ed.) - The Hagira is also certainly the era of the sons of Hagar, *bny hgr* or the Hagarenes, *mhgry'*.

[38] Cf. *L'Expansion nestorienne en Asie*, loc. cit., pp. 224-230. In general one uses too much rigor, in my opinion, in researching the sources of the Qur'an. It could only have been concerned with verbal sources, more or less digested or brewed. All the confusions therefore, remain possible and even probable. Cl. Huart emphasizes the influence of the old Arabic poets to peddle and recite just as our troubadours the chansons de gestes, *Journ. asiat.*, 10th series, vol. IV (1904), pp. 130-3 and 165-7. One also may not neglect the informal discussions of Muhammad. Concerning the later introduction of Judeo-Christian traditions in Islam, cf. C. Huart, Ibid., pp. 331-50.

[39] The defection, in the midst of battle, of the Banu Thenoukh, who seem to be the Jacobite Tanûkâyê, saved the Arabs for the first time, cf. below, p. 43, n. 80. The Arabs of the south, whom Sergius had not given their usual wage, were the first to defect and lead their fellow countrymen into Gaza, cf. Theophanes, ad ann. 623; they were defectors who taught the nomads the use of battle machines., Lebeau, *Histoire du bas Empire*, LVIII, 19. Everywhere there was only treason, Romain handed over Busra, Ibid., LVIII, 16; Josias handed over

Damascus, Ibid., LVIII, 25; another handed over the people of Tripoli, Ibid., LVIII, 32; another let the battle of Yarmuk be lost, which led to the defection of the Arabs of Ghassan, Ibid., LVIII, 44; Yukinna (doubtless an Arab, because his name is none other than *Yuhnna* = John) handed over numerous cities, Ibid., LVIII, 49-54; and divided the kingdoms among themselves, Ibid., LVIII, 24; the governors were jealous of one another and did not help one another; LVIII, 35; the others making treaties to their own advantage as Cyrus for Alexandria, LVIII, 63, and John for Osroene, cf. Theophanes, ad ann. 628. The Greek empire succumbed more from the blows of their own than from the blows of the inhabitants of the Hijaz.

[40] Cf. Bar Hebraeus, *Chron. eccl.*, II, 124-126. Quoting *Patr. orient.*, III, 58: Life of Marouta.

[41] *Chronicle*, II, p. 426.

[42] Mazoun was the name which was particularly given Sohar, and in general the region of Oman, cf. H. Lammens, loc. cit., II, 1907, pp. 400-401, and F. Nau, "Maronites, Mazonites et Maranites," in the *Revue de l'Orient chrétien* , vol. IX (1904), pp. 268-276.

[43] Others — at that moment of time — preferred to lose half their possessions. See also Bar Hebraeus, *Chronicle eccl.*, I, 338: "Les inhabitants du pays d'Alep (après 798) abandonnèrent leur foi tous en même temps, et se firent Arabes." - "The inhabitants of the land Alep all gave up their faith at the same time and became Arabs (after 798)."

[44] Cf. Rubens Duval, *Iso'yahb patriarchae III, Liber epistularum*, Paris, 1905, pp. 179-182, 192.

[45] *Chronicle* of John of Nikiou, ed. Zotenberg, in *Notices et extraits des manuscrits*, vol. XXIV, Paris, 1883, pp. 559, 562-563; cf. p. 570.

[46] *Le couvent des chétiens*, trans. E. Leroy, in *Revue de l'Orient*

chrétiens, vol. XIII (1908), pp. 198-199.

[47] The Greeks also made the political mistake of decapitating and dispersing the confederation of the Jacobite Arabs for reasons of religious confession. Cf. Michael, *Chronicle*, II, p. 350.

[48] We do not know if the Byzantine government was able to correct itself and stop being the representative of a single group and the oppressor of the rest of the Greeks and to grant all subjects of the empire equality at law and in treatment, because 300 years later (968), when Nicephorus Phocas retook Syria, which had been devastated and depopulated, he requested that the Patriarch John VII come live there and lead his co-religionists back there with him. He promised him religious freedom, but soon did not keep his promise, as he had the Jacobite Patriarch and four bishops brought to Constantinople and (after a two month-long discussion) demanded that they become adherents of the Council of Chalcedon. As a result of their refusal, they were imprisoned. Cf. Michael, *Chronicle*, III, 131; Bar Hebraeus, *Chron. eccl.*, I, 412-414; Assemani, *Bibl. or.*, II, 133-140; Lequien, *Oriens christ.*, II, 1378; & c. It was worse 50 years later (1029) under the rule of Romain, cf. Michael, *Chron.*, III, 140-145, 147, 166-167. To the contrary Michael praised the tolerance of "the Franks" often, Ibid., III, 222, 226, 249.

[49] Michael, *Chron.*, II, 412-413, and Bar Hebraeus, *Chron. eccl.* , I, 273.

[50] *Chronicle*, in notes and extracts of the manuscript, vol. XXIV, Paris, 1883, p. 560.

[51] Ibid, pp. 560, 562, 577.

[52] *Patr. orientalis*, I.

[53] Cf. Bar Hebraeus, *Histoire des dynasties*, trans. Pococke, Oxford, 1663, p. 114. One finds it somewhat strange that this volume is not

mentioned by any contemporaries, and one sees a motive for placing it in doubt, and not without reason.

[54] It was in this manner that the books of Severus bar Sakako were likewise carried into the public baths (δημόσιον) of the Sultan of Mosul, cf. Bar Hebraeus, *Chron. eccl.*, I, 411, (in the year 1241).

[55] Loc. cit., pp. 569, 577-578, 585.

[56] Loc. cit. p. 578.

[57] Loc. cit. p. 585.

[58] "Les Églises des chrétiens," in *Revue de l'Orient*, vol. XII (1907), p. 197.

[59] Ibid., p. 201.

[60] Ibid., p. 208.

[61] In 1178, for example, "driven by famine, a numerous (group of) people set themselves in motion and moved out of Arabia." But this "Hagira" did not find the same success of its predecessors, 100,000 people were killed, and the others drowned, as they tried to cross the Euphrates. Michael, *Chronicle*, III, 376.

[62] Michael the Syrian, *Chronicle*, III, 151-157, relates how the Turks left the south of Siberia, first as helpers of Persians or Arabs, and finally as invaders.

[63] I Maccabees 3:59; 9:10(b).

[64] "Descendants of Hagar."

[65] Without a doubt Syria, see Introduction , p. 18.

[66] Literally: "With the holy and God-honored Father and Lord and Patriarch of ours."

[67] 9 May 639, see Introduction, p. 33, n. 6.

[68] Nothing is said of the Arabs in this enumeration, it moreover appears from this discussion that the Gospel had not yet been translated into their language, and it was (translated) for the first time in May/June 639 (after the 9th of May and before the departure of 'Amr for Egypt).

[69] The Caliph 'Umar II also seems to have asked this question in his letter to Leo III by saying, "who was holding the heavens and the earth" while Jesus was on the earth?; see Gaudeul, "Leo and 'Umar," *Islamochristiana*, 10 (1984), p. 145, BNM 4944, l. 48 - ed.

[70] Exodus 24:18. - Cf. Qur'an 2:48 and 7:138 - ed.

[71] One will notice without coming to negative conclusions that the Qur'an is not referred to, but only the Pentateuch. The Muslims are very well "Hagarenes," the descendants and disciples of Abraham and "of Hagar." It is very interesting to see that Michael the Syrian, *Chronicle*, II, 403, has Islam originate from Judaism: "Muhammad attached himself to the faith of the Jews, who pleased him... He suggested it to his comrades and won some of them." As a result — because of the right of inheritance — he sent them to plunder the old land of the Jews, Palestine (Ibid). Theophanes informs us also (the year 622), that the Jews had joined Muhammad, because they accepted him as one of their prophets.

[72] The same reason (is given) in the homily of the LXX by Severus of Antioch, p. [303]. *Patr. orient.*, vol. XII, p.21.

[73] Deut. 6:4.

[74] The *Didaskalie* of Jacob (Sargis of Aberga), *Patr. orientalis*, vol.

8, pp. 711-780 (fasc. 5) is dedicated to the proof of this thesis. Moreover, it was written at approximately the same time (640).

[75] The Qur'an, and early Islamic tradition, mention neither the names nor the Books of the prophets, and it is quite certain that Muhammad knew nothing of them - ed.

[76] Gen. 19:24. This text is commented to in the same manner by Severus of Antioch, loc. cit. p. [308]. The Greek is: Καὶ κύριος ἔβρεξεν ἐπὶ Σόδομα καὶ Γόμορρα θεῖον καὶ πῦρ παρὰ κυρίου ἐξ οὐρανοῦ. The Syriac is: *wmry' 'ht 'l sdwm w'l 'mwr' kbrt' wnwr' mn qdm mry' mn shmy'.*

[77] Gen. 19:18, the Syriac gives the plural *mry,* but one should perhaps read: "The glorious name of the LORD and (a second time) of the LORD."

[78] The Masoretic text has been translated word for word in the Greek and Syriac: וַיהוָה הַמְטִיר ... מֵאֵת יְהוָה מִן הַשָּׁמַיִם. All of this seems to show that the Pentateuch had not been translated into Arabic, if not, then one would have based (his decision) — for or against — on this translation.

[79] See below, pp. 270-271 [deleted] on the subject of the "Patriarch John on inheritance." Very early on Roman laws were translated into the Syriac to regulate this casuistry. Land published one of these compilations according to a Syriac manuscript from the beginning of the 6th century, *Leges saeculares,* in *Anecdota syriaca,* I, Leyden, 1872, p. 128. - The preserved collections have been published by E. Sachau, *Syrische Rechtsbücher,* vol. I and II, Berlin, 1907 and 1908. - We quote the regulations of the edition of the laws of the Spanish Muslims, which was recently published: *Particion de Herencias entre les Musulmanes del rito malequi,* by José A. Sanchez Pérez, Madrid, 1914, in 8°, xvi-312 pp.

[80] These are the main three tribes of the Christian Arabs. See

their conversion and their praise in the "Life of Ahoudemmeh," *Patr. orient.*, III, 21-33. The 'Aqûlâyê, "that is, the people from Baghdad went from Haran to Mabbug and Hamath," writes Michael, *Chronicle*, II, 445. The three tribes seem to be "west of the Euphrates" (Ibid., II, 466-467). The most powerful Christian tribe seems to have been the Taghlibs who were stretched out from Oman and the banks of the Tigris to the valley of the Orontes and Damascus: one said as a proverb, "Without the introduction of Islam, the Taghlib would have invaded everywhere." Cf. H. Lammens, in *Mélanges de la Faculté orientale de Beyrouth*, 1908, III, 1, pp. 262-263. The Tanûkâyê are without a doubt the Benon-Thenoukh (the sons of Tanuk), who made an agreement with Khalid prior to 639 to desert in the midst of battle, cf. *l'Arabie* by Noël Desvergers, Paris, Didot, 1847, p. 235 (according to Kemal-Eddin, *Histoire d'Alep*). Because of this one understands why the "Tanûkâyê" were in the camp of the 'Amr. See in Michael, *Chronicle*, II, 481, the martyr of the leaders of the Taghlibs Mo'adh and Sam'alla, about 709. In Bar Hebraeus, *Chron. eccl.*, II, 123, (*Patr. orient.*, III, 57 quotes) "The Christian Arabs are the Taghlibs, who live in tents."

[81] Matt. 10:19-20 (with Luke 21:12b, paraphrase - ed.).

[82] This entire closing also shows that the discussion took place in 639, as the Arabian victories frightened all Christians, for their internal discord did not delay to begin again. After June, 659 there was a conflict before Mu'awiya in Damascus, between the Jacobite bishops Theodore and Sebokt and the Chalcedonian monks from Mar Maron, and Mu'awiya profited from imposing a monetary fine on the Jacobites. See F. Nau, *Opuscules maronites*, I and II, Paris, 1899 and 1900; E. W. Brooks, *Chronica minora*, II, Paris, 1904, p. 55.

[83] Or "the bishops," because the word *hsy'* is often reserved for them.

[84] Thomas, Severus and Sergius are mentioned in the *Chronicle* of Michael, vol. II, p. 412, in that they formed the entourage of the

Patriarch Athanasius, predecessor to John, when he went to find the Emperor Heraclius. It is natural that they escorted his successor John when he went to find 'Amr.

[85] In 940 (629) named as the bishop of Marga and Gomal, cf. Michael, *Chronicle*, II, 416, 419.

[86] This word appears to describe a superior in the monastery.

[87] Here is that which Michael relates, *Chronicle*, II, 432: "At that time 'Amr, the Amir of the Tayyâyê, forbade that the crosses appear even on feast days and rogation days. This pleased the Jews, and they gave themselves to taking the crosses out of the churches. Then a Christian, who was known by the Amir, was provoked by zeal as he saw how a Jew ran on top of the church of St. John the Baptist (in Damascus), to take away the cross, and went to 'Amr to meet with him and said. 'O righteous Amir! It is not right that you allow a Jew to make our mysteries a derision.' Then as God changed his heart, he said: 'I have not prescribed to take away the crosses, except for those which are displayed in the streets, on the walls...' This order ceased, and the Christians began to carry the crosses at the rogation days, on feast days and in funerals again. Meanwhile, in Emesa and Damascus, they never had this freedom since this edict of the Amir 'Amr was proclaimed."

[88] The manuscript of London, Add. 17265, is of the XIII century, that is, contemporary with Bar Hebraeus.

[89] The editor translated *Bar Chatibi ad sedem* (*'wmr'*) and corrected his writing, Ibid., I, 923.

[90] We have made the remark, *XIV. Congrès des Orientalistes*, Algier, vol. II, 1906, p. 62, that one also finds the date 960 or the word *ss* and since one reads *sm* or 940 (629), all synchronisms are satisfied.

[91] One reads in folio 127 v° that Simon Zaite "built a prayer house

for the Hanife" *bn' byt s'wt' 'hnp'* in the year 707, as the manuscript of London Add. 17265 gives: "He built the mosque, which is south of the church (of Mar Theodore in Nisibe), a house of prayer for the Arabs," *wbn' 'msgd' dmn tymnh d'dt' byt s'wt' 'th'.* Thus describes *Hanfo*, whose real sense means "pagan," but sometimes "the Arabs," as in a manuscript of Paris. - This construction will moreover be explained in detail, Ibid.; ms. 375, fol. 176. *wtwb mtl 'yqr' dmlk' dth' wdnbsm 'byhwn 'qwb'h. bn' 'l gbh d'dt' msgd' rb' wshpyr' wsbth tb myqr't wsm ptwr' dml' kl tkbyn dbmdynt'. wklhyn npqth mn 'dt' hy dshql hw'. wmnyh hw' bh 'k'hwn th' wpqyh' wms'yn' dsybyn hww.* "Thereupon to honor the King of Tayyâyê and to reconcile them with their hearts, (Simon Zaite) built a large and beautiful mosque next to the church (of Theodore of Nisibe about 708), and he decorated it with care and he erected a table, loaded with everything good which was in the city — he took the income of the church for this — and he restored all the Tayyâyê, faqihs and euchites who came."

[92] The manuscript gives "some fastings," the parallel passage, which is further below gives "some crosses" *slyb'*.

[93] Read *'dt'*.

[94] Cf. Bar Hebraeus, *Chron. eccl.*, II, 143, where one precedes a Metropolitan and sings *'wnyt'* and *m'nyt'*.

[95] Literally: "wanted for the Arabs."

[96] Muhammad imposed four *zouzes* for the poor, but twelve for merchants and the rich, cf. Bar Hebraeus, *Chron. eccl.*, II, 116-118.

[97] This probably means that Gabriel had requested the protection of the Arabs against the Kurds.

[98] *dr'* from *dr* or *dwr, circumivit*. Cf. Arabic *duran*, "procession."

LEO III'S
REPLY TO 'UMAR II

The text of Leo III's religious correspondence to 'Umar II, as found in Ghevond's *Armenian History*, was first translated into English by Arthur Jeffery in the *Harvard Theological Review*, Vol. 37 (1944), pp. 269-332. As Jeffery mentions in his article, an abbreviated version of the text has also been preserved in Latin in *Patrologia Graece*, Vol. 107, cols. 315-324, but he shows that the letter was originally written in Greek. Although the authenticity of the correspondence has been and continues to be a subject of discussion, Jeffery shows that a few early Christian historians refer to 'Umar's religious letter to Leo and some in turn to Leo's reply. What was not available to Jeffery at the time of his writing though, was any evidence of the religious correspondence in Islamic sources,[1] the future discovery of which, however, he thought to be a real possibility.[2]

In 1983, the Catholic priest Jean-Marie Gaudeul, while reading several works of Christian-Muslim dialogue which he considered to be from the 9th and 10th centuries, discovered two Muslim documents which fit the descriptions of 'Umar's letter as given in Ghevond's text of Leo's letter. Gaudeul published his findings in *Islamochristiana* 10 (1984), pp. 109-157. The two Muslim documents are: BNM No. 4944 of the National Library in Madrid (the edition of D. Cardaillac) which contains the first part of 'Umar's letter; and the "Anonymous Pamphlet," which contains a continuation of 'Umar's text discovered by D. Sourdel, cf. *Revue des Etudes Islamiques*, T. 34 (1966), pp. 1-33.[3]

Having compared all of the texts in question, Gaudeul shows the

letter of 'Umar as given by Ghevond to be a forgery, due to its brevity
and deficiencies.[4] He is also convinced that Ghevond's text of Leo's
letter is a faithful representation of an earlier manuscript.[5] Nevertheless, Gaudeul rejects the notion that either of the two letters could
have actually been written by 'Umar II or Leo III,[6] rather ascribing the
letters to two unknown writers, who both fancied to name themselves
'Umar and Leo in these manuscripts.[7] In dating the various manuscripts Gaudeul refers to Jeffery's opinion that Ghevond lived in the
9th or 10th centuries (see note 16 below) and that Leo's descriptions of
the Muslim sects (i.e. the Jahiziyya) also correspond to this time
period. Gaudeul then cites Sourdel's suggestion that the "Anonymous
Pamphlet" was also written 885-900 A.D.[8] and thus concludes that
neither of the letters could be genuine.

Yet one very peculiar feature of manuscript BNM 4944 is that it is
headed with the title: "This is the epistle that 'Umar b. 'Abd-al-Aziz,
king of the believers, wrote to Lyon, king of the Christian Infidels,"
which is followed by an *isnad* of three persons, all of whom are known
to have been respected Islamic scholars.[9] After showing that the isnad
as is stands is incomplete (the first transmitter Isma'il b. Ayyas was
born about the time of 'Umar's death), Gaudeul presumes that it was
fabricated, probably even before the document came to Spain.[10] In his
analysis of the various texts at hand, however, Gaudeul fails to consider
some of the remarkable *coincidences* concerning them. The Armenian
historian Ghevond gives what he alleges to be Leo's letter to 'Umar.
Another manuscript, preserved by Muslims at the opposite end of their
empire, claims to be 'Umar's letter to Leo. Both these manuscripts
just *happen* to fit the descriptions they give of each other. In addition,
secondary witnesses to this exchange can be found in the Latin for
Leo's letter and the Arabic "Anonymous Pamphlet" for 'Umar's. It is
known from both Islamic and Christian sources that 'Umar II and Leo
III corresponded with each other on other subjects,[11] and the chance
that letters written by unknowns (who independently conspired to
assume fictitious identities) should later receive so much respect as to
be consulted and translated as authentic by two cultures so diverse
from each other seems much more unlikely than the alternative that

the letters are actually genuine.

Jeffery is very cautious about regarding the authenticity of the text of Leo's correspondence. On the one hand he defends it against some of Beck's arguments for placing the letter in the 9th or 10th centuries;[12] yet on the other he prefers this dating for Ghevond.[13] The only real objection Jeffery voices against the letter's genuineness is that the text appears to describe Muslim sects which formed after the 8th century—specifically the *Basli* and the *Jahdi*, which Jeffery identifies as a group of the Mu'tazilites and the Jahiziyya, respectively.[14] But rather than discredit the authenticity of Leo's letter as Gaudeul assumed,[15] these inconsistencies are ascribed by Jeffery to textual changes made by Ghevond.[16] Indeed Jeffery himself writes that the identification of the Muslim sects mentioned in the text is not easy,[17] since the Arabic names were most probably translated from Greek into Armenian. If, however, the terms *Basli* and *Jahdi* were actually added to the text by Ghevond, and thus not translated from Greek at all, then he certainly should have been able to spell the words more exactly (the terms as they appear in the text do not match any of the names for Muslim sects known to have existed). The very fact that these words must be manipulated in order to identify the groups intended again points to an early dating for the text of the letter. There are also other possible alternatives to Jeffery's suggested interpretations of the names. *Basli* could also be *Basri*, in which case almost any of the early Mu'tazilite sects of Basra could be meant. The *Jahdi*, of whom it is said in the text that they do not believe in God or the resurrection, may refer to the Yazidis, who worship the Malak Ta'us and believe in the transmigration of souls. Though there are quite a few differing opinions as to the origins of this group, the most credible appears to be the account given by ash-Shahrastani *Kitab al-Milal wa n-Nihal*, ed. Cureton, I, 101)[18] tracing their origins to Yazid b. Abu Anisa whose sect broke off from the Kharidjites (again one of the earliest sects in Islam).[19] Indeed the paradox of the Yazidis being Kurdish and their scriptures being written in Arabic, would seem indicate that they were heretical Muslims and not Nestorians or Persian Zoroastrians as some assume. Consequently, if the *Jahdi* of are to be identified with the Yazidis,

Leo's letter would then represent the earliest reference to date which mentions them.

Theologically the letters of both Leo and 'Umar also possess characteristics which would have been typical in the very early stages of the Christian-Muslim dialogue. 'Umar not only mistakes something which Job said for a saying of Jesus,[20] but he also erroneously credits Jesus with another saying which later Islamic tradition attributes to a revelation of Muhammad.[21] Furthermore, 'Umar somehow neglects to mention the creed and the Hajj in his ennumeration of the rites which "Muhammad" (and not God) imposed upon them.[22] Were the text of 'Umar's letter actually written in the 9th or 10th centuries, the Muslim author should have at least known his own major hadith and subsequently, the five pillars, both of which were still being collected and developed in early Islam. Many of the the Bible quotations cited by 'Umar have been corrupted by him[23] to comply with Islamic doctrine, and some of his references were simply his own invention.[24] Such inferior tactics would not have lasted very long in the more developed discussions of the 9th and 10th centuries (the Caliph, who accuses the Jews and Christians of altering the Bible to suit their doctrines, himself turns out to be the corrupter of the Scriptures; Leo, parag. AI). 'Umar furthermore, paraphrases the Qur'an more than he actually quotes from it, something which would be quite rare in the later Muslim polemic. Both 'Umar and Leo use the phrase "you pretend..." to express the rejection of a certain idea for which they accuse the opposing party of having. This wording is somewhat unique in the history of the Christian-Muslim dialogue, and the directness of the accusation of dishonesty lends itself more to an earlier dating rather than a later.[25] Leo for his part never quotes the Qur'an in his letter, he only alludes to it, and as Gaudeul notes, Leo errs in thinking that Muslims bury their women when their husbands die.[26] As a rule the later Christian polemicists do quote the Qur'an and would have shunned using such material as Muslims could readily disprove.

The major polemical subjects of the correspondence have also been used as evidence either for or against an early dating. As mentioned above, 'Umar charges the Jews and Christians with altering the texts of the Torah, Zabur and Injil, and not a few Western scholars have thought this accusation to be a later development in Islam. But the notion of *tahrif* (rearranging the letters in a word) being practiced by the People of the Book is anchored in the Qur'an,[27] and a hadith quoting Ibn 'Abbas says that the People of the Book have changed *(baddala)* the their books and only the Qur'an should be consulted by Muslims.[28] The charge that the Jews and Christians have changed the Scriptures could well have been the natural reaction of Muslims who could not find the prophetic references to Muhammad in the Bible, which the Qur'an claims to describe.[29] This is also the nature of the accusation brought by the Caliph Mahdi in his discussion with the Nestorian Patriarch Timothy I (circa 781 A.D.),[30] and even John of Damascus (d. circa 752 A.D.) was familiar with the Muslim charge.[31] The Muslim references to Muhammad being described as the Paraclete in the Gospel of John and the camel rider of Isaiah were also some of the subjects of this early discussion.[32] In fact Timothy appears to have responded so quickly to Mahdi's vague reference to the latter of these, that one suspects the argument had already been in circulation for some time by then. It is quite obvious that the early Muslims knew tragically little of the text of the Bible. Even more amazing, in their search for a "prophet to come," they overlooked the wealth of Messianic passages in the Old Testament and settled for an obscure passage concerning the conquerors of Babylon in Isaiah. It is interesting to note that 'Umar in mentioning this alleged prophecy to Leo again assumes that it is a saying of Jesus:

> Convert, O Jerusalem, until the time when the one who rides on an ass comes to you. Then will come after him the one who rides a camel.[33]

In his reply to 'Umar on this point, Leo simply refers to it as "this vision of Isaiah"[34] and continues with an exegesis of the passage. It is therefore not totally incredible to think that the Muslims stumbled upon these verses either in this or similar exchanges with Christians. In any event the claim that Jesus and Muhammad are to be indentified in this passage shows up rather early in the Muslim polemic.

Aside from Islamic objections to the diety of Christ which are based
on the Qur'an,[35] we see that 'Umar also presented the question of how
God could live in the womb of a woman.[36] Not only did Leo respond
to this,[37] but John of Damascus also gives instruction on how to answer
this question.[38] The Muslim understanding of the veneration of the
cross as idolatry is expressed by 'Umar,[39] and the counter-accusation of
Muslim veneration of the Ka'ba can be found in both Leo[40] and John
of Damascus.[41]

Many of Leo's polemical attacks against Islam are remarkably similar
to those of the 8th century John of Damascus. Both recognize the
Muslim legal practice of demanding that witnesses confirm certain
events and then in turn ask Muslims for the prophetic witness concerning the advent of Muhammad.[42] Both attack Muslims with the Qur'-
anic mistake identifying Mary the mother of Jesus with Miriam the
sister of Aaron and Moses.[43] Both deny that the Ka'ba could have
been "the House of Abraham"[44] and attack the sensuality displayed in
the Qur'anic descriptions of Paradise.[45] Both assault Muhammad's
character in the events surrounding his marriage to Zaynab the wife of
Zayd[46] and denounce the Qur'anic passages which describe remarriage
after divorce[47] and women as tillable fields.[48]

If 'Umar did actually write to Leo and if Leo replied, then Leo's
answer would certainly have been sent to the Umayyad capital Damascus, when John of Damascus apparently still occupied a high position
in the Muslim government there.[49] The similarities in the style and
content of the polemic of Leo III and John of Damascus against Islam
appear to be more than just coincidental, especially for two men who
later shared no great love for one another's theological beliefs.[50] The
arguments of the Muslims as presented by both writers, not to mention
the evidence we have in 'Umar's letter, also represent the various
doctrines of early Muslims. So why do we not possess either the
opening of Umar II's letter in Arabic or Leo III's letter in Greek?
The answers may lie in the poor intellectual and theological qualities of
'Umar's correspondence, which left little for later generations of
Muslim polemicists to be proud of. As for Leo's letter, later Byzantine

theologians condemned his iconoclastic views,[51] and many of his arguments against Islam appear to be preserved in the works of his opponent John of Damascus.

The translation which follows by Arthur Jeffery was originally published under the title "Ghevond's Text of the Correspondence Between 'Umar II and Leo III," *Harvard Theological Review*, Vol. 37 (1944), pp. 269-332. Because of the more recent discoveries of the text of 'Umar's letter, the version given by Ghevond has been deleted and Jeffery's explanatory notes which accompanied it have been moved so as to correspond with Leo's responses. Since Leo's work gives a rather accurate description of the text of 'Umar's letter, we have not presented it here. For more information concerning the text of the various manuscripts involved, see Jean-Marie Gaudeul's "The Correspondence Between Leo and 'Umar," *Islamochristiana*, Vol. 10 (1984), pp. 109-157.

Notes:

[1] See below, p. 61.

[2] See below, pp. 98-99.

[3] Gaudeul, "Leo and 'Umar," *Islamochristiana*, 10, p. 110.

[4] Ibid. pp. 113-4.

[5] Ibid. p. 128.

[6] Ibid. p. 114.

[7] Ibid. p. 127.

[8] Ibid. p. 126.

[9] Ibid. p. 132.

[10] Ibid. pp. 126, 132.

[11] See below, p. 59.

[12] See p. 101, n. 13, and p. 106, n. 33.

[13] See p. 103, n. 19.

[14] See p. 114, n. 54.

[15] Gaudeul, "Leo and 'Umar," *Islamochristiana*, 10, p.119.

[16] See pp. 62 and 99, below.

[17] See p. 114, n. 54.

[18] Joseph, *Devil Worship*, p. 18.

[19] *Shorter Encyclopedia of Islam*, p. 248.

[20] Gaudeul, "Leo and 'Umar," *Islamochristiana*, 10, p. 133, BNM 4944, parag. 5; Leo, parag. C.

[21] Gaudeul, "Leo and 'Umar," *Islamochristiana*, 10, p. 153, "Anonymous Pamphlet," parag. 75; Leo parag. BD, *Sahih Bukhari*, The Book of the Beginning of Creation, ch. 7, hadith 467, Vol. 4, p. 306.

[22] Gaudeul, "Leo and 'Umar," *Islamochristiana*, 10, p. 155, "Anonymous Pamphlet," parag. 83.

[23] Ibid. p. 121; Leo, parag. AK.

[24] Gaudeul, "Leo and 'Umar," *Islamochristiana*, 10, p. 140, BNM 4944, parag. 29; p. 150, "Anonymous Pamphlet," parag. 66, etc.

[25] Leo, note 22.

[26] Gaudeul, "Leo and 'Umar," *Islamochristiana*, 10, p. 115, note 8; Leo, parag. AY.

[27] Qur'an 2:56; 5:16, 45.

[28] *Sahih Bukhari*, The Book of Monotheism, ch. 42, hadith 634, Vol. 9, p.461.

[29] Qur'an 7:156, 61:6.

[30] Timothy, parags. AS and CL.

[31] John of Damascus, parag. D.

[32] Timothy, pp. 169, 173.

[33] Gaudeul, "Leo and 'Umar," *Islamochristiana*, p. 139, BNM 4944, parag. 28.

[34] Leo, parag. BC.

[35] Gaudeul, "Leo and 'Umar," *Islamochristiana*, 10, p. 144, BNM 4944 and "Anonymous Pamphlet," parag. 45; p. 146, parag. 51.

[36] Ibid. p. 144, BNM 4944 and "Anonymous Pamphlet," parag. 47.

[37] Leo, parag. AT.

[38] John of Damascus, parag. M.

[39] Gaudeul, "Leo and 'Umar," *Islamochristiana*, 10, p. 149, "Anonymous Pamphlet," parag. 63.

[40] Leo, parag. AX.

[41] John of Damascus, parag. F.

[42] Leo, parags. G and AH; John of Damascus, parag. C.

[43] Leo, parag. AH; John of Damascus, parag. B.

[44] Leo, parag. AH and AJ; John of Damascus, parag. F.

[45] Leo, parag. BD; John of Damascus, parag. H.

[46] Leo, parag. AX; John of Damascus, parag. G.

[47] Leo, parag. AY; John of Damascus, parag. G.

[48] Leo, parag. AX; John of Damascus, parag. G.

[49] Savas, *John of Damascus on Islam*, pp. 43-4. It is quite well attested to that the early Muslims rarely knew any other language than Arabic (Suyuti, *el-Itkan*, Vol. 2, p. 440; Finkel, "Jahiz," notes 35 and 38) and that because of this many Christians and Jews were employed in the early Muslim governments due to their being multilingual (Finkel, "Jahiz," p. 696, below). Nevertheless, Gaudeul ("Leo and 'Umar," *Islamochristiana*, 10, p. 139, note 33) somewhat naively suggests that 'Ali b. Rabban al-Tabari (c. 855 A.D.) could have been the one 'Umar describes as being the "someone who knows your language and ours" (Gaudeul, "Leo and 'Umar," *Islamochristiana*, 10, p. 139, BNM 4944, parag. 27), who allegedly translated "Paraclete" to be equivalent to "Ahmad."

[50] Savas, *John of Damascus on Islam*, p. 6, note 2.

[51] Ibid. pp. 9-10.

GHEVOND'S TEXT OF THE CORRESPONDENCE BETWEEN 'UMAR II AND LEO III
by Arthur Jeffery
Columbia University

DIALOGUE

The UMAYYAD Caliph 'Umar II
and the
BYZANTINE Emperor Leo III
c. 719 A.D.

THERE is a persistent tradition in Eastern Christian Churches, often referred to by Oriental Christians even at the present day, to the effect that early in the 8th century there was an exchange of letters on the question of the respective merits of Christianity and Islam, between the Umayyad Caliph 'Umar II (717-720 A.D.) and the Byzantine Emperor Leo III, the Isaurian (717-741 A. D.), in which the Emperor gloriously refuted the claims of Islam. If this is so, it will represent one of the earliest documents in the Muslim-Christian Controversy known to us. Carl Güterbock rightly states that the beginnings of literary discussions concerning Islam among the Greeks can be traced back to the middle of the 8th century, when Leo III was succeeded by his own son Constantine V (741-775 A.D.),[1] but he begins his account of the Byzantine polemicists with John of Damascus (d. 754 A.D.) and his pupil Theodore Abu Qurra (c. 825 A.D.). A polemical epistle of Leo III to 'Umar II must have been written before 720 A.D., and would thus be earlier than any known Byzantine tractate on this controversy.

We have notices of this correspondence in various sources. The

Byzantine Chronographer Theophanes (d. 818 A.D), writing of the
second year of the Caliphate of 'Umar,[2] the year when there was a
great earthquake in Syria, and when 'Umar was making great efforts to
have the Christians of his realm accept Islam,[3] says - "he also sent a
theological epistle to the Emperor Leo, thinking that he might persuade him also to accept Islam," a statement which is repeated in
much the same words by Cedrenus (c. 1100 A.D.) in his *Historiarum
Compendium.* The Syrian writer Mahbub, Bishop of Manbij (Hiera-
polis), better known under his Westernized name Agapius, writing in
the middle of the 10th century his Arabic World History, the *Kitab
al'Unwan,* not only knows of 'Umar's letter attacking the Christian
religion and calling Leo to become a Muslim, but knows also that the
Emperor replied to it, refuting the Caliph's arguments, proving him the
perversity of his own Muslim beliefs and demonstrating the truth of
Christianity from the Scriptures, the laws of reason and the testimony
of the Qur'an itself.[4] Further, in Armenian literature, besides the
account of Ghevond, with which we shall be concerned presently, and
in which we are presented not only with a précis of the letter of the
Caliph,[5] but also with what purports to be the complete text of Leo's
reply; we have references to the correspondence in three later writers.
Thoma Ardzruni (c. 936 A.D.) in his History,[6] and Kirakos of Gandzac
(d. 1272 A.D.) in his History of Armenia,[7] both tell us that Leo's reply
was so full of sagacity that as to put to shame the Caliph, so that he set
about reforming many abuses among the Muslim people and from that
time on showed a much more benevolent spirit towards the Christians
of his realm. Finally, Vartan (d. 1272 A.D.) in his Universal History,[8]
mentions 'Umar's inquiry as to the seventy-two sects of the Christians
and quotes Leo's reply thereto. All three, however, may be dependent
on Ghevond, whose account, in any case, is the earliest and the fullest.

There is no a priori ground for rejecting the possibility of such an
exchange of letters between the two potentates. No one familiar with
the Arabic accounts of 'Umar's reign would find anything strange in
the story of such a letter to the Byzantine Emperor. 'Umar's zeal for
the propagation of Islam was as noteworthy as that of Leo for propagating a pure and undefiled Christianity. The Muslim accounts of this

Caliph's reign abound in eulogies of his piety and his interest in religion, which he was eager to spread even at the expense of the treasury.
His instructions to his governors in Khurasan to ease the conditions as
to tribute, a move which led to the people of that area flocking to
Islam, are famous,[9] and he apparently tried the same move in Spain
and when it failed, sought to reduce the influence of Spanish Christians
by dividing up their lands. But even more famous is his retort to an
official who objected that these numerous conversions, by reducing the
numbers of the non-Muslim body which supplied the tribute, were
adversely affecting the treasury, that Allah had sent His Prophet as a
missionary and not a tax-collector. That he was given to writing
epistles in the interests of his propaganda for Islam, is also clear. We
find accounts of how he wrote to the Princes of Transoxiana, inviting
them to accept Islam; of how he addressed a rescript to the Kings of
Sindh, to whom he promised all the privileges and immunities of Arabs
if only they would become Muslims; and of how he had great success
with the letters he wrote to urge the Berbers of North Africa to accept
Islam.

That he was actually in correspondence with the Byzantine Empire is
likewise evident, though this was in another connection. In the *Kitab
al-Aghani* we have the text of a letter he sent to the Muslim prisoners
at Qustantiniyya, who had been taken in the wars with the Byzantines,
consoling them in their affliction and assuring them of his care for
their families at home, while Baladhuri, in his account of Latikieh,
which was attacked and destroyed by a Byzantine raid about 718 A.D.
(= 100 A.H.), tells how 'Umar sent to the Greek Emperor (Taghiyah)
asking to be allowed to ransom the Muslim captives taken there. This
was not religious correspondence, but all that we learn from Muslim
sources about 'Umar favors the possibility of such a correspondence.

Nor is it difficult to believe that Leo should write or have written in
his name, a reply to such a letter from the Caliph. His interest in the
promotion of the Christian religion is one of the outstanding features
of his reign. His activities in connection with the iconoclastic controversy need not be more than mentioned, but he was also active in

promoting the baptism of Jews and Montanists, and not always, perhaps, by the most reputable methods. That he too indulged in lengthy
correspondence on points of theological disputation, is clear from his
correspondence with Pope Gregory II in Rome, in one of which letters,
indeed, he claims to be priest as well as Emperor.

Leo's relations with Muslim peoples had begun long before his elevation to the imperial throne. The Germanica of his childhood days is
the Arabic Mar'ash, in the far north of Syria at the border of Asia
Minor, and this Mar'ash was taken as early as 637 A.D. by Khalid ibn
al-Walid, who destroyed it. Then it was used as a base of operations
against the Byzantine Empire and was built up by the first Umayyad
Caliph, Mu'awiya (661-680 A.D.), who settled it with troops. Under
Yazid, the son and successor of Mu'awiya, the Greeks succeeded in
driving the Muslims out of it entirely, and from then on it was the
scene of almost constant battles between Muslims and Greeks and was
so badly damaged in the fighting that about 694 A.D. al-'Abbas, a
grandson of 'Abd al-Malik, had to rebuild and fortify it, moving into it
a great body of troops and building a notable mosque in it. In the days
of Leo's youth it probably contained more Muslims than it did Greeks,
so that he must have been in constant contact with Muslims at Mar-
'ash, while most of his active life as a soldier, whether as Spatharius on
the Lazian frontier, or as military commander of the Anatolic Theme
under Anastasius II, was spent in combating Muslim armies, long
before his brilliant relief of Amorium in 716 A.D., his relief of Constantinople from the Muslim fleet in 717 A.D. and his final defeat of
Maslama's armies in the winter of 717-718 A.D., gave him the name of
the champion of Christianity against the Muslims. It would not even
be surprising if Leo knew of Islam from direct acquaintance with
Arabic sources, as he claims in the text of his letter in Ghevond, for
though he is still called "the Isaurian," following our Greek text of
Theophanes, there is a good case for regarding him as a Syrian,[10] and
one Arabic source informs us that as a Christian citizen of Mar'ash he
could speak fluently and correctly both Greek and Arabic.[11] The Leo
who so obviously enjoyed his controversy with Pope Gregory and with
John of Damascus, we may well imagine would enjoy equally well a
similar controversy with 'Umar, the Caliph of the Muslims.

But though the possibility of such an exchange of controversial letters between Leo and 'Umar may be granted, whether it really did take place is another question. No Muslim source available to us makes any mention of it,[12] and of the Christian sources, the only one which supplies any detailed information about it is the Armenian history of Ghevond, which brings it in incidentally in the midst of an account of the wars between the Arabs and the Armenians.[13] In Migne's *Patrologia Graeca*, 107, cols. 315-324, we find the Latin version of an *Epistola Leonis Imperatoris Augusti cognomento Philosophi ad Omarum Saracenorum regem de fidei christianae veritate et mysteriis et de variis Saracenorum haeresibus et blasphemiis*, printed among the works of Leo VI (886-912 A.D.) the Philosopher. A comparison of this with the text of Ghevond makes it clear that the Latin, though much briefer and somewhat differently arranged, is really the same material meeting the same Muslim objections with essentially the same arguments. As there was no Saracen ruler 'Umar contemporary with Leo VI to whom that Emperor could have addressed such an epistle, the probability is that this is really a Latin summary of the letter elsewhere ascribed to Leo III, and wrongly attributed to his more theologically minded namesake.[14]

But if the Latin form is an abbreviated and somewhat corrupted text, the Armenian form in Ghevond, as we have it,[15] errs in the other direction, for it occasionally expands the argument with references to Islamic matters that can hardly be dated as early as the reigns of 'Umar and Leo III. A comparison of the two texts shows that it is not possible to regard the Latin as an abbreviation of the Armenian, nor to look on the Armenian as an amplification of the Latin, so that we are forced to assume a Greek document[16] purporting to give some account of the letter of 'Umar to Leo, and the text of Leo's reply, which in a considerably reduced form survived in a Latin translation in the West, and in a somewhat expanded form was preserved in an Armenian translation in the East. It may be noted that the Armenian translation, whether we accept an earlier or a later date for Ghevond, rules out the attribution of the letter to Leo VI.

The date of Ghevond (Leontius) is somewhat difficult to determine. Armenian writers generally include him among the historians of the 8th century, but Neumann in his *Versuch einer Geschichte der armenischen Literatur* (Leipzig, 1836), p. 129, lists him among the writers of the 10th century, and this later date, one must admit, would suit better the information he has about Islam. He is definitely quoted by Mekhitar of Airivank in the 12th century and is referred to by Stephen Asoghik, a 10th century writer, so that his work must be earlier than either of them. Chahnazarian, who first edited the text of Ghevond (Paris, 1854), makes a defence of the 8th century date by pointing to the facts 1) that his chronicle of the relations between Arabs and Armenians runs from 632 to 788 A.D., and one would imagine that he had brought it up to his own time; 2) that in telling of the battle of Arjish[17] between the Arabs and Armenians in 770-771 A.D., he speaks as though his account were drawn from eyewitnesses of that battle, for he says, "the enemies themselves have assured me of the fact saying," and again, "they have also told me." In the colophon of the St. Petersburg text we read that Ghevond's account was made at the command of the lord Shapuh Bagratuni. If this Shapuh is the brother of Ashot Msaker, as Chahnazarian and Petermann assume, then as he died in 824 A.D.,[18] Ghevond must have flourished in the 8th century.[19] But there was another Shapuh among the Bagratids, a son of Sembat the Confessor (d. 855 A.D.) and a brother of that other Ashot (d. 890) who was king of Armenia, so that if Ghevond's account was written for him it would give us a date in the latter half of the 9th or even the beginning of the 10th century, which would suit much better some of the Islamic references in the text, e.g., its mention on p. 61, among the Muslim sects, of the Jahiziyya, a sect which only developed after the death of al-Jahiz in 869 A. D., and so could hardly have been known to a writer in the 8th century.[20]

In the St. Petersburg edition of 1887, the letter of 'Umar and the reply of Leo are given in chapters 13 and 14 of Ghevond's History, pp. 43-99.

Ghevond's Text of the Letter of 'Umar to Leo has been deleted.

Ghevond's Text of the Letter of Leo III to 'Umar II:

(A) Flavian Leo, Emperor, the Servant of Jesus Christ and the sovereign of those who know Him, to 'Umar, Chief of the Saracens.

(B) What exact reply can I make to all the arguments you advance against me? It is God Himself who commands us to instruct our adversaries with kindliness, to see whether He will not grant them time to repent. Moreover, our ordinary laws by no means impose on us the duty of smiting with hard words, as with stones, those who manifest a desire to learn the marvelous mystery of the truth. But as your letter, in its opening, did not reveal even the least appearance of truthfulness, it is laid on us that we call not just that which is not. In your letter you say that we have discussed with you more than once the divine mysteries of our Christian religion,[21] but that you have not succeeded in being able to study its doctrines, which you refer to as imaginary.[22] These two statements, however, are not accurate. As a matter of fact, nothing would induce us to discuss with you our doctrines, since our Lord and Master Himself has bidden us refrain from exposing our unique and divine doctrine before heretics, for fear it be turned into ridicule, and least of all before those to whom the predictions of the prophets and the testimony of the apostles are as something strange. This is the rule we observe towards others. It is true that we have several times written to you, and we shall write to you again does necessity demand, but it has always been about mundane affairs,[23] never about affairs divine. Still, Holy Writ bids us reply to those who question us[24] and maintain silence before those who do not. With regard to you, however, we are not now for the first time learning about the substance of your beliefs, for we have been commanded of God to examine all, and hold fast to that which is good. So we possess historical documents composed by our blessed prelates who were living at the same epoch as your legislator Muhammad, and these writings[25] make it unnecessary for us to importune you on the subject of your religion. However, that you may not think we are ashamed to profess a religion so marvelous as ours, hearken, if it please you, and in hearkening to me, you will, as Isaiah says, eat of the good produce of the earth.[26]

(C) It is truly difficult to refute even the most palpable lie, when the adversary dreams only of obstinately persisting in it. Let me explain it to you this way. Suppose two men are standing near a fire. One of them recognizes that this element really is fire, but the other, driven by a spirit of contradiction, says that it is a spring of water, then the bad faith of the other is evident. Just so you advance that our Lord said in the Gospel - "We came into this world naked, and we shall quit it in the same state,"[27] whereas we do not find in the Gospels any such statement coming from our Lord,[28] though He does counsel us often to meditate upon death. On the contrary it was the just Job, who said, after having been tempted by Satan, "Naked was I born, and so shall I die. The Lord hath given, and the Lord hath taken away; blessed be the name of the Lord." (Job 1:21). It is thus that you are wont to elude and mutilate the evidence of the Holy Scriptures that you have not read, and will not read.[29] You love to make traffic of the things of God and of the faith, by catching hold in the Scriptures of some word which appears favorable to your opinions and employing it in your defence. Puffed up as you are in your despotism, nevertheless, hearken to my replies.

(D) You say that we have found in the Psalms of David and in the books of the prophets testimonies regarding our Lord,[30] but today is not the first time we have searched for and found such words of the Holy Spirit, who spoke them by the mouths of the prophets.[31] It is by such words as these, aided by the grace of God, that Christianity has been preached since its origin, has been founded, propagated and believed. It is by these words, I say, that it will still prosper, by the power of God the Creator. You write that we have contented ourselves with these words and that we have had faith in them, without paying due attention to what Jesus has said about His own person, regarding that as something doubtful and uncertain. It would be a desirable thing for you, following your own words, to have had faith in the infallible and positive statements of the Gospel, rather than any other. Now, although there exists no contradiction between the Old and New Testaments, seeing that God, the unique source of mercy, cannot at the same time produce both good and bad, truth and lies, yet God, to make easier to the Jewish people the acceptance of the incarnate Word, placed in the mouths of the prophets declarations, parables and clear predictions, so that His people should be instructed in advance and prepared to receive Jesus Christ, and not oppose Him as it has done. In the very same way, the Savior, in the Gospel, has borne testimony to His person, and having become incarnate, cited in the most express fashion all the testimonies which the prophets had given of Him before His incarnation.

(E) I propose, with the aid and by the grace of God, to show you all this,[32] point by point, in my present letter, attributing the most glorious of these predictions to His superhuman nature and the more humble ones to His human nature.

(F) You write that Jesus merits our confidence because, being near to God, He knew Him better than all those who have written about Him, and whose writings, for the rest, have been falsified by people whom we know not. I reply, that the truth cannot deny what is and at the same time affirm that which is not, whereas the lie is capable of anything, being able to deny not only things visible, but even the Creator Himself, by professing that there is no God. Consequently it is not astonishing that the lie should deny the existence of the Holy Scriptures or accuse them of defects.[33] Jesus is, indeed, worthy of confidence; not, however, as mere man and deprived of the Word of God, but as a perfect man and perfect God. Just as His commands, set forth by the mouths of the prophets, merit our entire confidence, not because they were pronounced by men, but because it was the Word of God which dictated them before His incarnation. And as it was that Word itself which inspired them in the Old and in the New Testaments, it is for that reason that no contradiction is found in them. As for what you affirm about falsification of these writings, if it is the head of your religion who taught you this, he has forgotten himself[34] and if it is some other, he only lied worse.

(G) Hearken then and reflect. The head of your religion admits that one must accept nothing without witnesses,[35] and he adds that the (Mosaic) Code held the same, and indeed, the Code does ordain that every testimony be confirmed by two or three witnesses. We know that it was Abraham who earlier received the promise of the mission of Christ, and it was to him that God said - "All nations of the earth shall be blessed in thy seed" (Gen. 22:18). Isaac, nourished on the same hope, blessed Jacob, and then he, with the same end in view, blessed Judah, saying - "The sceptre shall not depart from Judah, nor a legislator from between his feet, until Shiloh come, to whom will belong the assembly of the peoples" (Gen. 49:10). We know too, that Moses, to the same end, ordained and designated Joshua (Deut. 31:7,14,23). Recall also David, Solomon, the twelve prophets, with Samuel, Elijah, Elisha, Isaiah, Jeremiah, Daniel, Ezekiel, Job the just, John the Baptist, son of Zachariah. Add to these the twelve apostles and the seventy disciples of the Lord, in all a hundred and eleven persons in the Old and New Testaments. You despise then so many holy persons cherished of God, who have predicted the coming of Christ, people to whom Muhammad himself bore this testimony that they were holy servants of God,[36] that Muhammad may appear more worthy of faith than God speaking through them and than the Word of God manifest in the flesh. Well, I put to you this question, and I beg you to reply. Is the testimony borne by a hundred and eleven servants of God, speaking unanimously of the same Savior more worthy of faith than that of a dissident or heterodox, who while he lies he thinks that he is telling the truth? Remember that Muhammad in speaking of them, represents them as servants and as the favored minsters of God and compels you to regard them as such, whereas what God has said through them he himself rejects and prevents others from admitting.

(H) You ask how we can depend on the book of the Jews,[37] the Old Testament, as you maintain that we believe that this book was several times written and lost, until after long years some individuals undertook to recompense it after their own ideas. Thus, according to the opinion that you attribute to us, such work would have continued being done from generation to generation, while those who did it were exposed to all sorts of error and to the seductions of Satan, and those who by their hateful spirit resemble him. In reply I am much astonished, not only at your incredulity, but also at the manner in which, without a blush, you expose ideas which render you ridiculous, while you pretend to seduce us by our own words.

(I) Thus you commence your letter by citing one of our opinions, pretending to draw from it all that follows, as though that had emanated from us [presumably the misquote of Job 1:21 - ed.]. But if you believe in our opinions you must believe in them all together, because no one can base himself on a lie, and it is a lie to adopt part of a testimony and reject the other part. However, as you are not instructed, hearken and learn.

(J) When we say it was the Hebrews who composed the Old Testament, we do not mean to say they have produced it out of their imaginations, but that they composed it in the sanctuary, on the faith of authentic documents from holy and pious men of their nation and drawing from the works of the prophets themselves. The number of beings created by God during the first six days amounts to 22,[38] and so the Old Testament contains 22 books received by the Jews as well as by us. Their alphabet is composed of 22 letters, of which five may be doubled and that not without an important signification. That is by inspiration of God through the His prophets, that all the truths might be attested, the ones by the others. Of these 22 books, five are known under the name of the Law of the Code, and called by the Hebrews *Torah*, by the Syrians *Oratha* and by us *Nomos*. They contain teaching about the knowledge of God, and account of the creation of the world by Him, the prohibition of the worship of pagan divinities, the covenant concluded with Abraham, the goal of which was Christ and the laws concerning civil procedure and sacrifice, laws which put them far from the customs of that paganism for which they showed so much attachment. Then the books of Joshua, Judges, Ruth, the four of Kings, the Paralipomena, containing the marvelous works of God wrought from time to time and the exact genealogy of the just, descending regularly to Christ. They recount also the history of Israel, indicating what kings among them were agreeable to God, and those who were not; of how the Jewish people, because of their sins, were separated into two kingdoms, that of Judah and that of Israel; and finally of their captivity. Then the Psalms of David; the books of Solomon, called by the Jews Koheleth and Shir-ashirim, but by us Parimon and Samatan;[39] those of the twelve prophets, and of Isaiah, of Jeremiah, of Daniel and of Ezekiel, containing all the prophecies as to the coming of Christ. So if anyone among the Jews had wished to falsify herein, the number of books would have had to suffer some change, for the sacrilegious fellows would have had to suppress some or reduce them to one, two, or at the most three books and retrench the rest, because thus it would have been much easier to get rid of them.

(K) I suppose too, that you are not ignorant of the enmity which exists between us Christians and the Jews.[40] The sole cause of this is our belief in the divinity of Christ Jesus, whom we regard as the Christ, the Son of God, announced by the Prophets, while the Jews, while admitting the future coming of the Christ, have set themselves against the intimations of the prophets and have been unwilling to recognize the Son of God in the person of Christ. So how can one admit that those who might have falsified the books would have left there intact, or would themselves have added so many indubitable testimonies, which, no matter how much violence is done to them, cannot be applied to any other than the incarnate Son of God?

(L) Hear yet my third response. The captivity of the Jews took place long before the coming of Christ in the flesh, so how could it be that then, that is to say at the period of Christ, the temple, the Testament, the priesthood continued to exist, as the Gospel affirms, according to which the Lord Himself submitted to circumcision and the other ceremonies, precisely as you yourself confirm, and all that without doubt, with the object of proving that it was He Himself who had, by the mouths of the prophets, ordained these ceremonies, and that far from being disagreeable to Him they were very agreeable and served as solid testimonies to His purpose and mission? Did the Jews possess any other Testament than the books of the prophets, which, having traversed the double captivity of Judah and Israel, continued to exist up to the times of our Savior, and from which, in preaching to the hardened Jews, He drew the major part of His testimonies, as we see from His Gospel? The Jewish people was led into captivity by Nebuchadnezzar, yet the divine protection did not abandon them and did not permit them to be dispersed as we see in our own days. God established them entire in the land which He had decreed Not only did this people carry it with the Testament, but it was even accompanied by some of the prophets. Thus Ezekiel says that he found himself on the banks of the river Kebar in the midst of the captives. Also the blessed Ananians were cast into the fiery furnace in Babylon. Moreover the eminent Daniel commenced his prophetic career at Babylon, for it was there that he was cast into the lions' den. There also it was that the events of the history of Esther took place. To convince you that the captives took with them the Testament, I invite your attention to what the Holy Spirit says through the prophet in the Psalms relative to this enslavement of the Jews. This enslavement had not yet taken place, yet he announces it in an unmistakable manner in Ps. 136,[41] saying - "We were seated by the rivers of Babylon, and there we wept; we remembered Zion. We hung up our harps on the willows, when those who had taken us prisoners demanded of us that we sing songs and rejoice them by the sound of our harps that we had hung up, saying to us - 'Sing some of the songs of Zion.' "

(M) You pretend that the Testament was composed by human genius, and I know that you attack the second edition that Esdras composed.[42] Yet this man possessed the grace of the Holy Spirit, and all that he composed has the cachet of infallibility, as is proved by the fact that when all the people delivered from captivity came back to Jerusalem bringing with them the Testament, there was seen the marvelous work of God, for when it was compared with the edition of Esdras, this was found completely in conformity with the former.

(N) You have said that the writers of the Testament, in their quality as men, were exposed to faults of memory.[43] I admit that every man is always feeble in every respect; is imperfect and forgetful. Yet God, who is eternal, whose power is great and whose wisdom is without limitation, spoke to men by the prophets, His ministers. He who is exempt from forgetfulness and conjectures, He it is who speaks in the prophets without having need of human wisdom. But you, do you not regard your Muhammad as a man? Yet relying on the simple word of Muhammad, you disdain the testimonies of so many saints of God. You say further that Satan finds himself near the servants of God. As for God Himself, he does not approach Him, and reasonable people well know that he much rather approaches a person who is deprived completely of the testimony of the Holy Scriptures, than such holy and recommendable people. As concerns the Holy Scriptures this will suffice.

(O) In saying that there cannot be found in the Mosaic Code any reference to Paradise or Hell or Resurrection of Judgment,[44] you show your unwillingness to comprehend the fact that God has instructed man in the measure that his intelligence has developed.[45] God did not speak with a man a single time only, nor by a single prophet, as you assume in supposing that God would institute through the ministry of Moses all that was necessary. Not at all. What He commanded Noah He did not demand of those who preceded him. Not all that He commanded Abraham did He command Noah, nor all that He commanded Moses did He command Abraham. Not all that He commanded Joshua did He command Moses, and what He commanded Samuel and David and all the other prophets in each epoch, He did not command Joshua. And so on, since, as we have already said, God wished to reveal Himself little by little to men, who would have been unable to perceive and appropriate at one single step such marvelous knowledge. So, if God ought to have ordained all by a single prophet, why should He send others? And if He was going to let everything get falsified, as you pretend, why then ordain it? However, the revelation made by God to Moses was only a sort of preparation for the instruction of men, not a complete instruction. Nevertheless, God does therein make mention of the Resurrection, of Judgment and of Hell. As regards the Resurrection, God says - "Behold, now, it is I Myself, and there is no God beside Me. I make to die and I make to live, I wound and I cure, and no one is able to deliver out of My hand" (Deut. 32:39). As regards Judgment He says - "I sharpen the blade of

My sword, and if My hand seizes the judgment, I will make vengeance turn on My adversaries and will render it to those who hate Me" (Deut. 32:41). As regards Hell He says - "The flaming fire of My wrath will burn them unto the lowest hells" (Jer. 17:4). These doctrines received further development and illumination in what came later by other prophets.

(P) We recognize Matthew, Mark, Luke and John as authors of the Gospel, and yet I know that this truth, recognized by us Christians, wounds you, so that you seek to find accomplices for your lie.[46] In brief, you admit that we say that it was written by God and brought down from the heavens, as you pretend for your Furqan, although we know that it was 'Umar, Abu Turab and Salman the Persian who composed that, even though the rumor has got around among you that God sent it down from the heavens.[47] Recognize, then, in that the frankness of the Christians, as we profess it, how can you dare invent calumnies, pretending that since that time there have been introduced into the Gospel alterations,[48] whether by us or others? What could have hindered us from removing from it the names of the Evangelists, or from adding that it was God alone who sent it down from the skies? Further, give attention to this fact, that God has not willed to instruct the human race either by His own appearing or by the mission of the angels.[49] He has chosen the way of sending them prophets, and it is for this reason that the Lord, having finished all those things that He had decided on beforehand and having fore-announced His incarnation by way of His prophets, yet knowing that men still had need of assistance from God, promised to send the Holy Spirit under the name of Paraclete, (Consoler), to console them in the distress and sorrow they felt at the departure of their Lord and Master. I reiterate, that it was for this cause alone that Jesus called the Holy Spirit the Paraclete, since He sought to console His disciples for His departure and to recall to them all that He had said, all that He had done before their eyes, all that they were called to propagate throughout the world by their witness. Paraclete thus signifies "consoler," while Muhammad means "to give thanks," or "to render grace," a meaning which has no connection whatever with the word Paraclete.[50]

71

(Q) This blasphemy, in fact, is unpardonable, as the Lord Himself says in the Gospel - "Blasphemy against the Holy Spirit will never be forgiven" (Matt. 12:31). Can there be a blasphemy more terrible than that which consists in replacing the Holy Spirit by a person completely ignorant of the Holy Scriptures? To comprehend that the Lord, in this passage, was speaking of the Holy Spirit, give heed to what He says - "The Comforter, the Holy Spirit, whom the Father will send in My name, will teach you all things and will recall to your remembrance all the things that I have told you" (John 16:26). A little further on He adds - "whom the Father will send in My name," whereas your Muhammad did not come in the name of our Lord, but in his own name. Jesus promised the Holy Spirit to the saints, that is, to His own disciples, not to men in general, and you well know that His disciples did not live to see your Muhammad. I have already said that the Creator spread abroad the light of His knowledge by His prophets successively, little by little, and yet, even by them all, He did not achieve all the justice that was to come. By the ministry of the prophet Daniel God has pointed us to three periods whereby the world shall arrive at a really satisfactory knowledge of God. First it comes out of the shadows of idolatry, and it arrives at a certain degree of knowledge by the Law. From that it passes to the clearer light of the Gospel of Christ, and finally, from the Gospel to the perpetual light of the world to come. None of the prophets has announced to the world the fourth period, whether for doctrine or for the promises. On the contrary we are ofttimes warned by our Savior not to admit any other prophet nor any apostle after the death of His disciples.[51]

(R) You pretend, moreover, that after the death of the disciples of the Lord, we became divided into seventy-two sects.[52] This is not true, so do not think to console yourself by this lie. Let me explain this to you. According to your own people, it is a hundred years,[53] more or less, since your religion appeared in the midst of a single nation speaking a single language. Yet this religion, so young, and professed by a single nation, already presents numerous schisms, a few of which we shall mention here as having come to our notice. Look then at the Kouzi, the Sabari, the Tourapi, the Kentri, the Mourji, the Basli. Further the Jahdi, who deny both the existence of God and the Resurrection, along

with your pretended Prophet and the Hariuri. One group of these
sectaries is peaceable enough, but the others are so stirred up against
you that they consider you both as infidels and enemies, considering
the assassination of your persons preferable to any other justice and
regarding death at your hands as the foremost of meritorious works.
Such acts take place habitually amongst you. As for yourself, have you
no thought that by exterminating those who differ a little from your
opinions, you commit a crime against God?[54] If such acts take place
among you, who form one single people speaking a single language and
having at your head a single person, who is at the same time chief,
sovereign, pontiff and hangman, would it be astonishing that the
Christian faith, were it the invention of some human wisdom, should
become worse than yours? Yet it is now eight hundred years since
Jesus Christ appeared, and His Gospel has been spread from one end
of the earth to the other, amongst all peoples and all languages, from
the civilized countries of Greece and Rome to the furthest countries of
the barbarians, and if there is found some divergence among Christians
it is because of the differences of language. I have said divergence,
because there has never been among us that bitter hostility such as one
sees deeply rooted among you. It would appear that under this number seventy-two you must include all the voluptuous, impure, filthy,
impious people who conduct themselves like pagans, and among whose
number you count us. But these are people who disguise under the
name of Christ their own abominations, giving themselves out to be
Christians, but whose faith is only a blasphemy and their baptism only
a soiling. When such manifest their intention of abandoning their
detestable life, the Holy Church receives them into her bosom only
after administering baptism to them, just as to pagans. Indeed, God
has long since caused them to disappear completely, so that one no
longer sees them.

(S) As for us, we are accustomed to designate the Christians as
seventy races, which have all received holy baptism, the gage of eternal
life. If among them some questions of minor importance cause agita-
tion, especially among some of them who live far from us and speak a
tongue other than ours; above all those who have fallen under your
tyranny, yet they are none the less Christians and have no need to be

73

baptized anew. In any case it is nothing strange that Christians, who live as foreigners afar off, have not been able to acquire a closer acquaintance with the traditions of the truth, such as they ought to have. Yet the Scriptures are the same, conserved intact in each language; and the Gospel is the same, without any variation. I leave on one side then, the various languages in which the wondrous and salutary Christian religion has been spread abroad, after indicating a few of them - (1) our Greek language; (2) the Latin; (3) the Hebrew; (4) the Chaldean; (5) that of the Syrians; (6) that of the Ethiopians; (7) that of the Indians; (8) that of the Saracens, which is yours; (9) that of the Persians; (10) that of the Armenians; (11) that of the Georgians; and (12) that of the Albanians.[55] Suppose following what you say, that one or two of these peoples had introduced changes in the books in their respective languages, how can one suppose that these changes are to be found also in the books of other peoples, dwelling as you well know, far from us, and differing from us both in their language and their peculiar habits. As for you, you have already given us examples of such falsifications, and one knows, among others, of a certain Hajjaj, named by you as Governor of Persia, who had men gather up your ancient books, which he replaced by others composed by himself, according to his taste, and which he propagated everywhere in your nation, because it was easier by far to undertake such a task among a people speaking a single language. From this destruction, nevertheless, there escaped a few works of Abu Turab, for Hajjaj could not make them disappear completely.[56]

(T) Such a thing as this would have been impossible among us. First of all because God has forbidden us to dream of such an audacious enterprise. Secondly, because even if someone, in spite of God's prohibition, had dared so to act, it would have been impossible for him to have gathered up all the books spread abroad in so many different languages, procured and brought together skilled interpreters and have had these interpreters examine the books so as to add and subtract according to his idea. For the rest, as you are well aware, since you mention the fact, there exists among the Christians a sort of enmity regarding questions of little import, it is true, but sufficient to be capable of inspiring each nation with the notion of introducing changes into the books in its language according to its opinions. Yet no such thing has taken place, neither amongst those who find themselves far from us, nor among those who live in lands near us. Cease then to multiply such inanities, lest you nullify the little truth there is in what you advance.

(U) One thing about you indeed, astonishes me more than a little. It is that after you have shown such disdain with regard to the Gospel of our Savior, and the books of the prophets, regarding them as falsified and as recomposed by men according to their ideas, you nevertheless, in order to support your own inconstant opinions, cease not to draw citations therefrom, which you twist and modify at will. Whenever, for example, you come across the word *Father*, you replace it by *Lord*, or sometimes by *God*.[57] If you are making your researches in the interests of truth, you ought to respect the Scriptures before citing them. Or, if you disdain them as corrupt, you ought not to use them for citation, and if you do cite them, it is an obligation on you to cite them such as you find them in the books, without modifying them in the way you do.

(V) It is very difficult, as a matter of fact, for the servants of God who are under your command, to have any relations with you. Pagans, when they hear the names of the prophets or apostles, begin to laugh, but you, though you do not despise their names, turn their words into ridicule. Let us, however, cite to you the following passages addressed to Moses - "I am the Eternal... the God of Abraham, the God of Isaac, the God of Jacob" (Ex. 3: 14); "Let us make man in our own image, according to our resemblance" (Gen. 1:26); "Come then, let us go down and confound their language" (Gen. 11:7). Again - "The Eternal rained down from heaven, on Sodom and Gomorrah, sulphur and fire from the Eternal" (Gen. 19:24). These I quote from the books of Moses which you have not read, neither you nor your legislator. What! do you believe that it is to angels, who dare not look upon Him, that the Eternal is addressing the above-mentioned words? We do not permit ourselves to think, as you so often do, that such passages as these from Holy Scripture are empty and futile. To whom then could

75

it be that God is addressing these words, if it is not to His Word, the image of His substance, the ray of the light of His glory, and to the Holy Spirit who sanctifies and enlightens all? And yet we are accused by you of recognizing three gods.[58]

(W) Is the sun different from the rays which derive from it? Yes, without doubt. Yet take away these rays and there is no more sun. And if anyone says that the rays generate directly from the sun, and from it alone, without the concourse of any other power, in a way different from the generation of humans, which proceeds from the coupling of the sexes, that, in a word, it draws them out from its own proper substance, such an one so saying would not be deceiving himself. In effect, though the sun is other than its rays, their union does not make two suns.[59] Is not that your opinion too? So, if this light, visible and created, which the night obscures, which the height of buildings intercepts, seems to us to proceed from a birth so pure, what will be the purity of a divine birth which proceeds from a light whose eternal splendor nothing dims?[60]

(X) I was driven to make use of this example in order to convince you, because it seemed to me that you give little heed to what God orders us in the Holy Scriptures, as you prefer your own will to them. From them you take what pleases you, fearing not to modify them at your caprice, changing what is not in accordance with your views. Maledictions upon any man who admits two or three divinities emanating from different origins. For our part, we know only one God, the Creator of heaven and earth, a wise God, whose Word, holy and full of reason, created all things and governs them. And this word is not as ours, which, as long as it has not proceeded from our mouths, remains incomprehensible to others, and as soon as it has gone out, decomposes and dissipates. This Word is what we recognize as the Word of God, the ray of light that nothing dims, a ray which is not simply like those of the sun, but is of a quality so eminent as to disconcert the intelligence and evade explanation. It is this Word which Scripture calls the Son of God, engendered by Him not under the dominance of passion such as is of earth, but as the rays are born from the sun, as light goes out from fire, as the word emanates from the reason. In

sum, this is all that human language can say with regard to the
Word—God, emanated from God and as to their consubstantiality.

(Y) Now among creatures there is no being more precious before
God than man, as you yourself avow in mentioning that the angels
were commanded by God to bow the knee to Adam, a fact unknown to
the Holy Scriptures.[61] Adam was a man, and in rendering him such
homage, you have well evidenced your pride, so let everyone know
what place they ought to occupy, who are unwilling to render homage
to the Man, according to your own expression.[62] It is evident that
Adam was created in the image of God, but do you believe that it was
his material body full of infirmities which God created in His image?
Not at all. On the contrary, it was his soul, reason and word which
God created in the image of His Spirit and His Word. Man, being
created in this manner and receiving honor and independence, became
the image of God.[63] But later, deceived by the Tempter, he was
robbed of the honor for which he was destined by His Creator and
being now a despised creature because of his blameworthy forgetfulness, he abandoned himself to a life of most blameworthy debauchery
and luxury. Voluptuousness became his unique occupation, and his
whole life came to present nothing but a tissue of hatred, rapine,
assassination and avidity, and he ended up by plunging into idolatry,
which is the summation of all iniquities, and into such voluptuousness
as I am ashamed to speak of here. In this aberration he set about
worshipping not only fantastic visible entities, but even his vices,
adultery, sodomy, to which he rendered divine honors. Thus did the
Temper succeed in reducing humanity to such degradation, and he
rejoices in triumph at seeing himself adored under the form of the
idols of paganism and in exciting voluptuous man more and more to
this perverse cult by auguries and deceitful talismans.

(Z) God, however, seeing His image so degraded by this adoration
rendered the Tempter and by the abasement into which man had fallen
in doing that which was pleasing to Satan, was touched by compassion
for man's misery, for He alone is the true benefactor and friend of
humanity. And, as there existed no other road of salvation for man
than that of coming to know his Creator and to flee from his enemy,

He manifested Himself to man to this end, making Himself known at first through intermediaries, the prophets, His ministers, as by a light which shines little by little in the midst of the darkness of paganism. So great was the blindness of man's spirit that he could not contemplate fully all at once the whole of the knowledge of God, for which reason God commenced, as I have noted above, by illuminating it little by little, until the right time arrived. Thus God enlightened man by as much as He found good for him, but promised him in advance, through the prophets, the coming of His incarnate Word, who should clothe Himself with our flesh and our soul and all that is proper to man, save sin.[64]

(AA) As no one among men has been able to descend lower than He in humiliation, we attribute to Him all that has been said as to His lowering Himself; and, on the other hand, all that has been said as to His glory, we attribute to Him as to one who is veritably God. You will probably recall what we reported above from the books of Moses concerning the equality of the Word of God with God Himself. Hearken now, to what Moses further says relative to the future appearance of the Word clothed in a human form. "The Eternal, thy God, will raise up a prophet from among thy brethren, to whom you will hearken as to Me... and he will tell them all that I have commanded. And it will so be that whoever will not hearken to My words which he will speak in My name, I shall demand it of him" (Deut. 18:15,18,19). Everyone knows it is true that since the death of Moses, instead of but one single prophet, there have appeared a great number. Nevertheless the passage before us can apply but to one, namely, he who is the most powerful of them, and who announces things difficult to believe. Now I shall cite you a multitude of passages from the prophets indicating the coming of Christ, and I prefer to set before you first those which speak of Him in terms of humiliation, in the conviction that you will welcome such with much pleasure. In this manner, I hope that I shall succeed in raising you, if God will, as by a stairway, from the profound depths of this earth to places most elevated, even to the presence of God.

(AB) David, speaking of Him, says, as being in His place: "But I, I

am a worm, and not a man, opprobrious to men and despised of the
people. All those who see me make mock of me; they sniff at me, they
shake their heads. He abandons himself, they say, to the Eternal; let
Him deliver him and take him away since He takes pleasure in him"
(Ps. 22:6-8). This prophecy was not accomplished in David, but in the
person of the Lord, when He was hanging on the cross. The same
David speaks of Christ in eminent terms; "The Eternal has said to me;
Thou art My son, This day have I begotten thee" (Ps. 2:7). To indicate
the complete conversion of all the pagans to the Christian faith, the
same prophet adds: "The Eternal hath said to my Lord; Sit thou at My
right hand till I have made thy enemies the footstool for thy foot...
The people will be a people of free volition, in the day when thou
assemblest thy army with holy pomp: the dew of thy youth will be
produced for thee from the breast of the morning" (Ps. 110:1,2). The
same prophet expresses himself thus on the unity of the divine nature
(the holy Trinity seated in the heavens): "The earth is full of the
gratuity of the Eternal, and all their host by the breath of His mouth"
(Ps. 32:5,6).

(AC) Jeremiah expresses himself thus: "The Lord sent me and His
Spirit" (Isa. 48:16). He also says concerning the incarnation of the
Word of God: "He is our God, and He has found all the paths of
wisdom and has given it to Jacob His servant and to Israel His favorite;
then He appeared in the world and walked with men" (Baruch 3:35-
37). In this passage the prophet indicates two kinds of light; the first is
that of His extreme abasement, whereby He illuminated the entire
universe by propagating therein the rays of the knowledge of God; and
the second is that of the general resurrection that He announced to the
Hebrew people, exhorting it to remain faithful to the first rising of that
light and not to revolt against it (as really took place), for fear lest
strangers, that is to say pagans, should enter into possession of their
glory. He then says to them: "Return, O Jacob, and hold on to him
during the birth of his first light, and give not thy glory or interest to
another" (Baruch 4:2,3). I call your attention to this passage, for in it
the prophet announces not only the future incarnation of the Word of
God, but also predicts there in the clearest manner the future revolt of
the carnal people of Israel.

(AD) This prophecy does not prevent us from receiving yet another, made, in spite of himself, by a stranger and mentioned by Moses: "How beautiful are thy tabernacles, O Jacob, and thy pavilions, O Israel" (Num. 24:5), and a little further on he adds, "water will distill from its waters, and his seed will be among the grand waters, and its king will be elevated above Agag, and its kingdom very highly elevated" (v.7); and again, "I see him, but not now; I regard him, but not from near. A star will be born of Jacob, and a sceptre will be raised up in Israel; he will transpierce the chiefs of Moab and destroy all the children of Seth" (v.17). This prophecy speaks of Him as a man, yet you see well how in precise fashion it indicates the future domination He will exercise over the pagan; that is to say, all the peoples must believe in Him, as you see for yourself. Under the name of the chiefs of Moab, one may understand Satan and all his demons, who maintain the mendacious cult of idolatry among the peoples, finally beaten and superseded by Christ, since the polytheism of the Moabites and those people subject to their dominion was more detestable than that of all the other peoples, since they adored, among other things, the genitals of man and woman, instruments of the most detestable voluptuousness.[65] As for what he says about "he will be elevated above Agag," it is necessary to recall that, whatever may be the extent of Agag and his force, his power is but temporary, while that of Christ will be eternal.

(AE) That the empire of Christ really is such you will see if you give attention to the words of the Holy Spirit on this matter, when He says through David: "O God, give Thy judgments to the king, and Thy justice to the king's son" (Ps. 72:1). That shows that Christ was, by His divinity, Son of God the celestial King, and by His human character as son of David, terrestrial king, as we have often told you. A little further on the prophet adds - "They will fear Thee as long as the sun and moon endure throughout all ages... indeed, He will dominate from one sea to the other and from the river to the ends of the earth.... All kings also will prostrate themselves before Him, all nations will serve Him.... Prayers will be made continually for Him, and each day He will be blessed.... His renown will endure forever, His renown will go from father to son, as long as the sun shall endure; and people will be blessed in Him; all nations shall proclaim Him blessed" (Ps. 72:5,8,11,

15,17). Can one, after having heard expressions so sublime, attribute them without trembling to an ordinary man, a descendant of David, and not to Him who, in His human nature is son of David, but in His divine nature is Son of God and Word of God; and who in the end must reign, not by force of arms, or by pitiless effusion of blood, nor by enslaving, but by pacific faith. As is indicated still more clearly in the following passage of the Psalms: "In His time shall justice flourish, and there shall be an abundance of peace till there be no more moon" (v.7).

(AF) God also further announced the Messiah through Micah in these terms - "But thou, Bethlehem-Ephratha, although small among the thousands of Judah, from thee shall come out one unto Me to be he who dominates in Israel; and his issuing forth is from old, even from eternal days" (Micah 5:2). Is the issue of some simple man to be dated as from eternal days? Hear yet another prediction which God makes to us by the mouth of Jeremiah: "The heart is guileful and desperately wicked above all things, who can know it? O Eternal, Thou art the expectation of Israel. All those who abandon Thee will be ashamed. Those who turn away from Me shall be written in the earth, because they have left the source of living water, the Eternal One" (Jer. 17:9,13). Under the name Israel one must not understand the obstinate Jews, but those who have seen the Word of God and have believed that He was God engendered of God, because in the Hebrew language the word Israel signifies *clairvoyant*.[66] This explanation is given the word by God Himself in a passage in Isaiah, where He says - "The infant is born unto us, the son has been given us, the empire has been set on His shoulder, and His name shall be called Admirable, Counselor, God mighty and powerful, the Father of Eternity, the prince of peace, the Angel of the great mystery" (Isa. 9:5 - Septuagint - ed.). He is called *Angel* by reason of His human character completely pure and admirable; *Counselor* and *Mighty God*, are expressions of His divine nature. Then the prophet adds - "There shall be no end to the growth of His kingdom and prosperity on the throne of David, and on His reign to affirm it and establish it in justice and judgment, from now on and for always" (v.6). Now it is well known that Jesus did not mount the throne of David and did not reign over Israel, because this has no reference to a temporary throne, but to that of which God had spoken to David in these terms: "I will make thy prosperity eternal, and I will see to it that thy throne shall be as the days of the heavens" (Ps. 89:29). Someone may now ask, what is this throne of David? And how is it eternal and as the days of the heavens? Without doubt it is the celestial empire of Christ, who as to His human nature was a son of David, as had been announced in so precise a manner by Isaiah - "There shall be no end to the growth of His kingdom and prosperity on the throne of David and on His reign, to affirm it and establish it in justice and judgment from now on and forever" (Isa. 9:7). This passage leads us to see that the most powerful and glorious empire of Christ, the son of David by His human nature, will be in the heavens, where He will transport His eternal and inaccessible kingdom.

(AG) Nor must one neglect what Isaiah says in regard to this: "Behold, a virgin who will become pregnant and will bring forth a son, and his name shall be called Emmanuel" (Isa. 7:14). I have still many other passages I might cite on this subject, but, that I may not weary you, I have preferred to limit them. Nevertheless, I beseech you, hearken to some citations regarding His extreme humiliation in the sufferings which He voluntarily supported in accordance with the previous indication thereof by the prophets. The Holy Spirit, by the instrumentality of Isaiah, speaks thus: "I have not been rebellious and have not retired backwards. I have exposed my back to those who smote me and my cheeks to those who pulled out my hairs. I have not hidden my face from insults nor from being spat upon" (Isa. 50:5,6). Also through Zechariah He speaks: "And I said to them, if it seem good to you give me my hire; if not, give it me not. Then they weighed my hire, which was twenty pieces of silver" (Zech. 11:12). This prediction, along with all the others, was fulfilled in the person of the Savior. He was sold by His disciple and handed over to death, as the evangelists have preserved record, which you may examine as carefully as you wish and will find it such as we have presented it to you. Among many others David thus predicted the sufferings of Christ - "He who was at peace with me, whom I trusted and who ate my bread, has lifted up his heel against me" (Ps. 41:9). Isaiah speaks of the same subject in a more detailed manner, saying - (Here he quotes Isa. 53: 1-9 at length.)

(AH) Dare you then, relying on the bare word of your Muhammad, deny and give the lie to so many testimonies of the Holy Spirit, set forth by the prophets His ministers? You must at least conform to the prescription of your legislator, who commands that nothing be affirmed unless verified by two witnesses.[67] Indeed this is one of the more important regulations. How then, have you not shame, in dependence on the sole word of your Prophet, to utter so evident a blasphemy? Is it that you have forgotten, though maybe you are hardly aware of it, the tremendous imposture credited by your Prophet, according to whom Miriam the daughter of Amram and the sister of Aaron was the mother of our Lord,[68] whereas between the first Miriam and the second there was a space of 1370 years and thirty-two generations? If you had a countenance that was sensitive and not of stone, truly you would have had to blush at such impostures absolutely without foundation. The Christ, according to the promise of God, ought to come from the tribe of Judah, whereas Miriam the daughter of Amram belonged to that of Levi. Your objections are full of inconsequences and offer nothing but a multitude of gross and inadmissible falsifications. The source of so many such subterfuges and contradictions is naught but purely human invention, but I shall endeavor, by the aid of the little seal of truth, to bottle it up.

(AI) With regard to the Mosaic Code, the Psalms and the Gospel, you pretend that the Hebrews and ourselves have altered them,[69] though you recognize that these books are of divine origin. Suppose we admit for the moment that ours have been falsified and corrupted. Where, pray, our yours, in which you place credence? Show us other books of Moses or the prophets, Psalms of David or the Gospels, that we may see them.[70] This imposture is the most monstrous and most ignoble. At the very least you will have to admit that even you have never seen them. But do you, who lovest to pry into the Gospel that we possess in order to find some citations that you can them produce, after forcing them and altering them,[71] do you still pretend that we have falsified them? At least cite this Gospel which your legislator knew, and then I shall be convinced that you speak the truth.

(AJ) There is only one single faith you say. Yea, doubtless, there is but one faith, one baptism that which no other faith or commandment has been given men by God. Then you reproach us for not turning, when we pray, to the region indicated by the Code,[72] and for not communicating as the legislation ordains.[73] This object is completely vain and full of folly. The region to which the prophets turned when they made their prayers is not known. It is you alone who are carried away to venerate the pagan altar of sacrifice that you call the House of Abraham.[74] Holy Scripture tells us nothing about Abraham having gone to the place which afterwards, according to the order of Muhammad, became the center of adoration of your co-religionists. As to the sacrament of the Communion you will have my response later on.

(AK) Let us for the moment examine the different passages of the Gospel which are relevant to your pretensions. Jesus Christ, as God, had no need of prayers, but as man He made them in order to teach us how to pray, even us whose nature He partook, But in His praying He said nothing of all that which you attribute to Him. On the contrary He said: "Father, if Thou shouldest wish to put this cup far from Me; but in any case, not My will be done, but Thine" (Lk. 22:42).[75] He thereby gave evidence He was really man, since it is necessary to believe that the Word of God was both perfect man and perfect God, so that whosoever deprives Him of one or the other of these attributes, also deprives himself of the hope of attaining eternal life. The truth of the Gospel and the fidelity of Christians are manifested by conserving intact in equal measure both those traits in Him which are the most eminent and those which are the most humiliating, for had those who preceded us been able, or if we had the thought of introducing some changes into the Gospel, would not these humiliating traits have been suppressed? Jesus said: "The Son can do nothing of Himself, but the Father who dwells in Me, He it is who does the works" (John 5:19; 14:10). If then you believe that the Son can do nothing of Himself, you must also believe that the Father who dwells in Him is He who does the works. Similarly, if you believe in the fear which came over Him as He was being put to death alive and the sweat with which He was covered and which was not that of Adam and of which He had said before His incarnation - "Thou shalt eat thy bread in the sweat of thy brow" (Gen. 3:19), and if you believe in the assistance given Him by the angels,[76] though this was not to encourage Him, but to dissipate the idea of His disciples that He was a mere man, such an apparition making them realize that He was in many respects above the state of a mere man; if, I repeat, you believe all this, you must also believe what He said in the same book - "No one takes from Me my life, but I leave it of Myself; I have power to leave it and power to take it again" (John 10:18). Never did He say, as you pretend, that God sent Him into the world and that He returns to Him.[77] On the contrary He said that the Father who sent Him was with Him, and adds - "I came forth from the Father and am come into the world," and again, "I leave the world, and I go unto the Father" (John 14:28 and 31). As for you, in all these passages that I have cited, whenever you meet with the word "Father" you change it, and replace it either by the word "Lord," or by the word "God,"[78] and you think to be able to justify your position by thus doing. Meanwhile, among these shameful modifications you make in the Scriptures, there is one passage which you cite with some fidelity, though you put no faith in it. That passage is this, - "He who believes in Me, believes not merely in Me, but in Him who sent Me" (John 12:44).[79] The meaning of this is that it is not in His human and visible character that one believes, but in His divine character, inasmuch as He is the Word of God. Then He adds as follows -- "He who rejects Me, rejects Him who sent Me," and "He who contemplates Me, contemplates Him who sent Me" (John 12:45,48). He was sent as a man, and He sent His disciples as God, saying to them - "The Father is greater than I" (John 14:28), that is to say greater than My human nature, for otherwise He would not have said a little later on, "I and My Father are one" (John 10:30). Similarly, in His prayer, that you yourself report, Jesus said, "That they may know Thee the only true God and Him whom Thou hast sent, Jesus Christ" (John 17:3). In this passage we see Jesus Christ bearing the title of God. Had He been merely a prophet, needs must He have said - "That they may know Thee, the only true God and Moses with the other prophets and then Jesus."

(AL) Put aside, then, all these idle tales, for the fact is that Jesus, perfect God became, by the admission of a human nature, perfect man, to whom we attribute the humiliating expressions of Scripture as applying to man, just as the glorious expressions apply to a true God., as I have mentioned several times. Under the envelope of His human body He allowed Himself to be tempted by Satan, who, at the baptism of Jesus, when he heard the divine voice saying: "This is My beloved Son in whom I am well pleased," was seized with horror, not being able to make out to whom it was addressed. Meanwhile Jesus, by His fast forty days, as by the voice divine, proved that it was He alone to whom the voice was addressed. Then Satan, the declared enemy of those who practice virtue, desolated and devoured by jealousy, approached the person of the Lord and found in Him one who knew all that was passing in the mind of the Adversary, and who replied to him only by disdaining him as the enemy of humanity, refusing to reveal to him the mystery of His designs. But why have you not read what follows, how when Satan found his temptations useless he retired for the moment, and how the angels approached the Lord and adored Him? Did the angels adore Him as a man? It would appear that it is only the truth that you flee, exerting yourself to create all imaginable obstacles so as not to recognize our Lord as God, presenting Him always as a mere man, comparing Him to Adam, who, according to you, was created immediately by God, without having parents.[80]

(AM) As for His vivifying death, of which, as a matter of fact you are not ignorant of, you fabricate another imposture by saying that no one could put Him to death.[81] But I ask you, if Jesus were a mere man, according to you supposition, is it a thing incredible that a man should be able to die? Pay close attention and reflect on this. You accept with satisfaction all the humiliating traits in the life of our Lord, but you despise and reject all glorious traits. I invite you, therefore, to direct your attention to some points of the Gospel in regard to this matter. John the Evangelist, speaking of Jesus says: "He who believes in the Son has eternal life; but he who disobeys the Son will never see life, but the wrath of God dwells on him" (John 3:36). John the son of Zachariah says: "Behold the Lamb of God which taketh away the sin of the world" (John 1:29). Then John the Evangelist commences his

Gospel with these words, "In the beginning was the Word, and the Word was with God, and the Word was God. It was in the beginning with God. All things were made by it, and without it nothing of what was made was made" (John 1:1-3). The Word of God itself, having come into the world in flesh, expressed itself in the following manner - "He who has seen Me has seen the Father" (John 14:9), "As the Father knows Me, so know I the Father" (John 10:15), "the Father (who has sent Me) is with Me" (John 16:32), "I mount to My Father and your Father, to My God and your God" (John 20:17). He is His Father by His divine nature, our Father by grace, because "all those who receive Him to them gives He the right to be children of God, even to those who believe on His name" (John 1:12). He is His Son because of His human nature, which He has in common with us. In His quality as being man Jesus was sent and in His quality as being God, He sent His disciples - "as the Father hath sent Me, so send I you" (John 20:21). Thus all the passages of the Gospels are in accord on these points.

(AN) With regard to circumcision[82] and the sacrifice,[83] you pretend that we have changed things, altering the former into baptism and the latter into the communion in bread and blessed wine.[84] We have not altered or modified anything in these institutions. It was the Lord Himself who, in accordance with the prediction of Jeremiah, changed the type as laid down in the Old Testament and established the true law. Just listen to this prophecy. "Behold the days come, saith the Eternal, when I shall make a new covenant with the House of Israel and with the House of Jacob, not according to the covenant which I made with their fathers on the day when I took them by the hand to bring them out of the land of Egypt" (Jer. 31:31). What covenant did He make with their fathers, if not that of which one is reminded by the blood of the lambs on the day of Easter and which He had given to be kept in the midst of their people? (cf. Ex. 12:21-28).

(AO) So if the Children, then, were preserved from destruction by the blood of an unreasoning lamb, could not we be saved from eternal death by the blood of the immaculate Lamb? Jesus Christ, before His passion, took bread, which He blessed and distributed to His disciples.

He did the same with the cup filled with wine. These He called His body and His blood and commanded that we take and drink thereof in remembrance of Him, announcing thereby His death as the sacrifice of the Lamb, innocent and pure, a sacrifice often announced in the Old Testament. The Holy Scriptures, which you certainly can never have read, give Jesus different names, e.g., the Word, the Son, the Ray, the image of God, the image of the servant, God, man, angel, the Pearl, the Bait, Lord of Lords, the Servant, the Lamb, the Sheep, the Shepherd, the eldest among Brethren, the eldest among the dead, etc. Did I recognize in you one who seeks only for justice, nothing would hinder me from giving for each of these names a detailed exposition, indicating their true sense, signification and extent?

(AP) Regarding circumcision, you pretend that we have replaced it by baptism.[85] The mystery of circumcision, whereby God desired to treat of His covenant in this secret member and not in others more visible and glorious, remains unknown to you it seems. Is it that you are also ignorant of the further circumstance, that Abraham before he was circumcised drew to himself the favor of God and that he received the sign of circumcision only that it might serve as a sign of nothing other than his attachment to God? As for the principal reason why this secret member was chosen to serve this institution, you cannot know it, as I observed above. As for us, we have not received any command to circumcise our exterior members, but our heart, in a spiritual manner, as in the above cited promises of God announcing the re-establishment of a new covenant. Indeed, if the true law of Jesus Christ our Master had not completely destroyed circumcision, as well as the Sabbath and the sacrificial system, what new covenant could He be promising? You, on the other hand, ought to be ashamed of the fact that at so modern a time as ours, when God has delivered the human race by breaking the bonds of the law, you announce yourself as a defender of circumcision and in so doing have covered it with opprobrium. In the ancient law God ordered every male to be circumcised on the eighth day after birth, whereas among you, not only the males but also the females,[86] at no matter what age, are exposed to this shameful operation.

(AR) As for the divine institution of Baptism, it was announced to us by God long beforehand through the prophet Ezekiel, in these words: "I will pour out clean water upon you and ye shall be clean: I will cleanse you of all your uncleanness and all your idols" (Ezek. 36:25). This same baptism Jesus Christ commanded in His Gospel, saying to His disciples: "Go then and teach all nations, baptizing them into the name of the Father and of the Son and of the Holy Spirit" (Matt. 28:19). By this was fulfilled the prediction of the prophet - "I have established thee as a light to the peoples" and "the people that was sitting in darkness has seen a great light" (Isa. 42:6; 9:2).

(AS) Nor have we substituted Sunday for the Sabbath, as you pretend,[87] without having reflected that among yourselves the Friday has been set as the day for reunion, without any reason being apparent that can justify the choice. As for us, we assemble on the day of the resurrection of our Savior, who thereby has promised us resurrection, to say our prayers and render thanks to the Creator for so great a mystery. This is the day on which the Creator at the beginning said - "Let there be light, and there was light." It was on the same day that the light of the good news of the resurrection of human kind shone forth by the resurrection of the Word and of the only begotten Son of God in His human body. For the rest we have received no other command to cease work therein, or as the Jews, not to prepare our food. Yet for what reason do you, who manifest such incredulity, whether as regards the prophets or as regards our Savior, attach so much importance to the genuine traditions of the Christians? I imagine that it was for you and such as resemble you that God said by His prophet: "regard, you outrageous people, and you will be outraged and reduced yourselves. I am about to undertake in your times a work at which you would not believe if one told you thereof" (Habak. 1:5).

(AT) Nor have I forgotten the objection raised by you in these terms: "How is it possible for God to dwell in the womb of a woman, in the midst of blood and flesh and dirt?"[88] I suppose that you know that there is a multitude of things God has created by His simple command as Psalm 148 (v. 5) assures us in these words - "He commanded and they were created. He has established them forever and ever." Amongst these figures the sky with its sun, moon and other stars, celestial bodies and the earth with its vegetation and the animals. All these beings, it appears, occupy in your thought an eminently superior place and seem purer and more precious than man, who, though considered by you as an impure being, was nevertheless created, not by a simple command, as these above-mentioned things, but by the all-powerful hand of God and animated by His breath. Consequently human nature, created by the holy hand of the Creator and honored by Him with resemblance to Him, cannot be a filthy thing in His sight. Do not, then, offer insults to the good Creator, in whose eyes nothing of all that has been created by Him is unclean, save only sin, which not only was not created by Him in man, but was not even ordained. On the contrary, there is nothing more precious than man, for whom all things were created. God then, who has so honored man by creating him in His image, would not think it shameful to take man's image in order to save him, since, as I have said, there is nothing unclean in human nature save sin, and all those things in man which you consider filthy, have been organized so by God for our good. For example, the menses of the female serve in the reproduction of the human species, and the evacuation of the excesses of food and drink serve for the conservation of our life. It is you alone who consider them impure, whereas in the eyes of God it is pillage, assassination, blasphemy and other such crimes which are considered as defiling, rather than those things above-mentioned which are designed for the purpose of reproduction and the conservation of human life.

(AU) Beyond all that I have brought up so far, I have yet to observe to you another matter, namely, that if the bush flaming with divine fire at the time of Moses was not consumed, man must be considered as more precious than a bush and than all created things, for it is of holy men that God said: "I will dwell in their midst" (Ezek. 43:7), and again, "In whom will I dwell if not in men kindly and humble, and in those who fear My words?" (Isa. 66:2). It is here clearly to be seen that God calls just men His habitation, and that He is not offended by their natural infirmities, which you call filthiness, since it befits the everliving to have a living temple.

(AV) I submit to you also the following proposition, and the more willingly, as I perceive you to be envious of the glory of the saints of God and their relics, that God declared to be His dwelling. If God cares for all the bones of the human race in view of the general resurrection, how should He not take special care for those of His saints, of whom He has more than once spoken in such glorious and majestic terms, above all those who have suffered death in His cause? It is of these martyrs that the Holy Spirit says by the mouth of David that "every kind of death of the beloved of the Eternal is precious in His sight" (Ps. 116:15), and in another passage: "The just has ills in great number, but the Eternal delivers him from them all. He guards all his bones, and not one of them is broken" (Ps. 34:19-20). The divine power that dwells in His saints affirms that their bones will not be broken, yet we know that a great number of saints' bones have been ground to powder or by the fire reduced to ashes. As for you, child that you are, occupied with things that are visible, you do not think of that at all. The Holy Spirit speaks further in another passage: "God is marvelous to His saints," and Solomon speaks in these terms: "The just will live eternally and will receive their recompense from their Savior. Only in the eyes of the impious are they dead, for they enjoy repose" (Wisd. 3:1,2; 5:16). I presume that you are not ignorant of that history of the uncircumcised stranger, whose corpse, so soon as it was cast into "the sepulchre of the prophet Elias and touched his bones, came back to life and rose upon his feet" (II Ki. 13:21). Now, if divine power did not reside in the bones of the holy prophet, how could those of a simple dead man be able to revive a corpse? Thus we see that the living God does not consider that He is defiled by dwelling in the tomb of a dead person, for God judges of men in a way different from our own judgment. Yet what respect for the saints could one expect from you, when I see you, even now, excited by a species of fanaticism worthy of a pagan, exercising such cruelties toward the faithful of God with the purpose of converting them to apostasy and putting to death all those who resist your designs, so that daily is accomplished that prediction of our Savior: "The time will come when everyone who puts you to death will believe that he is serving God" (John 16:2). For you are far from thinking that in killing all those who resist you, you are putting yourself to an eternal death. It is thus that Muhammad, your uncle,[89] acted aforetime, when on the very day he went to immolate the profane sacrifice of the camel, at the same time had decapitated a number of Christians, servants of God, and mingled their blood with that if the animal which was offered in sacrifice. Yet you are annoyed when we gather together the remains of the martyrs who have sealed the profession of their faith by their blood, so that we may bury them in places consecrated to God.[90]

(AW) Further, in your letter are some words apropos of the cross[91] and pictures. We honor the cross because of the sufferings of that Word of God incarnate borne thereon, as we have learned from a commandment given by God to Moses and from the predictions of the prophets. The metal plate which Moses, bidden by God, placed on the forehead of the pontiff or high priest, bore the image of a cross having the form of a living being,[92] and it is in imitation of this sign that we Christians sign our foreheads with the cross, as of the Word of God who suffered for us in His human nature. The prophet Isaiah even indicates the wood out of which that cross should be made, the sublime crown in which the Church forever glories. "The fir tree, the pine and the box together, to render honorable the place of My sanctuary; and I will render glorious the place of My feet" (Isa. 60:13) Solomon speaks thus of it: "Blessed be the wood by which justice is exercised" (Wisd. 14:7) and in another place says: "It is the tree of life for all those who embrace it and who attach themselves solidly to it as to the Lord" (Prov. 3:18).

(AX) As for pictures, we do not give them a like respect, not having received in Holy Scripture any commandment whatsoever in regard to this. Nevertheless, finding in the Old Testament that divine command which authorized Moses to have executed in the tabernacle the figures of the cherubim, and animated by a sincere attachment for the disciples of the Lord, who burned with love for the Savior Himself, we have always felt a desire to conserve their images, which have come down to us from their times as their living representation. Their presence charms us, and we glorify God who has saved us by the intermediary of His only-begotten Son, who appeared in the world in a similar figure, and we glorify the saints. But as for the wood and the colors, we do not give them any reverence. But you, do you feel no shame to have venerated that House that is called the Ka'ba, the dwelling of Abraham, which as a matter of fact Abraham never saw nor so much as dreamed of in its diabolical arid desert? This House was existing long before Muhammad and was the object of a cult of your fellow citizens, while Muhammad, far from abolishing it, called it the dwelling of Abraham.[93] In order not to appear to wrongfully give you offence, I shall prove (its diabolical nature), by passages from the Holy Gospel and from your own history. Jesus Christ often drove out demons into that very desert. "He (the demon) goes by the desert places" (Matt. 12:43). These unclean spirits appear to you there under serpent form,[94] and sometimes they seem to indulge in evil relations with women, according to their custom, giving the appearance of making marriages. You, deceived by the illusion, and imprudently falling into the net, make yourselves their compeers here below and in the world to come, so far are you from understanding that in the other world it is forbidden them, by command of the Savior, to have such commerce.[95] Jesus Christ fettered here below their revolting violence, and though like their father Satan, they are constantly malevolent, yet they cannot openly cause harm to anyone, since if they dared to do this, or were able, they would inevitably have destroyed you as by fire in a single day. As it is they are able to do no more than draw you by occult machinations, to the loss of your souls. For example, by means of a stone that is called *rukn*,[96] that you adore without knowing why; by means of that carnage of demons from which the birds and the beasts flee with all haste and extreme aversion; by means of the stones cast, the flight, the having your head shaven and other such ridiculous superstitions.[97] Nor do I wish to pass over in silence the abominable authorization given you by your legislator to have with your wives a commerce that he has compared, I am ashamed to say, to the tilling of fields. As a consequence of this license, a goodly number of you have contracted the habit of multiplying their commerce with women as if it were a question of tilling fields.[98] Nor can I forget the chastity of your Prophet and the manner full of artifice whereby he succeeded in seducing the woman Zeda.[99] Of all these abominations the worst is that of accusing God of being the originator of all these filthy acts, which fact has doubtless been the cause of the introduction among your compatriots of this disgusting law. Is there indeed a worse blasphemy than that of alleging that God is the cause of all this evil?[100] As for the example of David, who took Uriah's wife, as you remind me,[101] it is well known that therein he committed a sin before the Eternal, for which he was grievously punished.

(AY) To sum up, the fact is that your legislator and all of you continue to resist the truth. In this you do well, for I know nothing worse than not holding sin to be such as it is, and that is what you really do in never seeking nor receiving pardon.[102] In the Gospel God has commanded the husband not to repudiate the wife save for the cause of adultery, but you act quite otherwise. When you are tired of your wives, as some kind of nourishment, you abandon them at your fancy. It had been my intention to conceal, if possible, the shamelessness with which you remarry, and how before retaking your repudiated wives you make them sleep in the bed of another.[103] And what shall I say of the execrable debauchery which you commit with your concubines? For you are prodigal with them of all your fortune, and then, when you are tired of them you sell them like dumb cattle. It is said that the serpent has intimate relations with the *murines*, the reptile of the sea, but on arriving at the seashore the serpent spits out its venom before entering on its love affair. But you are more venomous than the serpent, never putting any limits to your bad faith and not being able to satisfy your unleashed passions while still alive, at the hour of your death you violently put to death your wives, following the inspiration of the evil spirit.[104]

(AZ) In speaking of Satan and the souls of the just, you pretend that we have represented the former as the treasurer of God.[105] That is an error. We say, on the contrary, that Satan was most happy at seeing humanity, in the horror caused it by seeing death, plunge into the depths of despair, for he believed the just to be abandoned by God and lost after death. Filled with this thought and struck by the extreme humiliation of Christ, he believed that he also would be subject to the condition of men and so incited His disciple to betray Him and the Jews to put Him to death. But when he saw the Savior walk willingly towards the sufferings of the cross, he was seized with horror, and in order to hinder the salvation of the human race, he attempted to terrify by remorse the wife of the judge (Pilate). In spite of his artifices, however, the Word of God tasted death in His human nature, while remaining in His divine nature always immortal, though inseparable from His humanity, and as true God engendered from true God. He rose again, or rather resuscitated His human nature in accord with what was said by the prophet David: "Let God arise and His enemies will be dispersed" (Ps. 68:1) and according to another prediction made by one of the twelve prophets.

(BA) The Word of God being thus resuscitated, less for Himself, since He was Spirit, immortal and incorruptible, than for the human race whose nature He had taken upon Himself, He assured by this resurrection the resurrection of men and rendered certain the hope that the dead, delivered from the influence of the spiritual enemy, will be reclothed in new bodies, since souls obtain many graces from the Creator by the incarnation of His Word.

(BB) It is thus then that Satan, enfeebled, lost and led along by his own despair and that of his legions, sees himself at last reduced to the impossibility of leading any longer the world to those cults which are strange and contrary to the will of God. So he has nothing to expect but the punishment of the eternal fire.

(BC) Now it is time for me to explain to you this vision of Isaiah, where a rider appears to him mounted on an ass and a camel.[106] The sense is this. The aspect of the maritime desert indicates that it is your desert situated by the side of the sea, a neighbor to and a boundary of Babylonia. Presently the prophet says that he sees two riders mounted the one on an ass and the other on a camel. These two riders are really only one and the same, as the prophet himself clearly affirms in the passage itself. Under the name of "ass" the prophet means the Jewish people, which, although it has read the law and the prophecies, yet influenced by the teaching of Satan, has refused to submit and accept the Gospel destined to save the universe. It is this disobedience of the Jewish people that the same prophet complains of at the commencement of his book - "The ox knows his owner and the ass the crib of his master, but Israel has not known" (Isa. 1:3). Under the name "camel," the prophet designates the Midianites and the Babylonians, because among you these animals are very common. And the same enemy who led the Jews into error, under the pretext of conserving the law, has made you also fall into idolatry I have said above that the two riders really represent only one and the same man, as the prophet lets us know immediately after by saying: "I saw the same horseman who came mounted on two steeds. Lo, the horseman who appeared two before was only one and mounted on two horses."[107] He designates by these two horses the Jews and the pagans dominated by him. Whence then comes this man? What does he say? He comes mounted on two horses and cries at the top of his voice - "Babylon is fallen, and its works have been overturned." It was then the enemy who deplored its desolation, and who, not finding any refuge other than your desert, has led you to the horses of his iniquity, that is to say, the inconstancy of the Jews and the debauchery of the pagans. By the aid of these two elements he finally succeeded, by occult means rather than by the exercise of force, in drawing you into his error. It is thus that he has got you to circumcise yourselves, yet without admitting the divinity of the Son and of the Holy Spirit, the creators and sanctifiers.

(BD) As for divination and knowledge of the future and as to demons who lead only to the torments of hell,[108] you have the same faith in them as the pagans, whose abominable debaucheries are familiar to you. You call "the Way of God"[109] these devastating raids which bring death and captivity to all peoples. Behold your religion and its recompense. Behold your glory, ye who pretend to live an angelic life. As for us, instructed in and convinced of the marvelous mystery of our redemption, we hope, after our resurrection, to enjoy the celestial kingdom, so we are submissive to the doctrines of the Gospel and wait humbly for a happiness such that "eyes have never seen it, nor have ears ever heard it, but which God has prepared for those who love Him" (I Cor. 2:9).[110] We do not hope to find there springs of wine, honey of milk.[111] We do not expect to enjoy there commerce with women who remain forever virgin[112] and to have children by them, for we put no faith in such silly tales engendered by extreme ignorance and by paganism. Far from us be such dreams, such fables. "The kingdom of God consisteth not in eating and drinking" (Rom. 14:17), as saith the Holy Spirit, "but in justice," and "at the resurrection men will not marry women, nor women men, but they shall be as the angels" (Matt. 22:30). For you who are given up to carnal vices and who have never been known to limit the same, you who prefer your pleasures to any good, it is precisely for that reason that you consider the celestial realm of no account if it is not peopled with women.[113]

(BE) Behold the short reply that I address to you, For the sake of our unshakable and imperishable faith we have endured at your hands, and still endure, much suffering. We are even prepared to die, if only to bring to ourselves the name of "saint," a name precious and incomparable as predicted by Isaiah: "You will bear a new name that the Lord will give you" (Isa. 62: 2). The Lord Himself, when He was upon earth, told us beforehand of these sufferings, saying to us - "If they have persecuted Me, they will persecute you also; if they have kept My word they will keep yours also; they will do all these things to you for My name's sake, because they have not known Him that sent Me" (John 15:20,21); and again, "you will weep and you will lament" (John 16:20). Jesus Christ in His prayer addressed to the Father, said: "They were Thine, and Thou didst give them to Me.... They are not of the world, as I am not of the world" (John 17:6,16), "if ye had been of the world, the world would love that which belongs to it; but because you are not of the world, but I have chosen you out of the world, for that reason the world hates you" (John 15·19).

(BF) Because such is our hope, you continually menace us, you strike us with death, but we respond not to your blows with anything other than patience, for we count on neither our arm nor our sword to save us, but on the right arm of the Lord and on the light of His face. Should He will it we are prepared to suffer still more in this world, so as to be recompensed in the world to come. Yea let Him fix the hour and the mode of the torture, we are ready prepared.

(BG) As for you, persisting in your tyranny and your usurpations, you attribute to your religion the success with which heaven favors you.[114]

You forget that the Persians also prolonged their tyranny for 400 years.[115] What was the reason for so long a reign? God alone knows; but surely it was not because of the purity of their religion. As for us, we accept with eagerness all the sufferings and all the tortures which can happen to us for the glorious name of Jesus Christ, our Lord and Savior, so that we may arrive at the happiness of the future world with all those who have loved to see the coming of the great day of Judgment of God, for the praise and glory of His well-beloved. May we be worthy to contemplate then with them the unique divinity of the Father, the Word and His unique Son and His Holy Spirit, now and forever. Amen.[116]

The Emperor Leo sent this response by one of his intimate officers to 'Umar, sovereign to the Arabs.[117] After having read it, the Caliph was very confused. This letter produced on him a very happy effect. From this moment he commenced to treat the Christians with much kindness. He ameliorated their state and showed himself very favorable towards them, so that on all hands were heard expressions of thankfulness to him. As I have before mentioned, he gave entire liberty to the captives and gave back to them their effects without demanding any ransom. He showed himself also much more generous to his own subjects than any of his predecessors. He distributed to the troops great sums of money, which till then had been stored up in the coffers of the treasury. After all these beneficent acts he died.

The question remains as to the genuineness of this correspondence, and that really is a matter for the historians to argue on the basis of the material itself. The fact that both Byzantine and Oriental writers know of the correspondence and apparently know of it independently, may indicate a probability that there was such an exchange of correspondence on religious matters, as well as that on political matters for which we have Muslim evidence. That we have no Muslim evidence as yet to this religious correspondence is no serious objection, since so much of the early Muslim material is still unpublished.[118] One has only to think of the new light on many little points already shed by the recent start at the publication of the historical works of Baladhuri and Ibn 'Asakir, to realize that we might well find reference to this in Muslim sources were more of them available to us.

However, even if it were established that there had been an exchange of such letters between the two potentates, it would not follow that this text of Ghevond is the authentic text of Leo's side of that correspondence.[119] There are only too many instances of where enthusiastic writers have invented the text of documents they knew must have existed, so that Christian writers might quite as well have produced what they would have us believe was the text of Leo's letter to 'Umar, as Muslim writers have produced what they would have us believe is the text of Muhammad's letters to the surrounding potentates.[120]

We have to bear in mind, however, that we have a Latin text in the West and an Armenian text in the East, neither of which is derivable from the other, and both of which obviously depend on a common body of original material. The Scripture quotations in Ghevond seem conclusive evidence that original was in Greek, and the Armenian forms of some of the proper names also suggest that Ghevond read them, not in their Arabic form, but in Greek. While there is no denying that Ghevond has padded his material here and there, it seems clear enough that he was using an account of the correspondence and not creating it himself. To the present writer there seems sufficient evidence in his style to show that in these chapters he is translating and not freely composing as he is in the later chapters, though more profound Armenian scholars may disagree as to this. A Greek original, to provide a basis both for Ghevond in the East and the Latin in the West, could not have been composed very long after Leo's own time, if it were a later compilation and not the genuine correspondence.

The next step would seem to be to compare this material with the other correspondence of Leo on theological matters, but the present writer has no opportunity for that task, so he must be content for the moment to present this material as it is, in the hope that someone more fortunate may be able to make that comparison and add one more argument for or against its genuineness.

But whether it is the genuine correspondence of Leo with 'Umar or not, it is a sufficiently early document in the literature of Muslim-Christian controversy to provide extremely important evidence on the subjects of controversy and the methods of controversy prior to the well-known works of the later centuries and as such is deserving of the consideration of students interested in that little explored but not unimportant branch of theological learning.

\-

Notes:

[1] *Der Islam im Lichte der byzantinischen Polemik*, Berlin, 1912, pp. 7, 8.

[2] *Chronographia*, ed. de Boor, 1883, I, 399.

[3] Eastern Christian writers often speak of 'Umar's severity with Christians. Michael the Syrian XI, 19 (pp. 455, 456 of the text) tells at length how 'Umar legislated to ease the position of those who were willing to become Muslims and to increase the disabilities of those who unwilling to accept Islam. See also Bar Hebraeus' *Makhtebha-nuth Zabhne*, p. 117 (ed. Bedjan, Paris, 1880). But note Wellhausen's rejoinder in *Das arabische Reich und sein Sturz*, pp. 187 ff.

[4] *Kitab al-'Unwan*, ed. A. Vasilev in *Patr. Orient.*, VIII, 3 (Paris, 1912), p. 503.

[5] Ghevond's text of 'Umar II's letter has been deleted. See the editor's preface to Leo III's letter - ed.

[6] *Patmoui Arcreameac 'i 5 girs camn 996* (History of the Ardzrunids to 996 in 5 Books), ed. Constantinople, 1852, p. 116; ed. St. Petersburg,

1887, p. 105.

[7] *Patmoutiun iuroy zamanakim vasn arsanuanac Tartarac* (History of his own Times and the Invasion of the Tatars), ed. Venice, 1865, p. 37.

[8] Text in Muyldermans, *La Domination arabe en Armenie*, Paris, 1927, pp. 52, 53.

[9] Tabari, *Annales*, II, 1354; *Ibn al-Athir Kamil*, ed. Tornberg, V, 37.

[10] The statement of Theophanes, *Chronographia*, I, 391 τῇ ἀληθείᾳ δὲ ἐκ τῆς Ἰσαυρίας, is probably due to a confusion of Germanikeia in Comagene with Germanikopolis in Charicene, which latter might be called Isauria.

[11] *Kitab al-'Uyun* in *de Goeje et de Jong Fragmenta Historicorum Arabicorum*, I, 25. This writer informs us that when Leo was appointed Patricius of Amorium, the citizens of that place objected to his appointment on the ground that he was a Nabataean Arab.

[12] See the editor's preface to Leo III's letter - ed.

[13] Hildebrand Beck in a monograph "Vorsehung und Vorherbestimmung in der theologischen Literatur der Byzantiner" in *Orientalia Christiana Analecta*, CXIV (Rome, 1937), to which the Editors of the *H.T.R.* have called my attention, devotes a paragraph to "Pseudo Leo III" (pp. 43-46) in his section on "Die Polemiker gegen den Islam," and considers that the correspondence between Leo and 'Umar is not part of the original history of Ghevond, but was inserted therein by some later hand at the end of the 9th or the beginning of the 10th century. Obviously this correspondence does break the sequence of the history and reads like an insertion, but it would have been such even if placed there by Ghevond himself, and Beck's arguments against its being part of the original text of Ghevond are only valid if Ghevond, as

he assumes, wrote in the 8th century; but this, as we shall presently see, is an assumption which cannot be justified.

[14] Ehrhard in Krumbacher's *Geschichte der byzantinische Literatur [2]* (1897), p. 168, and the Abbé Vogt in *Camb. Med. Hist.* VI, 59, accept without question the attribution of the letter to Leo VI following its earlier acceptance as such by Baronius, Fabricius and Migne, and Wolfgang Eichner in *Der Islam* XXIII (1936), p. 142, by setting a date c. 900 for it, is obviously following the same opinion. Dom Ceillier had, however, seen that it must have been wrongly assigned to Leo VI, and Popov in his special study of the work of this Emperor, Императоръ Левъ Мудрый и его царствованіе въ церковно-историческомъ отношеніи, Moscow, 1892, shows that not only is the latter quite unworthy of his subtle pen, but in its Latin form it expressly supports the Roman Catholic side of the *Filioque* controversy, whereas in the genuine works of Leo VI he expresses himself definitely on the other side.

[15] My translation of the letters was made years ago from Chahnazarian's text, but in preparing this article I have only been able to use the text in the edition of St. Petersburg, 1887, edited by K. Iziants, a microfilm of which was put a my disposal by the kindness and courtesy of Professor R. Blake and the Librarian of Harvard University. Chahnazarian's edition was printed at Paris in 1857, and it was from this text that the Russian translation by Patkanian was made. Fortunately the 1887 edition includes the critical notes of both Chahnazarian and Patkanian.

[16] K. Schenk, however, in his article in *Byzantinische Zeitschrift*, V, 1896, p. 277 n. 2, considers the whole letter an invention, - "Was endlich den Bekehrungsbrief anlangt, so ist dieser wohl in das Reich der Fabel zu verweisen, da es Omar nicht einfallen konnte zu erwarten, dass der Kaiser, siegesfroh und stolz, Byzanz errettet zu haben, noch in demselben Jahre zum Glauben der geschlagenen Feinde übertreten werde. Die Erzählung wird erfunden sein zu dem Behufe, die Behauptung, Leon sei ein Freund des Islam, zu rechtfertigen." This is perhaps

being hypercritical, for the sending of such a letter is not at all out of character with the 'Umar who meets us in the Muslim sources. Brosset has a note on the correspondence in his *Deux Historiens Arméniens* (St. Petersburg, 1870), p. 34. H. Beck in *Orientalia Christiana Analecta*, CXIV, p. 44 n., adduces a number of little pieces of evidence to show that there was a Greek text underlying the Armenian; e.g., he refers to "our Greek language," calls the Torah νόμος, uses the LXX names for Chronicles and Canticles, etc.

[17] *Baladhuri Futuh*, 200.

[18] See Tableau II, B, "Les Bagratounis," in Muyldermans, *La Domination arabe en Arménie*, p. 148.

[19] Finck in the section on Armenian literature in "Die orientalischen Literatur," *Die Kultur der Gegenwart*, I, vii (1906), p. 289, accepts a date at the end of the 8th century, but H. Beck in *Byzant. Zeitschr.* XXXVII (1937), p. 436, who places the Greek original of the letter "aus der Wende des X. Jahrh.," obviously accepts the later date for Ghevond. Ernst Filler's *Thesis Quaestiones de Leontii Armenii Historia*, Leipzig, 1903, also supports an 8th century date, following Chahnazarian in making a special point that Stephen of Asoghik in his list of historians places Ghevond between Sebeos and the two 10th century writers Shapuh and Johannes Catholicos, while Kirakos places him between Sebeos and Thomas Ardzruni. This, however, would not obviate a late date in the 9th or early 10th century, and as a matter of fact Mekhitar of Airavank in his Tabula of the Armenian historians places him between Moses Arghovan and Oukhtanes, both 10th century writers (Brosset, *Histoire chronologique par Mkhitar d'Airavank*, St Petersburg, 1869, p. 25, in Tome XIII No. 5 of the *Mémoires de l'Académie impériale des Sciences de Saint-Petersbourg*, VIIe série). Filler raises objections to the general accuracy of Mekhitar, but it may be pointed out that his date agrees better with the fact that Ghevond on p. 61 of the text speaks of its "being now 800 years since Christ appeared," though Bosset in a note on p. 80 of his Mkhitar refers to Ghevond as "presque contemporain" with the events of Leo III's reign.

J. H. Petermann in his essay "De Ostikanis," *Arabicis Armeniae gubernatoribus*, Berlin, 1840, p. 9 had made Ghevond a contemporary of Thoma Ardzruni in the 10th century, and E. W. Brooks, "Byzantines and Arabs in the Time of the Early 'Abbasids," in the *English Historical Review*, XV (Oct., 1900), p. 731, judges that "the Armenian Leontius, though his history only comes down to 790, seems to have written in the later half of the ninth century," with which dating we agree.

[20] There have been two translations of the History of Ghevond, one by Chahnazarian, Paris, 1856, *Histoire des Gerres et des Conquetes des Arabes en Arménie, par l'eminent Ghévond*, vardabed arménien, écrivain du huitième siècle, traduite par Garabed V. Chahnazarian, and one by K. Patkanian, St. Petersburg, 1862 - Исторія халифовъ Вардапета Гевонда. писателя VIII вѣка. Переводъ съ армянсаго. Both these, however, are so rare as to be unprocurable.

[21] Cf. Gaudeul, "Leo and 'Umar," *Islamochristiana*, 10, p. 133, BNM 4944, parag. 3 - ed.

[22] This charge, which does not appear to be groundless when compared with 'Umar's letter as represented in BNM 4944 and the "Anonymous Pamphlet," indicates a rather early dating for this correspondence between the two - ed.

[23] This may be indirect confirmation of the fact that 'Umar wrote to the Emperor about the prisoners taken at Latikieh.

[24] Perhaps he is thinking of I Pet. 3:15.

[25] It is not impossible, of course, that Byzantine prelates, roughly contemporary with Muhammad, may have written some account of the new religion that had arisen in Arabia, but if they did we know nothing of it. The earliest Christian references to Muhammad and Islam so far known to us, e.g., those of John of Phenek and Sebeos, are bare historical notices, which tell us very little about the religion itself.

[26] Isa. 55:2. Perhaps a reference to the already mentioned promise of Muhammad to the Muslims, that if they were obedient to the new faith they would eat of the goodly inheritance.

[27] Cf. Gaudeul, "Leo and 'Umar," *Islamochristiana*, 10, p. 133, BNM 4944, parag. 5 - ed.

[28] The reference is to the voluntary poverty of Jesus and the disciples, who were people of no worldly account when they commenced their mission and had no worldly possessions when their ministry closed. Leo has quite mistaken the reference in his answer to this. Even to the present day the popularly read lives of Muhammad are at pains to demonstrate that, on the contrary, the Arabian prophet was of the noblest family and proudest lineage of the Arabs, and his companions among the best-born and most influentially connected at Mecca. Moreover, Muhammad promised his followers that they should inherit the rich possessions of the people surrounding them as a reward for their acceptance of Islam. The writers of the Eastern Church frequently remark on this. For example, the Armenian historian Sebeos (edition of 1851, p. 164, 165), in his account of Muhammad, tells of how the Prophet urged on his followers that they as Muslims were the true children of Abraham and so should go up and possess his inheritance. Ghevond has much the same story at the beginning of his history, and Michael the Syrian (ed. Chabot, p. 405 of the Syriac text) tells how the Prophet encouraged his armies with the promise that of they were faithful to Allah, He would give them a fine country as an inheritance.

[29] Cf. *Sahih Bukhari*, The Book of Monotheism, chap. 42, hadith 614, Vol. 9, p. 461 - ed.

[30] Cf. Gaudeul, "Leo and 'Umar," *Islamochristiana*, 10, p. 134, BNM 4944, parag. 9 - ed.

[31] *Researches into the books of the prophets and the Psalms.* A glance at the arrangement of the material in the early part of the "Epistola Leonis ad Omarum Saracenorum," in PG, CVII, will show

what he means. The early apologists, for example Justin Martyr in his apology for the Christians to Antoninus Pius, had set the example of assembling a great body of verses and fragments of verses from the Old Testament and particularly from the prophets and Psalms, which they judged to be clear cases of the foretelling of the coming life and work of the Christ, and apparently the earliest controversies with Islam brought out the same style of argument. This was probably true in the lifetime of the Prophet himself, for he would hardly have been so eager to see in the earlier Scriptures prophetic references to his own coming (cf. Qur'an 7:156 and 61:6), had he not heard the Christians of his day urging the Old Testament prophecies as grounds for their claims in their preaching of Jesus. What the Caliph is thinking of in his objection to this is firstly, that in the Qur'an Jesus bears witness to Himself while still an infant in the cradle (19:30-35), and secondly, that His witness is more worthy of acceptance than that of any prophet or psalmist, since in the Qur'an He is one "of those who draw near" (3:40 *min almuqarrabin*), a phrase used elsewhere of the Angels of the Presence (4:170), and of certain groups of the blessed in Paradise (56:11, 87; 83:21, 28), so that to seek witness from others rather than accepting the witness He bears to Himself savors of disbelief in Him.

[32] The assembly of Scripture witnesses what follows, as that in Latin 316-318, is his answer to the Caliph's charge against the Christians of making Jesus the associate and equal of God. The Caliph is merely following the Qur'an, for there (Qur'an 5:116, 117) Muhammad has God take Jesus to task for the claim of the Christians that He and His mother were gods beside God, and He denies that He had told His followers any such thing. Also in 5:76 the Qur'an makes Jesus proclaim that Allah alone is God to be worshipped, for those who associate anything with Allah will find paradise denied them. The use of terms in the Caliph's charge is worth noting - "associate," "equal," "unique," "all-powerful," all of them Qur'anic terms, so that it would be interesting to know what the Greek terms were. Perhaps the use in the Latin 315a, 317c of the title "Son of Mary," is because this title (ibn Maryam), is most commonly used for Christ in the Qur'an itself.

[33] *Falsification of the Scriptures.* Most Muslim works of polemic deal at length with this question of the corruption of the Jewish Scriptures, a question that is as old as the Clementine literature and the Manichaean controversy. In Muslim polemic it is the matter technically known as the question of *tahrif*. This word is the verbal noun from Stem II, *harrafa* - "to change the letters" (*harf*, pl. *huruf*), and the charge of *tahrif* is ultimately based on a passage in the Qur'an (2: 70; cf. 4:48; 5:16, 45), where the Jews are accused of altering Scripture. What Muhammad refers to in this passage seems obviously to be the naughty habit of some of the Madinan Jews, who, when he asked them about their Torah, would listen to it read in Hebrew and then garble it when they translated it to him, in order to make mock of him. In the polemical writers, however, it is more generally taken to mean that the Scriptures in the hands of the Jews have been deliberately altered by designing men, so that what the Jews (and Christians) now use as Scripture are not the original texts as revealed by God. Some Muslim writers commonly understand *tahrif* as meaning "false exegesis" of the Biblical passages, but the favorite meaning with the polemical writers, since Ibn Hazm's day, has been to take it as meaning deliberate tampering with the text. Ignazio di Matteo has a long discussion of this matter, "Il *Tahrif* od alterazione della Bibbia secondo i Musulmani" in *Bessarione*, XXXVIII (1922), 64-111, 223-260, Fritsch has a section on it, pp. 54-74 of his *Islam und Christentum im Mittelalter* (Breslau, 1930), and the word is discussed by Goldziher in ZDMG, XXXII (1878), p. 364 ff. Ibn Hazm of Cordova (d. 1064), Salih al-Ja-'fari (c. 1200) and al-Qarafi as-Sanhaji (d. 1285) all deal at length with this question. It was raised by al-Mahdi with the Patriarch Timothy - Mingana's text in Woodbrooke Studies, II, p. 55. This disposes of the objection of H. Beck in *Orientalia Christiana Analecta*, CXIV, 44n., that the Muslim argument concerning the Torah falsification by the Jews was only raised in this form in the 9/10th centuries - and it was one of the questions that has to be met by al-Kindi (*Risala*, ed. of 1880, pp. 138-140.). How much a part of the general Muslim outlook this doctrine of *tahrif* had become is well illustrated by the way the Jewish convert 'Abd al-Haqq al-Islami, who must surely have known better, feels obliged in his denunciation of his former co- religionists, to

charge that the Scriptures in their hands are only poor falsifications (M. Perlmann in *JQR* XXXI (1940), pp. 177, 181.). The reference to its having been recomposed we shall take up later. - The Muslim charge that the Jews had changed the Scriptures was also known by John of Damascus, see parag. D - ed.

[34] He is referring to the fact that in the Qur'an Muhammad himself, on more than one occasion, appealed to the testimony of the Scriptures in the hands of the Jews and Christians (Qur'an 3:87; 5:72; 10:94; etc. - ed.)

[35] Qur'an 5:105-107, 96; 65:2; 2:282; 4:7, 19 are the classical passages about the calling of witnesses, but in none of them is there any reference to this being also in the Torah of Moses, though the Commentators know of the regulation in Deut. 17:6. Leo later brings up again this question of Muhammad's demanding two witnesses as a ground for objecting to the Muslim rejection of the divinity of Christ on the single witness of Muhammad himself, whereas the Christians can produce many witnesses in favor of it from the Old and New Testaments - John of Damascus also used the argument of calling for witnesses, cf. John of Damascus, parag. C - ed.

[36] The reference is probably to such passages as Qur'an 19:59 and 6:84-87, which represent the prophets as rightly guided, and 61:14; 5:111, which refer to the Hawariyun (the disciples - ed.), who were the followers of Jesus.

[37] Cf. Gaudeul, "Leo and 'Umar," *Islamochristiana*, 10, p. 134, BNM 4944, parag. 10 - ed.

[38] This number 22 is no argument against the ascription of the letter to Leo on the ground that the Emperor, familiar with the Septuagint, would have used the orthodox list containing the Deuterocanonica, and on the other hand the usual Armenian lists of Ghevond's time would almost certainly have contained the extra books. See Beck's note and references in *Orientalia Christiana Analecta*, CXIV, 45 n.

[39] The *Kuhilet* for Koheleth, and *Sirtsirim* for Shir hash-Shirim, are fairly good equivalences, but *Parimon* seems to be a mistake, the subscription παροιμίαι from the book of Proverbs being taken for the superscription to Ἐκκλησιαστής. The *Samatan* doubtless represents part of the title ἄσμα ἀσμάτων.

[40] Cf. Mingana, "Timothy and Mahdi," *Bulletin of the Johns Rylands Library*; Timothy, parag. CN; al-Kindi, parag. CJ.

[41] Psalms 136 (Septuagint) = Psalms 137 - ed.

[42] He is referring back to the charge of the Caliph that the Old Testament was many times lost and at a later period recomposed out men's heads. The "many times lost" doubtless refers to the Rabbinic tale that at three different times in the history of the Jews the Torah was nearly forgotten, but each time a man from Babylon restored it. The first time it was restored by Ezra, the second by Hillel in the time of King Herod and the third by Rabbi Hiyya the elder, the disciple of and friend of R. Jehuda Hannasi, assisted by his sons Hezekiah and Judah (B. Sukkah 20a). The "recomposing," of course, is the legendary labor of Esdras and his scribes related in II (IV) Esdras cap. 14, a tale that occurs elsewhere in Muslim apologetic. The Latin 315b has the charge a little more explicitly - "*et iterum dicis, quia, cum lex Moysi in igne fuisset cremata et renovasset eam Esdras propheta ut potuit ei memoria cordis sui recordari, et non sine mendacio,*" and refers to it again in 321a, - "*quod autem dicis, legem Moysi esse crematam, et quod eam Esdras memoriter et mendaciter memoravit.*" A second reference by Leo (p. 55 of the Armenian text), also recognizes that the Caliph's reference is to the Ezra legend, "you attack the second edition which Esdras composed." The Ezra legend in II (IV) Esdras 14 speaks of the law as having been burned - "*lex tua incensa est*" (v. 21) and of Ezra's memory being the source of the dictation - "*spiritus meus conservabat memoriam*" (v. 40) and of course it was the Holy Spirit's descent which was to enable him to do the work - "*inmitte in me spiritum sanctum, et scribam omne quod factum est in saeculo ab initio quae erant in lege tua scripta*" (v. 22). Leo may have derived his knowledge directly

from the book in the Apocrypha, but the detail he adds about the confronting of the two texts is curious. His earlier insistence that the "Testament" (i.e. the Torah) went with them to Babylon is in accord with a Rabbinic tradition to the effect that a copy of the Torah with "crowns" had been buried under the threshold of the temple, where Ezekiel found it and carried it to Babylon with him, whence it was brought back by Ezra (Sefer ha Tagin in Ginzburg's *Massorah*, II, 680). As the tradition speaks of its being brought by back by Ezra himself, it is clear that an attempt is being made to identify it with "the Law of thy God which is in thy hand" of Ezra 7:14, 25, 26, so that the reading aloud of the Law mentioned in Nehem. 8 ff. may have been interpreted as the comparison of the old copy from Babylon with the new one produced by Ezra by way of inspiration. The Latin 321c makes the point that even though Ezra reproduced the matter from memory, this would be nothing against it, since he was a prophet and *"in prophetis Dei non est mendacium neque oblivio, quia Deus fit revelatio illorum,"* a sentiment which would be universally approved by orthodox Muslims, since according to their teaching one of the things which cannot be ascribed to prophets is "nisyan", i.e. "forgetfulness." - For 'Umar's remark which triggered this response, see: Gaudeul, "Leo and 'Umar," *Islamochristiana*, 10, p. 135, BNM 4944, parag. 10 - ed.

[43] Cf. Gaudeul, "Leo and 'Umar," *Islamochristiana*, 10, p. 135, BNM 4944, parag. 13 - ed.

[44] See the Latin 315b, 321b. - Jahiz, parag. T - ed.

[45] The Muslim finds so much detail in regard to eschatological matters in the Qur'an and the Traditions that it naturally struck him as very strange that he found so little descriptive matter in the Old Testament regarding the pains of hell, the pleasures of heaven, or details on the great day of Resurrection and Judgment, though there were passages more to his mind in the Gospels. This is not a subject generally raised by the polemic writers, though Perlmann in his account of the Moroccan Jewish convert to Islam, 'Abd al-Haqq al-Islami, mentions that one of the points he makes against the Jewish Scriptures

is that they contain no reference to paradise or hell, as they would if they were of divine origin (*JQR*, XXXI, 187). Leo makes little attempt to meet this charge, and the Latin in 315b, 321b, refers to the evidence of Esdras, which may mean the matter in II (IV) Esdras 7 & 8 (On the other hand, his Esdras may not refer to the book in the Apocrypha, but merely to Ezra as the restorer of the Old Testament).

[46] The Caliph's problem is that the Injil (εὐαγγέλιον) mentioned in the Qur'an as the book of Jesus, must, according to theory, be a book containing the revelations given by God to Jesus for Him to proclaim to the people, whereas the Gospel in the hands of the Christians consists of these four Evangelists' accounts of the "Good News" as proclaimed in the words and deeds of Jesus, which is a very different thing. - For 'Umar's comment on this, see: Gaudeul, "Leo and 'Umar," *Islamochristiana*, 10, p. 135, BNM 4944, parag. 13 - ed.

[47] The orthodox Muslim view, of course, is that the divine original of Scripture is in the heavens and that the material was revealed piecemeal by the angel Gabriel to the Prophet over a period of some twenty odd years, the Prophet reciting the passages to the people as they were progressively revealed to him. (Bukhari, ed. Krehl, II, 410. - *Sahih Bukhari*, The Virtues and Merits of the Prophet and his Companions, ch. 24, hadith 819, Vol. 4, pp. 526-7. - ed.) In very many passages Allah speaks of revealing this or that to the Prophet, and the common verb used in the Qur'an in connection with revelation is *nazzala, anzala, tanazzala,* from a root meaning "to come down," so that there is no doubt that the material was meant to be understood as "sent down from heaven." In the Qur'an itself, however, there are hints that Muhammad's contemporaries knew that he had informants of another faith giving him at least some of his material. In (Qur'an) 25:5,6 we have the charge of the Meccans that others had helped him with the production of the Qur'an, which they said was but "tales of the ancients" that he had put into writing as they were dictated to him morn and even; and in (Qur'an) 16:105 the Meccans hint that they know a certain person who taught him the things he claimed to receive by revelation. Numerous suggestions have been made, both by the Mus-

lim commentators and by Western students, as to who this "mentor" may have been, but in any case that would refer only to odd bits of information or material supplied to Muhammad for working up into his revelations, not that they were the authors of the book. The charge that 'Umar, Abu Turab and Salman the Persian were the authors of the Qur'an, however, is peculiar. By 'Umar he means 'Umar b. al-Khattab, the second Caliph. Abu Turab is 'Ali, the son-in-law of the Prophet and the fourth Caliph. The tractate "Contra Muhammad," printed at the end of Bartholomew of Edessa's *Confutatio* in PG, CIV, speaks (col. 1457) of 'Ali as having been the one through whom the Qur'an was put into circulation. Salman al-Farisi is one of the most curious figures of Islamic history and legend. That he was a historical person, need not be questioned. Possibly he was a Persian slave at Madina who embraced Islam and put his knowledge at the service of the new faith. His position as a non-Arab Muslim, however, made him as conspicuous as "the firstfruits of Persia in Islam," and attracted so much legend to his figure that even his connection with the famous Ditch is questioned by some critics. Part of this legend connects him with the production of the Qur'an.

[48] The commonest charge of alteration in the Gospel is that the name of Muhammad was there, but the Christians removed it. The remark about removing the names of the Evangelists refers to the Muslims claim, mentioned before, that Matthew, Mark, Luke and John prove the Gospels to be the words of men and not the word of God, or as the Muslim objector in Bartholomew of Edessa says (col. 1384c) - Διὰ τί τὸ κατελθὸν Εὐαγγέλιον ἐκρύψατε, καὶ νέον ἐγράψατε;

[49] In the Qur'an there are many references to the expectation that an angel should be the agent of revelation, or of instruction from God.

[50] The Caliph's question as to whether Jesus had not in the Gospel, in speaking about the Paraclete, referred to the coming of Muhammad, goes back to the Qur'anic verse 61:6, "And when Jesus, the son of Mary, said - O children of Israel, I am the messenger of Allah to you,

confirming the Torah now present and announcing a messenger to come after me, whose name is Ahmad." The name Ahmad is from the same root as the name Muhammad, both meaning much the same thing, "the praised," and the common supposition is that the statement refers back to the promise of the Paraclete in John 14:16, 26; 15:26; 16:7. But see the discussion by A. Fischer, "Muhammad and Ahmad, die Namen des arabischen Propheten," in *Berichte über die Verhandlungen der Sächsischen Akademie der Wissenschaften*, 84 (1932), Heft 3. Whatever the origin of this may have been, the claim that the promise of the Paraclete was fulfilled in Muhammad is prominent in Muslim thought. Timothy in his Apology before al-Mahdi (Timothy, parags. AN-AP) is at pains to prove the Muslim claim wrong, and almost every polemical writing in this field contains some account of the matter (see Fritsch, 90 ff.). Some sought to explain the reference as a deliberate deception of Muhammad by the renegade monk who was his mentor. Thus the Syriac writer Isho'yabb in the Christian Bahira Legend edited by Gottheil in ZA, XIII, tells us (on p. 213) how the scribe Kaleb (= Ka'b), who came after Sergius, taught the Muslims that Muhammad himself was the Paraclete. - For 'Umar's mention of this, see: Gaudeul, "Leo and 'Umar," *Islamochristiana*, 10, p. 139, BNM 4944, parag. 27 - ed.

[51] A fallacious claim by Leo. - ed.

[52] The Caliph's question was doubtless based on his memory of the Muslim tradition as to the seventy-two sects of the Christians, not on anything he had learned from Christian sources - cf. Wensinck, *Handbook, Sunan Abu Dawud*, Book of Sunna, chap. 1. - ed. The splitting up into sects is a matter for which the Jews and Christians are blamed in the Qur'an, indeed (30:31; 42:11), but the number seventy belongs only to the tradition. - For 'Umar's remark concerning this, see: Gaudeul, "Leo and 'Umar," *Islamochristiana*, 10, p. 135, BNM 4944, parag. 14 - ed.

[53] The hundred years since the religion of Islam appeared would be accurate for Leo writing in 718 (A.D.), for August 3rd of that year saw

the beginning of the year 100 A.H., a year specially marked by the Muslims, as we know from the Annalists, because it was to be a year of great portent for the Islamic religion and empire.

[54] The identification of these Muslim sects is not simple. The names are given in the same order, though with slight orthographical variations, in Vartan (p. 53 of the text as printed in Muyldermans, *La Domination Arabe*) who almost certainly took them from a MS of Ghevond. In each case we have to assume, of course, that the Armenian name is an attempt at transliterating a Greek form, which itself may not be a very accurate representation of the Arabic original. The *Kawzi* (Vartan *Kouzi*) are doubtless the Khawarij, as Chahnazarian suggests. They were the political puritans of Islam, who created much trouble all through the days of the Umayyad caliphate. The *Sabari* (Vartan *Sabri*), whom Chahnazarian would identify with the Jubba'ites, followers of Abu 'Ali al-Jubba'i (d. 915), are perhaps rather the Jabarites, who with the Murji'ites presently to be mentioned, formed one of the earliest known sects of Islam. The *Tourapi* (Vartan *Tourabi*) are doubtless some 'Alid sect, since 'Ali himself was known as Abu Turab (see Nöldeke in ZDMG, LII, 29 ff. on the name) and his Shi'ite followers often Turabiyya. - For a Muslim source on how 'Ali received this name, see al-Tabari, *History*, Vol. 7, pp. 16 ff. The *Kntri* may be, as Chahnazarian suggests, the Qadarites, who appear with the Murji'ites and the Jabarites as among the earliest sects of Islam. They were so named because they believed in free-will and that man had power (*qadar*) over his actions. They were the predecessors of the Mu'tazilites. The *Mourji* are quite obviously the Murji'ites or "postponers," who withheld judgment till they could see how Allah would pronounce on the Last Day. The *Basli* (Vartan *Basli*) must be the Mu'tazilites, or at least a group of them, the name deriving from the famous Wasil b. 'Ata' (d. 131 A.H. = 748 A.D.), whose separation from his master al-Hasan al-Basri is a story famous in the books of Muslim theology. - Another possibility is that the name refers to Basra itself, a city which became fertile ground for the opponents of orthodox Islam. As early as 'Uthman's Caliphate not a small number of Muslims in Iraq read the Qur'an according to the codex of Ibn Mas'ud,

which codex is known to have differed considerably from that of the orthodox recension of 'Uthman - ed. The *Jahdi* (Vartan *Jhdi*) would seem to be the Jahizites, the followers of the "goggle-eyed" Mu'tazilite teacher of Basra, Abu 'Amr b. Bahr al-Jahiz, who died in 869. It is hardly true to say, as Ghevond does, that he denied the existence of God and the resurrection, though the thoroughgoing philosophical skepticism of Jahiz and his clever mockery of much that the orthodox taught both about Allah and the hereafter, may well have sounded like a denial of both. - The term *Jahdi* might instead refer to the Yazidis, a group which ash-Shahrastani says was founded by Yazid b. Abu Anisa as a Kharijite sub-sect. The Yazidis, which still exist today as a group, pray to the Malak Ta'us, i.e., Satan, who is practically their object of worship. Though they do believe in God as Creator, theologically they accord the Malak Ta'us by far the greatest honor. Moreover, the Yazidis apparently believe in reincarnation and have no doctrine of eternal punishment (cf. Joseph, *Devil Worship*, pp. 18, 19 and 118-131; also SEI, pp. 248 and 641-645.) If indeed the Yazidis are meant here, it would not only be one of the earliest evidences of their existence, but would also confirm that they were originally an Islamic sect - ed. The *Hariuri* (Vartan *Hariri*) Chahnazarian would identify with the Khurramiyya, followers of Babak al-Khuarrami, the son of an Aramaic-speaking oil-seller of Ctesiphon, who appeared in 816 and for some twenty years terrorized W. and N.W. Persia, claiming to be a theophany and to reincarnate the spirit of Jawidan. Or failing this he would see in them the Hululite sects who taught that God's spirit continues to incarnate amongst men (see Baghdadi, *Farq*, 241 ff.). It is much more likely, however, that the reference is to the Haruriyya, a name for the Kharijites, or portion thereof, given them from the town of Harura or Haraura, outside Kufa, where the Khawarij retired when 'Ali returned to Kufa from the battle of Siffin. They are often called Haruriyya in the theological tractates and also in ordinary historical references. They would best fit the description of Ghevond of being so fierce against the orthodox that they would willingly kill them as infidels and enemies and consider it most meritorious to die fighting against them.

[55] This list of languages is that of the 1887 text, which differs somewhat from that of 1857.

[56] This is a rather confused reference to the work of al-Hajjaj on the text of the Qur'an. The orthodox Muslim theory assumes that the text as canonized by 'Uthman was the final canonization, but there is reason to believe that a recension of 'Uthman's text was made by the direction of al-Hajjaj, so that we only know of the text of 'Uthman in this later recension. This fact was apparently well known to Oriental Christian writers, for al-Kindi in his Apology (al-Kindi, Parag. CO), speaks of al-Hajjaj not leaving a single codex which he did not gather up and left out many things, and of how he sent out copies of his new recension and directed his attention to destroying the older codices. This statement of al-Kindi has always been looked at askance as a piece of Christian polemic, but we know from Ibn 'Asakir (*Tarikh*, IV, 82) that one of al-Hajjaj's claims to fame was his being instrumental in giving the Qur'an to the people, and from Ibn Duqmaq (*Intisar*, IV, 72) we know of the commotion in Egypt when a codex from those which al-Hajjaj had officially written out to be sent to the chief cities of the Muslim Empire reached that country. As there were stories about al-Hajjaj being connected with the earliest attempts at putting diacritical marks in the Qur'anic text to make its readings more certain (Ibn Khallikan, I, 183 quoting Abu Ahmad al-'Askari), and also with the earliest attempts at dividing the text into sections (Ibn Abu Dawud, *Kitab al-Masahif*, p. 119 in my *Materials*), it might be suggested that this recension of his was merely an improved edition of the 'Uthmanic text, which he had prepared and copies of which he had sent out as the edition to be officially used. Such a suggestion would also suit the story in the as yet unprinted *Mushkil* of Ibn Qutayba, that he ordered the destruction of all the codices representing a text earlier than that canonized by 'Uthman and (that) with his well-known enmity towards the text of Ibn Mas'ud (Ibn 'Akasir, IV, 69; Ibn al-Athir *Chronicon*, IV, 463). In Ibn Abu Dawud (pp. 49, 117), however, we have a list of eleven passages on the authority of no less a person than Abu Hatim as-Sijistani, where our present text is said to be that of al-Hajjaj and that this was well known to Christians of that day, and naturally exag-

gerated by them for polemical purposes. As this work would seem to
have been done by al-Hajjaj during his period of office under the
Caliph 'Abd al-Malik b. Marwan, who died in 86 A.H. = 705 A.D.,
there is no difficulty in supposing that Leo may have heard of it during
his official life in Syria. His remark about a few of the works of Abu
Turab having escaped may refer to works such as collections of proverbs, etc., which were ascribed to 'Ali, and as such circulated in the
East, or it may merely refer to codices of the Qur'an which he knew
had escaped the general destruction ordered by al-Hajjaj. - The reference to Abu Turab and al-Hajjaj on the part of the Christian polemicists may very well have been an argument which was adapted from
charges early Shiites brought against Sunni editions of the text of the
Qur'an; cf. Religious Dialogue, parag. I - ed.

[57] 'Umar appears to have misquoted Bible verses just as Leo accuses
him; for an example, see: Gaudeul, "Leo and 'Umar," *Islamochristiana*,
10, p. 137, BNM 4944, parag. 20 - ed.

[58] The Latin deals with this charge in 317a. Again it is a Qur'anic
charge that the Caliph is preferring, for in 4:169 the Christians are
bidden "say not three," and in v. 77 of the next sura, those who say
"Allah is the third of three," are classed among the unbelievers. The
wording of sura 5:116, "O Jesus, son of Mary, was it Thou who didst
say to the people - 'Take Me and my mother as gods apart from
Allah?' " suggests that Muhammad thought of the Christian Trinity as
parallel to the numerous Near Eastern triads of Father, Mother, Son.
In the Latin 317a the question of the engendering of the Son is brought
out a little more specifically - "Pater non est genitus, Filius est genitus,
Spiritus sanctus non est genitus necque ingenitus," apparently having in
mind the Qur'anic passage 112:3, "He begetteth not and is not begotten."

[59] The notion of using the sun as an example to explain the Trinity
is at least as old as Tertullian, c. 200 A.D. (*Apology* 21 as given in
Eerdmans' Handbook, p. 112) and as evidenced by Timothy, al-Kindi,
etc., see Appendix A; its use in early Christian-Muslim dialogues was

widespread - ed.

[60] This illustration from the sun is given somewhat differently by the Latin 316c.

[61] The story of the angels being commanded to bow down to Adam is in Qur'an 2:32 (cf. 17:63; 18:48; 20:115), which is the story of the fall of Iblis through his refusal to obey this command.

[62] This is the beginning of his argument in reply to the objection that the Christians are in error in adoring Christ. The Latin 320c on this points out that the Children of Israel adored the Ark (doubtless referring to II Chron. 5:6 ff.), and yet in so doing they were not adoring the wood of the Ark, but the Law, the Word of God, which was in the Ark (I Ki. 8:9), so since the angels were commanded to adore the newly created Adam, why should one not adore the Incarnate Word? Then it asks whether it is not better to adore Him than some deaf stone at Mecca, which is but a relic of ancient heathenism. The reference, of course, is to the shrine at Mecca with its sacred Black Stone. The *"idololatria illa qua adorabant Jaoh, Jaoc, Nazara, et Allac et Allogei et Mena, quidam ex eis erant dei in similitudine virorum, quaedam in similitudine feminarum,"* is a reference to Qur'an 53:19,20, which mentions the three goddesses Al-Lat, al-'Uzza and Manat, all of which were in female form, and Qur'an 71:23, which mentions the ancient Arab deities Yaghuth, Ya'uq and Nasr. His following sentence, however, is difficult to understand - *"Majores horum, dicebantur Alleubre, unde et sermo iste derivatur, Alacuiber, inter vos immolentes eis pecora et camelos in uno die pro unoquoque anno."* If we can suppose *Aleubre* to be a misprint for *Alcubra*, then the two words may be the two superlatives, masc. and fem. *al-kubra* and *al-akbar*, "the greatest," used in the titles of the original male and female deity of the shrine, i.e. the Hubal and 'Uzza whom we learn figured together in the pagan Mecca war-cry. The sacrifice of cattle and camels at the Meccan shrine in pre-Islamic times is well attested. He then goes on, *"et secuti estis consuetudinem paganorum super lapide illo, in Mecha, in angulo domus ipsius idololatriae, cui serviebat antiquitas paganorum, et immola-*

bat," referring to the Black Stone (*al-hajar al-aswad*), which is set in
the outside southern corner of the Ka'ba (Rif'at Pasha, *Mir'at al-Hara-
main*, I, 132 ff.; 300 ff.).

[63] The idea of using man as an example to describe the Trinity was
also used by Timothy and al-Kindi; see Appendix A - ed.

[64] The substance of the argument of God's remedy for the sad state
of sinful man is that of the Latin 319. The following Scripture "proof
texts," while by no means the same as are used in the Latin in 317 ff.,
(they) are of the same general type.

[65] That the Moabitish worship was of a licentious character is suggested by such Old Testament passages as Num. 25, and the Moabite
Stone with its reference to 'Ashtar-Chemosh, suggests the Baal and
consort worshipped with licentious rites at the "high places," but we
have no evidence to support the precise charge in the text as to the
forms of the images. Later Rabbinic writers commenting on Num.
21:29, tell us that the idol of the Moabites was a black stone in female
form (*Midrash Lekach Tob*, ed. Padua, Wilna, 1884, in loc.).

[66] The name יִשְׂרָאֵל = "may El strive," is explained in Gen. 32:28;
Hos. 12:4 as "wrestler with El," but from the later pronunciation of the
name, represented in the Greek and Syriac forms with initial א, there
grew up the conceit that it was made up of the three elements אִישׁ רָאָה
אֵל = "man who saw God." From Philo's Ἰσραήλ, ὅπερ ἑρμηνευθέν
ἐστιν . . . ὁρῶν θεόν - (*de Abrahamo*, 12, cf. de congressu eruditionis
gratia, 10), the idea passed to the Greek ecclesiastical writers, and was
doubtless the common understanding of the name in Leo's day.

[67] For this question of the two witnesses see p. 108, n. 35.

[68] The passages in question are Qur'an 19:29 where the mother of
Jesus is called the sister of Aaron and 66:12 where she is called "daughter of Imran." The Latin 315b. c. does not make this point about the
thirty-two generations that had elapsed between the two Miriams, but

merely says that the one Miriam died in the desert before they entered the promised land. It then goes on to make the further point that the first Miriam was of the tribe of Levi, whereas the mother of Jesus was of the tribe of Judah. - This subject was so popular in early Christian-Muslim dialogues, that it finds mention in *Sahih Muslim* as an objection of the Christians at Najran (Kitab al-Adab, ch. 891, hadith 5326, Vol. 3, p. 1169), see also: John of Damascus, parag. B - ed.

[69] See notes 33 and 42.

[70] In the Qur'an Jesus is represented as saying things which are not to be found in any Gospel, canonical or apocryphal, but which, according to Muslim theory, would presumably have been found in the Gospel to which Muhammad refers, which is why Leo further on asks that this Gospel be cited. The reason Leo mentions specifically the Torah, Psalms and Gospel is that these three alone are mentioned in the Qur'an, and the challenge to produce other books of Moses, David and Jesus, if those which are in the hands of the People of the Book are not genuine, must have been early made, for there have been attempts to answer the challenge by producing such. The point of the usual Muslim objection to the Scriptures at present in the hands of the Jews and the Christians, is that a Scripture should contain the "Word of God," i. e., in it God would be the speaker from beginning to end as He is in the Qur'an. In the Qur'an we find God addressing man all through, whereas in the Jewish and Christian Scriptures it is as often as not man addressing God. The genuine Torah or Zabur (Psalter) or Injil (Gospel), would thus, according to the Muslim idea, be similarly composed in verses of rhymed prose (*saj*, in which God would be addressing man.

[71] Numerous examples of "sayings of Jesus" are to be found in Muslim theological literature.

[72] The regulation concerning the Qibla, or direction to which the Muslims must turn in prayer, is given in Qur'an 2:136-140. The Ka'ba, of course, in pre-Islamic days had been a pagan shrine, and there can

be little doubt that many of the ceremonies thereat, the circumambulation, the kissing of the Black Stone, etc., which were taken over into the Islamic ceremonial of the Pilgrimage, derive from pagan practice, so that there is some color of truth to the charge that the Muslims venerate a pagan altar of sacrifice.

[73] Cf. Gaudeul, "Leo and 'Umar," *Islamochristiana*, 10, p. 137, BNM 4944, parags. 17, 18 - ed.

[74] Possibly this was a name used for the Ka'ba, though now the *Maqam Ibrahim* (which is mentioned in the Qur'an in 2:119; 3:91), is pointed out as a special place in the sanctuary area and has its own cycle of legends. - That the Scripture says nothing as to the direction in which the prophets prayed, is not accurate (I Kings 8:29; Dan. 6:10), and appears to show a little dishonesty on Leo's part. Early Muslims also used to pray toward Jerusalem before Muhammad had a falling out with the Jews and a "revelation" came changing the direction of prayer to the then still pagan shrine of the Ka'ba (Qur'an 2:136-145; al-Tabari, *History*, Vol. 7, pp. 24 ff.) - ed.

[75] Cf. Gaudeul, "Leo and 'Umar," *Islamochristiana*, 10, p. 137, BNM 4944, parag. 21 - ed.

[76] The Qur'an speaks of Jesus as having been aided by the Holy Spirit (2: 81, 254; 5:109), and as Gabriel was identified with the Holy Spirit (cf. 16: 104), it was commonly said that Jesus had angelic help and assistance, which is doubtless what is referred to here.

[77] The reference is probably to the statement in the Qur'an that Jesus was merely a "Messenger" (*rasul*, 5:111; 3:43; 4:156; cf. 43:59), i.e. one sent, just as other Messengers had been sent, and to the passages (3:48; 5: 117) which refer to how Allah took Him to Himself. The Latin 315a states the objection that adoration of Christ is out of place since He Himself brought testimony "*dicens quod missus sit a Deo,*" and quoting the promise in Matt. 10:32 about confessing before the Father those who would confess Him on earth and His statement

in John 20:17 about ascending to His God and their God, as clear evidence that He did not think of Himself as God. - Cf. Gaudeul, "Leo and 'Umar," *Islamochristiana*, 10, p. 138, BNM 4944, parag. 24 - ed.

[78] Cf. Gaudeul, "Leo and 'Umar," *Islamochristiana*, 10, p. 139, BNM 4944, parag. 27 - ed.

[79] Cf. Gaudeul, "Leo and 'Umar," *Islamochristiana*, 10, p. 138, BNM 4944, parag. 24 - ed.

[80] The argument from here on is an answer to the Muslim objection that Jesus was a mere man as Adam was. In the Latin 315a the objection is put quite simply, that Christ was in the sight of God such as Adam was, for He ate and slept as Adam did, This is again taken up there in 320b. The reference is to the Qur'anic passage 3:52, "Jesus, indeed, is as Adam in the sight of God. He created Him of dust *(turab)*." To which the Latin 320d, 321a objects - "*Ponitis facturam de luto, quae contradixit Deo suo, et non custodivit praeceptum eius, similem Verbo Dei et lumini ipsius, qui non est factus, sed per ipsum facta sunt omnia.*" The *de luto* of the Latin probably represents the *min tin* "of clay" of the Qur'anic stories of the creation of Adam (7:11 etc.). It would seem that Christians in their argument with Muslims used to make much of the fact that the birth of Jesus was without the agency of a human father, as is admitted in the Qur'anic accounts of the Annunciation. A favorite Muslim counter-argument is that mentioned by Leo here, that if Jesus is to be ranked high because of His birth from a mother without a father, then Adam must rank higher still, for he was produced without even a mother being necessary.

[81] Doubtless a reference to the famous passage in Qur'an 4:156, which replies to the Jewish boast that they had killed the Messiah by declaring that they had not killed Him nor crucified Him, but only someone in His likeness.

[82] Since all Muslims follow the ancient Semitic practice of circumcision, though it is not so much as mentioned in the Qur'an, it was a

peculiar grievance of theirs against the Oriental Christians that they did
not follow this custom and considered their baptism as a substitute for
it. The Caliph al-Mahdi urges this against the Patriarch Timothy,
Timothy, parags. AA-AB - ed.

[83] The Latin 321c leads up from the sacrifice of the two sons of
Adam, which is mentioned in the Qur'an itself (5:30), and so well
known to Muslims, to the sacrificial nature of the Eucharist. Then in
321d, 322a he quotes the strange account of the Last Supper and
institution of the Eucharist given in Qur'an 5:112-115. His knowledge
of the Qur'anic passage is probably from oral tradition and makes
curious comparison with the original -

Cum discipuli Filio Dei dixis-
sent, 'Invoca Deum ut dirigat
nobis manna de coelo?'; et
dixisset Christus, 'Timete Deum
si estis fideles,' discipuli
dixerunt, 'Volumus comedere
illud et credemus tibi et sci-
emus quia verbum locutus es
nobis, et testabimur quia Christus Deus es: dirige manna de
coelo, ut sit nobis festum sol-
umne, et posteris nostris sig-
num ex te: haec nobis tribue,
quia tu es dator donorum.' Et
Deus dixit, 'Dirigam illud vobis'; quod postquam negavit,
cruciaverunt eum cruciatione
qua nemo cruciatus fuit.

When the disciples said, 'O Jesus,
Son of Mary is your Lord able to
send down to us a table from heav-
en?' He said, 'Fear Allah, if you are
believers.' They said, 'We desire to
eat thereof, that our hearts may be at
ease, and we shall know that Thou
hast spoken the truth to us, and we
shall be witnesses thereto.' Jesus,
Son of Mary, said, 'Allahumma, our
Lord, Send down to us a table from
heaven, which will be to us a feast, to
be first of us and the last of us and a
sign from Thee. Do Thou make
provision for us, for Thou art the
best of providers.' Allah said, 'I shall
send it down to you, but whoever of
you afterwards believes, Him will I
punish with such a punishment as I
have never punished anyone in the
world.'

When he goes on to attribute this strange account of the Eucharist to a

Nestorian instructor - "*Et tamen hi sermones fuerunt Nestoriani cujus-dam haeretici, non sane de Christo sentientii, qui vos introduxit quasi ut aliquid de fide Christi intellegeretis, sed ut est ratio et varitas vobis non demonstravit,*" he is alluding once again to the commonly held idea that Muhammad was instructed in religion by a mentor from one of the other heretical sects.

[84] Cf. Gaudeul, "Leo and 'Umar," *Islamochristiana*, 10, p. 137, BNM 4944, parag. 18 - ed.

[85] See reference in note 84.

[86] Chahnazarian has a note about this charge of Leo's that among the Muslims the females also are circumcised, saying that he had not been able to find any ancient author who tells of this, so that he judges that what is said on this matter in Greek and Armenian authors must be put down either to inexact information or to prejudice and enmity. The practice is, however, well evidenced among Muslim peoples, though neither male nor female circumcision is referred to in the Qur'an. In the famous story in the *Arabian Nights*, entitled "The Muslim Champion and the Christian Maid," for example, we read - "so he expounded to her the tenets of the faith of Islam, and she became a Muslima, after which she was circumcised, and he taught her the ritual prayers." There is a discussion of the practice as applied to both boys and girls in the *Musnad* of Ahmad b. Hanbal, V, 75. - an early Muslim reference to female circumcision can be found in al-Tabari, *History*, Vol. 2, p. 72; al-Jahiz, parag. T - ed.

[87] See reference in note 84.

[88] The objection to the incarnation is not generally put as grossly as it is by 'Umar, but it was a common objection. In the Latin 321a the objection is put *quomodo Deus potuit ingredi in ventrem mulieris, tene-brosum et angustum et fetidum,* and the reply is given that the sun every day sends its rays down into all sorts of filth and ordures, yet far from being defiled thereby, it on the contrary cleanses everything. It then

continues with the illustration of the "burning bush" (Exod. 3:2-4),
adding - *nonne melius erat corpus Virginis quam illa spina rubi?* Very
curiously the Latin thinks that Moses was given the Law from the fire
in the bush, obviously confusing the call at Horeb to go and liberate
the Children of Israel, with the flame of fire at Sinai at the giving of
the Law - *qui ingressus in rubo qui erat in monte Sinai, et locutus est
servo suo Moysi, et legem ei dedit.* This is the more curious as the
Qur'an keeps the two events quite distinct, the experience of the bush
being at the vale *Tuwa* (20:9-35; 79:16), and the giving of the Law at
Sinai (7:138-142). The objection, of course, arises from the indignant
denial oft repeated in the Qur'an that the eternal God could have had
a son or daughters as the pagan Arabs asserted. The Latin 319a quotes
in this connection Qur'an 3:40, where the birth of Jesus is said to be "a
word from Him: His name shall be Messiah," but curiously says the
announcement was to Zachariah, getting it mixed up with Qur'an 19:7,
the succeeding verses of which also tell of the annunciation to Mary. In
320a, again, in speaking of Mary as *Mariam quam elegerat*, there is
apparently a reference to 3:37, where Mary is twice referred to as
"chosen" by Allah. In 320c the reference to the Jews *dicentes blas-
phemiae verba ad Mariam matrem ejus, cui pudor castitatis inerat*, is
doubtless to Qur'an 4:155, where the Jews are upbraided for having
"spoken against Mary a grievous calumny." The writer, however, has
slipped in his further reference - *et secundum vestrum sensum, Judaei
intelligentes de Christo, persequentes et comprehendentes, eum crucifixer-
unt*, for 4:156 expressly states, "But they slew Him not, nor crucified
Him, but only one in His likeness." - For 'Umar's remarks concerning
this, see: Gaudeul, "Leo and 'Umar," *Islamochristiana*, 10, p. 144,
BNM 4944, parag. 47.

[89] The reference is to 'Umar's uncle Muhammad b. Marwan, whom
Leo would have known only too well, for it was he who in the year 75
A.H. = 694 A.D. led the summer campaign which resulted in the
severe defeat of the Byzantines at Mar'ash, Leo's own home (Baladhuri, *Futuh*, 188). He was also the general governing Armenia under
the Caliphate of his brother 'Abd al-Malik (ibid. 205) and under his
successor al-Walid I and had the task of putting down the Armenian

rebellion which took advantage of the insurrection of Ibn az-Zubair to make a bid for freedom. His cruelties and evil deeds in Armenia had already been dealt with at length by Ghevond earlier in this book.

[90] There are a few hadith which show that Muhammad cursed the Jews and Christians for burying some of their dead in places of worship - *Sahih Bukhari*, The Book of Salat, ch. 55, hadith 427, Vol. 1, p.255; *Sahih Muslim*, Kitab al-Salat, ch. 197, hadith 1081, Vol. 1, p. 269. For 'Umar's comment on this, see: Gaudeul, "Leo and 'Umar," *Islamochristiana*, 10, p. 149, BNM 4944, parag. 62 - ed.

[91] It very natural for the Caliph to raise an objection to Christian veneration of the Cross. In Muslim tradition as to the Last Day we find an account of how Jesus will return before the end and become a Muslim, and among the particular acts He will then perform is that of breaking all the crosses, the reason, of course, being that the cross is an offence to the Muslims (cf. *Sahih Bukhari*, The Book of Sales, ch. 104, hadith 425, Vol. 2, pp. 233-4; and *Sahih Muslim*, Kitab al-Iman, ch. 72, hadith 287, Vol. 1, p. 92. - ed.). We have early attestation of Christians being reproved for their veneration of the Cross. The veneration of saints and relics, and the use of pictures and images are part of the regular arsenal of later Muslim polemical writers, but they must have been subjects of controversy and discussion in Leo's day, when the Iconoclastic controversy was raging, so that it is not surprising to see them appear in the Caliph's letter. The Latin 322a in dealing with this problem inserts the tale of Constantine's vision of the Cross in whose sign he should conquer, and the subsequent journey of his mother Helena to Jerusalem to seek out the Cross which the Jews had hidden, with the miracle whereby the true cross was revealed, and the Church was built over the sepulchre. The form of the legend as he gives it is very close to that discussed by Tixeront, *Les Origines de l'église d'Edessa et de la lègende d'Abgar* (Paris, 1888), 170-174. - For 'Umar's statements regarding this, see: Gaudeul, "Leo and 'Umar," *Islamochristiana*, 10, p. 149, "Anonymous Pamphlet," parag. 63 - ed.

[92] This is the *tsits* of Exod. 28:36-38, and of which we have divergent

descriptions by Josephus, *Ant.* III, vii, 6 and *BJ*, V, v, 7, and which, as evidenced also by Philo and the *Letter of Aristeas*, seems to have had on it the name of God engraved; but this idea that it had on it some foreshadowing of the crucifix, seems a Byzantine conceit.

[93] See note 74. This reply to the charge of veneration of the Cross etc. by a counter-charge of Muslim veneration of the Ka'ba, is commonly used, as e.g. by John of Damascus in PG, XCIV, 769 - John of Damascus, parag. F - ed.

[94] The story of the serpent connection with the Ka'ba is curious, cf. Ibn Hisham (*Sira*, ed. Wüstenfeld, p. 122). - Ibn Hisham, *The Life of Muhammad*, ed. Guillaume, p. 84. - ed.

[95] He seems to be referring in this passage to the "jinn," who in Muslim thought have a kind of intermediate place between angels and men, being made of fire, whereas angels are made of light and men and animals of clay. These *jinn* are of two sexes, inhabit the space between the earth and the vault of heaven, take on various forms and have relations with human kind, as is frequently illustrated by the tales of the *Arabian Nights*.

[96] This *rokounn* is the Arabic *rukn*, a name for the Black Stone, which is kissed by the pilgrims during the rites of circumambulation of the Ka'ba.

[97] All the references in this last paragraph are to the various ceremonies connected with the annual Pilgrimage, The "carnage of demons" refers to the sacrifice of animals at Mina; the casting of stones refers to the "stoning of the satans" on the 10th of Dhu'l-Hijja on the return from the visit to 'Arafat; the "flight" probably refers to the traversing of the Wadi Muhassir after leaving Muzdalifa, for this passage is directed to be done in speed. The head is shaven after the pilgrimage sacrifice has been killed, and in a measure restores the pilgrim to the freedom of normal life.

[98] Qur'an 2:223 - "Your women are to you as cultivated fields (*harth*); come then to your cultivated fields as you wish, but send forward something for yourselves," a verse which greatly exercised the (Muslim) Commentators. - cf. John of Damascus, parag. G - ed.

[99] *Zedai* is apparently a mistake for Zaynab, the wife of Zayd, the Prophet's adopted son, who divorced her that the Prophet, who had been attracted by her charms, might marry her. It is curious that Bartholomew of Edessa 1420b calls Muhammad's sixth wife Ζαιτέ, which is very much the same as this Zeda of the Armenian text. - cf. John of Damascus, parag. G - ed.

[100] What is in his mind is the fact that in the last resort the Muslim line of defence is that these things were commanded by Allah, who in the Qur'an is represented as explicitly settling these matters, as for example the case of Zaynab above mentioned. To the thought of the Muslim, of course, David's action with Bathsheba and Uriah would also have been under divine direction, since David was a prophet, and it would seem as though 'Umar had made that point in his correspondence with the Emperor.

[101] Cf. Gaudeul, "Leo and 'Umar," *Islamochristiana*, 10, p. 153, "Anonymous Pamphlet," parag. 78 - ed.

[102] Apparently there is here a reference to the characteristic doctrine of Fate, which holds that every action of man, even the least, whether of good or evil, was decreed before his birth, so that no act can really be labelled a sin to be repented of, since it was decreed beforehand that it should happen so, and what sense is there in seeking pardon for doing what we only did in accordance with Allah's decree? The Latin 324a takes this up in somewhat different words - *si ita est, non est illi gratia si bonum operetur, neque peccatum si male operetur; quia non ille operatur, sed quod praescriptum et praeordinatum est illi antequam nasceretur. Nam si ita est, ut cuilibet homini sit praescriptum antequam nascatur, ergo Deus impie videtur egisse.* The Qur'anic passages usually quoted in this connection are 54:52,53; 91:7,8; 17:14; i.e. the

passages concerning the decree and the passages where Allah asserts that whom He will He guides and whom He will He leads astray (14:4; 16:38; etc.). It is this question which is being raised by John of Damascus in PG, XCIV, 1589c, 1592a (John of Damascus, parags. R-AA - ed.), and Bartholomew of Edessa (PG, CIV, 1393b) draws from this idea the conclusion that God must be held finally responsible for both good and evil, as in our Latin.

[103] The marriage laws of the Qur'an are a frequent cause of adverse comment in the Christian polemic writings, as witness John of Damascus 769c (John of Damascus, parag. G - ed.) and the tractate *Contra Muhammad*, 1452a. The charge of ease of divorce is based on Qur'an 2:227 ff.; that of plural marriages in Qur'an 4:29; and the particular regulation that a man may not retake his divorced wife till she has cohabited with another man, in 2:230 violates both the Gospel, which says (Matt. 5:32; 19:9) that he who takes the wife put away by another is an adulterer, and the Law, where in Deut. 24:1-4 the regulation is that if a man wishes to retake a wife whom he has put away, he can only do this if no one else has touched her in the meantime, but 322d makes the further point that whereas the Muslims have a law forbidding them to salute those of another faith (apparently referring to Qur'an 6:54), yet they are permitted to take wives of the women of any faith, and in refusing to pray at the grave of such a non-Muslim wife they are really going contrary to their own law, which in 2:59 declares that all who are faithful, to whatsoever religion it may be, are with God. The usual Muslim burial service, of course, assumes that the corpse is that of a believer, and could not be used for a person of another faith, but Leo's idea of refusal to pray at the grave of an unbeliever is probably based on the Qur'anic passage 9:85 - "Pray not thou ever over any one of them who has died, nor stand at his grave, for they disbelieved in Allah and His Apostle, and died while they were reprobates," where the prohibition was probably meant for that particular occasion (whether referring to the laggards at Hudaybiya or Tabuk), and referred to Muhammad's participating in the pagan Arabian customs connected with burial, but has been taken as a prohibition of general import.

[104] This practice has no support in Islamic sources. - ed.

[105] Cf. Gaudeul, *Islamochristiana*, 10, p. 148, "Anonymous Pamphlet," parag. 57 - ed.

[106] The passage is Isa. 21:6,7 as it stands in the Peshitta text, and in it the Caliph is advancing one of the most famous cases of Old Testament passages in which the Muslims have found prophecies of the coming of Muhammad. Their case is that the watchman in his vision sees two prophets who are yet to come, and hears a great and long speech. The one whom he sees riding on a ass is Jesus, and was fulfilled at the entry of Jesus into Jerusalem (Matt. 21), while the one riding on a camel is Muhammad, and was fulfilled at the Hijra, when Muhammad left unbelieving Mecca and went by camel to Medina, where he organized his community. The great and long speech is a reference to the Qur'an, the sublime eloquence of which Muhammad was to bring to his people. - It is interesting to note that 'Umar apparently thought a quotation of one coming on a camel was a saying of Jesus: cf. Gaudeul, "Leo and 'Umar," *Islamochristiana*, p. 139, BNM 4944, parag. 28 - ed.

[107] This is a very free paraphrase of the LXX text, taking first the ἀναβάτας ἱππεῖς δύο of v.7, and then the ἀναβάτης συνωρίδος of v.9.

[108] Here again the reference would seem to be to the belief in *jinn*.

[109] This represents the Qur'anic *sabil Allah*, and since Allah summoned the Muslims to strive and fight "in the way of Allah," the military expeditions for the spread of Islam were said to be *fi sabil Allah*, whence the reference here.

[110] 'Umar seems to have thought this verse to be another saying of Jesus (cf. Gaudeul, "Leo and 'Umar," *Islamochristiana*, 10, p. 153, "Anonymous Pamphlet," parag. 75), although some rather famous

hadith consider this saying to be a revelation of Allah to Muhammad (*Sahih Bukhari*, The Book of the Beginning of Creation, ch. 7, hadith 467, Vol. 4, pp. 306-7.); see p. 663, n. 64 - ed.

[111] Qur'an 47:16, cf. John of Damascus, parag. H - ed.

[112] Qur'an 56:35 - ed.

[113] This question of the "heavenly spouses" (Qur'an 43:70; 36:56; 55:70 ff; 37:47) was continually raised in the Christian controversial writings, as indeed, the whole Qur'anic picture of a sensuous Paradise.

[114] Cf. Gaudeul, "Leo and 'Umar," *Islamochristiana*, 10, p. 155, "Anonymous Pamphlet," parags. 87, 88 - ed.

[115] The 400 years of Persian tyranny must refer to the Sassanian rule, which lasted from 226 A.D. when Ardashir succeeded in establishing the new national Persian dynasty on the throne in place of the Parthian Arsacids, till 652, when Yazdagird III was killed by the Muslims after the battle of Nihavend. Since the rule of the Sassanians virtually came to an end during the Arab invasions during the reign of Ardashir III (628-630), Leo's 400 years is a correct enough figure.

[116] This conclusion may be the padding of the monkish editor rather than the actual ending of the Emperor's letter.

[117] See 'Umar's remark concerning previous letters: Gaudeul, "Leo and 'Umar," *Islamochristiana*, 10, p. 133, BNM 4944, parag. 3 - ed.

[118] Cf. Gaudeul, "Leo and 'Umar," *Islamochristiana*, 10, pp. 109 ff. - ed.

[119] Ibid, p. 128.

[120] E.g. *Sahih Bukhari*, The Book of Revelation, hadith 6, Vol. 1, pp.

7 ff. - ed.

JOHN OF DAMASCUS
WORKS ON ISLAM

Perhaps none of the Greek Orthodox writers on Islam is as famous as John of Damascus (d. circa 752 A.D.), who is often credited with being the first to address this subject formally. Although this latter distinction may not rightly belong to him, his writings on Islam do appear to have enjoyed a great deal of influence among Byzantine polemicists simply by virtue of their being better preserved. John's role in the Iconoclastic controversy as an opponent of the Emperor Leo III is well known in church history, and in the end they were John's views on the matter which prevailed.

From history it appears that John's family, or more specifically his grandfather, was actively involved in surrendering the city of Damascus to the Muslims.[1] Furthermore, it is known that John's ancestors (and later he himself) held a rather high position in the early days of the Umayyad Caliphate.[2] John's works on Islam are preserved in a section of his work *De Haeresibus*, chapters 100 and 101, and *Disputatio Saraceni et Christiani*. Yet considering all of the knowledge and experience which John of Damascus should have had as one who had grown up and lived in a Muslim society, he transmits very little of this to us. It is apparent that John was familiar with the major "anti-Christian" doctrines espoused by the Qur'an, but his knowledge of the hadith and Islamic history seem to have been remarkably deficient. In many respects John's polemical arguments share an uncanny resemblance to those of Leo III,[3] and as a high official in the Muslim capital, John certainly would have known about any correspondence from Leo to 'Umar II.

The works of John of Damascus on the subject of Islam are instructional in nature, and even his example dialogues with Muslims fit this scheme. After giving a short introduction to Islam, in which he also accurately portrays Muslim Christology, John begins to show how various Islamic accusations can be countered. He warns his reader here and there about occasional pitfalls and traps which the Muslims of his day used on Christians and shows how such problems could have been avoided. The options suggested by John concerning the question of whether or not God's Word is created definitely point to his having some contact with Muslim groups on both sides of the Mu'tazilite issue. In the dialogues preserved by him, John rather oddly devotes approximately equal amounts of text to both defending the Biblical view of Christ and attacking the orthodox Muslim conception of predestination. In at least one passage John shows that he certainly knew of other Muslim objections to Christianity for which he offers no replies, e.g., he is aware of the Muslim accusation that the Bible has been altered,[4] but apparently he either did not know how to answer the question or he thought it to be of lesser importance. In asking Muslims for witnesses to Muhammad's future prophethood, John does not report on any of the Muslim attempts to find Biblical references to him, although this idea is Qur'anic[5] and thus intrinsic even to early Islam. John further misses some obvious Muslim contradictions; he knew that according to the Qur'an there is a river of wine in Paradise from which to drink,[6] but that "Muhammad" had forbidden the drinking of wine.[7] John's frequent paraphrasing of the Qur'an and particularly his choice of wording in some passages[8] also show that his works were intended to instruct Christians rather than to confront Muslims directly.

The brief dialogue of Theodore Abu Qurra is also included as it portrays an application of the Muslim doctrine of progressive revelation and a typical Melkite response according to the methods related by John of Damascus.

The following translations of the works of John of Damascus and Theodore Abu Qurra, were originally published by Rev. John W.

Voorhis in *The Moslem World*, vol. 24 (1934), pp. 391-398 and vol. 25 (1935), pp. 266-273. For a critical investigation of the life and works of John of Damascus on Islam, I recommend Daniel J. Sahas, *John of Damascus on Islam*, E.J. Brill, Leiden, 1972.

Notes:

[1] Savas, *John of Damascus on Islam*, p. 17.

[2] Ibid. pp. 28-9; 41 ff.

[3] Editor's preface to "Leo's Correspondence," p. 52, above.

[4] John of Damascus, parag. D.

[5] Qur'an 7:156; 61:6.

[6] John of Damascus, parag. H, Qur'an 47:16.

[7] Ibid. parag. J, Qur'an 2:216.

[8] Ibid. parag. H.

JOHN OF DAMASCUS
ON THE MUSLIM HERESY
John W. Voorhis

GENERAL INFORMATION
ON ISLAM / DIALOGUES

GREEK ORTHODOX CHRISTIAN
ANTI-ICONOCLAST
John of Damascus
d. circa 752 A.D.

John of Damascus (Johannes Damascenas), an eminent theologian of the Eastern Church, derives his surname from Damascus, where he was born about the close of the seventh century. His Arabic name was al-Mansur (the victor), and he received the epithet Chrysorrhoas (gold-pouring) on account of his eloquence.

His father Sergius, a Christian, held high office under the Saracen Caliph, in which he was succeeded by his son. John wrote (c. 730) several treatises in defence of image-worship, which the emperor, Leo the Isaurian, was making strenuous efforts to suppress. He then surrendered his worldly goods and betook himself to the monastery of St. Sabas, near Jerusalem, where he spent the rest of his life. He was ordained priest by the Patriarch of Jerusalem.

In his last years he travelled through Syria, contending against the Iconoclasts, and visited Constantinople at the imminent risk of his life during the reign of Constantine Copronymus. With him the "mysteries," the entire ritual, are an integral part of the Orthodox system, and all dogma culminates in image-worship. He died probably about 752.

One of his more important books is entitled *De Haeresibus* which, among other tractates, contains an account of Islam. According to Keller "this brief treatise was the armory for all future controversial writings against Islam in the Eastern church." The translation given below was made by the Rev. John W. Voorhis from the Greek text of J. P. Migne, *Patrologia Graeca*, Vol. 94, 1864, cols. 764-773; sec. 101, Latin text in parallel columns.

Professor Bell of Edinburgh University, in his book *The Origin of Islam in its Christian Environment*, refers also to John of Damascus pp. 207-211:

> As showing how that took place I take two things which occur in the works of John of Damascus. John's father was a Christian who was employed in an official position at the court of the Umayyad caliphs at Damascus. He himself in early life occupied a similar position and began his literary activity there before he withdrew to the monastery of Saba where the latter part of his life was spent. In the introduction to his great dogmatic work in which he treats of the heresies, he devotes a section to Islam. There is also included in his works a *Dialogue with a Saracen*, which is a kind of manual for the guidance of Christians in their arguments with Muhammadans. It is not the only work of that kind which has come down to us from that early time. It is not, perhaps, so interesting as we might expect from the situation to which it belongs. But the very fact of such a work having been composed is itself suggestive. It proves what in itself is inherently likely—that arguments of that kind were fairly frequent.

"Islam" in *On Heresies*

(A) There is also, prevailing unto now, the deceptive[1] error[2] of the Ishmaelites, a fore-runner of the anti-Christ. It takes its origin from Ishmael, who was born by Hagar to Abraham; for which reason they are called Hagarenes and Ishmaelites. But they call themselves Saracens, as those (sent away) empty by Sara, Σαρρα κενους[3] because of that which was said by Hagar to the angel. "Sara sent me away empty, Σαρρα κενεν."[4] These then, served idols and worshipped the morning[5] star and Aphrodite, whom they also named in their own tongue "Chabar,"[6] which indeed signifies "great." Accordingly until the time of Heraclius they openly served idols. From that time until now a false prophet arose for them surnamed Mamed, who having happened upon the Old and New Testament, in all likelihood through association with an Arian monk, organized his own sect. And when by a pretence of godliness he had gained the favor of[7] the people, he declared that a scripture[8] had been brought down to him from heaven. Wherefore when he had inscribed in his book[9] certain things worthy of ridicule, he gave it to them as as object to be reverenced.

(B) He says there is one God, maker of all things, not begotten nor begetting (Qur'an 112:3). He says that Christ is a Word of God and His Spirit (Qur'an 4:169), but created (Qur'an 3:52) and a servant[10] (Qur'an 43:59) and that He was born without seed from Mary, the sister of Moses and Aaron (Qur'an 19:29).[11] For the Word of God and the Spirit came in unto Mary and she bare Jesus (Qur'an 4:169; 19:16-21), a prophet and a servant of God (Qur'an 43:59); and that the Jews unlawfully determined to crucify Him, and when they seized Him, they crucified Him in appearance only (Qur'an 4:156);[12] but the Christ Himself was not crucified, nor did He die, for God took Him into heaven unto Himself (Qur'an 4:156) because He loved Him.[13] And this he says, that, when Christ had come up (Qur'an 5:116) into the heavens, God asked Him saying: "O Jesus, did you say, 'I am the Son of God and God'?" And Jesus answered, "Be gracious unto me, Lord; You know that I said not so, nor did I count myself above being Your servant (Qur'an 4:170); but erring[14] men wrote that I said this thing,[15] and spoke falsely against me and have been deceived." And God answered and said to Him, "I know that you did not say this thing."[15] And in this book he tells of many other marvels, worthy of ridicule, and he insolently boasts[16] that this scripture was brought to him from God. But then we say, "Who is the witness that God gave a scripture to him?[17] Who of the prophets foretold that such a prophet would arise?" And they are quite at a loss. (But we point out in contrast that) Moses received the Law when God appeared at Mt. Sinai in the sight of all the people [in cloud and fire, in darkness and storm; and that all the prophets, beginning with Moses and in succession, foretold the advent of Christ and that the Christ was God and that a Son of God would come in the flesh, be crucified, die and be raised up and that this one would judge[18] the living and the dead. And then we say,[19] "How is it that your Prophet did not so come with others bearing testimony concerning him; and how is it that God did not give him the scripture of which you speak, when you were present, as God gave the Law to Moses while the people looked on and the mountain smoked, that you also might have certainty?" They reply that God does as He wishes. This, we say, we know: but in what manner did this scripture come down to your Prophet, we ask. They answer that at a time[20] when he fell asleep the scripture came down upon him.[21] In jest we say to them that since he received this scripture while he was asleep and since he was not sensible of the divine influence, there was fulfilled in him (the saying) of the popular proverb[22] .....][23]

(C) Again we ask,[24] "How is it that when he commanded us (you?) in your scripture to do nothing or receive nothing without witnesses,[25] you did not inquire of him 'First, do you yourself show through witnesses that you are a prophet and that you have forth from God: and what scripture testifies of you?' They keep silent, having been put to shame. (Then we point out further) Forasmuch as it is not lawful for you to marry a wife without witnesses, or to do business, or to acquire (possessions); and (forasmuch as) you neither allow one to receive an ass or any beast without witnesses; but faith alone and scripture you receive without witness. For the one who delivered this scripture to you has no verification from any source, nor is any previous witness to him known; yet, while he was asleep, he received this (scripture)."

(D) And they call us "*Hetairiastai*" (Associators)²⁶ because, they say we set beside God an associate when we say that Christ is Son of God and God. To whom we say that the prophets and the Scripture transmitted this, and you receive the prophets as you stoutly insist. If then we say wrongly that Christ is the Son of God, it is they who taught and delivered this to us. And some of them say that when we have read such things into²⁷ the prophets, we then attribute such things to them. Others say that the Hebrews, because they hated us, deceived us by writing those things as though they had been written by the prophets in order that we might be destroyed.²⁸

(E) Again we say to them: "Since you say that Christ is Word of God and Spirit, how is it that you revile us as *Hetariastai*? For the Word and the Spirit are not separated one from the one in whom they are by nature. If therefore His Word is in God, it is evident that the Word is also God. But if the Word is outside of God, then according to you God is without reason and without life.²⁹ And so, fearing to provide an Associate for God, you have mutilated Him. It were better for you to say that He has an Associate than to mutilate Him and to treat Him as stone or wood or some insensible thing.³⁰ Wherefore³¹ you speak falsely of us when you call us '*Hetariastai*'; but we call you '*Koptai*' (Mutilators) of God."

(F) And they malign us as being idolaters because we bow before³² the cross, which indeed they despise. But we say to them: "How is it that you attach such significance to a stone in your Kabatha,³³ that you kiss it³⁴ and embrace it?"³⁵ And certain of them say that upon it Abraham had intercourse with Hagar; and others that to it he fastened his *camel* when he was about to sacrifice Isaac.³⁶ To them we reply, "The Scripture says that the mountain was wooded,³⁷ and pieces of wood were there, some of which, when he had split it for the burnt offering, Abraham laid upon Isaac; and that he left the *asses* behind with the servants. Why are you so foolish? For there is not much wood to be found there,³⁸ nor do asses travel through there."³⁹ They are put to shame. Nevertheless they say it is the stone of Abraham. Then when we say, "Let it be Abraham's (stone) as you maintain. But you are not ashamed when you kiss it simply because Abraham had intercourse with a wife[40] upon it or because he fastened a camel to it; yet you take us to task because we worship before the cross of Christ through which[41] the power of demons and the deceit of the devil have been destroyed?"[42] And this stone, about which they speak, is the head of Aphrodite whom they worship, whom they call Chaber; (for) upon this stone, even until now, an engraved image is apparent to those who scrutinize it carefully.

(G) This Mamed, as has been said, drew up many foolish sayings; and to each of these he gave a title, such as the passage[43] "Concerning the Woman." In this (passage) he permits by law that one may openly take four wives, and may take a thousand concubines if he is able, or as many as his hand can support beyond the four wives (Qur'an 4:3); and he permits by law that one divorce whomsoever he pleases and that, should he desire it, for such cause[44] one may take another. Mamed had a co-worker named Zeid.[45] This man had a beautiful wife whom Mamed desired. When they were seated together, Mamed said, "O thou, God has commanded me to take your wife." And he replied; "Thou art an apostle; do as God has said to you; take my wife."[46] Or rather, that we may tell it from the beginning,[47] he said to him; "God commanded me that you should divorce your wife." And he divorced her. After many days he said; "But God commanded that I should take her."[48] Then when he had taken her, and when he had committed adultery with her, he made such a law: "Let him who desires it, divorce his wife. But if after the divorcement he shall return to her, let another (first) marry her. For it is not lawful (for him) to take her, unless she shall have been married by another (Qur'an 2:230).[49] And if indeed a brother divorce her, let his brother, if he be willing, marry her." In the scripture[50] itself he declares such things; "Till the ground which God has given you, and beautify it; and do this thing and in such manner,"[51] — not to say, as he does, things altogether shameful.

(H) Again, there is a passage,[52] "Concerning the Camel[53] of God" (Qur'an 17:61; 26:155) of which it says, there was a camel from God; it drank the whole river and was not able to pass between two mountains because there was not sufficient space. Now, it says, there were people in that place and they drank the water on one day, but the camel drank on the next day (Qur'an 54:28). And when the camel had drunk the water, it nourished them, supplying milk instead of water. Then there arose certain evil men and they killed the camel, its offspring, which, (the passage) says, when the mother had been destroyed, cried out to God; and He took it to Himself. To them[54] we say, "Whence was that camel?" They say it was from God. And we say, "Was not another camel brought together with this one?" But they say, "No." "How," we say, "did it bring forth then? For (otherwise) we are confronted with a camel without father, without mother and without genealogy. But when it had brought forth, it suffered evil. Yet there does not appear the one who put the female to the male;[55] and the small camel was taken up. Your Prophet, then, to whom you say God spoke, why did he not learn regarding the camel, where it fed, who milked it and took the milk? Was it destroyed when it encountered evil men as the mother; or did it enter into Paradise as your forerunner, from which (camel) comes your river of milk about which you talk so foolishly? For you say three rivers flow for you in Paradise; of water, of wine and of milk.[56] If the camel, your forerunner, is outside of Paradise, it is clear that it has been destroyed by hunger and by thirst, or that others enjoy its milk. In vain therefore does your Prophet boast that he associated with God; for the mystery of the camel was not revealed to him. But if it is in Paradise, it drinks again the water; and you will dry up for want of water in the midst of the luxury of Paradise. But if you desire wine from the river flowing by, since there is no water, for the camel drank it all, in drinking unmixed wine you become inflamed, are overcome with drunkeness and fall asleep; and when you are heavy with sleep and debauched by wine, you miss the pleasures of Paradise.[57] How is it then that your Prophet did not consider these matters, lest perchance they should befall you in the Paradise of luxury? He has not even considered where the camel now lives. But neither did you ask this dreamer to tell you about the three rivers. But we plainly declare to you that your wonderful camel, your forerunner, had entered into the souls of asses, where you also, brutish as you are, are about to go. But there is outer darkness and punishment unending, a roaring fire, a worm that dieth not and demons of Tartarus."[58]

(I) Again Mamed says (in) the passage, "Concerning the Table," that Christ asked from God a table and it was given to Him (Qur'an 5:114). For God, it says, said to Him, "I have given to you and to yours an incorruptible table."

(J) Again (he gives) a passage, "Concerning a Heifer," and he says many other foolish things, worthy of ridicule, which, then it may be fitting to pass by on account of the multiplicity of them. Those who had wives he ordained by law should be circumcized,[59] and he gave commandment not to keep the Sabbath and not to be baptized; and he gave direction to eat some of the things which are forbidden on the law and to abstain from some of the others; but the drinking of wine[60] he forbade altogether.[61]

The Discussion of a Christian and a Saracen

(Translated from the Latin and Greek texts of J. P. Migne, *Patrologia Graeca*, Vol. 94, 1864, cols. 1885-1898.)[62]

(K) If you are asked by a Saracen: "What do you call Christ?" say to him, "The Word[63] of God;" nor think that you say amiss, for He is called in Scripture, the Word and the Arm of God and the Power of God and many such things. Moreover do you in turn ask him, "What is Christ called by your scripture?" Then he too will be eager to ask you another question, seeking thus to escape you. But by no means do you reply to him until indeed he has answered that which you will have asked him. For necessity will compel him to answer you by saying, "By my Scripture he is called the Spirit and the Word of God." Then again ask him, "By your Scripture is the word said to be created or uncreated?" If he will say, "Uncreated," say to him, "Behold, you agree with me. For everything not created, but (existing) uncreated, is God." If, however, he will have said that the Word and the Spirit is created, then inquire; "Who created the Word of God and the Spirit?" For if compelled by necessity he will reply "God Himself created (the Word and the Spirit)," then do you again say, "Therefore before God created the Spirit and the Word, He had neither Spirit nor Word."[64] When he hears this, he will flee from you since he has no answer.

(L) But if indeed *you* are asked by a Saracen "Are the words[65] of God created or uncreated?" for the Saracens set these problems before us, desiring to show more forcibly that the Word of God is created, which He is not; and if you say, "Created," he will say to you, "Behold, the Word of God is created." If however you say, "Uncreated," straightway he will reply to you; "Behold, all the words[66] of God are created, but they are not gods. And behold you acknowledge that Christ, since He is Word[67] of God, is not God;" wherefore say, neither created nor uncreated. But thus reply to him: "I acknowledge only one Word[68] of God Who is uncreated. But I do not call all scripture λόγοι, that is 'words' of God; but ῥήματα, that is 'formal words'[69] of God." And the Saracen (will say), "How then does David say, 'The words[70] of the Lord, pure words?'" Say to him, "Because he spoke figuratively[71] and not literally,[72] that is not with the normal and established significance of the words." And the Saracen will say: "What is figurative interpretation and what is literal interpretation?"[73] Reply: "Literalness refers to the established and fixed meaning of a thing. Figurative interpretation, however, involves a secondary[74] meaning." And the Saracen (will say), "Does this link the prophet with his own characteristic mode of speaking?" Say to him, "It was the custom of the prophets to speak figuratively, such as this, 'The sea saw and fled.'[75] Behold, the sea has not eyes, nor is it a living thing. And again in the same way the prophet addresses it as if it were alive, 'What is it to you, O sea, that you have fled?' and so forth. And again (here is) an illustration of our position. For God said to Cain, 'Cursed art thou from the earth which hath opened its mouth to receive the blood of thy brother from thy hand.'[76] See, there he has said 'mouth' figuratively. And, 'My sword shall devour flesh.'[77] For a sword cuts, it does not swallow down." And thus ῥήματα, that is, formal words, that which is able to be spoken and (formally) expressed, he has called λόγοι, that is concepts,[78] that is a meaning conceived inwardly in the mind or formed by thought;[79] but, as has been said, (the formal words or terms are) ῥήματα.[80]

(M) If the Saracen should say to you, "How did God come down into the womb of a woman?"[81] speak thus to him; "Let us use your Scripture and my Scripture. Your Scripture says that God first cleansed his Mary above all flesh of woman, and the Spirit and the Word of God descended upon her.[82] And my Gospel says, 'The Holy Spirit shall come upon you and the power of the Most High shall overshadow you.'[83] See, there is one voice and one mind in each saying. But perceive this, however, that according to our interpretation[84] the Scriptures speak of the descent and ascent figuratively, not literally. For He (God) is spoken of as descending and ascending literally [κυριολογική][85] according to the philosophers. However, God Who holds all things is (Himself) held by nothing. For a certain one of the prophets has said: 'Who measured the sea with his hand and the heaven with (the) span (of his palm) and the earth by a handful?'[86] And well (it is said). For all the seas are but cradled[87] in the hand of God; and His palm (measures) all the heaven; and all the earth (is but) a handful. How therefore can it be that He Who holds all things in His own hand descends and ascends?"[88]

(N) And if you should be asked by a Saracen, "If God was Christ, how did He eat and drink and sleep, and (how) was He crucified, and (how) did He die and such things?"[89] Say to him, "Because the eternal Word of God created all things, even as my Scripture and yours testify, He created from the body of the holy virgin a man, complete and living and intelligent; that one ate, drank and slept; (He was) indeed the Word, that is the Word of God; but the Word of God did not eat, drink or sleep; nor was He crucified, nor did He die; but the flesh which He assumed from the holy virgin, that (flesh) was crucified. For you know that Christ was two-fold [in nature], but one in person.[90] For it is not said, 'The Word of God is eternal and after the assumption of the flesh is *anypostaticum*,'[91] that is, He is not (divinely personal nor of divine) nature.[92] For a fourth person is not placed alongside the Trinity after the inexpressible union with the flesh."

(O) And if the Saracen should ask you, "He Whom you call God, did He die?" do you reply: "He did not die;" relying confidently on the proof of Scripture. For Scripture speaks concerning this. For natural death came against the memory of men, mastering it, that is, subduing all things even as in us. But the first man, in the state of perfection, slept,[93] and was deprived of a rib.

(P) And the Saracen (says): "Behold, I am wounded in some part of my flesh, and the pierced flesh forms a wound and in the wound a worm is made: who therefore formed it?" Say to him, as we have said before, that after the first week of the creation of the world, we do not find anything whatsoever, either a man forming (anything), or (anything)[94] that has been formed; but by command of God which He commanded in the first week, He finished (all) that which is made. However, after the transgression the earth was condemned to bring forth thorns and thistles. As our body also was condemned at that time even until this day it produces lice and worms."

(Q) Saracen[95]: What do you say is the cause of good and of evil?[96]

Christian: Of all the good [we say the cause] is God, but (God) is not the cause of evil.

(R) S: And what do you say is the cause of evil?

C: This is from our own rashness and from the cunning of the devil.

(S) S: How is this so?[97]

C: Because of free will.

(T) S: What then? Have you free will, and are you able to do whatever you wish?

C: I have been formed by God with free will.[98]

(U) S: [Why so?]

C: (That) when I do good, I fear not the law, but rather I am rewarded and granted mercy by God. In like manner also, the devil ....[99] and
he sinned and God thrust him forth from his estate. But perhaps you
will reply to us, [saying thus,] what sort of things are good and bad?

(V) S: Behold the sun and the moon and the stars are good; make
(good and evil) one from these.[100]

C: [Not for the sake of (attaining) this conclusion)] do I speak to
you;[101] because (on my own responsibility) as a man[102] I do good and
evil; good (for example) in praising God,[103] in prayer, in deeds of
mercy and in such things; and evil, in fornication and theft. But if you
say that good and evil are a consequence of [the commandment] of
God, then according to you God will be found unrighteous which He is
not. For since, as you say, God commands the fornicator to commit
fornication and the thief to steal and the murderer to kill, they are
worthy of honor; for they have done the will of God. And your lawgiv-
ers also will be found false; for they command that the fornicator and
thief be beaten and the murderer be put to death, though (according to
your point of view) they did the will of God.

(W) S: Who forms the unborn child in the womb of the mother?[104]
(This he asks) desiring to show that God is the cause of evil.[105] Behold, God is (made) a partner with the fornicator and adulterer.

C: We in no wise find the Scripture saying that after the first week [of
world creation] God formed or created anything. [And if you are
doubtful about this, point out anything whatsoever which has been
fashioned or created by God after the first week (of creation); but it is
not possible to do this.][106] For all the visible creation[107] was made in
the first week. For God made man in the first week and commanded
him to beget and to be begotten, saying, "Be fruitful and multiply and
replenish the earth." And because man had life within himself, having
seed with life within itself, he made seed to develop in his own life. So
that man begat [man] even as the divine Scripture says: "Adam begat
Seth, and Seth begat Enos, and Enos begat Cainan, and Cainan begat

Malaleel,"[108] and so forth. And it does not say, "God fashioned Seth,
or Enos, or any other." [And from that time until now we know that
men have been begotten and have begotten; and so by the favor of
God the world has continued since from the beginning,[109] all grass
produces and is produced: for God said;] "Let the earth bring forth
herbs of grass;"[110] and by command of God [each tree brought forth;
and so likewise both herb and plant had from itself seed and power (of
life); and (the) seed of every plant and herb, having life within itself,]
falling on the earth [of itself] or sown by another, again brought forth;
not fashioned[111] by anyone, but responding to the commandment[112] of
God. And behold I, as indeed I said at the start, since I am of free
will, whether I sow, whether[113] unto my own wife or unto one belonging
to another, I use[114] my own free will, and she brings forth and it comes
to pass in response to the first command of God; not that even now
God fashions each day and (creatively) works; since in the first week
God made the heaven and the earth and all the world in six days, and
on the seventh day ceased from all His (creative) works which He had
begun to do; even as my Scripture bears testimony.[115]

(X) S: How then does God say to Jeremiah, "Before I formed thee in
the belly I knew thee, and from the womb I sanctified thee?"[116] [Thus
certainly[117] God formed him in the womb.]

C: Adam, having in his own loins life and the power of generating
seed, begat Seth, even as I said; and Seth, Enos and each man, holding
in his loins his son, (begat him); and the son (in turn) begat until the
present. But in respect to the (statement), "From the womb I sanctified thee," [have in mind her[118] who truly begat children of God according to the testimony of the holy Gospel.]

(Y) S: Do you say those who do the will of God are good or evil?

[C: Do you wish to say that Christ suffered against His will? And if I
say to you (that those who do the will of God are) good, you will say
to me, "Come then, accept indeed the Jews as those who did the will
of your God."

(Z) S: Indeed I was intending to say this to you.

C: What] do you say is the will of God? I say it is forbearance and longsuffering.... When God said, "Thou shalt not steal, thou shalt not commit fornication, thou shalt not kill," did He will that we should steal or commit fornication or kill?

(AA) S: No; for if He (so) willed, [He did not say this.

C: Glory to God that you have confessed.] For see, you have agreed with me in this and that God does not will that we should steal or commit fornication or murder. And if now, rising up, I steal or commit fornication or kill, what do you say in regard to it? (Does the situation reveal) God's will or forbearance and longsuffering?

(AB) S: Which according to you is greater, the one who sanctifies or the one who is sanctified?[119]

C: When you come with your slave to the bath, when you are bathed and cleansed by him, who do you say is greater?[120] That pitiable slave, bought with silver, or yourself who have been cleansed by him [being also thus his master?]

(AC) From the controversies with the Saracens of one[121] (Theodore, surnamed Abucari, bishop of Cari) using[122] the language of John of Damascus.

(AD) Saracen: Tell me, O Bishop; was not the world full of idols before Moses proclaimed Judaism?

Theodore: Certainly.

(AE) S: When Moses was teaching men to practice Judaism, which part of the world seems to you to have shown piety; the part which received Judaism or the part which continued to worhip idols, unpersuaded by Moses?

T: The part which received (Judaism).

(AF) S: Then, when years after, Christ came proclaiming Christianity, which part seems to you to have shown piety, the part which received Christianity, or the part which continued unchanged in Judaism?

T: The part which received Christianity.

(AG) S: Then, when years after, Muhammad came proclaiming the Magarismos,[123] which part seems to you to have shown piety, the one which accepted the Magarismos or the part which continued in Christianity, unpersuaded by Muhammad?

T: The part which continued in Christianity.

(AH) S: The last conclusion you have not set forth in conformity with the preceding.[124]

T: Is it necessary for me to draw a conclusion from false premises? For Moses and Christ did not become worthy to be received (simply) because they were preaching and teaching, as you have assumed, so that Muhammad also should be believed because of his preaching and teaching; but consider the record concerning each which is trustworthy. [Here follows an account of the miracles of Mose's staff and the hand in his bosom (Ex. 4:1-8).] And God said to him, "If they will not believe the first sign, nor the second, make the water blood." And so after Moses had been sent, he did (thus); and his words were confirmed by his works. Is this so or not?

(AI) S: Entirely so.

T: Christ came confirming in Himself his mission from God; (for) testimony was borne (to Him) not only by the prophecy of Moses; but He establishes Himself by signs, wonders and mighty works after that prophecy.[125]

(AJ) S: By what things?

T: By birth without the aid of seed any by a mother unjoined to a man and by a birth from a virgin; by the change of water into wine; then after this, not obscure but very well known (are) the giving of sight to the blind, the cleansing of the lepers, the strengthening[126] of the palsied, the healing of various diseases, the manifestation of His deity upon the mountain, the driving out of demons, the satisfaction of many thousands from a few loaves and fish, the raising of the dead as from sleep and finally[127] the regeneration of sinful human nature.[128] What do you say to these things, O Saracen? Did Christ establish Himself by demonstrations less than the signs of Moses?

(AK) S: In no wise.

T: This one, who was foretold by Moses, who by so many and such signs has demonstrated that He came from God, declared to His disciples, saying, "The law and the prophets (were) until John the Baptist. He who has ears to hear, let him hear."[129] Where then is your Prophet? That is not obscure.

Notes:

[1] Lit. - "people-deceiving."

[2] σκεία taken as σκία. Figuratively, spiritual darkness or error. Cp. Mt. 4:16; Lk. 1:79; Jn. 1:5 and 8:12, I Jn. 1:5 and 2:8-11. The Latin text here uses "*superstitio*."

[3] Transliterated to English - Sara(k)cenous.

[4] Transliterated to English - Sara(k)cenen.

[5] Lit.- "morning-bearing."

[6] Arabic *akhbar* means "greater."

[7] Lit. - "put himself into the hands of." Thus, thrust himself upon. Perhaps, "foisted himself upon."

[8] Lit. - "a writing," and so regularly.

[9] Lit. - "in the book with him."

[10] Or - "but indeed a created servant."

[11] Leo, parag. AH - ed.

[12] Lit. - (they crucified) his shadow, form, outward appearance. Gr. σκίαν.

[13] Leo, parag. AM - ed.

[14] Lit. - "men, the transgressors."

[15] Lit. - word.

[16] The Greek verb (φυάττομαι) is properly used of spirited horses; to neigh or snort.

[17] Leo, parag. G and AH - ed.

[18] Lit. - "would be judge of."

[19] Lit. - "When we say - they reply."

[20] Lit. - "at such a time."

[21] *Sahih Muslim*, Kitab al-Salat, ch. 162, hadith 790, Vol. 1, p. 220 - ed.

[22] The proverb is wanting in all the authorities for the text. - Savas shows Lequien as suggesting Plato's: "You are spinning me in dreams." Cf. Savas, *John of Damascus on Islam*, p. 135, note - ed.

[23] That which is enclosed in brackets is lacking in 2 Reg. and in older translations.

[24] Lit. - "again we ask ... they keep silent."

[25] Qur'an 2:282; Leo, parags. G and AH - ed.

[26] "A name given to the Christians by the Muhammadans, because the former believe that God has a compeer." See Sophocles' *Greek Lexicon of the Roman and Byzantine Periods*.

[27] Lit. - "allegorized."

[28] Qur'an 2:56; 5:16, 45; etc. Leo, parags. H, J and K - ed.

[29] ἄλογος-ἄπνους - without word and breath (i.e., life or spirit).

The writer has just used above λόγος and πνεῦμα. The initial α has a negative force.

[30] Lit. - "some of the insensible (or senseless) things."

[31] Lit. - "so that."

[32] Lit. - "worship."

[33] probably for the Ka'ba.

[34] al-Kindi, parag. DI - ed.

[35] The Muslim accusation of the veneration of the cross was often countered by the Christian accusation of the veneration of the Ka'ba: Leo, parag. AX, Religious Dialogue, parag. AU - ed.

[36] This accusation does not seem to have any merit in any of the major Islamic sources. The Qur'an describes Abraham's relation to the Ka'ba differently - cf. 2:121 - ed.

[37] That is, with growing, living wood i.e., trees; in contrast to the following word that refers to cut wood, split pieces of wood.

[38] That is, around the Ka'ba.

[39] The Greek is simply, "travel through." Perhaps the meaning is, "travel through so far," i.e., from Palestine to Arabia.

[40] Hagar.

[41] The Greek could mean "through whom" i.e., Christ. But the Latin text reads "*crucem - per quam.*"

[42] Religious Dialogue, parag. AT - ed.

[43] Lit. - scripture.

[44] I.e., the mere desire to take another is sufficient cause.

[45] Zayd. - Zayd was Muhammad's adopted son (Qur'an 33:37) - ed.

[46] Leo, parag. AX - ed.

[47] I.e., completely.

[48] Qur'an 33:37 (rough paraphrase) - ed.

[49] Leo, parag. AY - ed.

[50] I.e., the Qur'an.

[51] Qur'an 2:223 (rough paraphrase), Leo, parag. AX - ed.

[52] Lit. - "scripture."

[53] Qualifying modifiers indicate the feminine gender for "camel" throughout the passage, i.e., "she-camel." - There is no sura known by this title. - ed.

[54] Lit. - "whom."

[55] ὁ βιβάσας - see Liddell and Scott *Lexicon*, unabridged, 8th ed.

[56] Qur'an 47:16; Leo, parag. BD - ed.

[57] John of Damascus misses an obvious contradiction here; he knew that Muhammad had forbidden the drinking of wine for Muslims (parag. J; Qur'an 2:216) and yet that wine would be drunk in Paradise (parag. H; Qur'an 47:16) - ed.

[58] It is extremely hard to believe that John of Damascus could have

said this to any Muslim and have survived the consequences. Peter the bishop of Maiuma was put to death for naming Muhammad a "false prophet" and "forerunner of the Antichrist" in 743 A.D. (Savas, *John of Damascus on Islam*, pp. 54, 68-9 quoting Theophanes) - ed.

[59] Leo, parag. AQ; Jahiz, parag. T - ed.

[60] See note 57 above - ed.

[61] The translator desires to acknowledge the helpful suggestions of Professor W. P. Armstrong.

[62] The Greek text for the opening part is fragmentary. This section is thus translated from the Latin text.

[63] Latin - *Verbum*; Greek - λόγος.

[64] The Greek πνεῦμα and λόγος have also the force of "life" and "reason." Thus, God originally would have been inanimate and unreasoning, - blind force.

[65] Latin - *verba*; Greek - λόγια, "sayings."

[66] Latin - *eloquia*; Greek - λόγια.

[67] Latin - *Verbum*. Note change in term from 66.

[68] Latin - *Verbum*; Greek - λόγος.

[69] The Greek λόγος does not represent a formal word or term alone, which is ρῆμα; but refers to the mental concept or idea which, expressed or unexpressed, is a λόγος.

[70] Latin - *eloquia;* but the parallel Greek term is λόγια. That is, David would seem to contradict the statement just made by the Christian.

[71] Latin - *tropologice*, a transliteration of the Greek term.

[72] And so also, Latin - *cyriologice*.

[73] The Latin is, *"Quid est tropologia et cyriologia?"*

[74] Latin - *infirma*.

[75] Psalm 114:3 - ed.

[76] Genesis 4:11 - ed.

[77] Deut. 32:42 - ed.

[78] Latin - *verba*; but here used with λόγια in reference to the inner meaning behind the expressed word. The formal term (ρῆμα) must be distinguished from the spiritual reality which, in figurative use, it may represent. The formal words of Scripture (ρήματα) are created; but the spiritual reality of Christ, figuratively called "the Word" (λόγος) may be uncreated.

[79] Latin - *ratione*.

[80] The Muslim's question as to whether the words of God are created or not points to the influence of the Mu'tazilites (Editor's Preface to Jahiz, note 3) - ed.

[81] Gaudeul, "Leo and 'Umar," *Islamochristiana*, p. 144, BNM 4944, parag. 47; Leo, parag. AT - ed.

[82] Qur'an 3:37, 40; 66:12 - ed.

[83] Luke 1:35 - ed.

[84] Latin - *proprietatem*, "proper signification."

[85] The Latin would be *cyriologice*.

[86] Isaiah 40:12 - ed.

[87] Latin - *simplex comprehensio manus Dei*.

[88] An allusion to Deut. 30:12,13 (Septuagint); Prov. 30:4; Rom. 10:6, 7 - ed.

[89] Cf. Qur'an 5:79 - ed.

[90] Latin - *hypostasis*, the word used of the Persons of the Trinity.

[91] Impersonal, transliterated from the Greek ἀνυποστατικόν; not hypostatical or personal in reference to the hypostases or Persons of the Trinity.

[92] This is what is *not* said. The meaning seems to be that the incarnation did not destroy the divine person or nature of the second Person of the Trinity. Or, the force may be that Christ was a true Being, i.e., Christ had a true Person and true natures (human and divine as stated in the preceding sentence); but this does not mean the Person of Christ's Being is distinct from the second Person of the Trinity. See the next sentence.

[93] I.e., did not die, as perfect man?

[94] Or, a man that has been formed.

[95] From this point the translation is based on the Greek text.

[96] Cf. Qur'an 14:4; etc.

[97] Lit. - because of what?

[98] Man has free will that he may be rewarded for the good and punished for the evil which he does. Cf. the fuller Latin text.

[99] The Latin text supplies: "deceived the first man through free will, and he sinned." The Greek text is broken and the Latin would indicate that "the one thrust forth" is man.

[100] Lit. - "make one from these." That is, make good and evil alike arise from the nature of creation. Or perhaps the meaning is, in the realm of nature all is good; there is no evil in nature and apparent evil there is good.

[101] Or, if we follow the second interpretation in the above footnote, the meaning might be, "not for the sake of discussing whether evil is inherent in nature (sun, moon annd stars) do I talk to you." The Christian wishes to discuss evil in the realm of man and personality.

[102] I.e., as one created with the capacity and responsibility of moral choice and action.

[103] Lit. - "in respect to" or "by" praise of God.

[104] The Greek forms are plural.

[105] The Greek text is broken. The Latin supplies: "For if you reply saying, 'God forms the unborn child in the womb of the mother,' the Saracen will say to you."

[106] Lit. - this is not possible to be pointed out.

[107] Lit. - visible created things.

[108] Gen. 5:3-12 (condensed) - ed.

[109] Lit. - from then.

[110] Gen. 1:11 - ed.

[111] I.e., created.

[112] I.e., the original commandment of God.

[113] Lit. - even if.

[114] Lit. - using my own free will, she brings forth.

[115] Gen. 2:2 (Septuagint) - ed.

[116] Jer. 1:5 (Septuagint) - ed.

[117] Greek, πάντως, "wholly."

[118] Could this be a reference to the Church? The Christian refers the prophecy of Jeremiah to spiritual birth, not to physical.

[119] The Latin supplies: C.- I know what you wish to say. S.- If then you know, answer me. C.- If I shall say to you, "the one who sanctifies," you will say to me, "Come then, worship John the Baptist, who baptized and sanctified your Christ." S.- Thus I was intending to say to you - cf. Religious Dialogue, parag. T - ed.

[120] Lit. - whom do you have to say is greater.

[121] Lit. - of him.

[122] Lit. - through the voice of.

[123] See Sophocles, *Greek Lexicon of Roman and Byzantine Periods*. The Greek μαγαρισμός (pollution, defilement) by a bitter linguistic trick is used in travesty by John of Damascus for Muhammadanism. Drop the first letter and we have ἀγαρισμός (same as ἀγαρισία), Greek for Muhammadanism, - derived from Ἄγαρ, Hagar. So John in his book *On Heresies* (Migne text, col. 764) refers to Muhammadans as

Hagarenes. The Latin text here has "Magarismum Eslamismumve."

[124] This is a good example of how the Islamic doctrine of progressive revelation was and still is being applied in dialogues with Christians - ed.

[125] See Appendix A - ed.

[126] σφίξις taken as σφίγξις (from σφίγγω), a binding tight. Thus the strengthening or tightening of relaxed muscles in palsy or paralysis to normal conditions of control.

[127] Lit. - in general, on the whole.

[128] Lit. - of the nature of sins.

[129] Luke 16:16, paraphrase - ed.

THE DIALOGUE OF
PATRIARCH TIMOTHY I
WITH CALIPH MAHDI

The following discussions between the Patriarch Timothy I and the Caliph Mahdi are the first examples of the Nestorian-Abbasid dialogue given in this collection. Shortly after coming to power, the Abbasids moved the capital of their empire from Damascus to Baghdad; a move which also took the court of the caliphs away from the religious influence of the Melkites (Orthodox) and Jacobites in the West and brought them into sphere of the Nestorians in the East.

The text of the following dialogue was translated by A. Mingana and published in 1928 from a copy of a Syriac manuscript written in the 13th century.[1] Apparently unknown to Mingana at that time, Fr. Cheikho had already published an Arabic text of this dialogue in 1923, of which L.E. Browne made mention in 1931 in *The Moslem World*.[2] Browne compares both the Syriac and Arabic texts of Timothy's discussion with Mahdi. Although Mingana and Cheikho are of the opinion that the original manuscript was written in Syriac, Browne believes the Arabic text to be a more faithful reproduction than the Syriac text which Mingana translated. Browne contends that some of the Bible quotations of the Syriac text are defective;[3] that the Syriac presents the Incarnation more in the Nestorian sense of God being "clothed" with humanity (whereas the Arabic even denies this at least once);[4] that the section on Christ paying the debt owed by men and angels is a Nestorian addition;[5] and that the Syriac denies the attribution of death to God (a Nestorian distortion denied in the Arabic).[6] But the very arguments which Browne advances in favor of the Arabic text of the dialogue, can be applied even more convincingly in favor of the Syriac text: in general, corrections of defective Bible quotations tend to be a feature of later copies; the Nestorian bias of the Syriac leans more in its favor since Timothy was himself Nestorian and it is thus more likely that the Arabic, which could well have been adapted by the Orthodox or Monophysites, contained deletions or changes of sections of the text which represented unacceptable doctrines. Browne is also skeptical of the authenticity of the second day of Timothy's discussion, since the Arabic does not contain it but has included some of the topics of the second day in the main body of the text.[7] But this could just as well be due to a deletion on the part of the Arabic text as to an addition by copyists of the Syriac, though there is little in the way of stylistic changes or anachronisms to betray this. Browne cites Cheikho in mentioning that other copies of the Arabic text of Timothy's apology are located in European libraries.[8]

Traditionally, it was the Nestorians who took the message of the Gospel to the peoples of the East, and it appears that what little direct contact Muhammad may have had with Christianity was also with the members of this group. In general the Nestorians were looked upon as being doctrinally nearer Islam than either of the Melkites or Jacobites, a feature mentioned in paragraphs FJ and FK of the following text; they seem to have been valued all the more by their Muslim rulers for their aversion for the Byzantines.

The text of the following dialogue between the Patriarch Timothy I and the Caliph Mahdi is believed by Mingana and others to have taken place about the year 781 A.D., i.e., about 60 years after the letter of Leo III to 'Umar II and some 40 years after John of Damascus may have written about Islam. In general, the tone of Timothy's dialogue with Mahdi is far from the polarized atmospheres of either Leo's letter to 'Umar or John of Damascus' writings concerning Islam, and largely due to the fact that Timothy's discussions with his ruler Mahdi were held face-to-face. Thus it should not come as a complete surprise that Timothy exalts the Arabs over the Jews[9] (after all but conceding that Christians do not accept the Qur'an, but the Old Testament), that he lauds Muhammad as having "walked in the path of the prophets"[10] (after admitting that Christians do not believe in him), or that he contradicts himself in the parable of the lost pearl by wishing to have a share in the hypothetical fortune of the Muslims (after he had already concluded them not to be in possession of such[11]).

Neither Timothy nor Mahdi seem to have had a very good knowledge of the other's religion. As Mingana mentions in his introduction to the dialogue, Timothy's information on the Qur'an appears to have been second-hand; moreover, he does not display any familiarity with the hadith or Islamic history. Mahdi's knowledge of the Torah and the Gospel also seem to have been from other sources, as he uses them mostly as evidence that Muhammad's coming was foretold in the scriptures. The major Biblical references Mahdi cites on this subject have to do with the Paraclete,[12] the rider of the camel[13] and the prophet described in Deuteronomy 18.[14]

Other accusations which Mahdi brings against the Christians are that they have corrupted the scriptures[15] and that the Christians reject Muhammad as the Jews rejected Jesus.[16] Mahdi also asks why Christians aren't circumcised as Jesus was,[17] don't pray in the same direction as Jesus did,[18] and he even opens a discussion based on the Islamic view of predestination, by which he attempts to clear the Jews of guilt in Jesus' execution.[19] Moreover, Mahdi makes use of his advantage of rulership in asking Timothy what he thought of Muhammad.

Timothy's reply to this question is most certainly a compromise,[20] though his answers to the matter of the prophet of Deuteronomy 18 and the contradictions in Mahdi's use of Islamic predestination are interesting. Timothy somewhat parallels Leo in showing that the enmity between the Jews and the Christians is the best guarantee that the scriptures could not have been corrupted[21] and makes frequent use of the ancient example of the sun as an illustration of the Trinity.[22] Timothy also uses the idea that the divine mission of the prophets is to be confirmed by miracles quite extensively,[23] and intends, of course, to point out Muhammad's deficiency in this respect.

Although Mahdi asks but few questions, Timothy (in the absence of a direct knowledge of Islam) constantly finds himself on the defense and thus in a no-win situation. Timothy also makes a few mistakes, especially in asserting that prophecy ended with Jesus[24] (only to later mention that Elijah is to return[25]) and by stating that Jesus abolished the Law[26] (whereas Jesus Himself said that He was to fulfill the Law[27]). But Mahdi (due to his own minimal knowledge of the Bible) was not in a good position to catch these shortcomings either; it is very likely that the Muslim doctrine of successive revelation was spurred on by such statements made by the Christians.

As Mingana notes, the Nestorian Apology of al-Kindi uses many of the same ideas and arguments as Timothy with Mahdi, yet both are somewhat different from the letter of Leo III and the writings of John of Damascus.

Mingana's English translation of Timothy's discussions with Mahdi originally appeared in "The Apology of Timothy the Patriarch Before the Caliph Mahdi," *Bulletin of the John Rylands Library*, vol. 12 (1928), pp. 137-226.

----

[1] Mingana, p. 173, below.

[2] L.E. Browne, "The Patriarch Timothy and the Caliph al-Mahdi," *The Moslem World*, vol. 21 (1931), p. 38.

[3] Ibid., p. 39; Timothy I, parags. BE and FH.

[4] Browne, "Timothy I and Mahdi," p. 41; Timothy I, parags. G, I, X, Y, AD, FD.

[5] Browne, "Timothy I and Mahdi," p. 41; Timothy I, parag. AD.

[6] Browne, "Timothy I and Mahdi," p. 41; Timothy I, parag. BC.

[7] Browne, "Timothy I and Mahdi," p. 42.

[8] Ibid., p. 38.

[9] Timothy I, parag. CT.

[10] Ibid., parag. DA.

[11] Ibid., parag. FO.

[12] Ibid., parag. AN; Leo III, parag. P, n. 50.

[13] Timothy I, parag. AV; Leo III, parag. BC, n. 106.

[14] Timothy I, parags. CA-CC.

[15] Ibid., parag. CL; (for the Jews) Leo III, parags. J and K; John of Damascus, parag. D.

[16] Timothy I, parag. AS.

[17] Ibid., parag. AA; Leo III, parags. L, AN n. 82, AP n. 85.

[18] Timothy I, parag. AD; Leo III, parags. AJ n. 73.

[19] Timothy I, parag. BH; John of Damascus, parag. Y.

[20] See note 10 above.

[21] Timothy I, parags. CN, CO, CR; Leo III, parag. K.

[22] Timothy I, parags. D, F, J, M, etc.

[23] Ibid., parags. AL, AP, AU, CC, etc., John of Damascus, parag. AH-AI.

[24] Timothy I, parags. DX and EF.

[25] Ibid., parags. CH-CI.

[26] Ibid., parags. AB-AC.

[27] Matthew 5:17.

WOODBROOKE STUDIES

PATRIARCH TIMOTHY I AND
THE CALIPH MAHDI

A. Mingana

DIALOGUE

The NESTORIAN Patriarch
Timothy I and
The 'ABBASID Caliph Mahdi

c. 781 A.D.

I give in the following pages the text and the translation — accompanied by a critical apparatus — of an official apology of Christianity.
The writer of the apology is the celebrated Nestorian Patriarch Timothy I. (780-823 A.D.), and the man to whom it was delivered by word
of mouth is no less than Mahdi, the third 'Abbasid Caliph (775-785
A.D.). There is reason to believe that it was delivered in this way
towards the end of 781 A.D. or at the latest 782. See below p. 220 *.

The apology is in the form of a theological discussion between Timothy and Mahdi. It is not necessary to suppose that every word in it was
uttered *verbatim*, but there are strong reasons for believing that it

contains as faithful an analysis as could possibly be made under the circumstances of the questions and answers of the Caliph and the Patriarch. This colloquy was naturally conducted in Arabic, but we have it now before us in the Syriac style of one of the most illustrious ecclesiastical dignitaries that have ever honored a high Patriarchal See of any Church either Eastern or Western.[1]

It is naturally very difficult to ascertain the duration of time that must have elapsed between the two days of the oral discussion of the two friendly antagonists, and the days in which that oral discussion was first written down in its present form by the Christian protagonist. From the nature of some phrases used in the text I am inclined to believe that that time could not have been very considerable, and I consider that 785 A.D. constitutes the lowest limit to which we might ascribe it with safety.

I have in my footnotes compared Timothy's Apology under Mahdi in the eighth century with two other apologies of the ninth century: that of 'Abd al-Masih b. Ishaq al-Kindi and that of 'Ali b. Rabban at-Tabari. Kindi's Apology — to which I refer by the word *Risala* — is in favor of Christianity and was written under the Caliph Ma'mun (813-833 A.D.)[2] and that of Ibn Rabban is entitled *Kitab ad-Din wad-Daulah*, is in favor of Islam and was written under the Caliph Mutawakkil (847-861 A.D.).[3]

I may here note that I believe that Kindi's Apology mentioned by the Muslim Biruni[4] and the Christian Nestorian 'Abdisho' of Nisibun[5] is a genuine and authentic work. His adversary, who Biruni tells us was 'Abdullah b. Isma'il al-Hashimi, informs us[6] that he had frequent discussions with the Patriarch Timothy, the author of the present Apology. The Apology itself makes mention of contemporary events that took place in the time of the author, such as the insurrection of Atabag al-Khurrami[7] and counts two hundred years from the time in which the Prophet lived down to the time in which it was written.[8] Kindi himself being decidedly a Nestorian could not possibly be confused with any other author of a hostile community from the beginning of the ninth to the end of the tenth century, such as the Jacobite Yahya b. 'Adi who died in 974 A.D. Kindi[9] quotes the Nestorian hymn, "Blessed be the One who created the light,"[10] explains the "sleep" of Lazarus through the Nestorian exegesis,[11] and clearly shows in many passages his adhesion to the Nestorian Christological belief in the mystery of the Incarnation.[12] No Jacobite author could possibly have done this.

Further, no other *milieu* was so favorable for the writing of a book of such an aggressive tone as that created by the Caliph Ma'mun,[13] and no author could have spoken in such a way of himself, of his adversary and of Islam in general except a man of a true and noble Arabian extraction as Kindi, on his own showing,[14] was.

As to the distinction between *sifat dhat* and *sifat fi'l* they are adaptations to Arabic and Islamic philosophy of the previously known Syriac terms of *dilaita dakhyana* and *dilaita de-sa'orutha*. Even the present apology of Timothy alludes to this distinction. I cannot, therefore, see why a Christian Arab author writing about 820 A.D. should not have made use of this philosophical notion which was at home within Christian circles of his time, and in my judgment the argument taken from the use of these two terms in favor of a later date for the Christian Apology[15] is scientifically unwarranted by the Nestorian philosophical studies of the time.

It has also been urged that another detail might suggest that the Christian apology was not composed by Kindi but by an author of the tenth century and that is the allusion that it makes to the fact that the name of Muhammad is believed by the Muslims to be inscribed on the base of the throne of God.[16] It has been said[17] that since Tabari, who died in 923 A.D., refuted an opinion similar to this held by the Hanbali Barbahari, the apology could not be ascribed to about 820 A.D. But is it not probable that such a belief was held also by some Muslims in 820 A.D.? What proof have we that it was the Hanbali Barbahari who was the first man to hold and enunciate such a belief? After a careful study of the subject I have come to — in my judgment — the only probable conclusion; that from the internal and external evidence Kindi's apology for Christianity is genuine and authentic in spite of some variants exhibited by the different Arabic and Garshuni MSS. that contain it. The contrary opinion is, I believe, a mistake which should be at once corrected.

To return to our present apology: I may state with some confidence that the Patriarch Timothy was well acquainted with the contents of the Qur'an, but his knowledge does not seem to have been acquired at first hand; it was rather derived from some Christians of his own community. It is very doubtful whether he was aware of the existence of a Syriac translation of the Islamic book. The phrase "I heard" and the Qur'anic Arabic words that he uses in this connection suggest that he was dependent upon an Arabic and not a Syriac text of the Qur'an.

The most important verses of the Qur'an which he quotes in a Syriac translation are 3:48; 4:156; 4:159; 4:170; 19:17; 19:34; 21:91 and 90:1-3. He is also aware of the existence of the mysterious letters found at the beginning of some suras. The usefulness of these quotations for the criticism of the text of the Qur'an is emphasized in my footnotes, but it will not be here out of place to put side by side the Syriac text of the Qur'an as quoted by Barsalibi — a text which I edited and translated in 1925[18] — and by Timothy. If both texts are identical, there would be strong reasons for believing that the Jacobite Barsalibi and the Nestorian Timothy were quoting from a text lying before them. On the whole, however, the balance is in favor of the opinion that Timothy's text is not Barsalibi's text.

Barsalibi	Timothy
l' qtlwhy wl' slbwhy 'l'	*l' qtlwhy wl' slbwhy 'l'*
mtdmyw 'tdmy lhwn hbn'	*mdmyw dmy lhwn hbn'*
	4:156
shlm 'ly ywm' d'tyldt wywm'	*shlm' 'ly bywm' dbh mtyld 'n'*
dm't 'n' wywm' dmtnhm 'n' hy'	*wywm' dbh m't 'n' wywm' dbh*
	mshtdr 'n' hy'
	19:34

'n' mmyt 'n' lk wmsq 'n' lk lwty	*h' mmyt 'n' lk wmdp' 'n' lk lwty* 3:48
Not in Barsalibi	*shdrnn lwth rwh' dyln* 19:17
wnphnn bh rwh' dyln	*wnphnn bh mn rwh' dyln* 21:91
l' ym' 'n' bhn' 'tr' ... *w'b' whw dylyd mnh*	*ym' 'n' bhn' twr' wylwd'* *wyldh* 90:1-3
Not in Barsalibi	*l' mstnkp mshyh' dnhw' 'bd'* *l' lh'* 4:170

The only old MS. that contains the present apology is the one pre-served in the Monastery of our Lady, near Alkosh,[19] which may be ascribed to about the thirteenth Christian century. From it are tran-scribed Seert 65,[20] Vatican 81,[21] Mardin 50[22] and Mingana 17.[23] Apart from Seert 65, which might have been ascribed to the eighteenth century all the other MSS. were copied in the nineteenth century, and if we have a faithful copy of the MS. of the Monastery of our Lady, we have practically all the other MSS.

For my present edition I give all Mingana 17 in facsimile (this has been deleted in the present edition - ed.). It was transcribed some thirty years ago by the very able copyist, the priest Abraham Shikwana of Alkosh from the above MS. of the Monastery of our Lady, and in my last journey to the East (in 1925) I collated it myself with the original MS. The reader has therefore every reason to rely on the accuracy of the text of the apology. In some passages my translation slightly deviates from the text for the sake of clearness. The editorial plural is sometimes maintained.

TRANSLATION.

With the assistance of God we will write the debate held by the Patriarch Mar Timothy before Mahdi, the Commander of the Faithful, by way of question and answer, on the subject of the Christian religion.

(A) On the one hand I feel repugnance to write to you lordship,[24] and on the other hand I am anxious to do so. *I feel repugnance*, on account of the futility of the outcome of the work. It is true that I could not have acquired a mature experience of such a futility from the single discussion herein mentioned, But I may state that I have acquired such an experience from discussions that took place before the one involved in the present lucubration.[25] *I am anxious*, in order to confirm and corroborate a traditional habit, inasmuch as the habit of friendly correspondence has acquired the right of prescription from very early times and has thereby received an additional title to existence; as a matter of fact it is born and grows in us from our childhood, nay even babyhood, and it is very difficult to shake a habit of such a duration. For the reason, however, stated at the beginning I sometimes infringe this law, especially when I am reminded by a wise man who says that it is useless to draw upon that which is difficult to inherit. This is also due to that fact that the subject is to me difficult and is even against my nature, but we know that habit conquers inclination, as a powerful thought conquers a weak one.

(B) We often see that a strong and well-rooted branch goes spontaneously back to its former and congenial state after it has been violently twisted, and we do find that when powerful torrents are diverted from their natural channels with violence, they return immediately to their natural and customary course, without the need of any violence. This happens to me in relation to your great wisdom; to put a stop to our correspondence we must needs make use of violence, but after the cessation of this violence, we go back to our natural state, while love conquers all between us and covers the weakness of the flesh which are full of shame and confusion and also many other human proclivities which are known to the mind, but which the speech conceals and hides under the veil of silence. Such are well known to your great wisdom, as if you were their father and originator, and are also known to all the members of the Orthodox Church. Love covers and hides all these weaknesses as the water covers and hides the rocks that are under it. But let us now embark on our main subject in the way sanctioned by our old habit and ancient custom.

(C) Let it be known to your wisdom, O God-loving lord, that before these days I had an audience with our victorious King, and according to usage I praised God and His Majesty. When, in the limited space allowed to me, I had finished the words of my complimentary address, in which I spake of the nature of God and His Eternity, he did something to me, which he had never done before; he said to me: "O Catholicos, a man like you who possesses all this knowledge and utters such sublime words concerning God, is not justified in saying about God that He married a woman from whom He begat a son."[26] - And I replied to his Majesty: "And who, O God-loving King, who has ever uttered such a blasphemy concerning God?" - And our victorious King said to me: "What then do you say that Christ is?" - And I replied to his Majesty: "O King, Christ is the Word-God, who appeared in the flesh for the salvation of the world." - And our victorious King questioned me: "Do you not say that Christ is the Son of God?" - And I replied to his Majesty: "O King, Christ is the Son of God, and I confess Him and worship Him as such. This I learned from Christ Himself in the Gospel and from the books of the Torah and of the prophets, which know Him and call Him by the name of 'Son of God,' but not a son in the flesh as children are born in the carnal way, but an admirable and wonderful Son,[27] more sublime and higher than mind and words, as it fits a divine Son to be."

(D) Our King asked then: "How?" - And I replied to his Majesty: "O our King, that He is a Son and one that is born, we learn it and believe in it, but we dare not investigate how He was born before the times, and we are not able to understand the fact at all, as God is incomprehensible and inexplicable in all things; but we may say in an imperfect

175

simile that as light is born of the sun and the word of the soul, so also Christ who is Word, is born of God, high above the times and before all the worlds." - And our King said to me: "Do you not say that He was born of the virgin Mary?" - And I said to his Majesty: "We say it and confess it. The very same Christ is the Word born of the Father, and a man born of Mary. From the fact that He is Word-God, He is born of the Father before the times, as light from the sun and word from the soul; and from the fact that He is man He is born of the virgin Mary, in time; from the Father He is, therefore born eternally, and from the mother He is born in time, without a Father, without any marital contact and without any break in the seals of the virginity of His mother."

(E) Then our God-loving King said to me: "That He was born of Mary without marital intercourse is found in the book,[28] and is well known, but is it possible that He was born without breaking the seals of the virginity of His mother?" - And I replied to him: "O King, if we consider both facts in light of natural law, they are impossible, because it is impossible that a man should be born without breaking the seals of his mother's virginity and is equally impossible that He should be conceived without a man's intercourse. But if we consider not nature, but God, the Lord of nature, as the virgin was able to conceive without marital relations, so was she able to be delivered of her child without any break in her virginal seals. There is nothing impossible with God,[29] who can do everything." - Then the King said: "That a man can be born without marital intercourse is borne out by the example of Adam, who was fashioned by God from earth without any marital intercourse - but that a man can be born without breaking his mother's virginal seals, we have no proof, either from book nor from nature."

(F) And I replied to his Majesty in the following manner: "That He was born without breaking the virginal seals of His mother we have evidence from book and nature. From book there is the example of Eve, who was born from the side of Adam without having rent it or fractured it, and the example of Jesus Christ, who ascended to Heaven without having torn and breached the firmament. In this way He was born of Mary without having broken her virginal seals or fractured them.[30] This can also be illustrated from nature: all fruits are born of trees without breaking or tearing them, and sight is born of the eye while the latter is not broken or torn, and the perfume of apples and all aromatic substances is born of their respective trees or plants without breaking and tearing them, and the rays are born of the sun without tearing or breaking its spheric form. As all these are born of their generators without tearing them or rending them, so also Christ was born of Mary without breaking her virginal seals; as His eternal birth from the Father is wonderful, so also is His temporal birth from Mary."

(G) And our King said to me: "How was that Eternal One born in time?" - And I answered: "It is not in His eternity that He was born of Mary, O our King, but in His temporalness and humanity." - And our King said to me: "There are, therefore, two distinct beings: if one is eternal and God from God as you said, and the other temporal, the latter is therefore a pure man from Mary." - And I retorted: "Christ is not two beings, O King, nor two Sons, but Son and Christ are one; there are in Him two natures, one of which belongs to the Word and the other one which is from Mary, clothed itself[31] with the Word-God."[32] - And the King said: "They are, therefore, two, one of whom created and fashioned, and the other uncreated and unfashioned." - And I said to him: "We do not deny the duality of natures, O King, nor their mutual relations, but we profess that both of them constitute one Christ and Son."

(H) And the King retorted: "If He is one, He is not two; and if He is two, He is not one." - And I replied to him: "A man is one, while in reality he is two: one in his composition and individuality, and two in the distinction found between his soul and his body; the former is invisible and spiritual, and the latter visible and corporeal.[33] Our King, together with the insignia of his Kingdom is also one King and not two, however great may be the difference that separates him from his dresses. In the same way the Word of God, together with the clothings of humanity which He put on from Mary, is one and the same Christ, and not two, although there is in Him the natural difference between the Word-God and His humanity; and the fact that He is *one* does not preclude the fact that He is also *two*. The very same Christ and Son is indeed known and confessed as *one*, and the fact that He is also *two* does not imply confusion or mixture, because the known attributes of His natures are kept in one person[34] of the Son and Christ."

(I) And our King retorted to me: "Even in this you cannot save yourself from duality in Christ." - And I demonstrated the fact to him through another illustration and said: "The tongue and the word are one with the voice in which they are clothed, in a way that the two are not two words nor two tongues, but one word, together with the tongue and the voice, so that they are called by all one tongue with the word and the voice, and in them *one* does not expel *two*. This is also the case with the Word-God; He is one with His humanity, while preserving the distinction between His divinity and His humanity. Christ is *one* in His sonship and *two* in the attributes of His natures."

(J) And our King said to me: "Did not Jesus Christ say, I am going to My God and to your God?"[35] - And I said: "It is true that this sentence has been said by our Savior, but there is another sentence which precedes it and which is worthy of mention." - And the King asked: "Which is it?" - And I said: "Our Lord said to His disciples, 'I am going to My Father and to your Father, and to My God and your God.' " - And our King said: "How can this be? If He says that He is His Father, He is not His God, and if He is His God, He is not His Father; what is this contradiction?"[36] - And I replied to Him: "There is no contradiction here, O God-loving King. The fact that He is His Father by nature does not carry with it that He is also His God by nature, and the fact that He is His God by nature does not imply that He is His Father by nature. He is, however, from His Father by the nature of the Word, born of Him from eternity, as light from the sun and word from the soul; and God is His God by the nature of the humanity of the Word born of Mary. Man is living and rational only by the nature of his soul, which has indeed received from God a living and rational nature, but he is said to be living and rational in his body also, through its association with this living and rational soul. In reality what he is by nature when his body and soul are separated, is not what he is in its composite state when his body and soul are united. In spite of all this, however, he is called *one* living and rational man and not *two*. In the same way God is called, and is, the Christ's *Father* by the nature of the union of the Word-God with our human nature, and on the other hand He is called His *God* by the nature of His humanity that He took from us in union with the Word-God.

(K) In this way He is then *one* Son and Christ and not two. He was not born of Mary in the same way as He was born of God, nor was He born of God in the same way as He was born of Mary. So the Son and the Christ are really one, in spite of His births being two, and the same Christ has God as Father by nature and as God: Father by the fact that He is Word-God and God by the fact of His birth from Mary."[37]

(L) Our King showed here marks of doubt as to the possibility of all the above explanations, and I removed his doubt through another illustration and said: "The letter of the Commander of the Faithful is one, both in the words that are written in it and in the papyrus on which the words are written, and our King, the King of kings, is called both the father and the owner of his letter. He is called its father through the words born of his soul, which have been impressed on the papyrus, and he is called its owner through his being the owner of the papyrus on which the words have been written. Neither the papyrus, however, is by nature, from the soul of the King, nor the words are by nature from the papyrus reed, but the words are by nature born of the soul of the King, and the papyrus is by nature made of the papyrus reed, i.e., from $\pi\dot{\alpha}\pi\upsilon\rho\sigma\varsigma$.[38] In this same way Christ is one, both in His being Word-God and in His humanity taken from us, but the very same God of Christ is both His Father and His God: His Father, from the fact that He was born before the times, of the Father, and His God from the fact that He was born in time of Mary. By nature, however, He is not a man from the Father, nor is the Word by nature from Mary, but He is the very same Christ both from the Father and from Mary, in the first case as God, and in the second case as man."

(M) Then our God-loving King said to me: "How can the spirit who has no genital organs beget?" - And I replied to him: "O God-loving King, how can the spirit then do things and create without possessing organs of creation? As He created the worlds without instruments of creation, so He was born without the medium of the genital organs. If He could not be born without the intermediary of the genital organs, He could not by inference have created without the intermediary instruments of creation. If He created without any instruments of creation, He was, therefore, born without the genital organs. Lo, the sun also begets the rays of light without any genital organs. God is therefore able to beget and create, although He is a simple and not a composite spirit; and without any genital organs and instruments of creation He begets the Son and makes the Spirit proceed from the essence of His person as the sun does for the light and the heat."

(N) And our King said to me: "Do you believe in Father, Son and Holy Spirit?" - And I answered: "I worship them and believe in them." - Then our King said: "You, therefore, believe in three Gods." - And I replied to our King: "The belief in the above three names consists in the belief in three Persons, and the belief in these three Persons consists in the belief in one God. We believe in Father, Son and Holy Spirit as one God. So Jesus Christ taught us, and so we have learned from the revelation of the books of the prophets. As our God-loving King is one King with his word and his spirit, and not three kings, and as no one is able to distinguish him, his word and his spirit from himself and no one calls him King independently of his word and his spirit, so also God is one God with His Word and His Spirit, and not three gods, because the Word and the Spirit of God are inseparable from Him. And as the sun with its light and its heat is not called three suns but one sun, so also God with His Word and His Spirit is not three gods, but is and is called one God."[39]

(O) Then the King said to me: "What is my word? It is something that vanishes and disappears." - And I replied to him: "As God does not resemble in His nature the Commander of the Faithful, so also the Word and the Spirit of God do not resemble those of the Commander of the Faithful. We men sometimes exist and sometimes do not exist because we have a beginning and an end, as we are created. This is the case also with our word and our spirit, which at one time exist and at another cease to exist and have a beginning and an end. God, however, who is higher and more exalted than all, is not like us in this respect, but He exists divinely and eternally, and there was no time in which He was not, nor will there be a time in which He will not be. He has no beginning and no end, because He is not created. In the same way are His Word and His Spirit, who exist divinely and eternally, that is to say without beginning and without end, as God with God, without any separation."

(P) Then our King said to me: "Are the Word and the Spirit not separable from God?" - And I replied: "No; never. As light and heat are not separable from the sun, so also (the Word) and Spirit of God are not separable from Him. If one separates from the sun its light and its heat, it will immediately become neither light-giver nor heat-producer, and consequently it will cease to be the sun. So also if one separates from God His Word and His Spirit, He will cease to be a rational and living God, because the one who has no reason is called irrational,[40] and the one who has no spirit[41] is dead. If one, therefore, ventures to say about God that there was a time in which He had no Word and no Spirit, such a one would blaspheme against God, because his saying would be equivalent to asserting that there was a time in which God had no reason and no life. If such adjectives are considered as blasphemy and abomination when said of God, it follows that God begat the Word in a divine and eternal way, as a source of wisdom and had the Spirit proceeding from Him eternally and without any beginning, as a source of life. God is indeed the eternal source of life and wisdom; as a source of wisdom He imparts by His Word wisdom to all the rational beings, and as a source of life He causes life to flow to all the living beings, celestial and terrestrial alike, because God is the Creator of everything by means of His Word and His Spirit."

(Q) And our powerful King said to me: "Tell me from which books you can show me that the Word and the Spirit are eternally with God." - And I replied: "We can demonstrate this first from the books of the prophets and afterwards from the Gospel. As to the prophets, David said first thus: 'By the Word of the Lord were the heavens made and all His hosts by the Spirit of His mouth.'[42] In another passage he glorifies the Word of God as if it were God, in the following terms: 'I shall glorify the Word of the God.'[43] Further, in speaking of the resurrection of the dead, he said of God, 'Thou sendest forth Thy Spirit and they are created, and Thou renewest the face of the earth.'[44] The prophet David would not have glorified a created being, nor would he have called creator and renewer some one who was created and fashioned. In another passage he speaks of the Word of God as itself God, without a beginning and without an end, because he writes:[45] 'Thou art forever, O Lord, and Thy Word standeth in Heaven;' he teaches here that as God is forever in heaven, so also the Word of God is in heaven for ever and without an end, because he who is without an end is also without a beginning, and he who has no beginning has no end.

(R) "Afterwards comes the prophet Isaiah, who speaks of the Word of God in a way similar to that of David, in saying thus: 'The grass withereth and the flower fadeth, but the Word of our God standeth forever.'[46] Other prophets also speak of this point in several passages. So as far as the Gospel is concerned, we gather the same conclusion from the following passage: 'In the beginning was the Word, and the Word was with God, and the Word was God.'[47] We are taught here two things: that the Word is eternal and that the same Word is God by nature. All these the Gospel teaches about the Word, and it teaches us also the same thing concerning the Spirit in the very same chapter, 'In Him was life,'[48] *i.e.*, in the same Word-God was 'life' which means '(in Him) was Spirit' or 'He was it.' In saying of the Word in the first passage that He 'was,' does not refer to any beginning, and so is the case with regard to the second passage referring to the Spirit. Indeed the Gospel in using this 'was' is not speaking of His creation, but of His eternity. If Spirit is life and life is eternally in God, the Spirit is consequently eternally in God. And Jesus Christ is the Spirit of God and the life and the light of men.

(S) "In one passage Christ said to His Father, 'And now, O Father, glorify Thou Me with Thine own Self with the glory which I had with Thee before the world was.'[49] He said here, 'with the glory which He *had* before the world was,' and not which *came* to Him;' if He had said, 'With the glory which *had come to me* with Thee before the world was,' He would have taught us that He was a created and made being, but since He said 'with the glory which *I had* with Thee before the world was' He clearly taught us that while all the world was created He alone was without a beginning, as the Word of God.

(T) "In another passage, while He was about to ascend to Heaven He said to His disciples, 'Go and teach all nations and baptize them in the name of the Father and of the Son and of the Holy Ghost.'[50] Jesus Christ would not have allowed Himself to count created and made beings with the One who is uncreated and unmade, and temporal beings with the One who has no beginning and no end.[51] As the wise men do not mix promiscuously with one another in one count sun, stone and horse, nor pearl, gold and brass, but say, for instance, in a separate way: three pearls, or three stars, as these are similar in nature and resemble one another in everything, so also would the case be with Jesus Christ, who would have never allowed himself to count with God His Word and His Spirit, if He did not know that they were equal to God in nature. How could He have made equal in honor and royal power the one who was not God in nature with the one who was, or the one who was temporal with the one who was eternal? It is not the servants who participate in royal honor, but the children."[52]

(U) Then our King said to me: "What is the difference between the Son and the Spirit, and how is it that the Son is not the Spirit nor the Spirit the Son? Since you said that God is not composite, there should not be any difference with God in the fact that He begets and makes proceed from Himself." - And I replied to our King as follows: "There is no difference, O King, between the persons in their relationship to one another, except that the first is not begotten, and the second is begotten, and the third proceeds; and God consists in Father, Son and Holy Spirit; and He begat that former and made the latter proceed

from Him from eternity without any bodily cleavage and separation in
the organs and places that are fit for generation and procession. God
is not composite and has no body, and since the terms 'cleavage' and
'organs' imply a body — because all bodies are composite — it follows
that 'cleavage' and 'organs' do not apply to God; indeed God being
without body and not being composite, is thought of without any notion
of 'cleavage' and 'separation.' Reason comes out of the soul — because
mind comes out of the soul — but it comes out of it without any suffering, without cleavage and without the instrumentality of organs. The
very same sun begets light and makes heat come out of it, without any
cleavage or bodily separation, and in a way that all the light is from all
the sun and all the heat from all its spheric globe.

(V) "All the reason and all the mind are from all the soul, the former
by process of birth and the second by that of procession, as all the heat
and all the mind are with the sun and with the soul respectively, and all
the heat and all the reason are with the soul, with the sun and with
ourselves, while light does not become heat nor heat light. This very
method applies to the Word and the Spirit: the former is begotten and
the latter proceeds from God and the Father, not through any material
cleavage and any suffering, nor from a special organ, but as from an
uncircumscribed being: an uncircumscribed one in an uncircumscribed
fashion, and one who is all in all without space and time, in a way that
the Son is not the Spirit, nor the Spirit the Son in qualifications and
attributes.

(W) "From the whole of an apple the whole of the scent and the
whole of the taste are begotten and proceed in a way that the apple
does not make the scent proceed from one part of it and beget the
taste from another, but scent and taste come out of all the apple.
While scent and taste are mixed with each other and with the apple,
they are nevertheless separate in a way that taste is not scent and scent
is not taste and are not confused with each other, nor separated from
each other, but are so to speak mixed together in a separate way and
separated from each other in a mixed way, by a process that is as
amazing as it is incomprehensible. In this very way from the uncircumscribed Father the Son is begotten and the Spirit proceeds, in an

uncircumscribed way: the eternal from the eternal, the uncreated from the uncreated, the spiritual from the spiritual. Since they are uncircumscribed, they are not separated from one another, and since they are not bodies, they are not mixed and confused with one another, but are separated in their persons in a united way, so to speak, and are united in their nature in a separate way. God is, therefore, one in nature with three personal attributes."

(X) And our King said to me: "If they are not separated by remoteness and nearness as they are uncircumscribed, the Father therefore, and the Spirit clothed also themselves with the human body, together with the Son; if the Father and the Spirit did not put on human body with the Son, how is it that they are not separated by distance and space?" - And I replied to his Majesty: "As the word of the King clothes itself with the papyrus on which it is written, while his soul and his mind cannot be said to do the same, and as his soul and his mind, while not separated from his word, cannot nevertheless be said that they clothe themselves with the papyrus, so also is the case with the Word of God; because although He put on our human body without having been separated from the Father and the Spirit, yet the Father and the Spirit cannot be said to have put on our human body.

(Y) "Further, the word that is begotten of the soul clothes itself with the voice that is caused by the vibration of the air, and yet it is not separated from the soul and the mind, and the soul and the mind are not said that they clothe themselves with the voice, and no man ever says that he heard the mind and the soul of so-and-so, but he does say that he heard the word of so-and-so, and this in spite of the fact that the word is not remote from the mind, nor the mind from the soul, and are not separated from one another. In this very way the Word-God clothed Himself with a body from ourselves, without having been separated in the least from the Father and the Spirit, and in this way also the Father and the Spirit are not said to have put on human body with the Word.

(Z) "Finally, the body is believed to be and actually is the temple and the clothing of the soul, but it is not believed and actually is not the temple of and the clothing of the word and of the mind, in spite of the fact that neither the word nor the mind are remote from the soul, nor is the soul itself remote from the word and the mind. In this way the Word alone is spoken of as having put on our human body, while the Father and the Spirit are not said to have put it on, in spite of the fact that they are not remote from the Word in distance and locality." The objections and the difficulties raised by our Sovereign have been rebutted and explained in the above way.

(AA) After these the King said to me: "Who is your head and your leader?" - And I replied: "Our Lord Jesus Christ." - And our King asked me: "Was Jesus Christ circumcised or not?"[53] - And I answered: "He was." - And our King asked me: "Why do you not then circumcise yourself? If your head and leader is Jesus Christ, and Jesus Christ was circumcised, you should also by necessity circumcise yourself." - And I spoke thus: "O King, Jesus Christ was both circumcised and baptized. He was circumcised eight days after His birth according to injunction of the Law, and He was baptized while He was about thirty years of age, and by His baptism He annulled circumcision.[54] I do not follow the Law as the Christ followed the Law;[55] I follow the Gospel, and that is why I do not circumcise myself in spite of the fact that Christ circumcised Himself, but I baptize myself with water and spirit like Him. I believe in Jesus Christ, and since Jesus Christ was baptized, I consider baptism as an urgent necessity for me.[56] I leave the image and cleave to the reality."

(AB) And our King asked me: "How did Jesus Christ abolish circumcision, and what is the meaning of the 'image' you have spoken of?" - And I replied: "All the Torah was, O King, the image of the Gospel. The sacrifices that are in the Law are the image of the sacrifice of Jesus Christ, and the priesthood and high-priesthood of the Law are the image of the high-priesthood of Christ, and the carnal circumcision is the image of His spiritual circumcision. As He abolished the Law by the Gospel, and the sacrifices by His sacrifice, and the priesthood of the Law by His priesthood, so also He abolished and annulled the carnal circumcision which is performed with the work of the hands of men by means of His circumcision which is not performed by the work of the hands of men, but by the power of the Spirit, and it is the sacrament[57] of the Kingdom of Heaven and of the resurrection from death."

(AC) And our King said: "If Christ abolished the Law and all its requirements, He is, therefore, its enemy and its adversary. We call enemies those who destroy and contradict one another." - And I replied to him: "The light of the stars is abolished by the light of the sun, and the light of the latter is not for that the enemy of that of the former; the functions of childhood are also abolished by those of manhood, and man is not for that the enemy of himself; an earthly kingdom is also abolished by the heavenly Kingdom, and the Kingdom of God is not for that the enemy of men. In this very way Jesus Christ abolished and destroyed the Law by the Gospel, while He is not for that the enemy and the adversary of the law."[58]

(AD) And our King said to me: "Where did Jesus Christ worship and pray in the years that elapsed between His birth and His ascension to Heaven? Was it not in the house of holiness[59] and in Jerusalem?" - And I replied: "Yes." - And our King asked: "Why then do you worship God and pray in the direction of the East?"[60] - And I replied: "The true worship of the Omnipotent God, O King, will be performed by mankind in the Kingdom of Heaven, and the image of the Kingdom of Heaven in the earth is the paradise of Eden; now as the paradise of Eden is in the east, we therefore worship God and pray rightly in the direction of the east in which is the Paradise which is the image of the Kingdom of Heaven. There is also another reason for our conduct: Jesus Christ walked in the flesh thirty-three years on the earth, O King, In the thirtieth year He repaid to God all the debt that the human kind and angels owed to Him. It was a debt that no man and no angel was able to pay, because there has never been a created being that was free from sin, except the Man with whom God clothed Himself and became one with Him in a wonderful unity."[61]

(AE) "After having then paid to God the debt of all the creatures and abrogated, annulled and torn the contract containing it, He went to the Jordan, to John the Baptist, and was baptized by him, and thus the

One who was the image of the Kingdom of Heaven placed this baptism of His in the forefront of the Christian life. From the day of His baptism to that of His ascension to heaven there are three years, and it is in these three years that He has taught us all the economy of the Christian religion: baptism, laws, ordinances, prayers, worship in the direction of the East and the sacrifice that we offer. All these things He practiced in His person and taught us to practice ourselves. Because He wished to proclaim to the world through His disciples: the Gospel, the baptism, the sacrifice and the worship and prayer to God; He performed and fulfilled them all in His own person, in order that His disciples might fulfil themselves what they had seen Him practicing Himself, and that they might teach others to do the same.

(AF) "Further, the worship of God started at the beginning in the East, it is indeed in that Adam and his children worshipped God, because the Paradise is in the direction of the east.[62] Moreover, Noah, Abraham, Isaac, Jacob and Moses used to worship God and pray while turning toward the east and Paradise, that is towards the direction and the place in which God had been worshipped from the beginning by Adam and his children, as we have just now said. It is for this reason that Jesus Christ taught His disciples to worship God and pray towards the east. Because Adam transgressed the commandment of God, he was driven out of Paradise, and when he went out of Paradise he was thrown on this accursed earth. Having been thrown on this accursed earth, he turned his face away from God, and his children worshipped demons, stars, sun, moon and graven and molten images. The Word of God came then to the children of men in a human body, and in His person paid to God the debt that they were owing Him. To remind them, however, of the place from which their father was driven because of his transgression of the commandment, He made them turn their faces towards Paradise in their worship and prayer, because it is in it that God was first worshipped.

(AG) "Because Jesus Christ saved men from the depredation of Satan, and the Word of God freed them from the worship of idols, He rightly turned also the direction of their sight and their minds towards God and towards Paradise where He was first worshipped. He simply brought back the one who was going astray to the house of his father. This is also the reason why the angel Gabriel, when announcing to Mary the conception of Jesus Christ, appeared to her from the direction of the east as it is written in your book.[63] Finally, we worship God in the direction of the east, because being light He is more congruously worshipped in the direction of the light."

(AH) Our King them said to me: "Did Christ then worship and pray?" - And I answered his Majesty: "He did worship and pray." - And our King retorted saying, "By the fact that you say that He worshipped and prayed, you deny His divinity, because if He worshipped and prayed, He is not God; if He was God, he would not have worshipped and prayed."[64] - And I replied: "He did not worship and pray as God, because as such He is the receiver of the worship and prayer of both the celestial and the terrestrial beings, in conjunction with the Father and the Spirit, but He worshipped and prayed as a man, son of our human kind. It has been made manifest by our previous words that the very same Jesus Christ is Word-God and man, as God He is born of the Father, and as man of Mary. He further worshipped and prayed for our sake, because He Himself was in no need of worship and prayer."

(AI) And our King said to me: "There is no creature that has no need of worship and prayer." - And I replied: "Has Jesus Christ, the Word of God, sinned or not?" - And our King said: "May God preserve me from saying such a thing!"[65] - And I then asked: "Has God created the worlds with His Word or not?" And our King replied in the affirmative and said: "Yes." - And I then asked: "Is the one who is neither a sinner nor in need of anything, in need of worship and prayer?" - And our King answered: "No." - And then I said to him: "If the Christ is a Word from God and a man from Mary, and if as a Word of God He is the Lord of everything, and as a man He did not commit any sin as the book and our King testify, and if He who is the Lord of everything and a creator is not in need, and he who is not a sinner is pure, it follows that Jesus Christ worshipped and prayed to God neither as one in need, nor as a sinner,[66] but He worshipped and prayed in order to teach worship and prayer to His disciples, and through them to every human being.

(AJ) The disciples would not have yielded to His teaching if He had not put it into practice in His own person. There is no creature that has not sinned except Jesus Christ, the Word of God, and He is the only created being who in His own humanity appeared above the dirt of sin. As He was baptized without having any need of baptism, and as He died on the cross, but not because of His own sin, so also He gave Himself to worship and prayer not for His own sake, but in order to impart their knowledge to His disciples."

(AK) Our God-loving King ended the above subject here and embarked on another theme and said to me: "How is it that you accept Christ and the Gospel from the testimony of the Torah and of the prophets, and you do not accept Muhammad from the testimony of Christ and the Gospel?"[67] And I replied to his Majesty: "O our King, we have received concerning Christ numerous and distinct testimonies from the Torah and the prophets. All of the latter prophesied in one accord and harmony in one place about His mother: 'Behold a virgin shall conceive and bear a son,'[68] and taught us that He shall be conceived and born without marital intercourse like the Word of God. It is indeed fit that the One who was born of the Father without a mother should have been born in the flesh from a virgin mother without a father, in order that His second birth may be a witness to His first birth. In another place they reveal to us His name: 'And His name shall be called Emmanuel, Wonderful, Counsellor and Mighty God of the worlds.'[69]

(AL) "In another place the prophets reveal to us the miracles that He will work at His coming in saying, 'Behold your God will come...He will come and save you. Then the eyes of the blind shall be opened, and the ears of the deaf shall hear. Then shall the lame man leap as an hart, and the tongue of the dumb shall be loosed.'[70] Yet in another place they disclose to us His passion and His death, 'He shall be killed for our transgressions and humbled for our iniquities.'[71] Sometimes they speak to us about His resurrection, 'For Thou hast not left my soul in Sheol, nor hast Thou suffered Thy Holy One to see corruption,'[72] and 'The Lord hath said unto me, Thou art my Son; this day have I begotten Thee.'[73] Some other times they teach us concerning His ascension to Heaven, 'Thou hast ascended on high, Thou hast led captivity captive, and Thou hast made gifts to men,'[74] and 'God went up in glory, and the Lord with the sound of the trumpet.'[75]

(AM) "Some other times they reveal to us His coming down from heaven in saying, 'I am one like the son of men coming on the clouds of heaven,[76] and they brought Him near before the Ancient of days, and there was given Him dominion, and glory and a kingdom that all peoples of the earth should serve Him and worship Him. His dominion is an everlasting dominion, and His kingdom shall not pass away or be destroyed.'[77] These and scores of other passages of the prophets show us Jesus Christ in a clear mirror and point to Him. So far as Muhammad is concerned, I have not received a single testimony either from Jesus Christ or from the Gospel[78] which would refer to his name or to his works.

(AN) And our benevolent and gracious King made a sign to mean that he was not convinced, then he repeated twice to me the question: "Have you not received any?" - And I replied to him, "No, O God-loving King, I have not received any." - And the King asked me: "Who is then the Paraclete?"[79] - And I answered: "The Spirit of God." - And the King asked: "What is the Spirit of God?" - And I replied: "God, by nature; and one who proceeds, by attribute; as Jesus Christ taught about Him." - And our glorious King said: "And what did Jesus Christ teach about Him?" - And I answered: "He spoke to His disciples as follows: 'When I go away to Heaven,[80] I will send unto you the Spirit-Paraclete who proceedeth from the Father, whom the world cannot receive, who dwelleth with you and is among you, who searcheth all things, even the deep things of God, who will bring to your remembrance all the truth that I have said unto you, and who will take of mine and show unto you.' "[81]

(AO) And our King said to me: "All these refer to Muhammad."[82] - And I replied to him: "If Muhammad were the Paraclete, since the Paraclete is the Spirit of God, Muhammad would therefore be the

Spirit of God; and the Spirit of God being uncircumscribed like God, Muhammad would also be uncircumscribed like God; and he who is uncircumscribed being invisible, Muhammad would also be invisible and without a human body; and he who is without a body being uncomposed, Muhammad would also be uncomposed. Indeed he who is a spirit has no body, and he who has no body is also invisible, and he who is invisible is also uncircumscribed; but he who is circumscribed is not the Spirit of God, and he who is not the Spirit of God is not the Paraclete. The Paraclete is from Heaven and of the nature of the Father, and Muhammad is from the earth and of the nature of Adam. Since Heaven is not the same thing as earth, nor is God the Father identical with Adam, the Paraclete is not, therefore, Muhammad.

(AP) "Further, the Paraclete searches the deep things of God, but Muhammad owns that he does not know what might befall him and those who accept him.[83] He who searches all things even the deep things of God is not identical with the one who does not know what might happen to him and to those who acknowledge him. Muhammad is therefore not the Paraclete. Again, the Paraclete, as Jesus told His disciples, was with them and among them while He was speaking to them, and since Muhammad was not with them and among them, he cannot, therefore, have been the Paraclete. Finally, the Paraclete descended on the disciples ten days after the ascension of Jesus to Heaven, while Muhammad was born more than six hundred years later, and this impedes Muhammad from being the Paraclete. And Jesus taught the disciples that the Paraclete is one God in three persons, and since Muhammad does not believe in the doctrine of three persons in one Godhead, he cannot be the Paraclete. And the Paraclete wrought all sorts of prodigies and miracles through the disciples, and since Muhammad did not work a single miracle through his followers and his disciples, he is not the Paraclete.[84]

(AQ) "That the Spirit-Paraclete is consubstantial with the Father and the Son is borne out be the fact that He is the maker of the heavenly powers and of everything, and since He who is the maker and creator of everything is God, the Spirit-Paraclete is therefore God; but the world is not able to receive God, as Jesus Christ said,[85] because God is uncircumscribed. Now if Muhammad were the Paraclete, since this same Paraclete is the Spirit of God, Muhammad would therefore be the Spirit of God. Further, since David said, 'By the Spirit of God all the powers have been created,'[86] celestial and terrestrial, Muhammad would be the creator of the celestial and terrestrial beings. Now since Muhammad is not the creator of Heaven and earth, and since he who is not creator is not the Spirit of God, Muhammad is, therefore, not the Spirit of God; and since the one who is not the Spirit of God is by inference not the Paraclete, Muhammad is not the Paraclete.

(AR) "If he were mentioned in the Gospel, this mention would have been marked by a distinct portraiture characterizing his coming, his name, his mother, and his people as the true portraiture of the coming of Jesus Christ is found in the Torah and in the prophets. Since nothing resembling this is found in the Gospel concerning Muhammad, it is evident that there is no mention of him in it at all, and that is the reason why I have not received a single testimony from the Gospel about him."[87]

(AS) And the God-loving King said to me: "As the Jews behaved towards Jesus, whom they did not accept, so the Christians behaved towards Muhammad, whom they did not accept." - And I replied to his Majesty: "The Jews did not accept Jesus in spite of the fact that the Torah and the prophets were full of testimonies about Him, and this renders them worthy of condemnation. As to us we have not accepted Muhammad because we have not a single testimony about him in our books." - And our King said: "There were many testimonies but the Books have been corrupted, and you have removed them."[88] - And I replied to him thus: "Where is it known, O King that the Books have been corrupted by us, and where is that uncorrupted Book from which you have learned that the Books we use have been corrupted? If there is such a book let it be placed in the middle in order that we may learn from it which is the corrupted Gospel and hold to that which is not corrupted.[89] If there is not such a Gospel, how do you know that the Gospel of which we make use is corrupted?

(AT) "What possible gain could we have gathered from corrupting the

Gospel? Even if there was mention of Muhammad made in the Gospel, we would not have deleted his name from it; we would have simply said that Muhammad has not come yet and that he was going to come in the future. Take the example of the Jews: they cannot delete the name of Jesus from the Torah and the prophets, they only contend against Him in saying openly that He was going to come in the future, and that He has not come yet into the world. They resemble a blind man[90] without eyes who stands in plain daylight and contends that the sun has not yet risen. We also would have done likewise; we would not have dared to remove the name of Muhammad from our Book if it were found anywhere in it; we would have simply quibbled concerning his right name and person like the Jews do in the case of Jesus. To tell the truth, if I had found in the Gospel a prophecy concerning the coming of Muhammad, I would have left the Gospel for the Qur'an, as I have left the Torah and the prophets for the Gospel."

(AU) And our King said to me: "Do you not believe that our Book was given by God?" - And I replied to him: "It is not my business to decide whether it is from God or not. But I will say something of which your Majesty is well aware and that is all the words of God found in the Torah and the prophets and those of them found in the Gospel and in the writings of the Apostles, have been confirmed by signs and miracles; as to the words of your Book they have not been corroborated by a single sign or miracle.[91] It is imperative that signs and miracles should be annulled by other signs and miracles. When God wished to abrogate[92] the Mosaic law, He confirmed by the signs and miracles wrought by the Christ and the Apostles that the words of the Gospel were from God, and by this He abrogated the words of the Torah and the first miracles.[93] Similarly, as He abrogated the first signs and miracles by the second ones, He ought to have abrogated the second signs and miracles by third ones. If God had wished to abrogate the Gospel and introduce another book in its place, He would have done this, because signs and miracles are witnesses of His will; but your book has not been confirmed by a single sign and miracle. Since signs and miracles are proofs of the will of God, the conclusion drawn from their absence in your Book is well known to your Majesty."

(AV) And our King asked: "Who is then the rider on an ass and the rider on a camel?"[94] - And I replied: "The rider on an ass is Darius the Mede, son of Assuerus, and the rider on a camel is Cyrus the Persian, who was from Elam. The King of Elam destroyed the kingdom of the Medes and passed it to the Persians,[95] as Darius the Mede had destroyed the kingdom of the Babylonians and passed it to the Medes."

(AW) And our King said to me: "From where is this known?" - And I replied: "From the context. In the preceding passage the prophet said, 'Go up, O Elam, and mountains of Media.'[96] By the words 'mountains of Media' Darius the Mede is meant, and by the word 'Elam' the kingdom of the Persians is designated. The Book says also in the words that follow, 'And one of the horsemen came and said, 'Babylon is fallen, is fallen,' and shows clearly that the passage refers to Darius and Cyrus, because it is they who destroyed the kingdom of the Babylonians."

(AX) And our King said: "Why did he say that the first was riding on an ass and the second on a camel?" - And I replied: "The reason is that asses are generally more in use in the country of the Medes, while in the country of the Persians and Elamites camels are more in evidence. Through animals the prophet referred to countries, and through countries to the powers and kingdoms which were to rise in them. Further, because the kingdom of the Medes was to be weak and indolent while that of the Persians or Elamites was to be strong and valiant, God alluded to the kingdom of the Medes through the weak ass, and to that of the Elamites and Persians through the valiant camel. In the book of Daniel also God alluded to the kingdom of the Medes through the indolent bear and to that of the Elamites and Persians through the valiant leopard.[97] Again, in the vision of the King Nebuchadnezzar God symbolized the kingdom of the Medes in the malleable silver, while that of the Persians and Elamites in the strong brass.[98] In this same way the prophet alluded to the kingdom of Media through the ass, and to that of Elam through the camel."

(AY) And our King said to me: "The rider on the ass is Jesus and the rider on the camel is Muhammad."[99] - And I answered his Majesty: "O our God-loving King, neither the order of the times nor the succession of events will allow us to refer in this passage the riding on the ass to Christ and the riding on the camel to Muhammad. It is known with accuracy from the order and succession of the revelations to the prophets that the ass refers to the Medes and the camel to the Elamites, and this order of the revelations and this succession of events impede us from ascribing the words of the scripture to other persons. Even if one, through similarity between adjectives and names, does violence to the context and refers the passage dealing with the ass to Jesus on account of a different passage: 'Lowly and riding upon an ass, and upon a colt, the foal of an ass,'[100] yet it is not possible to refer the passage dealing with the camel to Muhammad."[101]

(AZ) And our King said: "For what reason?" - And I replied: "Because the prophet Jacob said, 'The sceptre of the kingdom shall not depart from Judah, nor an utterer of prophecy from his seed, until Jesus Christ come, because kingdom is His, and He is the expectation of the peoples.'[102] In this he shows that after the coming of the Christ there will be neither prophet nor prophecy. And Daniel also concurs in saying that for putting an end to all vision and prophecy and for the coming of Christ the King, seven weeks and threescore and two weeks will elapse, and then the Christ will be killed and there will not be any more kingdom and prophecy in Jerusalem.[103] In this he showed that visions and prophecies will come to an end with the Christ. And the Christ Himself said: 'The prophets and the Torah prophesied until John.'[104] Every prophecy, therefore, ended with the time of Christ, and after Christ there was no prophecy, nor did any prophet rise.[105] All the prophets prophesied about Jesus Christ, and the Christ directed us to the Kingdom of Heaven, and it is superfluous that after the knowledge that we have of God and the Kingdom of Heaven, we should be brought down to the knowledge of human and earthly things.

(BA) "As to the prophets, they prophesied sometimes concerning the earthly affairs and kingdoms and some other times concerning the adorable Epiphany and Incarnation of the Word-God. As to Jesus Christ, He did not reveal to us things dealing with the law and earthly affairs, but He solely taught us things dealing with the knowledge of God and the Kingdom of Heaven. We have already said that all prophecy extended as far as Christ only, as Christ Himself and the prophets asserted, and since from the time of Christ downwards only the Kingdom of God is being preached, as Jesus Christ taught, it is superfluous that after the adorable Incarnation of Christ we should accept and acknowledge another prophecy and another prophet. A good and praiseworthy order of things is that which takes us up from the bottom to the top, from the human to the divine things and from the earthly to the heavenly things; but an order which would lower us from top to bottom, from divine to worldly and from heavenly to earthly things, is bad and blameworthy."

(BB) And our victorious King said to me: "Why do you worship the cross?"[106] - And I replied: "First because it is the cause of life." - And our glorious King said to me: "A cross is not the cause of life, but rather of death." - And I replied to him: "The cross is as you say, O King, the cause of death; but death is also the cause of resurrection, and resurrection is the cause of life and immortality, and this is the reason why through it, as a symbol of life and immortality, we worship one and indivisible God. It is through it that God opened to us the source of life and immortality, and God, who at the beginning ordered light to come out of darkness, who sweetened bitter water in bitter wood, who through the sight of a deadly serpent granted life to the children of Israel — handed to us the fruit of life from the wood of the cross and caused rays of immortality to shine upon us from the branches of the cross.

(BC) "As we honor the roots because of the fruits that come out of them, so also we honor the cross as the root of which the fruit of life was born to us, and from which the ray of immortality shone[107] upon us. As a decisive proof of the love of God for all, luminous rays of His love are those that shine from the rational beings. This love of God can then be demonstrated from all creatures visible and invisible, but the most luminous rays of the love of God are those that shine from the rational beings. This love of God can then be demonstrated from all creatures and from the ordinary Divine Providence that is manifest

197

in them, but the great wealth of His love for all humanity is more
strikingly in evidence in the fact that He delivered to death in the flesh
His beloved Son for the life, salvation and resurrection of all. It is only
just, therefore, O our victorious King, that the medium through which
God showed His love to all, should also be the medium through which
all should show their love to God."[108]

(BC) And our King said to me: "Can God then Himself die?"[109] - And
I replied to his Majesty: "The Son of God died in our nature, but not
in His divinity. When the royal purple and the insignia of the kingdom
are torn, the dishonor redounds to the King: so also is the case with
the death of the body of the Son-God."[110] - And our King said to me:
"May God preserve me from saying such a thing.[111] They did not kill
Him and they did not crucify Him, but He made a similitude from
them in this way."[112] - And I said to him: "It is written in the *Surat
'Isa*,[113] 'Peace be upon Me the day I was born and the day I die and
the day I shall be sent again alive.' "[114] This passage shows that He
died and rose up. Further, God said to 'Isa (Jesus) "I will make Thee
die and take Thee up again to Me."[115]

(BD) And our King said: "He did not die then, but He will die after-
wards." - And I replied to him: "Therefore He did not go up into
Heaven either, nor was He sent again alive, but He will go up to
Heaven afterwards and will be sent again alive in the future. No, our
King, Jesus did go up to Heaven a long time ago and has been sent
again alive, as your book also testifies. If He went up it is obvious that
He had died previously, and if He had died, it is known that He had
died by crucifixion, as the prophets had stated before His coming."

(BE) And our King said to me: "Which prophet said that He died by
crucifixion?" - And I replied to his Majesty: "First the prophet David,
who said, 'They pierced my hands and my feet, and my bones cried;
and they looked and stared upon me; they parted my garments among
them and cast lots for my vesture.'[116] The Gospel testifies that all of
these were fulfilled. And Isaiah said, 'He shall be killed for our sins
and humbled for our iniquity.'[117] And the prophet Jeremiah said,

'Wood will eat into His flesh and will destroy Him from the land of the living. I gave my body to wounds and my cheeks to blows, and I did not turn my face from shame and spittle.'[118] And the prophet Daniel said, 'And the Messiah shall be killed, but not for Himself.'[119] And the prophet Zechariah said, 'And smite the shepherd of Israel on his cheeks,' and 'O sword, awake against my shepherd.'[120] Indeed numerous are the passages in which the prophets spoke of His death, murder and crucifixion."[121]

(BF) And our King said: "He made a similitude only for them in this way." - And I replied to him: "And who made a similitude for them in this way, O our King? How did God deceive them and show them something which was not true?[122] It is incongruous to God that He should deceive and show something for another thing. If God deceived them and made a similitude for them, the apostles who simply wrote what God had shown to them, would be innocent of the deception and the real cause of it would be God. If on the other hand we say that it is Satan who made such a similitude for the apostles, what has Satan to do in the economy of God? And who dares to say about the *hawari-yun*[123] that Satan was able to deceive them? The apostles drove and cast away the demons, who shouted and ran away from them on account of the divine power that was accompanying them. If crucifixion was only an unreal similitude and if from it death took place, even death would be an unreal similitude; then out of this resurrection there has been ascension to Heaven, which would also be unreal and untrue. Now since the resurrection precedes the ascension, this resurrection is also a reality and not a similitude; and since death was a reality and not a similitude, and since death is preceded by crucifixion, this crucifixion is consequently a reality also and not an illusion or a similitude."

(BG) And our King said: "It was not honorable to Jesus Christ that God should have allowed Him to be delivered to Jews in order that they might kill Him." - And I answered his Majesty: "The prophets have been killed by the Jews, but that not all those who have been killed by the Jews are despicable and devoid of honor[124] is borne out by the fact that none of the true prophets is despicable and devoid of honor in the sight of God. Since it is true that the prophets have generally been killed by the Jews, it follows that not all those who have been killed by the Jews are despicable and devoid of honor. This we assert for the prophets. So far as Jesus Christ is concerned, we say that the Jews crucified only the Christ in the flesh, which He delivered to them voluntarily, and His murder was not imposed forcibly upon Him by them. Because He, Jesus Christ said, 'I have power upon My soul to lay it down, and I have power to take it again; and no man taketh it from Me.'[125] In this He showed that He should suffer out of His own free will, and not out of His own weakness or from the omnipotence of the Jews. He who when hanging on the wood of the cross moved the heavens, shook the earth, changed the dazzling sun into darkness and the shining moon into blood-redness, and He who rent the stones and the graves, raised and resuscitated the dead, could not be so weak as not to be able to save Himself from the hands of the Jews. It is therefore out of His own free will that He approached the suffering on the cross and death, and He did not bear the death of the crucifixion at the hands of the Jews out of abjection and weakness on His part, but He bore both crucifixion and death at the hands of the Jews out of His own free will."

(BH) And our King said: "No blame attaches, therefore, to the Jews from His death, if they simply fulfilled and satisfied His wish."[126] - And I answered his Majesty: "If the Jews had solely crucified Him in order that He might raise the dead and ascend to Heaven, they would naturally have been not only free from blame, but worthy of thousands of crowns and encomia of all kinds, but if these same Jews crucified Him in order not that He might rise up again from the dead and ascend to heaven, but in order that they might intensify His death and obliterate Him from the surface of the earth, they would with great justice be worthy of blame and death. Indeed they crucified Him not in order that He might go up to heaven but go down to Sheol; God, however, raised Him up from the dead and took Him up to Heaven."

(BI) And our God-loving King said to me: "Which of the two things would you be willing to admit? Was the Christ willing to be crucified or not?[127] If He was willing to be crucified, the Jews who simply accomplished His will should not be cursed and despised. If, however, He was not willing to be crucified and He was crucified, He was weak and the Jews were strong. In this case, how can He be God; He who found Himself unable to deliver Himself from the hands of His cruci-fiers whose will appeared to be stronger than His?"

(BJ) And I answered these objections by other questions as follows: "What would our King, endowed with high acumen and great wisdom say to this: When God created Satan as one of the angels, did He wish this Satan to be an angel or not? If God wished him to be Satan instead of an angel, the wicked Satan would, therefore, simply be accomplishing the will of God; but if God did not wish Satan[128] to be Satan, but an angel, and in spite of that he became Satan, the will of Satan became stronger than the will of God. How can we then call God one whose will was overcome by the will of Satan, and one against whom Satan prevailed?

(BK) "Another question: Did God wish Adam to go out of Paradise or not? If He wished to drive him out of Paradise, why should Satan be blamed, who simply helped to do the will of God in his driving Adam from Paradise.[129] On the other hand, if God did not wish Adam to go out of Paradise, how is it that the will of God became weak and was overcome, while the will of Satan became strong and prevailed? How can God be God, if His will has been completely overcome? The fact that Satan and Adam sinned against the will of God does not affect the divinity of God and does not show Him to be weak and deficient, and the fact that God had willed Satan to fall from Heaven and Adam to go out of Paradise does not absolve Satan and Adam from blame and censure, and the fact that they did not sin to accom-plish the will of God but to accomplish their own will are a good analogy to the case of Jesus Christ. He should not indeed be preclud-ed from being God, nor should He be rendered weak and deficient in strength by the fact that the Jews sinned but not by His will and that in their insolence they crucified Him; and the fact that the Christ wished to be crucified and die for the life, resurrection and salvation of all should not exempt the Jews from Hell and Curse.

(BL) "The Jews did not crucify the Christ because He willed it, but they crucified Him because of their hatred and malice, both to Himself and to the One who sent Him. They crucified Him in order that they might destroy Him completely, and He willed to be crucified so that He might live again and rise from the dead and be to all men the sign and proof of the resurrection of the dead.

(BM) "Another question: What would our victorious and powerful King say about those who fight for the sake of God?[130] Do they wish to be killed or not? If they do not wish to be killed and are killed, their death has no merit, and they will not go to Heaven;[131] and if they wish to be killed, are their murderers blameworthy or not? If they are not blameworthy, how is it that unbelievers who killed Muslims and believers are not blameworthy, and if they are blameworthy, why should they be so when what they did was simply to fulfill the wish of the victims? The fact is that the murderers of the men who fought for the sake of God are not exempted from Fire and Hell; indeed, the murderers do not slay them so that they may go to Heaven, but they do it out of their wickedness and in order to destroy them. In this way also the Jews will not be exempted from the eternal fire by the fact that Jesus Christ wished to be crucified and die for all. They did not crucify Him because He wished to be crucified, but because they wished to crucify Him. They did not crucify Him in order that He might live again and rise up from the dead, but they crucified Him in order that He might be destroyed once for all. Let this suffice for this subject.

(BN) "Jesus was also able to save Himself from the Jews, if He had wished to do so. This is known first from the fact that on several occasions they ventured to seize Him, but because He did not wish to be seized by them, no one laid hands on Him. It is also known by the fact that while He was hanging on the cross, He moved the heavens, shook the earth, darkened the sun, blood-reddened the moon, rent the stones, opened the graves and gave life to the dead that were in them. He who was also able to do all these things in such a divine way, was surely able to save Himself from the Jews. And He who rescued from the mouth of Sheol in such a wonderful way the temple of His humanity, after it had lain therein for three days and three nights, was surely able to save and rescue the very same temple from the unjust Jews, but if He had saved it, He would not have been crucified, and if He had not been crucified, He would not have died, and if He had not died, He would not have risen up to immortal life, and if He had not risen up to immortal life, the children of men had remained without a sign and a decisive proof of the immortal life.

(BO) "Today because of the resurrection of Jesus Christ from the dead, the eyes of all the children of men look towards an immortal life, and consequently, in order that this expectation of the immortal life and of the world to come might be indelibly impressed upon mankind, it was right that Jesus Christ should rise from the dead; but in order that He might rise from the dead, it was right that He should first die, and in order that He might truly die, it was imperative that His death should have been first witnessed by all, as His resurrection was witnessed by all. This is why He died by crucifixion. If He were to suffer, to be crucified and die before all, when He had to rise from the dead His resurrection would also be believed by all. Immortal life is thus the fruit of the crucifixion, and the resurrection of Jesus Christ from the dead — a resurrection which all believers expect — is the outcome of the death on the cross.

(BP) "If He had delivered Himself from the hands of His crucifiers, He would have brought profit to Himself alone and would have been no use to the rest of mankind, like Enoch and Elijah, who are kept in Paradise beyond the reach of death for their exclusive benefit, but now that He delivered Himself into the hands of the crucifiers, and they dared to kill Him on their own account, He conquered death after three days and three nights, rose up to immortal life and brought profit first to His own self and then to all creatures, and He became the sign and proof of resuscitation and resurrection to all rational beings. He put His wish into practice in an economy full of wisdom, and His crucifiers cannot be absolved from blame any more than the brothers of Joseph can be absolved from blame.

(BQ) "When Joseph was sold by his brothers as a slave to some men, and he afterwards rose up from slavery to the government of Egypt, it was not the aim of those who sold him that he should govern Egypt. If they had dreamed of this they would never have sold him into slavery. Indeed, those who were unable to bear the recital of Joseph's dreams on account of their intense jealousy and violent envy, how could they have borne seeing him at the head of a government? They sold him into slavery, but God, because of the injustice done to him by his brothers, raised him up from slavery to power. This analogy applies to the Jews and to Satan their teacher: if they had known that Christ would rise again to life from the dead and ascend from earth to Heaven after His crucifixion, they would never have induced themselves to crucify Him, but they crucified Him out of their own wicked will."

(BR) "What would you say to this, O King of kings: If your Majesty had a house and wanted to pull it down in order to rebuild it again, if an enemy came and pulled it down and burned it with fire, would you give thanks to that enemy for his action in pulling down the house, or would you not rather inflict punishment on him, as on one who had demolished and burned a house belonging to your Majesty?" - And our King replied: "The one who would do such a thing would deserve a painful death." - And then I answered; "So also the Jews deserve all kinds of woes, because they wished to demolish and destroy the temple of the Word of God, which was anointed and confirmed by the Holy Spirit, which was divinely fashioned without the intervention of man from a holy virgin, and which God raised afterwards to Heaven. God showed in all this its thorough distinction from, and its high superiority over, all else. As the heaven is high above the earth, the temple of the Word of God is greater and more distinguished than all angels and children of men. If Jesus Christ is in Heaven and Heaven is the throne of God, it follows that Jesus Christ sat on the throne of God."

(BT) And our King said to me: "Who gave you the Gospel?" - And I replied to his Majesty: "Our Lord Jesus Christ." - And our victorious King asked: "Was it before or after His ascension to Heaven?" - And I replied to him: "Before His ascension to Heaven. As the Gospel is the narrative of the Economy of the works and the words of Jesus Christ, and as the works of Jesus Christ were done, and His concrete words were uttered before His ascension to Heaven, it follows that the Gospel was delivered to us before His ascension to Heaven. Further, if the Gospel is the proclamation of the Kingdom of Heaven, and this proclamation of the Kingdom of Heaven has been delivered to us by the mouth of our Lord, it follows that the Gospel was also delivered to us by the mouth of our Lord."

(BU) And our King, invested with power, said to me: "Was not a part of the Gospel written by Matthew, another part by Mark, a third part by Luke and a fourth part by John?"[132] - And I replied to his Majesty: "It is true, O our King, that these four men wrote the Gospel. They did not write it, however, out of their own head, nor from the fancies of their mind. Indeed they had no literary attainments of any kind, and by profession they were generally fishermen, shoemakers or tentmakers. They wrote and transmitted to us what they had heard and learned from Jesus Christ, who had taught them in actions and words during all the time He was walking with them in the flesh on the earth and what the Spirit-Paraclete had reminded them of."

(BV) And our King said to me: "Why are they different from one another and contradict one another?" - And I answered his Majesty: "It is true that there is difference between their words; as to contradictions there is not any between them, not even in a single case. Different people write differently even on the creation of God, the Lord of all: some of them speak of the great height of heaven, some others of the brilliant rays of the sun, some others of the wonderful phases of the moon, some others of the land and sea and some others of some other topics. Further, among the people who write on heaven alone, some speak of its immense height and some others of the swiftness of its movement, and among those who speak of the sun alone, some write on the high and dazzling resplendence of its light, some others on its heat, some others on the roundness of its sphere, some others on its purity and clearness and some others on its multitudinous powers and effects.

(BW) "Let your Majesty order some men to write on the topic of the resplendent glory of your Majesty and some others on the great quantity of your gold and silver and some others on the lustre of your pearls and precious stones and some others on the beauty and fine features of the face of your Majesty, and some others on the power, might and strength of your kingdom and some others on the wisdom and intelligence of your Majesty and yet some others on your gentleness, virtue and piety. In what they will write there might be differences of words in their statements of facts, but there will not be any contradiction between them, not even in a single item. They will all be right in all that they will write, although some of them might omit some items, because there is no one who is able to speak with accuracy of everything dealing with the works of God, nor with the greatness of the glory of your Majesty. The above applies to what the evangelists wrote concerning the words, deeds and natures of Jesus Christ. There are here and there differences in their statements, but as to contradictions there are none whatever. The four of them write in the same way and without discrepancies and differences on the main topics of His conception, birth, baptism, teaching, passion on the cross, death, burial, resurrection and ascension to heaven."

(BX) And our powerful King said to me: "You should know, O Catholicos, that as God gave the Law through the prophet Moses and the Gospel through Christ, so He gave the *furkan*[133] through Muhammad" - And I replied: "O my victorious King, the changes that were to take place in the Law given through Moses, God had clearly predicted previously through the prophets whom we have mentioned. God said thus through the prophet Jeremiah and showed the dissolution of the Law of Moses and the setting up of the Gospel, 'Behold the days come, saith the Lord, that I will make a new covenant with the house of Israel and with the house of Judah: not according to the covenant that I made with their fathers in the day that I took them by the hand to bring them out of the land of Egypt, which covenant they nullified, and I also despised them, saith the Lord: but this shall be the covenant that I will make with the house of Israel. After those days, saith the Lord, I will put my law in their minds and write it in their hearts and will be their God, and they shall be My people. And they shall teach no more every man his neighbor nor his brother saying, "Know the

Lord," for they shall all know Me from the least of them unto the greatest of them.'[134] In the above words God demonstrated both the dissolution of the Law of Moses and the setting up of the Gospel.

(BY) "Through another prophet, called Joel, God disclosed the signs which would occur at the time of the dissolution of the Torah and the setting up of the Gospel, and the signs concerning the Spirit-Paraclete which the apostles, the commanders of the army of the Gospel, were to receive, because He said through him, 'And afterwards I will pour out My Spirit upon all flesh, and your sons and your daughters shall prophesy, and your old men shall dream dreams, and your young men shall see visions. And on My servants and on My hand-maidens I will pour My Spirit in those days.'[135] This is said of the Spirit-Paraclete who descended on the apostles after the ascension of Jesus to heaven, according to the promise that He had previously given. And the prophet adds, 'And I will show wonders in the heavens and the earth, blood and fire and pillars of smoke. The sun shall be turned into darkness and the moon into blood.'[136] All this took place at the passion of Jesus Christ on the cross. And he further adds, 'Before the great and terrible day of the Lord;' he calls the 'great and terrible day of the Lord,'[137] the day on which the Word-God will appear in our flesh with great power and glory of angels and the day on which the stars will fall from heaven, as Jesus Himself said in the Gospel.'[138] And the prophet further adds, 'Whosoever shall call on the name of the Lord shall be saved,' that is to say whosoever shall receive the Gospel of God shall live an everlasting life.

(BZ) "God, therefore, pointed clearly to the transition from the Law to the Gospel when He showed us a new covenant and signs witnessed by men, that appeared in heaven and earth, in sun, moon and stars, and when He showed us the gifts of the Holy Spirit which He imparted to the apostles: wonders, signs and miracles. God nowhere showed such irrefragable signs for the transition from the Gospel to something else. The Law that was given by Moses was the symbol of the Gospel, and the Gospel is the symbol of the Kingdom of Heaven, and there is nothing higher than the Kingdom of Heaven."

(CA) And our powerful King said to me: "Did not God say clearly to the children of Israel, 'I will raise you up a prophet from among your brethren like me'?[139] Who are the brethren of the children of Israel besides the Arabs,[140] and who is the prophet like unto Moses besides Muhammad?" - And I answered his Majesty: "The Israelites have many other brethren besides the Arabs, O our Sovereign. First of all the six sons of Abraham by Keturah are nearer to the Arabs than to the Israelites, then the Edomites composed of three hundred clans are also nearer to the Israelites than the Arabs. Jacob, from whom descended the Israelites, and Esau, from whom sprang the Edomites are indeed brothers and sons of Isaac, and Isaac, from whom the Jews descended, and Ishmael, from whom the Arabs spring, together with Zimran and Jokshan[141] and their brothers, the sons of Keturah, are children of Abraham. If the sentence of the prophet Moses refers to the brethren of the children of Israel and not to their own twelve tribes, it would be more appropriate to apply it to the Edomites, because it has been shown that they are nearer to the Israelites than the Arabs. It is not only the Arabs who are the brethren of the Israelites but also the Ammonites and the Moabites.

(CB) "Further, Moses said to the children of Israel that God will raise up from their brethren a prophet to themselves and not to the Arabs, because he says that the prophet whom the Lord your God will raise up will be from among yourselves and not from outside yourselves, from your brethren and not from strangers, and then that prophet will be similar and not dissimilar to him in doctrine, This Biblical passage resembles that other passage in which God said to them concerning a king, 'I will raise up for thee a king from thy brethren.'[142] As in the subject of a king, God does not refer to the children of Ishmael by the word 'their brethren,' so also in the subject of a prophet He does not refer to them through the same word.

(CC) "Further, you assert that Muhammad has been sent as a prophet to his own people.[143] We must examine in this respect the construction of the words. It is said: a prophet from yourselves, from among your brethren, and like unto me. If Muhammad be a prophet like Moses, Moses wrought miracles and prodigies; and Muhammad, who would in this case be a prophet like Moses, should have wrought many miracles and prodigies. And then, if Muhammad be a prophet like Moses, since Moses practiced and taught the Law that was given to him on Mount Sinai, Muhammad should similarly have taught the Torah and practiced the circumcision and observed the Jewish Sabbath and festivals. Muhammad did not teach the Torah, and Moses taught the Torah, the prophet Muhammad is not, therefore, like unto Moses, because the one who was to be a prophet like unto Moses, would not have changed anything from Moses, and the one who is different in one thing from Moses is not a prophet like unto Moses. The prophet Moses spoke the above words concerning the prophets who from time to time rose after him from this or that Jewish tribe, such as Joshua son of Nun, David, Samuel and others after them, who from generation to generation were sent to the Israelites."[144]

(CD) And our victorious King said to me: "What is the punishment of the man who kills his mother?" - And I replied to his Majesty: "And what is the punishment of the man who does not respect the honor of his mother?" - And our King said to me: "Strokes, fetters and death." - And I said to his Majesty: "The decision of your Majesty is just. And the man who kills his mother is also liable to the same punishment." - And our King said to me: "Jesus Christ is therefore liable to the same punishment, because He let His mother die and so killed her." - And I asked the King; "Which is the highest, this world or the world to come?" And our King answered: "The world to come." - And I then replied to his Majesty: "If Jesus Christ let His mother die, and through death He transferred her to the next world, which as your Majesty asserts is better then this one, He therefore invested His mother with a higher dignity and more sublime honor; and since the one who honors his mother is worthy of all blessings, Jesus Christ, who transferred His mother from the mortal life to the immortal one and from the land of troubles to the Kingdom of Heaven, is, therefore, worthy of all blessings.

(CE) "What should Jesus Christ have done? While He takes up everybody from earth to heaven, and while, as God said, He causes them to be immortal after having been mortal, should He only have left His own mother in this mortal life? This would have been a great disgrace, but her death which took place like that of every other human being, was only natural and did not bring the smallest disgrace to her. As it was not a dishonor to her to have been born from a womb, so also it was not a dishonor to her to have been born again to eternal life from death and earth.[145] If Mary had not died, she would not have risen; and if she had not risen, she would have been far from the Kingdom of Heaven, and it is fair that Mary, the mother of Jesus Christ through whom the Kingdom of Heaven was revealed, should have been raised up first to heaven, It was, therefore, imperative that she should have died. He who demolishes a house in order to renew it and ornament it, is not blame worthy but praiseworthy."

(CF) And our King said to me: "Is Jesus Christ good or not?" - And I replied to his Majesty: "If Jesus Christ is the Word of God, and God is good, Jesus Christ is, therefore, good. He is one nature with God, like light is one with the sun." - And our King said: "How then did Jesus say, 'There is none good but one, that is one God?' "[146] - And I replied to him: "Was the prophet David just or not?" - And our King said: "He was just and head of the just." - And I said then: "How then did the prophet David say, 'There is no one that is just, no not one,' "[147] - And our King said: "This saying does not include David. It has been said of the wicked ones." - And I said: "So also the sentence, 'There is none good but one' cannot possibly include the Christ. As the sentence, 'There is no one that is just' embraces many others to the exclusion of David, so also the sentence, 'There is none good' embraces many others to the exclusion of Jesus Christ, and as David did not include himself when he said, 'There is no just man, no not even one,' so also the Christ did not include himself when he said, 'There is none good but one, and that is one God.'

(CG) "The very same Jesus Christ who said about Himself, 'I am the *good* shepherd,'[148] could not have said the above sentence, 'There is none good' about Himself. Indeed, He said this sentence about the one whom He was addressing. The latter was thinking this in his heart: how difficult are the laws that Jesus Christ is establishing?

There is none good but one God who gave us all the good things found in the land of promise. As to Jesus Christ, He disclosed to him his hidden thoughts and showed to him that his words were in flagrant contradiction with his thoughts, in calling Him in his words 'good master' while in his thoughts he was saying, 'This one was no good,' and wishing to rebuke him He disclosed his thoughts and said to him, 'Why callest thou me good with thy tongue while in thy thoughts thou sayest about me, "This one is no good, because He orders me to squander my fortune; there is none good but one that is God" '? Jesus Christ makes mention both of a *good* man and a *good* tree.[149] How is it possible that there is a good man and a good tree, and Jesus Christ alone is not good? How can this be possible?"

(CH) And our King said to me: "If you accepted Muhammad as a prophet your words would be beautiful and your meanings fine" - And I replied to his Majesty: "We find that there is only one prophet who would come to the world after the ascension of Jesus Christ to Heaven and His descent from Heaven.[150] This we know from the prophet Malachi and from the angel Gabriel when he announced the birth of John to Zachariah."

(CI) And our King said: "And who is that prophet?" - And I replied: "The prophet Elijah. The prophet Malachi, who is the last of the prophets of the Law, said, 'Remember ye the Law of Moses my servant, which I commanded unto him in Horeb for all Israel, with the statutes and judgments. Behold I will send you Elijah the prophet before the coming of the great and dreadful day of the Lord. And he shall turn the heart of the fathers to the children and the heart of the children to their fathers, lest I come and smite the earth with a curse.'[151] And the angel Gabriel, when announcing to Zechariah the birth of John reminded him of these very words, because he said to him, 'Fear not, Zechariah, for thy prayer is heard, and thy wife Elizabeth shall bear thee a son, and thou shalt call his name John. And thou shalt have joy and gladness, and many shall rejoice at his birth. For he shall be great in the sight of the Lord and shall be filled with the Holy Ghost even from his mother's womb. And many if the children of Israel shall he turn to the Lord their God. And he shall go before him in the spirit and power of the prophet Elijah, to turn[152] the hearts of the fathers to the children and the disobedient to the wisdom of the just and to make ready a people prepared for the Lord.[153]

(CJ) "Think, O our victorious Sovereign, how the angel called Jesus 'the Lord their God.' It is this prophet Elijah who, as we have learned, will come into the world after the ascension of Jesus to Heaven. He will come to rebuke the Antichrist and to teach and preach to everybody concerning the second apparition of Jesus from Heaven. As John, son of Zechariah, came before His apparition in the flesh and announced Him to everybody in saying, 'Behold the Lamb of God, which taketh away the sin of the world,'[154] 'He it is that shall baptize with the Holy Ghost and fire,'[155] 'He is the one the lachet of whose shoes I am not worthy to unloosen.'[156] — so also the prophet Elijah is going to come before the divine apparition of Jesus Christ from Heaven in order to announce beforehand to all His glorious apparition and to make them ready for His presence.[157]

(CK) "Both messengers, John and Elijah, are from one power of the Spirit, with the difference that one already came before Christ, and the other is going to come before Him, and their coming is similar and to the same effect. In the second coming He will appear from Heaven in a great glory of angels, to the effect the resurrection of all the children of Adam from the graves. As the Word of God, He created everything from the beginning and He is going to renew everything at the end. He is the King of Kings and the Lord of Lords, and there is no end and no limit to His Kingdom."

(CL) And our highly intelligent Sovereign said: "If you had not corrupted the Torah and the Gospel, you would have found in them Muhammad also with the other prophets." - And to set his mind at rest on this subject I replied to him: "To the mind of your Majesty, O my illustrious Sovereign — you to whom God has granted that intelligence and broad-mindedness which are so useful for the administration of public and private affairs of the people, and you who speak and act in a way that is congruous with the dignity of your Majesty — it is due to inquire why and for what purpose we might have corrupted the books. Both the Torah and the prophets proclaim as with the voice of thunder and teach us collectively the divinity and humanity of Christ, His wonderful birth from His Father before the times, a birth which no man will ever be able to describe and comprehend. It is written, 'Who shall declare His generation?'[158] and, 'His coming out is in the beginning, from the days of the worlds'[159] and, 'From the womb before the morning-star I have begotten Thee' and, 'His name is before the sun.'[160]

(CM) "So far as His temporal birth is concerned, it is written, 'Behold a virgin shall conceive and bear a son and shall call his name Emmanuel.'[161] David and Isaiah and all the other prophets reveal to us clearly and distinctly the signs and miracles that He was going to perform in His appearance in the flesh and the accurate knowledge of God with which the earth was going to be filled through this appearance. They tell us about His passion, His crucifixion and His death in the flesh, as we have demonstrated above. They tell us about His resurrection from the dwelling of the dead and His ascension to Heaven. Finally they enlighten us concerning His second appearance from Heaven and concerning the resurrection of the dead which He is going to effect and the judgment which He is going to hold for all, as one who is God and the Word of God. O our Sovereign, while all the corpus of the Christian doctrine is embodied in the Torah and the Gospel[162] like a clear symbol and mirror, for what reason could we have dared to corrupt these living witnesses of our faith? They are indeed the witnesses of our truth, O our Sovereign, and from them shines on us the resplendent light of the duality of the natures of the divinity and humanity of Christ and that of His death, resurrection and ascension to Heaven, It could never have been possible for us to stir ourselves against ourselves and tamper with the testimony of the Torah and the Gospel to our Savior.

(CN) "Even if we are able to corrupt the books of the Torah and the Gospel that we have with us, how could we have tampered with those that are with the Jews? If one says here that we have corrupted those that are in our hands while the Jews themselves corrupted those that are in theirs, how is it that the Jews have not corrupted those passages through which the Christian religion is established? The Christians never have had and will never have such deadly enemies as the Jews; if the Jews had, therefore, tampered with their book, how could we Christians induce ourselves to accept a text which had been corrupted and changed, a text which would have shaken the very foundations of the truth of our religion? No, the truth is that neither we nor the Jews have ever tampered with the books. Our mutual hostility is the best guarantee to our statement.[163]

(CO) "If the Christians and the Jews are enemies, and if there is no possibility that enemies should have a common agreement on the line that divides them, it was therefore impossible for the Christians and the Jews to agree on the corruption of the books. Indeed the Jews disagree with us on the meaning of some verbs and nouns, tenses and persons, but concerning the words themselves they have never had any disagreement with us. The very same words are found with us and with them without any changes. Since the Torah and the prophets teach the truth of Christianity, we would have never allowed ourselves to corrupt them, and that is the reason why, O our victorious Sovereign, we could have never tampered with the Torah and the prophets.

(CP) "The very same reason holds good with regard to the Gospel, which we could not and would not have corrupted under any circumstances. What the ancient prophets prophesied about the Christ is written in the Gospel about the Christ. The ray of light that shines on the eyes of our souls is the same from the Torah, from the prophets and from the Gospel. The only difference is that in the first two books the light is in the words uttered in advance of the facts, while in the last book it is in the facts themselves. What the prophets had taught us about the divinity and humanity of Christ and about all the economy of the Word-God in the flesh, the Gospel proclaimed to us without corruption in a glorious manner. Further, God, the giver of both the Torah and Gospel is one, and if we had changed them in any way, we would have changed those things which according to some people are somewhat undignified in our faith."

(CQ) And our victorious King asked me: "And what are those things which you call undignified in our faith?" - And I replied to his benevolence: "Things such as the growth of Christ in stature and wisdom; His food, drink and fatigue; His ire and lack of omniscience; His prayer, passion, crucifixion and burial and all such things which we are believed by some people to be mean and debasing. We might have changed these and similar things held by some people to be mean and undignified; we might have also changed things that are believed by some other people to be contradictory, such as the questions dealing with the times, days, verbs, pronouns and facts, questions which appear to some people to furnish a handle for objections that tend to some extent to weaken our statement. I submit that we might have been tempted to alter these, but since we did not induce ourselves to alter them, how could we have dared to tamper with whole passages revealed by God? Not only could we not dream of tampering with them, but we are proud of them and consider them as higher and more sublime than others. From such higher and more sublime passages we learn that Jesus is an eternal God, and we believe that He is consubstantial with the Father, and from the passages that are believed by some to be mean and undignified, we learn that this same Jesus is a true man and having the same human nature as ourselves.

(CR) "No, our victorious Sovereign, we have not changed not even one iota in the divine book, and if the name of Muhammad were in the book, how we would have expected his coming and longed for it, as we expected with an eager desire to meet those about whom the prophets wrote, when they actually came or they were about to come. Further, what closer relationship have we with the Jews than with the Arabs that we should have accepted the Christ who appeared from the Jews while rejecting the Prophet that appeared from the Arabs? Our natural relationship with the Jews and with the Arabs is on the same footing. Truth to tell, the Jews, before the appearance of Christ, were honored more than all other nations by God and by men, but after the sublime appearance of the Word-God from them, since they shut their eyes in order not to rejoice in the light that came to enlighten the world, they have even been despised and dejected, and they thought of God as other people did.

(CS) "A shell is kept in the royal treasuries as long as it contains a pearl, but when the pearl has been extracted from it, it is thrown outside and trodden under the feet of everyone. In this same way are the Jews: as long as Christ had not appeared from them, but was hidden in them as a pearl is hidden in a shell, they were respected by all men, and God showed them to others, as a glorious and enlightened people, by means of the numerous signs and wonders that He performed among them; but after the appearance from them of the Christ-God in the flesh and their rejection of His revelation and their turning away from Him, they were delivered to slavery among all other peoples.

(CT) "The Jews are, therefore, despised today and rejected by all, but the contrary is the case with the Arabs, who are today held in great honor and esteem by God and men, because they forsook idolatry and polytheism, and worshipped and honored one God; in this they deserve the love and the praise of all; if, therefore, there was an allusion to their prophet in the books, not only we would not have introduced any changes in it, but we would have accepted him with great joy and pleasure, in the same way as we are expecting the one of whom we spoke, and who is going to appear at the end of the world. We are not the correctors but the observers of the commandments of God."

(CU) And our Sovereign said with a jocular smile: "We shall hear you about these at some other time, when business affairs give us a better opportunity for such an intimate exchange of words."

(CV) And I praised God, King of Kings and Lord of Lords, who grants to earthly Kings such a wisdom and understanding in order that through them they may administer their empire without hindrance. And I blessed also his Majesty and prayed that God may preserve him to the world for many years and establish his throne in piety and righteousness for ever and ever. And in this way I left him on the first day.

HERE END THE QUESTIONS AND ANSWERS OF THE FIRST DAY.

THE QUESTIONS AND ANSWERS OF THE SECOND DAY.

(CW) The next[164] day I had an audience of his Majesty, Such audiences had constantly taken place previously, sometimes for the affairs of the State, and some other times for the love of wisdom and learning which was burning in the soul of his Majesty. He is a lovable man, and loves also learning when he finds it in other people, and on this account he directed against me the weight of his objections, whenever necessary.

(CX) After I had paid to him my usual respects as King of kings, he began to address me and converse with me not in a harsh and haughty tone, since harshness and haughtiness are remote from his soul, but in a sweet and benevolent way.

(CY) And our King of kings said to me: "O Catholicos, did you bring a Gospel with you as I had asked you?" - And I replied to his exalted Majesty: "I have brought one, O our victorious and God-loving King." And our victorious and Sovereign said to me: "Who gave you this book?" - And I replied to him: "It is the Word of God that gave us the Gospel, O our God-loving King." - And our King said: "Was it not written by four apostles?"[165] - And I replied to him: "It was written by four apostles, as our King has said, but not out of their own heads, but out of what they heard and learned from the Word-God. If then the Gospel was written by the apostles, and if the apostles simply wrote what they heard and learned from the Word-God, the Gospel has, therefore, been given in reality by the Word-God. Similarly, the Torah was written by Moses, but since Moses heard and learned it from an angel, and the angel heard and learned it from God, we assert that the Torah was given by God and not by Moses.

(CZ) "In the same way also the Muslims say that they have received the Qur'an from Muhammad, but since Muhammad received knowledge and writing from an angel, they therefore affirm that the book that was divulged through him was not Muhammad's or the angel's but God's. So also we Christians believe that although the Gospel was given to us by the apostles, it was not given as from them, but as from God, His Word and His Spirit. Further, the letters and official documents[166] of your Majesty are written by the hands of scribes and clerks, but they are not said to be those of scribes, but those of your Majesty and of the Commander of the Faithful."

(DA) And our gracious and wise King said to me: "What do you say about Muhammad?" - And I replied to his Majesty: "Muhammad is worthy of all praise by all reasonable people, O my Sovereign. He walked in the path of the prophets and trod in the track of the lovers of God. All the prophets taught the doctrine of one God, and since Muhammad taught the doctrine of the unity of God, he walked therefore, in the path of the prophets. Further, all the prophets drove men away from bad works and brought them nearer to good works, and since Muhammad drove his people away from bad works and brought them nearer to the good ones, he walked therefore in the path of the prophets. Again, all the prophets separated men from idolatry and polytheism and attached them to His cult, and since Muhammad separated his people from idolatry and polytheism and attached them to the cult and knowledge of one God, beside whom there is no other God, it is obvious that he walked in the path of the prophets. Finally Muhammad taught about God, His Word and His Spirit, and since all the prophets had prophesied about God, His Word and His Spirit, Muhammad walked therefore, in the path of all the prophets.[167]

(DB) "Who will not praise, honor and exalt the one who not only fought for God in words, but showed also his zeal for Him in the sword? As Moses did with the Children of Israel when he saw that they had fashioned a golden calf which they worshipped and killed all of those who were worshipping it, so also Muhammad evinced as ardent zeal towards God and loved and honored Him more than his own soul, his people and his relatives. He praised, honored and exalted those who worshipped God with him and promised them kingdom, praise and honor from God, both in this world and in the world to come in the Garden.[168] But those who worshipped idols and not God, he fought and opposed and showed to them the torments of hell and of the fire which is never quenched and in which all evildoers burn eternally.

(DC) "And what Abraham, that friend and beloved of God, did in turning his face from idols and from his kinsmen and looking only towards one God and becoming the preacher of one God to other peoples, this also Muhammad did. He turned his face from idols and their worshippers, whether those idols were those of his own kinsmen or of strangers, and he honored and worshipped only one God. Because of this God honored him exceedingly and brought low[169] before his feet two powerful kingdoms which roared in the world like a lion and made the voice of their authority heard in all the earth that is below heaven, like thunder, viz., the kingdom of Persia and that of the Romans. The former kingdom, that is to say, the kingdom of the Persians, worshipped the creatures instead of the Creator, and the latter, that is to say the kingdom of the Romans, attributed suffering and death in the flesh to the one who can not suffer and die in any way and through any process.[170] He further extended the power of his authority through the Commander of the Faithful and his children from east to west and from north to south. Who will not praise, O our victorious King, the one whom God has praised, and will not weave a crown of glory and majesty to the one whom God has glorified and exalted? These and similar things I and all God-lovers utter about Muhammad, O my Sovereign."

(DD) And our King said to me: "You should, therefore, accept the words of the Prophet." - And I replied to his gracious Majesty: "Which words of his, our victorious King, believes that I must accept?" - And our King said to me: "That God is one and that there is no other one besides Him." - And I replied: "This believe in one God, O my Sovereign, I have learned from the Torah, from the prophets and from the Gospel. I stand by it and shall die in it." - And our victorious King said to me: "You believe in one God, as you said, but one in three." - And I answered his sentence: "I do not deny that I believe in one God in three and three in one, but not in three different godheads, however, but in the persons of God's Word and His Spirit. I believe that these three constitute one God, not in their person, but in their nature. I have shown how in my previous words."

(DE) And our King asked: "How is it that these persons whom you mention do not constitute three gods?" And I answered his Majesty: "Because the three of them constitute one God, O our victorious King, and the fact that He is only one God precludes the hypothesis that there are three gods." - And our King retorted: "The fact that they are three precludes the statement that there is only one God. If they are three, how can they be one?"- And I replied: "We believe that they are three, O our Sovereign, not in Godhead, but in persons, and that they are one not in persons, but in Godhead." - And our King retorted: "The fact that they are three precludes the statement that they are one, and the fact that they are one precludes the statement that they are three. This everybody will admit." - And I said to him: "The three in Him are the cause of one, and the one that of three, O our King. Those three have always been the cause of one, and that one of three." - And our King said to me: "How can one be the cause of three and three of one? What is this?" - And I answered his question: "One is the cause of three, O our King, because this number one is the cause of the number two, and the number two that of the number three. This is how one is the cause of three, as I said, O King. On the other hand the number three is the cause of the number one because since the number three is caused by the number two and this number two by the number one, the number three is therefore the cause of the number one."

(DF) And our King said to me: "In this process the number four would also be the cause of the number five and so on, and the question of one Godhead would resolve itself into many godheads, which, as you say, in the doctrine not of the Christians, but of the Magians." - And I replied to our King: "In every comparison there is a time at which one must stop, because it does not resemble reality in everything. We should remember that all numbers are included in the number three. Indeed the number three is both complete and perfect[171] and all numbers are included in a complete and perfect number. In this number three all other numbers are included, O our victorious King. Above three all other numbers are simply numbers added to themselves by means of that complete and perfect number, as it is said. It follows from all this that one is the cause of three and three of one, as we suggested." - And our King said to me: "Neither three nor two can possibly be said of God." - And I replied to his Majesty: "Neither therefore one." - And our King asked: "How?" - And I answered: "If the cause of three is two, the cause of two is would be one, and in this case the cause of three would also be one. If then God cannot be said to be three, and the cause of three is two and that of two one, God cannot, therefore be called one either. Indeed this number one being the cause and the beginning of all numbers, and there being no number in God, we should not have applied it to Him. As, however, we do apply this number to God without any reference to the beginning of an arithmetical number, we apply to Him also the number three without any implication of multiplication or division of gods, but with a particular reference to the Word and the Spirit of God, through which heaven and earth have been created, as we have demonstrated in our previous colloquy.[172] If the number three cannot be applied to God, since it is caused by the number one, the latter could not by inference be applied to God either, but if the number can be applied to God, since this number one is the cause of the number three, the last number can therefore be applied also to God."

(DG) And our victorious King said: "The number three denotes plurality, and since there is no plurality in Godhead, this number three has no room at all in Godhead." - And I replied to his Majesty: "The number one is also the cause and the beginning of all number, O our King, and number is the cause of plurality. Since there cannot be any kind of plurality in God, even the number one would have no room in Him." - And our King said: "the number one as applied to God is attested in the book." - And I said: "So also is the case, O our King, with a number implying plurality. We find often such a number in the Torah, in the prophets and in the Gospel, and as I hear, in your book also, not, however, in connection with Godhead, but in relation to humanity. So far as the Torah is concerned, it is written in it, 'Let us make man in our image, after our likeness;'[173] and 'The man is become as one of us';[174] and, 'Let us go down, and there confound their language.'[175] As to the prophets, it is written in them, 'Holy, Holy, Holy is the Lord of hosts';[176] and 'The Lord God and His Spirit hath sent me';[177] and 'By the Word of the Lord were the heavens made, and all His hosts by the Spirit of His mouth.'[178] As to the Gospel, it is written in it, 'Go ye and teach all nations, baptizing them in the *name* of the Father and of the Son and of the Holy Ghost':[179] As to your book, it is written in it, 'And We sent to her our Spirit,'[180] and 'We breathed into her from our Spirit,'[181] and, 'We fashioned,' 'We said,' 'We did,' and all such expressions which are said of God in a plural form. If the Holy Books refer these words to God in a plural form, what the books say concerning God we have to say and admit. Since we had to preserve without change the number one as applied to God, we had also by inference to preserve without modification the number three, that is to say plurality, as applied to Him. The number one refers to nature and Godhead, and the number three to God, His Word and His Spirit, because God has never been, is not and will never be without Word and Spirit."[182]

(DH) And our wise Sovereign said: "The plural form in connection with God, in the expressions 'We sent,' 'We breathed,' 'We said,' etc., has been used in the books not as a sign of persons or of trinity, but as a mark of divine majesty and power. It is even the habit of the kings and governors of the earth to use such a mode of speech." - And I replied to the wealth of his intelligence: "What your glorious Majesty has said is true. To you God gave knowledge and understanding along with power and greatness, more than to all other countries and kings. The community of all mankind, whether composed of freemen or of subjected races is personified in the kings, and the community of mankind being composed of innumerable persons, the kings rightly make use of the plural form in expressions such as, 'We ordered,' 'We said,' 'We did,' etc. Indeed the kings represent collectively all the community of mankind individually. If all men are one with the king, and the king orders, says and does, all men order, say and do in the king, and he says and does in the name of all.

(DI) Further, the kings are human beings, and human beings are composed of body and soul, and the body is in its turns composed of the power of the four elements. Because a human being is composed of many elements, the kings make use not unjustly of the plural form of speech, such as 'We did,' 'We ordered,' etc.[183]   As to God who is simple in His nature and one in His essence and remote from all division and bodily composition, what greatness and honor can possibly come to Him when He, who is one and undivided against Himself, says in the plural form, 'We ordered,' and, 'We did,'?   The greatest honor that can be offered to God is that He should be believed in by all as He is.   In His essence He is one, but He is three because of His Word and His Spirit.   This Word and this Spirit are living beings and are of His nature, as the word and the spirit of our victorious King are of his nature, and he is one King with his word and spirit, which are constantly with him without cessation, without division and without displacement.

(DJ) "When, therefore, expressions such as, '*We* spoke,' '*We* said,' '*We* did,' and '*Our* image and likeness,' are said to refer to God, His Word and His Spirit, they are referred in the way just described, O King of kings.   Who is more closely united to God than His Word through which He created all, governs all and directs all?   Or who is nearer to Him than His Spirit through which He vivifies, sanctifies and renews all?   David spoke thus: 'By the Word of the Lord were the heavens made, and all His hosts by the Spirit of His mouth';[184] and, 'He sent His Word and healed them, and delivered them from destruction';[185] and 'Thou sendest forth Thy Spirit and they are created, and Thou renewest the face of the earth.'[186]

(DK) "If one asserts that the expressions, '*Our* image' and '*Our* likeness' used by Moses, and the expressions, '*We* made,' and '*We* breathed,' used by Muhammad,[187] do not refer to God but to the angels, how disgraceful it would be to believe that the image and the likeness of God and those of the angels, that is of the Creator and the created, are one!   How dishonorable it would be to affirm that God says, orders and does with the angels and His creatures!   God orders and does like the Lord and the Creator and orders and does in a way that transcends that of all others; but the angels being creatures and servants, do not order with God, but are very much created by God.

223

The angels are what David said about them, 'Who maketh His angels spirits and His ministers a flaming fire.'[188] In this he shows that they are made and created.

(DL) "As to the Word and Spirit of God, the prophet David says that they are not created and made, but creators and makers:[189] '*By* the Word of the Lord were the heavens made,' and not His Word alone; and 'the heavenly hosts were created *by* His Spirit' and not His Spirit alone; and, 'Because He said and they were made, and He commanded, and they were created.'[190] It is obvious that one who 'says,' 'says' and 'commands' by word, and that the word precedes the action, and the thought precedes the deed. Since God is one without any other before Him, with Him and after Him, and since all the above expressions which denote plurality cannot be ascribed to angels, and since the nature of God is absolutely free from all compositions — to whom could we ascribe then all such expressions? I believe, O our victorious King, that they refer to the Word and the Spirit of God. If it is right that the expression 'One God' is true, it is also right that the expression 'We ordered,' 'We said,' and 'We breathed from our Spirit' are without doubt true and not false. It is also possible that the three letters placed before some suras in the Qur'an, as I have learned, such as A.L.R. and T.S.M. and Y.S.M. and others, which are three in number, refer also in your book to God, His Word and His Spirit."[191]

(DM) And our victorious King said: "And what did impede the Prophet from saying that this was so, that is that these letters clearly referred to God, His Word and His Spirit?" - And I replied to his Majesty: "The obstacle might have come from the weakness of those people who would be listening to such a thing. People whose ears were accustomed to the multiplicity of idols and false gods could not have listened to the doctrine of Father, Son and Holy Spirit, or to that of one God, His Word and His Spirit. They would have believed that this also was polytheism. This is the reason why your Prophet proclaimed openly the doctrine of one God, but that of the Trinity he only showed it in a somewhat veiled and mysterious way, that is to say through his mention of God and of His Spirit and through the expres-

224

sions 'We sent our Spirit' and 'We fashioned a complete man.'[192] He did not teach it openly in order that his hearers may not be scandalized by it and think of polytheism, and he did not hide it completely in order that he may not deviate from the path followed by Moses, Isaiah and other prophets, but he showed it symbolically by means of the three letters that precede the suras.

(DN) "The ancient prophets had also spoken of the unity of the nature of God and used words referring to this unity in an open and clear way, but the words which referred to His three persons they used them in a somewhat veiled and symbolical way, 'Go ye,' said He to His disciples, 'and baptize all nations in the name of the Father, and of the Son and of the Holy Ghost.'[193] Moses also uttered the same thing in a way that means both one and three, 'Hear, O Israel,' said he, 'The Lord your God is one Lord.'[194] In saying He 'is one,' he refers to the one nature of the Godhead, and in saying the three words, 'Lord, God and Lord' he refers to the three persons of that Godhead, as if one was saying that God, His Word and His Spirit were one eternal God. Job also said, 'The Lord gave, and the Lord hath taken; blessed be the name of the Lord.'[195] In blessing the single name of the Lord, Job used it three times, in reference to one in three."

(DO) And our King said to me: "If He is one, He is not three; and if He is three, He is not one; what is this contradiction?" - And I answered: "The sun is also one, O our victorious King, in its spheric globe, its light and its heat, and the very same sun is also three, one sun in three powers. In the same way the soul has the powers of reason and intelligence, and the very same soul is one in one thing and three in another thing. In the same way also a piece of three gold denarii is called one and three, one in its gold, that is to say in its nature, and three in its persons, that is to say in the number of denarii. The fact that the above objects are one does not contradict and annul the other fact — that they are also three, and the fact that they are three does not contradict and annul the fact that they are also one.

(DP) "In the very same way the fact that God is one does not annul the other fact that He is in three persons, and the fact that He is in three persons does not annul the other fact that He is one God. Man is a being which is living, rational and mortal, and he is one and three, one in being one man and three in being living, rational and mortal, and this idea gives rise to three notions not contradictory but rather confirmatory to one another. By the fact that man is one, he is by necessity living, rational and mortal, and by the fact that he is living, rational and mortal, he is by necessity one man. This applies also to God in whom the fact of His being three does not annul the other fact that He is one and *vice versa*, but these two facts confirm and corroborate each other. If He is one God, He is the Father, the Son and the Holy Spirit; and if He is the Father, the Son and the Holy Spirit, He is one God, because the eternal nature of God consists in Fatherhood, Filiation and Procession, and in the three of them He is one God, and in being one God He is the three of them."

(DQ) And our King said to me: "Do you say that the nature of God is composed of the above three, as the human nature is composed of its being living, rational and mortal, and as the sun is composed of light, heat and sphericity, and as the soul is composed of reason, intelligence and as gold is composed of height, depth and width?" - And I denied this and said: "No, this is not so." - And our King said to me: "Why then do you wish to demonstrate with bodily demonstrations One who has no body and is not composed?" - And I answered his Majesty: "Because there is no other god like Him from whom I might draw a demonstration as to what is a being that has no beginning and no end." - And our King said to me: "It is never allowed to draw a demonstration from the creatures concerning the Creator." - And I said to him: "We will then be in complete ignorance of God, O King of kings."

(DR) And our King said: "Why?" - And I answered; "Because all that we say about God is deduced from natural things that we have with us; as such are the adjectives: King of all Kings, Lord of all Lords, Mighty, Powerful, Omnipotent, Light, Wisdom and Judge. We call God by these and similar adjectives from things that are with us, and it is from them that we take our demonstrations concerning God. If we remove Him from such demonstrations and do not speak of Him through them, with what and through what could we figure in our mind Him who is higher than all image and likeness.?"

(DS) And our victorious King said to me: "We call God by these names, not because we understand Him to resemble things that we have with us, but in order to show that He is far above them, without comparison. In this way, we do not attribute to God things that are with us, we rather ascribe to ourselves things that are His, with great mercy from Him and great imperfection from us. Words such as: kingdom, life, power, greatness, honor wisdom, sight, knowledge and justice, etc., belong truly, naturally and eternally to God, and they only belong to us in an unnatural, imperfect and temporal way. With God they have not begun and they will not end, but with us children of men they began and they will end."

(DT) And I replied to his Majesty: "All that your Majesty said on this subject, O our victorious King, has been said with perfect wisdom and great knowledge; this is especially true of what you have just now said. It was not indeed with the intention of lowering God to a comparison of His creatures, that from the latter I drew a comparison concerning Him who, in reality, has no comparison with the created beings at all. I made use of such similes solely for the purpose of uplifting my mind from the created things to God. All the things that we have with us compare very imperfectly with the things of God. Even in saying of God that He is one, we introduce in our mind division concerning Him, because when we say for instance one man, one angel, one denarius, one pearl, we immediately think of a division that singles out and separates one denarius from many denarii, one pearl from many pearls, one angel from many angels, and one man from many men.

(DU) "A man would not be counting rightly, but promiscuously if he were to say: one man and two angels, one horse and two asses, one denarius and two pence, one pearl and two emeralds. Every entity is counted with the same entities of its own species, and we say: one, two, or three men; one, two, or three angels; one, two, or three denarii; one, two, or three pearls, as the case may be. With all these calculations, in saying 'one' we introduce, as I said, the element of division, but in speaking of God we cannot do the same thing, because there are no other entities of the same species as Himself which would introduce division in Him in the same sense as in our saying: one angel, or one man. He is one, single and unique in His nature. Likewise when we say three we do not think of bodies or numbers, and when we say: Father, Son and Holy Spirit, we do not say it in a way that implies division, separation or promiscuity, but we think of it as something high above us in a divine, incomprehensible and indescribable way.

(DV) "Our fathers and our children were born from marital union and intercourse, and their fatherhood and filiation have a beginning and an end. Further, a father was a son before becoming a father and all relationships are liable to natural dissolution and cessation. As to Fatherhood, Filiation and Procession in God, they are not in a way similar to those of our humanity, but in a divine way that mind cannot comprehend. They do not arise from any intercourse between them, nor are they from time or in time, but eternally without beginning and without end. Since the above three attributes are of the nature of God, and the nature of God has no beginning and no end, they also are without a beginning and without an end. And since He who is without a beginning and without an end is also unchangeable, that Fatherhood, therefore, that Filiation and Procession are immutable and will remain without any modification. The things that are with us give but an imperfect comparison with the things that are above, because things that are God's are above comparison and likeness, as we have already demonstrated."

(DW) And our victorious King said: "The mind of rational beings will not agree to speak of God who is eternally one in Himself in terms of Trinity." - And I answered "Since the mind of the rational beings is created, and no created being can comprehend God, you have rightly affirmed, O King of kings, that the mind of rational beings will not agree to speak of one God in terms of Trinity. The mind, however, of the rational beings can only extend to the acts of God, and even then in an imperfect and partial manner; as to the nature of God, we learn things that belong to it not so much from our rational mind as from the books of revelation, i.e., from what God Himself has revealed and taught about Himself through His Word and Spirit:

(DX) "The Word of God said, 'No one knoweth the Father but the Son, and no one knoweth the Son but the Father,'[196] and, 'The Spirit searcheth all things even the deep things of God.'[197] No one knows what there is in man except man's own spirit that is in him, so also no one knows what is in God except the Spirit of God. The Word and the Spirit of God, being eternally from His own nature — as heat and light from the sun, and as reason[198] and mind from the soul — alone see and know the divine nature, and it is they who have revealed and taught us in the sacred books that God is one and three, as I have already shown in my above words from the Torah, the prophets, the Gospel and the Qur'an according to what I have learned from those who are versed in the knowledge of your book.

(DY) "Were it not for the fact that His Word and His Spirit were eternally from His own nature, God would not have spoken of Himself in the Torah as, *Our* image and *Our* likeness;'[199] and 'Behold, the man is become as one of *us*';[200] and 'Let us go down and there confound their language';[201] and the Qur'an would not have said, 'And *We* sent to her *Our* Spirit';[202] and '*We* breathed into her from *Our* Spirit';[203] and '*We* did,' '*We* said,' and so on. By such expressions (The Qur'an) refers to God and His Word and His Spirit as we have said above. Has not the mind of the rational beings, O our victorious Sovereign, to follow the words of God rather than its own fanciful conceptions? The inspired books are surely right, and since we find in them that one and the same prophet speaks of God as one and as three, we are compelled by the nature of the subject to believe it."

(DZ) And our powerful Sovereign said to me: "How does the nature of the subject compel us to believe it?" - And I answered: "Because my Sovereign and King granted full freedom to his obedient servant to speak before him, may I further implore your Majesty to be willing that I ask more questions?" - And our King said: "Ask anything you want." - And I then said: "Is not God a simple and uncircumscribed Spirit?" And our King said: "Yes." - And I asked his Majesty: "Does he perceive in an uncircumscribed way with all His being, or does He perceive like us with one part only and not with another?" - And our King answered: "He perceives with all its nature without any circumscription." - And I asked: "Was there any other thing with Him from eternity, or not?" - And our King answered: "Surely not." - And I asked: "Does not a perceiver perceive a perceived object?" - And our King answered: "Yes."

(EA) And I then asked: "If God is a perceiver and knower from the beginning and from eternity, a perceiver and knower perceives and knows a perceived and known object, and because there was not created thing that was eternally with God — since He created afterwards when He wished — in case there was no other being with Him, whom He might perceive and know eternally, how could He be called a perceiver and knower in a divine and eternal sense and before the creation of the world?"

(EB) And our King answered: "What you have said is true. It is indeed necessary that a perceiver should perceive a perceived object, and the knower of a known one, but it is possible to say that He perceived and knew His own self." - And I asked: "If He is all a perceiver without any circumscription, so that He does not perceive and know with one part and is perceived and known with another part, how can a perceiver of this kind perceive Himself? The eye of man is the perceiver and it perceives the other objects, but it can never perceive its own self except with another eye like itself, because the sight of the eye is unable to perceive itself. If the sight of the composed eye cannot be divided into parts so that a part of it perceives itself, and the other part is perceived by itself, how can we think of God, who is a Spirit without body, without division and without parts that He perceives Himself and is perceived by Himself?"

(EC) And our intelligent Sovereign asked: "Which of the two do you admit: does God perceive Himself or not?" - And I answered: "Yes; He perceives and knows Himself with a sight that has no limits and a knowledge that has no bounds." - And our King asked: "How is it that your argumentation and reasoning concerning divisions, separations and partitions do not rebound against you?" - And I replied to him: "God perceives and knows Himself through His Word and the Spirit that proceeds from Him. The Word and the Spirit are a clear mirror of the Father, a mirror that is not foreign to Him, but of the same essence and nature as Himself, without any limits and bounds. He was perceiving His Word, His Spirit and His creatures, divinely, eternally and before the worlds, with this difference, however, that He was perceiving and knowing His Word and His Spirit as His nature, His very nature, and He was eternally perceiving and knowing His creatures not as His nature, but as His creatures. He was perceiving and knowing His Word and His Spirit as existing divinely and eternally, and His creatures not as existing then, but as going to exist in the future. Through His Word and His Spirit He perceives and knows the beauty, the splendor and the infiniteness of His own nature, and through His creatures the beauty of His wisdom, of His power and of His goodness, now, before now, and before all times, movements and beginnings."

(ED) And our King asked philosophically: "Are they parts of one another and placed at a distance from one another, so that one part perceives and the other is perceived?" - And I replied to his Majesty: "No, not so, O King of kings. They are not parts of one another, because a simple being has no parts and composition; nor are they placed at a distance one from the other, because the infiniteness of God, of His Word and of His Spirit is one. The Father is in the Son and the Son in the Spirit, without any break, distance and confusion of any kind, as the soul is in the reason and the reason in the mind without break and confusion; and as the spheric globe of the sun is in its light, and this light in its heat; and as the color, scent and taste are in the apple, without any break, confusion and promiscuity. All figures, comparisons and images are far below that adorable and ineffable nature of God, so there is fear that we may be falsely held to believe in the plurality of Godhead."

(EE) And our powerful and wise King said: "There is such a fear indeed." - And I said: "O King of kings, this would arise in case we diminished something from Godhead, just as well as if we added something to it. As it is a blasphemy to add something to Godhead, it is also a blasphemy to diminish something from it in our belief, and as it is not allowed to add anything to the sun or to the pearl, so it is not allowed to diminish anything from them. He who divests God of His Word and His Spirit, resembles the one who would divest the sun of its light and its heat, and the soul of its reason and its mind, and the pearl of its beauty and its luster. As it is impossible to conceive a pearl without luster, or a sun without light, or a soul without reason and mind, so it is never possible that God should be without Word and Spirit. If, therefore, Word and Spirit are God's by nature, and God is eternal, it follows that the Word and the Spirit of God are also eternal. They are not added to Him from outside that one might think of the plurality of Godhead, but it is of the essence of God to possess both Word and Spirit."

(EF) And our victorious King said: "In your previous words you said that the perceiver perceives the one that is perceived, and the one that is perceived perceives also the one that perceives; and that if they be near a thing they are all there at the same time, because the Word and the Spirit of God are the object that is perceived by God and are eternal like the perceiver; and if there is no perceiver, there is no perceived object either, and if there is no perceived object, there is no perceiver. Did you say these things or not?" - And I answered: "I did say them, O victorious King." - And the King of kings said: "But it is possible that God was perceiving His creatures before He created them." - And I said: "O our victorious King, we cannot think or say otherwise. God perceived and knew eternally His creatures, before He brought them into being."

(EG) And our King said: "The nature of the subject will not compel us, therefore, to believe that if the perceiver is eternal, the perceived should also be eternal, because the fact that God is an eternal perceiver of the creature does not carry with it the necessity that the creature which is perceived by Him is also eternal, and the fact that the creature is also perceived does not carry with it the necessity that He also is the perceived object like it. As such a necessity as that you were mentioning in the case of the creature has been vitiated, so also is the case with regard to the Word and the Spirit."

(EH) And I said: "O our King, it is not the same kind of perception that affects the creature on the one hand, and the Word and the Spirit on the other. This may be known and demonstrated as follows: it is true that God was perceiving the creature eternally, but the creature is not infinite, and God is infinite, the creature has a limited perceptibility, and the perception of God has no limits. Further, the nature of God having no limits, His knowledge also has no limits, as the divine David says, 'His understanding is infinite.'[204] If God, therefore, has any perception, and if He is infinite and unlimited, and if His perception is infinite, it perceives a perceived object that is likewise infinite; but the perceived object that is infinite being only the nature of God, it follows that His Word and His Spirit are from His nature, in the same way as the word and spirit of a man are from human nature. It is, therefore, obvious that if God is an infinite perceiver, the Word and the Spirit that are from Him are also infinite.

(EI) "God knows His Word and His Spirit in an infinite way as His knowledge and His perception are infinite, but He perceives and knows His creature not in the same infinite way as are His perception and His knowledge, but in a finite way according to the limits of the creature and of the human nature. He perceived His creature only through His prescience and not as a substance that is of the same nature as Himself, and, on the contrary, He perceived the Word and the Spirit not through His prescience but as a substance that is of the same nature as Himself. This is the reason why the prophet David said, 'Forever, art Thou O Lord, and Thy Word is settled in heaven';[205] and likewise the prophet Isaiah, 'The grass withereth and the flower fadeth, but the Word of our Lord shall stand forever.'[206] In this passage Isaiah counts all the world as grass and flower, and the Word and the Spirit of God as something imperishable, immortal and eternal.

(EJ) "If, therefore, God is an infinite perceiver, the object that is perceived by Him has also to be infinite, in order that His perception of the perceived should not be incomplete in places. And who is this infinite-perceived except the Word and Spirit of God? God indeed was not without perception and a perceived object of the same nature of

Himself till He brought His creature into being, but He possessed along with His eternal perception and eternal knowledge a perceived object that was eternal and a known object that was also eternal. It is not permissible to say of God that He was not a perceiver and a knower, and if His Word and His Spirit were perceived by Him divinely and eternally, it follows that these same Word and Spirit were eternally with Him. As to His creatures, He created them afterwards, when He wished, by means of His Word and His Spirit."

(EK) And our King said to me: "O Catholicos, if this is your religion and that of the Christians, I will say this, that the Word and the Spirit are also creatures of God, and there is no one who is uncreated except one God." - And I replied: "If the Word and the Spirit are also creatures of God like the rest, by means of whom did God create the Heaven and the earth and all that they contain? The books teach us that He created the world by means of His Word and His Spirit — by means of whom did He then create this Word and this Spirit? If He created them by means of another word and another spirit, the same conclusion would also be applied to them: will they be created or uncreated? If uncreated, the religion of the Catholicos and of the Christians is vindicated; and if created, by means of whom did God create them? And this process of gibberish argumentation will go on indefinitely until we stop at that Word and that Spirit hidden eternally with God, by means of whom we assert that the worlds were created."

(EL) And the King said: "You appear to believe in three heads, O Catholicos." - And I said: "This is certainly not so, O our victorious King. I believe in one head, the eternal God the Father, from whom the Word shone and the Spirit radiated eternally from the single nature of God, together, and before all times, the former by way of filiation and the latter by way of procession, not in a bodily, but in a divine way that befits God. This is the reason why they are not three separate Gods. The Word and the Spirit are eternally from the single nature of God, who is not one person divested of Word and Spirit as the weakness of the Jewish belief has it. He shines and emits rays eternally with the light of His Word and the radiation of His Spirit, and He is one head with His Word and His Spirit. I do not believe in God as stripped of His Word and Spirit, in the case of the former without mind[207] and reason, and in the case of the latter, without spirit and life. It is only the idolaters who believe in false gods or idols who have neither reason nor life."

(EM) And our victorious King said: "It seems to me that you believe in a vacuous God, since you believe that He has[208] a child." - And I answered: "O King, I do not believe that God is either vacuous or solid, because both of these adjectives denote bodies. If vacuity and solidity belong to bodies, and God is a Spirit without a body, neither of the two qualifications can be ascribed to Him." - And the King said: "What then do you believe that God is if He is neither vacuous or solid?" - And I replied to his Majesty: "God is a Spirit and an incorporeal light, from whom shine and radiate eternally and divinely His Word and His Spirit. The soul begets the mind and causes reason to proceed from it, and the fire begets light and causes heat to proceed from its nature, and we do not say that either the soul or fire are hollow or solid. So also is the case with regard to God, about Whom we never say that He is vacuous or solid when He makes His Word shine and His Spirit radiate from His essence eternally."

(EN) And our victorious King said: "What is the difference in God between shining and radiating?" - And I replied: "There is the same difference between shining and radiating in God as that found in the illustration furnished by the fire and the apple: the fire begets the light and causes heat to proceed from it, and the apple begets the scent and causes the taste and savor to proceed from it. Although both the fire and the apple give rise, the former to light and heat and the latter to scent and savor, yet they do not do it in the same manner and with an identical effect on the one and the same sense of our body. We receive the heat of the fire with the sense of feeling, the light with the eyes, the scent of the apple with the sense of smell and the sweetness of its savor with the palate. From this it becomes clear that the mode of filiation is different from that of procession. This is as far as one can go from bodily comparisons and similes to the realities and to God."

(EO) And the King said: "You will not go very far with God in your bodily comparisons and similes." - And I said: "O King, because I am a bodily man I made use of bodily metaphors, and not of those that are without any body and composition. Because I am a bodily man, and not a spiritual being, I make use of bodily comparisons in speaking of God. How could I or any other human being speak of God as He is with a tongue of flesh and lips fashioned of mud and with a soul and mind closely united to a body? This is far beyond the power of men and angels to do. God Himself speaks with the prophets about Himself not as He is, but simply in the way that fits in with their own nature, a way they are able to understand. In His revelations to the ancient prophets sometimes He revealed Himself as man, sometimes as fire, sometimes as wind and some other times in some other ways and similitudes.

(EP) "The divine David said, 'He then spoke in visions to His holy ones';[209] and the prophet Hosea said on behalf of God, 'I have multiplied my visions and used similitudes by the ministry of the prophets';[210] and one of the Apostles of Christ said, 'God at sundry times and in divers manners spake in time past to our fathers by the prophets.'[211] If God appeared and spake to the ancients in bodily similitudes and symbols, we with stronger reason find ourselves completely unable to speak of God and to understand anything concerning Him except through bodily similitudes and metaphors. I shall here make bold and assert that I hope I shall not deserve any blame from your Majesty if I say that you are in the earth the representative of God for the earthly people; now God maketh His sun to rise on the evil and on the good and sendeth His rain on the just and the unjust.[212] Your Majesty also in the similitude of God will make us worthy of forgiveness if in the fact of being earthly beings we speak of God in an earthly way and not in a spiritual way like spiritual beings."

(EQ) And our victorious King said: "You are right in what you said before and say now on the subject that God is above all the thoughts and minds of created beings, and that all the thoughts and minds of created beings are lower not only than God Himself but also His work. The fact, however, that you put the servant and the Lord on the same footing you make the Creator equal with the created, and in this you fall into error and falsehood."

(ER) And I replied: "O my Sovereign, that the Word and the Spirit of God should be called servants and created I considered and consider not far from unbelief. If the Word and the Spirit are believed to be from God, and God is conceived to be a Lord and not a servant, His Word and Spirit are also, by inference, lords and not servants. It is one and the same freedom that belongs to God and to His Word and Spirit, and they are called Word and Spirit of God not in an unreal, but in a true sense. The kingdom which my victorious Sovereign possesses is the same as that held by his word and his spirit, so that no one separates his word and his spirit from his kingdom, and he shines in the diadem of kingdom together with his word and his spirit in a way that they are not three kings and in a way that he does not shine in the diadem of kingdom apart from his word and his spirit.

(ES) "If it please your Majesty, O my powerful Sovereign, I will also say this: the splendor and the glory of the kingdom shine in one and the same way in the Commander of the Faithful[213] and in his sons Musa and Harun,[214] and in spite of the fact that kingdom and lordship in them are one, their personalities are different. For this reason no one would venture to consider, without the splendor of kingdom, not only the Commander of the Faithful, but also the beautiful flowers and majestic blossoms that budded and blossomed out of him; indeed the three of them blossom in an identical kingdom, and this one and the same kingdom shines and radiates eternally in the Father, the Son and the Holy Spirit, or if one prefers to put it, in God, His Word and His Spirit, and no one is allowed to give to any of them the name of servant. If the Word and the Spirit are servants of God, while they are from God Himself, the logical conclusion to be drawn I leave to a tongue other than mine to utter."

(ET) And the King said: "It is very easy for your tongue, O Catholicos, to prove the existence of that Lord and God, and the existence also of that cosubstantial servant and to draw conclusions sometimes or to abstain from them some other times, but the minds and the will of rational beings are induced to follow not your mind, which is visible in your conclusions, but the law of nature and the inspired books."

(EU) And I replied: "O our victorious King, I have proved my words that I have uttered in the first day and today both from nature and from book. So far as arguments from nature are concerned, I argued, confirmed and corroborated my words sometimes from the soul with its mind and its reason; sometimes from fire with its light and its heat; sometimes from the apple with its scent and its savor; and some other times from your Majesty and from the rational and royal flowers that grew from it: Musa and Harun, the sons of your Majesty. As to the inspired books, I proved the object under discussion sometimes from Moses, sometimes from David and some other times I appealed to the Qur'an as a witness to prove my statement.

(EV) "God said to the prophet David and caused him further to prophecy in the following manner concerning His Word and His Spirit, 'I have set up My King on My holy hill of Zion.'[215] Before this He had called Him His Christ, 'Against the Lord and against His Christ.'[216] If the Christ of God is a King, it follows that the Christ is not a servant, but a King. Afterwards David called Him twice Son, 'Thou art My Son, and this day have I begotten Thee,'[217] and, 'Kiss the Son lest the Lord be angry and ye perish from His way.'[218] If the Christ, therefore, is a Son, as God called Him through the prophet David, and if no son is a servant, it follows, O King, that the Christ is not a servant. In another passage the same prophet David called the Christ 'Lord,' 'Son' and a priest for ever,' because he said 'The Lord said unto my Lord, Sit Thou at My right hand.'[219] And in order to show that Christ is of the same nature and power as God, he said on behalf of the Father as follows, 'In the beauties of holiness from the womb I have begotten Thee from the beginning.'[220] God, therefore, called Christ 'a Lord' through the prophet David, and since no true Lord is a servant, it follows that Christ is not a servant.[221]

(EW) "Further, Christ has been called through David one 'begotten of God' both 'from eternity' and 'In the beauties of holiness from the womb.' Since no one begotten of God is a servant, the Christ, therefore, O King of kings, is not a servant and created, but He is uncreated and a Lord. God said also through the prophet Isaiah to Ahaz, King of Israel, 'Behold a virgin shall conceive and bear a Son, and His name shall be called — not a servant — but Emmanuel, which being interpreted is, God with us.'[222] The same Isaiah said, 'For unto us is a Child — and not a servant — is born, and unto us a Son — not a servant and a created being — is given, and His name has been called Wonderful, Counsellor, the Mighty God of the worlds.'[223] If the Christ, therefore, is the Son of God, this Son of God, as God Himself spoke through the prophet Isaiah, is the 'mighty God of the worlds,' and not a servant in subjection, but a Lord and a Prince. It follows, O our victorious King, that the Christ is surely a Lord and a Prince, and not a servant in subjection.

(EX) "As your Majesty would wax angry if your children were called servants, so also God will be wrathful if anybody called His Word and His Spirit servants. As the honor and dishonor of the children of your Majesty redound on you, as also, and in a higher degree the honor and dishonor of God's Word and Spirit redound on Him. It is for this reason that Christ said in the Gospel, 'He that honoreth not the Son, honoreth not the Father who hath sent Him,'[224] and, 'He who honoreth not the Son shall not see life, but the wrath of God shall abide on him.'[225]

(EY) "The above is written in the Gospel. I heard also that it is written in the Qur'an that Christ is the Word of God and the Spirit of God,[226] and not a servant. If Christ is the Word and the Spirit of God, as the Qur'an testifies, He is not a servant, but a Lord, because the Word and the Spirit of God are Lords. It is by this method, O our God-loving King, based on the law of nature and on divinely inspired words and not on pure human argumentation, word and thought, that I both in the present and in the first conversation have demonstrated the Lordship and Sonship of Christ and the divine trinity.[227]

(EZ) Our victorious King said: "Has not the Christ been called also several times a servant by the prophets?" - And I said: "I am aware, O my Sovereign, of the fact that the Christ has also been called a servant, but that this appellation does not imply a real servitude is borne out by the illustration that may be taken from the status of Harun, the blossom and flower of your Majesty. He is now called by everybody 'Heir Presumptive,'[228] but after your long reign, he will be proclaimed King and Sovereign by all. He served his military service through the mission entrusted to him by your Majesty to repair to Constantinople against the rebellious and tyrannical Byzantines.[229] Through this service and mission he will not lose[230] his royal sonship and his freedom, nor his princely honor and glory and acquire the simple name of servitude and subjection like any other individual. So also is the case of with the Christ, the Son of the Heavenly King. He fulfilled the will of His Father in His coming on His military mission to mankind, and in His victory over sin, death and Satan. He did not by this act lose His royal Sonship and did not become a stranger to divinity, Lordship and Kingdom, nor did He put on the dishonor of servitude and subjection like any other individual.

(FA) "Further, the prophets called Him not by what He was, but by what He was believed by the Jews to be. In one place the prophets called Him, according to the belief of the Jews, 'A Servant, a Rejected one, one without form or comeliness, a stricken one, a smitten one, a man of many sorrows.'[231] In another place, however, it has been said of Him that, 'He is the fairest of the children of men,[232] the Mighty God of the worlds, the Father of the future world, the Messenger of the great counsel of God, Prince of Peace, a Son and a Child,[233] as we demonstrated in our former replies. The last adjectives refer to His nature, and He has been spoken of through the first adjectives on account of the mission that He performed to His Father for the salvation of all, and in compliance with the belief of the Jews who only looked at Him in His humanity, and were totally incapable of considering Him in the nature of His divinity that clothed itself completely with humanity.

(FB) "Some ignorant Byzantines, who know nothing of the kingship and sonship of your son Harun, may consider him and call him a simple soldier and not a Prince and a King, but those who know him with certainty will not call him a simple soldier, but will consider him and call him King and Prince. In this way the prophets considered the Christ our Lord as God, King and Son, but the unbelieving Jews believed Him to be a servant and a mere man under subjection. He has indeed been called not only a servant, on account of His service, but also a stone, a door, the way and a lamb.[234] He was called a stone, not because He was a stone by nature, but because of the truth of His teaching; and a door, because it is through Him that we entered into the knowledge of God: and the way, because it is He who in His person opened to us the way of immortality; and a lamb, because He was immolated for the life of the world. In this same way He was called also a servant, not because He was a servant by nature, but on account of the service which He performed for our salvation and on account of the belief of the Jews.

(FC) "I heard also that it is written in your book that the Christ was sent not as a servant, but as a son, 'I swear by this mountain and by the begetter and His Child.'[235] A child is like his father, whether the latter be a servant or a freeman, and if it is written, 'The Christ doth surely not disdain to be a servant of God,'[236] it is also written that God doth not disdain to be a Father to Christ, because He said through the prophet about Christ, 'He will be to Me a Son'[237] — and not a servant — and, also 'I will make Him a first-born — and not a servant — and will raise Him up above the kings of the earth.'[238] If Christ has been raised by God above the kings of the earth, He who is above the kings cannot be a servant, Christ is, therefore, O King, not a servant and one under subjection, but a King of Kings and a Lord. It is not possible that a servant should be above angels and kings.

(FD) "God said also about the Christ through the same prophet David, 'His name shall endure for ever, and His name is before the sun. All men shall be blessed by Him, and all shall glorify Him.'[239] How can the name of a servant endure for ever, and how can the name of a servant be before the sun and other creatures, and how can all nations be blessed by a servant, and how can all nations glorify a servant? God said to His Word and His Spirit, 'Ask of me, and I shall give Thee the nations for Thine inheritance and the uttermost parts of the earth for Thy possession. Thou shalt shepherd them with a rod of

iron. Be wise now, O ye kings and be instructed, ye judges of the
earth. Serve the Lord with fear and hold to Him with trembling. Kiss
the Son, lest He be angry and ye stray from His way when His wrath is
kindled but a little. Blessed are all they that put their trust in Him.'[240]
If all the nations and the uttermost parts of the earth are the inheritance and the possession of Christ, and if he who has under his authority all the nations and the uttermost parts of the earth is not a servant,
the Christ therefore, O our victorious Sovereign, is not a servant, but a
Lord and Master; and if the kings and the judges of the earth have
been ordered by God to serve the Christ with fear and to hold to Him
with trembling, it is impossible that this same Christ who is served,
held to and kissed by kings and judges of the earth should be a servant.

(FE) "It follows, O our victorious Sovereign, that the Christ is a King
of Kings, since kings worshipped and worship Him; and a Lord and
Judge of Judges, since judges served and serve Him with fear. If He
were a servant, what kind of a wrath and destruction could He bring
on the unbelievers, and what kind of a blessing could He bestow on
those who put their trust in Him? That He is a Lord over all and a
Master over all, He testifies about Himself, and His testimony is true.
Indeed He said to His disciples when He was about to ascend to
Heaven and mount on the cherubim and fly on the spiritual wings of
the seraphim, 'All power is given unto Me in Heaven and in earth.'[241]
If Christ has been given all the power of Heaven and earth, He who is
constituted in this way in Heaven and in earth is God over all, and
Christ, therefore, is God over all. If He is not true God, how can He
have power in Heaven and in earth; and if He has power in Heaven
and earth, how can He not be true God? Indeed He has power in
Heaven and in earth because He is God, since anyone who has power
in Heaven and earth is God.

(FF) "The archangel Gabriel testified to this when he announced His
conception to the always virgin Mary, 'And He shall reign over the
house of Jacob and of His Kingdom there shall be no end.'[242] If the
Christ reigns for ever, and if the one who reigns for ever there is no
end to his kingdom, it follows, O our Sovereign, that Christ is a Lord
and God over all. The prophet Daniel testified also to this in saying, 'I

saw one like the son of men coming on the clouds of heaven, and they brought Him near before the Ancient of days, Who gave Him dominion and glory and a kingdom, that all nations should serve Him and worship Him. His dominion is an everlasting dominion, and His kingdom shall not pass away and be destroyed.'[243] If the kingdom of Christ shall not pass away and be destroyed, He is God over all, and Christ is, therefore, God over all, O our King: over the prophets and the angels.[244]

(FG) "If Christ has been called by the prophets God and Lord, and if it has been said by some people that God suffered and died in the flesh, it is evident that it is the human nature that the Word-God took from us that suffered and died, because in no book, neither in the prophets nor in the Gospel, do we find that God Himself died in the flesh, but we do find in all of them that the Son and Jesus Christ died in the flesh. The expression that God suffered and died in the flesh is not right."

(FH) And our victorious King asked: "And who are those who say that God suffered and died in the flesh." - And I answered: "The Jacobites and Melkites say that God suffered and died in the flesh, as to us, we not only do not assert that God suffered and died in our nature, but that He even removed the possibility of our human nature that He put on from Mary by His impassibility, and its mortality by His immortality, and He made it to resemble divinity, to the extent that a created being is capable of resembling his Creator. A created being cannot make himself resemble his Creator, but the Creator is able to bring His creature to His own resemblance. It is not the picture that makes the painter paint a picture in its own resemblance, but it is the painter that paints the picture to his own resemblance; it is not the wood that works and fashions a carpenter in its resemblance, but it is the carpenter that fashions the wood in his resemblance. In this same way it is not the mortal and passible nature that renders God passible and mortal like itself, but it is by necessity God that renders the passible and mortal human nature impassible and immortal like Himself. On the one hand, this is what the Jacobites and Melkites say, and on the other, this is what we say. It behooves your Majesty to decide who are those who believe rightly and those who believe wrongly."

(FI) And our victorious King said: "In this matter you believe more rightly than the others. Who dares to assert that God dies? I think that even demons do not say such a thing. In what, however, you say concerning one Word and Son of God, all of you are wrong." - And I replied to his Majesty: "O our victorious King, in this world we are all of us as in a dark house in the middle of the night. If at might and in a dark house a precious pearl happens to fall in the midst of people, and all become aware of its existence, everyone would strive to pick up the pearl, which will not fall to the lot of all, but to the lot of one only, while one will get hold of the pearl itself, another one of a piece of glass, a third one of stone or of a bit of earth, but every one will be happy and proud that he is the real possessor of the pearl. When, however, the night and darkness disappear, and the light and day arise, then every one of those men who had believed that they had the pearl, would extend and stretch his hand towards the light, which alone can show what every one has in hand. He who possesses the pearl will rejoice and be happy and pleased with it, while those who had in hand pieces of glass and bits of stone only will weep and be sad and will sigh and shed tears.

(FJ) In this same way we children of men are in this perishable world as in darkness. The pearl of the true faith fell in the midst of all of us, and it is undoubtedly in the hand of one of us, while all of us believe that we possess the precious object. In the world to come, however, the darkness of mortality passes and the fog of ignorance dissolves, since it is the true and the real light to which the fog of ignorance is absolutely foreign, In it the possessors of the pearl will rejoice, be happy and pleased, and the possessors of mere pieces of stone will weep, sigh and shed tears as we said above."

(FK) And our victorious King said: "The possessors of the pearl are not known in this world, O Catholicos." - And I answered: "They are partially known, O our victorious King." - And our victorious and very wise King said: "What do you mean by partially known, and by what are they known as such?" - And I answered: "By good works, O our victorious King, and pious deeds and by the wonders and miracles that God performs through those who possess the true faith. As the luster of a pearl is somewhat visible even in the darkness of the night, so also the rays of the true faith shine to some extent even in the darkness and the fog of the present world. God indeed has not left the pure pearl of the faith completely without testimony and evidence, first in the prophets and then in the Gospel. He first confirmed the true faith in Him through Moses, once by means of the prodigies and miracles that He wrought in Egypt, and another time when He divided the waters of the Red Sea into two and allowed the Israelites to cross it safely, but drowned the Egyptians in its depths. He also split and divided the Jordan into two through Joshua, son of Nun, and allowed the Israelites to cross it without any harm to themselves, and tied the sun and the moon to their own places until the Jewish people were well avenged upon their enemies. He acted in the same way through the prophets who rose in different generations, viz.: through David, Elijah and Elisha.

(FL) "Afterwards He confirmed the faith through Christ our Lord by the miracles and prodigies which He wrought for the help of the children of men. In this way the disciples performed miracles greater even than those wrought by Christ. These signs, miracles, and prodigies wrought in the name of Jesus Christ are the bright rays and the shining luster of the precious pearl of the faith, and it is by the brightness of such rays that the possessors of this pearl which is so full of luster and so precious that it outweighs all the world in the balance, are known."

(FM) And our victorious King said: "We have hope in God that we are the possessors of this pearl, and that we hold it in our hands." - And I replied: "Amen, O King. But may God grant us that we too may share it with you, and rejoice in the shining and beaming luster of the pearl! God has placed the pearl of His faith before all of us like the shining rays of the sun, and everyone who wishes can enjoy the light of the sun.

(FN) "We pray God, who is King of Kings, and Lord of Lords, to

245

preserve the crown of the kingdom and the throne of the Commander of the Faithful for multitudinous days and numerous years! May He also raise after him Musa and Harun and Ali[245] to the throne of his kingdom for ever and ever! May He subjugate before them and before their descendants after them all the barbarous nations, and may all the kings and governors of the world serve our Sovereign and his sons after him till the day in which the Kingdom of Heaven is revealed from Heaven to earth!"

(FO) And our victorious King said: "Miracles have been and are sometimes performed even by unbelievers." - And I replied to his Majesty: "These, O our victorious King, are not miracles but deceptive similitudes of the demons and are performed not by the prophets of God and by holy men, but by idolaters and wicked men. This is the reason why I said that good works and miracles are the luster of the pearl of faith. Indeed, Moses performed miracles in Egypt, and the sorcerers Jannes and Jambres performed them also there, but Moses performed them by the power of God, and the sorcerers through the deceptions of the demons. The power of God, however, prevailed, and that of the demons was defeated.

(FP) In Rome also Simon Cephas and Simon Magus performed miracles, but the former performed them by the power of God, and the latter by the power of the demons, and for this reason Simon Cephas was honored and Simon Magus was laughed at and despised by everyone, and his deception was exposed before the eyes of all celestial and terrestrial beings."

(FQ) At this our victorious King rose up and entered his audience chamber, and I left him and returned in peace to my patriarchal residence. *Here ends the controversy of the Patriarch Mar Timothy I with Mahdi, the Caliph of the Muslims. May eternal praise be to God!*

Notes:

[1] On his remarkable zeal in the spread of Christianity in Central Asia see my *Early Spread of Christianity in Central Asia*, 1925, pp. 12-17, 30, 74-76. See also my *Early Spread of Christianity in India*, 1926, pp. 34 and 64.

[2] I use in my references the Arabic text published in Cairo in 1912 by the Nile Mission Press.

[3] My references are to my own edition and translation of the work in 1922-1923.

[4] *Athar*, p. 205 (edit. Sachau).

[5] Catalogue in Assemani *Bibl. Orient.*, iii. 213.

[6] See p. 387, below.

[7] See p. 430, below.

[8] See p. 438, below.

[9] Ibid., parag. DD.

[10] In Bedjan's *Breviarium Chaldaicum*, i, ii and iii, p. 47.

[11] See p. 438, below.

[12] See p. 481, below.

[13] See pp. 488-489, below.

[14] See pp. 463, 489, below.

[15] *Encyclopedia of Islam*, ii, 1021.

[16] In al-Kindi, parags. J and BX - ed.

[17] *Encyclopedia of Islam*, ii. 1021.

[18] *An Ancient Syrian Translation of the Qur'an*.

[19] No. 90 (7°) in A. Scher's catalogue in *J.A.*, 1906, p. 57. The reference to No. 96 in Baumstark's *Gesch. d. Syr. Lit.*, p. 217, is a misprint.

[20] In Scher's catalogue. In my last journey to the East in 1925 I was informed on the spot that this MS. was among those which had been destroyed by the Kurds in the world war of 1914-1918.

[21] In *J.A.*, 1909, p. 263 and in *Zeit. f. Assyr.*, ix, p. 363.

[22] In *Revue des Bibliotheques*, 1908, p. 80. No special mention, however, is made of the Apology.

[23] In the custody of the Rendel Harris Library, Birmingham.

[24] The correspondent of the Patriarch. He was possibly either Sergius, priest, monk and teacher of the monastery of Mar Abraham, or Sergius, Metropolitan of Elam.

[25] These sentences amplify a little the original.

[26] The Christian apologist Kindi refutes an objection of his adversary, 'Abdullah b. Isma'il al-Hashimi, which was in almost identical terms: "We never say about the Most High God that He married a woman from whom He begat a son." al-Kindi, parag. BL.

[27] Cf. Is. 9:6.

[28] Qur'an 3:41; 21:91.

[29] Luke 1:37; Qur'an 3:41, etc.

[30] This doctrine has no direct Biblical support, and thus the remark of Timothy is somewhat misleading here - ed.

[31] Note the semi-Nestorian expression of "putting on, clothing oneself with" as applied to the union of God with man in the Incarnation. In the following passages we shall not attempt to render this expression into English at every time.

[32] Browne mentions that the Arabic version of the text as shown by Cheikho does not contain this "Nestorian bias." Browne, "The Patriarch Timothy," *Moslem World*, vol. 21 (1931), p. 41 - ed.

[33] The example of man as being both singular and plural in explanations of the Trinity was also used by others. Leo, parag. Y and al-Kindi, parag. BO - ed.

[34] *Parsopa* = πρόσωπον.

[35] John 20:17.

[36] The Arabic *muhal*.

[37] Browne states that the Arabic text of Cheikho has but one short sentence dealing with the duality of Christ's nature whereas the Syriac text is much longer. Browne, "The Patriarch Timothy," *Moslem World*, vol. 21 (1931), p. 41 - ed.

[38] There is no doubt therefore that the official letters and documents of the early 'Abbasids were written on papyrus and not on parchment. The Arabic word *Qirtas* seems by reference to indicate papyrus in the majority of cases, if not always.

[39] The example of the sun was very widely used in explanations of the Trinity, and dates at least as far back as Tertullian, *Apology*, 21. Leo, parag. W, etc.; see Appendix A - ed.

[40] In Syr. the same root *milltha* is used to express both "reason" and "word." The author plays on this identical root in a constant manner.

[41] In Syr. "spirit" which also means "soul."

[42] Ps. 33:6 (Peshitta).

[43] Ps. 56:10 (Peshitta).

[44] Ps. 104:30.

[45] Ps. 119:89 (Peshitta).

[46] Is. 40:8.

[47] John 1:1.

[48] John 1:4.

[49] John 17:5.

[50] Matt. 28:19.

[51] Timothy evidently misses the argument that the word "name" is singular whereas the persons of the Godhead are plural - ed.

[52] Most of the above Biblical passages are quoted also by the Christian apologist Kindi; see al-Kindi, pp. 423, 496.

[53] This question was also posed by 'Umar II, cf. Leo, parags. AN n.

82, AP n. 85 - ed.

[54] The idea that Christ came to annul the Law and its rites, seems to have been prevalent at this time period, though it is in direct contradiction of the words of Jesus, see Matt. 5:17. Cf. Leo, parag. AP, al-Kindi parag. DG - ed.

[55] Cf. Matt. 5:17.

[56] This objection about the circumcision of Christ and the uncircumcision of Christians is also mentioned and refuted by the Christian apologist Kindi. al-Kindi, parag. DG. It is likewise alluded to by the Muslim apologist 'Ali Tabari, *Kitab ud-Din*, pp. 159-160 of my translation. - See also Leo, parag. AP, Jahiz, parag. T - ed.

[57] The same Syriac word means both "mystery" and "sacrament."

[58] See note 54 above - ed.

[59] I.e., Temple. Syr. *baita d-makdsha* from which the Arab. *bait al-makdis*.

[60] This question was also asked by 'Umar II, see Leo, parag. AJ n. 73 - ed.

[61] This teaching is that of Theodore of Mopsuestia. - As this passage does not read the same in the Arabic text given by Cheikho, Browne considers the Syriac version given here to be a later addition by Nestorian Christians. Since Timothy was himself Nestorian, however, it is more likely that the passage was later changed by non-Nestorian Christians. See "The Patriarch Timothy, " *Moslem World*, vol. 21 (1931), p. 41 - ed.

[62] That the Paradise of Eden was situated in the direction of the East is the opinion of the majority of Eastern fathers, many of whom believe also that it is found in the firmament. To it, according to them,

the souls of the just go till the day of resurrection.

[63] Qur'an 19:16.

[64] This question was also asked by 'Umar II, see Leo, parag AK n. 75. The reply given to this question by the monk in The Religious Dialogue of Jerusalem was to cite Qur'an 33:56, wherein Allah is said to pray for Muhammad; Religious Dialogue, parags. AJ, AM - ed.

[65] The Arab. *a'udhu billahi*.

[66] The Islamic doctrine of the sinlessness of all the prophets probably resulted directly from Muslims being confronted with the Biblical teaching of the sinlessness of Jesus. See Religious Dialogue, AR - ed.

[67] That the name of Muhammad is found in Jewish and Christian books is the claim made by the Prophet himself in Qur'an 7:156. "The *ummi* prophet whom they found written down with them in the Torah and in the Gospel." See also 61:6.

[68] Is. 7:14.

[69] Is. 7:14 and 9:6.

[70] Is. 35:4-6.

[71] Is. 53:5.

[72] Ps. 16:10.

[73] Ps. 2:7.

[74] Ps. 68:18.

[75] Ps. 48:5.

[76] Browne shows that the Arabic text of Cheikho gives the quotation of this verse more completely. See "The Patriarch Timothy," *Moslem World*, vol. 21 (1931), p. 39 - ed.

[77] Dan. 7:13-14.

[78] Browne shows the Arabic text of Cheikho to say: "I never saw a single verse in the Gospels or the Prophets or elsewhere bearing witness to Muhammad." See "The Patriarch Timothy," *Moslem World*, vol. 21 (1931), p. 39 - ed.

[79] 'Umar II also asked this question. See Leo, parag. P n. 50 - ed.

[80] Browne states that the Arabic text of Cheikho gives "When He ascended..." instead of "When I go away to Heaven..." See "The Patriarch Timothy," *Moslem World*, Vol 21 (1931), p. 40 - ed.

[81] John 14:16,26; 15:26; 16:7; I Cor. 2:10.

[82] The Muslims have always ("always" is a bit to strong here, but this belief certainly shows up early in the Christian-Muslim dialogue - ed.) believed that the Paraclete spoken of in the Gospel refers to Muhammad. See *Kitab ad-Din* of Ibn Rabban (pp. 546-547, below), who even corroborates his statement by an appeal to the numerical value of the letters of the word. Many other writers (such as Yahsubi in his *shifa*) counts the name of the Paraclete among the names of the Prophet.

[83] Qur'an 6:50; 7:188; 11:33, etc.

[84] The method of searching for miracles as a confirmation of prophethood is definitely Biblical (John 10:37-38; Acts 2:22; etc.) and was used frequently in the early Christian-Muslim dialogue, see John of Damascus, parags. AI-AJ; Appendix A - ed. This idea of miracles accompanying prophets also occurs in the Qur'an (6:109; 20:133; 21:5; etc.) though Muhammad in essence admits to not being able to per-

form them (6:109; 29:49; etc.). See note 93 below - ed.

[85] John 14:17.

[86] Ps. 33:6; 104:30 (both Peshitta).

[87] The bulk of the Muslim testimony, based on Qur'an 7:156, is to the effect that the name of Muhammad is found in the Gospel. Almost all the work of Ibn Rabban entitled *Kitab ad-Din wad-Daulah* has been written for the purpose of showing that this name is found in Jewish and Christian scriptures. (See especially pp. 77-146 of my translation) Cf. Ibn S'ad's *Tabakat*, i. ii., 89, and i. i., 123, and see the commentator Tabari on Qur'an 7:156 and the historians Ibn Hisham and Tabari.

[88] The Muslim charge that the Torah, Psalms and Gospel have been corrupted is prevalent in the early stages of the Christian-Muslim dialogue and still is used in our own day. See Leo, parag. K; John of Damascus, parag. D - ed.

[89] This reply to the challenge was also made by Leo, see parag. AI, and likewise appears to have remained unanswered. With the exception of the spurious *Gospel of Barnabas*, which though considered original by many Muslims can rather easily be shown to be a forgery, Muslims have failed to produce any evidence that the Torah, Psalms and Gospel at one time coincided completely with the testimony of the Qur'an - ed.

[90] Read *samya* in sing.

[91] See note 84 above.

[92] Read *d-nishré*. - The idea that the Law was abrogated by the Gospel, is in contradiction to the Gospel itself. See note 54 above - ed.

[93] Muslim tradition, somewhat against Qur'an 29:49, etc., is full of

miracles of all sorts attributed to the Prophet. All these miracles have apparently been invented in order to answer the objection of the Christians to the effect that since Muhammad performed no miracle, he was not a prophet. Pp. 30-60 of my edition of Ibn Rabban's *Apology*, the *Kitab ad-Din wad-Daulah*, have been written for this purpose. The extent to which later tradition amplified this fabulous theme may be gauged by the references given in Wensinck's *Handbook of Early Muhammadan Tradition*, pp. 165-168. The theme of the lack of miracles on the part of the Prophet is emphasized by the Christian apologist Kindi, pp. 435sqq. and 439, below.

[94] The Muslim use of this verse from Isaiah as a reference to Muhammad also appears rather early in the Christian-Muslim dialogue, see: Leo, parag. BC n. 106. Browne also considers the change of subject in the Syriac too abrupt to be original and favors the text of the Arabic which introduces this new subject, see: "The Patriarch Timothy," *Moslem World*, vol. 21 (1931), p. 39 - ed.

[95] Read *l-Parsayé*.

[96] Is. 21:2.

[97] Dan. 7:5-6.

[98] Dan. 2:31 sqq.

[99] 'Umar II also used this argument, see Leo, parag. BC, n. 106.

[100] Zech. 9:9.

[101] A great deal is made of this prophecy of Isaiah concerning the rider on an ass and the rider on a camel in Ibn Rabban's *Apology* the *Kitab ad-Din* (pp. 95-97 of my edition). The author concludes his references to it in the following words of my translation: "Are not men of intelligence and science among the *People of the Book* ashamed to attribute such a clear and sublime prophecy to some rude and barba-

rous people?... Did not the adversaries fall ashamed in saying that the rightly guided prophets of the family of Isaac prophesied about the Kings of Babylon, Media, Persia and Khuzistan, and neglected to mention such an eminent Prophet and such a great and Abrahamic nation?"

[102] Gen. 49:10 (Peshitta with slight changes).

[103] Dan. 9:24 sqq.

[104] Matt. 11:13.

[105] The last of the prophets, according to Muslim apologists, is Muhammad: "If the prophet had not appeared, the prophecies of the prophets about Ishmael and about the Prophet who is the last of the prophets would have necessarily become without object." Ibn Rabban's *Apology*, the *Kitab ad-Din*, p. 615, below *et passim*. - Other Christian apologists also used this idea that prophecy ended with the advent of Jesus (see, John of Damascus, parag, AK; al-Kindi, parag. *) very much to the contrary of what is written in the New Testament, as Ibn Rabban even noticed and pointed out, see note 150 below - ed.

[106] This question was very popular among Muslim apologists, see Leo, parag, AW n. 91; John of Damascus, parag. F - ed.

[107] Read *we-azlegh* with a *waw*.

[108] This subject of worship of the cross is also alluded to at some length by the Christian apologist Kindi in his *Apology*, parag. EA.

[109] See, John of Damascus, parag. N-P; Leo, parag. AM - ed.

[110] Browne considers this passage to be corrupt, as he feels it contains Nestorian bias, whereas the Arabic version of the text maintains the orthodox view that death was attributed to God in the death of Christ. See, *Moslem World*, vol. 21 (1931), p. 41 - ed.

[111] Here as above on p. 167 the Arab. *a'udhu billahi*.

[112] Qur'an 4:156. The *Qurra* apparently read the verb as *shabbaha* and not *shubbiha* in the time of the Patriarch Timothy.

[113] There is, of course, no sura named "Surat 'Isa;" the sura referred to here is Surat Maryam (Qur'an 19) - ed.

[114] Qur'an 19:34.

[115] Qur'an 3:48. The Syriac *marfa* from Arab. *wa-rafi'uka*.

[116] Ps. 22:16-18 (Peshitta).

[117] Is. 53:5 (Peshitta).

[118] Cf. Lam. 3:4 and 30, etc.

[119] Dan. 9:26. Read *laih*.

[120] Zech. 13:7.

[121] Browne states that the Syriac here "quotes part of a verse from Jeremiah (which he mistranslates) and with it a verse from Isaiah; and attributes them to Isaiah; and he mistranslates quotations from Daniel and Zechariah." The Arabic version, according to Browne, quotes all of these verse accurately and so must be closer to the original. See, *Moslem World*, vol. 21 (1931), p. 39 - ed.

[122] Browne gives the Arabic version of the Caliph's question as, "The prophets thus made ambiguous statements (i.e., caused misunderstanding) about Christ in this way," and feels the Arabic to be more in harmony with flow of the dialogue that the Syriac. See, *Moslem World*, vol. 21 (1931), p. 40 - ed.

[123] The Arabic word often used in the Qur'an to express "apostles" is of Ethiopic origin.

[124] The word "Jew" has been, and is often in our days a term of derision in the East, where also it indicates weakness and powerlessness.

[125] John 10:18.

[126] See, John of Damascus, parag. Z - ed.

[127] See John of Damascus, parag. Z; Religious Dialogue, S - ed.

[128] The Arabic Qur'anic word *iblis*.

[129] See, Religious Dialogue, parag. S - ed.

[130] The Arabic: *mutawwa'in bi-sabil il lahi*.

[131] Syr. *ganntha* from which the Qur'anic Arabic *jannah*.

[132] See, Leo, parag. P, n. 46, 48 - ed.

[133] I.e., the Qur'an. This Qur'anic word is the Syriac *furkana*, "salvation."

[134] Jer. 31:32-34. This prophecy is with much ingenuity ascribed to Muhammad and to Islam by the Muslim apologist 'Ali b. Rabban Tabari, who concludes his statement as follows: "These meanings cannot be ascribed to any other besides the Muslims." *Kitab ad-Din*, p. 125 of my translation.

[135] Joel 2:28-29.

[136] Joel 2:30.

[137] The Cod. repeats inadvertently.

[138] Cf. Matt. 25, etc.

[139] Deut. 18:18.

[140] Lit. Ishmaelites.

[141] Cod. Joktan *ex errore*, see Gen. 25:2.

[142] Cf. I Kings 14:14; Jer. 30:10.

[143] Arab. *kaum*.

[144] Great ingenuity is shown by the Muslim apologist 'Ali b. Rabban Tabari to ascribe this prophecy to Muhammad. We will quote him here in full: "And God has not raised up a prophet from among the brethren of the children of Israel except Muhammad. The phrase, 'from the midst of them' acts as a corroboration and limitation, viz., that he will be from the children of their father and not from an avuncular relationship of his. As to Christ and the rest of the prophets, they were from the Israelites themselves; and he who believes that the Most High God has not put a distinction between the man who is from the Jews themselves and the man who is from their brethren, believes wrongly. The one who might claim that this prophecy is about the Christ would overlook two peculiarities and show ignorance in two aspects; the first is that the Christ is from the children of David, and David is from themselves and not from their brethren; the second is that he who says once that the Christ is Creator and not created, and then pretends that the Christ is like Moses, his speech is contradictory and his saying is inconsistent." *Kitab ad-Din*, pp. 621ff., below.

[145] The following pronoun and verb are probably to be used in feminine: *lah* for *lan*, *tithiledh* for *nithiledh*.

[146] Mingana gives Matt. 19:17 here as a reference, but Luke 18:19

better fits the quotation - ed.

[147] Peshitta version (Ps. 14:3).

[148] John 10:11.

[149] Luke 6:43, etc.

[150] That the line of defence of the Christians against the Muslims of the eighth and ninth centuries was to the effect that no prophet will rise after Christ is borne out by the Muslim apologist 'Ali b. Rabban Tabari, who in his *Apology* (*Kitab ad-Din*, pp. 15, 17-18 of my edition) quotes against the Christians, Acts 9:24; 13:1; 21:9, in which St. Luke speaks of prophets. On the Christian side it is well emphasized by the apologist Kindi in his *Risalah*, p. 78. - Here Timothy contradicts himself. After stating that there would be no prophecy or prophet after Jesus in paragraph AZ, Timothy now says that Elijah is yet to come. According to the book of Revelation, which was generally avoided by early Christian commentators, two prophets are still expected, one of whom may turn out to be Elijah, see Rev. 11:3-14 - ed.

[151] Mal. 4:4-6.

[152] Read *d-naphne* with *Dalath*.

[153] Luke 1:13-17.

[154] John 1:29.

[155] Matt. 3:11.

[156] Luke 3:16.

[157] Browne notes that this sentence is missing in the Arabic version of the text, see *Moslem World*, vol. 21 (1931), p. 40 - ed.

[158] Is. 53:8.

[159] Cf. Is. 51:9, Prov. 8:23-24.

[160] Cf. Ps. 2:7; 72:17; Is. 44:2, 24. This prophecy of David, "His name is before the sun" is referred to by the Muslim apologist, 'Ali b. Rabban Tabari to Muhammad himself. *Kitab ad-Din*, pp. 624, 644, below.

[161] Is. 7:14.

[162] Since the Arabic text contains the phrase "Torah and the Prophets," and all of the scripture references in this passage are from the Old Testament, Browne is of the opinion that the word "Gospel" in the place of "Prophets" represents a later substitution in the text. See *Moslem World*, vol. 21 (1931), p. 39 - ed.

[163] That the Jews and Christians are enemies and that this enmity is a guarantee of the genuineness of the Biblical text is also emphasized by Kindi in his *Risalah*, p. 150. - See also Leo, parag. K - ed.

[164] Or possibly: On another occasion.

[165] Here also the Qur'anic Arabic word *hawariyun*.

[166] Arab. *tumar*.

[167] Browne states that although the Arabic text does not contain the second day of discussion, this section in praise of Muhammad is found in the Arabic. Browne assumes that this section was probably deleted by an early Syrian, only to be added in a second day discussion by a later hand, see, *Moslem World*, vol. 21 (1931), p. 42. All things considered, Browne's arguments in support of the greater authenticity of the Arabic version can be much better applied in favor of the Syriac version, cf. pp. 163-164, above - ed.

[168] The Paradise of the Qur'an.

[169] Put a *waw* before the verb.

[170] Allusion to the Jacobites and Melkites.

[171] Cf. the medieval Latin adage: *Omne trinum perfectum*. - See al-Kindi, parag. * - ed.

[172] The Christian apologist Kindi (*Risalah*, p. 35) develops this same idea of number one and number three to his adversary 'Abdullah b. Isma'il al-Hashimi and concludes as follows: "In number (also God is one because) He embraces all sorts of numbers, and number in itself is not numbered. Number, however, is divided into an even number and an odd number, and both even and odd numbers are finally included in the number three." al-Kindi, parag. BJ.

[173] Gen. 1:26.

[174] Gen. 3:22.

[175] Gen. 9:7. The very same argument taken from the plural of majesty to prove the Trinity is used by Kindi in his *Apology* for Christianity (al-Kindi, BN sqq.), where the same Biblical verses are quoted to the same effect.

[176] Is. 6:3.

[177] Is. 48:16.

[178] Ps. 33:6 (Peshitta).

[179] Matt. 28:19.

[180] Qur'an 19:17 (read *luathah* in fem.).

[181] Qur'an 21:91 (read *bah* in fem.).

[182] The idea that there was no time in which God could have been devoid of mind and life or otherwise of word and spirit is developed also by Kindi in his *Apology* for Christianity, al-Kindi, parag. M.

[183] Put a *waw* before *d-akh*. This idea is developed by Kindi in his Apology (*Risalah*, p.42) on the same lines.

[184] Ps. 33:6 (Peshitta).

[185] Ps. 107:20.

[186] Ps. 104:30.

[187] This Qur'anic use of the plural *we* in connection with God is also taken as an argument in favor of the Trinity by the Christian apologist Kindi, parag. BO.

[188] Ps. 104:4.

[189] It would perhaps be better to put the verbs and pronouns of this sentence in plural.

[190] Ps. 148:5.

[191] The Patriarch refers here to the mysterious letters placed at the beginning of some suras of the Qur'an. It is highly interesting to learn that the Christians at the very beginning of the 'Abbasid dynasty understood them to refer to the Holy Trinity. In the Qur'an of our day the letters A.L.R. are found before suras 10, 11, 12, 14 and 15, and the letters T.S.M. before suras 24 and 28, but the three letters Y.S.M. are not found before any sura at all, but sura 36 has only the two letters Y.S. Why this last change in our modern Qur'an? There is no question of a copyist's error in the Syrian text, because the letters are in words and not written in figures only.

[192] Qur'anic expressions.

[193] Matt. 28:19.

[194] Deut. 6:4.

[195] Job 1:21.

[196] John *passim*.

[197] I Cor. 2:10.

[198] Here also the same Syriac word *milltha* means "word" and "reason." - See note 39 above - ed.

[199] Gen. 1:26.

[200] Gen. 3:22.

[201] Gen. 11:7.

[202] Qur'an 19:17. (Here also read *lwathah* in fem.)

[203] Qur'an 21:91. (Here also read *bah* in fem.)

[204] Ps. 147:5.

[205] Ps. 119:89 (Peshitta).

[206] Is. 40:8.

[207] The author is constantly playing on the Syriac word *milltha* which means both "word" and "reason."

[208] Cod. *is;* the reading *ith laih* seems, however, to be better than

ithauh. The Caliph's objection bears on the fact that since God begets, something goes out of Him and He is consequently vacuous.

[209] Ps. 89:19 (Peshitta).

[210] Hos. 12:10.

[211] Heb. 1:1.

[212] Matt. 5:45.

[213] The Caliph Mahdi himself.

[214] Harun is of course the future and famous Harun ar-Rashid. About Musa, the other son of the Caliph Mahdi, see Tabari, *Annales*, iii, 1, pp. 452-458. (see Tabari, *History*, 30:3-59 - ed.).

[215] Ps. 2:6.

[216] Ps. 2:2.

[217] Ps. 2:7.

[218] Ps. 2:12.

[219] Ps. 110:1 and 4.

[220] Ps. 110:3 (Peshitta).

[221] The Muslim apologist 'Ali b. Rabban Tabari argues that the term "lord" in Syriac *mara* is applied sometimes in the Bible to men, and therefore in Deut. 33:23; Is. 40:10-11; and 63:14-16 the word designates Muhammad. See *Kitab ad-Din*, pp. 622, 632, 644, below. The idea that the word *mara*, "Lord," refers sometimes in the Bible to men is of course taken by Tabari from Syrian commentators whom he knew perfectly.

[222] Is. 7:14; Matt. 1:23.

[223] Is. 9:6.

[224] John 5:23.

[225] John 3:36, where "believeth" for "honoreth."

[226] Qur'an 4:169. Cf. 3:40.

[227] Some of the above Biblical verses are quoted also by the Christian apologist Kindi in his *Apology*, pp. 496-498, below.

[228] Arab. *wali al-'ahd*.

[229] This expedition of Harun, son of the Caliph Mahdi, against the Byzantines led by Nicetas and governed by the Empress Irene and Leo (d. 780 - ed.) is told at some length on the Muslim side by Tabari under the year 165 A.H. (781 A. D.), *Annales*, iii. i. pp. 503-505. Cf. also the historians Ibn Khaldun, iii. p. 213, and Muqaddasi, p. 150, etc.

[230] It appears that this second conversation between Timothy and the Caliph took place in 781 A.D., while Harun, the Caliph's son, had not returned yet from his expedition against the Byzantines. The sentences used in the text do not seem to yield to another interpretation.

[231] Is. 53:2-4.

[232] Ps. 45:2.

[233] Is. 9:6.

[234] All these adjectives are known to the Muslim apologist Ibn Rabban. *Kitab ad-Din*, p. 83 of my edition.

[235] Qur'an 90:1-3, is interpreted by late Muslim commentators to mean: "I do not swear by the Lord of the land... nor by the begetter and what He begets." In the early Islam the first word was evidently read as *la-uksimu*, "I shall swear" (with an affirmation), instead of *là-uksimu*, "I shall not swear" (with a negation). I believe that the ancient reading and interpretation preserved in the present apology are more in harmony with the Qur'anic text.

[236] Qur'an 4:170. The author is using the Arabic word *istankafa* as in the Qur'an.

[237] II Sam. 7:14; Heb. 1:5.

[238] Ps. 89:27.

[239] Ps. 72:17 (Peshitta). See above, n. 160, how Ibn Rabban, the Muslim apologist refers this verse to Muhammad.

[240] Ps. 2:8-12 (Peshitta).

[241] Matt. 28:18.

[242] Luke 1:33.

[243] Dan. 7:13-14.

[244] About two words are missing in the MS.

[245] A third son of Mahdi, nicknamed ibn Ritah. See Tabari, *Annales*, iii. iii. pp. 137, 501, 522, 1035. The Cod. has erroneously 'Alah.

THE RELIGIOUS
DIALOGUE
OF JERUSALEM

In contrast to the other discussions in this collection, *The Religious Dialogue of Jerusalem* appears less to represent a historical meeting between a monk and the Amir of Jerusalem, as it claims, than to be a religious pamphlet, whose theological ideas have been cloaked in the form of a dialogue. So why have we included this dialogue? Though there are several reservations against considering it to relate a historical encounter, there is good evidence that *The Religious Dialogue* itself was written sometime in the 9th century. Moreover, the lack of authenticity concerning the setting of the discussion does not mean that the arguments it puts forward were either invalid or unknown. Indeed, at least two of the accusations against Islam which are brought up in this dialogue, and are moreover unique to it in this collection, are known to have generally caused a great deal of concern for Muslim theologians.

As Vollers mentions in the text which follows, there are actually several versions of a dialogue between a monk named Ibrahim of Tiberias and a Muslim official. In the list of Steinschneider,[1] referenced by Vollers, some compositions of the dialogue show the Muslim official to be the Caliph 'Abdul Malik b. Marwan[2] and others to be 'Abdarrahman b. 'Abdul Malik b. Sâlih.[3] Furthermore, as mentioned by Vollers, some versions of the dialogue give the location as Damascus rather than Jerusalem, and show the monk to be Nestorian rather than Jacobite.[4] As has been demonstrated with the texts of the Patriarch Timothy I's dialogue with the Caliph Mahdi, and al-Kindi's

Apology (both of Nestorian origin and apparently tampered with by Jacobites in their transmission), the text of *The Religious Dialogue* also seems to have been known and used by Jacobites and Nestorians, whose alternate claims of authorship can hardly be verified now due to the lack of genuine historical evidence.

Vollers presumes a date of 800-850 A.D. for the authorship of the version of the dialogue which was in his possession,[5] though other manuscripts of the text, i.e., those mentioning the Caliph 'Abdul Malik, would have had to have been at least 100 years older. In spite of the unlikelihood of a mere monk's dialogue with a powerful caliph escaping the notice of both Christian and Muslim historians, it would be highly improbable that copyists should have later changed the discussion with a caliph into a dialogue with an amir. Thus Vollers' version and dating for the text of the discussion appear to have substantial merit.

Theologically *The Religious Dialogue* shares suspicious similarities to the Patriarch Timothy I's discussion with the Caliph Mahdi. God's quality of being without beginning and end[6] and His not being able to exist without His Word and His Spirit[7] is used by Timothy and the monk in making a case for the Trinity. The statement that all the prophets murdered by the Jews were not outcasts,[8] and that the Jews were not stronger than Jesus[9] were used by both Timothy and the monk to counter Muslim objections with respect to the Gospel accounts of Jesus' death. The Muslim arguments that predestination would absolve the Jews of guilt in the death of Jesus are also found in John of Damascus,[10] but both Timothy and the monk respond to this by using the examples of the creation and rebellion of Satan and the creation and rebellion of Adam.[11] In defence of the Bible's not having been corrupted, Timothy, the monk, and (previous to them) Leo challenge their Muslim counterparts to produce what they consider to be the true Gospel, without result.[12] Timothy and the monk also similarly counter Muslim remarks to the effect that as the Jews rejected Jesus, the Christians rejected Muhammad.[13] In defence of praying toward the East the examples of the Garden of Eden, light and the Annunciation are used by Timothy and the monk.[14] Granted that some of the arguments may have originally been common to Jacobites and Nestorians, e.g., the reasons for praying toward the East, others, especially those concerning Islam, probably became known to both through transmission. Since the dialogue between the Patriarch Timothy I and the Caliph Mahdi seems to possess the advantage of historical authenticity, it is only logical to consider *The Religious Dialogue* as subsequent to it in time and theological content.

As already mentioned above, *The Religious Dialogue* uses some arguments which are unique to it in comparison to the other discussions in this collection. In countering the Muslim accusation that Jesus could not have been God because He prayed, the monk responds by showing that the Qur'an portrays God as praying for Muhammad.[15] The monk later asks for a general explanation for this verse,[16] but the Muslim changes the subject. In contrasting the lives of Jesus and Muhammad, the monk replies to the Muslim contention that Muhammad was also sinless, by pointing out that the Qur'an presents him as having previous and future sins.[17] Though these ideas may not have been original with the author of *The Religious Dialogue*, their widespread circulation, as we will see later, did affect several major changes to Islamic doctrine as early as the middle of the ninth century.

The monk appears to be adequately versed in the Qur'an, but his knowledge of Islamic hadith and history seem to be relatively deficient; he only twice refers to hadith.[18] With respect to the early editions of the Qur'an, the monk mentions those of 'Uthman and Hajjaj[19] without giving much further elaboration. Biblically, either the monk or later copyists appear not to have been terribly careful in their citation of verses, and we see much the same situation in al-Kindi's Apology.

With the exception of the passages which very closely resemble Timothy I's dialogue with Mahdi (see above), the polemic of the various Muslim characters in *The Religious Dialogue* is rather flat and passive. Aside from the unsupported Muslim claim that Muhammad was sinless (something which Vollers also mentions as noteworthy), the dialogue

as a whole contains no new Muslim arguments against Christianity.
Indeed, whereas the monk is granted lengthy monologues, his Muslim
antagonists rarely speak more than one or two sentences at a time;
even the Caliph Mahdi was more active in challenging the arguments
of the Patriarch Timothy I than either of the Muslim "theologians"
al-Manzûr or al-Basri are in countering those of the monk.

The manner in which the miracles and the immediate conversion of
the Amir and those present are described[20] further solidifies the suspicion that *The Religious Dialogue* does not describe a historical event.
If something of this nature had really taken place, at least the Christian
historians of that day would have certainly made mention of it.

The text which follows was first translated into German by K. Vollers
and published in *Zeitschrift für Kirchengeschichte*, 29 (1908), pp. 29-71,
197-221. The English translation of the dialogue from the German is
the work of the editor. Vollers used the mark "-?-" for passages, and
"(?)" for words, which could not be determined; words or phrases
enclosed by parentheses serve to make the text more understandable in
German or English and were employed by both Vollers and the editor.

Notes:

[1] Steinschneider, *Polem. und apolog. Literatur*, pp. 82-83.

[2] Ibid., p. 82; the codices Vatic. Karshun. 208 and Florintine Med.
68.

[3] Ibid., pp. 82-83; the codices Vatic. 99, Paris 88; and those mentioned by Vollers, Paris 215 (new catalogue) and C.V. (Codex-Vol-
lers).

[4] See references in note 2 above.

[5] Religious Dialogue, p. 279.

[6] Timothy, parags. N and O; Religious Dialogue, parag. M.

[7] Timothy, parags. EE and EL; Religious Dialogue, parag. M.

[8] Timothy, parags. BG and BH; Religious Dialogue, parag. Q.

[9] Timothy, parag. BI; Religious Dialogue, parag. S.

[10] John of Damascus, parag. Y.

[11] Timothy, parag. BK; Religious Dialogue, parag. S.

[12] Timothy, parag. AS; Religious Dialogue, parag. V; Leo, parag. AI.

[13] Timothy, parag. AS; Religious Dialogue, parag. Z.

[14] Timothy, parags. AD-AG; Religious Dialogue, parag. AA.

[15] Religious Dialogue, parag. AJ; see the reference in note 99 for the problematical explanations of later Islamic theologians.

[16] Religious Dialogue, parag. AM.

[17] Religious Dialogue, parag. AR, n. 148.

[18] Religious Dialogue, parag. AJ, n. 101; AT, n. 153.

[19] Cf. Leo, parag. S; al-Kindi, parags. CO and CP.

[20] Religious Dialogue, parags. AV and AW.

THE RELIGIOUS DIALOGUE OF JERUSALEM
by Kurt Vollers

DIALOGUE

Hypothetical Discussion
Between a JACOBITE Monk
and an Amir of Jerusalem
written c. 800 A.D.

THE FOLLOWING translated text is of a manuscript which I bought several years ago in Egypt. It is a parchment manuscript of 97 leaves (numbered 2-98), measuring 18 x 25.5 cm, and which consist of, for the most part, 21-23 lines. The beginning and end of the work are missing. An explanation concerning the history of the volume is given to us in a very early, if not the original handwriting of one of its custodians; it contains 2a: folio 2; 12a:3; 24a:4; 36a:5; 48a:6; 60a:7; but then 74a:8; further information is lacking. Moreover, we are missing all of the first folio and two leaves of the second. Nothing definite can be said about the close of the work; it is probable, however, that the volume concluded with the translated text given here. The last leaf (98) has been torn in such a manner that not much more than the right upper third of the same remains. This tear, which had been recent to the time of my purchase, seemed to have been done intentionally by the next-to-the-last seller (a Bedouin?) in order to conceal the origin of the volume.

It is a Christian-Arabic collection, which according to the script, belongs to the tenth century of our era. Briefly, its contents are as follows: 2a-4a: the close of an unknown writing, containing the names of months of the Syrian calendar with superstitious remarks; 4a: John Chrysostom on the birth of John the Baptist; 6a: the same on the beheading of the latter; 9a: a letter of Anba Musa to a brother of like office; 13b: an admonition of John Chrysostom; 17b: the sayings of holy teachers; 55a: the true Orthodox creed; 57b: Theophilus, patriarch of Alexandria on the holy mysteries which take place on great Thursday; 61b: John Chrysostom on the saying of Paul that the blood of Christ has reconciled heaven and earth; 65b: "The Story of Life" and how it should be for God's servants, the story begins: "There was a noble man in Rome named Euphemianus (Euthymianus?), who had a distinguished position among all the princes of Rome. He had 3000 slaves who wore silk and golden belts...," etc. 67a: an admonition of John Chrysostom; 69a: the story of a certain Girgis (Georgios); and the end of the work is composed of the religious dialogue which I have translated.

Even though the text in question here is also preserved in other manuscripts, my codex[1] has the distinction of being far older. Not only in that the copy is several hundred years older than any other known manuscript, but also the text is more ancient and complete. Of the manuscripts that Mor. Steinschneider[2] collected several years ago, only two of the manuscripts belonging to the Bibliothèque Nationale in Paris[3] were consulted for comparison. Here I insert the physical description of the volumes as given in the new catalogue: the signature of No. 214 has been expanded by a later writer, and reads: "the end of Ba'una 1254 M"[4] (27th of Muharram 945 AH or 25th of June 1538 A.D.). The writer calls himself Gurgi al-Ya'qubi (114a), but then later Girgis al-Ifengi (125b). The religious dialogue here forms the second part (leaves 26a-47b) of the folio collection. The other (No. 215) Volume 8°) was copied out on Wednesday, 2 Hator 1306 M (1590 A.D.), and is accompanied by a note of collation. Here our text also forms the second part (50a-82a). The relationship to C.V. can be explained briefly as follows: aside from considerable abridgements, the texts in Paris modify the older form of the disputation with respect to its rhetoric and content in a manner consistent with their age. The transmission of the texts has been loose in regard to the names of the leading personalities. The name of the author in C. V. "al-Maqdisi" is missing in the manuscripts in Paris, and apparently in all others as well. The real name of the amir " 'Abdarrahman" is distorted in the Karshuni manuscript in the Vatican and the Florentine manuscript; the writers appear to have thought of the Umayyad caliphs. The monk, who in C. V. is anonymous, is later called Abraham (Ibrahim). The Florentine manuscript gives Damascus, rather than Jerusalem, as the place of the dispute, and shows the monk to be Nestorian, whereas the C.V. places the unity of Syrian Christendom over the dogmatic schisms with good intentions. In that the interest in the theological and historical elements of the text outweighed those of its philology, I think this general description to be sufficient. In light of my work, it would be easy to show the close relationship between the texts of Rome and Florence to that of C.V.[5] I plan to handle all of the philological questions with regard to the text elsewhere.

It appears that the "Religious Dialogue" presented here lacks evidence of authenticity. While one can hardly find a single argument which speaks in its favor, the reasons for assuming that we are dealing with fictitious literature here abound. The anonymity of the composition, even as often as this appears in oriental literature, already gives us reason to consider its intent. The naming of an Arab amir, who is well-known in the history of the early caliphs, at first appears to be favorable, but after closer examination turns out to be just the opposite. We know of 'Abdarrahman b. 'Abdul Malik b. Salih, a relative of the 'Abbasids, as being in military and administrative posts shortly before and after 800 A.D. We learn nothing though, of his rule in Jerusalem, which says nothing then as to whether he had an interest in the subject at hand. In 175 AH. (791 A.D.) he arrived on Crete with his father (as it appears) for battle with the Byzantines, one year later he took over a fortress in Anatolia independently and six years later he is said to have advanced as far as Ephesus. After ten or eleven years (193 AH. = 808/9 A.D.) we find him in the easternmost part of the empire in Marw and later in Nishapur. The date of his death appears to be unknown. What should strike us most is that Christian historians who wrote in Arabic also know nothing of his stay in Jerusalem or about the "Religious Dialogue." The assumption, based on the silence of the witnesses mentioned above, that this is a fictitious work, are strengthened by other observations. The names of places and people in the dispute are, for the most part, typical, and whenever an non-captious name is used, the external evidence abandons us, as in the case of the Amir, who leads the discussion. This is true in the case "al-Mansûr (Manzûr) b. Ghatafan al-Qaisi" (C.V. 77a, l. 1), who is not insignificantly misrepresented in P. 214.

Moreover, "the monk" from Edessa is a poor representative of Christian wisdom, as is "al-Basri," who appears in C. V. 88b, of Islamic learning. In P. 215 we read "al-Bahili" for the latter, who is from the tribe of the Bahili in northeastern Arabia. This name can also produce the same state of affairs in that one of the most celebrated speakers of early Arabia, Sahban, is often thought to be from the Bahili. If we consider his tribal name in relation to the other speakers, we see the dispute wishes to show that even the most accomplished eloquence of Islam is defeated by the Christian dialectic. It is also the same in the case of description of the writer in C. V. "al-Maqdisi" (al-Muqaddasi), that is "of Jerusalem."

Otherwise there is nothing unusual about the geographical names. Jerusalem is a holy city for all three religions, Tiberias was the seat of Jewish, heathen and Christian learning and Edessa the seat of Syrian Christianity. Who could the anonymous author have been? It is certain that he was a man of exceptional intelligence and education. He knows the holy books of all three religions, i.e., both the New and Old Testament of the Bible and the Qur'an, and the dogma of his time no less. It appears that the holy traditions (hadith) were not unknown to him. The monk, his mouthpiece, receives the witness of the Amir for having a thorough knowledge of higher Arabic. He knows the unlimited appreciation of the art of rhetoric by the Arabs. He is very familiar with the impious factionalism which shook the oldest caliphates. The mention of the 'Antar legend (C.V. 77a) shows a taste for belles-lettres. If we accept the chronological data given in C.V. 76a,[6] that the Arab empire had not yet existed 200 years, we arrive at approximately the time of 'Abdarrahman, who is said to have been the cause of the dispute. I do not wish to date the author much later than 800 A.D., perhaps 850 A.D., because we find nothing which would indicate a later time period. Had he experienced the signs of the political downfall of Baghdad, which began shortly afterward, we would have expected to see an allusion to them in C.V. 75b. It is without doubt that the author was Syrian, even if "Arabized." His geographical horizon is exactly that of Aramaic Christendom: the Palestine triangle, Diar Mudar (which approximates old Osrhoene) and Babylonia (al-Iraq). Aside from Jerusalem and Tiberias in Palestine, he also mentions ar-Ramia, which appears to have its background in Egypt. Aside from Edessa in Diar Mudar, ar-Raqqa on the Euphrates is also named. In Babylonia al-Basra is mentioned only indirectly in the name of the Basran, and in addition to this the more or less "Arabized" inhabitants of the province (an-Nabat) on the other side of the eastern mountains from the ill reputed inhabitants of Khuzistan. Babylon is not described as well as the other lands. Perhaps because of this we should consider it the homeland of the author, who wanted to remain unknown. In favor of this view, one could make good the contention (at least in P. 215), as the departing victorious monk explains, that he wishes to go to Babylon, even though he lived in Edessa and sought his spiritual welfare in Jerusalem. The remarks of the Parisian manuscripts also concur with C. V. 88b that the monk comes from Syria, but lives in Babylonia.

Due to his comprehensive education mentioned above, I do not want to look for the author among the intellectually narrow-minded, physically wasting-away Syrian clergy. I am more apt to think it was an independent layman who had acquired a complete Christian and Islamic education in his time. The dispute over questions regarding the Trinity and Christology, which is unsavory for us, was for him, in that Islam presented a newly created situation, contemporary and fashionable. The beautiful pictures, with which he (C.V. 72b, 73b) portrays the development of a genuine Christian life, would perhaps permit us to think of him as a well-educated landowner who, in the quietness of country life, paid homage to the thoughts of his time. Up until the present, people of this sort are by no means rare in Egypt and Syria, but rather are more numerous than most of the fleeting visitors

279

of these regions might suppose.[7]

It can hardly be a coincidence that with respect to the layout and development of the composition, certain parallels between our Religious Dialogue and the book of Job are noticeable. In the former as well as the latter the introduction gives us the impression that we are dealing with something which has historical foundation.[8] One difference is that in the book of Job the personality who is described in the beginning remains the hero of the narration, whereas the Amir only initiates everything to later cede the main role to the monk. The three or four opponents of the hero in the book of Job are represented here by the Amir, the faqih, the Basran (or al-Bahili) and in a subordinate role the Jewish scholar. In both compositions the conclusion is not an intellectual balance, but rather is brought about by a drastic effect; here in the trials of poison and fire; in Job in the speech of God which brings all arguments to naught.

There is no need for an elaborate proof, rather it will become clear to every unbiased reader that we are dealing with a literary performance here, whose background is far superior to that of the miserable monasterial productions. Even though he was a glowing follower and a polished defender of the Christian faith, the author had observed his environment only too well, and had compared his faith with that of the lord of Islam sufficiently enough to recognize that the common foundation with regard to its physical and ethical aspects, was much broader than the confessional groups on both sides wanted to admit. This permits the monk (72a) to present Christianity in such a manner, that the Amir believes to have recognized Islam therein. The three major groups of the Syrian church of that day were summarized without showing their differences, and no authority on these dogmatic differences is allowed to speak. The monk alone is the representative of Christendom in this ethical summit; and only in this manner was it possible for him to hit his opponents, who were strengthened by his staunch determination, in his own weak point: unfruitful ritualism. The outcome would be full of suspense if Syrian Christendom had not possessed the weapons of its Hellenistic education, which were lacking in Asiatic Islam; I mean the dialectic on the good side, the hard logical method of proof, and on the bad side sophism, which always found the way out of a jam. The simpler and healthier Islamic mentality was not adequately prepared, and after a courageous fight of honor had to withdraw from the field, if it had not already admitted defeat and given up. Thus the final outcome was brought about by tactless miracles.[9]

All of the pride of Christendom, which felt itself to be mentally superior to the Islamic lords found expression (C.V. 93a). As the Basran was catching his breath in the rhetorical skirmish, the monk informed him: "... your (the Muslim's) area (of strength) is politics and party conflicts, ours is the intellect and dialectic." It will quickly be evident to anyone who knows the orient of the present, that all of the major themes, which came to the agenda in the contact between the monk and the Islamic speakers, are the same ones we still observe in such events today. The Amir is the fore-runner of the educated, benevolent and power-conscious Turkish Pasha. The reaction of the Christian cleric change according to the situation at hand; at times showing subjugation and flattery, at times obstinate and arrogant, at times showing cunning and intrigue. Moreover, some of the remarks of the monk are of the sort that they also give witness to the non-historicity of the dispute, which I have already defended above. On paper it looks good, but in reality the monk would have been punished for certain of his insolent remarks against the ruling religion, in spite of his guaranty of safety, which he essentially knows how to abuse. I find another confirmation of my view in that the author says: "in other places" (is this or that explained) a few times. Here the author betrays that the speaker would have expressed himself otherwise in Arabic.

Often the monk plays with didactic narrations of things, which in light of the context, must still be known works. It is thus in C.V. 77a, where someone unfaithfully abandons his comrade, and in 80b, in the story of the physician who drinks a poison and is not harmed. The wise instruction on how one should act before princes and leaders (C.V. 74b, 76b) is also of this sort. All told one gets the impression the we are dealing with works which came out of India or the Far East. Even with the help of my friend V. Chauvin (Liège) I was not successful in establishing their origin. I wish to leave the discussion of the Christian dogmatic views, which appear in the dispute, to those who have a competent knowledge of the oriental church. From Islamic dogma I only want to remark that the Basran describes the prophet (Muhammad) as sinless (95b).

From an exegetical standpoint there are two passages which deserve mention. They are: Luke 9:35, which the monk quotes five times C.V. 86a, 93b, 95b in the old style: "My Son and My beloved," 90b as: "My beloved Son," and 88b just: "My Son."[10] In the Parisian manuscript we find the common wording: "My beloved Son." Further P. 214 (see C.V. 94b) gives a reading which deserves attention for the much-disputed last phrase of Luke 2:14 (compare Merx on this).

None of the passages of C.V. which remain unclear are of the type so as to impair either the theological or historical meaning of the text.

THE TRANSLATION

(A) In the Name of God the merciful, the compassionate. A copy of the book of Maqdisi (Muqaddasi) of the disputation which took place in the presence of 'Abdarrahman b. 'Abdul Malik b. Sâlih al-Hâshimi concerning the religion of the Christians, and with the Jew with respect to the difference between them and the Christians.

(B) At the time of his stay in Jerusalem 'Abdarrahman b. 'Abdul Malik b. Sâlih al-Hâshimi turned his attention toward that which concerns Christianity,[11] their customs and their intelligence and their science in (various) things and their steadfastness — in spite of all of the bad consequences — in remaining in the religion of Christianity and their persistence, and their confession that God exists in three beings (persons)[12] and that the Messiah (Christ) is the Son of God. In that he was not satisfied in wanting to know more about them, he called his tutor[13] and made his thoughts known to him. The tutor answered him: "Do not wonder about this too much, that you do not trouble yourself, rather call together people from the Christians and Jews that have knowledge of your subject, and command them (?) to dispute so that you may learn what spiritual possessions they have at their disposal." 'Abdurrahman answered: "Why should I then bring the Jews here, since God has covered them with shame, and cursed and humiliated their religion?" The tutor: "It is certainly as you say with respect to them and even worse, but we want to bring a few of their men here, who understand the books of the prophets, and know their content, in order to learn whether or not the Christians have added or left out anything, and if the original is in the hands of the Jews and they insist on this, that the Christians (72a) have either added to or left out, then they, the Jews, will accuse them of lying, because they are their opponents and enemies."[14]

(C) Then 'Abdarrahman commanded to summon the Byzantine patriarchs and the bishop of the Jacobites and the bishop of the Nestorians[15] who lived there. As they stood before him then, he said to them: "I have been thinking about things concerning your religion, I have collected my thoughts and would like have an explanation about your confessions with respect to the doctrine that God exists in three substances and that Christ is the only Son of God." In that they feared this was a trick of his directed against them, they answered him discourteously and said: "You should ask those who know the books of the prophets and the Gospel thoroughly, so that you can make yourself familiar with the prophecies and their content, one after the other, in every book." Then he called those to himself who had converted to Islam through his effort, namely three of his clients, of whom two were formerly Christians, the third though, a Jew; ones who understood the scriptures and knew their contents, and (aside from these) a young physician who was with him and who was also a Christian. He commanded these then to dispute about the matters of the Christian religion in his presence, but they restrained themselves from this out of fear (?) that it might be trick of his against them.

(D) As he gazed onto the roadway outside, from the vantage point of his chair he saw a monk who appeared in that moment, as he came toward them. He commanded that he should be brought, and as the monk was there and stood before him and the greeting was finished, he

said to the monk: "What is your name, and why have you come here?"
The monk answered and said: "I belong to the servants of God and to
the children of Adam. I was born in Tiberias,[16] Syria, the mine of
science and tradition.[17] I stayed in the monastery of -?- in ar-Ruha[18] in
the land of Mudar,[19] and since I am too ill to work, I have come here
as a pilgrimage to the most holy Temple, full of a longing for God and
in the hope of attaining compassion from God, who is full of grace.
Now in this hour I find myself in a well built fortress, and in clean
(fine) company, before an illustrious prince, who shines as the moon.
May God permit him a long reign as Amir, and let him be near joy
and far from suffering!" 'Abdarrahman answered him: "Good, O
monk! You are a skillful speaker and your Arabic is excellent! You
should also know about religious matters!" The monk: "Of a truth, it
is so, but I deserve no praise in this, and before the representatives of
intelligence I need no excuse for my deficient understanding." 'Abdarrahman: "Well, which religion is the best, and which are the most
honored before God?" The monk: "Each question has its manner of
explanation and every explanation finds an answer, but this is a standpoint for which I find neither explanation nor answer, because I see
three men from the community of the Christians in your presence, who
belong together. I do not doubt that they could defend the matters
whereof you inquire. (72b) If you consider this good, permit them to
speak; let it be done so!" 'Abdarrahman: "No, I want to give you the
duty to answer this question. Where not, I will permit you to speak,
and command to answer. Above all I will grant you safety, and want to
inform you that I am one of tolerance, generosity and benevolence;
that I possess knowledge and understanding, and that I speak the
truth." The monk: "Your words have still not reached the limit of that
which you know, because the holy family belongs to you, distinguished
by nobility and insight. For you are the sons of Islam, and the light in
its darkness, the moon of its esteem and the sword of its power; in this
rests its science and the security of its (non-Muslim) subjects and the
paradise of its products. You are those who live according to its
commandments and the steadfast position of its traditions, and God in
His omnipotence said concerning religion, as I have noticed: The
distinguished religion is the one which God in His eminence has
chosen, with which He has made the angels joyful, which He has

selected for His servants, with which He has distinguished His saints and those who obey Him, through which He has given nobility to His prophets, to which His messengers (apostles) have been assigned, which He has preserved for His pure ones, through which He has brought the peoples and nations to Himself without sword, without compulsion, without awakening a desire for earthly things, in which He adorned His traditions with virtues, forbearance and forgiveness, which He made to be a science, light and example, and to be a guidance for all of His servants in all lands, in which the excellent community practices its religion, which fast continually, pray at all hours, distribute numerous alms, proclaim the verses of the truth day and night, who sacrifice themselves and their goods in obedience to God, who endure severe injustice and (even) the spilling of their own blood together with all manner of torture (just) to preserve their religion and out of love for their Lord and Creator."

(E) 'Abdarrahman: "If you know all this, why do you remain in another (religion)?" The monk: "No, truly I remain in no other, I hold fast to it, believe in it, think about it and persist in it, because I have been planted in its soil; in it my plant has sprouted and my fruit budded. I want my life to end in it; I want to return to my relatives in it, and be resurrected to my Creator." 'Abdarrahman: "Which religion have you meant, and which confession have you described?" The monk: "The religion of Christianity, the faith in Christ, the religion of truth, the community of the Christians." 'Abdarrahman: "You have canceled (all of your claims) and have accredited Christ with idolatry, because Christ[20] was neither Jew nor Christian (73a), but hanif,[21] surrendered to God (Muslim); in thought you are far from Him and He from you, because you worship Him, without God, though He was created and is the son of a created woman, the prophet of God, a humble servant of God, whom God made strong by His Word (Logos) and His Spirit, and whom He has sent as a token and as (a proof of His) mercy for humanity." The monk: "One can speak at length about what you say of Christ and our matters. A strong mind, a fine comprehension, determined ears and a broad heart are needed to understand the matter. The proof for comprehension will only be sure on the day of the resurrection, therefore hold your spirit free if you demand an

explanation for it." 'Abdarrahman: "We have never sought for this
without having opened our minds for this. This is alone the form of
Islam and the true religion, which God has chosen for His creatures; as
He said:[22] '... and whoever follows another religion aside from Islam, it
will not be accepted of him, but he will belong to the lost.' And it is
the manner of Muhammad, the seal of the prophets and the lord of the
apostles, and the community which has found mercy (in God) and
those who love their prophets and the holy family and their book,
which is the Qur'an, the bond of the compassionate ones, which He
has revealed as guidance and light and mercy, and this the apostle of
God composed (put together), who can be accused of no lie, of whom
they extol because of the acknowledgement of the unity of God in the
formulation: 'There is no god beside Allah alone, who has no partners,
and that Muhammad is His servant and apostle.' And the manner of
the ruler of the believers, to whom God has given esteem, by whom
God has stood in every respect, whom He has guarded day and night."
The monk: "If you want us to stand by you in these statements, against
our own opinions about them, — and that we should say: 'The Amir is
right' — we will do this. If you would rather that we answer, as is
proper on the grounds of the (promise of) safety granted me, we will
do this also. The matter is so: when there are two opponents and one
of them goes to the judge and accuses (the other) and weeps and
speaks as to address him with a wounded heart, and wails and appeals
to the compassion of the judge and those present. Then he pronounc-
es judgment according to that which he heard from him, not with a
decided genuine judgment. If both opponents are there though, the
vain accuser will (be brought) to dishonor, and for the wailer his
wailing will be disastrous. If every speech must find its answer (then
the following cases are possible).[23] There are those among the rhetori-
cians whose speech needs no answer. These are the best, those of
intelligence, of understanding, of excellence, of tolerance, of prudence,
of godliness, righteousness and justice. One need only hear their word
and accept their word. One need (only) ask them for the explanation
and can trust in their word. There are others for whom only the
answer is needed and the defence of his standpoint. (73b) These are
(also) the sensible, understanding, excellent, tolerant, righteous, just,
patient ones. Again there are other speakers whom one should not

only answer, but also give honor and glory, out of fear of them, out of fear of their attack. These are the possessors of sovereignty, high nobility and power, because they are hasty, easily excited and impatient in that which they hear. Finally there are those whom one need not answer at all, those whom one may scorn and treat as unimportant. These are they who are in error, unbelief and of vanity, ignorance, shame, lewdness, rebellion (against God) and are (under a) curse. But you (God grant you esteem) belong to those who are far from this last quality (group), so choose (God grant you strength) to which of the three other qualities (groups) you wish to belong, so that I can answer you accordingly. If you wish, then gather those to yourself and try (?) them with respect to fairness and -?- to them what you wish so that no harm, shame or failure come upon us."

(F) 'Abdarrahman: "How beautiful are your words and (at the same time) how dumb are your actions! This comes about in that you speak with the people of deeds with words, but in knowledge you find yourself on the standpoint of fools. Lay all jest and youthful talk aside, and trust in God to whom you will one day return; become a Muslim before me, and if you do this, I will give you a prominent position with me." Then the monk was silent and did not answer a word. 'Abdarrahman: "Why are you so silent? Are you not able to speak and to answer me? Well then, I want to excuse you (let you go)." The monk: "By God, I am not silent because I could not speak or answer, for the place to which I return is spacious, and its pasture and their feed is abundant. The roads are comfortable, and my horse is noble. The fear thereof is no error; this all with the help of God. But I find myself, thank God, in a good leading, in the light and in an undifficult position with respect to the knowledge of my own situation (my standpoint). To the contrary, I wonder about the expression of the Amir, in that he counts me with the fools, and handles the speech between ourselves as a joke and youthful talk. Why shouldn't I be so (silent) then, not because of the weakness of my arguments and not because of a deficiency of knowledge, but rather I (feel) like one of the weak animals (in the meadow), which are opposite a giant lion, who fear his attack upon them and that he will snatch one of them away, who are then restless and disconcerted, out of fear for their own lives."

287

'Abdarrahman: "You are right, (74a) in your metaphors, only that we
know the lions, who really bag their prey, but who out fear of God and
consideration for humans cause no additional damage. I am such a
lion, whose influence one fears, who has given you a great measure of
security and has made your way level with righteousness and justice.
So trust God, and leave your standpoint, because you know that that to
which I invite you, is better than that in which you find yourself. You
know this in all certainty, so do not belong to those whose hearts and
eyes are sealed,[24] so that they remain without understanding." The
monk: "Now I know that the discussion between us was a joke and
youthful talk, because you say, recognize it and in recognizing it accept
it! Yes, those whose hearts and eyes are sealed, so that they do not
believe, are the Jews, because of that which their hands have done,
whose weak-mindedness and estrangement is obvious. Also your book
gives witness against them and you see them (as being far) away from
belief. But I belong to neither these nor those, rather to the worship-
ers of Christ and His followers. (May) God let the Amir continue in
faith, and reward him with good, and forgive him, and save him from
the snare of Satan, because he (the Amir) rewarded me with good, and
has summoned me to accept his standpoint, in which he has found his
pleasure. He has shown himself excellent (against me) and has not
made me envious because of the standpoint chosen by him. Even so it
is the duty of those, who proclaim a religion and invite others to it, that
he not make them envious to share his own possessions with him, from
which he hopes for the mercy of God. But, by God, I feel no need of
that to which you call, and (I have) no desire, because I do not covet,
rather I am happy in my possession, and if I did not esteem you, then I
would lead another discussion, because God has taught us something
other than what you have said. If it appears good to you (may God
have mercy upon you) to give me liberty to go, then I will do this, for I
have no (proper) position here."

(G) 'Abdarrahman: "How amazing it is, O monk, that you shake
poisonous arrows over me, you regard my words as unimportant, seek
to refute my religion, maintain that your matters are better than mine
and then you bid me let you leave! You have been prejudiced by an
illusion. By Him who sent Muhammad with the truth, you will not

escape without becoming a Muslim; whether forced or willingly. Or you must bring me a proof from God of your statement and the statement of your comrades in faith; that He consists of three persons and that Christ is God's Son. And you must revoke your description of my religion and must answer me chapter for chapter, letter for letter, and you may not entertain any other thoughts." The monk: "Every sin finds its repentance. (74b) I expressed my unthoughtfulness before I saw a way out (to escape). If you would like to impose a penitence, I will perform it and will boast of it (or: to have your recognition). But you have sworn that I should not come away without having become a Muslim and without having brought you a confirmation from God of my statement and the statement of my comrades in faith, that He consists of three persons and that Christ is His Son, and (that) without the revocation of my description of your religion and your comrades in religion. Concerning Islam, I have no need of it, and (even) if I should be dismembered limb by limb, I would not deny Christ. What concerns my religious matters, Christ and the persons of the trinity, if I were in a position to answer you (May God grant you esteem) I would bring a clear proof in each chapter, which would put out every other light and lamp, because it belongs to that which cannot be hidden. Its manifestation cannot be thwarted by a prince or normal humans, and it is not permitted to hide it. Finally, concerning the revocation of my description of your religion and your prophet, (as you know), that one is shy before your great people, and fears your low (common) people, because of the dominion and the respect; therefore I release myself (to describe) this quality."

(H) 'Abdarrahman: "You are correct in your metaphoric speech, whoever does not have the true religion, and does not leave it (his old religion), he injures (only) himself. However, whoever has the true religion and abandons it desiring goods, worldly honor or out of the fear of being killed, he is poor in both worlds. Whoever conceals his religion is a sinner. Concerning your conversion to Islam, I do not need to maintain the demand only because I wish it. But you must absolutely clarify your statements regarding the persons of the Trinity and regarding Christ to me. What you have said, that one need fear even our small people, by my life, it is so, but it is not bad for you, because we will not give you over into the hand of a Muslim either small or great, after we have provided for your protection. So now trust in that which we have guaranteed you, and calm yourself, because I will remain to be your protector, God willing." The monk: "The wise say: 'In all (events) beware of association with princes in all circumstances,' but if you come into unfavorable contact with them, and want to come out well, then lower your gaze, so that you do not see their shamefulness, and keep their secret well in the audiences. (Always) act so, in order to flatter their desire. Be sincerely well-minded in their service. In (your) association with them remain quiet and prudent, in all of this do not think to be safe from their anger, because it is not far away. Between them is a close association: they are angry, as children they attack as an armed man.[25] I therefore absolve myself of this demand!"

(I) 'Abdurrahman: "Your words blaze within me as fire,[26] because you have said that God knows my religion and the community of my Prophet differently than my words sound! But only trust in my surety, because I have held the cords of my rule and power lax for you, and have left you open doors on all sides; so enter in where you wish in the protection of God and my person, without having to suffer harm." (75a) The monk: "The confessors of Islam disdain magnificent honor and highly treasure the trivial and disrespectful. Thus they have an oath for which there is no expiation; if they have sworn it once, they will keep their word. If you intend to keep the word of honor you gave me, then say it (this oath) or freely let me leave." As 'Abdurrahman heard this, he swore without reservation, that he would keep his word to him and that he (the monk) should not suffer ill. The monk withdrew in the same evening, and those present dispersed. But on the next day they came again, and the monk had a book with him, of which he said: "First you claim (God grant you esteem) that Christ was a hanif Muslim, and that I have ascribed polytheism to Him. Rest sure in the knowledge that all have to do with idol worship and polytheists in the name of the hanif, thus Christ, in the Gospel, ordered and declared: 'Travel not in the way of the heathen[27] (hanif), and do not enter the cities of the Samaritans!' Now your (other) claim, that I am far from myself, and that He has nothing to do with me, how is it

possible that He says to His apostles there: 'Believe on Me and on
Him who sent Me, for I am in My Father and My Father is in Me, and
whoever believes in Me, I am in him and he in Me.' (conglomerate
paraphrase) I believe on Him as the apostles believed on Him. Now,
your (further) claim, that I worship Him without God — no, truly, it is
not so, but I honor Him in God and God in Him. And He, the highly
praised, has said: 'I am in My Father, and My Father is in Me,' (John
14:10a, Diatessaron) and 'I and My Father are one.' (John 10:30,
Diatessaron) 'Whoever has seen Me and believed on Me, he has seen
My Father and believes on Him.' (John 12:44,45; John 14:9b; paraphrase) The confirmation of this is found in your expression, that God
strengthened Him with His Word (Logos) and His Spirit. Whoever
God has strengthened with His Word and Spirit,[28] how can he be just a
prophet or a simple human? He is more (than this), He is God, who
deserves worship, and (He is) the judge of humans on the day of
judgment. Your (further) claim: Whoever desires another religion
besides Islam,[29] it will not be accepted of him. Then know that your
book testifies that all creatures are Muslims, for it says:[30] 'Everything
gives itself to Him, whatever is in heaven and on the earth, willingly or
unwillingly.' (The book) doesn't give any precedence to angels or
humans over demons and animals; thereby you have rebelled against
Islam and have charged the Bedouins with a lie as they said:[31] 'We are
believers.' but you say: 'No, only Muslims, for the faith has not pene-
trated your hearts.' Your (further) claim, that your Prophet is the seal
(the last) of the prophets, [is wrong] because he is barely called a
prophet. He is but an angel (messenger), whom God chose and whom
He filled with His word together with all His sons (75b), whom He had
given Abraham, to make Ishmael into a great people. Your (further)
saying: 'the community on which God shows mercy' (is wrong), because
God includes all creations, and they doubt it not, because they see it
with their eyes, (namely) the rising of the sun and the falling of the
rain and the abundant provision of sustenance for believers and unbelievers, without showing partiality of one before another. For the next
time, however, in the future, it will be fitting (?) for his creations:
When He will forgive, it will be of His grace, when He will punish, it
will be because of the past actions and because of His righteousness
against them. Your (further) statement: 'the community of their

prophets and his family, which helped them, loves' - well, if you want, then I will tell the truth, when you know otherwise, namely that they spilled the blood of the family of their Prophet and all of his companions, who were his helpers (ansar), and that they laid their abodes and homes waste and plundered their goods! Neither you nor another can refute what I have said. Which community is more wonderful than this when they reward him, who was supposedly their prophet, and who gave them dominion over the world, and allowed them more than what is allowed others who honor God, and who permitted them to marry a number of (genuine) wives, together with the maids in their hand, be it few or many, and through whose intercession they are assured Paradise, by murdering his family! Can this (virtue) belong to any one of the peoples who are your enemies, without their being subject to two alternatives? In both instances (it is so): whether they be people, who complain about their neighbors and hold this to be allowed for him and his family; because it is not possible than that one relate it to another (?) out of fear of the power over their life and blood; thus they slander their master (leader) out of love for the goods of this world. Or it is the people of the worst evil in that they return evil for good and evil deeds for good deeds. And in both cases the proof turns itself against them in full clarity, because they, who(ever) they are, prohibit the entrance into heaven for themselves and then invite the others to their religion, although they claim what is without a doubt forbidden among them. And he who called them to this religion and has promised them paradise, the same has told them:[32] 'I and your fathers are either in the guidance (of God) or in clear error.' And he said further: [33] 'I do not know what will be done to me and you.' (76a) And further:[34] 'Except for God you have no intercessor nor helper.' And further:[35] 'Be patient, practice patience and remain steadfast and trust on God, so it will go well with you.' And:[36] 'O people, we have created you of man and wife and have made peoples and tribes of you, so that you know each other. The most reverend among you is he who is most honored before God.' Concerning your claim that God has given the ruler of the believers esteem and power, there is no honor in it, rather God has already given esteem many of the unbelievers, polytheists and idolaters of the Arabs and others and has helped them against their enemies, for He deals with His creatures as He wills. Further, the claim that he is safe day and night, if you wanted to prove this you would realize that when the ruler of the believers (God grant him strength) sleeps with his children, brethren and relatives he must fear assassination and murder. This is confirmed thereby in that although your reign has not yet existed 200 years, so many caliphs have been murdered without an enemy or opponent of Islam having done it. And what you have said about the Qur'an, well, if you (God grant you long life) ask about its destiny and remain true, you will realize that a prophet has really brought it, but that after his death many of his companions have written (it) down, among them Abu Bakr, 'Umar, 'Uthman, 'Ali, 'Abdullah b. 'Abbas and Mu'awiya b. Abu Sufyan. The revelation had come, but 'Uthman was not satisfied with it, concerning that which one had agreed, until he had written it again and had corrected it according to his own desire, leaving out whatever did not please him. Then came al-Hajjaj b. Yusuf [37] and collected the Qur'ans from all the provinces and destroyed the copies and distributed the Qur'ans corrected by him to the people. And you (God grant you esteem) know that one party of the Muslims claim that the honor of a prophet belongs to 'Ali b. Abu Talib, and this party is called: (the) children of 'Ali, (the) sons of the Prophet and (the) sons of (God's) messenger. Another party seeks to belittle Abu Bakr and 'Umar and speaks badly of them; yet another party curses 'Ali and 'Uthman in the pulpit, and a group of them curses the children of 'Abbas and approves of the spilling of their blood. And most of the Muslims curse Mu-'awiya and say to curse him is as good as the (payment) of the community tax. And most (76b) Muslims say likewise that al-Hajjaj belongs to those who inhabit hell, because he changed the Qur'an and threw down the holy house with catapults and stones and then rebuilt it. If you (God grant you esteem) think about that which I have spoken of in this area and are a just governor, you will surely recognize that a just governor cannot give preference to a book with respect to that in which often so many differences exist among a group of believers in the questions which lie between them and the family and the companions of the Prophet, and (with respect to) everything the book has suffered in changes, additions and omissions. Further, concerning the confession of God's unity, God had already revealed this to Moses and made the understanding of this expression easier for the children of Israel so that they might believe in God, that He is a God (in unity), but He had not yet said anything about the persons (of the Trinity), because they did not understand it, but rather deviated from faith daily and rebelled against Moses and Aaron and likewise against the prophets after them."

(J) The monk said further: "By God, [38] (May He grant you esteem) I have not said what I have said because Islam -?- and because it is imperfect (?), I only wish to take this position and request immunity from you, but you have frightened my efforts as a snake is afraid of heat, thus I find no way to free myself." 'Abdarrahman: "Leave the past and remain in that which concerns us now. I would like God to strike you down because of your unbelief and your bitterness against God, because you have filled up my heart with that which has disappointed (?) me entirely." The monk: You (I?) have looked at -?- -?-, the contact of whom (which?) I am ashamed, and by which I am discouraged, and a point has escaped me to which I can refer to give you honor. Because the wise man says: 'Reprove no man who guards his tongue in front of the rulers,[39] because in their presence the knee shakes, the eyes become darkened, the forelocks of the forehead stand on end, one loses his composure, the ways of escape to help one's self disappear and the tongues shutter, because God has given the princes the power to be feared, which takes away the hearts of men and gives them (the princes) majesty. But you (God grant you long life) belong to those whom God prefers in all situations of life, if you (I give myself for you) want to free me from the dispute, then do so, if you do not want to, then give me one single man with whom (I) can dispute and who (can) dispute with me in your presence; that would be more pleasant and calmer for me and would leave me my composure." 'Abdarrhman: "I concur with your wish and summon a faqih who is knowledgeable in religion and disputation."

(K) (77a) He was called al-Mansûr[40] b. Ghatafan al-Qaisi and he (the governor) summoned him, (to) where they stood and explained the preceding (discussion) to him. Then the faqih was angry about it and turned to the monk and said. "What do you want then, that you speak these worthless things, that you boast yourself with polytheism and lies against God? Retrieve your head, if you have lost it, and attend to that which you say, and know that you have met with a fire which cannot be extinguished!" The monk: "I see you are a malicious fellow, who left his comrades in the village and who drags himself out of an unpleasant situation by flight, but I notice none of the works of 'Antar[41] in you, rather I see stuttering, fearful(ness) and suspicions; that you belong to those who when evil breaks out over them cry: 'I will be quicker than they with the call of attack so that they will flee!' Trust only in God, because you have nothing to fear, but are in safety and esteem. If you are a fire, as you claim, then I am a sea whose depth is unfathomable and when one as I meet your fire, I will extinguish it." The Muslim: "God is the only strength! Tell me what you have to say of God!" The monk: "Every building in which the foundation is missing, cannot be built high and will not be stable." The Muslim: "And what is the foundation of this building?" The monk: "The books of the prophets." Now there was a Jewish man among them, who heard them speaking, because the Jews know the books of the prophets. The Jew said: "Nothing of the newer books can be accepted." The Muslim: "Neither the new, nor the old books can be accepted; we do not recognize them." Then the monk said to both of them: "If you both wanted to, you could well accept (?) it with me, but we do not want to be too rash, because the way of sophism will not achieve anything for me or you, and I bring the proof against you only -?-, because either as a whole or singly the books are -?-, since you are both my opponents." The Muslim: "Why?" The monk: "Will you not bear witness to me Mansûr that Christ is the Word (the Logos) of God and His Spirit, that He was born of Mary, the pure virgin (and that she is of the children of Israel, of the tribe of David) without intercourse, without a man's seed and that He performed signs and wonders and is ascended up into (77b) heaven and will come again and destroy the anti-Christ and that aside from Him there is no Christ?" Mansûr: "The Muslims know and say all of this of Him, as you have said." The monk: "As truly as אהיה אשר אהיה[42] is, and as truly as the ten commandments exist, which were revealed to Moses on Mount Sinai, and as truly as Moses and Aaron and all the prophets are, do you know if God prom-ised Ishmael (the ministry of) prophecy, or that out of his descendants would come a prophet or apostle, or that Muhammad is mentioned in

the Torah or in the books of the prophets?" The Jew: "As truly as
faith is, by that which you have made me swear (I bear witness) that
none of these is in the books of the prophets, rather, only that he
(Ishmael) will have dominion and power and many descendants."
'Abdarrahman: "You have lied you -?- -?- -?- May God curse you!"
The monk and Mansûr said: "(Let us) remain in the subject in which
we are."

(L) Mansûr: "You monk, from whom do you have the tradition that
God consists of three persons?" The monk: "From the trustworthy
apostles." Mansûr: "What have the apostles said about it?" The monk
(they said): "We, all peoples and nations served idols without ceasing
before the appearance of Christ, but when He appeared the apostles
believed in Him, and (when) the time of His ascension was come, He
commanded the apostles to call mankind to faith in Him and he who
was willing, to baptize (him) with water and (the) Spirit: In the name
of the Father and the Son and the Holy Spirit, the one God. As we
then viewed the day of their naming these names with shyness and
mistrust, they said: 'Do not be shy, because those are the names of the
persons of God, and it is not as you think, rather God is only recognized in the name of the Father, and the Son and the Holy Spirit, that
is, God and His Word (Logos) and His Spirit, one God and one substance, and when you say, God's Son, this is not as the relationship (?)
of a child to a father and mother, rather He appears from Him without
division,[43] He (God) is not older than His Word and His Spirit, neither
is His Spirit nor His Word younger than He, rather the Word is of
God,[44] uninterrupted Light of God's Light, truth from God, true Son of
Truth, He is His Son, begotten of Him and no one else, the only Son
of the only Father, who (otherwise) has no Son, perfect, not having
become (perfect), from a perfected, (Father) without flaw, visible God
from a visible God, benevolent Spirit from a loving God, wise God
from a compassionate Lord, praiseworthy Spirit from a God worthy of
worship; and when we say: Father (78a), it means God the Almighty,
the All-powerful, without beginning and end, without change and
without transitoriness. When we say, the Son, this means God, the
Word without beginning which has never ceased, nor ever will. When
we say Holy Spirit though, this means God the Creator, the Merciful,

the All-compassionate. But God did not make three names known all
at once, rather first through the apostles, those who followed Christ, as
they were shown and distributed (?) the books of the prophets. But
we, the followers of Christ, and His disciples have brought it to you, so
accept it, because we have sent it especially to the peoples and nations
as a sign of God's mercy for you and bring the Torah and the books of
the prophets together, because you see the confirmation of our statements in the witnesses of them, which are not dark. If not, if you do
not accept these books from us, we say to you: 'May God reward you
with good, you have become guilty!' We bring you then the Torah, the
books of the prophets and the Gospel, and the first (thing you) see
when we open the Gospel is that in the beginning of it is written: 'The
Word (the Logos) was always from earlier, and God was the Word and
the Word was always with God.' (John 1:1, slight paraphrase)[45] And
when we open the Torah, it is written in the beginning: 'And the Spirit
of God hovered (fluttered) over the water.' (Gen. 1:2b) And when we
open the Psalms, it is (written): 'Heaven and earth were created by the
Word of God and the host of the angels by His Spirit.' (Ps. 33:6) The
waters of the seas gathered themselves by the power of God and the
wisdom of His Word, the mountains and the hills solidified, and the
ground rose on the water and the shrubs and fruits began to appear,
and the darkness was contaminated, and the light of the lanterns (of
Heaven) became manifest. Thus says the prophet David: 'Why do the
peoples raise themselves and the nations show a vain striving? The
kings of the earth and their rulers gather themselves against the Lord
and His anointed One and say: "We want to put off their chains from
us and throw off their yokes." He in Heaven enthroned laughs at them
and the Father makes fun (of them).' (Ps. 2:1-4) He meant thus the
everlasting Persons (of the Trinity). Likewise says the prophet David:
'He sent His Word and healed them and freed them out of the net.'
(Ps. 107: 20) And he says further: 'I will praise the Word of God' (Ps.
56:4,10); and further: 'You were from ever, O Lord, and Your Word
was in Heaven.' (Ps. 119: 89, Peshitta) And God spoke to Moses: 'Go
to Pharaoh and say to him: "Let My Son, the first-born, Israel, free so
that he may serve me on the holy mount." ' (Ex. 4:22,23; paraphrase)
(78b). As Moses said: 'O Lord, when Pharaoh asks me of your name,
what should I tell him then? Then God answered him: 'Tell him אהיה

אֶהְיֶה אֲשֶׁר sent me.'(Ex. 3:13,14; paraphrase) And Moses said: 'Our Lord and our God is one God.' (Deut. 6:4; paraphrase) And David said: 'May God bless us, our God, the One, and we will be blessed.' (Ps. 67:6; paraphrase) And Moses says of God in the Torah: 'We will create man in our own image and our likeness.' (Gen. 1:26a) And God put it in the hearts of the angels that God is one. And the angels said: 'Today God will show us His form and likeness.' (non-Biblical) So, pay attention, O listener, to the Word of God, how it guides those with insight and understanding, and how it clarifies the three Persons and that He is but one God, when He says: 'We will create a man'; and the angels: 'Today God will show us His form (image).' When God created Adam, He set him in paradise, then as he ate from the tree, He said: 'Adam has become like one of us'(Gen. 3:22a); not (that) Adam had become one of the Persons (of the Trinity), but that another would come from Adam's race and would be God, the eternal Word, the Son of God the Father, in that He united Himself with him and rose to Heaven and sits on the throne of glory. And therefore God said: 'See, Adam has become one of us.' And Moses says of God in the Torah: 'Come We will go down (to the earth) and divide the languages.' (Gen. 11:7a) So understand, if you have insight, that the expression: 'Come We will go down' is the name of the praised and exalted, who cannot be described with rising and descending, rather He only says this that His worshippers know that He, His Word and His Spirit are one God and one substance. And Solomon, the son of David, says: 'He who created the Heaven and earth and that which is between (them), what is His name and that of His Son? If you have insight!' (Prov. 30:4; paraphrase) And Job the faithful says:[46] 'The Spirit of God created me and has taught me wisdom and insight,' (Job 33:4a and Job 32:8b) and by His Word He rules (over) everything, and by His Spirit He divides all creatures. And the prophet Jeremiah says: 'You children of Israel, do not mock my words, because I tell you nothing new of myself, but God's Spirit speaks with my tongue.' (non-Biblical) And the prophet Isaiah says: 'The reed (?) dries up, the people (?) fade,[47] and the creation changes itself, but the Word of God lasts in all eternity.' (Is. 40:7,8; paraphrase) Job the faithful says further: 'God continually spreads out the sea as land by His Word and His Spirit.' " (non-Biblical)

(M) Then 'Abdarrahman said to those around him: "Is that true what the monk has said?" They answered him: "Of course it is true, and more than this is in the books of the prophets." Then the monk said to the Jew: " What do you say, is it true, the Word of God to His prophets?" The Jew answered: "There is no one (79a) who could contradict you, that God, His Word and His Spirit are one God, (if so) it would have to be one who did not comprehend the words and did not understand the scriptures." Then the monk said to the Muslim: "What do you say then, O Muslim?" The Muslim: "We believe in God and His messengers, but we know that a father is always older than his son." The monk: "Every father is older than his son with the exception of God, the great and exalted, because He is with His Word and His Spirit, and the Word is begotten of Him without having become (someone) new thereby, and His Spirit has appeared from Him without increase, and this should not be so immense (a thing), because you also hear of a being begotten without age difference, because you know that the sun, the moon and the fire were created and that the power of their rays is from them without having become something new thereby, and their heat appears from them without increase or decrease. Their substances are not older than their rays and heat and this (heat) is not younger than the substances, and the substances are only manifest in the rays and glowing, and these again only in the substances. So is God, His Word and His Spirit, between them is no division and no mixture; He is not older than His Word and His Spirit and these are not younger than He; He is only known through His Word and His Spirit, and they only through Him. Were there a difference between God, His Word and His Spirit, He must then have beginning and end."[48] The Muslim: "You do not divide God, His Word and His Spirit then?" The monk: "No, they are not divided and are not lessened. Just as the rays and the glow do not divide from the sun, so God does not divide from His Word and His Spirit. If a division between the sun, the rays and the heat would come about, it would destroy it, and it would not be called the sun any longer.[49] Even so God would perish, if He would divide Himself from His Word and His Spirit, and He would not be God any longer, rather He would be without life and without speech,[50] because the prophet David says:

299

'Praise the Word, God!' (Ps. 56:10, paraphrase) Further he says: 'He has sent His Spirit to rebuild (?) them and to renew them.'[51] (Ps. 104:30; paraphrase). And the Son of the Father is He who knows no boundary, the Son, the Word which has neither beginning nor end, and He has revealed His Spirit as without end (79b), and without difference, both eternal, from one eternal (Father), both Creators from an uncreated and un-?- (God). And none is separable from the other as takes place in bodies because they are 'Persons,' unlimited, indescribable with qualities and bodily limitations."

(N) The Muslim: "Did not Christ say to His disciples: 'I go to My Lord and your Lord and My God and your God.'?" (John 20:17b) The monk: "You have distorted the words, Christ, the praised, only said: 'I go away to My Father and your Father and My God and your God.' The meaning of His words is this: 'My Father,' because in His mercy and His goodness to the apostles He grouped them with Himself, and in His humbleness to them He named them prophets and His brethren. From the perspective of the select humanity as the sprout of David he said: 'My God and your God.' When He says: 'My Father and your Father.' that is said as to a high lord, to say to the godly honorers of God: 'My son,' because he is near Him, not that he is (really) His son. In this manner Christ also named the apostles: the sons (children) of God; and when He says to Himself: 'My Father,' this is a statement of clarity (a confirmation), not something unthinkable, because God is His Father in truth."

(O) The Muslim: "If He is His Father, then He is not His God, and if he is His God, then He is not His Father." The monk: "In the respect in which He is His Father, He is not His God, and vice versa; He is His Father by the substance of the Word, which is begotten of Him without having become something new. He is God through His select human nature as the sprout of David, as son of the virgin Mary; we have to -?- Him, but we no longer divide the Word and the human nature after they have united themselves, as soul and body are not to be divided." The Muslim: "How does it befit God, who is powerful enough to provide recognition for His command, since He sits on the throne, that He chose this man, as you claim, in order to renew His creatures through Him?" The monk: "I am amazed at your limited knowledge of various expressions that you have Him sit down upright on the throne,[52] and then you back away from our claim that He united Himself with a man in an unlimited and indescribable manner, so bring (back) your expression again: 'He held Himself upright on the throne.' Does He say thereby that He was away from the throne for a while and then sat down upright and rigid thereon? That the throne was unoccupied by Him for a time and then (He) sat down upright and rigid thereon? For all these things represent the limited functions of a created being, give me a just answer concerning this! (80a) And know that the expression, 'He sat Himself down upright,' requires a 'from' and a 'to,' just as you have expressed it, that is, as a rider. Every rider is a limited being and that where upon he rides is alone stronger and more powerful than he. Do not describe God in such a manner, but rather, return back to your expression that He has power to carry out His matters (commands). He is certainly Almighty and All-powerful, but also invisible, indescribable, incomprehensible and unlimited. No created being can hear His Word or look at Him, as Moses and the other prophets and apostles received knowledge. When God saw that the hearts of mankind were corrupted and their thoughts were increasingly evil without intermission in contradiction of the truth, and when he summoned and scolded them and had to call them to believe on Him, in that God the Father revealed His Word in becoming flesh and resemblance to God in all long-suffering so as not to force mankind to believe, since He would reward and punish them in all righteousness. Thus Christ, the Word of God, was an example to them in honoring God and a leader, who was to lead them so that they should let Him lead them out of error to belief on the three eternal Persons. This Christ led those who honor God (as a shepherd) in His patience, generosity and compassion and saved them out of error, idolatry and the honor (worship) of the images of the devil and led them to the truth. Since God had not revealed the Word in His own substance and did not change Himself concerning His immortality and did not go from one place to another where He had not been before and the throne did not remove itself from Him, neither did the heaven and earth and that which is between them and (that which is) underneath the ground and above, outside of, not inside of, inside of, not outside of, indescribable, unbounded, unlimited, unmixed and undivided. Then His nature unified itself with mankind, without bounds, without limits, without division, without mixing; only by love, power and esteem."

(P) The Muslim: "But mankind showed Christ no honor, rather subjected Him to the humiliation of the cross, as you confess." The monk: "No, certainly only those humans accepted Him whom God had chosen and those on whom He had mercy and those He had made of His group. Those who accepted Him and believe on Him are more numerous than the unbelievers. So do not say: 'Mankind did not accept Him, rather those who did not accept Him and subjected Him to the previously mentioned humiliation, they are the Jews, the accursed. So look at the deep economy of God, the highly praised, because He made known His signs and wonders, because He did not dare to call the humans to His matters without bringing the argument of His signs and wonders against them. So He called all of mankind to believe in Himself and that He is the Son of the living God. Because of their extraordinary evil and hardness of heart and stubbornness the children of Israel did not receive His Word, did not listen to Him and did not consider that which He had done for them and revealed to them. (They) did not turn to that which is in the scriptures so that they could believe in Him, and all this (took such a course), not because He was incapable of holding His own, or to punish them and not because of His weakness to do it, rather He in His patience gave them a fixed time, and because He would practice a certain economy with them and His believers, He did not hurry this with them, because they would not escape Him (anyway). But Christ turned His majesty into shame at the time of His crucifixion and resurrection on the third day after His death, and they did not attain their goal (?) with that (by) which they sinned against Him and dealt with Him in enmity. Also the people coveted nothing of belief from Him, but the believers were increasingly joyful and the unbelievers increasingly alienated and sadder. And the King (God) says that He has not done this to them because He was weak towards them, but because He wanted to grant His matters more esteem and reveal His power even more, that He provided them with a fixed time thereby and endured their foolishness in many respects. I want to relate a parable here if you want to accept the contents of the scriptures. One says there was a man who gave out that he was a physician and that he had a medicine which he asked the people to take. He used to say that if a person took this medicine, that not even poison would harm him. Many people passed by him and held him for a liar and said: 'What you praise as your medicine is not right, no one would have the courage to take deadly poison in the hope of receiving an advantage and salvation from this medicine, unless he had previous experience with your medicine. But you understand this best and have the most trust, so you take the deadly poison, drink it, and when it begins to take effect, then try your medicine to see whether others believe you.' Then the physician said: 'We will make a contract among us, bring me a deadly poison so that I (can) drink it; and if I die from it, then you are not guilty of my death. If I am healed by my medicine, then I can do with you as I will.' They agree with this and brought him a poison, he drank it, but the poison did not harm him. Under which circumstances was the physician more credible for you? As he took the poison and drank it, or if he had held back and not have taken it? I do not think anyone doubts that he was stronger and more awed after taking the poison. That means if he had not taken it, they would have (81a) doubted his medicine and would have ridiculed him. Thus we say when the Jews wanted to crucify Christ our Lord, He did not fail among them, and He did not avoid and keep away from them. It is the custom of rulers and governors to subject their enemies to crucifixion and being put to death. When the unbelievers had vented their anger on Christ, and thought that He had disappeared from them and would not return, He rose from the grave by the power of His deity and conquered death through His death without having something which His enemies had done to Him harm Him. But if Christ had not tolerated that which was done to Him for the sake of mankind, from being struck by Satan, and if He had avoided death and crucifixion, then He would not have been able to proclaim these miracles of Himself, and He would have made lies of the prophecies of the prophets, that which they had predicted of Him. But by this He was able to unify several things, one of which is that He confirmed the word of the prophets, secondly, that He conquered death without being conquered by its power, while I must -?- Him as all the other dead, and the matter of the resurrection was made clear, third and fourth, that it is a wonderful thing when men relate that a man was killed and crucified is -?- living God, living without end."

(Q) The Muslim: "Christ would have had more esteem with God if He had not been delivered into the hands of Jews that they should kill Him. Do not insult Christ so, and do not make Him into an outcast!" The monk: "You also know that the Jews killed the prophets and the apostles in various manner, and if because of their being killed these are outcasts, as you maintain, then all of the prophets murdered by the Jews are outcasts![53] But God would guard against any of the prophets being considered an outcast by God. So is it with the matter of the prophets. But concerning Christ, the Jews crucified Him according to His human nature, but could not realize their intents against Him with respect to destruction (?), for He delivered Himself into their hands. If He had not willed that this take place and that they do to Him what they did, then so would this have come about according to His will. And He said many a time before He was crucified: 'I am come to give My life and to receive it (again), but none can take it from Me.' (John 10:18; paraphrase) And He taught us that He endured this only according to His inclination and will and that this did not occur because of His weakness or incapability, or because the Jews were too powerful for Him. The proof thereof can be found as He hung on the cross and (81b) the sun and the moon were darkened over the whole world and the earth shook and the mountains split and the light of the sun changed to darkness and the light of the moon shone as blood and the graves opened themselves and the dead therein were resurrected. He who could bring about such deeds, could He be too weak to turn back His enemies and rescue His (own) life out of their hands? No, but He tolerated all of this only by His long-suffering to save the world from the -?- of death."

(R) The Muslim: "God forbid, that Christ should have been crucified, we only wish to oblige and say: 'If He was crucified with His (own) approval and willingly, as you say, then the Jews should not be blamed, because they only carried out what He wanted and willed.'"[54] The monk: "They committed all the more and were even more wanton, because they did not know that after their murder of Him, He would be resurrected and would attain this high position, rather they thought to destroy Him by murdering Him and to extinguish the remembrance of Him. Through this they earned God's wrath and curse. Your book also bears witness that they intended to kill Him, and likewise (about) His death and ascension to Heaven when it says:[55] 'O Jesus, son of Mary, I bring you to Me and raise you to Me and give you superiority over the unbelievers until the Day of Judgment.' "

(S) The Muslim: "Leave off with these words! Did Christ want to be crucified or not? If Christ wanted this, then the Jews only fulfilled His desire and are not outcasts then. If He did not want to be crucified, then He was too weak and the Jews were stronger then He.[56] How could He wish to be called God if He could not once save His life from the cross?" The monk: "Which point is better on which to hold fast? When God created the devil and took (him) from the angels, did He want him to be Satan or not? If He wanted this, then Satan only did God a favor when He became Satan, and (therefore) does not deserve reprimand. If God had not wanted him to become Satan, then the will of Satan conquered the will of God, and He could not wish to be called God, because the will of the accursed was stronger than the will of God. And I will present another example: Did God want to (82a) drive Adam out of Paradise or not? If He did not want to, then God was too weak and Adam too strong for Him, and He (would) not deserve to be called God anymore. If He wanted to have Adam (driven) out, then Adam did not fail if he unwillingly left Paradise only to fulfill God's will.[57] So it is with your question, only we make known to you that as God did not expel (Adam) of His deity, majesty and power, what Adam and the devil did in their obstinacy and insubordination against His command, He should not be thought of as weak, because He did not rejoice over their sins, but they sinned (of themselves). Adam and the devil are not free from guilt thereby, because God rejoiced over (these things), I mean over the devil's fall from Heaven and over Adam's leaving Paradise, because they did not sin in order to make God happy, but to follow their (sinful) desire and out of (their) joy in insubordination. Likewise the sacrilege and crucifixion of the Jews does not force Christ out of His deity. He should not be considered weak because the Jews were so sacrilegious, rather Christ was to be crucified and die to save all mankind from the sin of Adam, which had brought death upon him and them."

(T) The Muslim: "If you only think that Christ is God because He resurrected the dead, Elisha, Ezekiel and the other prophets did the same with God's permission, so they would have to be called God and be worshipped." The monk: "We do not consider Christ God only because He resurrected the dead, but because He told us that He is the Son of the living God, the Light of the world and the Good Shepherd and that He will resurrect the dead again and that He is the Judge of all mankind, who comes to everyone who wills and turns from his sins, and that He punishes those who persist in their sins, because He did signs and wonders by His irresistible Word, without being asked (to). Whoever has done such wonderful things, because He is God, His command must be accepted, one must hear Him and He may not be measured against others. But what you have said of the things of the prophets, we do not deny it, but what a difference there is between the works of the prophets and those of Christ, because each single prophet, when he wanted to perform a deed (wonder), used to fast and entreated God more than usual for this and prayed. He first performed his intercession then and requested that which he wanted. But Christ did not stand on this level, but rather at all times, whether in the bazaars or somewhere else, He performed signs and wonders of Himself, without especially having to fast, pray or entreat for them. But the prophets did not have the authority to do signs at any time they wanted to without asking (God), and they carried out the mysterious (hidden) only when God commanded them, in that they made them known to mankind; but Christ raised the dead, opened the eyes of the blind, gave hearing to the deaf, healed the sick, cleansed the leper, cured infirmities, satisfied many people with little food by His power, made known the secret thoughts of many people, spoke out the hidden and also proclaimed that which was in the future. If the prophets had said (it), may God reward us, it would have sounded as if the people had accepted their word due to the excellent qualities which they had shown that day. But they did not use to lie and measure themselves (by) that which was not right, rather they said: 'We are only God's servants.' But Christ said: 'I am God's Son,'thus He said that truth and the prophets also."

(U) The Muslim: "How can you be so insolent to God and say that
Christ is God's Son and (yet) was crucified? Do you not realize that
God gave over His Son to the crucifixion, but that -?- something was
shown them -?-."[58] The monk: "How can you just admit that the Jews
believed to have crucified Christ and yet you say that this was only
shown them and that another than He was crucified? Admit it, the
matter was unclear to the sacrilegious Jews and not the less to the
apostles, rather the error was of God! May God forbid! He does not
lead His servants into error! And further, you correct (?) the apostles,
because they have borne witness that they looked at Christ crucified,
and He died and was laid in the grave for three days, then He rose
again and came to them several times after His resurrection and spoke
to them; He remained with them for 40 days, then He ascended up to
Heaven before their eyes (83a) as they looked upwards. How could
this have (only) been shown them? And how can you accuse the
apostles of lies and your prophets and the others of the Jewish scholars
who testify of them that they were God's helpers and that they only
spoke what God gave them? Do you think that God made them
believe worthless things to lead His servants into error? God forbid
that something of the such take place! We do not accuse the apostles
of the Messiah of lying." The Muslim: "I do not wish to belittle Christ
and (do) not (want) to accuse the apostles of lying, to the contrary, I
wish to give Him and them preference, because it is worthier of Him
and them than what you say!" The monk: "The case is just the opposite, for when you make the king and the lord of a man and take the
noble man from his father, then you have done the utmost in belittling,
because you call Christ, who is highly testified of, a wretched human
(and say) that He is not the Son of God, and you count the word of
the prophets as a lie, which testify this of Him."

(V) The Muslim: "What you say, you report only out of your Gospel
and out of your new books; but the first genuine Gospel is among us,
we have received it from our Prophet, and this is in contradiction with
that which is in your hands, for John and his comrades have edited the
Gospel after the ascension of Christ to Heaven and arranged that

which is in your hands as they themselves wished; thus our Prophet narrated (it) to us." The monk: "If the matter is so as was said, then I call for the genuine books and the genuine Gospel, which is among you, so that we may compare it with ours, thus it must be clear to you what we have distorted. Then we will accept the genuine and do away with the distortion.[59] But how can you maintain that your Prophet proclaimed such a thing, since he also testified of them that they were the helpers of God to whom He revealed? Thus he says in your book, '...but if you doubt that which I tell you, then ask those who have received a revelation before you.'[60] If the book and all the other books were distorted, then God could not speak in them as you maintain, for you doubt that which lies before you. So turn back to Him and to (83b) those who have received a revealed book so that it will become clear to you and them what it is about and that which you doubt. Further, how did the princes, the philosophers and all the nations since John and his comrades accept the book which you maintain has been distorted and contains polytheism? Will you maintain that they let themselves be led by the desire for their goods, the fear of their troops, the fear of their swords or by the alleviation of their ordinances and the comfort of their law and tradition? If you maintain these, you and all other humans know that the apostles had no riches and that they were examples of austerity, humility and the toleration of disgrace and that they did not acquire any goods. If any of them had something, he distributed it to the poor. If you recognize all these things in their preaching, which are necessary for accepting the lie, by means by which people try to win liars over to their side, then these people at that time had to be as they called the peoples to their religion, their book and their God, shown in a -?- power on that day and magnificent things which urged (?) these people to be the object of their preaching, so that they recognized the truth, wisdom and genuineness of their prophecy about God's being, and to let themselves be led to their preaching. For you know with all certainty that the kings and other people did not accept this Gospel out of a desire for their goods and not out of the fear of the sword and not out of the fear of their greater numbers and not out of an inclination towards an alleviation of their ordinances, rather they bowed down and humbled themselves only to the object of preaching due to the extraordinary things which were revealed by them and because they performed such miracles as the resuscitation of the dead, the casting out of demons from the possessed, the opening of the eyes of the blind, the cleansing of leprosy and the healing of all illnesses and all infirmities. If not, then have insight, you, who produce lies against the true religion of God and blaspheme the Gospel, in that you explain the Gospel thus, of which you maintain it has been distorted from the original, see which of the two is nearer righteousness as the text demands, which has stricter regulations and which ordinances are harder to fulfill: the one in our hands or the one in your hand? I think that you will only speak that truth and say that that which (84a) is in our hands has stricter regulations and harder ordinances, for example continual fasting, praying, alms, abstention from all pleasures such as eating, drinking and intercourse, and the distribution of goods to the poor. And you know the superiority of that which is in our hands above that which you and others maintain is in your hands, and this is not so very wonderful, because God proclaimed in all the books of the prophets and apostles, that out of the loins of David and the seed of Abraham a man and a ruler of Israel should go forth out of the loins of David as a Savior of mankind from error and unbelief. Mankind has always hoped for this Deliverer from generation to generation, from one epoch to the next and waited on the days in which He was born until the times were fulfilled. As He appeared and performed the signs and wonders, He then fulfilled only the books of the prophets and verified their word. But you have remained unbelievers and have not found pleasure in Him. Yes, you have even offered resistance to His believers and have gone so far as to -?- and maintain of Him that your Prophet enjoys more esteem with God than He!"

(W) The Muslim: "Does not our Prophet have more esteem with God than Adam and his descendants?" The monk: "No, certainly not, I do not know thereof, but that the Heaven is higher than the earth and His power is nobler and honored by God than the inhabitants of the earth, and I know that Christ is the highest in Heaven and your Prophet as all the other prophets under the earth in dust, not less that Heaven is the throne of God and His domicile and that Christ sits on the throne of glory at God's right (hand) over the angels, as our Lord Christ (Himself) has said. How can he who is under the earth be more powerful and honored than He who is in Heaven on the throne of glory at the right (hand) of God?" The Muslim: "Have you not maintained that Christ knows the hidden and inner (thoughts) of the heart? Why did He deny this then as His disciples asked Him when the Day of Resurrection would be? He said to them: 'No one knows that but *God* alone!' " The monk: "(84b) Most of all (you should) know that you have taken this word from Christ. He, however, said to them that no man knows the day but only the *Father*, not even the Son knows it; whomever the Father wants to make it known, He does it. So He has ascribed this knowledge to the Father, for it was not useful that He know the time, therefore He answered the question thus. Then He said: 'And whomever the Father wants to make this known, He does it.' Now concerning His word, that this knowledge is with the Father, this is the truth, but this does not exclude the Son from the knowledge of the Day of Judgment, in that He and the Father are one in substance, power and force, and everything which is created is created by His Word, for Christ has said that He and the Father are one and that He is in the Father and His Father is in Him and that He will be Judge on the Day of Judgment. How could He be this if He did not even know the day? He just did not want to give the apostles knowledge thereof, because He would scare them and the other believers, if they would wait for Him in knowledge thereof, and their lives would not be joyful any longer."

(X) The Muslim: "We do not accept these words from you without the surety of them being made clear to us." The monk: "Tell me about the place where God told Adam, when he sinned against Him and was in Paradise and knew the appearance of his -?- and hid himself, and He called him as Moses says of God in the Torah: 'Adam, Adam, where are you?' Then Adam said: 'Here I am!'[61] Did not God know in this case that he was there or what?" The Muslim: "Of course He knew where he was." The monk: "Why did He ask of that which He knew? That is a complement to the hindrance of Christ to let the apostles know when the resurrection would be; and how did He not know when it would be? Since He made known the signs and miracles which would precede these days, so that we would see all with our eyes, which He said would come."

(Y) 'Abdarrahman: "O monk, what is the Paraclete?"[62] The monk:
"The Spirit of Light, deity, knowledge, insight, nobility, wisdom, it is
God according to substance, without plural, in appearance coming out
of, flowing out of the Father, out of God, and with this (85a) special
quality I mean the Spirit, as our Lord Christ has said." 'Abdarrahman:
"And what does Christ say about the Spirit?" The monk: "Christ said
to His disciples: 'I go to My Father who has sent Me, to send you the
Paraclete, who comes out of the Father. The children of the world
cannot accept Him, but He is with you and among you, who knows
everything of the divine economy, He will remind you of everything
which I have taught you, He will teach you that which is hidden and
will bear witness of Me, as I of Him, and you will afterwards bear
witness to the believers of that which I have taught you.' "[63] 'Abdarrahman: "He meant only our Prophet thereby." The monk: "The
Paraclete is the Spirit of God, the Holy Spirit, uncreated, unlimited, as
God is also unlimited, invisible, indescribable in human qualities. He
is in Heaven, knows the secret and hidden and is the Paraclete, as
Christ said to the apostles, 'He will be with you' and He was with them
and taught them as He came upon them ten days after the ascension of
Christ into Heaven, then He taught the disciples that God, even as one
according to substance, is of three persons as Christ also taught, and
the Paraclete performed miracles through the apostles. And in the
Torah He said by the tongue of Moses in the mention of the creation
of beings that the Spirit of God hovered (fluttered) over the waters
before time, and the prophets and apostles also testified of Him that
He is the creator of everything. It is not so with your Prophet; he is
the son of 'Abdullah b. 'Abdul Muttalib and his mother is Amina the
daughter of Wahb b. 'Abdmanaf. He was born 600 years after Christ
and His ascension to Heaven, is created, the son of a created being, his
is not reckoned with the three Persons (the Trinity), because there is
only one God, one Creator, one worthy of praise, he did not belong to
the apostles, mankind saw him, he married, was a father, did not know
the hidden, as he also testifies of himself, because he said he did not
know what would become of himself and his followers.[64] But Christ
said: 'I send you the Paraclete, who comes from the Father,' if your

Prophet (85b) is the Paraclete, then he is sent by Christ, and that the
Father of Christ has sent Him, how can your Prophet be the Paraclete,
because he gave no sign of himself and manifested no miracles. But if
you admit that he was sent by Christ, whom He sent, then there is a
certain connection with a part of the question."

(Z) 'Abdarrahman: "No, our Prophet is the Paraclete, he is ruler, but
you do not believe in him, (just) as the Jews did with Christ."[65] The
monk: "The Jews do not believe on Christ, even though the Torah and
all the books of the prophets speak thereof, and even though the truth
and light shine bright in the testimonies and confirmation of our word,
at the present though, the unbelievers are more numerous than the
believers, and the Jews have loaded the curse and the wrath of God
upon themselves thereby. Concerning ourselves, we strive against your
Prophet because we do not find him mentioned in the books and (do
not find) any witnesses for him. If we had found him mentioned, then
we would want to distance ourselves from him and say: 'He has not
come, he who has come, as the Jews, may the curse and shame be
upon them,[66] say of Christ that He has not come yet, rather will yet
come."

(AA) 'Abdarrahman: "What is the reason that the Christians turn to
the East when they pray, while Christ turned to Jerusalem to do
this?"[67] The monk: "There are six reasons (points). First, because
God is light, and it is fitting to hold the direction toward Him from
whom light comes. Secondly, the Paradise from which Adam was
driven out is in the East, and we hope to return to that place from
which our father was driven out, to our Lord Christ. Thirdly, as
Gabriel appeared to Mary and announced the birth of Christ to her, he
only appeared to her from the East. Fourthly, When our Lord Christ
comes at the end of the days, to resurrect the dead and retrieve the
dead from the graves, He will only come from the East. Fifthly, God
said to the priests of the children of Israel: 'Have the eastern gate
blocked, because the God of Israel will go in and out of it.'[68] And
(sixthly) the prophet David said in one of his Psalms: 'Praise the
highest in heaven, because He lets His voice sound loudly from the
East.' "[69]

(AB) 'Abdarrahman:[70] "O monk, is baptism only a custom or an unbreakable (86a) obligation?" The monk: "No, it is obligatory and (an) unbreakable duty, for it is a light whereby hearts approach (to God) and the soul receives peace. It is so that our Lord Christ was born in two manners, firstly of His mother Mary, secondly by baptism in the waters of the Jordan by John the Baptist. As He came out of the water, a cloud overshadowed Him and He heard a voice say: 'This is My Son and My beloved[71] in whom I have joy: obey Him!' Thus He was born for the second time in this manner after the birth from the mother, and he who is born the second time in baptism is spiritual and thereby Christ lets His light illuminate mankind. Just as the pearl also has two beginnings, the one out of the sea and the other out of the mussel, which is encapsulated by water, and whoever attacks it does not know what is in the mussel until he investigates it more exactly and the light of the pearl shines on him. So it is also with the Christian. When he is born of flesh and blood, he does not yet possess the light and the luster, rather like a strong fortress there is a wall of division between him and the believers of Christ. If he has received baptism though, he takes possession of grace and binds himself to the light and love of the believers of Christ."

(AC) Now one of the Bedouins was in the assembly, who was a Christian who had accepted Islam. As he heard the words of the monk and the Muslim and that they were not nearing each other, he said to the monk: "You Christians say monstrous things when you maintain that the eternal Word of God lives in Christ inwardly and outwardly and that Jesus was crucified on the stake and was pierced through with a lance and that His hands and feet were fastened with nails. Do you then say that the Word of God was opened with the piercing of the lance and the nails being driven in, or that the Word (did not)[72] suffer in the pain and anguish of death as Jesus suffered? You are liars in both cases, because you maintain that the 'Word' lived in Jesus, outwardly and inwardly, undivided." The monk: "I will make known to you how it stands correctly, how the Word of God lived in Jesus outwardly (86b) and inwardly, without participating in the pain and anguish as the body of Jesus. Tell me rather how it is that the breathing in the spirit (breath of life) into the embryo in the womb occurs without the mother feeling pain or knowing thereof."[73] The Muslim: "God sends an angel to her with the spiritual breath of life for the child and breathes it into him (the child) in the womb." The monk: "Is the angel created and unlimited or not?" The Muslim: "Of course, he is created and limited." The monk: "Does everyone have such an angel with him who is assigned to him to bring him to God on the Last Day or not?" The Muslim: "Of course, he is assigned to him to bring him to God on the Last Day." The monk: "We are with many together in this assembly and have our angels with us. If this assembly would fall upon us to kill us, who would take our souls then?" The Muslim: "The angel assigned to us." The monk: "If the Amir would become wroth with one of us and commanded that he be boiled in oil and ordered a large kettle and had him, with whom he was angry, lie in the kettle and then (had) oil poured over him so that it covered him, closed the kettle and had it soldered closed with lead, would the angel assigned to him remain in the kettle, or go out?" The Muslim: "No, he would remain with him inside and outside and would take his spirit with him." The monk: "How is that possible since he is created and limited? Do you maintain that the angel is outside of the womb and then, when the child comes out of the mother breathes the breath of life into him, or that he clings to the child in the narrowness (of the womb) and in the kettle (for the man)? Likewise you maintain that the angel who was with us and who is assigned to us leaves us when the house caves in and takes our souls to themselves at death, or that they are with us at all times, come what may, and that everything befalls them as it befalls us, since they are created and limited and are bound to us. Likewise (do you maintain) that (87a) the angel, leaves him who is boiled in oil, and when he (the man) dies and the kettle is opened, takes his spirit to himself, or that he participates in all the pain and anguish in the death of the one boiled, since he is bounded and created?" The Muslim: "God created the angel as a spiritual being, indescribable and unlimited, He creates what He wishes." The monk: "You must admit though that two cases are impossible here. Either the angels leave people at the coming of pain, or they share in them." The Muslim: "No. I maintain that the angels are with people, unlimited, indivisible and uncombined, but they do not share in the sufferings and joy of mankind." The monk: "You have admitted that angels are created and limited and (when they are) with people (they are) unlimited and indescribable, and that they do not share in the sufferings and joys of mankind. How can you force me to describe the eternal Creator, who has created everything by His power, who is unlimited and indescribable, who cannot be comprehended and who is without peer? Concerning your words, that He shared in the pain of the lance and the incision (?) of the iron weapon, thus (I note): What do you say about the young camel which one brings and makes to kneel in the sun and slaughters, then brings a lance and dismembers its limbs. Did the piercing of the lance and the dismembering of the young animal push itself between the sun, its movement and its power (influence), or was something of the sun also dismembered that part of it fell off. Did the sun also have to suffer in the cooking kettle as it (the flesh) did?" The Muslim: "No, truthfully it (the sun) does not suffer by any means the same as the sacrifice and as the bottom of the cooking kettle does." The monk: "One of the two cannot be refused, either the sun pulls itself back from the sacrifice when (it is) slaughtered and dismembered, or the sun suffers the same as the sacrifice and as the bottom of the cooking kettle." The Muslim: "What you say delves into that which is undefinable. The sun does not suffer as the young animal and just as little as the bottom (of the kettle)." The monk: "I know for certain that as the angel is unlimited, undivided, uncombined and does not suffer as people do, that it is also the same with the eternal creative Word of God, who unified Himself with the chosen man of the body of the virgin Mary and (with Him) has become one Christ, and at the time of His birth (He) was in the body of His mother and He shared in the suffering (87b) and joy and hung on the cross and was pierced with the lance and was cut by the nails and lay in the grave, and yet (as Christ) was undivided, uncombined and without material limitation and as Word did not share in suffering and joy, God the worshipped and highly named!"

(AD) The Muslim: "What does this mean that the Christians do not wash themselves at every prayer and do not cleanse themselves from the ritual impurity?"[74] The monk: "What do you understand to be impurity?" The Muslim: "By pollution or by the intercourse of a man with his wife or maid servant." The monk: "Has God dictated that these two things make one impure?" The Muslim: "No, but He has commanded us to cleanse ourselves from every impurity and to wash ourselves at the time of prayer." The monk: "But this is no impurity, and the confirmation thereof is that God said: 'The community of the believers is sanctified before God,'[75] thus pollution is no sin or shame for man, rather impurity is in the committing of sins. But we do not want to leave (?) you, the ones who most transgress in this matter, in blindness (darkness) concerning that which is more distinguished with you: faith or Islam." The Muslim: "Faith is Islam and Islam is faith, the two are inseparably bound together," The monk: "Your book refutes you, for it says:[76] 'Fear God with genuine fear and die not without having become a Muslim.' Now I say: 'O Prophet of God, who is strong enough for this?' Then he told you:[77] 'Fear God as best as you can,' thereby he has taught you that faith is stronger and harder than Islam, and since you are not strong enough in faith, he commanded Islam for you. Likewise, because you are not strong enough in the washings of faith, you command the rinsing with water." The Muslim: "Independent of water, what is the washing of faith?" The monk: "So says the Word of truth concerning the washing of faith: it is the abandoning of prostitution, that you do not commit intercourse which is forbidden, and the washing of the hands is the (abstention) from theft, and the washing of mouth should mean from lies, and the washing of the face should mean to protect one's gaze from the forbidden, and the washing of the ears should mean to deafen them to the speech of the ridiculer, and the rubbing of the face is as collecting one's spirit before God, and the washing of the feet is to restraint them that they not walk in the way of wantonness, and the washing of sexual impurity means the genuine repentance after committing unchastity and deceit; that is the washing and cleansing of Faith!"

(AE) The Muslim: "What a glorious explanation, it is true! But God designated water for purifying (88a), for it cleanses people and opens the gates of prayer and brings (us) nearer to God." The monk: "And what do you say about a group of Muslims who went on a journey and rode for three days into the desert, so that the ritual washing must end, and some of them were ritually impure, because they had no water but that which they needed for their existence;[78] and what should they do at the time of prayer?" The Muslim: "Whoever of them wanted to perform his need, should take a stone to clean himself -?-,[79] he should rub himself with sand, and he who was overcome by sexual impurity, he could also rub himself with earth." The monk: "And when God brought them out of the desert and they came to water and washed themselves and -?-[80] would they have the duty to perform each prayer again which they performed in the desert or not?" The Muslim: "They would not be obligated thereto, for God had already accepted their prayers and their matter was taken care of, just as God wished it." The monk: "I do not comprehend (how) the water has a preference, as you say, that it opens the gates of prayer and brings (us) nearer to God, since earth and stone with which one rubs himself also take the place thereof. Do not boast against us with the ablution, because water does not bring the wanton nearer to God, neither do the earth and stones separate the believers from Him."

(AF) 'Abdarrahman: "O monk, Do you not say that Christ was created, the son of a created (being)?" The monk: "According to the substance of His Father, He is eternal Creator, but according to the substance of His mother, He was born, the son of a created (being), but (He is) one Christ, without division according to the unification of the divinity with humanity." 'Abdarrahman: "Must not one born, the son of a created (being), kneel down in prayer?" The monk: "I find a community which knelt down before a created (being), even though they were esteemed by God, and I will bring (my proof) here (to the point) to describe them. They (said): 'We do not want to kneel down before a created (being)'; then God was angry with it and it was the most wretched being before Him." 'Abdarrahman: "Which of the two communities do you mean?" The monk: "Do you not confess that it says in your book:[81] 'When we said to the angels: 'Fall down before Adam,' then they fell down, with the exception of the devil (Iblis, diabolos), for he refused and showed himself to be full of pride and (therewith) belonged to the liars.' " The Muslim: "Of course, that is God's Word, truly, without a doubt." The monk: "Were the angels then polytheists, when they obeyed God and bowed down before Adam? And were the devil and his host believers when they offered

Him spite and did not bow down before Adam? God, however, showed Himself friendly to the angels and disinclined toward the devil and his host, He, the strong and noble." (88b) 'Abdarrahman: "No, truly, it is not so, rather the angels are believers, obedient, the devils are insurgents, accursed." The monk: "Then know with full assurance that God the Father did not create the beings and did not reveal any wonders and signs earlier by the hands of the reverend prophets and apostles except due to the grace of the Messiah. Until He had appeared, no one who believed in Him entertained doubt and misgiving. And as He said to the angels: 'Fall down before Adam,' and whoever of them fell down, was very honored of Him, whoever refused and rebelled, was an idolater, so said He to the angels and other eyewitnesses of Christ, that is: 'This is My Son,[82] in whom I have joy, listen to Him, follow Him and -?-[83] not!' And I do not doubt that whoever listens to Him, obeys Him, follows Him and falls down before Him, has chosen the best and has nothing to fear, without a doubt! For fear, unpleasant things and curse(s) come upon them who distance themselves from Him and rebel, for we do not doubt that Christ is more honorable, excellent, higher and more distinguished than Adam before God. And Christ is true God, as we have shown in various instances."

(AG) Then 'Abdarrahman laughed and said: "O monk, by God, you are far off from the way!" Now there was a man of the Basrans[84] who had come to Jerusalem as a pilgrim. He met Mansûr in the mosque and greeted him. Then Mansûr told him: "Is it not unusual that the Amir is obstinate in examining the religion of the Christians with a purpose therein? He has a monk with him with whom he disputes, and we are there and also dispute with him, but he (the monk) is not softened and is not tired thereby," Then the Basran asked: "Where is he from?" al-Mansûr answered: "Born in Syria;[85] he relates that he grew up in Diâr Mudar and lives in the mountains of Edessa."[86] The Basran: "Do you not want to take me to him that I may speak to him?" al-Mansûr did this after he had admonished him not to accept any statements which concerned the (holy) scriptures. Then several Christians who had become Muslims were there and showed that they were united concerning his (the monk's) knowledge and excellent examination of the scriptures.[87] Then the Basran bound himself (i.e., with an oath) not to dispute with the monk about the scriptures.

(AH) The Basran: "O monk, you say that Christ is the God of the created and that they are all His servants, (what about) the Jews and the others?" The monk: "Of course, Christ is the God of the created and they are all His servants." The Basran: "But He paid the Jews two drachma, which they required of all men." The monk (89a): "Of course, His disciples paid them for Him." The Basran: "How can He be God then, because He humbled and lowered Himself to pay a tax which His servants required of Him?" The monk: "No, truly He did not humble and lower Himself, rather, He condescended in His generosity, mildness and excellent economy. I wish to inform you how He paid this, and what the reason for this was. Our Lord Christ used to perform signs and wonders at all times. When He wanted to do this one time, He was together with those who collected the two drachma. Then He said to His disciple Simon,[88] who is known as Peter: 'Go out to them!' As he was gone out, they said to him: 'Your master does not pay the two drachma, which according to custom He must pay.' As Peter then turned to our Lord and met Him, He then asked him what they had said; and he reported everything to Him. Since He wanted to proclaim His condescension and toleration to His disciples, to strengthen his (Peter's) heart and their hearts, due to that which they saw of Him, He said to Simon: 'Take up your hook and go to the sea and throw it in, then you will catch a fish. Open its mouth and take four drachma out, and pay them for Me and you.' Then the believing disciple, who trusted in the word of his Lord and his God, went and did as He had commanded him and caught the fish, opened its mouth and took the drachma out. And behold, they were new pieces of the coin of Caesar, for they gave the tax to the Caesar and his people accepted no other coinage, because it was obligatory and because the Jews had no other coinage on which the dinar of dirhem was stamped.[89] And God laid this degradation upon them due to their (evil) deeds.[90] Then the disciple paid the two drachma, then he thought to himself and said: 'Our Lord, who possesses glory and power, could have done what He wanted with the two drachma, now He allowed (it) to give them to these unbelievers and doubters as a tax, while we are worthier.'[91] This and similar things were to strengthen the hearts of the disciples, because they called mankind to lowliness, tolerance, humility and perseverance in the suffering of injustice, but we do not honor a God who lowers and humbles Himself, rather a strong, powerful, mighty (one), who knows everything hidden, who has created everything according to His will, who brings silver out of the sea (89a) and out of the body of the fish,[92] as He told His disciple, before he saw with his eyes, to teach him and all mankind, that He is the Lord of the sea and the land and that that which is in it and outside of it submits to His word." The Basran: "And how do we know that the drachma came from there as related?" The monk: "The proof thereof is the pure Gospel of God and the witness of the apostles, the helpers of God, who cannot be suspected of lies, whom no one can slander nor -?- -?-, they all testified that Christ is the Word of God and that He performed signs and wonders, for example the resurrection of the dead, overcoming the demons and healing the ill of all sorts of infirmities. He fed many people with little food in a desert far away from any settlement and He changed the conditions of some people from what they had before.[93] Whoever has done these magnificent, noble and wonderful things, should one deny Him, that He brought out a drachma out of the mouth of a fish and made (this) place known to one of His disciples to get them?"

(AI) The Basran: "Do you not claim that Gabriel once said to Mary: 'I hail you, you (who are) full of grace, the Lord is with you!'? Was then this embryo of Mary, the God of creation and her leader?" The monk: "Certainly it is as you have said, and we have it thus from the apostles." The Basran: "If an accident had occurred to Mary and the child in her womb had died, who would have ruled mankind?" The monk: "Do you not believe on that which your book[94] relates about the prophets? He is the one of whom it is said: 'The powerful, He placed Himself straight up in the highest point of Heaven, then He came nearer and let Himself down and was two bow shots away (from me) or less, and revealed to His servant what He wanted.' Is He the God of the created and their leader?" The Basran: "Of course, He is the God of creation." The monk: "If He then slipped off His highest point, fell, shattered and then died, who would then be the God of creation?" The Basran: "God, the praised and noble cannot be described in this

manner, but Christ was squeezed in the womb of His mother." The
monk: "No, this description is limiting and restrictive, because you say:
'On the highest point in Heaven,' so He must be there and not in the
place to which He came nearer, and to whom He came down to, and
whoever comes nearer, must move himself from the place where he is,
to the (other) place which (90a) he nears, and whatever lets itself
down, must be high and fall. What do you think about your word from
your Prophet what he says? Will you say that God the praised and
noble (only) held Himself fast to the highest point of Heaven and let
His head and hands down? This is rather the description of a limited
being, and you still say: 'If an accident occurred to Mary and she and
Christ in her womb died, who would then rule the world?' I will
answer you according to your manner: If He were fallen down from
the highest point and then died, who would then rule the world? And
you know very well if 'it were so,' 'it was not so,' 'it is not' and 'O but
that' that these are all qualities of mankind, and is used in speech only
with relationship to three things, one covetous of knowledge, or one
who splits hairs (fault-finder, sophist) or by an instructor. Concerning
the question of the teacher and learner, every smart person has an
answer (already) prepared for him. But the question of the splitter of
hairs deserves no answer whatsoever, but rather only a similar question; and this question belongs to the splitter of hairs."

(AJ) The Basran: "What do you say of Christ, did He pray or not?[95]
Because the Gospel testifies of Him that He prayed and entreated
God." The monk: "Of course He prayed." The Basran: "God prays
to none other, for prayer is the obligation of created man to his Lord.
If you say that He prayed, then you give Him the character of a servant
of God. But if you say that He did not pray, then you accuse yourself
and the Gospel of lies." The monk: "You ask questions as a man who
brings accusation and at the same time is judge and answerer, but God
forbid that I accuse the Gospel of lies, that do alone the Jews, the
people of the curse and hypocrisy and who do not believe in God at
all.[96] But I say that our Lord Christ prayed to God the Father in
truth." The Basran: "Why do you want to exclude Him from the
sphere of God's servants and worship a God who Himself worships?
And if one say to you that you are polytheists, then you draw back,

while your (worship of) many gods is very clear! (90b) For only God is
worthy of worship, whoever worships a worshipper, he is a polytheist."
The monk: "We are not polytheists, rather, we have bound God with
His foreknowledge of these people, the elect, who was made of our
matter, and by Him God has instructed us that He is of three persons
and likewise to distinguish between good and evil and that the resurrection and afterlife are before us and that Christ is the Son of the
living God. We as Christian people have not invented this word, rather
God, the mighty and noble said: 'This is My beloved Son,[97] on whom I
have My joy, hear Him'; then we obeyed and heard (Him). And our
Lord Christ said: 'I and the Father are one,'[98] the angels standing near
God proclaimed this, the prophets prophesied of Him, who were sent,
the apostles have made known among all peoples, the blessed prophets
referred to Him, we then are not polytheists, unless it be in that we
bind God together in one Being, as you correctly say, which did not
pray and does not pray." The Basran: "You lie, God did not associate
Himself with anyone, and He is never pleased with Him who associates
one with Him, I remain by your words that God did not pray and prays
not." The monk: "How clear is the truth, how illuminating the argument and how strong the matters of Christ for him who has set himself
free from defiance and rebellion (against God). Tell me then to whom
the believing worshippers of God pray!" The Basran: "God is raised
above that to which you accredit Him. God has not prayed and does
not pray to anyone, rather to Him -?- (are) the prayers of all the
angels and mankind." The monk: "If you now admit that God did not
pray and prays not, you prove this, that you have accused your book of
lies and that which your Prophet has brought, because they testify of
Him, that He prayed and that prayers come to him (the Prophet),
because it is (written) in the Qur'an (33:56) that God and His angels
pray over the Prophet: 'O you believers, pray (91a) over him and hail
him!'[99] Your book shows that God and His angels say a prayer over
your Prophet with this verse. If this matter is correct, then only one of
the two can be God, to whom the angels and those who honor him
pray and whom they entreat in the matter of His prophet. Whoever
says this is damned in both worlds. If you say this again and yet say
that God did not pray and prays not, you accuse yourself and your
book of lies." The Basran: "The prayers of God are not like those of

the angels and the other creatures, rather they are only mercy and
forgiveness from Him for the prophets and apostles." The monk:
"You have not left your Lord any superiority above the angels and
other worshippers with this word; you have not given Him any honor
and you have left no distance between Him and them, rather you have
handled the three levels as one in the expression when you say that god
and the angels pray over the Prophet: 'O you believers, pray over him
and hail him'; that is the same manner of speech (for all these three
levels). If the prayer of God is only mercy and forgiveness, then your
word about your Prophet does not apply anymore. If it means that he
is the lord of the children of mankind[100] and that the intercession
belongs to him,[101] because he, to whom the intercession for others
belongs, does he have need of the angels and mankind, that they
should have compassion on him and to request forgiveness for him and
entreat God for him? This proves that you have loosed him from both
categories. But we do not reprimand you for this, rather (we) show
ourselves friendly to you and say with you: If the prayers of God are
forgiveness and mercy, according to you, then the prayers of Christ, the
eternal Word of the Father, are also forgiveness and mercy. So God
prayed and the prophets and the messengers of God repeated it (91b)
according to your witness of your Prophet, your Qur'an; and Christ, the
Word of God, prayed and the apostles, the reverend and all believers
repeated it." The Basran: "You wretched monk, God has not become
(to exist), not limited, and squeezed into the womb of a woman and
was neither begotten nor weaned, He neither ate[102] nor drank, nor
fasted, nor prayed, nor praised (God), rather praise and prayer belongs
only to all the angels and humans!" The monk: "And likewise it (the
Word of God) suffered nothing, it neither suffers, nor does it praise,
nor does it pray toward the same side (direction) as angels and humans, rather praise, glory and holiness are due to Him with the Father
and the Holy Spirit from all angels and humans." The Basran: "And if
the Gospel of Christ testifies of the Word of God and His Spirit that
these qualities have affected Him and have worked in Him that He
bowed Himself and entreated God, the powerful and the noble?" The
monk: "And how will you free God from these human qualities and yet
impose them on His eternal creative Word, which was begotten of Him
without procedure. Will you extinguish the light of God with these

words? God lets His light shine, and has confirmed His truth by His Word! And how will you add these (qualities) to His Spirit, to the Holy Spirit, to the Paraclete, who created all beings by His grace and led them by His wisdom whom He formed and forced by His power, who surrounds them with mercy and embraces them with His goodness?"

(AK) The Basran: "Is there no difference between God and His Word?" The monk: No, between God, His Word and His Spirit there is no distance or difference according to being, might and pre-eminence, and to every other aside from you, the books of God are the proof that your view and statement (that) there is a distance and a difference (92a) between God, His Word and His Spirit according to substance and might, (is in error!)[103] So tell us then whether the Word of God and His Spirit are of one substance or of a different one." The Basran: "I know and recognize nothing except that God is alone without associates!" The monk: "Your statement 'I do not know' is no argument to your advantage. In meetings with intelligent and instructing men (it is) not acceptable, rather it is the word of one incapable with a weak argument, who refuses the struggle with thin excuses, or even the word of a boastful mocker, or of one who does not know how to give an explanation. And of you, I think that you have no joy in having one of these qualities placed upon you. Now if the Word of God and His Spirit are of one substance, and if God is Creator, eternal without beginning, without end, without changing from state to state, and without transitoriness, then it is the same with His Spirit and His Word likewise, and they are eternal with Him. But if you say that there is a distance and difference between God, His Word and His Spirit, are not the Word and the Spirit then not of His substance? And one may not attribute that which does not belong to it to this distinguished noble substance, which has no peer, as one may not attribute to man or to the sun or the fire that which is not of their substance. Likewise it is not just to apply to God what is not of His substance, if you do this, however, you commit polytheistic (sin), for one does not say that pearls and hyacinth (stone) belong to the substance of man or (that) musk, amber, glass pearls of other things belong to the substance of man. Even less one (does not) say that iron belongs to the substance of the sun or halfa grass to the substance of fire, rather one says: the clay of man or his life, the rays of the sun and its heat, the brilliance of the fire and its glow. It is also thus with a statement about God the powerful and noble, His Word and His Spirit with respect to division and difference, for the Word and Spirit are of no other substance than God. One also does not say: the ear of God and His Spirit, rather the word of Adam and his spirit and the word of Gabriel and his spirit." The Basran: "If God proclaimed (to us) that His Spirit was created? For when our Prophet was asked about the Spirit of God, God spoke to him:[104] 'When they ask you about spirit, say: "the spirit is by the commandment of my Lord! But only a few of you are instructed." Thereby He made clear that His Spirit exists by His command. Whatever is by command, is less than He, and whatever is less than, is less than He, that is, created.' " The monk: "You err you stupid fellow, and speak without having been instructed, for they did not ask him about God's Spirit and not about the Holy Spirit, the Paraclete, rather about Gabriel the faithful, because when God revealed this angel to your Prophet and by him his people and his tribe, the Quraysh and gathered his helpers from the Yemenites, he spoke: 'I am the Prophet of God and His messenger because God sent down the faithful spirit with the revelation, with Gabriel.' When he spoke to them much about the spirit, they asked him: 'What is the spirit then?' He said: 'The spirit is by the command of my Lord!'[105] And he was right in this, for Gabriel is of spiritual form and is by the command of God. But if the Word of God and His Spirit should be by His command, this is blasphemy, for He commands neither His Spirit nor His Word, because they both belong to the three Persons of the one eternal God, who is without beginning and without end, the Father, the Son and the Holy Spirit, one substance, and all creatures, angels, humans and all others are by the command of God, but His Word and His Spirit are not separate from Him in substance, unlimited, indescribable, without end."

(AL) The Basran: "If you only worship Christ because He is the Word of God and His Spirit, Adam is also the Word of God and His Spirit, because God, the exalted and powerful says in the Qur'an: 'We breathed our Spirit into him.'[106] This proves that he is of His Spirit

and His Word, so worship Him as you worship Christ!" The monk: "It
is not enough for you to be unknowledgeable, rather you yet lie,
slander and mistrust! That should not be allowed you! If Adam were
the Word of God and (part) of His Spirit were breathed into him, then
he would have conquered the evil motives and desires as Christ did,
but Adam is not the Word of God and is not His Spirit, that is, (part)
of His Spirit was not breathed into him, rather he is by the command
of the Word of God, which creates everything but God. You say
likewise, that God said to him:[107] ' "Be!" and he was,' but it was only
the breath of life which was breathed in his face, and thus he became a
living reasoning, but created, living being. And everyone with insight
knows that Adam is not the Word of God and that nothing of His
Spirit was breathed into him. If something of God's Spirit were in
him, then the devil, the accursed, would not have set about to deceive
him, so that he followed and obeyed him and transgressed God's
command and (therefore) died. And he never recovered from this fall,
until our Lord Christ redeemed him from (93a) his sins, which had
brought death over him and his descendants. And it is the same with
your statement about Adam as with that about Gabriel [and Mary]:
'And We sent her our Spirit, and he stood before her as a well-built
man.'[108] For if Gabriel were the Spirit of God, he would be eternal
Creator; but he is neither God's Spirit nor a human spirit, also the
Spirit of God was not breathed into him, rather both are by the command of God, His Word and His Spirit."

(AM) Then the Basran bowed his head and began to look at the
ground. The monk said to him: "What is wrong? You are silent and
will not answer. This is no meeting for intrigues, politics and business,
which is followed by conflict, rather this is a meeting for the purpose of
disputation, for every word an answer must be ready, if not, then you
end the dispute, so say then what you think, and when the evening
comes to you, then begin to reflect and consider, make known to us
about the words in the Qur'an: 'God and His angels pray over the
Prophet, O you believers, pray over him and hail (him), as is fitting![109]
Is this a revelation from God, or an empty fabrication?" The Basran:
"This can only be a revelation of God to the Prophet by Gabriel the
faithful spirit." The monk: "If this suffices you, then you have opened

the gate (?), if it is a fabrication, then only one could have done it, who senses your and your comrade's joy in another's misfortune concerning their enemies who feud with them, or rather, if you claim that God consented with His angels and humans to pray over your Prophet, then you have no proof thereof in the books of the prophets, we also hear nothing of the truth of this in earlier or later scriptures. No angel is known, no prophet was ever sent, over whom was prayed aside from your Prophet; if you do not want to accuse and criticize yourself and your prophets, then likewise you should do this to Christ, when you claim that God selected Jesus the son of Mary, to mankind and that the Son, who is united with Him, born of Him, eternal and creative Word so that the two eternal substances and the new (one) become one Christ and one Son, Father God in truth; and they have witnesses thereof in the books of the prophets and your book, which your Prophet brought, where he testifies to us that there is only one Christ." The Basran: "Will you dispute with me out of the Qur'an? Will you admit that it is a revelation of God, which He sent to our Prophet?" The monk: "No, by all means, I do not admit to any of that, and also not that your Prophet is a genuine prophet, rather he is only an angel, in whom God found pleasure, and fulfilled His promise through him (93b) which (promise) He had given Abraham concerning Ishmael, for prophecy and revelation were taken away after John the son of Zacharias, and David and Christ testify of this, but I do not want to argue with you as Christ did with the ridiculers, namely from their words where He said to them: 'By your word I will judge you,'[110] by your admission and with your book, with which you boast I will dispute with you when you say it is from God."

(AN) The Basran: "By God, you lie. According to the Qur'an Christ is not Creator, but created, the son of one created." The monk: "Do you not know that in the Qur'an it is (written):[111] 'As the angels said to Mary: "O Mary, God has chosen you of all other women and has purified you." ' " The Basran: "That is the Word of God in truth, not disprovable, incontestable." The monk: "He chose her and our Lord Christ received a body of her pure flesh and her pure blood, by the power of the Holy Spirit she bore him, as women do after nine months. He did not change Himself thereby, this pure cleansed seal did not fall to its opening and the angels said to her:[112] 'We hail you full of grace, our Lord is with you!' Then later he says in your Qur'an:[113] 'As the angels said to Mary: "O Mary, God proclaims good to you by a Word from Him; His name is Christ, Jesus, (the) son of Mary, the Word of truth concerning whom you argue." ' " Thereby He made known that His Word (and) Jesus is one Christ. God the powerful and noble laid the sun in His hand and created it as a likeness of Christ out of two substances into one sun, that means that He created light on the first day and as the fourth day came He created the disc of the sun and concentrated the sunlight of two substances into one. Likewise Christ, the eternal creative Word of God, unified Himself from man and the new -?- to a Son of God the Father and to one Christ, this is the Word of truth, over whom you argue, and he continues in your Qur'an and says:[114] 'Jesus is only a sign for mankind and mercy, so follow Him and do not argue!' And he says further:[115] 'Jesus the son of Mary is only a sign for the hour (of the Judgment), do not argue about Him, rather follow Him!' And in the Gospel He tells us that He said to the angels and people with a loud voice from Heaven: 'This is My Son and My beloved[116] in whom I have joy, hear Him and follow Him, and do not dispute concerning Him!' Even though it was said to you, 'follow Him and do not argue concerning Him,' you resist the Word of your Lord from the mouth of your Prophet and the statement of the Qur'an and doubt, dispute and resist those who believe therein in contradiction to everything which is right!"

(AO) The Basran: "You lie! Christ is not God's Son and not God (Himself) and not the Judge of the world, rather He is only one of the worshippers of God and one of many prophets and the same as Adam, whom God created of earth and said to him:[117] ' "Be!" and he was.' (94a) But God honored Him, raised Him to Himself and has made this known in the Qur'an, where He says:[118] 'Christ did not disdain to be a worshipper of God, as low as the angels who stand near God.' " The monk: "Truly He whom God honored and exalted to Himself and has given Him a rank as no other than Him, this must one also admit and must set Him over all mankind. It is (thus) not so, as you say, rather you twist (the scriptures) and slander, even in contradiction to that what God alone has commanded! Tell me, where is Adam, his children and his contemporaries, where is Noah, his children and his contemporaries, where is Abraham, his children and his contemporaries, where is Moses and the prophets and the messengers, witnesses, reverend ones and the holy and excellent man, where is the son of your Prophet and his community, of whom you claim that God created nothing more distinguished than them." The Basran: "All you have mentioned and named lie under the earth, but our Prophet, as we said previously, none of the honorers of God is as distinguished as he!" The monk: "And where are the angels who stand near God?" The Basran: "In Heaven!" The monk: "No, in the air under Heaven. All of the honorers of the scriptures testify to this and there are many of them among us!" Then all of the Muslim present said: "He is right, there is no other created (being) in Heaven aside from Jesus, the son of Mary."

(AP) The Basran: "It is as you say!" The monk: "I do not dispute about anything without you admitting that all created beings are between heaven and earth." The Basran: "Good, all creatures are there where you say, with the exception of the angels whom God exalted to Himself according to His will." The monk: "And where is Christ, concerning whose domicile there can be no doubt according to the Qur'an which your Prophet brought?" The Basran: "In Heaven, because God has honored Him and exalted Him to Himself." The monk: "Pull yourself together and decide for yourself or admit it in spite of pride[119] and decide against yourself, that if Christ were as Adam, He would be with Adam where he is, and if He were as the other prophets, then He would be there where they are, and if your Prophet were honored by God, as Christ, then He would not have exalted Christ and set Him next to Himself on the throne of glory. But He left your Prophet under the earth where the reverend one and pure ones are. And how is it that God exalted Him to Himself, whom you attribute the character of a (mere) servant, and clothed Him with fame and glory, clothed Him -?-,[120] covered Him with light, revealed His knowledge to all angels, prophets and reverend of the believers, that the dead and the living confess concerning Him, has given Him the dominion over all creatures, provided Him with eminence and power over them, has perfected His matters according to what the prophets prophesied of Him and the angels proclaimed of Him, and thereby He distinguished the prophet David as he said:[121] 'The Lord said to my Lord, sit at My right hand, so that I may lay your enemies down as a footstool under your feet,' and he said:[122] 'You are since the beginning of time, O all-knowing!' And likewise says the Lord:[123] 'The Lord says: "You are My Son, today I have begotten You," ' and likewise he says:[124] 'Who is the Man on whom You think, O Lord, and the Man in whom You have found pleasure, You have lowered Him a little under the angels -?- by death, then later You have clothed Him with honor and made Him glorified with magnificence, You have given Him power over (Your) handwork and have laid everything under his feet!' Likewise he says:[125] 'Your throne O God is established continually (94b) in all eternity, the pillar of your Kingdom stands upright:[126] You have loved godliness and hated wantonness, therefore God, Your God, anoints You with the oil of joy, more than Your fellows.' He says the same in another place:[127] 'All kings bow before You, and all of the peoples worship You.' And the prophet Isaiah, who is celebrated among the prophets, says:[128] 'A child was born unto us, and a Son was given us, He who is called: Wonderful, Savior, God, Powerful, Sign, Prince of peace, Great King, whose dominion has no end.' "

(AQ) Then the monk continued: "Do you not know, you man; if you had a virgin maid and said to her: 'You maid, I will not let you free, but every child you give me, will be free,' when she then bears a boy, then he is accounted illegitimate, and not free, since he was born of a maid." Then the crowd said: "No, he is free, no one can do him harm." And the monk said: "And in compliance with your admission, according to God the name of a 'servant'[129] for Jesus the son of Mary rolls out of the mouth of Gabriel before His mother was pregnant with Him, for when Gabriel announced the reception to Mary, he did not say to her: 'God proclaims His servant to you,' rather he said to her: 'God proclaims His Word to you'; and he did not say: 'The servant of God is with you!' rather he said to her:[130] 'You are hailed, you, rich in grace, our Lord is with you, you will receive and bear a son, and He will be called Jesus, He will be (very) holy and be called the Son of God.' And God has removed the name of 'servant'[131] from Him in all

scriptures.[132] Then Mary went and visited Elizabeth the mother of
John the son of Zachariah, and as she came near to her and greeted
her, and Elizabeth received the words of Mary, John moved in the
womb of his mother and bowed down to Mary. Then Elizabeth raised
herself and said: 'Where does this honor come to me that the mother
of my Lord comes! You are hailed, O blessed among women and
blessed is the child of your womb! Truly I say to you in that moment,
as your voice hit my ear, the child moved in my womb, you (ruling)
lady of mankind, and He who comes out of you, is the same of whom
the prophets of the Lord have proclaimed, and your book testifies to
this, as it says:[133] 'O Zacharias, God (proclaims) John (to you) to confirm His Word from God, and He is in the womb of His mother, a
prophets among the reverend. 'As Christ was born, the angel descended and appeared to mankind to bow down and say:[134] 'Praise be to God
in the highest and peace on earth and to mankind glorious (exuberant)
hope.'[135] Then the angels proclaimed it to some shepherds and said to
them:[136] 'I proclaim to you today great joy which will be shared with
the world, today in the city of David is a Savior born unto you, a
Messiah and the Lord of mankind.' And at the time of His birth God
drove the rulers of East, who sent their messengers to Him, trustworthy people who had valuable gifts with them, God showed a star to
them, which went before them, and they wandered over the high and
low places of the land until they came to Jerusalem. When they
arrived there, the star disappeared before them, who was their leader,
so that they had to enter the city to ask concerning the King born to
the Jews. Then the news got to Herod, the ruler of Jerusalem, whom
it worried greatly; and the news spread further to all the region around
Jerusalem; then Herod gathered all the leaders of the priests (95a) and
all the learned men and said to them: 'Who among you knows where
the King of the Jews should be born?' Then they said;[137] 'In Bethlehem,
the place of David, according to the prophecy of Micah, for he says:
"And you, Bethlehem in Judah, you are in no wise the smallest among
the Princes of Judah, for a ruler should come out of you, who will
make my people Israel graze, whose beginning is before the created
existing world, the eternal God in all times (?)," ' and as Christ had
entered riding on the foal of a donkey, the city came to motion because of His entrance, and the young people and all the others came to

331

meet Him and children not of age[138] spoke, and all called out of one
mouth:[139] 'Blessed is he who has come and who comes in the name of
the Lord, to Him be praise in the highest!' Then some of the priests
of the Jews came to Him and said to Him: 'What do we hear that
these children not of age speak?[140] Command them to be quiet!' Then
Christ said to them:[141] 'Have you not read the scriptures for a long
time? "Out of the mouths of children and sucklings you have prepared
the Lord praise!" Truly I say to you: If these sucklings be quiet, the
stones would say what they say!' Yes, the stone which the builders left
out, has become the cornerstone and thereby is the covenant completed by the Lord! And every witness, even when it is a miracle for the
world, has been brought by the Holy Spirit. Christ was spoken of
through the mouth of David and all the prophets, of the creative
eternal Word of God and that praise should be given Him and that He
has led all peoples and nations back to honoring God, and praise
should be given Him, after they lingered so long in error and in the
dominion of the evil spirits over them and in the worship of idols. And
all scriptures testify of Christ of that which He has said in the Gospel,
namely, that He is God's Son and that He and the Father are one
regarding rank of rulership, but you will not accept Him, rather you
are prideful; how could it be possible then that He should be called a
man (God-honorer)?"[142]

(AR) The Basran: "You have spoken till you bore (us), you monk!"
Then al-Manzûr[143] said to the Basran: "You have spoken thereof and
only asked him whether Christ prayed or not, as he answered: Yes!
You left the question and entered into unnecessary things about which
we had already disputed with him; now ask him how Christ prayed, if
He is the Son of God, as he claims, eternal, Creator, uncreated." The
monk: "O Manzûr, nothing else in the dispute held me up from telling
how Christ prayed except for the circumstance that I know you only
intend sophism and contention, therefore I was on the guard against
you, because you ask about something which most men are not grown
up to and that which only one can know who possesses a healthy
intellect and who is established in his matters. Now I will explain the
most necessary of this to you, O Manzûr. Just as you cannot describe
the sun, and no one can fasten on to its rays, and its existence can only

be defined by its light and warmth, so God, the praised and noble, is only definable, describable and comprehendible by that which the prophets say of Him in their scriptures and by the believers that God and His Word and His Spirit are one God (95b). Further I will tell you, O man, yes, Christ did pray, who is the Word of God become flesh, as we have shown it to you in various places, without having need to pray, and as He let the baptismal,[144] I mean the baptism[145] occur without having needed it, either the one or the other, only to purify the water (?) by His baptism and to open the way of baptism to us. Likewise He prayed, without having needed it, only to be helpful to His disciples thereby, since they were publicans, fishers and old people, whom He wanted show how one must act so that they could repeat in deed what they saw and so that (they could) call mankind to believe in Christ, the Son of God the Father, so that their preaching might not be according to hearsay, rather according to that which their eyes had seen and their hands had handled." The Basran: "There is no one created who does not need to pray so as to serve the Creator by prayer." The monk: "God, the Word, the eternal Creator deserves to be bowed down to (and deserves) the prayer and the praise of all angels and mankind, because He is too high and too powerful to be able to commit a sin. He also has no need to pray, but by His goodness and mercy and the prayer performed by Him, He led mankind out of error and to belief in God." The Basran: "This our Prophet also committed no sin, and fasted as well as prayed, without having needed to." The monk: "Such words are not spoken by one who understands and belong to no one who understands without condemning them and the speaker, with such come only those who are not skilled in rhetoric and argumentation, as the people from Khuzistan[146] and Nabateans[147] and the backward fellows, because they would accept this of you, without searching for the truth and without seeking the genuine religion, rather they only look for outward esteem, (the) warding off of injustice and the tax, without doing what is theirs in the relationship between them and the Creator, so know now with all assurance that your Qur'an testifies of your Prophet that he has sinned and will sin as it says:[148] 'O Muhammad, We have forgiven you of your past sins and what is yet to come'; this proves that he sinned and had need of forgiveness, thus God says to him, as you also maintain, that vengeance will be his share."

(AS) The Basran: "The angels have not sinned and yet they worship and bow down without needing to do so." The monk: "You are right, but God, the praised and noble, did not say to any angel what He said to our Lord Christ: 'You are My Son, today I have begotten You.' Like wise He did not say to any angel: 'This is My Son and My beloved[149] in whom I have joy,' much the less He did not say to any angel: 'Sit at My right (hand), so that I may lay Your enemies as a footstool under Your feet,' much the less: 'Kings and peoples and nations bow down before You and in the created You find their blessing and every tongue praises You,'[150] and He exalted none of the angels to give him domin-ion, power, glory and majesty; and He did not say to any angel:[151] 'You are the place of My joy,' but all of this was said of Christ. When the angels pray, God gives this to them in grace without needing their praise. (96a) But they speak (?) of Christ due to His exalted name."

(AT) The Basran: "What is that to mean that you worship the cross and that you bless yourselves therewith?"[152] The monk to 'Abdarrah-man: "O Amir, may God grant you esteem, do you say as he says that we worship the cross?" He answered: "Yes, we maintain them both." The monk to him: "Those who do it should not be reprimanded for it, because without knowing it they call on the same (one) as you. At times they do the wrong thing; at times the right thing. But you, O Amir, with that which God has given you of esteem, glory, insight and majesty, and by that which has preceded you from the word of your Prophet:[153] 'Give the Quraysh precedence and do not place yourselves in front of them!' And you know something of the Quraysh and yet do not know them. If a Quraysh saw me, then he would see me -?- and if he did not look on his brother, due to that which they are in God; and only those who find themselves in this situation, he will accept their word without insight and believe that the Christians worship the cross. If we did this, then we would have done nothing else but painted it on the wall, set it on the mountain tops and on each hill and in each desert,[154] in streets, alleys and on vessels, that it may please (?) all. And he uses them for every purpose[155] so that it be -?- among them and -?- for each adversary. But none may blame the Christians for

334

this, because they love the cross, kiss it and desire it, because through it great and noble things are revealed to them, whose number is immeasurable, and because it is the banner of victory and the conquest of all its enemies and because it saves from error and idolatry, and if the Christian believer in Christ wanted to, who has sincere faith, who is pure of sins, who is perfected in goodness and godliness, he would turn away the harm of deadly poison, if he is ill from it or is forced to drink it for God's sake, and he would drive the demons out with force and stomp out the blazing fire by the name of Christ our Lord and our God, who was crucified on the stake. Thus the believer who brings this about without having to suffer when he made the sign of the cross thereby."

(AU) When the monk finished speaking, they all said: "Now the liberation has come, God has laid everything in your hand, know that if you do these things, or one of them, you have aided your matters to victory and you have conquered every adversary." The monk: "I and most of the Christians, in whom the things described by me are found together with the (right) faith, they accomplish it with the help of God by the power of blessing of the cross of the holy, but if you maintain that the truth is in your hands, then it is fitting for you to accomplish such things in the name of your God, the Black Stone, the rukn,[156] the maqam[156] and the (holy) tombs[157] and those which are in them and other things which you honor highly, if not, then the truth of the Christians has become manifest by that which comes to pass of signs and wonders by their hands, and (also) if nothing of this sort is done by your hands." The Basran: "Which miracle should I show you?" The monk: "I will not make this matter too difficult for you; I request that you heal a blindness or to cure one who is ill with a fever, so that the fever leaves him (96b), or to rest[158] his limbs through the power of blessing of the things which you honor highly." The Basran: "Go to Mecca with me, and I will show you there how your proposal will be solved by the power of the blessing of the Black Stone." The monk: "Now is not the God to whom you call and whom you request to perform a sign by the blessing of the Black Stone, is He not everywhere, so that no place is empty of Him? And does He not hear the voice of every single person and He -?- of him, who -?- and hinders no one near or far from requesting (of Him) sincerely and believing? But you wish something in which you do not trust and that which you are not certain of, and you have no security that it has taken place or will take place. To the contrary, I say that the wood on which our Lord Christ was crucified[159] is in Constantinople, and when we, be it in the East or West, ask for something and hope in the name of Christ and the sign of the cross, it will be given us. But we do not request this without saying to him who asks us,[160] and if we need something for ourselves, then we go to Constantinople, or to the place where the relics of our Lord Christ are, to take care of our matter there. But I will make the matter easy for you: You say that God is one, undivided, and that Muhammad is the Prophet of Islam, the true religion, and that the Qur'an is the book of God and that the holy house (in Mecca) is God's house and that Gabriel brought the Black Stone from Paradise and that the relics which you honor highly are there and that God will be honored by all this." The Basran: "Testify to the truth of all that which you have said and believe that God has no pleasure in anything besides Himself!" The monk: "And what do you say of those who deny what you just said?" The Basran: "I say that he is damned (wretched) in this world and that and has nothing (good) at all to expect." The monk: "I call God as a witness to me and His angels and all those present that I deny all of what you have said! Is there any among you who is resentful because of this and wants to give his life in death and wants to show me himself that it is so with the religions as the people say? Now, if he does this, we know that his word is true and he will carry more desire for your religion and will feel happy therein, if not, then he will bring to naught your claims to light, and he should not call the Christians, the believers of Christ, polytheists any longer. And if you will, O Basran, and you, O noble one, will you do all this yourselves for me? You trust in your religion and are firmly established therein." The Basran: "Truly, I find nothing in you but insolence toward God; it is as if you trusted that He could not prohibit you, your belief in the resurrection and the revival (of life) is sufficient for what you request, so it is you with whom we will begin to produce a miracle of your religion." The monk: "Truly I trust in my religion and beliefs in the resurrection and the revival (of life), because our Lord Christ proclaimed it to us and let us see it in Himself with (our) eyes, and the resurrection of the dead worked. But you and the Jews do not have any hope in the resurrection and the revival (of life), and you do not have any assurance (?)" The Basran: "Why?" The monk: "The resurrection (97a) takes place and God will resurrect those in the grave; but Moses died and was not resurrected and not revived. Your Prophet came and said the same to you, and he died likewise without being resurrected and without being revived.[161] Then our Lord Christ came to us before you and said to us:[162] 'Do works for God which are able to bring you closer to Him and do not remain by the things of old, because they are temporal (?), but the resurrection will take place and God will resurrect all of those who are in the grave, and each man will be rewarded according to his works; if he was good, with good, or when he was bad, with bad.' Then He died and was buried and stood up, was resurrected and went up into Heaven and He will come again to resurrect the dead, then He will reward them, the good with theirs and the bad with punishment. It is certain for us what our Lord proclaimed and what we saw with (our) eyes; but you are in doubt of that which Moses brought and your comrade."

(AV) The Basran: "O Amir, is there not anyone in the prisons who deserves death?" He answered: "Yes, there is one there who incited the Bedouins against us, he was a highwayman between ar-Ramla and Egypt[163] and he deserves death and the cross." The Basran: "What if the Amir would command to bring him and to impose upon him to suffer that which the monk maintains he would do by trusting in Christ and the cross? If he trust in the things of Islam and all of its benefits, then we would have something in hand, we who mean well with the matters of our religion, to disprove the word of the monk; and it would be finished with his denial. Then the Amir should give the command and make preparations to free the man and show him good as a reward for his patience and persistence. But if he die, then that is come upon him which he deserved as a punishment for robbery." Then 'Abdarrahman had the man called to be brought and imposed on him all of what the monk said, and he agreed to that which was told him and answered (that) he could bring what he would, (adding) 'I will obey him.' " The monk: "O Amir, grant us, and let us bring deadly poison." Then the Amir called his physician and commanded him to bring poison. As he was bringing it, he said to the monk: "Let him who will, taste thereof." Then he took some of those present and gave (?) it (to them), then he gave it to the monk, who took it and said: "In the name of Christ, the Son of the living God, whom the Jews cruci- fied, who was buried and resurrected from the dead." Then he made the sign of the cross over it, drank it, washed the cup three times and drank it. The monk said: "O Amir, (to whom God grant esteem), what (97b) if the Muslim were also given of the poison as it was given me?" Then the Amir said to the physician: "Give it to him as it was given to the monk, because he must make the sign of the cross over each medicine to cure one, even though he knows it is deadly poison, but one of you, in whose hand it is, should give it to him and speak out the name of the unchangeable,[164] of the Black Stone, of the Prophet, of the rukn, of the maqam[165] and of the (holy) grave and all prophets whom you know. Then your God should -?- by love of these, then he should drink it so that the difference of that on which you call and that on which we call will be clear to you and us, and so that we may bring the truth to day (light)." As the man answered: "I will give it to myself," they gave him the poison, he took it and drank it after he had spoken out everything by name, which the Muslims honor and to that which they hold fast. As the poison took effect on his body, the cup fell out of his hand and he fell down dead; his flesh mutilated.[166] Then the Amir commanded to bring a piece of garment, had him wrapped and buried somewhere.[167] As this occurred, 'Abdarrahman said: "My brother gave me a female slave of ar-Raqqa; I was in love with her, but for some days something has struck her with a demon, and you claim that the disciples of Jesus drove out the demons in the name of Christ and the cross. Will you do it, and can all who have surety and trust in God and faith in Christ and honor the cross, do so, as when they are pressured to? If you are able to do it, then heal my female slave from her suffering, we have brought her." The monk: "O Amir, command her to come." As she was there and stood before the monk, he made the sign of the cross between her eyes; then the girl cried out: "O Lord, he has a sword and wants to behead me, O God, O God!" Then he spoke:[168] "You evil spirit, you unclean, filthy! It is determined of you that you are to come out of this daughter of Eve by the word of Jesus Christ, the Son of the living God, through whom heaven and

338

earth exist, and that you have nothing more to ruin in her and never will return to her." Then the accursed cried out of the mouth of the girl and said: "Travail upon You, Jesus Christ, son of Mary, and upon you disciples; we do not know where we should flee before you and ye!" The monk: "I drive you out only through Christ, the Word of God the Father, who drove out the strongest of you out (98a) of those in whom you sought refuge, and she was let to flee to the entrance in the strong (God)." He commanded it now, that it should not be allowed to speak without leaving the girl. Then the girl shook and he (the spirit) fell out of her toe as smoke.[169] Then the monk raised her up, held her hand and had her sit down, he then ordered a cup for her, poured into it and took a cross, which he had with him and two (other) crosses from the Christians and washed them and gave the girl to drink of the water [170] and washed her face; then she stood there as an idol (98a)[171] and praised God and thanked Him for the good deed He had done.

(AW) Then the Jew, al-Manzûr and al-Bahili said: "Full assurance rests only in the fire." Then the monk spoke to the Amir: "Be so good and do as you will; you have already hindered me in so many things which I needed." The Amir had firewood brought and had a fire made therewith, and as it became glowing coals, the monk stepped up to the oven and spoke: "What do we have, O Lord, what do we have aside from Your name, give us honor and glory, let us see Your power, and come to our rescue so that the adversaries recognize that You are in truth Christ, the Son of God!" Then he made the sign of the cross and put his hand entirely in the fire and turned it over and over and jested with it.[172] As the Jew, al-Bahili, al-Manzûr, the Amir and all of the members of the assembly saw this, they fell down[173] and bowed themselves, kissed his feet and spoke: "We believe on Christ, the Son of the living God, whom we had denied until now." Then the Amir spoke to those who were present: "These are strong miracles which are confirmed by the hand of the monk."

(AX) In the evening he had the monk summoned and spoke to him: "Truly, if you desire, then live in our land, we will give you land and a dwelling and will honor you and provide everything for you." Then the monk said: "I only want to go to Babylonia." Then he gave him presents and let him go to Babylonia.[174]

Notes:

[1] Later abbreviated as C.V. (= Codex Vollers)

[2] *Polem. u. apolog. Literatur,* (1877) p. 82ff.

[3] The new "Catalogue" (1883f) No. 214 (A. F. 88) and No. 215 (Suppl. 107; St. Germain).

[4] M = The Coptic era of the Martyrs - ed.

[5] I was almost finished with my work, when I was made aware that the Sachau collection of the Royal Library in Berlin also had a Karshuni manuscript of the text (*Handschriften Verzeichnisse XXIII*, 1899, p. 652, No. 199, 19). The Berlin text contains only a fraction of the disputation, of which the beginning is preserved, but otherwise ends abruptly during the discussion concerning the guilt of the Jews in the crucifixion of Jesus (C. V. 81b). The leaves 190-191 have nothing to do with this text. Of the passages shown from the Sachau manuscript in the large Berlin *Verzeichnis* (1899) p. 646ff. it has been noted that: p.647a, line 28 reads "muta'allimin" and p. 653a, line 33 reads al-Hajjaj. It is very striking in the handwriting style of this manuscript to see how the letter "n" is used. Parting with the Arabic usage of expressing the "an" of the accusative with a double fata line, the copyist takes the liberty of using the consonant "n" here and in other cases also. Examples of this are: ibn (son), idhn (permission), Qur'an, haitan or haitin (because), shibyan (youngsters), jinan (garden). The writing of vowels is very careless; I am not going risk saying to what extent "common speech" can be assumed here. I suspect religious piety where the word "God" is enclosed in ornamental brackets in the Muslim's argumentation that Jesus couldn't be God (188b, l. 7) and a later writer wrote next to it: "gawur" ("sacrilege"), and further (189a, l. 3) where the

name "Meryem" ("Mary") is furnished with three ornamental symbols, Greek crosses (?). For the most part the Berlin manuscript repeats what was said in the Paris texts, on the one hand it gives a very abbreviated form of the text found in Codex Vollers, and on the other hand it contains additions according to the "taste" of the time period or copyist. I would like to classify as weak the manner in which 186b characterizes the three persons of the Trinity, that is as follows: " ... when we say 'Father,' we mean the benevolent God, who has neither beginning nor end; when we say 'the Son,' it is to say 'eternal God'; when we say 'the Holy Spirit,' it means 'the God of all-encompassing power.' " Where C. V. mentions that "several" caliphs were murdered, 183b as P. 214 have "seven." "Mansûr al-Qaisi" has become (185a) "al-Mansûr al-'Abbasi." In two instances we find Syriac glosses, which are perhaps the work of later copyists: (180b) where the example of the roaming lion and the poor sheep is written in the margin in Syriac and (186a, l.1) where in an obvious fashion the well-known "faqat" is explained by using "balhoudh." I see the carelessness of the copyists in the following passages: (179b, l. 1) where we find "bilmahisan" for "bilmahasin," and (188a , l. 7) where the expression "God" or "Father" has been left out. On p. 180a, l. 1 we notice the correction of a later copyist, who tried to blot out the Arabic article.

[6] C.V. 85a places the birth of Muhammad 600 years after Christ; P. 215 more exactly, after the ascension of Christ.

[7] In the LCB 1903 No.31 Col. 1053, I have also assumed that a well-to-do, mostly belles-lettres educated Christian from a merchant background was the author of the narration "Sul and Sumul."

[8] Vollers openly shows a liberal inclination in his assertion about the book of Job, which lacks credible argument.

[9] Vollers makes a mistake in his logic here, in that after maintaining the superiority of the Syrians and inferiority of the Muslims remarks that in order to be conclusive, the dispute had to end with miracles.

[10] Vollers errs in applying these quotations to Luke 9:35. 86a - Gives a composite of Matthew 3:17 and 17:5; in any event a gross error on the part of the monk. 88b, 90b and 93b - approximate Matthew 17:5. 95b - approximates Matthew 3:17.

[11] P. 214 begins: "In the name of God, who is one in being, three in person and quality, do we begin with the help of our Lord and God and Savior Jesus Christ, with the transcript of the dispute which took place between the holy father Anba Abraham the monk and 'Abdarrahman the Muslim with the blessing of God, Amen! He says that 'Abdarrahaman etc., as he was overcome with musing about the things of the Christians." P. 215: "In the name of the Father and Son and the Holy Spirit, the one God! This is the disputation of the monk Ibrahim from the monastery in Edessa, from Tiberias in Syria, in the conference of 'Abdarrahman etc., who governed Jerusalem, with the help of God, Amen! He said that the Amir 'A. thought to himself etc."

[12] The Arabic expression "uqnum" pl. "aqanim," comes from the Syriac "qenoma"; this is to be understood as the οἰκονόμος, οἰκονομία of the Greek Christology.

[13] According to P. 214; 215 where "al mu'addib" is thought to be the same as the house philosopher of time of the Roman emperors. C.V. gives "al mu'adhdhin," the muezzin.

[14] The idea of using the enmity between the Jews and the Christians to resolve the question of whether or not the Bible had been corrupted, was also used by other Christian polemicists; cf. Leo, parag. K; Timothy, parag. CN; al-Kindi, parag. CJ - ed.

[15] P. 214, 26b: "the patriarch of the Christians and Mar Elia, the bishop of the Nestorians."

[16] P. 214 adds: "of Qahtan's children" and instead of Tiberias: "al-Akrach, the mine of knowledge, etc."

[17] P. 214 also names the monk Abraham here.

[18] ar-Ruha, present-day Urfa, Greek Edessa, compare 88b.

[19] This area named Diar Mudar came about as a planned settle-ment of Bedouins under the first caliphs. Al-Muqaddasi (c. 980 A.D.) names ar-Raqqa as the capitol of this area, which C.V. 97b will also mention; Yaqut (II, 637) c. 1220 A.D. names the cities Harran, ar-Raqqa, Simsat (Arsamosata), Sarug and Tell Mozan in this area.

[20] Qur'an 3:60 - this is said of Abraham.

[21] P. 214, 28a: Hanafi (!).

[22] Qur'an 3:79. C.V. reads "ittaba'a" - "follows", for "yabtaghi" - "desires", below 75a though: "ibtagha".

[23] The following explanation of the monk is missing in P. 215.

[24] Compare Qur'an 2:6.

[25] P. 215: "and their sensitivity is that of wild animals."

[26] P. 214: "in the firewood of the Ghada bushes."

[27] The monk depicts the Hanife according to the Syrian form for "heathen" (but) the Amir in the Qur'anic sense as the separatists, the forerunners of Islam.

[28] The last sentence is in the margin in C.V. - The writer seems to have confused Qur'an 2:81 and 2:254 with 4:169 - ed.

[29] Compare the other reading: C.V. 73a. - See note 21 above - ed.

[30] Qur'an 3:77.

[31] Qur'an 49:14.

[32] Qur'an 21:55 says: "you and your fathers are clearly in error."

[33] Qur'an 46:8.

[34] Qur'an 2:101.

[35] Qur'an 3:200.

[36] Qur'an 49:13.

[37] For other references to Hajjaj b. Yusuf on the part of Christian polemicists, see Leo, parag. S; al-Kindi, parag. CO - ed.

[38] The monk conforms to Islamic practice rather than the teaching of the Bible in the matter of swearing (Matt. 5:33-37) - ed.

[39] Or according to P. 215: "lets (himself) be muted."

[40] Later he is called al-Manzûr. P. 214: "al-Manzûr b. 'Affan al-'Absi."

[41] P. 215 has the name distorted to "ghair," P. 214 to the contrary is the same as C.V. The mention of the pre-Islamic poet in this context makes a noteworthy connection between the historical poet and the medieval Roman figure. Compare briefly: H. Thornbecke, *'Antara*, p. 31; Brockelmann, *Arabische Literatur*, II, 62.

[42] Here the mysterious designation of Ex. 3:14 is used as a personal name, as the Syrians and Samaritans use it. Cf. 78b.

[43] I read "fasl" instead of "fadl," preference in C.V.

[44] The argument of the persons of the Trinity being described as Father, Word and Spirit, in somewhat of a reference to Qur'an 4:169, was quite popular among Christian polemicists; Leo, parags. V, X, Y, AA; John of Damascus, parag. K; Timothy, parags. D, N, O, P; al-Kindi, parags. BL, BN, BP; etc. - ed.

[45] John 1:1 is the first verse of the Diatessaron - ed.

[46] The speaker in this passage is Elihu and not Job - ed.

[47] I cannot bring these words into harmony with Is. 40:7,8; either in the text or in the translation.

[48] Cf. Timothy, parags. N and O - ed.

[49] The use of the example of the sun to explain the Trinity was quite common among early Christian polemicists; cf. Leo, n. 59; Timothy, n. 39; etc. - ed.

[50] Cf. Leo, parag. W; Timothy, parags. EG and EN - ed.

[51] P. 215: "He resuscitated her and renewed the countenance of the earth."

[52] Qur'an 7:52, etc.

[53] Including the reference to John 10:18, this entire section of the discussion shares an uncanny resemblance to The Patriarch Timothy's dialogue with the Caliph Mahdi; see Timothy, parags. BG and BH - ed.

[54] This argument was frequently used by early Muslim polemicists; see John of Damascus, parag. Y and Timothy, parag. BH - ed.

[55] Qur'an 3:18.

[56] Cf. Timothy, parag. BI - ed.

[57] The examples of Satan and Adam were also used by Timothy; see Timothy, parag. BK - ed.

[58] P. 215: "but a child of the devil (ibn Iblis) was crucified..."

[59] The Muslim charge of the scriptures having been changed by the

Christians was and continues to be prevalent in such dialogues; the Christian challenge for the Muslims to produce the genuine Gospel less so; cf. Leo, parag. AI, n. 70; Timothy, parag. AS, n. 89 - ed.

[60] Qur'an 10:94a - ed.

[61] Gen. 3:9,10; paraphrase - ed.

[62] In their attempt to find prophecies concerning **Muhammad** in the Gospel, as the Qur'an (7:156; 61:6; etc.) describes, early Muslims sought to identify the Paraclete in John (14:16,26; 15:26; 16:7) with Muhammad; cf. Leo, parags. P and Q; Timothy, parags. AN-AP - ed.

[63] John 14:16,17,26b; 15:26b,27a; paraphrase - ed.

[64] Qur'an 46:8, see note 32 above - ed.

[65] Cf. Timothy, parag. AS - ed.

[66] Unfortunately, most of the early Christian polemicists were extremely anti-Jewish; see Leo, parag. BC; Timothy, parag. BG; al-Kindi, parag. CJ; etc. - ed.

[67] Cf. Timothy, parag. AD; Leo, parag. AJ - ed.

[68] Ezek. 44:2; Peshitta or Septuagint - ed.

[69] Ps. 68:32,33; Peshitta, paraphrase - ed.

[70] P. 215 adds the question of whether or not Jesus was circumcised.

[71] Cf. 88b, 90b, 93b, 95b

[72] Was added by me (Vollers).

[73] Cf. Hübschmann, *Jahrbuch für protestantische Theologie*, V, 211, concerning this explanation in Bundehes.

[74] Ganâba.

[75] This appears to be a generalization reminiscent perhaps of verses such as I Pet. 2:9 - ed.

[76] Qur'an 3:97.

[77] Qur'an 64:16 - ed.

[78] P. 215: as a hose (?) full.

[79] The page of C.V. has been punched out here.

[80] A hole in C.V.

[81] Qur'an 2:32.

[82] Cf. 86a.

[83] A hole in C.V.

[84] P. 215, 71a: "a man of Basra, who was called al-Bâhili"; in P. 214 al-Bâhili is already named in 39a, the Basran though in 39b for the first time.

[85] P. 214, 215 add: "He comes from Syria, but he was born in Babylonia."

[86] Cf. 82a.

[87] In P. 215 it is said that the Christians have falsified the scriptures; P. 214 says "harraqa," "to burn" instead of "harrafa," "to falsify."

[88] P. 215 as in C.V.: "Semûn"; P. 214: "Sam'ân."

[89] Cf. Matt. 17:24-27; the monk confuses the tribute tax, to the Romans, with the temple tax, for the Jewish temple - ed.

[90] P. 214, 40b: "The Jews were always the subjects of foreigners."

[91] P. 214, 215 add: "of the well-wishing (of grace)."

[92] P. 215: "He creates silver and stamped the coins in the body of the fish, while they live in water and praise God."

[93] P. 214, 215 explain this so: "who made apes and swine of the Jews and made a bird of clay live (by) saying the word 'fly!' "; cf. The Infant Gospel.

[94] Qur'an 53:6 ff.

[95] Cf. Leo, parag. AK, n. 75; Timothy, parag. AH - ed.

[96] See note 65 above - ed.

[97] Cf. 86a, 88b.

[98] John 10:30 - ed.

[99] For a clarification of this expression, cf. I. Goldziher, *ZDMG*, 50 (1896), pp. 97 ff.

[100] Cf. al-Kindi, parag. E, where Muhammad is said to be the "lord of mankind." - ed.

[101] The Qur'an (6:51; 39:45; etc.) oddly enough mentions God as intercessor, which for Islamic theologians poses the difficult question of between whom. Later dogma presents Muhammad as intercessor; e.g. *Sahih Muslim*, The Book of Faith, ch. 84, hadith 381, vol. 1, p. 133; cf.

al-Kindi, parag. AU, where Muhammad is also said to be the intercessor for Muslims - ed.

[102] Cf. Qur'an 5:79 - ed.

[103] Was completed by me (Vollers).

[104] Qur'an 17:87.

[105] This explanation of the monk is not in agreement with Muslim sources regarding the circumstances of this verse; cf. Ibn Ishaq, *Life of Muhammad*, trans. Guillaume, pp. 136 ff. - ed.

[106] This statement Qur'an 21:91; 66:12 applies to Mary.

[107] Qur'an 3:52b - ed.

[108] Qur'an 19:17.

[109] Cf. 90b, 91a. - Qur'an 33:56 - ed.

[110] Cf. Lk. 19:22a - ed.

[111] Qur'an 3:37.

[112] Lk. 1:28 - ed.

[113] Qur'an 3:40. - and Qur'an 19:35 - ed.

[114] Qur'an 19:35 where there is a variant of "tamtarûna" for "jamtarûna."

[115] Qur'an 43:61.

[116] Cf. 86a, 88b, 90b.

[117] Qur'an 3:52b - ed.

[118] Qur'an 4:170.

[119] P. 215 is as C.V., but P. 214 "without pride."

[120] P. 214, 215: "in magnificence"; cf. p. 177, n. 31 - ed.

[121] Ps. 110:1 - ed.

[122] Ps. 93:2b with an addition - ed.

[123] Ps. 2:7a - ed.

[124] Ps. 8:4-6 - ed.

[125] Ps. 45:6,7; with slight variation - ed.

[126] "Stands on a razor."

[127] Ps. 72:11 - ed.

[128] Is. 9:6, Peshitta with variations - ed.

[129] Servant = God-honorer, worshipper, man.

[130] Lk. 1:28 ff. - ed.

[131] Same as note 128 above - ed.

[132] The monk errs in this regard, e.g. Is. 53:11b - ed.

[133] Cf. Qur'an 3:34.

[134] Lk. 2:14 with some variation - ed.

[135] Sentence according to P. 214; C.V. is unintelligible, but can be

constructed from the text of P. 214.

[136] Lk. 2:10,11 - ed.

[137] Matt. 2:5,6 with variation - ed.

[138] P. 215: "The children in the wombs of their mothers."

[139] Matt. 21:9 with variations - ed.

[140] Cf. al-Kindi, parag. EO, n. 164 - ed.

[141] Matt. 21:15,16 with additions by the monk - ed.

[142] Cf. with the expression: 94b.

[143] Earlier al-Mansûr (77a, above).

[144] "Sibgha."

[145] " 'amudiya" (commonly "ma'mudiya"). This expression is borrowed from Syrian Christians, the other from the Abyssinians.

[146] "Elymais," the עילם of the O.T. For the characteristics of the people, cf. *Al-Muqaddasi*, ed. de Goeje, 403.

[147] Here the rural people of Babylon.

[148] Qur'an 48:2.

[149] Cf. 86a, 88b, 90b, 93b.

[150] This Bible references are given in paragraph AP above - ed.

[151] Or perhaps "in whom I have joy," see note 148 above - ed.

[152] P. 214, 215: "It is only a piece of wood, which neither harms nor profits."

[153] Cf. *Sahih Muslim*, Kitab al-Imara, ch. 754, hadith 4473 ff., vol. 3, pp. 1009 ff. - ed.

[154] Or according to P. 215: "Cave, cavern." Instead of "hill" C.V. gives "corner, angle."

[155] Concerning the purification ritual of the Oriental Christians, cf. the MS. Leizig-Vollers No. 1061.

[156] Holy things in Mecca.

[157] In Medina.

[158] P. 215: "an eye illness, which you can cool, or a cut which you can allay." P. 214 adds "a fever."

[159] Cf. the life-giving cross of the MS. Leipzig-Vollers, No. 1063, III.

[160] It appears there is a deficiency here.

[161] Cf. al-Kindi, parag. CF - ed.

[162] Extreme paraphrase and generalization - ed.

[163] P. 214, 215 leave out the place names.

[164] "as-Samad," the name of God; Qur'an 112:2; "everlasting refuge."

[165] Cf. 96a.

[166] P. 214 gives a similar expression; P. 215: "as they held him, he

was as a black garment; or when wants to hold tôb as tôb, he was (already as stiff) as a burned brick."

[167] P. 214, 215: "in a cattle stall."

[168] Regarding the formulae of exorcism of Basil the Great in the East; see the MS. Leipzig-Vollers No. 1061, 22.

[169] Cf. S.J. Curtis, *Ursemitische Religion*, pp. 172 ff.

[170] Since C.V. is unintelligible from here on, due to the previously mentioned damage to the page, this last section is given from P. 215.

[171] P. 215 "sanam." The point of comparison appears to be the beauty, as the synonym "dumiya" is used for "beautiful woman," (see) for example, Ma'n b. Aus, ed. P. Schwarz, 1, 15, etc. P. 214: "as if nothing bad had happened to her." - Vollers gives 98a twice, which appears to have been a misprint - ed.

[172] A similar test of fire is related from old Persia in Yaqut, 1, 86, 11 ff.

[173] "Charru," as in similar situations in the Qur'an.

[174] While P. 215 ends with only one formulation of reverence, P. 214 gives at the conclusion: "The disputation (al-mugâdala) which is known as (that of) Ibrahim, the monk of Tiberias, is ended."

| AL-KINDI'S
APOLOGY |
| --- |

An Arabic text of the correspondence between 'Abdullah b. Ismail al-Hashimi and 'Abd al-Masih b. Ishaq al-Kindi was re-discovered in the 19th century by American missionaries in Egypt.[1] Another manuscript (also in Arabic) containing the text was later found in Istanbul.[2] Anton Tien edited both of these manuscripts, and the result of his work was subsequently published by the Turkish Mission Aid Society in 1880.[3] In 1882[4] the Society for Promoting Christian Knowledge published the first English translation of parts of this correspondence in the booklet *The Apology of Al Kindy* by Sir William Muir. Tien, with the exception of a passage he felt to be distasteful,[5] then translated the complete text of the two letters into English apparently sometime between 1882-1885.[6] For some reason, however, he never completed, and thus never published his manuscript.

In 1991 while searching for early works in the Christian-Muslim dialogue, the present editor discovered a listing for Tien's translation manuscript in the catalogue of the School of Oriental and African Studies in London.[7] After obtaining a microfilm of the text, it was obvious that the manuscript was still in the form of an early draft. After comparing portions of the manuscript with the Arabic text printed by the SPCK in 1885 and *The Apology of Al Kindy* (ed. Muir, 1887), some minor mistakes were corrected and endnotes were added. Tien's introduction to the Apology has been deleted. The translated text of al-Kindi's Apology which follows is essentially Tien's manuscript which has been re-edited.

It is somewhat strange that the text of al-Kindi's Apology should have been re-discovered in the East. Peter of Toledo seems to have been the first to have translated the text (from an Arabic manuscript written in Syriac characters) into Latin in 1141, and Bibliander published the text of the correspondence in 1543.[8] However, it was not until Tien's edition of the Apology appeared in 1880 that al-Kindi's work became well-known among Western scholars of Islam, whose first doubts concerned the authenticity of the text.

Two rather early objections to a 9th century dating for the correspondence were that the Christian's text could have been authored by the famous Muslim philosopher Abu Yusuf b. Ishaq al-Kindi[9] and that the matter of Muhammad's name being written on God's throne was argued about among Muslims in the 10th century.[10] Muir responds to the former question in his essay on the age and authorship of the Apology (which follows this introduction),[11] and Mingana addresses the latter in his introduction to Timothy I's discussion with al-Mahdi.[12] It may be sufficient here to say that based on the internal evidence of the correspondence, both Muir and Mingana believed the work to be an authentic production of the early 9th century.

In its present form the text of al-Kindi's reply seems to be corrupt in a few places.[13] Though there is good evidence that al-Kindi was Nestorian, the text of his correspondence could well have been transmitted to us through non-Nestorian groups, in much the same manner as the Patriarch Timothy I's dialogue appears to have been altered. Moreover al-Kindi seems to quote the Bible quite freely in some passages, and this although he is aware that al-Hashimi has read the scriptures. It could have been that al-Kindi was at times quoting from memory, but more plausible explanations may be that he let his anti-Islamic zeal get the best of him or that these shortcomings are also the work of later copyists. In some passages it is obvious that al-Kindi was quoting from the Peshitta and in others that he was citing the Diatessaron, rather than a Syriac or Greek version of the New Testament. By way of contrast, though some paraphrasing appears to have been done by both sides, al-Kindi and al-Hashimi, in general, quote the 'Uthmanic recension of the Qur'an rather faithfully.[14]

As far as the Muslim polemic is concerned, al-Hashimi is very mild in his attacks on Christianity. The Muslim writer for his part offers none of the traditional charges on the scriptures having been corrupted by the Jews and Christians and does not even attempt to show that Muhammad's coming was foretold of in the Bible. One reason for this could very well have been due either to his deep friendship with al-Kindi, his wish to abide by the Qur'anic injunction governing discussions with Jews and Christians[15] or, less likely, because they had already spoken of various issues at previous meetings.[16] After saying that he was familiar with the beliefs and rites of Christians, al-Hashimi proceeds to explain the rites of Islam, the pleasures of Paradise and the torments of Hell by way of the Qur'an. Not once does he quote the Bible in inviting his friend al-Kindi to Islam, he simply insists that al-Kindi and Christians in general are in error.[17]

Al-Kindi, to the contrary, uses the guarantee of security promised him to speak his mind about Islam. Shortly following his brief introduction, al-Kindi begins his attack on Islam by attempting to show that the "orthodox faith" of Abraham as described in the Qur'an, was nothing less than the paganism of the Sabeans as was practiced in Haran. Al-Kindi's claim lacks credible evidence though, and betrays somewhat an attitude that his goal of wishing to discredit Islam should justify the means he applies. The natural arguments which al-Kindi uses in support of the Trinity very much resemble those of the Patriarch Timothy I,[18] and al-Kindi's Biblical approach of showing God, His Word and His Spirit to be one were already in widespread use among Christians.

Where al-Kindi exhibits a certain uniqueness is in his knowledge and exploitation of early Islamic sources. By virtue of a common language, similar culture and his position in al-Ma'mun's court, al-Kindi appears to have had access to many materials not available to others. Whereas Leo III's and Timothy I's information on the Qur'an may well have been second-hand, al-Kindi not only demonstrates a better knowledge of that book than John of Damascus, but he is also one of the few early major Christian polemicists to have made extensive use of Islamic traditions. Indeed, the writer Jahiz complains about the Christians of his day citing the hadith in their polemical discussions with Muslims, but by way of attempting to justify Islam, he adds that the isnads in the traditions cited by Christians are defective.[19] It is interesting to note that if al-Kindi's Apology was written c. 820 A.D., as its internal evidence rather strongly suggests, not even the first of the six most trusted editions of hadith had yet been collected.[20] However, many of the traditions to which al-Kindi refers in his Apology can be found in either *Sahih al-Bukhari* or *Sahih Muslim*, and this, from an Islamic standpoint, precludes the notion that these hadith could have had defective isnads. Furthermore, the majority of the remaining material which al-Kindi cites, can be found in the standard works of Ibn Hisham, al-Tabari, an-Nadim and Suyuti.

Drawing mainly from Islamic sources, al-Kindi displays no mean skill in measuring the alleged prophethood of Muhammad against the records of the Old Testament prophets. He shows that because Muhammad did not give any prophecies, the latter could not have been a prophet in the original sense of the word.[21] Additionally, al-Kindi takes the typical Christian argument of this time period, that prophethood must be confirmed by signs and miracles, one step further, by exhibiting Qur'anic evidence that signs were lacking in Muhammad's case and consequently exposing the witness of later hadith to his miracles as forgeries.[22] Al-Kindi's contention that Muhammad had claimed he was to be raised from the dead in a manner similar to Jesus, is not totally incredible, even though, quite understandably, there appear to be no direct Islamic sources for Muhammad saying this.[23] In comparing the raids of Muhammad with the battles waged by Moses and Joshua, al-Kindi rightly maintains that Muhammad lacked any divine command and challenges his opponent to produce evidence to the contrary.[24]

In dealing with the origin of the Qur'an, al-Kindi seems to have believed that the Jews played a more direct role in its composition[25] than is generally accepted; the mention of the influence of the Nestorian monk, though commonly referred to in another works, appears to contain a corruption in manuscripts of the Apology used by Tien.[26] Al-Kindi's knowledge concerning the collection, redactions and some of the codices of the Qur'an, though tainted here and there with 'Alid traditions, is not only relatively accurate, but appears to have surpassed that of any of his predecessors.[27] After presenting his array of accusations against Islam, al-Kindi excuses himself by appealing to his use of Islamic sources:

> We have confirmed nothing on our authority which is not confirmed by the traditions of your own scholars, men of weight among you. We have kept to what is generally accepted and held as a matter of faith on this and other points on their authority.[28]

Again it was this approach which evidently became (or was) so popular among Christians and effective against Islam that Jahiz felt the need to respond to it.[29]

Al-Kindi portrays the use of foreign words in the Qur'an as being incompatible with its claim to have been revealed in Arabic[30] and attributes his friends' boast that Arabic is the richest of all languages, to their ignorance of any other language.[31] In responding to the invitations of al-Hashimi to Islam, al-Kindi addresses the issues of circumcision,[32] the prohibition of pork (contrary to Biblical sources), the circumcision of women (evidently from Islamic tradition),[33] the pagan origin of the Ka'ba and the Hajj,[34] the divorce and re-marriage sequence in Islam,[35] the visitation of shrines[36] and the Jihad.[37]

Al-Kindi's defence of the worship of the cross does not vary considerably from that of his predecessors other than that he mentions two events in which al-Hashimi had himself made the sign of the cross in time of danger.[38] In his defence of Christianity, al-Kindi also shows himself not to be immune to making errors; he alleges that the tetragram appears twice in Ps. 110:1 and confuses the event of John 5:5-8 with that of Luke 5:24.[39]

By way of contrast to other Christian polemicists, al-Kindi defends the incorruptibility of the Bible by showing the belief in its being changed to be in contradiction to the Qur'an.[40] In relating the life of

Jesus, al-Kindi reverses the order of the coming of the shepherds and the magi to visit the child Jesus and His temptation in the wilderness with the beginning of Jesus' public ministry.[41] Al-Kindi also takes some verses out of context to make a point which could have just as well been proven otherwise.[42] Two paragraphs of the text, which are rather inconsistent with al-Kindi's style and even his tendency to paraphrase, appear to have been corrupted by at least one copyist whose goal of disproving Islam far outweighed his commitment to being faithful to the Biblical texts.[43] Al-Kindi's explanation for why the miracles of the monks of his day were not as abundant as those of the apostles seem to have been, is somewhat naive.[44] Towards the close of his letter, al-Kindi requests that al-Hashimi "compare point with point" of the things he wrote.[45]

The text of the Apology of al-Kindi which follows is from Anton Tien's translation manuscript No. 25190 in the library of the School of Oriental and African Studies in London. Sir William Muir's essay on the age and authorship of the Apology are taken from the book *The Apology of Al Kindy* which he edited and which was published by the SPCK in London in 1887, pp. 13-38; Muir's reproduction of the Arabic text of the Apology have been deleted in some passages.

The present editor wishes to kindly thank the School of Oriental and African Studies in London for their permission to publish Tien's translation in this collection of Christian-Muslim discussions.

Notes:

[1] See Tien's Preface, p. 382.

[2] Ibid.

[3] *Enzyklopedia des Islams*, "al-Kindi, 'Abd al-Masih b. Ishak," vol. 2, (1927) p. 1097.

[4] Ibid.

[5] See parag. DG, n. 119.

[6] Tien's manuscript does not contain any date as to when it was written, but in his introduction to the text of al-Kindi's Apology, which is not included in this book, Tien writes: "The first achievement of British diplomacy during the past century has been the regeneration of Egypt due to the able administration of of Lord Cromer and now crowned by the easier and more hopeful task of administration in the Sudan..." It is obvious that Tien must have been writing after the occupation of Egypt in 1882 and before the disaster at Khartoum in 1885.

[7] The manuscript is listed as " 'Abd al-Masih ibn Ishaq, al-Kindi, The Apology of al-Kindy (translated from the Arabic by Anton Tien, with an introduction and notes. The translation and notes are in typescript and the introduction in manuscript.)" 52 pp. manuscript and 297 pp. typescript, No. 25190.

[8] *Enzyklopedia des Islams*, "al-Kindi, 'Abd al-Masih b. Ishaq," vol. 2, (1927), p. 1097.

[9] Muir, *Apology of Al Kindy*, p. 19.

[10] *Enzyklopedia des Islams*, "al-Kindi, 'Abd al-Masih b. Ishaq," vol. 2, (1927), p. 1097.

[11] See Muir, pp. 367ff., 376.

[12] See Mingana, p. 171.

[13] Al-Kindi, parags. CN, ER.

[14] Notable exceptions being found in al-Kindi's description of pre-'Uthmanic codices of the Qur'an, some of which were still extant in his

day; see parags. CP and CQ.

[15] Qur'an 29:45; see parags. E and I.

[16] In parag. EA, al-Kindi alludes to a former discussion over which the Caliph allegedly presided.

[17] See parag. AY.

[18] Cf. al-Kindi, parags. BI and BJ; Timothy I, parags. DE and DF.

[19] See Jahiz, parag. P.

[20] Al-Bukhari was born in 810 A.D. and Muslim was born in 817 or 821 A.D. (*Shorter Encyclopedia of Islam*, pp. 65 and 417, respectively).

[21] See parags. CA and CB.

[22] See parags. CC and CE.

[23] See parag. CF, n. 48.

[24] See parag. CJ. The famous injunction of Qur'an 9:5 against the polytheists was revealed towards the end of Muhammad's life, long after his raids had taken their course.

[25] See parag. CN.

[26] See parag. CN, n. 62.

[27] See parags. CP and CQ.

[28] Parag. CR.

[29] Jahiz, parag. P.

[30] See parag. CT.

[31] Parag. CT. It is rather well known that because most Muslim scholars only knew Arabic, many of the translators for the Muslim caliphs were Christians. See Finkel, p. 699.

[32] Parag. DG.

[33] Parag. DH.

[34] Parag. DI.

[35] Parag. DJ.

[36] Parag. DK.

[37] Parags. DM, DO, DQ, DR and DC.

[38] Parag. EA.

[39] Parag. EE.

[40] Parag. EF.

[41] Parags. EH and EJ respectively.

[42] Parag. EN, n. 163.

[43] Parags. EQ and ER.

[44] Parag. EV.

[45] Parag. EW.

THE APOLOGY OF AL-KINDI

An Essay on its Age and Authorship

by Sir William Muir

Read before the Royal Asiatic Society

Al-Biruni, in his *Vestiges of Ancient Nations*, written A.D. 1000 (A.H. 390), while describing the customs of the Sabeans, cites the authority of *Ibn Ishaq al-Kindi, the Christian*, in these words:

> Likewise Abd al-Masih b. Ishaq al-Kindi, the Christian, in his reply to the epistle of Abdullah b. Ismail the Hashimite, relates of them (the Sabeans) that they are notorious for human sacrifice, but that at present they are not able to practice openly the same.[1]

A work answering the same description has recently been published by the Turkish Mission Aid Society, in Arabic, under the following title: "The Epistle of Abdullah b. Ismail the Hashimite to Abd al-Masih b. Ishaq al-Kindi, inviting him to embrace Islam; and the reply of Abd al-Masih, refuting the same, and inviting the Hashimite to embrace the Christian Faith."

The book, we learn from a note at the end, was printed from two MSS., obtained, one in Egypt, the other in Constantinople. Neither has the name of the copyist, nor the year of transcription. They are both said in this note to be full of errors and discrepancies, but the book has been edited with care and intelligence, and as a whole may be regarded as a correct reproduction of the original. The editor (Dr. Tien) deserves great credit for the way in which the task is executed. I proceed to give a brief account of the work.

The letters, themselves anonymous, are preceded by a short preface: [see text below].

The Hashimite's letter follows immediately on this. He reminds his friend that he, though a Muhammadan, is himself well versed in the Scriptures and in the practices and doctrines of the various Christian sects; and he then proceeds to explain the teaching of Islam and to press its acceptance on him. He begs of his friend to reply without fear or favor, and promises the guarantee of the Caliph that no harm should befall him for any freedom of speech in discussing the merits of their respective faiths. The reply of al-Kindi is introduced thus: [see text below].

This note is wanting in the Constantinople MS. It is no doubt an addition to the treatise as originally put forth; but of what antiquity and authority there is no ground for saying.

It is otherwise with the short preface, which is the same in both MSS., and probably formed the introduction to the discussion as it at the first appeared. Excepting, however, that it gives the name of the caliph, this preface adds nothing to what we gather from the contents of the epistles themselves of the personality of the disputants, namely, that both lived at the court of the caliph; that the Muhammadan was the cousin of the caliph, a Hashimite of the 'Abbaside lineage; and that the Christian was a learned man at the same court, of distinguished descent from the tribe of the Banu Kinda and held in honor and regard by al-Ma'mun and his nobles. But the names and further identification of the disputants are withheld, from motives of prudence — "in case it might do harm."

From the passage in al-Biruni, however, it is evident that in his time (A.H. 390) the Apology was currently known under the title, "The reply of Abd al-Masih *ibn Ishaq* al-Kindi, to the epistle of Abdullah *ibn*

Ismail al-Hashimi." The epithets Abdullah and Abd al-Masih are of course *noms de plume*. It is possible that the other names (in italics) are so also; Ishaq and Ismail symbolizing, under their respective Patriarchs, the Christian and Muslim antagonists.

Whether this be so or no, the name of *ibn Ishaq al-Kindi* has occasioned the surmise in some quarters that our apologist was the same as the famous "Philosopher of Islam," Abu Yusuf b. Ishaq al-Kindi, who also flourished at the court of Ma'mun and his successor. There can, however, be little or no doubt that the famous al-Kindi was a Muhammadan by profession. As a *Failsuf*, or philosopher, he was, it may be, not a very orthodox professor; but, at any rate, there is no reason to suppose that he had any leaning towards Christianity: on the contrary (as we shall see below), he wrote a treatise to refute the doctrine of the Trinity. The father of this ibn Ishaq, or his grandfather, was governor of Kufa, a post that, in fact, could be held by none other than a Muhammadan; and al-Ashath, the renowned chief of the Banu Kinda, who was converted in the time of Muhammad and married Abu Bakr's sister, is said to have been his ancestor; whereas our apologist glories in his Christian ancestry.

On the philosopher al-Kindi, de Sacy gives us an interesting note. After showing that D'Herbelot was mistaken in calling him a Jew,[2] and citing the authority Abul Faraj and Ibn Abu Usayba for regarding him as a Muslim, he mentions three considerations which might be urged against this view. *First:* In the catalogue of his writings there is none relating to the Qur'an or to Islam. *Second:* Al-Kindi was one of the translators of Aristotle, familiar with Greek and Syriac; and men of that stamp were mostly Christians. *Third:* In the "Bibliothèque Impériale" there is a MS. (257), entitled "A Defence of the Christian Religion" (apparently identical with our Apology), written in Syriac characters, but in the Arabic language, the author of which is named *Yacub Kindi*.

Of these objections (continues de Sacy) the last alone merits attention; but it may be met by these counter-considerations. In the preface the author is not named. The work is only said to have been by a person attached to the court of al-Ma'mun, a Christian of Kindian descent. It is called "The Treatise of al-Kendy, *the Jacobite*."[3] It is most likely by a misunderstanding, or with the view of increasing thereby the value of the work, that it has been ascribed to the authorship of Yakub Kindi. This suspicion acquires greater force, as in the catalogue of Syrian writers, written by Ebed Jesu, we find a certain Kindi named as the author of a religious treatise; and the Kindi in question — the same, without doubt, as the writer of our Syrian MS. (257), or at least whose name has been assumed as such — lived, according to an historian cited by Assemanus, about 890 A.D. (280 A.H.), a date to which it is little likely that Yakub Kindi survived.... For the rest we may suppose that Kindi, in pursuit of his philosophical studies, had embraced opinions opposed to Muhammadan orthodoxy, and that this led to his faith being suspected — a thing which has occurred to many Christian philosophers, and among the Jews happened to the famous Maimonides.[4]

But this *Kendi* mentioned by Ebed Jesu, whoever he was, could not possibly have been our apologist, for he flourished towards the end of the third century of the Hagira, whereas the Apology (as I hope establish below) was certainly written during the reign of al-Ma'mun, near the beginning of that century. The passage from Assemanus, referred to by de Sacy, consists of a note on chapter cxlii. of Ebed Jesu's Catalogue (in Syriac verse) of Christian authors. The verse and note are as follow:

[Verse]-CANDIUS *fecit ingens volumen Disputationis et Fidei.*

[Note.]-Candius *Ibn Kndy*, Ebn Canda, hoc est Candiae filius; who flourished under the Nestorian Patriarch Joannes IV, A.D. 893. Others refer the authorship to Abu Yusuf Yacub b. Ishaq al-Kindi; but he, according to Pococke and Abul Faraj,

was a Muhammadan. ...But the Candius whom Ebed Jesu
mentions was a Nestorian, not a Muhammadan, and wrote in
the Syrian language, not in Arabic.[5]

If any doubts were entertained of the religious principles of Ibn Ishaq
al-Kindi, they must be set at rest by the fact that he wrote a treatise to
disprove the doctrine of the Trinity. It was answered by Yahya b. 'Adi,
a Jacobite writer, whose pamphlet appears as No. 108 in Steinschneider's list.[6] The same is in the Vatican Library (Codex, 127, f. 88), and
was kindly copied out for me by Prof. Ign. Guidi. In this tract the
attack of Ibn Ishaq is quoted and replied to passage by passage; and
the tenor of the writing leaves no doubt of the antagonism of the writer
to Christianity.

On all these grounds we must clearly look for the author of our
Apology elsewhere.[7] But before doing so, it may be expedient to
notice the conjecture of de Sacy that the Apology may have been
ascribed to Ibn Ishaq al-Kindi either by a misunderstanding, or as a
pious fraud with the view of gaining for it greater celebrity and weight.

As to the supposed misunderstanding, it seems doubtful whether, in
reality, the Apology ever was so ascribed, excepting as a mere conjecture in modern times. The misunderstanding, whatever it may have
been, has arisen apparently from the similarity of name and tribe as
given in the quotation of al-Biruni.

The notion that, with the view of gaining greater weight, a paper
purporting to be in refutation of Islam and (for the) establishment of
Christianity, should have been ascribed to a Muhammadan philosopher,
will hardly, I think, be seriously held. What possible advantage could
have been expected from an attempt to palm off a polemical work of
the kind on an enemy of the Christian faith — a writer, moreover, who
had himself attacked one of its cardinal doctrines? There is, besides, no
trace in the Apology itself of any design to rest upon the authority of a
great name. The author's identity, as we have seen, is carefully suppressed. The only thing common to the "Philosopher" and the author,

which appears throughout the work is that both were learned and both went by the tribal title of al-Kindi; but that tribe was surely numerous and distinguished enough to produce more than one man of letters and noble birth at the court of al-Ma'mun.[8] Leaving now the "Philosopher," we may proceed, therefore, to consider the internal evidence furnished by the book itself of its age and authorship.

I have said that the name of al-Ma'mun, though given in the preface, occurs nowhere in the epistles themselves. But the manner in which the Caliph is throughout referred to in both, accords entirely with the assumption that they were written at his court. He is spoken of as the paternal cousin of the Muslim writer; his just and tolerant sway is repeatedly acknowledged by al-Kindi; the descent of the dynasty from the family of Muhammad is over and again referred to, and our author prays that the Empire may long be perpetuated in his patron's line. All this is perfectly natural, and in entire consistency with the ascription of the work to a courtier in the reign of al-Ma'mun.

Not less remarkable are the propriety and accuracy of all the historical notices. For example, when tracing the fate of the four exemplars of the Qur'an deposited by 'Uthman in the chief cities of the Empire, our Apologists tells us that the copy at Medina disappeared "in the reign of terror, that ism in the days of Yazid b. Mu'awiya"; and that the manuscript of Mecca was lost or burned in the sack of that city by Abu Saraya, "the *last attack* made upon the Ka'ba."[9] This is exactly what a person writing some fifteen years after the event, and in the reign of al-Ma'mun would say; for the siege of Mecca was then, in point of fact, the last which had taken place under the insurgent Abu Saraya in the year 200 A.H. Had the Apology been written later on, say in the fourth century, the "latest attack" on Mecca would not have been that of Abu Saraya, but of Sulayman Abu Tahir in 317 A.H. So also, in illustrating the rapine and plunder of the early campaigns, al-Kindi mentions, as of a similar predatory and ravaging character, the insurrection of Babak Khurramy and the danger and anxiety it occasioned thereby "to our lord and master the Commander of the Faithful." This rebellious leader, as we know, had raised the standard of revolt in Persia and Armenia some years before, routed an army of the Caliph and long maintained himself in opposition to the imperial forces; and the notice, as one of an impending danger then occupying men's minds, is precisely of a kind which would be natural and apposite at the assumed time and at no other.[10] Once more, in challenging his friend to produce a single prophecy which had been fulfilled since the era of Muhammad, he specifies the time that had elapsed as "a little over 200 years" and uses the precise expression to denote the period which one would expect from the pen of a person writing about the era 215 A.H., when we assume the work to have been written.[11] While the incidental references to dates and historical facts are thus in exact and happy keeping with the professed age of the work, there is throughout not a single anachronism or forced and unnatural allusion — which in a person writing at a later period and travelling over such large a field would hardly have been possible.

Still more striking are the aptness and propriety of the political allusions. These are, in the strictest affinity, not only with the traditions of the 'Abbasid dynasty, but of a court which had become partisan of the 'Alid faction, which freely admitted Mu'tazilite or latitudinarian sentiments and which had shortly before declared the Qur'an to be created and not eternal. The Umayyad race are spoken of with virulent reprobation; the time of Yazid is named the "reign of terror," and Hajjaj, with his tyranny and the imputation of his having corrupted the Qur'an, is referred to just in the bitter terms current at the time. Abu Bakr, 'Umar and 'Uthman are treated as usurpers of the divine right of succession which (it is implied) vested in 'Ali. I need hardly point out how naturally all this accords with the sentiments predominating at the court of al-Ma'mun; but which certainly would not have been tolerated some forty or fifty years later.[12]

The freedom of our author's treatment of Islam would have been permitted at none but the most latitudinarian court. He casts aside the prophetical claims of Muhammad, censures some of his actions in the strongest language, reprobates the ordinances of Islam, especially those relating to women and condemns Jihad with scathing denunciation. It

is difficult to conceive how such plain speaking was tolerated even at
the court of al-Ma'mun; at any other the Apology would have had
small chance of seeing the light, or the writer of escaping with his head
upon his shoulders. That the work did (as we know) gain currency can
only have been due to its appearance at this particular era.

These remarks apply with very special force to the section on the
Qur'an, since it seems highly probable that the Apology was written
shortly after the famous edict of al-Ma'mun which denied the eternal
existence of the Muslim scripture. The composition of the Qur'an is
assailed by our author in the most incisive style. First, a Christian
monk who inspired it, and then Rabbis interpolated it with Jewish tales
and puerilities. It was collected in a loose and haphazard way. Besides
the authorized edition imposed by the tyranny of 'Uthman (and subsequently depraved by Hajjaj)[13] — 'Ali, Ubayy b. Ka'b and Ibn Mas'ud
had each their separate exemplars. Having been compiled, if not in
part composed, by different hands and thrown unsystematically together, the text is alleged to be in consequence full of contradictions,
incoherencies and senseless passages. A great deal of this section was,
no doubt, very similar to the kind of arguments held, though of course,
in less irreverential language, by the rationalistic Mu'tazilies of the day
and favored by al-Ma'mun. For we know that it was after a hot and
prolonged discussion that the Qur'an was proclaimed by al-Ma'mun to
be created. It is therefore altogether in accord with the probabilities of
the case that this particular phase of the argument should have been
(as we actually find it) treated by our author at great length and with a
profusion of tradition possessing little authority, although popular in
that day — a kind of rank mushroom growth springing out of (the)
'Abbaside faction and forced by its success. The tables were soon
turned on this free-thinking generation, who in their turn suffered
severe persecution and never before or afterwards did such an opportunity occur, as our apologist enjoyed, under the very shadow of a Caliph's court to argue out his case with his enemy's weapons ready to his
hand.

Al-Kindi makes a strong point of the hypocrisy of the Jews and
Bedouins who lived at the rise of Islam, their superficial conversion

and the sordid and worldly motives by which, when the great apostasy followed immediately on the Prophet's death, they were brought back to Islam, "some by fear and the sword, some tempted by power and wealth, others drawn by the lusts and pleasures of this life." It was just the same, he said, with the Jews and Magians of the present day, and to make good his point, he proceeds to quote from a speech of the Caliph made in one of the assemblies which he was in the habit of holding. The passage is so remarkable and so illustrative of the character of al-Ma'mun, that at the risk of lengthening my paper, I give it here in full: [See text below]

It may appear strange that the Caliph should have expressed himself in this outspoken way regarding many of his courtiers in a public assembly. But, certainly, the sentiments are in entire accord with what we know of the character and principles of al-Ma'mun and also with the social and religious elements prevailing at Marw, where he first assumed the caliphate, as well as at Baghdad, where he shortly after fixed his court. It is difficult to believe that any one would have ventured to fabricate such a speech; or, supposing it genuine, that it should have been quoted by other than a contemporaneous writer.

I proceed to notice what evidence there is in the epistles themselves that the disputants were what they profess to have been, that is, persons of some distinction at the court of al-Ma'mun. The Apology, it is true, from its antiquity and rhetoric, may well stand upon its own intrinsic merit; but, undoubtedly, the controversy is invested with fresh life and interest when we know that the combatants were not fictitious, but real personages.

First, as regards *the Hashimite;* it is conceivable, of course, that he is an imaginary person, set up to be aimed at as the representative of Islam; a mere catspaw to draw forth the Christian's argument. This is the surmise of one of the learned Ulema from Constantinople, to whom I showed the book; but his chief reason for so thinking was that the argument for Islam was weakly stated, and that a much better case might have been made out.[14] In opposition to this view, it may be observed that the personality and character of the Muslim are sustained consistently throughout both epistles. Every notice and allusion is in keeping with his assumed Hashimite and 'Abbaside descent, his relationship to the Caliph, his friendship for our Apologist and the guarantee of freedom and safety obtained by him for the discussion. There is besides more than one incident of personal life. Thus we have a curious passage on the use of the cross, in which al-Kindi reminds his friend that repeatedly in circumstances of danger he had used the sign, or ejaculated an appeal to the cross, admitting thus the virtue of the same; and on one of these occasions, he specifies the place (Sabat al-Medayn) where it occurred. Elsewhere he refers to words used by his friend in another discussion about "the soul." In ridiculing the notion that the name of Muhammad is written on the heavenly throne, the Christian says that none even of his friend's own party held to that conceit. And, again, he apologises for the warmth of his language by reminding his friend that it was *he* who began the controversy.[15]

As regards *al-Kindi* himself, his personality transpires throughout the whole Apology. With a strong attachment to the Nestorian faith, he ever displays a violent aversion from Jews and Magians, on whom, upon all occasions, he bestows the most contumelious epithets. While giving honor to the Hashimites as chief amongst the Quraysh, he not the less vaunts the superior and kingly dignity of the Banu Kinda, as the blue blood of the Arabs, acknowledged to have been supreme over the whole Peninsula; and he apologizes from his own standpoint as an Ishmaelite, whenever the argument leads him to prefer the lineage of Isaac to that of Ishmael. The repeated assertion of his own learning, experience and knowledge of mankind and of the various systems of religion and philosophy, is also in keeping with the vein of conscious superiority, tinged with a slight spice of vanity, which runs throughout the Apology.

Add to this that, amidst much that is crude in our view, and even illogical, the work is characterized throughout by a singular command of the Arabic language and that the argument rises at times — as in the passage on Jihad and martyrdom — to a high pitch of impassioned eloquence, and it must be evident that the writer was a man of remarkable learning and attainments. The Apologist, therefore, could have been no obscure individual. There seems not any ground whatever for doubting that he was in reality what he professes to naturally and consistently throughout the Apology to be, a scion of the noble Kinda tribe, belonging further to a branch which had clung unwaveringly to their ancestral faith. For the suspicion of a pious fraud in the assumption of that character, there is not, so far as I can see, any reasonable ground whatever; nor (even if the internal evidence admitted the hypothesis) would there have been any sensible advantage in adopting that position.

To sum up then; I hold that the work may take its stand on the internal evidence as a composition certainly of the era at which it professes to have been written. Further, there is the strongest probability, amounting almost to certainty, that it is the genuine production of a learned Christian, a man of distinction at the court of al-Ma'mun, bearing the tribal title of *al-Kindi*. And still further, there is a fair presumption that the Apology was written as a reply to the Appeal which is prefixed to the Apology — an apology addressed *bona fide* to his friend by the Muslim, Abdullah al-Hashimi, the Caliph's cousin.

There are good grounds for this belief apart altogether from the evidence of al-Biruni. But that evidence, as we have seen, is conclusive of the fact that the work was current in the fourth century of the Hagira and that it was so under a title corresponding with the account of the authorship as recited in the brief preface to the Apology. Al-Biruni's testimony is, to my mind, chiefly valuable as serving to remove a doubt which must occur to the most casual reader; and that is whether anyone could have dared, at the metropolis of Islam, to put forth a production written in so fearless and trenchant a spirit against Islam; and whether, this having been done, the obnoxious treatise would not have been immediately suppressed. Religion and the civil power are, in the Muhammadan system, so welded together, that the *laese Majestas* of the State is ever ready to treat an attack on Islam as high treason of an unpardonable stamp. But the evidence of al-Biruni shows that, having survived, our Apology was actually in circulation, in a Muhammadan country a century and a half after the time at which it first appeared. This is almost a greater marvel than that it should even been written in the first instance; for, under the tolerant sway of the free-thinking al-Ma'mun that was possible, which a few years later would have been utterly impossible. And one may be very certain that when the orthodox views again prevailed, every effort would be made to suppress and exterminate an Apology, obnoxious not only for its attack on the religion of the State, but also for the political sentiments therein advocated as to the divine right of 'Ali, the usurpation of Abu Bakr and the manner in which the Qur'an was compiled. But the work had in all likelihood, from its intrinsic excellence, already so spread during the reign of al-Ma'mun and his immediate successors (who shared his Mu'tazilite views), that its entire suppression became, no doubt, on that account, impossible. And so copies survived, although stealthily, here and there in Muhammadan countries. But why this remarkable book was not better known and valued in Christian countries is very strange — indeed, to my mind, altogether unaccountable.

Admitting all that has been advanced, it will still remain a question a rare interest who this unknown "al-Kindi the Christian," was. In a letter from Dr. Steinschneider to Professor Loth a suggestion is thrown out which might possibly lead to the identification of our author. The trace is there given of a *Eustathius al-Kindi*, mentioned among other Christian and Jewish names by Casiri in his *Bibliotheca Arabica* as one of the translators of Aristotle or copyists of Greek works. May this not have been our apologist?[16]

Further inquiry on this, or some other similar direction, might possibly throw more certain light on the authorship of our Apology. Other MSS. of the same, whether in the East or in our European libraries, might also with advantage be compared with the printed version so as to elucidate the purity of the text and especially of such passages as appear to be imperfect or obscure in the MSS. from which this edition was printed.[17]

The inquiry is not unworthy (of) the attention of the most eminent of our Oriental scholars. The Apology is absolutely unique of its kind. In antiquity, daring, rhetoric and power, we have nothing in the annals of the Muhammadan controversy at all approaching it. And any research that might throw light upon the origin of the argument, the life and circumstances of our author, the authenticity of the work and the genuineness of the text handed down to us, must possess not only a literary interest, but in some respects a practical and important bearing on the same struggle, which is being waged today, as engaged the labors of Abdullah the Hashimite and Abd al-Kindi, the Christian, in the days of al-Ma'mun.

I have to express my acknowledgments to Prof. Ignatius Guidi of Rome, to Dr. Fritz Hommel of München and to Dr. Steinschneider of Berlin for their very kind assistance in the prosecution of this inquiry. To the first I feel specially grateful for his goodness in copying out for me the entire controversy in which Abu Yusuf al-Kindi appears as an opponent of the doctrine of the Trinity.

Notes:

[1] *Chronology of Ancient Nations*, p. 187, by Dr. Sachau, London, 1879. [Arabic deleted]

[2] On this, see notes in Slane's "Ibn Khallikan," vol. i, pp. xxvii. and 355.

[3] *kt'b 'l-kndy 'l-yaquby*. This, of course, is a mistake, as our apologist was a staunch Nestorian. There may have been some other Kindi, a Jacobite; or rather the epithet *ibn Yaqub* has been so misunderstood and misapplied.

[4] "Relation de L'Égypte par Abd Allatif," by M. de Sacy, Paris, 1810, p. 487.

[5] *Bibliotheca Orientalis*, Assemani, A.D. 1725, vol. iii. p. 213. The assumption that he wrote in Syriac is unfounded. But the treatise was probably translated into that language, as well as transliterated from the original into Syriac writing.

[6] *Pol. und Apolog. Literatur in Arab. Sprache*, Leipzig, 1877, p. 126.

[7] Those who care to prosecute the inquiry further, will find an elaborate article in *Al-Kindi der Philosoph der Araber, Ein Vorbild seiner Zeit und seines Volkes*, by Dr. G. Flügel, Leipzig, 1857. The paper is founded mainly on the authority of Ibn Abu Usayba and Ibn Kufti and is learned and exhaustive. A curious astrological treatise by the same al-Kindi is given by Dr. Otto Loth, p. 261, *Morgenländische Forschungen*, Leipzig, 1875. The cycles of Arabian history are there ascribed to astronomical conjunctions, and the essay closes with a prophecy of the eventual ascendancy of Islam over all other faiths. There is also a short article with an exhaustive list of Ibn Ishaq's works by Ibn Joljol, the Spanish writer, in the *Bibliotheca Escurialensis*, Casiri, Matriti, A.D. 1760, vol. i, p. 357.

[8] Muir here makes reference to the following remarks from his preface in *The Apology of Al Kindy:* "(The Banu Kinda) formed a great clan of themselves, who, advancing from the south spread over the center and north of Arabia, and had, in the fifth and sixth centuries of the Christian era, a distinguished role in the history of the Peninsula (see, *Life of Mahomet*, 1st edition, vol. i, p. clxxiii. et seq.). At the rise of Islam, though the greater part of the tribe, headed by the celebrated al-Ashath, passed over to the faith of Muhammad, still a respectable minority appear to have continued their attachment to the Christian religion; and in the time of al-Ma'mun, this remnant must have afforded ample numbers to produce other men of distinction bearing the tribal title of *al-Kindi*, besides the great philosopher."

[9] al-Kindi, p. 457, below.

[10] al-Kindi, p. 430, below. The name is erroneously printed *Atabk l-Khzzmy* but there can be no doubt that *Babk Khrrmy* is the correct reading.

[11] *lan hdh nyf wm"ta snh qd mdt mn zlk 'l-wqt.* The words imply "two hundred and odd years," or a little over 200. The edict against the dogma of the eternity of the Qur'an was issued, I think, about the year 211 or 212 A. H.; and our discussion took place probably about a year of two later, say 215 A.H.

[12] See my Rede lecture on the *Early Caliphate*. Smith & Elder, 1881, p. 21.

[13] The action of al-Hajjaj (who has been sufficiently misrepresented and abused by the 'Abbasid faction) appears to have been mainly confined to certain additions in the way of diacritical marks. See Slane's *Ibn Khallikan*, vol. i, p. 359, and note 14, p. 364. But it was natural at an Abbside court to vilify that great but stern and cruel Viceroy of the Umayyads.

[14] He also objected to the word *Qarib* (al-Kindi, p. 383, below, "neighbor, near") as applicable by a Muhammadan to a Christian.

[15] See al-Kindi parags. J and BX - ed.

[16] Dr. Steinschneider's letter will be found at page 315 of the *Zeitshrift der Morgenländischen Gesellschaft*, vol. xxix. The passage referred to in Casiri is as follows: *'l-kndy ktab ala la hyat... whd 'l-hruf nqlha bstash, Bibliotheca Arab. Hisp. Michaelis Casiri*, Matriti, A.D. 1760, vol. i, p. 310.

[17] There is the MS. in Paris referred to by de Sacy as No. 257 of

the "Bibliothèque Orientale." And there is also that mentioned by Steinschneider, No. 112, "*Kindi*, Jacob? Vertheidigung der christlichen Religion gegen den Islam, in Karschunischen MSS." See his *Polemische und Apologetische Literatur in Arabische Sprache*, Leipzig, 1877, p. 131. In this last, the letter of al-Hashimi (we are told) is given in an abridged form.

THE APOLOGY OF AL-KINDI

by Anton Tien

DIALOGUE

The 'ABBASID
'Abdullah b. Ismail
al-Hashimi

and

The NESTORIAN
'Abd al-Masih b. Ishaq
al-Kindi

c. 820 A.D.

Al-Kindi lived in Baghdad at the court of Ma'mun, son of the famous Harun ar-Rashid, about the year 820 A.D. (205 A.H.) He belonged to the royal tribe of Kindi in Arabia — the only Arabian tribe which retained the Christian faith after the advent of Islam. The genial and liberal-minded Caliph gathered round him the learned and gifted of all lands, and among them al-Kindi naturally found his place. While in the royal service he formed a friendship with 'Abdullah, a cousin of Ma'mun, with whom he was in the habit of discussing the respective merits of Christianity and Islam. The result of these discussions was a correspondence between the two protagonists, famous in its day, a double record of which has been discovered, first of all by the American missionaries in Egypt, and later in the north of Turkey. The complete text of the correspondence has been published by the Society for Promoting of Christian Knowledge, and a full translation is now, for the first time, offered to English readers in the belief that it will prove of interest to many. The chief value of the correspondence lies in the fact that it enables us to see Christianity, not through Western spectacles, but as presented to Orientals by one who was himself a child of the East.

THE APOLOGY OF AL-KINDI

(A) In the name of God, the Merciful, the Compassionate.[1]

(B) It is said that in the reign of 'Abdullah al-Ma'mun, there lived a man of noble descent, a Hashimite and, I believe, an 'Abbasid,[2] known far and near for his scrupulous piety and for his devotion to the faith of Islam. He was wholly absorbed in the discharge of religious duties. This man had a friend, one of the best of men, a man of breeding and culture, belonging to the Kindi tribe; a member of the caliph's suite and placed near to his person, equally distinguished for his attachment to the Christian faith. Between these two there reigned a great kindness and affection. They had perfect confidence, each in the sincerity of his friend, as was known to the caliph and all his court. For various reasons I prefer not to mention their names, but the Hashimite wrote a letter to the Christian in the following terms:

THE MUSLIM'S SUMMONS

(C) In the name of God, the Merciful and Compassionate.

(D) Let me begin my letter by wishing you mercy and peace, after the manner of my master, the lord of the prophets, Muhammad, the messenger of God, on whom may God be gracious, Heaven's blessing rest on him! Our best authorities, trusty men, on whose word we may rely and to whom we owe our knowledge of the Prophet, tell us that it was his custom, when he entered into conversation with any, to begin by wishing them mercy and peace in their intercourse with him. He made no difference between his own people and strangers,[3] between the faithful and idolaters; but rather, he wished to say that God had disposed him well to all men, and that his mission was not one of harshness and severity. In acting thus he appealed to the example of God, saying that "God is kind and pitiful to His faithful people." In the same way, when I have been at the Court of our Imams,[4] the caliph's enlightened and upright men, God be gracious to them one and all, I have noticed that, as one result of their perfect breeding and exalted rank, their magnanimity and generous dispositions, they followed the example of the Prophet, on whom Heaven's blessings rest! They know no distinction, nor did they favor one above another. I desire to follow in their steps and to imitate their example, claiming for myself some share in the admirable qualities I admire in others. I begin then by wishing you mercy and peace; lest my letter should fall into the hands of the Recording Angel, and he should disown me.[5]

(E) I am stirred up to show my regard for you by the fact that my master, Muhammad, on whom Heaven's blessing rest, has spoken of friendship as next neighbor to religion and faith, and you know I have subscribed myself an obedient servant of the Prophet of God, Heaven's blessing rest upon him! I am impelled to this course when I consider the excellent services you have rendered, your loyalty to us, and the kind and friendly feeling you have not only cherished, but manifested to us. I have further noticed how my cousin, our lord, the Amir of the Faithful,[6] may God aid him, honors you and keeps you near his person, confiding in you and speaking well of you. Must I not commend to you what I commend to myself, to my own household and my family? Must I not counsel you in all sincerity and with perfect frankness, placing before you those great religious verities which we hold by the grace of God? Nor has He committed them to us alone, but to all His creatures, promising therein a great reward at the Resurrection, and immunity from the penalties of sin in the future state.[7] For, saith He, the most High and ever Blessed, "Abraham was of the orthodox faith" (Qur'an 2:129).[8] Again He speaks, most Glorious and Great, whose word is truth, "They who believe in our signs, they are Muslims." (Qur'an 27:83). And further, confirming this He saith, "Abraham was neither a Jew nor a Christian, but an orthodox Muslim. He was not one of the idolaters." (Qur'an 3:60) I wish then for you what I wish for myself. My heart yearns over you when I see your high breeding and perfect culture, the exquisite refinement and grace with which religion has stamped your every feature, the repute in which you are held and the progress you have beyond most in your religion; in a word, your loyalty to such light as you have. I said, I will put before him what God has graciously revealed to us. I will teach him in the kindliest and gentlest way, what I believe; thus following the commandment of God, who is Glorious and Great, and has said, "Do not dispute with the People of the Book excepting in the kindliest way." (Qur'an 29:45). I will use only the most courteous of terms and the gentlest of tones. I will speak kindly to you that, if possible, you may be roused and return to the Truth, quickened into a desire by what you hear from me of the Word of God, the Glorious and Great, which was sent down to that seal of the prophetic order, that lord of mankind, the Prophet Muhammad, on whom Heaven's blessing rest. I do not despair of you, but cherish the hope that God, who directs as He wills, may make me His honored instrument in this good work. I find Him, ever Blessed and most High, saying in His sure word, "The only religion God acknowledges is Islam." (Qur'an 3:17) Confirming this He says further: "Whatever men may invent for themselves, in the way of religion besides Islam, it shall not be accepted of them, they shall suffer in the world to come." (Qur'an 3:79) This He further confirms in one decisive word; "Oh ye who believe, fear God in sincerity, and do not die till ye are within the fold of Islam." (non-Qur'anic)

(F) Now may God save you from the ignorance of unbelief and open your heart to the light of truth; you know that for many years past I have been immersed in the study of comparative religion. I have read the literature of many nations, particularly the scriptures of your own Christian community. I have read through the scriptures of the Old and New Testaments, which God sent down to Moses and Christ and the other prophets, Heaven's blessing rest on them. The scriptures of the Old Testament comprise the Law, the book of Joshua the son of Nun, the book of Judges, the two books of Samuel the prophet, the two books of Kings, the Psalms of David the prophet, the Wisdom of Solomon, his son, the book of faithful Job, the book of Isaiah the prophet, the books of the other twelve prophets, the book of Jeremiah the prophet, the book of Ezekiel the prophet, the book of Daniel the prophet, these are the Old Testament scriptures. The New Testament scriptures are these: the Gospel in four parts, the first by Matthew, the tax-gatherer, the second by Mark, the nephew of Simon who is called Cephas, the third by Luke the physician, and the fourth by John the son of Zebedee. Of these four Gospels two were written by members of the Apostolic band,[9] men who were in constant attendance on Christ, on whom Heaven's blessing rest, viz., those of Matthew and John. Two were by men who were numbered with the seventy whom Christ, Heaven's blessing rest on him, sent forth to preach the Gospel among the nations; viz., those of Mark and Luke. Next in order we have the Acts of the Apostles, what they did and taught after the ascension of Christ, as written by Luke; and the fourteen epistles of St. Paul, all of these I have read and studied. I have read of Timothy and the rapid steps by which he obtained primacy[10] among you, distinguished not only by his administrative powers, but by his intelligence and understanding.

(G) I have read of the three principal sects into which the Christian church is divided. First, there are the Melkites, who accepted Marcianus as their king, at the time of the schism which took place between Nestorius and Cyril; these are the Roman party. Secondly, the Jacobites, the most heretical of all, wanton and mischievous and, surely, furthest from the truth; who assent to the teaching of Cyril the Alexandrian, Jacob Baradaeus and Severus, bishop of Antioch. Thirdly, the Nestorians; these are your own party; and, on my honor, in their views they most strongly resemble the truth as conceived by men who speak reasonably. They are most favorably disposed to us of the Muslim community.[11] Muhammad spoke very highly in their praise and gave them special conditions and securities. He constituted himself and his people their guardians, and gave them deeds, signed and sealed, after

he came to power and when his power was established. They came to
him, and put themselves under his protection, recalling to his mind
how they had helped him by advertizing his claims and declaring the
divine powers committed to him — God be gracious to him. Heaven's
blessing rest on him! That is to say, even before he was ever himself
conscious of inspiration, the monks bore testimony to the powers which
were divinely entrusted to him, and for that reason he, God be gracious to him, Heaven's blessing rest on him, was very friendly to them,
and sought intercourse with them, and held prolonged conferences with
them when he travelled in Palestine and other places. The monks and
hermits honored him, and preached obedience to him, telling the
people that it was the purpose of God to exalt him and to give him a
famous name.[12] As a body, the Christians inclined to him. They
warned him of the intrigues of the Jews and the heathen Quraysh; how
they meant mischief and sought to do him hurt. They did this because
of their affection for him, and the honor in which they held him and
his friends; and, when he was inspired, God bore witness to them,
through him, in the Qur'an saying: "You shall find that the Jews and
the idolaters, i.e., the Quraysh, are the most bitter enemies of the
faithful; the nearest and most friendly to them, you shall find those
who say, 'We are Christians.' It is because they are under ecclesiastical
rule; they are not proud." (Qur'an 5:85). Our Prophet, Heaven's blessing rest on him, knew by inspiration the sincerity of their purpose and
intent. They were the true followers of Christ, walking in his ways and
receiving his precepts. They did not allow murder, or acknowledge the
right of private property. They did not overreach one another, or act
wrongfully, or practice guile. They sought peace; they abjured envy
and hate, and were, in these respects, superior to other men. On this
account our Prophet gave them special terms and securities, and
constituted himself and his people their guardians and gave them a
charge; while God showed him, as He did, their real worth and the
purity of their domestic life. We acknowledge all this; we do not
dispute or deny it. We have regard to what are facts; and desire to
maintain the same relations with them, and to accept the same respon-
sibilities.

(H) I have myself met many of these monks, noted for their extreme

abstinence and great learning. I have been their guest in their cloisters
and churches. I have been present at the long prayers, or offices,
seven in number which they make Matins, Lauds, Prime, Tierce, Sext,
or Midday. None towards afternoon, and Vesper, said at sundown,
prayers of intercession, which they say at the evening hour, and those
prayers which they offer before they take their nightcap. I have witnessed the wonderful zeal they display, their prostrations and genuflexions, when they touch the earth with their cheeks and beat their brows
and cross their arms while they are praying. All this they do in private.
On Sunday and Friday nights, and on feast days, they keep vigil,
standing upright praising God, repeating the Sanctus and singing
Psalms the whole night through. At break of day, too, they offer
prayers. In all this they make mention of the Father, Son and Holy
Ghost. On certain days, as at Easter, they throng the churches and
stand there with bare feet, in sackcloth and ashes, weeping floods of
tears and sobbing in a wonderful way. I have seen the preparation of
the sacred wafer; how carefully, and with what cleansing rites, it is
baked; and the long prayers made while it is offered , with extraordinary protestations, during the act of elevation at the altar in what is
known as "the Shrine," along with flagons of wine. I have seen how
the monks in their cells, on certain days, observe feasts, the greater and
the lesser fast, and so forth. I have been present with them at these
services and a witness of all this; and I know well what I say.

(I) I have conversed with their Metropolitans and bishops famous for
ripe scholarship and fine culture, and not less for their Christian
character and the rigor of their abstinence. In all my intercourse with
them I have tried to be impartial, aiming only at truth. I have put
aside, as unworthy of me, anything like insistence or acerbity. I have
not lorded it over them, nor stood on my dignity with them. I have
allowed them perfect freedom to make good their cause, and to speak
out their minds, without fear. I have never taken them to task for this,
nor have I cavilled at anything they might say. That I leave to others —
the rabble rout. Fools I call them, though they are of my own persuasion. The root of the matter is not in them nor any reason to which
one might appeal; neither religion nor good manners restrains them,
but they are disputatious, arrogant, overbearing. With them, pride of

Empire takes the place of argument. I must confess that in my intercourse with the Christians, when I have questioned them, inquiring as to their ideas and convictions, they have always given me a satisfactory answer. There has not been a suspicion of insincerity on their part in our discussions; but I have always found them, on close acquaintance, as I had heard of them at a distance. I have written all this at full length, after profound and particular research, lest you should imagine that I am ignorant of the matter under discussion. I wish those who may read what I write to realize that I am intimately acquainted with the Christian case in all its bearings.

(J) And now, God grant it to you, by all the knowledge which I have of your religion, and by all my old affection for the Truth as God has revealed it, and which I have adopted as my own, I summon you to the true Faith. Paradise is yours; nor need you fear the fires of hell on condition that you worship the one God, Sole, Eternal, neither begetting nor begotten, nor has He any peer. Such is the definition He, the most Glorious and Great, has given Himself; nor is He known to any of His creatures but to Himself alone. I summon you to the worship of the one God, as thus defined. Nor do I add, in this, by one jot to what He has said of Himself, whose name is Glorious, exalted in His memorial, lofty, great, without peer. This was the religion of your father and ours, Abraham, God be gracious to him, who also was an orthodox Muslim. Still further I summon you to bear witness, and confess the prophetic rank of my master, the lord of mankind, friend of the Lord of the universe, seal of the prophetic order, Muhammad, son of 'Abdullah the Hashimite, of Quraysh descent, an Arab of the country and town of Mecca,[13] master of the rod and the pool and the camel[14] who intercedes for us, friend of the Lord of power, companion of Gabriel the faithful spirit. God sent him to preach and teach all men everywhere, "with good guidance and true religion, to enlighten him on all religious matters, however the idolaters may repudiate him." He summoned all men everywhere, East and West, by land and sea, mountain and dale, in mercy and kindness, with good works and kindly dispositions and, in gentleness. Won by his gracious ways, they responded everywhere to his summons, and bore witness that he was the messenger of God, who is Lord of all, to all who accept His teaching.

All men confessed and paid him homage when they saw the absolute
sincerity of his teaching and the soundness of his cause, the clear and
indisputable evidence he furnished in a book inspired of God; the like
of which no man or Jinn could produce. "Say, if man or Jinn should
conspire to produce such a book as this, they could not, though they
stood back to back." (Qur'an 17:90)[15] Here, surely, is proof enough of
his mission. So then he summoned them to the worship of the one
sole eternal God, and they embraced his religion and submitted to him.
They were not scornful or overbearing, but humbled themselves,
confessing him, and seeking light and guidance at his hand. In his
name power was given them over those who disputed his claims, and
denied his mission in an antagonistic and self-righteous spirit. God
gave them power over the nations, and humbled the peoples under
their yoke. None were excepted save those who received his doctrine
and professed the faith, and testified. These saved their lives and
property and families, paying tribute and accepting humiliation. Now,
God be gracious to you, this witness was borne by God before the
world was made. Written on His throne are the words: "There is no
god but God; Muhammad is His Messenger."[16] By God, there is no
God but He who is Lord of the throne of Omnipotence.

(K) I summon you still further, to the five prayers. He who offers
them shall have interest, and be reckoned among the winners in this
world and the next. Religious duties, you understand, are of two sorts:
those imposed by God, and those imposed by His Prophet, such as the
free-will prayers. Those imposed by the Prophet comprise three acts
of devotion: after late evening, two at daybreak, two in the afternoon
and two after sunset. He who omits any of these shall lose his reward;
and he who omits them for days is open to correction and must make
good the omission. Further imposed are seventeen acts of devotion
covering the whole day: two at dawn, four at noon, four in the afternoon, three at sunset and four at the late evening — "Atamah" it was
called, but the Prophet of God forbade that name, and called it rather
"late evening" or "its close."[17]

(L) I summon you further to the fast of the month of Ramadan, the
sacred month when the Qur'an was sent down.[18] The month of which

God bears witness that it brought in the Night of Doom better than any thousand months. You may fast all day from food and drink and sexual intercourse till the sun's disk touch the horizon and the night begins. Then you may eat and drink and have intercourse all the night, till you can distinguish a white thread from a black. This you may do lawfully and without limit, in ease and comfort; it is God's decree. If you observe this Night of Doom with sincerity of purpose, you shall gain thereby in this world and the next. Thus saith God the Most High: "O ye who believe, fasting is imposed on you as on those before you; it may be ye will fear God. Appointed days ye shall fast; and if any of you be sick or on a journey, ye shall fast the same number of other days; and for those who could, and would not fast, the ransom shall be the maintenance of a poor man. If you obey freely, it shall be well with you; and if ye fast, it shall be well with you, if ye know it. Ye shall fast during the month of Ramadan, on which the Qur'an came down to you with guidance for life and clear proof and decision; he who is at home, let him fast; and if one is sick or on a journey, let him fast the same number of other days. God requires of you what is easy, and not what is hard; therefore ye shall fulfil the number, and glorify God who has given you guidance; it may be ye will be thankful. Should any of my servants inquire of Me — I am here; I hear the prayers of him who directs his prayer to Me. Let them respond to Me and believe; it may be they will be rightly guided. During the night of the fast ye may have intimacy with your wives; they are a covering to you, and ye to them; God knows how in this ye deny yourselves. He will turn to you and pardon you. Now, have free intercourse with them, and desire what God hath decreed for you. Eat and drink till you can discern a white thread from a black in the dawn; then continue your fast until the night comes, and abstain from them. Be diligent in attendance at the mosque; this is God's decree; come not near them. Thus God makes manifest His signs to men; it may be that they will fear Him." (Qur'an 2:179-183) The Prophet of God, on whom Heaven's blessing rest, advanced the hour for breaking the fast, and delayed the hour for resuming it as far as he could.

(M) Then I summon you to the Pilgrimage to the House of God, the Sanctuary in Mecca, and to visit the shrine of the Apostle of God, where he stepped, and where he stood; to fling the pebbles in Mina, and to cry "Labbaik, Labbaik," and to wear the pilgrim's dress and to kiss the black stone.[19]

(N) Then I summon you to wage war in the ways of God, i.e., to raid the hypocrites and to slay the unbelievers and idolater with the edge of the sword; to capture and plunder till they embrace the faith and witness that there is no god but God and that Muhammad is His servant and Apostle, or else pay the tribute and accept humiliation. "Slay those who do not believe in God or in the Day of Judgment, who consider not as unlawful what God and his Apostle have forbidden, nor do they hold the true faith; slay, till they pay tax and are humbled."[20] And I summon you to confess that God quickens the dead and is the righteous Judge who rewards good with good and evil with evil. All His saints and faithful people, who confess the one God, and that Muhammad is His servant and Apostle, and believe in the inspiration of the Qur'an, He will lead into Paradise where all good awaits them. So He promised them: "Behold, God will lead those who believe and do what is right into Paradise with its flowing rivers. They shall be adorned with bracelets of gold and pearls, and they shall be dressed in silk." (Qur'an 22:23)

(O) And they said: "Praise be God who hath removed sorrow from us; He is our Lord who pardons and repays. He hath given us, by His grace, everlasting abodes to dwell in, where we shall know no weariness nor fatigue." (Qur'an 35: 31,32)

(P) "There sure provision shall be made for them; even fruits. And they shall be held in honor, amid gardens of delight. They shall face each other seated on couches. Cups shall be handed round, filled from the well; a pure delight to those who drink. In them shall lurk no intoxication nor madness. Languishing[21] eyes shall be turned on them, gleaming like the white of an egg." (Qur'an 37:40-47)

(Q) "For those who fear the Lord, they shall be builded hall above hall, with rivers flowing beneath. God has promised, who never changes His word." (Qur'an 39:21)

(R) "Oh my servants, fear not that day; be not anxious, those who believe in our signs, they are Muslims. Enter into Paradise ye and your husbands with whom ye were so happy. They shall hand you golden goblets and cups full of what your hearts and souls desire and your eyes delight in, and ye shall dwell there forever." (Qur'an 43:68-71)

(S) "See, they who fear God have an enduring habitation, even Paradise with its fountains. They shall be clothed with linen and brocade, and shall face each other; and We shall wed them to black-eyed beauties. They shall call for all kinds of fruits without fear. They shall not taste death, save the first death; for the punishment of Hell shall not come to them. By the favor of their Lord this shall be their great gain." (Qur'an 44:51-57)

(T) And the Glorious and Great One has said: "Like Paradise, which is promised those who fear Him. In it are rivers of sweet water and rivers of milk never sour; rivers of wine, delicious to drink. Rivers of pure honey and all kinds of fruits shall be theirs with pardon from their Lord; while he who is in Hell fire shall drink hot water which rends the bowels." (Qur'an 47:16, 17)

(U) The Glorious and Great One has said: "This is the record; and those who fear God shall have a happy return, a garden of delights with open gates. Seated there, they shall call for fruits of many kinds and for drink, surrounded by languishing eyes of dear ones of their own age. This is what is promised them in the day of reckoning. Lo, this provision is made for us; it has no end." (Qur'an 38:49-54)

(V) Said the Glorious and Great in the description of Paradise: to him who fears the Judgment of his Lord shall be: "Two gardens; which then of the signs of your Lord will ye deny? Planted with shady trees; which then of the signs of your Lord will ye deny? Through each of them flow two fountains; which then of the signs of your Lord will ye deny? In them are all kinds of fruits, in pairs; which then of the signs of your Lord will ye deny? All sit on couches lined with brocade, and

with the fruits of two gardens near at hand; which then of the signs of
your Lord will ye deny? In them are languishing eyes of pure virgins
whom man nor Jinn hath known; which then of the signs of your Lord
will ye deny? Gleaming as if they were sapphires or pearls; which then
of the signs of your Lord will ye deny? The reward of the good is
good; which then of the signs of your Lord will ye deny? And besides
these there shall be two other gardens; which then of the signs of your
Lord will ye deny? Darkened with leafy shrubs; which then of the
signs of your Lord will ye deny? In them are fountains bubbling over;
which then of the signs of your Lord will ye deny? In them are fruits,
dates and pomegranates; which then of the signs of your Lord will ye
deny? In them are choice and beautiful ones; which then of the sign s
of your Lord will ye deny? Black eyes languishing in pavilions; which
then of the signs of your Lord will ye deny? Man hath not profaned
them, nor Jinn; which then of the signs of your Lord will ye deny?
Seated on the ground with pillows of akbar,[22] beautiful; which then of
the signs of your Lord will ye deny? Blessed be the Name of our
Lord; the Glorious and Great." (Qur'an 55:46-78)

(W) Said the Glorious and Great: "Those who fear their Lord shall be
driven to Paradise in troops, till they reach it and the gates thereof
shall be thrown open to them, and the porter shall say: 'Peace be to
you, ye have done well, enter and dwell forever.' " (Qur'an 40:73)

(X) "They shall be met by happiness and joy. For their patience thcy
shall inherit Paradise with silk garments. They shall be stretched on
couches where the sun shall not smite them, nor the winter's wind.
Low lie the shadows round them, branches shall drop over their heads.
Vessels of silver shall be handed round and cups and goblets made to
hold as much as they please; and they shall drink cups of wine mixed
with ginger from the well that is called Selsabil." (Qur'an 76:11-18)

(Y) "Those who fear God shall have the better part; they shall have
gardens with clusters of grapes and swelling bosoms of dear companions of their own age; and cups filled to the brim. No idle talk nor
false alarm shall break their repose. Their reward from their Lord
shall be beautiful gifts." (Qur'an 78:31-36) "Those who fear God shall

live in delightful gardens; they shall enjoy what their Lord hath given
them, and their Lord shall deliver them from the punishment of Hell,
Eat and drink in comfort the reward of your labors, seated on couches
arranged in rows. We shall wed them to black-eyed beauties. They
who believed and their children who followed them, We shall re-unite;
nor shall We deprive them of their reward in aught. Every man shall
be pledged for that which he hath done.[23] We shall spread out fruits
sufficient such as they love. They shall hand round cups in which no
idle talk nor evil is lurking. And youths shall serve them in order,
whose beauty gleams like pearls, and they shall face each other and
pledge each other. They shall say: 'See, we were formerly of the
people who obtained mercy. God was gracious to us and delivered us
from the torment of the fireblast. See, we formerly called on Him; He
is righteous and merciful.' " (Qur'an 52:17-28)

(Z) Those who went before and have precedence, they shall be near
in the Paradise of delight. Troops of the former,[24] but only a few of
the latter. They shall lie on couches, stretched out with cups, flagons
and glasses of spring water. Nothing shall molest their perfect repose.
With fruits such as they choose and flesh of birds and what they desire
with black-eyed beauties like gleaming pearls their reward shall be
according to their deeds. No idle talk nor false alarm shall break their
repose. It shall be said, 'Hail! Hail!' And ah! What companions on
the right hand among the lotus trees stripped of their thorns and the
acacia with fruits piled up on it; shady alleys and flowing streams,
various kinds of fruit, no end, no restraint, couches heaped up, see, We
create them a new type of womanhood, dear and of meet age to their
master at their right hand. Troops of the former and troops of the
latter. (Qur'an 56:10-39)

(AA) This, God bless you, is the description of Paradise as prepared
by God for those who fear Him and His Apostle. For them He has
prepared its delights; eating and drinking, all sorts of fruits and scents
and charms of black-eyed beauties like gleaming pearls. There is no
end to it, no limit. All they wish, they have; all their eye delights in.
Honor shall be shown them there, and life. They shall sit on couches,
resting in verandas with soft silk robes, behind curtains strewn with

pearls. On their faces shall be written the radiance of their day. Youths too, shall move in graceful circles; young men and maids who, in their own way, are like gleaming pearls. They shall hand them cups from which to drink, full of wine mixed with water from the well Taenim. Those who are near to God drink of it. In it they shall pledge each other to all that is kind and good. It shall be said to them: "Eat and drink and enjoy yourselves; have comfort in the fruit of your labors." No idle talk shall disturb, nor hunger gnaw, nor fatigue, and they shall dwell in all this comfort without fear, in confidence and perpetuity. But the unbelievers who worshipped other than the true God, and set up rivals to Him and did not believe His messenger and denied His signs, forbidding what He allowed and fighting against Him, they shall be condemned to the fire. The fire that cannot be quenched shall blow up in their faces and all the whirlwinds of Hell. There they shall dwell forever. The skin shall be flayed from off them only to grow again. Hell shall be their home; they shall drink of the slime and feed on the deadly tree. The Devil and his angels shall be their companions and everlasting misery their doom. "See, those who did not believe in God's signs, who slew His prophets without right, murdered those who taught them the truth and preached the judgment to come, these are they whose works perish in this world and in the next. These have no helper." (Qur'an 3:20,21)

(AB) "Behold, these who denied God and His Apostle, they said: 'Some of these things we will believe, but not others, and they tried to pick and choose their way; these in very deed are unbelievers. We have prepared for them punishment and disgrace." (Qur'an 4:149,150) "Those who do not believe, Hell fire is reserved for them; to it, no end, to them no death, nor shall their torment be lightened; such shall be the reward of all unbelievers." (Qur'an 35:33)

(AC) "The tree of Zakum we have planted as a curse to the evildoers, a tree that springs up from the roots of Hell and rises high as the Devil's head. They shall eat of it, and fill their bellies with its food. Not water shall be poured over for them. Ever their way leads back to Hell." (Qur'an 37:60-66)

(AD) "Alas for those who disbelieve in Hell; if they persist, evil shall be their latter end. They shall be flayed in the fire; foul shall be their bed. They shall taste of hot water with putrid stuff." (Qur'an 38:56,57)

(AE) "Over them fire shall spread like a canopy, and under their feet, darkness." (Qur'an 39:18)

(AF) "On the day of Resurrection, thou shalt see those who denied God; their faces shall be blackness, is not the abode of the proud in Hell?" (Qur'an 39: 61)

(AG) "Those who believed not in the signs of God, are they to suffer loss." (Qur'an 39:63)

(AH) "Unbelievers shall be driven into Hell in troops; when they reach the gates, these shall be thrown open to them, and the wardens shall say to them: 'Did no messenger come to you and recite to you the signs of your Lord?' They shall answer: 'Yea, but the sentence of doom is justly pronounced on unbelievers.' " (Qur'an 39:71)

(AI) "These in the fire said to the wardens of Hell, 'Pray for your Lord that He may lighten our day of torment.' They replied: 'Did He not warn you of this by His messengers?' They answer: 'Yea,' They said: 'Pray then.' But the prayers of the unbelievers are themselves errors." (Qur'an 40:52,53)

(AJ) "Do you not see that they who oppose the signs of God have no way to turn? They deny the scripture and the message we sent by our messengers; verily they shall know. Behold, collars shall be on their necks, and they shall be dragged in chains through the pitch; thus they shall be flayed in the fire." (Qur'an 40:71-73)

(AK) "To the unbeliever painful torment is appointed. You shall see evildoers when they face the torment that awaits them, saying: 'Is there no way of return?' You shall see how they meet it, crouching low, casting furtive glances at it." (Qur'an 42:42-44)

(AL) "Those who do wickedly shall be forever in the pain of Hell. No respite is theirs but blank despair. We have not wronged them; they have wronged themselves. They cry: 'Oh Angel, pray thy Lord that He put an end to our miseries.' But he shall say: 'Abide where you are.' " (Qur'an 43:74-77)

(AM) "This tree Zakum shall be the sinner's meat; like boiling pitch in their bellies; like boiling hot water. It will be said to the tormentors: 'Take him and drag him through the midst of Hell, then pour boiling hot water over his head to torment him.' saying: 'Drink of it, thou mighty and honorable one. See, once you did not believe in this.' " (Qur'an 44:43-50)

(AN) "They shall be ever in the fire and drink hot water till their bellies split. And this is because they loathed what God had given. They said: 'This we might accept, but not that.' God knows their secret and how shall it be when the Angel takes them, beating them on the face and back? And this because they followed what displeased God and loathed what He liked; therefore their works come to nothing. Do they whose words are not right suppose that God will not bring to light their hate?" (Qur'an 47:17-19)

(AO) "Alas! On that day for those who accused the prophets of lying! Have We not made the earth sufficient for the living and the dead? We have placed in it the stable and lofty hills and given them sweet water to drink. Alas! On that day for those who accused the prophets of lying. Go ye, to prove what ye denied! Go ye into the gloom branching out into three directions, where there is no shelter nor relief from the flames. They shall be pelted with sparks like castles for size, murky like the camel's hide. Alas, in that day for the unbelievers. On that day they shall say nothing, no excuse shall be permitted them. Alas! On that day for the unbelievers, this is the day of decision. We have gathered you and those who went before." (Qur'an 77:24-38)

(AP) Now God save you, my friend! Heard you ever a description more wonderful than that? So we tempt you and solemnly charge you and woo you as with a lover's kiss.[25] Here are hopes and fears, promises and threats for the stouthearted and obstinate; nay, for all, whether they will hear or forbear, whether they believe or disbelieve, whether they affirm or deny. If only thus, by what I have said, you are moved to fear, great will be the gain; and if only thus, by the fires and torments of Hell, you are moved to fear, it were cruel to spare your pain. God, most High and ever Blessed, hath said: "Warn them, for warning profits the faithful." (Qur'an 87:10)

(AQ) "If thou shalt see them rush in where angels fear to tread, turn thou from them until they turn in some other direction, and if Satan cause thee to forget, sit not with evildoers, when thou art admonished." (Qur'an 6:67) "Shall We warn them, whom the faithful messenger hath already warned?" (Qur'an 44:12)

(AR) "Let him remember and the admonition shall profit." (Qur'an 80:4)

(AS) "Warn them, and the warning shall profit." (Qur'an 87:9)

(AT) "On that day Hell shall be brought nigh, and men shall remember, but how shall memory profit them?" (Qur'an 89:24)

(AU) Thus we have warned you, and if you believe and receive the testimony of our book, you shall profit by the admonition we have written. And if nothing will content you but to abide in your unbelief and error, opposing the truth, we at least are sure of our reward; we have done His behest. But, if God wills, the truth shall come into its own with you. May God enlighten your mind as to the actual facts of the true religion, its precepts and signs and maxims. When you have embraced it and confessed it and borne witness, when you have embraced the law of light, these convincing signs and wholesome maxims to which we summon you, then you will be one of us. High indeed shall be your station in this world and in the next. For see, our Prophet, on whom Heaven's Blessing rest, has said: "On the day of Resurrection everyone, Prophet and angel alike shall be absorbed in himself; but he shall say: 'My house! My tribe!' and he shall receive an answer,

first for his house, and then for his tribe. The Merciful One shall say
to the angels: 'I am ashamed to refuse the intercession of Mine elect,
My friend.' "²⁶ Then, of course, we shall require of you what is due.
You shall pray toward the qibla, which God has given us, and offer the
five prayers after due ablutions. If you are well, standing on your feet,
but, if you are weak or sickly, sitting; if you are on a journey, half of
the number of what you offer when at home. "Offer thy prayers and
give alms. Those to whom we have given the earth, offer prayers and
give alms. Those to whom we have given the earth, offer prayers and
give alms and practice benevolence and desist from what is forbidden.
God rewards what men do."²⁷ Now alms are the fourth of the tithe,
when you come to divide the spoil, and it shall be in the hands of its
owner, a single unit, for a division. The tithe shall be given to the poor
members of the community and the indigent among them. You may
marry whom you please; it is no crime. For is there blame or offence
or reproach, if you marry them in (the) presence of his magistrate and
with witnesses, and give us a dowry what seems good to you and them
out of your abundance? In the same way, if you have four wives and
divorce them, because you dislike them, or you are tired and have
(had) enough of them, it shall not be held as a crime to take back
anyone of them you please, after you have given her to another. If you
still like her and your soul cleave to her. "If ye divorce, it is not
unlawful to have her till she have intercourse with another; if he have
divorced her, it is no crime to them if they come together again, if they
think they can do God's will, This is God's decree; may He make it
plain to the people who have understanding." (Qur'an 2:230)²⁸ But
abstain from captive maids when ye get possession of them. Circumcise them according to the rite of Abraham our father, the friend of
God, who is merciful, and of Ishmael our father and yours;²⁹ let them
purify themselves from defilement. Then, if you can, you will fast in
the month of Ramadan; but, if not, if you break the fast for any reason, sickness or a journey, afterwards you shall make a point of fulfill-
ing it.

(AV) God wills not for His servants what is burdensome, but what is
light. If you break an oath which you have made according to the
command of God, God will not punish you for a slip of the tongue; but

God will punish you for the evil you treasure up in your hearts. He is forgiving and kind. Among us Muslims the expiation of an oath which has been broken is the maintenance of ten poor men of your own tribe; or else (to) clothe them, or, if they be slaves, (to) ransom them. He who cannot do any of these, let him fast three days. This is the expiation for the breach of an oath; when you have sworn, guard your oath. Thus God makes plain to you His signs; perhaps ye will be thankful. You will, of course, make the pilgrimage. "In it are manifest signs; here stood the feet of our father Abraham, and he who enters there is safe." This is the duty which a man owes to God; whoever is fit for the road, let him make the pilgrimage. If you are not in debt, you can easily meet the expense of a camel and ride. Then you will go forth to fight: here is immediate profit in this world, and great interest reserved for the world to come. God has given easy terms to His faithful people; yet will He have us put our whole heart into His service. If there were nothing else in Islam but comfort and safety in submission to the Word of God, and quiet confidence in the promise He has freely given, that He will enrich us in the next world with a great reward, and will lead us into that delightsome Paradise where we shall abide forever; even so, great were the gain.

(AW) Thus now I have spoken to you the Word of God. His is a voice of truth, who never breaks His promise, nor belies His Word, what has been briefly stated may suffice. Away then with your present unbelief, which means error and misery and calamity. Will you any longer cleave to what you must admit is a mere medley? I mean your doctrine of Father, Son and Holy Ghost, and the worship of the cross? I have grave doubts on your behalf. What has one of your knowledge and reputation to do with so mean a conception of the divine? I find God saying: "God will not pardon those who worship more Gods than one; any other offences He may pardon, but he who worships more Gods than one lies against God with a grievous sin." (Qur'an 4:51) Again He says: "He is an unbeliever who says that Jesus the son of Mary, the Messiah, is God. The Messiah himself said: 'O children of Israel, serve God and my Lord, He who worships other gods, God has shut on him gates of heaven;' his dwelling place is the fire; the evildoers have no helpers. They are unbelievers who say that God is the

third of three, whereas there is no God but one; if they do not desist
from what they say, terrible punishment shall overtake those who do
not believe. Or will ye not return to God and plead for pardon? God
is forgiving and merciful. The son of Mary, the Messiah, is only a messenger. There were others before him, and his mother is a true
woman; both lived by bread. See how we have made plain our signs;
then see how they turn aside to lying." (Qur'an 5:76-79)

(AX) Away then with this error, this misplaced and wearing seal, this
practice of an ascetic life, this infliction on yourself of continuous
privations and protracted penances in which you spend your life.
There is no profit in all this, but only a weariness of the flesh and
vexation of the spirit. Come, enter the true fold; strike out into the
easy way; embrace the faith that brings assurance. Here is the good
law, the law of liberty which God has graciously granted to His servants. Thus I have spoken my mind to you, my friend, in the spirit of
goodwill and sincere affection. Fain would I breathe into you my very
soul, that we might be of one mind in this matter. Thus saith my Lord
in His faithful Word: "They who are unbelievers, whether they be
People of the Book or idolaters, shall be consigned to everlasting fire;
they are reprobates. But they who believe and do rightly, they are the
elect people; their reward shall be with their Lord in the delightsome
Paradise, where flows forever the river of life. God is well pleased
with them and they with Him, this is their lot who fear their Lord."
(Qur'an 98:5- 7) And again: "Ye are the elect people sent forth
among men to teach the practice of kindness and to desist from evil
and to believe in God; and, if the People of the Book believe us, it
shall be well with them. Some of them believed, but the majority of
them are evildoers." (Qur'an 3:106) Now, may God save you, for I
yearn over you; fearful lest you be of the reprobates and doomed to
hell fire. I trust by the good hand of God on you, you may yet be
among the faithful, in whom God delights as they delight in Him; these
are the elect people. I trust you may yet be among those who are sent
forth among men. But if you have no mind save stubbornly adhere to
your ignorance, persisting in your present defiant unbelief; if you reject
our appeal and will have none of the truth we have laid before you, so
that your efforts prove thankless and barren; at least let me hear what

are your views on this great question. What do you hold as Truth, and by what argument do you establish it? Write to me without fear and restraint, and do not hold back anything that is in your heart, as if you were afraid of me. I only wish to hear what you have to say. I shall be patient, submissive, responsive, as the case may require; ready to yield without dispute or demur. I have no fear. Only let us compare what you have to say with what I have already advanced. I shall leave you free to make what comments you like upon it. But do not blame us, as if fear of us had made you dumb. Do not plead in defence of a bad cause, that you held your tongue and had no freedom to state your case! Perfect freedom you shall have; only you must not blame us as if we were overbearing or accuse us of injustice or undue pressure. That is not in our line. But do you, as God may help you, make the best of your case. Say what you will, and say it as you will; let us have whatever you think may tend in the direction of a final settlement.

(AY) Come, let us appoint an imperial umpire, one who shall decide the case between us without partiality or undue pressure, and will not swerve from the truth, whichever way the wind may blow. Reason shall be the umpire between us. Reason, the attribute of God Himself, the arbiter of human actions. For ourselves, we have sought to deal fairly with you; we have given you every possible security. We shall be satisfied with the decision of reason, for or against us. Let no man's conscience suffer constraint. If we summon you thus, it is in all submission and in the name of the Truth which we hold; but we know that you are in the gall of iniquity. Peace be with you and mercy from God and blessing.

Notes:

[1] "Eternal" - Samad: "The person to whom one repairs or has recourse in an exigency; or, a Lord whose Lordship has attained to its utmost point or degree, i.e., a being who continues forever." (Lane)

[2] "Hashimite": Hashim was the great grandfather of the Prophet.

'Abbas, his uncle, was ancestor of the family who, in the person of Abul 'Abbas, attained to the caliphate (749-754 A.D.) and retained it to the close (1258 A.D.). The Hashimites include both 'Abbasids and 'Alids, and are opposed to the Umayyads (Tien refers the reader to his introduction, which has been deleted here - ed.).

[3] "His own people and strangers": The former (Ahl-Az-Zummah) are the free non-Muslim subjects of a Muslim government who pay tribute and are entitled to protection. The Ummi is one - "in the natural state of his people" (Ummah) i.e., uneducated (so applied to the Prophet himself); or, without a revealed religion, i.e., a Gentile or a heathen, or one with no relation to the Muslim rule. "Idolaters" are those who associate another with God as the subject of their worship, i. e., Polytheists. In the majority of cases we may render as above.

[4] "Imams": The imam is one who stands in front of the people, facing the qibla at prayer. After the Prophet's death the office descended to his successors. The civil and religious power is thus united in the caliph. When necessary the caliph could depute another to hold office as imam, e.g., on the field of battle.

[5] "Recording Angel": According to Islam two angels are told of to act the part of Minos and try the dead. One is called Nakir, the other Munkar. The process as described in the Qur'an is rough, but presumably effective. (See Qur'an 7:35 and 47:29.)

[6] "The Amir of the Faithful": Literally "the leader." The name was first given in 623 A.D. (2 A.H.) to 'Abdullah b. Jahsh who was deputed with seven of the refugees to lead against the Meccan caravan. The name was assumed in after days by the caliphs.

[7] "Resurrection - Future Life": Two words are used (Ma'ad and Ma'ab), both meaning "Return"; as at the close of a long journey. The latter word is used of the place which camels come for watering at evening. It is a primitive conception of the future life, which recalls the beautiful Scotch proverb "E'enen brings a' home." "When the heavens

shall be cloven in sunder and when the stars shall be scattered, and when the seas shall be suffered to join their waters, and when the graves shall be turned upside down, every soul shall know what he hath committed and what he hath omitted." (Qur'an 82:1-5)

[8] "Orthodox Faith": The point of the quotations which follow is this: Abraham stands as the representative of the earlier revelation which finds its further development in Christianity and Islam. The Christians are therefore bound, like him, to accept Islam. (For the original use of the word, see Introduction [deleted]). One may compare with this passage the use St. Paul makes in his epistles of the person and religious experiences of Abraham to widen out the scope of revelation so as to include the Gentile world. The word I have translated "Orthodox" is "Hanifite." It comes from the verb meaning to turn or bend and was used of one who inclines from a false to a true religion. "According to Akh, it was applied in the times ignorance to one who performed the pilgrimage to the Sacred House and was circumcised, because that was all they knew of the religion of Abraham." (Lane) Margoliouth thinks it may originally have been a tribal name. By Muslim writers it is regarded as a term of honor synonymous with orthodoxy. The Christian writer, as we shall see, regards it, from his standpoint, as synonymous with idolatry.

[9] "Apostolic Band": The word used "Hawariyy" means "the one who washes clothes," a Fuller. The disciples may have been so called (a) because that was supposed to be their trade, or (b) figuratively, as men cleansed from vice, or (c) as men who had stood the test and been found trusty (from "Har': "to return"). See Lane.

[10] "Primacy": The word is the Greek Katholikos as indicating the highest, i.e., universal authority in the church. Under the Katholikos came the Patriarch, then the Metropolitan and then the diocesan Bishops.

[11] The 5th, 6th and 7th centuries were marked by a succession of keen controversies in the church, the central point of which was the Person of Christ. The ancient Ebionite heresy, which denied the deity

of Jesus, and the Gnostic heresy, which denied His humanity, had been outgrown. A further stage in the discussion had been reached. What was the relation of the two elements (the human and divine) in the Person of our Lord? Nestorius, the Patriarch of Constantinople, affirmed the reality of the two natures, but in such a way as seemed to some to impugn the unity of the Person. At the Council of Ephesus (431 A. D.), summoned by the Emperor Marcianus, and presided over by Cyril the Alexandrian, he (Nestorius) was (condemned) as a heretic. Some twenty years later Eutyches went to the opposite extreme, affirming the unity of Christ in such a way as seemed to some to deny the reality of the two natures. They were condemned by the Council of Chalcedon (451 A. D.). Still a third possibility remained. A branch of the Syrian church in Lebanon, known as Maronites, taught that while the Nature of our Lord was dual, His will was single. This monothelite heresy was condemned by the Council of Constantinople (680 A.D.). Nestorius particularly objected to the use of the term Theotokos (Mother of God) as applied to the virgin. On his deposition he withdrew into private life. His followers founded a seat of learning at Nisibis, not far from the ancient Nineveh, and their missionaries carried the knowledge of letters into Central Asia and spread to the north, to India, Ceylon and Malabar. A branch of the Nestorian Church was found in China in 636 A. D. Naturally the Muslim writer gives the preference to the theological views of Nestorius. The Melkites were so called because they accepted the creed of Marcianus, the Roman Emperor or King (Melek) who favored the party of Cyril. The credit of maintaining the influence of the Monophysite party is Syria is due to Jacob, a man distinguished by indefatigable zeal. With great rapidity, and often amid many dangers, he traversed the Syrian province in the guise of a beggar; hence he was called "Baradaeus," "the man in rags" (Neander, vol. 4). Severus, another of the Monophysite leaders, played an important part in these disputes, and secured for himself the See of Antioch.

[12] For the relation in which Muhammad stood to the Christian monks, see Introduction [deleted]; - see Appendix A - ed.

[13] "Meccan": Two words are used - "al-Abtahy" and "at-Tahamy."

The former comes from Batha, the open field in which Mecca lies.
Tahama is the old name of Mecca. (According to Sir Muir "a broad
margin of low land between the coast of Arabia and the receding
mountains.")

[14] "Master of the Rod, the Pool and the Camel": The Prophet
seems usually to have carried a staff. On one occasion in (a) token of
special gratification with 'Abdullah b. Umayys, who had assassinated
the chief of the Lahyan, he presented him with this staff. This, said he,
shall be a token between me and thee on the day of Resurrection. The
Pool is Cawther which God created for the Prophet and his followers
in Paradise. " 'While I was looking about', said the Prophet, 'I came all
of a sudden on a river; on both banks are domes, each consisting of a
hollow pearl.' I asked Gabriel, 'What is this?' He said, 'This is Cawther which God hath given thee.' Then I perceived that the ground was
of pure musk and of a piercing fragrance. The pond is square and one
month's journey in circumference, being as long as Arabia. The water
is as white as milk and sweeter than honey; he who drinks of it thirsts
no more." (Sprenger, English version). The stories about the Prophet's
camel, "Al-Caswa," on which he escaped from Mecca and which he
rode ever after, are known to all.

[15] "Jinns": Often rendered "genii"; familiar to all readers; beings of
supernatural order. A whole sura of the Qur'an is devoted to them.
Before the coming of the Prophet, we are told, it was their custom to
eavesdrop at the gate of heaven and even to occupy a vacant chair
there. But afterwards, "We found the gate guarded by a strong body
of angels, and whoever listens now finds a flame of fire in ambush for
him." (Qur'an 72:8,9)

[16] This question of the shahada being written on the throne of God
has often been used as an argument for a 10th century dating for
al-Kindi's Apology. Mingana responds to this issue in his introduction
to the dialogue of the Patriarch Timothy and the Caliph Mahdi, see his
notes 16 and 17 (p. 171) and note 25 (p. 522) to al-Kindi's letter below
- ed.

[17] The prayers of Muslims are of two parts, (a) those imposed by the Qur'an, i.e., by divine authority, known as Fard and (b) those imposed by authority of the Prophet, known as Sunna. The latter are enumerated first in the text. "An act of devotion" consists of the utterance of certain words, accompanied by prostrations ("rak'ahs") in which the head is bowed so that the palms of the hands touch the knees, while the back is bent so that a glass of water, if placed on it, is not spilled. In addition to the Fard and Sunna there are the free-will prayers alluded to in the text, known as "al-Witr," i.e., "the prayers," with an odd number of rak'ahs. The Muslims following as they believe the practice of Allah, attach special importance to the odd number; "Verily, God is one only, He loveth the odd number, therefore perform ye the prayer (an) odd number, ye people of the Qur'an." (*Shorter Encyclopedia of Islam* [p. 634] shows this saying to be based on tradition and gives Ahmad b. Hanbal, i, 110 as a reference - ed. This particular act of devotion is optional and is performed at night; the later the better.

[18] After the Prophet left Mecca for Medina and saw the Jews there holding their annual fast on the Day of Atonement, he adapted the custom and imposed it on his people. At the same time he turned in prayer to the Temple at Jerusalem, as his qibla. But, after the breach with the Jews, he turned in prayer to Mecca and instituted a Muslim fast in the month of Ramadan. The original fast was held in the winter and entailed no great suffering; but, after the change of the calendar and the introduction of a lunar year, the season for the fast gradually shifted till it fell in the heat of summer, when, of course, the days are long and the heat is great and the suffering involved correspondingly greater. It is said that the fast is observed with absolute fidelity all over the Muslim world. - Liberal Muslim groups (e.g., the Bektashis) do not keep Ramadan at all - ed.

[19] Once at least in his lifetime the Muslim must make the pilgrimage to Mecca. The pilgrims meet near the city during the months of Shawal and Dhu'l Ka'ada and are obliged to be there by the beginning of Dhul Hajja , which is the sacred month. They put on the Ihram, or

sacred dress, consisting of two woolen wrappers, one thrown over the shoulder, the other wrapped about the loins; heads are bare, the feet shod with a slipper that covers neither the heel nor the instep. Great prominence is given to the prayer of invocation which precedes these rites, known as Labbaik. The origin of the word is doubtful; it may come from the word "Lubb" (the heart) and signify devotion. Here is the cry:

> Labbaik, oh Lord, Labbaik, Labbaik.
> There is no other God but Thee; Labbaik.
> Praise, blessing and dominion be to Thee, Labbaik.
> No one therein may share with Thee; Labbaik, Labbaik.

The sacred House or Ka'ba is surrounded seven times, the first three times with a quick short step, then with slow measured paces. This sevenfold circle, no doubt; points back to the original worship of the seven planets in pre-Islamic Arabia. Each time he passes the Rakan, or corner of the House, the pilgrim kisses, or at least touches the black stone which, originally white, fell from heaven when Adam fell, and has grown black with the world's sin. Close to the Ka'ba is the Stone, or Station of Abraham, on which he is said to have stood when he built the Ka'ba.; also the well of Zamzam from which Hagar is said to have given Ishmael drink. He then proceeds to Safa and Marwa, two hills near the city, and runs from one to the other seven times, in imitation of Hagar asking water for her child. He then moves on to the Valley of Mina. On the morning of the 9th Dhul Hajja he goes to Mount Arafat, where Adam is said to have been introduced to Eve, and spends a day in devotion there. The next day he returns to the Valley of Mina and throws stones at the devil in imitation of Abraham who was tempted to disobedience there by the evil one. Then come the sacrifices and the feast. Heads are shaved and nails pared; and the solemnities are at an end.

[20] For a criticism on this passage the reader is referred to the Christian's reply. In Qur'an 2:186,187 it is written: "Fight for the religion of God against those who fight against you; but transgress not, for God loveth not the transgressor; and kill them wheresoever you

find them, and turn them out of that whereof they have dispossessed you. War is enjoined."

[21] Most writers render the word "averted" as if expressive of modesty. It seems to me more true to the word, as well as more satisfactory to the Muslim bridegrooms to render it as above, i.e., expressive of passion. Compare the Biblical phrase, "Eyes that fail for longing."

[22] A town in Yemen where cloths, garments and carpets of variegated stuffs were made. It is also a place of which the Arab says, "It is in the land of the Twns." A pillow of akbar is therefore one made of fabulous stuff, i.e., of incredible beauty.

[23] i.e., "Every man is pledged unto God for his behavior; if he does well, he redeems the pledge; if ill, he forfeits it." (Sale)

[24] "The Former": i.e., "...either the first converts to Islam or the prophets who were the respective leaders of their peoples." (Sale)

[25] A characteristic Arabic expression. The verb means to sip or suck, and is used of a lover who seems to suck the sweetness from the lips of her whom he kisses.

[26] This reference is non-Qur'anic, but is similar to some hadith, see: *Sahih Muslim*, The Book of Faith, chap. 83, hadith 378, vol. 1, p. 131 - ed.

[27] The idea is difficult to grasp, unless we have an echo of St. Paul's great saying: "Let every man prove his own work, and then shall he have rejoicing in himself, and not in another; for every man shall bear his own burden." (Gal. 6:4,5) Muhammad claims to be an exception to the rule.

[28] The other is known as Mustahil. Sir W. Muir quotes from Burckhardt the proverb: "A thousand lovers rather than one Mustahil."

According to the Muslim Law a person who thrice divorces his wife cannot remarry her till she has been married to another man who becomes her legitimate husband, cohabits with her for the night and divorces her the next morning; afterwards the first husband may again possess her.

[29] Islamic sources attempt to show the rite of circumcising women as a practice instituted by Sarah, see al-Tabari, *History*, vol. 2, p. 72; see also Leo, parag. AQ; al-Jahiz, parag. T - ed.

THE CHRISTIAN'S REPLY

(AZ) In the Name of God, the Merciful, the Compassionate.

(BA) May my Lord help and not hinder; may He perfect what is good.

(BB) To - son of - , from - son of - , least of the servants of Christ, peace, pity and goodwill! Every blessing be yours in particular and in general, with all mankind through the abundance of His grace. Amen.

(BC) To proceed. I have read your letter, and give thanks to God for the favor He has granted me with our master, the Amir of the Faithful. I pray God, who disappoints none who call upon Him with a true heart, to lengthen the days of our master, to satisfy him with His favor, and to continue to him His grace. May He encompass him with salvation, according to His goodness and mercy. I am very grateful to you for his goodwill and consideration you have shown, for your graceful courtesy and for the kindly interest you have displayed to me personally. The friendship which has existed between us from the first has been confirmed, I think I may say, intensified, by the spontaneous expression on your part of so much solicitude for my spiritual welfare. I cannot thank you as I ought; and you have not exceeded what one might expect from your natural kindliness and splendid antecedents! I pray God, whose Name is Glorious, in whose Hand is all good, to recompense you on my behalf, as it is well in His power to do. Nothing is impossible to Him, may He handsomely reward you for your good intentions. In good sooth you have spared yourself no pains on my behalf, nor have you been lacking in any single point. I should indeed be grateful to you, for I am sure you have acted from the purest motives of friendship, your one incentive has been the warmth and kindness of your heart. I know (may God give you to know all good, and guide you into the way of uprightness!), I say I know all you have set forth in your letter. You have gone into the matter very fully, you have set before me your own religious convictions, and summoned me to embrace them with a great deal of persuasive power. And of course I know, God bless you, that you have been impelled to the discharge of these friendly offices by the fact that I enjoy the friendship of my master, your cousin, the Amir of the Faithful. For all this I cannot thank you enough. I can only look to God, whose help most humbly I invoke, praying to Him to recompense you on my behalf, as He is well able to do, for He has all power.

(BD) Now in regard to this question which you raise as to the religion you profess, "the orthodox faith"[1] as you are pleased to call it; you protest that you are of the faith of our father Abraham, and affirm that he was an orthodox Muslim. Here let my invoke the aid of Christ my Master, the Savior of the world, who has given us His word of promise, and pledged Himself when he says: "When they bring you unto synagogues and unto magistrates and powers, take ye no thought how or what thing you shall answer, or what ye shall say, For the Holy Ghost shall teach you in the same hour what ye ought to say." (Luke 12:11)

(BE) I have perfect confidence in what Christ has said in His Holy Gospel as to the fulfilment of His promise; and therefore I enter on this discussion with you, imploring His divine aid and dependent on Him alone. And though I am not sufficient for anything of myself, yet I do not hesitate. The entrance of His word gives light; His service brings its own reward. I begin this discussion in dependence on Him whose wont it is to inspire His servants with sound speech and wholesome doctrine. By His help I trust to prove victorious.

I : Doctrine of God

(BF) And, first of all, you tell me that you have read the scriptures and studied the sacred canon, particularly the Law, as revealed to Moses by God Most High, who imparted to him those mysteries which are contained in the first book, of Genesis. You know then that Abraham dwelt with his father in Haran; it was their home; but when he was 90 years old, God Most High revealed Himself to him. "And Abraham believed God and it was accounted to him for righteousness."

Now we know, God be gracious to you, that Abraham dwelt in Haran for 75 years, worshipping the idol called al-'Uzza, known in Haran as the moon god, according to the custom of the people there. The cult survives among them to this day, with no pretensions of concealment or disguise except in one point. Human sacrifices are no longer legal; they are therefore offered, not in public, but on the sly and secretly. This idol was worshipped with Abraham along with his father and forefathers and the people of the land. Yet you, an orthodox believer, claim that he was orthodox in so doing, and cite in evidence the following passages: "And he believed the Lord and it was accounted to him for righteousness." (Gen. 15:6). "For what saith the scripture, Abraham believed God and it was accounted to him for righteousness." (Romans 4:3). "... and the scripture was fulfilled which saith, Abraham believed God and it was accounted to him for righteousness." (James 2:2). That is to say, he abandoned an "orthodoxy" which meant the worship of idols, and became a worshipper of the one God, and a true believer. For we find what you call "orthodoxy" is described by the Word of God as idolatry.

(BG) The doctrine of the unity of God was bequeathed by Abraham as a precious legacy to Isaac, the child of promise, who had been offered to God on Mount Moriah and redeemed with a ram caught in a thicket. "It came to pass after these things that God did prove Abraham, and said to him, 'Abraham,' and he said, 'Behold, here am I.' And He said, 'Take now thy son, thine only son Isaac, whom thou lovest, and get thee into the land of Moriah and offer him there as a burnt offering on one of the mountains I will tell thee of.' " (Gen. 22:1,2). From this Isaac, child of Sarah the free woman, sprang Christ, the Savior of the world. Under such circumstances the doctrine of the unity of God was revealed to man. Isaac bequeathed it to his son Jacob, God's Israel, and he in turn bequeathed it to the 10 tribes; and so the sacred legacy was handed down by the children of Israel, till they entered Egypt on the invitation of Joseph. There, very slowly, through successive generations, it died down till it disappeared; as it had disappeared once before in the days of Noah. For, first of all, the unity of God had been revealed to Adam, and by him bequeathed to Seth, and so to Enos, who was the first to publish it and summon men to the faith. Thus Noah bequeathed it to his son, and his son begat a son; so as the true faith disappeared from among men till the time of Abraham, when it revived and continued with renewed power till the birth of Jacob. A second time it disappeared from among men, once more to be revived by the mission of Moses. And the angel of the Lord appeared unto him in a flame of fire from the heart of the bush. And "Moses said to God, 'Who am I that I should go to Pharaoh and bring out the children of Israel from Egypt?' And God said, 'I will be with thee... when thou hast brought the people out of Egypt ye shall worship God in this mountain.' And Moses said to God, 'If I go to the children of Israel and say to them, "The God of your fathers hath sent me to you," they will say to me, "What is His name?" What shall I say to them?' And God said to Moses, 'I AM THAT I AM,' And He said, 'Thus shalt thou speak to the children of Israel, The God of your fathers, the God of Abraham, the God Isaac, the God of Jacob hath sent me to you. This is My Name forever and this is my memorial to all generations.' " (Exodus 3: 11-15). Now, in this passage He republishes the doctrine of unity, but at the same time suggests the mystery of the Trinity; for He says, "The God of Abraham, the God of Isaac and the God of Jacob." By the repetition of the phrase, He indicates a three-fold personality, while He maintains the essential unity as at the first; the one in three persons, without a doubt. In the phrase, "The God of your fathers," He proclaims the unity, and then proceeds to repeat the glorious name three times. Do you suppose there are three gods? Or one three times affirmed? If we should say there are three gods, we should be polytheists, using pernicious (?) and misleading language; whereas if we say there is one God thrice affirmed, we do justice to the truth as it is written. For He might well enough have said, "I am the God of your fathers Abraham, Isaac and Jacob," but He repeats the word "God" so as to indicate that in this passage there lies a mystery. And what is it if not the one God in three persons? How can the point be proved more plainly? It is clear as daylight to anyone who is not determined to resist the truth and eager to deceive himself, who is not blind and deaf. God enshrined this mystery in the scriptures as written by the prophets, which are still, God be gracious to you, in the hands of those who read the Law. Yet what was the result? It was not understood till Christ our Lord came, Master of all mysteries, and discovered it to us. Well then, we have learned that Abraham for 75 years from his youth was what you call "orthodox," but really a worshipper of idols, and that afterwards he attained to the true faith of God. And now you summon me to the religious faith of Abraham, I should like to know, to which of these two phases of his religious experience you summon me, and by which of them you would have me abide. Shall I follow him in his "orthodoxy" when he worshipped the idol al-'Uzza, or shall I worship (as he) who abandoned this so called "orthodoxy" and professed the unity of God and obeyed Him as when He bade him leave his home, and he turned his back on home and Haran, that city of destruction? I do not suppose you will think it reasonable or consistent with that knowledge of the scriptures of which you boast, to summon me to follow Abraham as an idolater. But if you summon me to follow in that later phase, when faith was reckoned to him for righteousness, and when he worshipped the one true God, I must point out to you that the Jews, who are Abraham's children, were before you in this. They are the true heirs of Isaac who inherited the doctrine of the unity of God. He certainly takes precedence (before) you in this. And if so, why all this bluster, this vehemence and exaggeration? Why do you make a claim which you cannot substantiate, while at the same time you base your whole case on justice and brand it with that sacred name? Why your own master, of his own accord, put it thus: "Say, I am commissioned to be the first professor of Islam, and be ye not idolaters." (Qur'an 6:14)

(BH) Do you not see? If he first publishes Islam, then Abraham and others like him, who lived centuries before were not Muslims. And your master affirms it; he is the first professor of Islam. I think I have sufficiently answered you on this point; and have said enough to satisfy any sensible person. But if nothing will content you but to pose as the champion of the Jews and to plead for them; then you must understand what is required of you in this discussion with us. We shall suppose that the Jews accept you as their champion, so that that point is settled; while we, too facile and indulgent perhaps, accept your assurance that you are definitely and deliberately committed to the Jews in this controversy. I do not myself see how, having regard to your dignity and reputation, I could impose on you such a task, or place you in such a position. But if you have imposed it upon yourself, then I must ask you, in regard to this One, whose unity you now summon me to acknowledge, how do you understand He is one and in how many senses may it be said of one that He is one? Tell us that and we shall judge of your sincerity when you summon us to the worship of the One. If you are found ignorant on this point, where is your penetration? Do you not know that one cannot be said to be one except in one of three senses, either generically, specifically or numerically. I have not met anybody who could instance or conceive any other than these three; that is to say, if he was a person of sense and understood what he said. I write to you in this way and put this to you as a man of reason with profound insight into the inwardness of things. You know and understand what you say and are not, in my judgment, one of the people who, when you confront them with a question on some obscure point, making it easy for them, because they are dull and boorish in mind, are yet unable to comprehend you, and break off without giving you any answer. How can they? They have nothing to say but, "God be praised." And, no doubt, God shall be praised, and that forever, in this world and in the next; praised by every tongue that wags and every lip that breathes.

(BI) Well then, when you say of God, the Glorious and Great, that He is the One, in which of the various senses we have mentioned is He One? Generically, specifically or numerically? If you say He is generically one, then, as one genus, He includes various species; for the category of generic unity is that which includes an indefinite number of various species. But such reasoning is inapplicable to God, most High. If you say He is specifically one, then He is the one species which includes various individuals; for the category of the species includes within it a plurality of individuals. But, if you say He is numerically one, you contradict your own affirmation that He is one, sole, eternal. I do not doubt, if I were to ask you of yourself, and to inquire how many you are, you would not say that you are one, sole. And how can you reasonably accept a definition of the Deity which gives Him no preference over the rest of His creatures? I should like to know why, if you are going to describe Him numerically, you do not proceed to divide Him and subtract from Him as well. Do you not see, with all of your literary attainments, your wide reading, your intercourse with people of various faiths and the knowledge you have thus acquired; do you not see, that the single unit is only part of Number as a whole? For the perfect number is that which includes all the various powers of Number, of which the unit is but one. Here then you are guilty of a contradiction in terms. And, if you affirm He is specifically one, to the species belong various individuals, not a single unit.

(BJ) If, on the other hand, you suggest that He is one in essence, we must further interrogate you. In your judgment does specific unity exclude numeric unity; or do you hold that the specifically one is numerically one as well, in as much as He is all-inclusive? If you say that they exclude each other, we must remind you that in the judgment of all who are versed in the laws of language and the rules of logic, the category of specific unity is regarded as including various individuals, whereas, taken one by one, each stands for itself. Do you then affirm that God is one in essence as including various persons, or do you affirm Him a single personality? If you mean that the specifically one is numerically one, then I insist that you have not yet told us what specific unity is, or how it is constituted. So we return to your original statement that God is numerically one, a description applicable to His creatures, as we have pointed out. And if you ask, How could you possibly describe the Deity as numerically one, when, according to your own showing, such numerical unity implied plurality and excludes the idea of perfection, then we reply that we describe Him as One, perfect in essence, threefold in His personality. The definition of God is only complete when both aspects are included. In regard to essence, we affirm His unity, i.e., His exaltation, Glorious and Great, above all His creatures, over all things sensuous and non-sensuous. No one resembles Him, nor is He involved in other than His own, whether simple or complex. He is the Father of all existence in virtue of His essence, without mingling, merging or composition. So then, as to His number, because He is the Universal, including all the powers of Number, for His number cannot be reckoned. And since numbers are of two kinds, odd and even, both kinds enter into each of the three Persons. And whichever way we describe God, as one or three, we do not detract from what is due to His perfection in any way, as indeed is fitting. But we make it plain that when we predicate the unity of God, it is not in your sense of the phrase, and we hope that this may satisfy you and anyone who may look into what we have written, provided only that he examine it, as God grant he may, with an impartial eye.[2]

(BK) You must understand that we might have made our statement under this heading much more involved, in such a connection that were easy enough. But we are anxious that what we have to say may be easily apprehended by all who read it, and that the hearing of it may not be overweighted, lest the mind recoil. You must understand that our contention on this point is the contention of brethren, sharers in a common estate left them by their Father, each having an equal interest in it, neither having preference over the other. So, in our discussion you and I are on equal terms. If any bitterness has been introduced into our reply, under compulsion of the truth, you must bear with it patiently. We have no other alternative but to push our argument to the uttermost in refutation of those who make our plea and our cause void, thereby doing us grievous hurt.

(BL) Of course when you protest that God never took Him a wife,[3] gat a son, or had a peer, you say what is absolutely true. Such candor becomes you; it is worthy of you. You protest solemnly, and indeed you speak truly and argue logically when you affirm that he who imposes on God the necessity for friend or fellow, blasphemes Him and virtually imposes on Him the necessity of taking a wife, begetting a son and having a peer. But, God bless you, we do not say that God has a wife, or has gotten a son; we do not impute to the Deity such puerilities and vanities, predicating of God what is true of man. You credit us with these gross anthropomorphisms on the authority of the Jews, who sought to deceive you in this way, patching up idle tales which they tell at the corners of the streets and in the market places. They speak loosely and profanely. Whereas you, who have read the scriptures, know that such things are never named in them. They are not imposed on our reason; nothing of the sort is hinted at. It is in the Qur'an that these profanities are multiplied against us. Now, in prayer and intercourse with Christ my Lord, the Savior of the world, I have no need of reserve, but I am unwilling to burden our correspondence with such matters as these. I do not wish to give currency to a story by contradicting it. I will not trace it back to its source in the cunning of Wahb son of Manba, 'Abdullah son of Salam and Ka'b, the notorious Jewish doctor, cunning and crafty fellows every one of them. These men insinuated these and other blasphemies of the same sort against us and against you. If you have really examined your own book on this point, you must know the truth about it. Certainly we have never said, nor will ever say, that God, ever Blessed and most High, took a wife or gat a son. We do not even say that He "has" that Son, who is rather the creative Word breathing through men even when they utter such follies as these. And you also know how much profanity and contradiction is implied in such a phrase, and how entirely they misrepresent God, His Word and His Spirit. What we say is that His Word is eternal, (and) never ceases to be kind and patient. We attribute to Him, ever Blessed and most High, mercy and kindness, the Kingdom, the Glory and the Power, Sovereignty and Dominion with whatever attributes may resemble these by which He reveals Himself in His divine activities. In regard to these, reason instructs us to trace them back to their source in Him as their Author. The are rightfully referred to Him, as the sum of reality, and so is all else by which He is known, in so far as He is author of it. As to that which touches His essence, we believe that, co-essential and co-eternal with Him are His Word and Spirit, alike transcendent, exalted above all attribute and predicate.

(BM) At this point perhaps we should consider whether the attributes of wisdom and knowledge are to be regarded as proper and positive[4] terms, or as relative terms which indicate the relationship of one thing to another. And first of all, it is useful to make quite clear the difference between positive and relative terms. As to positive terms they are such as one uses when he speaks of earth or heaven, light or water, or anything of that sort which may be named, no one of which involves anything else than itself. Relative terms involve such a connection, e.g., we speak of knowledge and the knower, of wisdom and the wise, and so forth. It is clear that he who knows, knows in virtue of his knowledge, and knowledge must be known. So too, wisdom involves the wise man. The subject in each case corresponds to the predicate, and is strictly confined to it lest the term be unduly extended. Now, having explained the difference between proper and relative terms, we must ask whether, when we speak of God as living and knowing, the predicate inheres in the subject necessarily and eternally, or whether it is voluntarily assumed and belongs to Him only from some given point, as you may say of Him that He had a world after the world had been made, and so on with a great many other forms which I shall not enumerate, standing for attributes by which the agent reveals Himself in His actions. Now if it is said that God existed without any world until such time as He chose to create one, it might appear reasonable to say of Him in the same way, that He was without life, knowledge and wisdom till life, knowledge and wisdom came to birth within the Godhead, and were found in Him. But that were an abuse of terms. How could God for a single second be lacking in life or knowledge? If you retract your previous statement, nothing hinders you from arriving at the blasphemous conclusion, that the world existed for God before He had made it. We, on the contrary, affirm that there are just two ways of it; either God is alone eternal, creating all else about Him, or else the world and the creature were also eternal and were not made. Of course you would contradict anyone who used such terms of the creature. So then it follows, and there is no way out of it, that God was when there was no creature existing along with Him. How can we ascribe a world to the Deity when He had not yet created one, and/or till such a time as it pleased Him to create it? Perhaps you think that, on the ground that He always had power to create when He chose, we should affirm in an eternal act of creation; but then, why not affirm a similar eternal act by which He raised and quickened the dead, and summoned those who were in their graves and caused the righteous to enter into Paradise and filled hell with those who deserved it? No man of common sense will say such things; we must return to a more reasonable conclusion. We now see that the attributes of God are of two different sorts, those which are natural and essential and therefore inalienable in Him, and those which are spontaneous and describe His activities. These last are such as mercy and grace; the former such as life and knowledge. God does not cease to be the living and the knowing; nay rather, by your leave, life and knowledge are eternal in Him, without doubt.

(BN) As a result of what has been promised, we assert that God with His Word and Spirit, is one; three persons in the one substance or essence. This is the definition of the One we worship. He is the definition He has been pleased to give of Himself, indicating to us the mystery of the Trinity in the canonical books by the mouth of the prophets and apostles. First of all He communicated it to Moses, when He told him how He made man. "In the beginning God made the heavens and the earth." (Genesis 1:1) This passage points to the trinity of persons in the unity of nature. For he says God (Elohim) using the plural number, hinting thus at the trinity of divine persons, while he adds "made" in the singular number, indicating the unity of the nature and essence in which they inhere. Again He says: "Let us make man in Our likeness and image." (Gen. 1:26a) He does not say: "I will make man in My image." Again in the second chapter, when He proposed to make Eve: "It is not good for man to be alone, let Us make him a help-meet like himself." (Gen. 2:18) He did not say: "I will make." Again: "Man has become like one of Us," (Gen. 3:22a) when He rebuked him because of his sin in eating the fruit of the tree of which God had said: "Thou shalt not eat of it." (Gen. 2:17, para-phrase). He did not say: "Like Me." Again: "Come, let Us go down and confound their tongues, that they may not understand each other's speech." (Gen. 11:7) This was because they had conspired to build a tower whose top should reach heaven. God saw the weakness of their folly and purpose when they thought to build a tower high enough to be a shelter and a refuge for them should a second deluge overtake them. He knew that He had pledged Himself to Noah that the deluge should not return. How idle then, and silly, to talk of building a tower! So He confounded their speech, that they might fail to achieve their purpose, meaningless as it was. He did not say: "I will go down and confound their speech."

(BO) Now then consider the mystery of the three persons in the Godhead as imparted by God. Moses first confirmed it by signs and wonders, clear and convincing, beyond the power of man to achieve and then publish it among us as God had made it known to him. Do you suppose that we will surrender it, and accept in its place the words of your master, without reasons annexed or signs or wonders to convince or illuminate? Why, first of all he says that God is sole, eternal, and then he turns and contradicts himself, speaking of God and "His Word and Spirit," and thus he preaches the unity and the trinity without knowing it. I do not think you will consider that as compatible with the fairness which you affect toward us. In the same way the prophet Daniel tells us in his book how God, speaking to Nebuchadnezzar, said: "O Nebuchadnezzar, to thee We have spoken."[5] He did not say: "To thee have I spoken." In your own book are phrases like these which we have quoted from the lips of Moses and Daniel concerning God most High; e.g., "We have done..."; "We have created..."; "We have revealed..."; and others of the same kind. Now can you doubt that in such language we hear the voice of the many, not of the one? Possibly you argue that the Arabs allow such language and use it in conversation, merely as a matter of courtesy. You are certainly very ingenious, but here is our reply. If the Arabs alone had originated such a usage, your remark might have had some relevancy; but, as a matter of fact, the Hebrews, Syrians and Greeks were before them in this; nor is it possible in such cases to think of collusion, so that your argument from custom proves nothing. Then I ask you, under what conditions do the Arabs allow this usage? You will tell us, of course, it is allowed when a man, being one, yet uses such a phrase as "we order" or "we say," etc. Precisely, and that means that such language is allowed in regard to beings composed of various unlike parts. For example, man, being one, is yet many: soul, spirit and body; and the body is built up of many parts; and so it is customary to use the language we have described, though, as pointed out, the man is one. Yet you affirm that such language is used of God by way of honoring Him who is Glorious and Great, to whom belongs the majesty and the power, as when it is said: "We said..."; "We inspired..."; I reply, on my faith, what you say might pass if such language were never used except by those who are worthy of honor!

(BP) Let us rather say that God, in order to teach us that He, being one, is yet many persons, uses both forms of speech; e.g., "I have made" and "We have made." The former of these is clear proof of the unity of essence and the second of the plurality of persons. Proof of this may be found in what prophet Moses records of God in the Law, as revealed to him; how God appeared to Abraham at a place called the Oak of Mamre when he was seated at the door of his tent in the heat of the day. He lifted up his eyes and saw three men standing over against him, hastened to meet them and said: "My Lord, if I have found grace in Thy sight, pass not from Thy servant." (Gen. 18:3) You see that Abraham saw three men, yet talked with one. He addressed Him as "My Lord," in the singular, while he humbled himself and invited Him to turn in. The number three insinuates the threefold personality; while the welcome given, "My Lord," suggests the single essence, so that we have here the one and three, just as we put it. So also Moses tells us that God said to him: "Hear, O Israel, the Lord Thy God is one God." (Deut. 6:4) The meaning of this is that God, revealed in His threefold personality, is yet one Lord. David the prophet says of God in Psalm 33 (v. 6): "By the Word of God the heavens were made, and all the hosts of them by the breath (i.e., Spirit) of His mouth." Here, clearly and explicitly David speaks of the three persons when he mentions God, the Word and the Spirit. Have we said anything in advance of this? In another Psalm he solemnly affirms that the Word of God is God Himself: "I will praise the Word of God." (Ps. 56:10, Peshitta, paraphrase) Do you suppose that David praised what was not God? I am sure you believe nothing of the sort. In another Psalm he says: "Blessed be God, even our God, who daily beareth our burdens." (Ps. 68:19, paraphrase) Did David desire that the one God should be praised by him, or three gods? Does he not rather in his Psalms hint at the three persons who yet are one God? Isaiah the prophet praised God most High in chapter 61 of his prophecy, saying: "From the beginning I spake not in secret, and from the former time I was there; and now the Lord has sent me and His Spirit." (Is. 48:16)[6] This is just as we have said, there are three persons yet one God and one Lord. We have not gone beyond God's own word, nor have we added to or taken from it, nor have we altered or falsified it, though you say we have done so. We do not mean to end our discussion with you by tampering with the sacred text. Anyone with a grain of sense if he look at what we have written, will see that in this you have wronged us and accused us of that which we are innocent. This we shall maintain in your teeth and to the end, if God most High so will.

(BQ) So now we return to the matter in hand; for we are unwilling to leave it until we have exhausted it, and put you before the witness of the scriptures and the sacred canon as to the accuracy of our statement. The truth of what we hold and the integrity of our dealings with you; in which high task heaven be our help! Notice then that Isaiah the prophet describes how God appeared to him surrounded by the cherubim who cried saying: "Holy, Holy, Holy, Lord God of Hosts." (Is. 6:3) The fact that the cherubim do this three times over, ascribing holiness to Him, and yet confining themselves to the number three, neither exceeding it or falling short of it, is surely meant to suggest that they praise three Persons, one God, one Lord. This is their very being; for this end they were created, nor shall they fail or cease so to do to all eternity. How easily, if I chose, I might rain proofs on you from the holy scriptures to affirm and enforce my statement, that in the one God there are three persons. But I am unwilling to lengthen my discourse. You tell me in your letter that you have searched the scriptures; if so, the little I have written you may indicate how much there is in our sacred books concerning the mystery of the Trinity in unity.

(BR) And now having, by the help of God, put my case before you in such a way as must confirm it in your memory and, I trust, demonstrate it to your reason, I summon you to the worship of this one God whom I have thus declared to you; one yet three; three yet one. I do not follow your example, nothing here has been slurred over, nothing is ambiguous, obscure or contrary to reason. And now, as God may give you light, fulfill the solemn pledges which you gave me; apply your reason and your mind, as before God. It is necessary that you understand what I have said, and see what it implies; you must not pervert my meaning. I summon you to the worship of the one God in three persons, perfect in His Word and Spirit — one in three; three in one. You must on no account think of Him as if He were the third of three. So indeed your master misrepresents us as saying: "They are unbelievers who say that God is the third of three; and if they do not cease from what they say, sore punishment will overtake the unbelievers; or will they return to God and seek His pardon? He is merciful and forgiving." (Qur'an 5:77,78) So says your master; but, God be gracious to you, I should like to know who they are who teach that God is a third of three. Are they the Christians, or not? You claim some knowledge of the three Christian sects, and indeed they are the most prominent sects. Do you know any who say that God is the third of three? I am sure you do not, unless you mean the sect known as Marcionites, who speak of three substances which they term divine yet distinct, one of which represents justice, the other mercy and the other for an evil principle. But these Marcionites are not Christians, nor are they known by that name. The Christian community, on the other hand, are innocent of this heresy; nay they reject and disown it. They teach the one God in whom is the Word and the Spirit, and that without any distinction. Your master himself confessed this. Did he not commend you to the faith of Christ, Lord of the universe and the Savior of mankind, and enjoin it on you, saying: "O People of the Book, do not go beyond the mark in your religion, say not of God save what is true. Jesus the Messiah, the son of Mary, is a prophet of God and His Word whom He sent to Mary, from Him is the Spirit, believe in God and the prophets and say not there are three gods. Cease from this that it might be well with you; verily God is one." (Qur'an 4:169) You see how he imposes on you the faith of God as one with the Word and Spirit; and declares that Christ, the Word of God, took flesh and became man. Need we add proof or exposition to this? Then he sets a seal to his own word; saying, "Nor must you say there are three gods." How can such a thing be imagined of God, the Glorious and great? Cease from it, and then it shall be well with you, as long as you do not follow the lead of that cur, Marcion, an ignorant fellow who says there are three gods. I have expounded to you what is our way of it, and what we mean when we say that in the one God are the Word and Spirit; one yet three. All this I have made abundantly clear to you. God grant you the willing heart and the discrimination that you may profit thereby.

II. The Life and Claims of Muhammad Examined

(BT) And now we pass to the second part of our letter which also must be dealt with. I think that I may say I understand the claim you make, and the witness you bear to your master. You affirm that he is the Apostle and Prophet of God and that you hold him high in honor.

That you honor him and maintain his cause I do not deny; nor have I any right to object. So far as that goes I have no choice but silently to accept the fact (that) you ought best know those who are so nearly related to you. But we join issue with you when you summon us to admit his prophetic office as genuine and binding on all men. If it is genuine and binding on all, then, of course, we have no right to reject it or to take umbrage at it. No one will reject the truth unless he is headstrong, pugnacious and utterly ignorant of its real value. On the other hand, if it is not genuine, then you have no right to assert it, and why should you invite us to accept it? If you do so, you wrong yourselves first of all, and certainly you prove yourself no friend to those whom you invite to embrace a lie. Let us lay aside all prejudice and begin by examining the history of your master. Let us review it from first to last; let us subject it to a searching scrutiny. Let us be fair, and guard against that partiality which looks at truth with an eye of infatuation and passion. We cannot overrate the importance of the undertaking. Great are the issues at stake; high is the enterprise on which we enter. May the argument and the inquiry be worthy of it, patient and thorough.

(BU) Well then, you know that this man was an orphan in the care of his uncle, Abu Talib, who took him in charge at the death of his father, brought him up and befriended him; and that he worshipped the idols al-Lat and al-'Uzza as did his father's kindred and family in Mecca. He tells us this in the Qur'an: "Did He not find thee an orphan and took thee in? Did He not find thee in error and lead thee to the truth? Poor and enrich thee?" (Qur'an 93:6,7) You see how in this passage he admits that he was a homeless orphan, that he was in error and (was) guided into truth, that he was poor and made rich. So he grew up till he entered the service of Khadija as a camel driver, working for her as an hireling and travelling in her interests to and from Syria and other places till that happened which you know. He married Khadija. Backed by her fortune he conceived the idea of claiming power and headship over his tribesmen, but they were not well disposed to him, nor did they follow him except a little handful of men whom he swept off their feet by his artifices.[7] You know the bitter feeling of the Quraysh and the hostility with which they resented any assumption of authority. And when he despaired of what he really desired, then he claimed to be a prophet and an apostle. The first step in this direction was taken so warily that men scarcely saw what he was aiming at. They did not know how to test an adventurer like him; nor did they realize the calamities he was bringing on them. They were Arabs, men of the desert, and did not know the conditions of apostleship or the signs of a prophet. How should they, to whom a prophet was never sent? In taking these initial steps, he was prompted by one who constituted himself his director, one whose name and story I will relate further on. His next step was to hire a crew of idle fellows, raiders who infested the roads according to the custom of the country still current among them. This band joined him and sent out scouts to choke up the wells. They anticipated the arrival of the caravans from Syria, laden with merchandise, at the various stations along the route. They took possession of these stations, and then, sweeping down upon the trains, spoiled the baggage and killed the men. The first suggestion of this course of action was given when he went out one day and saw a camel train coming from Medina to Mecca, the property of Abu Jahl. This was called a raid, after the fashion of the Arabs of the desert when they go out to plunder travellers and infest the roads. For this reason he had to leave Mecca for Medina[8] when he was 53 years of age, 13 years after he first made claim to be a prophet. Before this he had met with every form of opposition and insult from the people of Mecca. They knew him well, and gave out that he was banished because he claimed to be a prophet. But their purpose was confirmed when it was made certain to them that he was thus infesting the roads. He went with his companions to Medina, then a desolate place with no inhabitants but feeble folk, mostly Jews, wholly without spirit. When there, by way of inaugurating his prophetic claim and demonstrating the justice of it, he took possession of a stable which belonged to two young orphans of the Banu Najjar and turned it into a mosque.[9] Then he sent out his first mission, Hamza the son of 'Abdul Muttalib, with 30 raiders to el-'Is, in the country of Juhayna to intercept the train of the Quraysh as it returned from Syria. Abu Jahl, son of Hisham, with 300 men from Mecca met him, but Hamza gave him the slip, because he had only 30 men and feared to meet Abu Jahl. He fled, and on this occasion there was no fighting.[10] Now, in God's name, is there any

427

indication here of what God said in the Law, when He promised to lead the children of Israel, whom He had brought out of the land of Egypt, into the land of the Amorites, that is Syria, saying: "One of them shall chase 100, and two of them shall chase 10,000; for I have put the fear of you and the dread of you in their hearts." (composite paraphrase of Deut. 2:25 and 32:30, with "100" for "1000"). This He did by the hand of Joshua, who led the children of Israel, and brought them into the land of promise and defeated the Philistines. And is not this the standard by which we must test the evidence of your master's prophetic office? As you have nothing to reply to this, but by your silence admit that we have the better of you, we shall proceed. Either it was true that Hamza was the messenger of a prophet, and his cousin too, and sent by him, and that he went out, with 30 riders in his name and convinced of the justice of his cause, yet broke up camp and gave Abu Jahl the slip, though he was an unbeliever and a heathen, because he had 300 men with him, who also were unbelievers and heathen, preferring peace to war with these idolaters. Or we have here a confutation of your statement that Muhammad was a prophet, sent by God, and that the angels helped him and fought for him as they fought for Joshua the son of Nun.[11] "Joshua said to him, 'Art thou of our friends or of our foes?' And the angel said to him, 'As the captain of the Lord's hosts, am I come.' And Joshua fell on his face on the earth and worshipped him and said, 'What saith my Lord to His servant?' And the captain of the Lord's hosts said: 'Take thy shoes from off thy feet, for the place where thou standest is holy ground;' and Joshua did so." (Josh. 5:13-15) In this word of the angel to Joshua there is a mystery which he did not yet understand. At that time Joshua was besieging Jericho, and seven days after(ward), took it without terms or conditions and slew all who were in it, both male and female, as the angel had bidden him. I am afraid you will find very little to help you here; for indeed you are wholly without a case. Let us then proceed to the second of your master's raids; possibly you may find something in it to help you. On this occasion he sent 'Ubayda, son of Harith, with sixty riders, doubling their strength so as to put more courage into them, to Batn Rabi', between Abwa and Jahafa, and Abu Sufyan, son of Harb, met him. Abu Sufyan had 200 riders and blood was shed between them as you know; so they returned.[12] Still I do not find that a single angel came to help them in their need; whereas you know that Gabriel in human shape rode on an ashen gray camel wearing a green mantle while Pharaoh and his host of 4000 horses pursued after Israel. And when the children of Israel were in the midst of the sea, Gabriel rushed in at their heels on his camel crying: "On then my braves," and the horse on which Pharaoh and his people rode followed in his wake. So Israel were saved and Pharaoh and his men drowned. You are a witness of this and confirm one of the signs wrought by Moses.[13] But your master has no such witness to bring. Again there is no help for it; we must proceed to the third raid. You must endure as best you can, with good grace or bad. Your master's next move was to send Sa'd, son of Waqqas, to Harrar outside of Jahafa with 20 men; and they came to the place. But the caravan got there before them by a day. Once more they were disappointed, and returned balked of their desire.[14] This is the very opposite of the sign of a prophet as given by Samuel to Saul. You know the story, as you have studied our scriptures carefully. You remember how Kish had lost his asses and sent Saul to find them. And Saul came to Samuel and said to him (it was a mere aside, and before he had told him the object of his visit): "As for the asses, they have returned to thy father's house, and he hath left caring for them and careth only for thee." (I Sam. 10:2) That was truly the sign of a prophet, with insight to see things both past and future, one who can publish them, predicting them before they can come to pass, and heralding them before their advent, as the Holy Ghost may teach and inspire. Christ our Lord in His Holy Gospel says that a true and faithful witness is that borne by two or three faithful men; such witness must be received. Now we have adduced three witnesses, surely this is sufficient for you.

(BV) After the three raids which went out at the command of your master, in which they turned and fled, let us look at those in which he himself took part. First of all he went out aiming at the camel train of the Quraysh and reached Waddam, where he was met by Majshiy, the son of 'Umar, but on this occasion he returned without any booty.[15] A second time he went out to Buwat on the road to Syria in pursuit of the train of the Quraysh in charge of Umayya, son of Khalf, and again returned without achieving anything.[16] A third time he went out, this time also in pursuit of the train of the Quraysh going to Syria. This was the train on whose account on their return journey was fought the battle of Badr.[17] But for the third time he returned empty handed, achieving nothing. Now judge of these instances and say honestly, is it on such grounds you hold your master to have been a prophet? What has a prophet to do with plunder and raids, infesting of roads, intercepting and taking the property of men? What has your master left for thieves and highwaymen to do? What is the difference between him and Atabek?[18] You know the stories that have reached us as to the crimes committed by this fellow. Answer me if you have any answer to give; but I know well enough you have none, nor are you worse off in this than your neighbors. And thus your master continued up to the end. If he went out against a tribe and found them weak and defenceless, he drove away their trains, took their merchandise and killed as many as he could of their people. If he found them in considerable numbers or entrenched in a strong position, they very soon saw the last of him; he turned and fled. So on it was till his death. Sixty-six in number were the raids in which he personally took part, besides Saraya or night forays and columns sent out by day, as well as expeditions, in nine of which he spread death about, while with the rest he sent out his friends.[19]

(BW) And certainly I wonder at the baseness of his conduct, the impudence and barbarity of the man who could send his messengers again and again to assassinate his victims; as when he sent 'Abdullah b. Rawaha to kill Usayr the Jew at Khaybar, and he assassinated him.[20] So he sent Salim to Abu Afak the Jew,[21] an old and quite harmless man, and killed him treacherously, while he was asleep in his bed, secure and comfortable, giving as his reason that the man had slandered him. But in God's name, tell me in what book you have ever read such a thing; by what judgment did he condemn the man to death because of slander? It was in his power to punish the old man if he had done wrong without slaying him treacherously by night, when sleeping in his bed. He is said to have slandered him; but, if he spoke the truth, it surely was not necessary to slay him because he spoke the truth, and, if he had trumped up a lie about the prophet, well, it was not necessary to slay him because of a lie. Why not afflict some chastisement upon him, so that he should not do it again? By heaven, do you not know that it is not lawful to hurt even a bird while in its nest by night; and what of an old man whom he sent to slay while in his bed, simply because he had slandered him? Might he not have done something else than (have) killed him? Such deeds are nowhere allowed, either by the Law of God or by the judgment of reason and nature. By my faith, so did the Devil from of old, aiming at man and his seed ever since the fall. What now of your statement that the Prophet was sent to all men in mercy and goodwill? Did he not send 'Abdullah, the son of Jahsh, the lion-hearted, to Nakhla, i.e., the garden of Abu Amar, with 20 of his companions, that they might bring him news of the Quraysh? There they met Amr the Hadhramite, with the train of the Quraysh and their merchandise which they were just bringing from Yemen, and they slew Amr and drove the train to Medina.[22] And when they arrived there, 'Abdullah and his companions brought 1/5 of the spoil and handed it over to the Prophet. I do not decide whether that was lawful or not; let every fairminded man judge for himself. Then there was the affair with the Banu Qaynuqa',[23] whom he attacked, though there was no fault on their part, nor any motive for such action except greed of gain. He shut them up within their lines till they surrendered at discretion. Only on the intercession of 'Abdullah, the son of Ubayy, did he consent to spare their lives and banish them to Adzraat, confiscating their property which he divided among his companions. But the 5th part of it he kept for himself, saying, "This is what God has allowed to His Prophet." I should like to know how he justified such conduct. With what sanction did he confiscate the property of men who had done him no wrong, with whom he had no quarrel, only judging them to be defenceless as, certainly, they were very rich. Not so does the true prophet of God, nor anyone who believes in God and the day of Judgment. There are other matters which I will not enumerate here lest I unduly extend my letter. The reader would only turn from them in weariness and disgust. We content with thus sampling of the deeds of your Prophet.

(BX) Let me linger over the battle of Uhud with its memorable incidents. The Prophet's front tooth, right side lower jaw, was broken, his lip slit, his cheek and forehead gashed by the hand of 'Utba. Ibn

Qami'a struck at him with his sword while Talha, son of 'Ubaydullah, defending him on his right side had his finger broken.[24] How different is all this from that of our Lord, the Savior of the world. When one drew sword in His presence against another and smote his ear and cut it off, Christ replaced the ear and made it whole as the other. Now, when the hand of Talha was injured while he defended his master at the risk of his own life, if the Prophet had prayed God and restored the hand whole as before, that would have been a sign that he was a prophet. Why was his front tooth broken, his lip slit and his cheek gashed? Where was the angel to help and protect him, the friend and messenger of God? Earlier prophets were protected. Was not Elijah protected from the minions of King Ahab, and Daniel from the lions of Darius, and Abin Hananiah and his brethren from the furnace of Nebuchadnezzar and others of the prophets and saints of God in the same way? Yet you say that God made man in your master's account and that his name is written on the folds of the Throne; such is your claim![25]

(BY) Let us have done with this and insist on another point. We assert that this action of your master proves the opposite of what you say, that he was sent in goodwill to all men. Indeed he was a man who had no thought or caring save for beautiful women whom he might marry, or men whom he might plunder, shedding their blood, taking their property and marrying their wives. He himself says that God gave him two passions: one for perfume and one for women.[26] Are we to hold him as a prophet because God gave him strength of loin to deal with as many women as forty ordinary men?[27] By my life, this is a proof of the prophetic character quite peculiar to himself. And what of that affair between him and Zaynab?[28] I have no wish to dwell on it here. I have too much respect for the paper on which I write to mention it; were it not for a matter which he has himself noticed and which he asserts was told him from above. Here it is: "Remember when thou didst say to him when God favored and thou too hast favored him (i.e., Zayd), keep thy wife for thyself and fear thou God; and thou didst guard as a secret what God had done for thee. If thou fearest man, God is worthier that thou should fear Him. So, when Zayd severed his connection with Zaynab we married her to thee, lest it should be

432

regarded as a crime in the faithful if they take the wives of their adopted sons, when they have been divorced. God's command must be fulfilled. It is no crime in the Prophet that God gave him license beyond those who had been before him. God's will is doom and fate." (Qur'an 33:37) Every man of sense must judge for himself as to this affair; it will not deceive anyone with understanding. Similar to this is the affair of 'Aisha and what took place between her and Safwan when they were returning from raiding the Banu Mustaliq. She, you will remember, was left behind the army and arrived with him the next day about noon, (she was) riding on his camel while he led her. On this account she was slandered by 'Abdullah, son of Ubayy, and Hasan, son of Thabit, and Musta, son of Ataba, and Sa'id, son of Rafaa, and Hamna, sister of Zaynab. 'Ali retailed to the Prophet what these gossips were saying and how they were blaming her, and how the story was going and growing.[29] And after nibbling and hinting at the facts so as to practically publish the whole story, he wound up by saying: "O Prophet of God, God hath laid no restrictions on thee; there are plenty of women as good as she." But he did not incline to this view of the matter, because of his passionate love for 'Aisha, (for) she alone of all the wives he married was a virgin, and she was the youngest of them all. She had a warm place in his heart and had quite captivated him. This was the occasion of a life-long feud between 'Ali and 'Aisha. Yet the Prophet proclaimed her innocence in the notorious sura Nur with these words: "See, they come to thee with lies conspiring against thee." (Qur'an 24:11)[30] You know the story well enough, the tale is widely told and freely commented on, so that I do not need to enlarge.

(BZ) According to report, the Prophet's wives were 15 in number with two concubines.[31] Let me enumerate them: first Khadija the daughter of Khuwaylid, next 'Aisha (the) daughter of Abu Bakr, next Sawda, then Hafsa daughter of 'Umar, between whom and 'Aisha that wonderful affair took place, then Umm Salma, whose name was Hind, whom he deceived. When she refused his offer and excused herself on the ground that she was naturally jealous,[32] he said he would take from her all ground of jealousy. When she pleaded that she was already a mother, and that her people might not approve of the new connection, he promised to bring up her children. He pledged himself to her that he would stand by her in this, so that she consented; and then he did not keep his word. He sent her as a marriage gift two stone jars, a hand mill and a leathern cushion stuffed with palm fiber. These and doubtless other advantages she obtained in this world and in the next through her connection with him. And then Zaynab, the wife of Zayd, to whom he sent a portion of flesh three times over, and she flung it in his face, so that he shunned not her only, but all his wives on her account, and swore that he would not go near them for a month. Alas! he could not contain, in 29 days he was back.[33] And Zaynab (the) daughter of Khuzayma and Umm Habiba whose name was Ramlah (the) daughter of Abu Sufyan (the) sister of Muswiya, and Maymuna (the) daughter of al-Narat, and Tuwayra the Mustalkite, and Safiya (the) daughter of ibn Hayy, the Jewess, whom he taught to boast over his other wives when they reviled her birth, saying that she was (a) daughter of Aaron, niece of Moses and wife of Muhammad. And Fatima (the) daugher of Abu Dahak, of whom it is reported that she was the daughter of Yazid Umra, and Anna (the) daughter of Dhil-Haiyya, and the daughter of Numan, who was disgusted with him when he said to her: "Give yourself to me." and replied: "Do queens marry traders?"[34] and Muleika (the) daughter of Ka'b, of whom so many stories are told, and Mary the mother of Ibrahim, his son, and Rayhana the Jewess. These were the wives whom he married and his two concubines. Now St. Paul, a true apostle, has said: "If a man have a wife, his utmost efforts are directed to please her, but if he have no wife he aims at pleasing his Lord." (I Cor. 7:32,33, paraphrase) A true word and well said! For a man must contrive to please his wife, and as the Lord has said: "A man cannot please two masters." (Matt. 6:24a) There is no help for it, he must cling to the one and despise the other. Now if a man cannot serve one wife and please her without forgetting his Maker, how much less can he bend all his energies to please 15 wives and two concubines? Besides he was, as you know, absorbed in other pursuits; I mean the management of ware, plans for taking the lives of his enemies, the capture of women, plunder of property and the dispatch of scouts. There were troops to be handled, roads (to be) infested and raiding parties (to be) sent out. Now, while he gave due attention to such constant claims, how could he find time to fast and pray, to collect his thoughts and to turn himself to other matters which were involved in his sacred duties? Certainly we have here a novel and original conception of the prophetic office.

(CA) But, leaving this count, let us consider next those credentials of a true prophet which compel us to recognize the claims of those who produce them, and then consider those of your master, and ask how far these correspond with those, and whether we are bound to admit his claims, or rather reject them. To begin with, the word "prophet" means "one who prophesies," i.e., tells us of things which no one else had told us, and that before they come to pass; or else one who tells us things which have already been, but whose origin is wrapped in mystery. In doing this he wins our confidence for the truth of his statements by signs which confirm his words and bear witness to their truth. So it was with Moses, who taught us in the book of Genesis how the earth was created, how God made Adam and Eve, the story of Cain and Abel, the people of Noah, the deluge and the story of Abraham and Isaac; a continuous narrative down to his own time when God appeared to him in the bush. Then follows the story of Israel and Pharaoh, and so we are brought down to the death of Moses. Mixed with all this, which deals with actual facts, there is also much concerning the divine purpose concerning Israel and the land of promise. Thus history and predictions are intertwined. First of all what he told them of the past was confirmed by signs and wonders, which he wrought among them. Thus he convinced them of the truth of what he taught and that he was a prophet sent by God. Here was a guarantee that he could teach men of things that were yet to come. But again, the truth of what he taught as to things still future was put beyond question by the plain and complete fulfilment of earlier prophecies, when the children of Israel entered the land of Canaan led by God's strong hand. In this way the certainty of things to come was guaranteed. Now, having this two-fold guarantee, we are compelled to acknowledge Moses as a prophet in very deed. But when one predicts events before they come to pass, such predictions may be fulfilled in either of two ways: either speedily in the prophet's lifetime, of after an interval and length of days. In such a case the proof and certification of the prophet are to be found in the signs and wonders of his mission. Thus Isaiah prophesied to Hezekiah the King when Sennacherib King of Nineveh went against him with an army, besieged him and wrote him an outrageous letter, full of threats and wild boasting. Hezekiah made his complaint to the Lord and God said to Isaiah: "I have heard the prayer of Hezekiah, and now go and say to him, Thus saith the Lord, one night's provision shall suffice for Sennacherib." (Isaiah 37:33-35, extreme paraphrase) That night God sent an angel and slew the army of Sennacherib, 185,000 men, and when he arose in the morning and saw what had befallen his people, he turned and fled. And then, there is the word which Isaiah spoke to Hezekiah when he was ill. "In those days Hezekiah was sick unto death and Isaiah came to him and said, Thus saith the Lord, set thine house in order for thou shalt die. And he turned his face to the wall saying, O my Lord remember how I have walked before you Thee in truth and with a perfect heart, and have done right in Thy sight, and Hezekiah wept bitterly. And before Isaiah had come into the city, the word of the Lord came unto him saying, Return and say to Hezekiah, Thus saith the Lord, God of David thy father; I have heard thy prayer and seen thy tears, behold I have healed thee. On the third day thou shalt go up to the House of the Lord, and I will add to thy days 15 years, and will save thee from the King of Assyria and will defend this city for David's sake. And Isaiah said, Take a lump of figs, and they took it and put it upon the boil and it was healed. And Hezekiah said to Isaiah, What is the sign to thee from the Lord, Shall the shadow advance 10 degrees or return 10 degrees? And he said, It is a little thing that the shadow be lengthened 10 degrees, let it rather return 10 degrees. And the prophet prayed, and the shadow went back 10 degrees on the dial of Ahaz." (Isaiah 38:1-8) And Hezekiah recovered from his sickness and did not die till the 15 years were completed. Now here you have the fulfilment coinciding with the sign and proof. On the other hand, you have the Isaiah's prediction of the coming of our Lord the Christ, how He should be born of a virgin and how they should call His name Immanuel, that is, God with us. Many other things were seen and foretold by him as to the future dispensation and the days to come after the destruction of Jerusalem; all of which came to pass as he had foretold. So we have the words of Jeremiah the prophet concerning the destruction of Jerusalem, the advance of Nebuchadnezzar, the captivity of Israel and their removal to Babylon where they remained as exiles 70 years. In part this prediction was fulfilled in the prophet's own life-time; and when the 70 years were over it was fully realized, and men knew that he had spoken to them in the name of the Lord. So too Daniel prophesied of the return of the children of Israel to Jerusalem. "Then was sent forth the finger of a hand, and this writing was written, MENE, MENE, TEKEL, UFARSIN; and this is the interpretation of it; God hath numbered thy kingdom, thou art weighed in the balance and found wanting, thy kingdom is divided and given to the Medes and Persians." (Dan. 5:25-28, paraphrase). In the same way he predicted the death of the Messiah, and how, after His death, there should be no continuance to the Jews. He told how they should be utterly scattered, and their kingdom brought to an end; and all this came about as stated. And so spake all the prophets and those who deserved the prophet's name. And so it was that kings and peoples dealt with those who claimed prophetic honors, they never recognized any of them, except after rigorous test and prolonged investigation as to the ground on which they based their claims. Those who had good and sufficient proof to give were recognized, but those who had no such evidence were treated as impostors and made examples of. If any other course had been adopted, any man who talked nonsense or spread gossip, any sorcerer or augur or soothsayer might have been enrolled among the prophets. Kings took this matter in hand and carried it through by the help of God. And so we come to the Messiah, the Savior of the world, exalted above all the prophets, as His rank is higher than theirs. He takes precedence of them all inasmuch as they were servants of God, but He is the beloved Son, the all-creating Word. It was He who sent the prophets of God with their message, and sent the apostles, and finally as the incarnate Word set His seal to their ministry. "The Word became flesh and dwelt among us, and we beheld His glory." He prophesied to the Jews and to His disciples during His ministry. He proved to them with indisputable clearness that He could read their secrets and knew what lay buried in their hearts. He could interpret providence, and knew what was to be before it came to pass. Thus when the disciples gathered round Him showing Him the temple buildings and admiring their perfect beauty and strength, He said to them: "Verily I unto you, not one stone of these buildings shall be left upon another." (Matt. 24:2b) He told them of the destruction coming

437

upon them, forty years after His glorious ascension. And then He told the Jews what was in their minds when they sought to slay Him. Again He said to His disciples: "Our friend Lazarus sleepeth." (John 11:11) The disciples, who knew that Lazarus had been sick, said unto them: "Lord, if he sleeps, he shall do well." (John 11:12b) For when a man falls into a deep sleep after the violence of a fever, it is a sign that he is recovering. But, when they could not understand what He meant, He said frankly to them: "Lazarus is dead." (John 11:14b) Once more, He spake to Simon on the last night of His sojourn, when He said: "All ye shall forsake Me this night." (Matt. 26:31a, Diatessaron), Simon said to him: "Though all men forsake Thee, I will never forsake Thee." (Matt. 26:33, Diatessaron) But Christ replied: "Verily I say unto thee, This night, before the cock crow, thou shalt three times deny that thou knowest Me." (Luke 22:34, Diatessaron) Simon was exceedingly sorrowful, and yet the cock did not crow once that night before three times in three different places, he had denied his Lord, swearing a great oath. And the Lord looked on him, and Simon remembered his word and went out and repented.

(CB) Such are the conditions and proofs of a true prophet. And now as to what you have found of your master, tell us, when did he ever prophesy? How does he prove himself to you and others like you to deserve a prophet's name? Have you any evidence to give in support of his claims? If you say that he gives us information about the prophets who were before him, e.g., Noah, Abraham, Moses and Christ; all I have to say is this, (and I do not think that you can dispute or deny my statement) that he told us what we already know. Our young people, even our children learn it at school. If you instance the story of the Aad, the Thamud and the camel, the masters of the elephant[35] and such like, we can only describe it as poor stuff, idle tales of bearded dotards with which they while away their days and nights. To maintain these is no proof that he was a prophet. Thus one of the guarantees which might compel our consent to his claim is found lacking. If, on the other hand, you tell us that he told us of things to come, we must hold you bound to substantiate this statement. Two hundred years and more have passed since his day, and if he made any such prediction it should have been confirmed and fulfilled among you, long ere now.

But you know he came not by this gate to his goal. He never claimed to have this faculty of foreknowledge, and thus the second of the guarantees of his prophetic office is gone. He has taught us nothing either of the past or of the future, while the signs and wonders by which a true prophet is verified were denied him.

(CC) As to this point, on which I must dwell, let us inquire if he really produced any signs. We affirm that in the Qur'an he asserts that is was said to him: "What prevents us from sending signs, except that those of earlier days denied them?" (Qur'an 17:61a) Now what is that but to say: We might have furnished you with these signs, but your contemporaries would deny them! On my honor, no one who knows what it is to argue would give such an answer. You know, we all know that your master disowns all claims to be a worker of miracles, simply because he had no such power. Fair-minded men like yourself cannot shirk the truth.[36]

(CD) It may be you advance, as evidence of the prophetic office of your master, the conquests which he achieved, and the fact that his companions, whilst still few in number and with no resources, over-threw the Persian Empire with all its power and prestige, its well-ordered allies, its stable government and all its stores of arms and men.[37] If so, we answer you in the words spoken by God to the children of Israel: "It is not because God loved you more than other nations that He has given you power over the Amorites and Perizzites to slay them, but because of the transgression of these nations, has God given them into your hands." (Deut. 9:4,5; extreme paraphrase) And so He did to Jerusalem, which He had chosen from the rest of the earth and set His name there and established it with signs and wonders. He caused His chosen prophets to dwell there, there Psalms and hymns were sung day and night in His honor, and prayer, offered toward that Holy Place received their answer because it was the place of blessing. Yet when this people proved refractory, when they brought their idols into His temple, despising His grace and disowning His signs, then He gave them over into the hands of the ill-starred Nebuchadnezzar, himself an idolater. This man brought them low, he slew the sons of God, His elect, the choice of His creation. Do you call Nebuchadnezzar a prophet because he conquered Jerusalem and wreaked his rage on it and its people? Did not this rather happen for the reason already assigned? It was not otherwise with the history of your master, and the conquest of the Persians by his companions. The Persians were Magians, unclean and defiled, they were the off-scouring of the nations and the most ignorant of men. They worshipped the sun and fire, they married their own daughters, sisters and mothers. They knew no bounds, but opposed the truth and boasted of their ignorance. They claimed a supremacy which God had never granted them; they abused His grace denying and opposing it. They roved through the earth in wantonness and violence, they behaved themselves haughtily as though they had established an empire by their own prestige and power. So God took His favor from them and set over them those who sacked their cities, slew them and carried their children captive. There was not left a woman who was not ravished, nor a child who was not enslaved. Thus they perished by the anger of God and His wrath.

(CE) But to return to mention these signs which secure for all who can display them, the admission of their prophetic claims. On this point we must institute a searching inquiry. We say that in the Qur'an no mention is made of such signs, rather as we have already shown, he asserts that because of the unbelief of earlier ages God was unwilling to furnish him with signs merely to provoke men to denial. Is this a satisfactory reason or valid reply? Can it pass with sensible people or win the (consent) of the learned and philosophic of men who are fastidious as to what they say and critical as to the origin and authority of what they believe? Yet this is the witness borne by the Qur'an. No doubt the Jews denied the signs of their prophets and rejected them; but what Arab could deny the signs of a prophet, when no prophet was ever sent to them? If he had furnished them with signs, perhaps after all they would have believed them. We see that many responded to his call even without a sign. But you know that this excess is trumped up and quite unfit to pass muster. As to the apocryphal legends to which you appeal, they are idle tales and old wives' fables. For example, they say that one of his marvelous signs was that a wolf stood by him howling, and that he turned to his companions and said to them: This is an ambassador from the lions; if you wish to lay any command on him, he will not disobey, but if you prefer, let be and stand off from him. They said: We do not wish to have anything to do with him; whereas the Prophet signed to the beast with his three fingers to make off, and it fled and disappeared.[38] Now by my life, this was a wonderful sign! No one ever heard the like of this or saw anything so wonderful. Here is something to mislead the intelligence of a philosopher and wise man, to perplex the learned, cunning and the subtle. Your master understood the howling of a wolf, he knew that it was an ambassador from the lions of the field. But tell me this, supposing he had told them that the wolf was a messenger from the Lord of all, could they have refuted his statement? My dear friend, it is clear as noon day; he was imposing on a simple and credulous people, who were not accustomed to testing the truth of such statements. They say that the wolf spoke to Aban the son of Aus, and that at once he professed the true faith.[39] Now if he had said that Aban had reported that a lion had spoken to him, that would have been, in my judgment, more remarkable, besides making things equal between them both; but he gave him the preference over himself. And so when the wolf howled, he claimed to understand its meaning; whereas in Aban's case, the wolf spoke articulately and, no doubt, in good Arabic! But what is not surprising of all this is that two such miracles both occurred in connection with the wolf, which is known as the robber beast. So help you God, stories of that sort are not going to take in a sensible fellow like you. Is there need any further to enlarge on it? Similar to this is the story of the ox creeping along; of which they say that it talked to him in its leisurely way when he struck it.[40] But the Qur'an is witness that the Arabs are impious and irreligious. And then there was the sheep of Umm Ma'bad whose udder he stroked.[41] Along side of these are many other wonderful tales, as when he called a tree and it hastened to meet him, ploughing up the soil.[42] We do not linger over that as there is some doubt about it, and many Muslims, whose opinion has weight, do not accept it, but reject it as inauthentic. Then there is the story of the poison which Zaynab daughter of al-Harith, the Jewess, the wife of Sallam put into the shoulder of boiled or grilled mutton. The shoulder of mutton, we are told, spoke up, yet ibn al-Bishr ate of it at the Prophet's table and died.[43] No doubt the poison, which did not cease to work in the Prophet himself, was ultimately the cause of his death.[44] Now I should like to know, did he alone hear the shoulder of mutton when it spoke, or did the whole company hear it? If he alone heard it, why did he not forbid ibn al-Bishr to eat of the poisoned food so that he, who remember was one of his own friends and an invited guest at his table, should not die? How could it be lawful to conceal from others this confession of the shoulder of mutton, that it was poisoned? If, on the other hand, the whole company heard the remark, how comes in that ibn al-Bishr did not refrain from eating, if he really heard the shoulder say: "Let no man eat of me for I am poisoned?" Why did the Prophet himself refrain from eating and allow this poor wretch to eat of the poisoned food? Was he not practically his murderer? There is but one alternative, either he alone heard it, and concealed the fact, or the whole company heard it, and yet ibn al-Bishr did not refrain from the food. The one heard and did not die, the other ate of the poisoned food and died. Ah! perhaps he ate of it, feeling secure as the guest of the Prophet, one whose prayers were certain to be answered, the messenger of the Lord, who was heard by his Lord in every petition he offered! Then why did not the Prophet call on the Lord, that he might grant his request, as was often the case with prophets whose intercession availed even to raising the dead to life? Elias (Elijah) raised the son of the widow Sarepta (Zarephath), and Elisha raised the son of the Shunammite. Many times did the prophets work such wonders; and even after death there was virtue in their bones so that when they placed a dead man over the bones of Elisha, he lived. You know that the story is true; you have read it in the book of Kings. There is no variance in this point between Jew and Christian, however otherwise they differ. Why did not your Prophet eat of himself, and yet take no harm? That would have been a sign worthy of a prophet. For we hold that all the prophets were protected by the providence of God, Glorious and Great. He protected them from the injuries which unbelievers sought to inflict on them and on the saints of God. So Christ has said: "If ye drink any deadly poison, it shall not hurt you." (Mark 16:18, paraphrase) That is just what happened, they tested this word again and again, and the truth of their message was confirmed by experiment and proof. Therefore it was said that Gentile kings accepted their teachings while wise men and philosophers, men of learning, skill and judgment followed suit. They were not driven by the rod or scourge, nor by sword or dart, nor by force of numbers, nor by worldly sanction, nor by the charm of eloquent speech, nor by skill, nor by reasoning, nor by any inducement in the way of concessions offered them. But, when they saw these men in the light of day working such wonders, they laid aside their royal state and pomp, and they abstained from the science and wisdom of the world abandoning a life of ease with all its claims to precedence, that they might follow those who, in outward appearance were only fishermen and tax gatherers, men with neither rank nor distinction to boast of, save only that they were the first to follow Christ who gave them power and authority to work such wonders. And that, God bless you, was the seal of their prophetic rank and dignity. These men could prove that they were sent by God most High. In this respect they differed from your master, who presses a claim which is destitute of support. As for the vessel, of which they say that when he thrust his hand into it the water overflowed till all had drunk;[45] this is a tale told by Muhammad b. Ishaq, but it has no authority with historians;[46] your own friends are not sure of its truth. Whatever you think, none of these stories about your master will go down. They have no probability and cannot authenticate themselves in any single case. Indeed your master is before hand with us; he has cut the ground from under your feet. He himself makes no claim to have wrought such signs, so that those who press the claim in his interest have no ground to stand on. Rather, he was sent with the sword, enforcing his pretensions and those who did not confess that he was a prophet were slain or paid a heavy fine.

(CF) Now, may God be your guide, can you wish clearer or more conclusive evidence than you have here, or a more complete refutation of your master's claims? You yourself affirm that he said: "There has never been a prophet about whom his own people did not invent lies, and how should I escape the general lot? What is told about me, you must test by the written word which I have left you with... If there is anything like it or any mention of it, there you must believe that I said it and did it; otherwise, I am not responsible for it. It is a lie handed down about me."[47] Now, looking at the tales we have cited from the memoirs of your friends, can you find any authority for them in the

Qur'an? If they are ever mentioned there, then on my honor, they are true; so did the Prophet, so said he. But if he is not responsible for them, they are idle tales attributed to him. Still worse is yet to come. They say that during his lifetime he told them not to bury him when he died. He said that God would raise him to heaven, as Christ our Lord was raised, and that he was too dear to God to be left on earth more than three days. They cherished this hope, and when he died on the Monday, the 12th night of the first Spring month in the 63rd year of his age, after an illness of 14 days, they laid him out, believing that he would be raised to heaven as he had said. But when the third day had come, corruption had already set in, and their hope failed. They despaired of his vain assurance, and buried him in the earth on the 4th day.[48] Some said that when he had been ill 7 days with pleurisy and was wandering in his mind, he spoke confusedly and uttered impious words. 'Ali was wroth at this and flatly contradicted them. When the Prophet recovered he told him what had happened and in consequence he gave orders that no one should be left in the house with him save Abbas his uncle.[49] When the 7th day of his sickness came, he died, and his body swelled and the little finger of his left hand bent. Damram says that during his illness he lay on a red mat and that when he died, he was wrapped in it and rotted in the ground unwashed and unshrouded. But according to Amram, the son of Qadir, he was washed and wrapped in three sheets of white Sahuli[50] cloth from Yemen. After his death the charge of affairs was committed to 'Ali and Fadal son of Abbas, his uncle. But all his adherents revolted and forsook the faith, except a little handful of personal friends, members of his own family who were desirous of sharing in the empire he had built up.[51] Abu Bakr, originally known as the ibn Abu Kuhafa, had such remarkable powers of organization and was so gentle in his ways and so conciliatory that after his master's death he was invested with the sovereignty. 'Ali was greatly offended at this. He felt as one would naturally feel who had confidently expected that the power would pass into his hands, whereas it was entirely taken from him, (in) spite of his ambition. Abu Bakr on the other hand, maintained his kindly and courteous demeanor, handling those who had revolted with such tact and kindness, such fair speeches and tempting offers and playing so skillfully on their various passions, that one and all were won back. Sometimes this end was accomplished by terror and fear of the sword, sometimes by inducement to worldly power and possessions, or might be by license allowed in carnal lusts. But those who returned did so apparently, not really.

(CG) I do not doubt that you remember what happened quite lately at the council table of the Amir of the faithful. It was told of one of his most distinguished courtiers that he had professed Islam, but was really a Magian. You remember his reply. "By God, I know that this one and that one (here he enumerated a long list of his courtiers) professed a faith of which they are destitute, meaning to impose on me. I know that they are really the opposite of what they seem. The reason is that they have embraced Islam with no appreciation of its religious worth, simply because they wish to be connected with us to share in the prosperity of our empire. They have no insight into the truth which they have professed; it is with them according to the proverb: 'A Jew is never more a Jew, than when he professes to be a Muslim.' So with these Magians. I know that this one and that one (again he enumerated a long list of his courtiers) is a Christian at heart and became a Muslim under compulsion. That is to say, he is neither Muslim nor Christian, but a deceiver. Now can I help it? What can I do? God's curses be upon them all! Of course when they left their faith, whether it was the Magian, horrid and dreadful as it is, or whether it was the Christian, which is nearest to the light and leading of Islam, they ought heartily to have embraced the new faith which they have adopted; whereas they only professed to believe and pretended conversion. But here as always I take the Prophet as my example, Heaven's blessing rest upon him. The majority of his companions, even his most intimate friends, professed to be his followers and allies, yet he knew that they were hypocrites.[52] This was quite evident to him. They did not cease from their efforts to compass his ruin; they plotted evil against him and planned his fall. They backed the heathen party openly against him. A company of them lay in ambush in a mountain pass, hoping to frighten his mule, that she might throw him and kill him, but God preserved him from their wiles.[53] So he continued till God took him, maintaining the most perfect courtesy toward those who were his enemies, yet ever on his guard. Shall I not follow in his steps? During his lifetime he had a numerous following, but after his death they revolted. No one maintained his allegiance.[54] They raised the standard of revolt, hoping to break up the State and so end it. With this aim, spoken or unspoken, in public or private, they continued to work against him. But he, with the help of God, drew the hearts of men to himself and inspired them with the ideal of a great earthly empire. Thus in time the constitution was established, faction was conciliated and a union consummated by his tact. Thus God accomplished His purpose with him, for all of which the praise and thanks are due, not to him, but to God alone. I too decline to repeat what I have seen and heard about my people. God visit them in His anger! I will not cherish any feeling toward them but that of courtesy and patience till God shall decide between me and them. Is not He the best judge?"

(CH) Now unless my lord the Amir had chosen to speak thus frankly in open court and in (the) presence of his great councilors, who naturally repeated the story to those who were not present, I certainly could not have related it here. You are a witness that I have not exaggerated but simply stated what took place, and not so very long ago. I have dwelt on the incident only to impress on you the fact of the general apostasy, and of the half-hearted way in which the people returned at last to their allegiance, moved rather by the desire to establish the Empire than by loyalty to the Prophet. I think these who read what I have written with any degree of intelligence will admit that I have fairly answered you. God grant it be so.

(CI) To return to the point from which we stared, we have said that the life of the prophet lasted 63 years, of which 40 had passed before he claimed prophetic dignity, while 13 were spent in Mecca and 10 in Medina.[55] I do not think this statement is open to question. The whole narrative as I have given it to you, from first to last, is borrowed from the principal authority on these matters, one in whom you have implicit confidence.[56]

(CJ) But perhaps you reply, it may be said of Moses and Joshua that they too fought against the Philistines and smote them with the sword, burned their villages and plundered their goods doing in this way just as we have denied that our Lord did or taught. Let me then reply. Moses and Joshua acted under special directions from God, that He might establish his purpose and fulfill the warnings directed against those who had rebelled and transgressed. In so doing He meant to chastise them as a fond father chastises his children. You will say what proofs have we that Moses and Joshua could plead the command of heaven in what they did, while your master had no such authority? Here is our reply. We know that Moses was a prophet by the signs and wonders which he wrought in Egypt in the presence of Pharaoh, Israel's oppressor. He brought the children of Israel out with a high hand, dividing the sea and leading them through its depths. He smote the senseless rock, and twelve streams of water gushed out, from which he made them to drink. He brought down manna from heaven and fed them with quails. Such things as these he did, beyond the reach of man, impossible save to one whom God had given supernatural powers. These are the arguments and proofs we offer, surely sufficient to convince us that he acted by the authority of heaven. We have no doubt then, that the slaughter of the Canaanites, the burning of their houses and the plundering of their property was decreed by God. So with Joshua, who made the sun stand still in mid heaven, till he had exterminated the nations. Scripture is witness that there was "no such day before or since" (Joshua 10:14a); a sign and a seal set to his mission, of Joshua that it might be a witness and a glory to him to the end of time. There are other events like these which I have not time to enumerate; besides, you have said that you have read the book of Joshua and studied it carefully. We Christians and the Jews, differing as we do on many points, are agreed as to the truth of these narratives, and that without any collusion on the testimony of Holy Scripture. Now will you kindly furnish us with any, even the smallest sign of proof, or any remarkable suggestion that your master acted under such authority. Let us have the witness of his own writings that we may acknowledge his prophetic dignity and rank, then we shall feel sure that when he slew men, carried them captive and plundered their goods, that he was acting by command of God, as those old heroes did. But we know in good sooth you have no answer to give, you can adduce nothing such as we require. Therefore you must not inveigh against us if we reject your statement and repudiate the claim you make, if we affirm that God never sent your master and never gave him a commission to wage such inexpiable war against any. We affirm on the contrary that he was a despot pressing his claims in his own interest and backed by his friends and family. No blame or penalty attaches to those who protest against your view and reject it. You have yourself justified their objections, you have credited them with a lofty temper, far removed from those headstrong and inconsistent utterances which have no witness but themselves, and thereby are proved untrustworthy. You know that reason and justice forbid the use of lies. They are, happily, not natural to you. They are the weapons of those ignorant and unbelieving Jews. Lies are their stock in trade, the sum and substance of their arguments; the keystone of the arch they build.[57] In this they resemble their father, who is a liar and the inventor of lies, as Christ our Lord witnessed against Him in His Holy Gospel. And so to resume, and let us, by God's help, come to the point once more. What am I to say? How shall I put my case most reasonably before you? Do you suppose that I can receive your statement without reason of proof? I am sure you agree with me, the thing is out of the question. Christ our Lord has said: "All the prophets prophesied till the time of My coming, and at My coming prophecy ceased, and no prophet shall arise after Me.[58] Those who come after Me and claim to be prophets are thieves and robbers; ye shall not hear them."[59] Alas, my friend, can I prove false to the command of my Lord, the Savior of the world, and receive any falsehood you may trump up, any affirmation you may make, any inducements you may offer, specially as though they center in this present passing world; and that without proof or reason? I do not believe a man of understanding would approve a course of conduct so gross; certainly I am not prepared to adopt it, nor does it commend itself to me. Do justice to my point, try to think clearly, be done with this assumption of superiority, this affectation of a little brief authority. Let me advise you with all tenderness, let me remind you of what you have read in the Gospel whereof our Lord says to His disciples: "Many prophets and kings have desired to see what you see, and saw not; and to hear what you hear, and heard not." (Luke 10:24) After all your reading and research must you swerve from the truth and give your heart to the world, although you know that it must fail and soon pass away? At least you now understand that we acknowledge the prophets and receive their testimony, because they bring with them the credentials of a prophet. They do not impose their authority by force, with partiality or passion, nor with overpowering pretensions, nor with overwhelming prestige, nor with overflowing wealth. Certainly they did not offer any concessions, or allow any license in the way of sensual pleasures. But they confront us with wonderful signs, far beyond the power of men to reach, evidently the finger of God, as are the signs of a true prophet and the miracles of our Lord and of His first apostles, before which the philosopher's reason and all the wisdom of the wise must bow. And because they furnish us with such indisputable witness, therefore we accept their teaching and confess in their honor that they are from God. Documentary evidence for this is still in our hands. We can follow their steps; they have left unmistakable marks of their presence, such as none can deny who are not willfully opposed to the truth, embracing falsehood and blinding their own eyes.

(CK) What we have just written makes it necessary that we inquire somewhat minutely into the laws and judgments imposed on you by your master, whom you honor as a prophet. Now we say that all laws and judgments are of three sorts; by no ingenuity can you add to them or take from them. First there is the law which is divine, the Law par excellence, and therefore beyond reason and nature. It pertains to God, Glorious is His name, and to none but Him; nor is there any like it. Then there is the law of nature, based on reason, innate in man's mind so that it appeals to the understanding with a certain convincing power not to be understood. This is the law of justice. And then there is the law of Satan; I mean the law of violence, opposed alike to the law of God and contrary to those of nature. Now the divine law, which transcends any other and is par excellence the law, was revealed by Christ, the Savior of the world, of whom your master affirmed: "We sent in their steps Jesus (the) son of Mary testifying to what was before him of the Law, and We gave him the Gospel, in which is light and leading, testifying to what was before of the Law, with leading and direction for the devout." (Qur'an 5:50) And so said Christ of Himself: "Verily I say unto you, love your enemies, bless them that curse you, do good to them that hate you, and pray for them that despitefully use you and persecute you. So shall ye be children of your Father which is in heaven, for He maketh the sun to rise on the evil and on the good, and sends rain on the just and the unjust." (Matt. 5:44,45; Diatessaron with slight paraphrase) This Law is divine, above nature, higher than reason. Here are mercy and forgiveness and all that corresponds to the divine nature. The second law is that of nature, based on reason, making itself felt in the instincts of fallen man. This is the law of which Moses wrote when he said: "An eye for an eye, a tooth for a tooth, a life for a life, and a wound for a wound." (Lev. 24:20, Peshitta, paraphrase) This law of nature which is enshrined in the dictates of reason, is the law of justice and equity. "Thou shalt do to another as he hath done to thee. Treat him as he hath treated thee; well if well, but if ill then ill." Of course this does not agree with the divine law, nor with that prescribed by our Lord who was merciful and pitiful toward His creatures. The third law is that of Satan, the reign of violence and wrong, pure and simple.

(CL) Now you must not blame me if I enforce my argument at this point. You know ever since we entered on this discussion I have not shirked the issue, nor will I cease to press as far as the spiritual weapons at my command enable me, in defence of the faith of God to which we look for help and victory over our enemies. If you blame me for this, you do me wrong, and I do not regard your blame in this matter. So as to return to the point at issue, I pray God that He may inspire you with the love of justice and the voice of truth showing you which of these three laws just enumerated and which of these precepts your master imposed. If you say that we owe to him the Law of God; I reply that Christ was 600 years before him in so doing, if we go back to His glorious ascension. And ever since and up to the present time, His followers have been applying and enforcing it as they will continue to do till the end of time. I have not seen any of your coreligionists who seemed to have an inkling of it, or a flavor of it, even if we go back to your master's lifetime. If you affirm (though I hardly think you will) that we owe to him the law of nature, with its precepts of justice and maxims of equity, we reply that Moses was before him in so doing, for he instructed us and established us therein and taught it plainly as from God in the Law. No one else can claim to be the author of it;

for he speaks always for himself alone, and bears witness in his book. By heaven, he who makes any such claim is manifestly a boaster, high-handed and false-hearted, dealing with what is, as clear as day-light, God's truth in the hands, heads and hearts of men, trying to wrest it and desiring by falsehood to claim it for his own. So far we know to whom we owe our knowledge, and we confess our duty and obligation to them. There is left the third, i.e., the law of Satan with its precepts of violence. Now consider, as God may help you, carefully and with an open mind such as neither bias nor prejudice can affect, and tell us who represents this third law, who backs it up, and embraces and practices its precepts? Or to put it otherwise, what was the law your master brought, and what precepts did he enforce, if not those of the third law as we have expounded it to you? Let us have the truth, if truth you have to tell, that we may accept it at your hands, and we will follow your lead. We would not fight against the truth nor reject from whatever quarter it may come. But perhaps you are prepared to affirm that your Prophet imposed both these laws, i.e., that of Christ and that of Moses, and enforced them in his book. You may appeal to the passage: "A life for a life, an eye for an eye, a tooth for a tooth, a nose for a nose" (Qur'an 5:49a), evidently based, you say, on the Mosaic Law, followed by words which just as clearly breathe the spirit of Christ: "If ye forgive, it is nigher unto piety." But you can see for yourself that the passage is self-contradictory; as if we should say of a friend, "He is sitting and standing, is blind and can see, is well and yet ails," at one and the same time. I do not suppose that you desire that such a style of speech should be generally used. It is absurd; nor can anyone who follows the argument so escape the conclusion that we have here phrases filched from different quarters; I mean, of course, the Law and the Gospel. If you were to confess both these laws and to claim them for your master, the adherents of each in turn, both Jews and Christians, would disown you; because it is their faith which they eagerly embrace and jealously guard to the rejection of your claims. Have they not inherited it? Do they not hold it fast, devoted to it as to the truth? They will say to you: "You are no friend of ours. Off! Hands off! Will you rob us of that inheritance which you yourself acknowledge to be ours, even while you are scheming to take it from us?" Give us some substantial proof that we may know that you are sincere in your claim. Are you not forced back on the third law, of which it is so abundantly proved that it has been practiced and supported by you? How can you deny what you affirm, maintaining it, defending it, and pleading for it as the law by which you live? Your whole system is built on it; yet, whenever it suits you, you turn round and disown it. You can hardly be content to claim for your master that he was a humble follower of Moses and Christ, whereas you place him far above both. You rank him with the Lord of All, and protest as if you were in the secrets of the Almighty, that, but for your master the world had never been created nor man made. Surely, my friend, it is incredible folly to press such a claim, and at the same time admit as you do, that he had no power to work miracles. We have made no provision for this in our plan of history; nor was it any part of his role to adorn his cause with miracles. Consider then Moses and Christ anticipated your master in promulgating the first and second laws; only the third is left, for we know of no fourth. Does not it follow that we must identify his name with the third, i.e., the law of Satan? Which of these two views suggested by you am I to take? I do not know. To which of them must I reply? Make up your minds and do not allow things to slip. That be far from you. In religious questions, beyond all others, slackness or hesitancy are forbidden. An earnest and thoughtful soul will recognize the duty to press the quest to the uttermost.

III. Origin and History of the Qur'an

(CM) I take it then that as your final ground and proof, you are forced to appeal to the Qur'an. This book you hold in your hand and the proof that it is divinely inspired is that it contains old-world stories about Moses, the prophets and our Lord the Christ. You urge that your master was an illiterate person,[60] not in any way conversant in such matters, and you ask how could he have composed such a book if he had not been inspired? You allege that such a book was never before written by man or jinn: "Say, if all men and all jinns should inspire to produce anything of the kind, they could not succeed, though they stood shoulder to shoulder." (Qur'an 17:90) You quote the passage: "If you are in doubt as to what we have brought down to our servants, produce something as good; summon your witness other than

God, if you are true men." (Qur'an 2:21) You quote that other passage: "If we had brought the Qur'an down to a mountain, you should
have seen it cleave in twain and confess the truth, for fear of God. We
use such figures in dealing with men so as, if possible, to make them
think." (Qur'an 59:21) In your judgment trifles such as these constitute
the strongest proof and clearest evidence of the prophetic office of
your master. It seems to you that in such proofs of inspiration you
may find a parallel to the wonders wrought by the earlier prophets, as
when Moses clave the sea, Joshua stayed the sun and Christ raised the
dead to life again. Is this the sort of thing which has misled multitudes? On my honor, you are content to rest your case on very frail
foundation, a crazy substructure, a rotten bottom. We have not far to
seek for an answer, nor will you have long to wait for it. It appears,
however, that I must open up this whole question. If in the process we
occasion pain, if festering wounds must be reopened, the patient must
brace himself to bear it like a man. When the iron has probed the
wound, he will quickly find relief, comfort and healing. The truth will
then be made plain to you, and the meaning of this figure as it applies
to yourself.

(CN) First of all, then I must put before you the origin of the Qur'an;
afterwards you may press your claim if you can — a false claim which
cannot abide the truth or stand examination. Well then, there was a
certain Christian monk named Sergius[61] who had perpetrated some
offence for which his companions disowned him and excommunicated
him, refusing him as was their wont, access to their churches and
intercourse with themselves. Repenting of what he had done and
anxious to expiate the offence and conciliate his Christian brethren, this
man travelled to the country of Tehama, and reached Mecca. There
he found a prosperous city divided between two religious sects. The
majority were of the Jewish faith, the rest were idolaters. So kindly
and skillfully did he handle your master that he quite won his heart.
Among his new friends he was known as Nestorius, hoping by this
change of name to strengthen the Nestorian heresy[62] which he had
embraced. He continued imparting instruction to your master, in
repeated conferences he insinuated point after point of the new doctrine, till at length his pupil ceased to worship idols. So he drew him

to confess the religion of Nestorius.[63] When the Jews perceived this, they revived an ancient feud and poured abuse upon him, as was the custom between them and the Christians. Still his influence grew stronger, with the result familiar to you. This is the explanation of the fact that Muhammad mentions the Messiah and the Christian faith in the Qur'an, defending them and protesting that Christians are "friendly disposed" (Qur'an 5:85b) and "that they are not under ecclesiastical rule and are not proud." (Qur'an 5:85b) When the Christian cause was strong and this Nestorius on the point of death, 'Abdullah (the) son of Salam and Ka'b, well known among the Jewish doctors, two crafty fellows, arose and gave your master to understand that they agreed with his views and accepted his teaching. They persisted in this artful and dishonorable course, bearing themselves so as to conceal from him what was all the time in their hearts, till after his death they found their opportunity. Then your master was no more, the people revolted, and the power came into the hands of Abu Bakr. 'Ali, meantime, was doing his best to seduce the people from their allegiance. Here at last was the opportunity they had waited for so long and aimed at from the first. They insinuated themselves into the confidence of 'Ali and suggested that he should claim the prophetic office, undertaking to see him through, just as Muhammad had been coached by Nestorius the Christian. Why should he accept a lower role than that of a prophet? 'Ali was aware of the influence wielded by Nestorius the monk, though he was only a youth during his master's lifetime. They recommended him not to divulge the situation or give a hint of it to any of the people. He, a mere youth, consented, inclining to their doctrines in the simplicity of his heart, as was natural to his tender years and inexperience. But God did not prosper their plans or permit of their realization. A hint of what they were after was confirmed to Abu Bakr, who at once sent for 'Ali and reminded him of their relationship. 'Ali perceived how entirely Abu Bakr had the upper hand, and abjured the treasonable designs on which he had entered. But already the Jews had tampered with the book, based on the teaching of the Gospel, which his master had committed to 'Ali's hands. They had introduced passages from their own Law and material from the literature of their own country. In this way they corrupted the whole, taking from it and adding to it as they chose, insinuating their own blasphemies into it.

Take the passages the Jews say that Christianity is built up on nothing, and the Christians say that Judaism is built on nothing, and yet they read the book. Those who were ignorant spake just like them, but God will be the judge between them in the last day on this point in which they differ (Qur'an 2:107). Many are the wonderful tales as to which no one can fail to see that they are the utterances of rival sects, each contradicts the teaching of the other. Let me mention the sura 16 (The Bee); 27 (The Ant) and 29 (The Spider) and other(s) of the same sort.

(CO) Well then, when he despaired of the caliphate, 'Ali went to Abu Bakr after forty days (though some say after 6 months), and gave him his allegiance. Abu Bakr said to him: "Ah, my friend Abul Hasan,[64] what kept you back from joining us?" 'Ali replied: "I was busy collecting the sacred writings as the Prophet charged me."[65] Now my dear Sir, you are a fair-minded man, just think what that means. "He was collecting the sacred writings." And you know that Hajjaj (the) son of Yusuf[66] also collected the sacred writings, but omitted many of them. My friend, be not deceived, God's word is not made up in that way, nor can you drop parts of it. I am simply narrating the facts, there is no denying them. We have them on the best authority, from sources the veracity of which it is impossible to dispute.

(CP) From the same authorities we learn that the original copy of the Qur'an was that which was held by the Quraysh. At a later period during his Caliphate, 'Ali took possession of it lest it should be tampered with. There you have the Qur'an in its purity, modelled after the precepts of the gospel as taught by Nestorius, who by the way was known among his friends sometimes as Gabriel and sometimes as "the faithful spirit."[67] But to return, when 'Ali, still paying homage to Abu Bakr, confessed that he was collecting the sacred writings, they replied: "You have some passages, we have others, why should not the sacred book be compiled?" So they united their efforts and put together the fragments which had been preserved in various quarters, e.g., the Sura Barat, which they wrote down from the Arabs of the desert, and other portions gathered from scattered tribes, as well as what they found written on white stones and the leaves of palm trees, on shoulder

bones and so forth. They did not combine these in a single volume,
but wrote them on loose leaves and rolls, after the manner and at the
instigation of the Jews. Thus it came about that different texts were in
use. Some read the text of 'Ali, and to this day they sware by him.
Others read the version whose origin we have just described.[68] Others
read according to the text of the Arabs who came from the desert
saying: "We to have a verse more or less, and someone wrote it down,
without inquiry as to its history or authority. A select circle read the
Qur'an of Ibn Mas'ud."[69] You remember your master's words: "If you
wish to read the Qur'an pure and undefiled, as it came from heaven,
read the Qur'an of Ibn Umm Mahad."[70] He himself perused it every
year and in the year of his death he read it over twice. Some read the
Qur'an of Ubayy b. Ka'b, as it is said: "Ubayy is the best reader[71] of
you all." The Qur'an of Ubayy and that of Ibn Mas'ud very nearly
correspond. The result was that in the Caliphate of 'Uthman it was
discovered that there was no consent as to the true text. Meantime
'Ali was conspiring against 'Uthman and aiming at his overthrow.
Undoubtedly it was his purpose to kill him. One man, then, read one
version of the Qur'an, his neighbor another, and differed. One man
said to his neighbor: "My text is better than yours," while his neighbor
defended his own. So additions and losses came about and falsification
of the text. 'Uthman was told that various versions were in use, that
the text was being tampered with, and that strife, with all the mischief
of party spirit, was being engendered. They said: "We do not believe
that matters can continue as they are, it is an affair of urgency; they
are slaying one another, the sacred book is corrupted, a second apostasy is imminent."[72] So 'Uthman sent and gathered all the leaves he
could secure and the various scraps, as well as the original text. They
did not interfere with the manuscript in the hands of 'Ali, nor with
those who adhered to him. The new rescension did not affect them.
Ubayy (the) son of Ka'b was dead before it was made, while Ibn
Mas'ud refused to give up his copy of the Qur'an, so they drove him
from his post in Kufa, and appointed Abu Musa as governor in his
place.[73] The next step was to commission Zayd (the) son of Thabit,
one of the Helpers, and 'Abdullah (the) son of Abbas (but some say
Muhammad, son of Abu Bakr) to carry through the enterprise, compil-
ing the Qur'an and rejecting what was corrupt in the text. These two

men were both young, but they were told that if they disagreed on any point as to a letter of a word, they must render it according to the dialect of the Quraysh.[74] Naturally they differed on quite a number of points, e.g., the word "tabut" which Zayd pronounced "tabuh," while the son of Abbas pronounced it "tabut"; so they adopted the form in use among the Quraysh, and so on other occasions. When the revision had been completed according to the various manuscripts, four copies were made in large text, one of which was sent to Mecca, a second remained in Medina, a third was sent to Syria and is today in Malatya. The copy in Mecca remained there to the days of Abu Saraya when in the year 200 A.H. occurred the last siege of Mecca.[75] Rumor says that Abu Saraya did not carry it away from the siege, but that it perished in the fire. The copy at Medina was lost during the reign of terror in the days of Yazid. A fourth copy was placed at Kufa, which was then the capital of Islam and the center of the Refugees and friends of the Prophet. This copy is said to be still in existence, but that is not so; it was lost in the days of Mukhtar.[76] Next 'Uthman gave directions that the leaves and sheets of the Qur'an should be gathered in from the provinces. He ordered his agents to collect all that they could lay their hands on and destroy them[77] till it should be certain that not a sheet remained in the possession of any private individual. Heavy penalties were threatened against the disobedient. All the leaves they could secure were shredded and boiled in vinegar till they were sodden, nothing remained, not even the smallest fragment that could be deciphered. It is said that the Sura Nur was originally longer than the Sura Baqara, and that the Sura Ahzab in its present form is curtailed[78] and incomplete. In the same way they say that the Sura Barat was not originally separated from the Sura Anfal, that they were not distinguished from each other by so much as the usual heading: IN THE NAME OF GOD: THE MERCIFUL. So of the two final suras which were included in his revision,[79] Ibn Mas'ud said: "Add not to it what is not in it."[80] On the other hand, 'Umar speaking from the pulpit said: "Let no man say that the verse about stoning is not in the sacred book, for I have myself read it. The man and woman who have committed adultery, stone them both. And if it were not that men would say that 'Umar had added to the Qur'an what was not in it, I would restore it with my own hands"[81] In another address he said: "I do not know how

457

anyone can say that the ordinance of al-Mut'a is not in God's word; we have ourselves read it there, but it dropped out.[82] God will not reward with blessing him who has omitted it. It was committed to him as a charge, but he was not faithful to the trust nor loyal to God and His Prophet." Much that had been added to the Qur'an was dropped,[83] and so again 'Umar says: "God deals kindly with man and has sent Muhammad with an easy religion."[84] Ubai b. Ka'ab said that there are two suras which they used to recite (he was speaking of the first recension and did not refer to the latter) these were al-Kanut and al-Witr, beginning with the words : "O God we ask Thy help, we invoke Thy pardon and guidance, we trust in Thee and commit ourselves to Thee."[85] — and so on to the end of al-Witr. And so with al-Mut'a, which 'Ali caused to be dropped.[86] It is said that when he heard a man reciting it in his time, he had him scourged with whips and commanded men not to read it. This was one of the things for which 'Aisha reproached him on the Day of the Camel. Among other things she said that 'Ali scourged men and beat them because of it, and altered and falsified it.[87]

(CQ) The copy of 'Abdullah (the) son of Mas'ud remained in his own hands and was bequeathed as a heirloom to the present day.[88] In the same way the copy of 'Ali remains among his own people.[89] Then followed the affair of Hajjaj who would not give up his material but put it together, omitting many things among which they say were verses concerning the sons of Umayya and the sons Abbas with names mentioned. Five copies were made of the version approved by Hajjaj, one of which was sent to Egypt, one to Syria, one to Medina, one to Mecca, one the Kufa and one to Basra. All copies of earlier additions on which he laid his hands he boiled in oil till they were sodden, and so made an end of them, following the example of 'Uthman. You are yourself witness to the truth of this. You have read the Qur'an and know how the material has been put together and the text corrupted, a sure sign that many hands had been busy on it, and that it has suffered additions and losses. Indeed each one wrote and read as he chose, omitting what he did not like. Now by the grace of God, are these what you consider the marks of an inspired book?

(CR) Besides, your master was an Arab by descent, dwelling in the desert, thinking his own thoughts and then throwing them in to verse. With these he betook to the desert-folk and established relations with them, of whom it is witnessed in their own book that "they are an impious and irreligious people."[90] Now then shall we receive the mysteries of God, His the sacred word and the faith as revealed to the Prophet at the hands of such people? You know what happened between 'Ali, Abu Bakr, 'Umar and 'Uthman, how they hated each other and quarrelled and corrupted the text; how each one tried to oppose his neighbor and to refute what he (had) said. Pray, how are we to know which is the true text, and how shall we distinguish it from the false (one)? Hajjaj too tampered with it; you know his methods and how he went to work. How can you appeal to him or cite him as an authority? Why, in every possible way he associated with the Umayyads! And still further the lying Jews had their hand in the pie. Some of them pretended to embrace the faith; but they did so with an intent to corrupt it. They tried to get control of the new movement, simply to wreck it. All this, God help you, must be clear enough, unless ignorance has blinded your mind and darkened your heart. How could it be put more forcibly or stated more frankly? Were it not that you read our sacred books and study them, and that I know the soul of justice that is in you, I would not have put the matter thus before you, perhaps causing you momentary pain, but, as I trust, for your comfort in (the) days to come. For this reason we have allowed ourselves this license. Bear patiently, I beseech you, the little pain inflicted by the physician, that you may enjoy your reward to the full in the relief he brings. We have said nothing more than your own writings allow. We have confirmed nothing on our authority which is not confirmed by the traditions of your own scholars, men of weight among you. We have kept to what is generally accepted and held as a matter of faith on this and other points on their authority. You do not suppose that they favored any particular sect. We have asserted only what they have well established, when we affirm that the Qur'an is loosely put together often without any meaning, and that again and again it contradicts itself. It is well known that those to whose authority we appeal, believed what they had handed down and, were it not that we are unwilling to prolong this discussion, we might enlarge still further

459

on the contradictions and the divergent readings of the Qur'an and the story of the origin of this strange farrago.

(CS) What ignorance could be more dense than his who appeals to such a book as evidence and proof that its author was a prophet sent by God![91] Is there anything here parallel to the cleaving of the sea by Moses; the raising of the dead and the cleansing of the lepers by Christ our Lord? This can approve itself only to the incurably ignorant who have never learned to collate and compare. I do not think that anyone of penetration or discrimination could venture to think it, much less defend it. Scarcely could he dream of it unless he were beside himself, out of his senses or weak in intellect. Or will you, in God's name I ask it, make an attempt to defend such a book by force of reason, by subtlety of thought and weight of learning, knowing what you do of its origin and how the authority of its text has been broken down before the inquiry we have instituted? I am accustomed to such studies, versed in textual criticism, and such fictitious narratives and "cooked-up" stories will not pass with me.

(CT) Now tell me about that utterance of your master: "If man or jinn should conspire to produce a book like this, they could not, though they stood shoulder to shoulder." (Qur'an 17:90) Do you affirm that the vocabulary of the Qur'an is specially rich? Our reply is that the Greek language is also rich and so is Zand in Persia and Syria among the people of Edessa and the Syrians, and Hebrew in Jerusalem among the Jews. In fact any language seems richer to than any other to those who can use it only.[92] They have a large vocabulary on which they draw. You may count them as barbarians, but remember, your Arabic rich as it seems to you, is barbarious enough in their ears. So we dismiss your assertion as to the rich vocabulary of the Qur'an. As a matter of fact, he has a rich vocabulary whatever language he uses, who does not need to borrow from other sources in conversation or discourse. But we see that your master had to borrow from other languages, and this though the book claims to be inspired: "We sent him down the Qur'an; it may be he will take heed." (Qur'an 12:2) Others, who were masters of the purest Arabic, eloquent orators and models of style have used it too. Yet he borrows such words as "istabrik" (brocade), "sindas" (linen), "abarik" (jars), "namarik" (saddle-cloths), which are all of Persian origin, and "mishkat," an Abyssinian word for "window." There are others of the same kind in his book. Was the Arabic lexicon too confined for his purposes? Was there not wealth in it to make him independent of other languages? Yet you say in was "sent down" from the Lord of the Universe by the hand of Gabriel. Clearly you must impute the defect either to the message or the messenger. If it lay with your master, it must be because he did not know the Arabic equivalent for these words, and therefore could not use them. Yet such words are used by Amru-l Qays, and others of the poets, eloquent orators and writers of former and later days, more in number than I can reckon. They occur in the vocabulary of orators and eloquent men before the coming of your master, more eloquent and refined, more subtle in thought than himself; as he confessed when after an argument he wound up by saying: "They are a disputatious lot." (Qur'an 43:58b) Disputatious they were, but at the same time with a greater power of reasoning and more eloquence than his own. So that at times he attributes their argument to nothing less than sorcery. Well then, if he is responsible for the Qur'an and the barbarous words it contains, there is only one alternative, either Arabic proved too poor for your master's use (though we know that it is the richest of all languages) or these additions must have been imported into the Qur'an by other hands. This is precisely what happened, as we have proved in our review of its history, where we have seen the many different hands at work. But which of these alternative do you prefer? Tell us, for there is no escape from one or the other of them, and you know what is implied in your choice when you have made it.

(CU) If you say there is nothing like the Qur'an in point of style and ornamentation, we reply that the style of our great poets is genuinely poetical, their rhythm is so perfect that, however difficult and subtle the thought, it is never broken at any point. Their diction is pure and chaste and from the choicest Arabic; while the most beautiful ideas are woven together in a way not only perfect in conception but equally perfect in execution. The Qur'an on the other hand, is broken in its style; hybrid in its diction and, while high-sounding, often destitute of meaning. If you protest that it has a very good meaning; we ask you what far-fetched meaning you have found? Let us have it; expound it to us, gladly will we learn of you. What interpretation have you discovered which fills you with admiration of the new light it brings? Let us see it; educate us into it. What have you to tell us that we do not already know; which we have not already read in some old book from which you are content to borrow? Do we not understand it without your help and claim such a knowledge of it as belongs only to the expert few? Is there in it any wonder or sign transcending human understanding, compelling us to admit your master's claim and accept his teaching as inspired? If there is, point it out.

(CV) Such was the origin of your sacred book, passing current with all of its falsifications and misrepresentations, its eloquent periods, its exquisite style, its choice Arabic. Forsooth: "Nor jinn could produce the like," but then it came to an illiterate race, Nabateans,[93] the off-scouring of the people, great in their own eyes, proud in their own esteem. If I misrepresent the matter, inquire for yourself, you can easily verify the story from its beginning. Thus were others who did as your master did, Musaylima the Manifite, Alswad and Tahayla. When I read the Qur'an of Musaylima I have to admit that, if he had your master's backing, his revolt might have proved much more serious than it did. But these men lacked the support at your master's command.[94]

(CW) So far as I can judge, you are driven to stake your case on this argument from style. You boast of it, and treat it as if it were private property; an ambush behind which you may safely shelter. As a matter of fact, it is common rather than private property. We share and share alike here. You have nothing to advance which we cannot advance you, nor can your knowledge stand you in stead against us. You are good enough to confess that we belong to an Arab tribe which can trace its descent by its language to Yored (the) son of Ishab, (the) son of Nabat, (the) son of Ishmael, our great ancestor, but the argument is futile, the claim is not valid. The Nabateans might claim the same, yet they are the off-scouring of all the people, barbarians, indolent and imbecile, without knowledge of the Arabic language, which is still a foreign tongue to them. When they meet anything in it they did not understand, they credit it at once and accept it in their barbarous simplicity. The pure Arabs of the desert have a common tongue, their dialect is one and they all understand each other. As for the townsfolk, who grow up in the streets and mix with alien races, on my honor, they do little else but corrupt each other by intercourse and interchange of customs. To mention language then, is no argument, nor is there anything there to which you can appeal. If you say that the Quraysh are the most eloquent of the Arabs, the knights errant of eloquence, we oppose to you a fact, the truth of which you can scarcely deny or dispute, viz. that Muleika (the) daughter of Naaman, the Kindi, when Muhammad asked for her hand, and she married him, she said: "Shall Muleika marry a trader?"[95] We both know that the Quraysh are the merchants and traders of the Arabs, while the Kindi were a royal race, who ruled the rest of the Arabs. I do not mention this fact to boast of the nobility of my own birth, or to establish my descent from a pure Arab stock, but to remind you that the Kindi were the most powerful and literary tribe in the kingdom, distinguished for their eloquence and poetry, leaders of armies, owners of cattle, distinguished for their virtue, ever the barbarians of Rome and Persia sought relationship with them, and boasted that their daughters were at our service; a boast such as only the brutish could make. No doubt the Quraysh also excelled in point of influence and natural gifts, particularly the Hashimites, as no one can deny who is not blinded by envy. And so, in my judgment, are all the Arabs and the rest of the nomads; high spirited, excelling in point of virtue and natural gifts, as God has endowed them beyond other barbarians.

(CX) If you argue that the Arabic language is enshrined in its poetry, and its vocabulary limited thereby, so that such a word as "namarik" (saddle cloth) is not found in it, we grant you that it is so. But the argument hardly bears on the matter in hand. It cannot escape the notice of a student that that word is foreign, and so the argument based on it, is refuted and fails to win the sanction of a thoughtful man. The passionate is seldom pure and what is irregular and foreign in origin usually affects the poetic form. When we compare such poetry to other poetry in pure Arabic of the desert, we do not find any great differences between them. It follows the same lines and pursues the same course. And as this is so, we conclude that the poetic form of Arabic literature, and the necessary limitations it involves, are not arguments in connection with the sacred books, at least if we have any desire to argue reasonably. It does not follow that a passage was originally poetic in form, because it resembles old Arabic poetry. Corruptions and alterations have taken place, additions and losses; and the poetic form is never an argument with a man of insight. It is not a matter on which one may dogmatize; indeed, by the erudite and philosophic, it is regarded as a trifle which pleases the foolish. And though (we) as Arabs by descent give preference without hesitation to the poetic form and affirm its superior beauty and celebrate its praises, knowing well the refining influence, exquisite art, the thrilling interest of our Arabic literature, still, taking everything into consideration, we cannot doubt that it is often corrupt. Much has entered into it which does not belong to it. It is a kind of speech that is not to be taken seriously! Widely circulated, its concepts are those of shallow minds, the common property of all. If it suits you, there it is! It is used by those who desire to cultivate the society of the great, and aspire, in this way to establish relationships with them.[96] In this way it is possible that corruptions entered, alterations, additions and losses. And, in fine, poetry is no argument at all in dealing with the divine mysteries, unless it be contrary to reason and defective in composition. In God's name, do not wrong your reason and rob it of its rightful sway over party feeling. That is too much the way with the herd, people wanting in intellect, who are not educated to read books, or versed in the history of earlier times.

(CY) Of this type were some of the rudest of the Arabs, who used to eat lizards and chameleons, reared in stint and wretchedness among the desert tribes. The hot wind beat on them and the desert blasts. They were in the extreme of hunger, thirst and nakedness. Sometimes a great longing seized them when they heard of rivers of wine and milk and all kinds of fruits, supplies of flesh and other dainties, of couches of satin, silk and brocade, free intercourse with women whose eyes gleamed like pearls, while boys and girls served them and they drank spring water and sheltered beneath trees.[97] The vision of such happiness stirred their hearts. Some of them had glimpses of it when, in their march, they passed through Persia. It winged their feet with joy;

they deemed that already they saw realized before them the dream of former years. Their spirits rose. To obtain all this, they fought the Persians and beat them too. You remember how, in the course of a long battle, when they obtained possession of stores and confections from the Persian larders, they said to one another: "By God, if there were no heaven to fight for, we might well fight for this."[98] But the people they fought with were corrupt and abominable; stubborn rebels against the Most High, therefore He, who is Great and Glorious, set over them a people of whom they had never heard. They were slain or driven into exile, because they had shed innocent blood; the judgment of heaven lay on them. Thus it fared with the race of evildoers, the one scourged the other for his sins.

(CZ) Such too were the Nabatean, a people of no resources, reared in wretchedness, growing up like cattle in herds; such too the peasants with no education or refinement. Sometimes they speak Arabic and talk with the utmost freedom; but at heart they are mongrel still. They lord it over their fellows; some of them profess Islam by word of mouth, but in heart they are heretics; either Jews or Magians. They do not know who made them; if you put before them the difference between themselves and their Maker, they cannot understand, nor have they any moral standards so as to distinguish (them). They are like cattle, like the beasts that creep on their faces; they are moved by every breath of wind. They do not apprehend the truth which they have embraced, as distinguished from that which they abjure. And so with the idolaters, the Magians and the Jews, with their meanness and profanity. Their ambition is to establish an empire; to lord it both in word and deed over races that were born to rule, the children of the free-born, better men than themselves, ennobled by religion, education and humanity. They are restrained from the commission of crime and the indulgence of lust which God has forbidden only by the principles of the Christian religion. These men will believe and embrace your faith for the sake of the license it offers them. So too those who allowed themselves liberty in low and sensual pleasures, inclining to the world with its deceptions and delights, seeking a little short-lived glory, grasped only to be lost, while they trust from them a great and abiding prize, that good part which shall never be taken from them. These also are to be reckoned with among the converts to your faith; which they are very pleased to accept as a rope or ladder by which they may lift themselves within the reach of objects which they desire. For indeed I know of no more subtle master under heaven than is religion's self,[99] whether it be to turn from the world or to it. No doubt to rule the world is to possess it, an open way to the commission of many and daring crimes. Finally, among your converts you may reckon those who make merchandise of religion, seeking thereby to gain an adequate livelihood and coveting that freedom from earthly cares which it insures.

(DA) In God's name, do you not see, has it not been told you? No man with religious instincts, no man of science, knowledge or administrative power, no one who has read the books, mastered the facts or grasped truths, no man who loves closely reasoned philosophic statements, was ever led to embrace any other religion but Christianity. With that exception, no man ever left his own religion, except it were for worldly reasons and under pressure of necessity, as e.g., that within the fold and empire of Islam, he may safely indulge in these crimes and sordid passions on which his heart is set. From these the Christian religion debar him; it denies him all liberty in that direction. Those who were denied the powers and practice they desired, embraced a religion which made it easy to do as they pleased, and offered under aegis of your empire, perfect security in return for outward profession. And that, God be gracious to you, is the powerful argument, with those whom you see professing your faith and accepting its doctrine. The majority of them believe the opposite to what they outwardly profess. Some of them go the length of slandering your master, questioning the dignity of his descent; some curse him.[100] Some of them assert that another[101] than your master deserved to rule, and that it was by a mistake he came to power. Some say that the Holy Spirit is divided into three parts, one of which rested on Jesus, one on Moses and one on another whom I forbear to mention;[102] your master had no share in it. But these surely are the most ignorant of mankind. They profess Islam and boast of it openly that they may lord it over the Christians, men of true heart who are among them as lambs among wolves. Did not our Lord Christ forewarn them and foretell how it should fare with these?

(DB) But I must not lengthen out my description of the views of your friends. God forbid they should be our friends; let me rather say, the devil's friends; his company and crew. Nor will I say more of what they say; it is enough to make a mountain blush. They circulate lies, first about God and then about your master whom they slander. God is not responsible for this, your master is blameless of it all. What say you to this? They say that when they desire to establish a point, they invent a story to make it good; or what do you say of those who report such a story as this, that God sent to Abu Bakr saying: "O Abu Bakr, I am well pleased with you, I hope you are with me"?[103] You surely do not need more to refute such follies as this which they invent about God. By my life, your master spoke truly when he said: "There never was a prophet whom his people did not misrepresent, and my people will misrepresent me also."[104] But I never knew any people (who) so misrepresent their own prophets, as the Jews do, nor do I know what to say about their lies.[105]

(DC) In many points their teaching conflicts with the truth, e.g., in regard to the call to prayer, funeral rites, confession and supplication, the fast, the takbhir, divergent texts, postponements,[106] judicial decisions and so forth; the story is too long to tell. Yet unless I knew you were well versed in such matters and in the criticism to which they have given rise (and) able to judge for yourself of their defects, I must have gone carefully into the matter, but I am well aware you understand it already. I draw a veil therefore over such questions as government, outward professions of religion and the name of Islam, the use of it merely as an ornament, the marvels they believe, the falsehoods they circulate and finally the hypocrisy which underlies all this, the professions that they are pure in heart and upright in purpose, while they play fast and loose with God and His prophets. When they say such things, how is it that the whirlwind does not sweep them away and the heavens fall on them in indignation and vengeance? They talk loftily, yet He does not cease to be long-suffering toward them and patient. For indeed God, whose name is Great, fears not the future. If they will only return to Him before the day when all secrets are revealed,

He will be gracious to them. God forbid that we should be among the evildoers.

(DD) Now as to what you say that those words are written upon the Throne: "There is no God but God, and Muhammad is His prophet,"[107] I wonder how, with your powers of reasoning and insight, you can allow such an idea to gain possession of your mind. How did you ever conceive it, that you should insinuate it to one like me, knowing as you do the strength of my convictions and the energy of my faith? On this point I reply that you deceive yourself and degrade your intellect. Why, if you believe that you can leave nothing for the anthropomorphism of the Jews. They describe God as seated on the Throne. Not satisfied with seating Him there, you must write His name upon the Throne along with that of a mortal. I should like to know, did He write it there Himself, or was it written for Him? And why did He write it there? For Himself, lest He should forget His own name, or that the angels might know it? But the angels knew it. When He proposed to create the light, when He said: "Let there be light," (Gen. 1:3a) and light was, then the angels praised Him saying: "Blessed be the Author of light."[108] They knew that they were created, and that there was a Creator, and this knowledge in them was constant and unintermittent. He had made them and they had no need that there should be a writing for their eyes to see, something to remind them lest they should forget the name of their Maker. They praised His name saying, "Holy," and that unweariedly; with every breath that is within them they fulfilled His behests. If, on the other hand, it was written for man's learning, they have little profit of it, for they cannot see the Throne, nor read what is written there. You cannot well suppose that it was written there for man that they might read it on the Resurrection Day and that it remains there as proof that evidence quite uncontrovertible, against us; for you know that on the Resurrection Day, all men shall have a perfect knowledge given them of their Maker. All doubts shall be dispelled, mere opinions shall yield to secure convictions. On that day when every man shall have his reward which he has earned and be absorbed in Himself. It is vainly spoken, it is a foolish idea, that these words were written on the Throne of God. As a matter of fact, I do not find any of your own people who agree with you on this point, They all, and specially those who know most, treat it as a foolish idea. They say that it is absurd, and that no such thing is mentioned in the Qur'an. I should like to know where you get the idea. God be merciful to you, you have taken it from some ugly story of the Jews, and they have much else of the same kind, which they have insinuated amongst you. Such is their skill, their delicate finesse, with such arts do they achieve their evil purpose and sow tares among men. When you have grasped the truth you will see quite clearly that the thing is impossible. God in His providence does not do the absurd or meaningless. Besides, I have found in your gatherings that the man will rise to preach and begin his sermon with an invocation. He seems to think that words can go no further than this. "O Lord, bless Muhammad and his seed, as Thou didst bless Abraham and his seed." So you think you have done your utmost for him, when you pray that he may be blessed like the people of Abraham. But this is sheer profanity that a man, whose name is written on the Throne of God in letters of light conjointly with that of God, who is Great and Glorious, a man, but for whom (at least, so you say!) no man, nor even the world itself had been created, should be associated in your prayers with one of the children of Abraham whose name I cannot bring myself to mention in this place.[109] Yet the Qur'an, which is inspired, confirms this witness saying: "O children of Israel, remember My kindness which I did to you, how I preferred you before all My creatures." (Qur'an 2:44,116) This passage compels you to admit that the children of Israel were favored beyond yourselves and any others you can name in point of virtue. You understand that in dealing with such profanities, I am aiming at those confounded Jews. I do not suppose that a sensible Muslim will be convinced by such things. Our answer to you is what we have already written. So far as it is possible for words to go, we have endeavored to make justice arbiter in our discussion with you. We have avoided any tendency toward arrogance and pride, nor have we made any boast of birth. For surely, when we come to know ourselves, we see that no one has any advantage over another in that respect. Do we not all return to one father and one mother? Are we not all made of common clay? One flesh is not fairer than another, nor is one blood better than another. Any preference or privilege there is must be in point of understanding and knowledge. That, I think, has been well expressed thus: "A man's worth is as he thinks and as he does."[110] I greatly admire that saying, and have embodied it in this passage though perhaps it is not germane to the matter we are discussing. I am anxious that no one who reads what I have written with any care or attention, even if he reads it with that evil eye which is the fruit of prejudice and ignorance, should have a chance, however mentally weak and infirm he may be, to suppose that I do not know what is due to you, the people of the house,[111] or that I do not accept my obligations or realize what they are; for indeed I do. But I apply here the dictum of one of your learned men who said: "If your answer is lacking in the proper place, you stammer and outrage reason."[112] Now I do not wish even to appear to outrage reason. I therefore pay no regard to the criticism of such ill-disposed persons, but put their words behind my back, and do not consider them in light save as my enemies. Much less do I intend to take counsel with them.[113]

IV. (Islamic) Customs

(DE) But now, when you summon me to the five prayers, and to the fast of the month of Ramadan, my answer is your own confession; the words you have written as to the prayers which we Christian offer, the fasts we hold and the zeal with which we prosecute them. You have been present and taken part in these sacred offices and now you summon me to what are fictitious and counterfeit offices. Be content with what you have seen, and let this be my answer to you.

(DF) But then you invite me to prostrations, purifications and to circumcision, with a view to establish the ordinances of our father Abraham. Here I answer you in the words of Christ our Lord. When the Jews asked Him why do not Your disciples wash their hands before meat, He replied: "What profit is there to a dark house, if a lamp is burning outside? So it is the inner life of the heart that must be cleansed from impure thoughts and sinful passions. As for the surface of the body, what is the use of laboriously cleansing it? Hypocrites pay attention to the surface which is like a grave with (a) marble front, enshrining the corruption of death, as ye do when ye wash your bodies while your hearts are defiled by sin." (Luke 11:38-40, extreme paraphrase) What is the use of washing the hands or feet or standing to pray,[114] while the heart is fixed on slaughter and plunder? See how our Lord replies: "It is needful that man first of all have his heart cleansed; when this is pure and his conscience void of offence, then let him wash his body in water." (Paraphrase) May God give you understanding of this word, apply your reason to the consideration of it.

(DG) As to circumcision, you must understand its history before you encourage men to the practice of it. If they quote the example of Abraham, then I say that God, when about to bring the children of Israel, Abraham's seed, into the land of Egypt, knowing well how, in the bitterness of their affliction they might be tempted to uncleanness such as He had forbidden, and to the immoralities of the land, set His seal on them, so that if any of them should incline to commit uncleanness with any of the women of the land, she might see this mark of circumcision on his body, and refuse to gratify him. He sealed them with a sign for this purpose.[115] But why do you summon men to circumcision, when you know that your master was not circumcised? So say your own friends, on the authority of the learned.[116] They say that he was not circumcised at all, and compare him in this respect to Abraham, Seth and Noah. If you affirm that Christ was circumcised, we reply that He was circumcised to confirm the precepts of the Law, lest it should be thought that He despised it or sought to discredit it. Whereas He confirmed it when He said: "I am not come to destroy the Law, but to fulfill." (Matt. 5:17) So too said the apostle Paul: "If ye are circumcised, it shall profit you nothing, nor shall uncircumcision be any loss, so long as you have true faith in God and a pure heart." (Gal. 5:6, paraphrase) Were it otherwise, it would be necessary to go the whole length, to offer sacrifices, to keep the Sabbath, to hold the Passover so as to conform to all the precepts of the Law, because forsooth, Christ kept them.[117] But He did this for our relief. He fulfilled the Law perfectly and to the last letter that He might exempt us from the burden of its fulfillment.[118] In place of it He has given us good laws, divine and spiritual precepts, imposing these instead of those of which God said: "I have given you precepts which are not

good, and which ye cannot bear." (Ezek. 20:25, paraphrase) Now if
you do us justice, you must confess that circumcision is not imposed on
us by way of necessity, for the Qur'an, to which you appeal as your
directory, affirms that it is not binding but rather that "he who approves it with his heart honors it, and he who dislikes it, rejects it."[119]
Those of your own friends who are circumcised and multiply their
ablutions do this not because it is imposed as a binding duty, leaving
them no choice but to comply, but rather because it is a common
custom of their time, and that they may conform to a current usage.
Some of our own customs touching personal cleanliness require the
same explanation..."[120] It is not otherwise if we refuse to eat the flesh of
swine or of the ass or of the camel. This is not forbidden, for God has
not made anything unclean. He Himself has said: "God saw all that
He had made, and behold it was very good." (Gen. 1:31a) Shall I
venture to say of anything He has made, that it is unclean or forbidden? If I did, I should be fighting against God; far be it from me to
do so. Anything He has made, I, you, any man may enjoy with perfect
freedom, so long as we receive it in faith, and find it agreeable to our
nature. There is only one exception, viz., the eating of blood, and of
the diseased and all things offered to idols. When anything was forbidden of God, it was by special decree. Now there was a good reason
why the children of Israel were forbidden to eat the flesh of swine. Let
me point it out. When they dwelt in Egypt, they saw the Egyptians
serving idols in the form of birds and oxen. Do you remember what
Moses said to Pharaoh: "We may not offer to God in the presence of
the Egyptians. If we offer in sacrifice what they worship and hold as
divine, what should hinder them from stoning us? Have we not offered
their gods, and made sacrifices of them?" (non-Biblical) Here is proof
that the Egyptians worshipped birds, oxen and rams. Another passage
points in the same direction. When Moses tarried on the mount, the
children of Israel came to Aaron saying, "Make us gods that we may
serve them, for as for Moses, we know not what has become of him."
(Ex. 32:1b, paraphrase) So he made an idol in the shape of a calf,
after the fashion they had seen in Egypt. Well then, the Egyptians
worshipped animals after this kind and offered in sacrifice to them
others (swine, asses, camels and other animals), which they regarded as
a lower order. Therefore it was that God, in giving the Law of sacri-

fice, commanded the people to offer birds, oxen, sheep and nothing
else; swine, asses and camels were forbidden, that the people might
reckon them as unclean and not eat of them, much less offer them in
sacrifice. He taught them, on the other hand, to abstain from the
worship of swine, camels and asses and so forth, and to shun them as
unclean and impure. These they must not even sacrifice, and on no
account must they worship any. They were not forbidden to eat the
flesh of birds, oxen, swine, camels or asses, but they were forbidden to
worship them, or adopt them as gods instead of Him who made all.
So long as we do not worship them, so long as we do not regard them
as divine, or associate them with the worship of idols, they are neither
taboo nor impure. We may eat of the flesh of birds, oxen, sheep,
swine and camels. These are food given of God, and it is good that a
man should eat freely, so long as he eats in faith and finds it agreeable
to his nature. If you see a brother eat any or all of these, impelled by
appetite, do not blame him. Your master, while permitting the use of
camel flesh for food, or with that of the ass or horse for sacrifice,
makes an exception in the case of swine's flesh. But for that we have
to thank 'Abdullah (the) son of Salam and Wahb (the) son of Manba,
both Jews, who would have wrecked the world and ruined the whole of
the race if they could. Here your master is not to blame.[121]

(DH) We must touch on the circumcision of women,[122] the history of
which is follows: Sarah (the) wife of Abraham, when she found that
her husband was smitten with the charms of Hagar her maid, gave her
to him, and allowed their intercourse. Then jealousy, so natural to
woman, came over her and she humbled her maid and did her best to
disfigure her and dishonor that of her which she supposed Abraham
most admired. She did this to put disgrace on Hagar and to get satisfaction out of her. Then Hagar came to the country of Tehama, and
when Ishmael was married, she took his wife in hand and humbled her,
lest she should insult her on this account.[123] She made her suppose
that this was customary in Abraham's house. Whenever a child was
born to Ishmael, he took the male children in hand, and his wife took
the females and circumcised them, and this sign remains, so that it
corresponds with the circumcision of the males. Proof of this is that
the custom is still practiced by the Arabs, though there is no mention

of it in any of the inspired books. Unless, in my judgment, religion had been above such considerations of a physical and temporary nature, I might have been silent on these matters, being myself a son of Ishmael. But I am a Christian, and in that religion I find a precedence which to me is all that pride of birth can be. I am proud of it and boast of it and pray heaven even I may die in it. Indeed all the hope I cherish is that by God's grace and goodness and the abundance of His mercy, I may escape the punishment of hell fire.

(DI) Next you summon me to take the pilgrimage to Mecca, to throw stones at the devil and to cry "Labbaik," and to kiss the Black Stone. I ask you what can you mean? This is mere drivel. You talk like a child, you talk like a fool; you babble when you should reason. Do we not know the whole story of the temple in Mecca, how it originated and grew to its present sanctity? To begin with, the Brahmans and fire-worshippers in India do the same. They call it devotion to the idols, and observe the same rites as the Muslims today. They shave, they strip themselves, they put on the pilgrim dress. Then they go round their temples. You have not improved or altered the ceremony by a jot. Only you do it once in the year at different seasons, while they do it twice in the year at appointed seasons. They do it at first when the sun enters Aries, and again when he enters Libra. That is, they do it at the beginning of summer and winter. They sacrifice early in the morning, just as you do, and perform the same devotions. Such is the origin of your pilgrimage with its stations and all its marvelous rites. You know that the Arabs performed this devotion long ago and ever since the house was built. When your master instituted Islam, he altered nothing, save that because of the toil and the length of the journey, he imposed one pilgrimage in the year[124] and omitted the profanities which were mingled with the prayers of invocation. Otherwise it remained as it was, the same as the devotions paid to their idols by Brahmans and fire worshippers in the cities of India. I quite approve that saying of 'Umar when he fell before the Black Stone and the station[125] of Abraham, "By God," said he, "I know that you are both stones, you cannot help or hurt, yet I have seen the Apostle of God kiss you, and I will do the same."[126] Whether the authorities from whom I quote, and who were no doubt honorable men, coined this story or not, I do not much care. What they said about the stone is certainly true.[127] If 'Umar said it, he said the truth. If he did not, he might have said it without going beyond the bounds of truth. As to those who are inclined to rebuke their neighbors when they shave their heads and race round, behaving like men demented and as if they were possessed by Satan, we, while allowing such criticism, might excuse you to them on the ground that the thing is done as an act of worship. But they reply that God is not worshipped by His creatures with degrading and immoral rites, revolting to the reason, but by rites which the understanding approves, i.e., according to those simple rites which God has Himself imposed on His servants. They say that men ought to worship Him, and draw near to him thus; otherwise, why do they condemn the Magians as immoral when they marry their mothers and daughters and practice their detestable rites? If these things are horrid in Magian worship, why do you in turn practice shaving and (kissing?). Why do you fling stones and race around?

(DJ) Still more dreadful than all this is the custom that a woman, when divorced, should have intercourse with another man who is known as her mustahil. He tastes her sweetness and thereafter she returns to her husband.[128] Not improbably she has children, noble men and fine women with houses of their own. Her husband may be a man of exalted position and highest rank. That such an indignity as I have hinted at should be inflicted on one who is reckoned as refined by her people, a woman of honor and possibly of wealth, surely this is more detestable and immoral than the doing of those abhorred Magians! Do you not see that you summon me to a practice which even beasts abhor? I am quite sure that if they had the power to speak, they would pronounce very strongly on such a practice as immoral and detestable. They would instruct us that by our concession to such practices we should be doing violence to reason and nature. May I never be among the evildoers.

(DK) But then you tell us that you visit the shrine of the Prophet of God, and present yourself at these "wonderful and blessed places." In God's name, you do not err in describing them as wonderful places, for what could be more wonderful to anyone with understanding than a place where such practices are allowed? But you call them "blessed" as well as wonderful places. Tell us then what you find there in the way of blessing. What sick man has gone there and returned healed of his disease? What palsied man has been carried there, and returned free of his palsy? What leper has visited them and found his leprosy leave him? What blind man have you brought thither and restored to him his sight? What person possessed of the devil has been led there, and been made sound in body and mind? I do not believe that you, even you alone, will venture to say that there is any such power in the place, much less can you point to one who has been thus restored. There is not one who holds your faith and worships the Prophet in whose honor you make this pilgrimage; there is not one man on the face of the globe, roofed in by the encircling dome of heaven, who could make such a claim from his own experience, unless indeed he professes the Christian faith. You cannot dispute the point I make, and what sense is there in talking of blessing and sanctity and associating such ideas with this place? We know that blessing rests where God is really worshipped, in the dwellings of the righteous, of holy men and saints who have devoted themselves to His service day and night, never ceasing from their toils. These men have trampled the world under their feet, and are free from it. They have put from their hearts the desire of it and all anxiety about its affairs. They are worthy that blessing should descend from God on them and on their dwellings, worthy that He should minister healing and help through their hands. What they ask of Him He bestows, when they intercede, He accepts their intercession, and answers their prayers. For His promises never fail, nor does help perish from His hand for those who do well. "The righteous seek and find," (Luke 11:9a, paraphrase) "The Lord is nigh unto them that call on Him; He fulfills the desire of those who fear Him." (Ps. 145; 18a, 19a) "Ask and ye shall receive, seek and ye shall find." (Luke 11:9a) Now God has kept His promises. He has made good the light and leading He sent us in His Gospel. There has never been one burdened, afflicted or (of) wounded soul, one sick man or suppliant asking in good faith and with a steadfast mind, in Christ's name, whose burden of sorrow and grief has not been dispelled. Comfort and healing have come down to him from God, through His saints. Blessing has come in answer to the prayers of His servants, to those who prayed in Christ's name, and sought help from whence help comes. I refer of course to the shrines maintained in the churches and all places where they celebrate the name of Christ, the Savior of the world, and where the monks find an asylum. These are rich in blessings so as to overflow on all who come about them to pray with a pure mind and a perfect heart. There you may cultivate the acquaintance of these holy men, and receive alms of what they have to give. Freely they give, and ask no equivalent from anyone, nor any regard, no recompense is sought, none is received. For Christ has said: "Freely you have received, freely give." (Matt. 10:8b) These men follow in His steps, and He, our Shepherd, hears their prayers and sends down healing and mercy by their hands on all men. If any are excepted, it is those only who reject the truth. They suffer loss because they turn aside and pervert the fear of God. They suffer loss, yet if they return in, He welcomes them as a father the son whom he loves. So it was with the prodigal son who wandered from his father's house till chiding his own folly he returned as penitent, sorry for his sin and acknowledging the debt too long unpaid. He confessed his follies and purged himself of his guilt. And then all the pity in his father's heart went out to meet him. He welcomed him right heartily and rejoiced to have him back, accepting his apologies and gladly restoring him in his old place at home. He did not chasten him, but rather embraced him,[129] in all the folly and ignorance of his youth. He said, "See thou wert dead, but art alive; thou wert lost, but art found; wert led astray, and hast found the right road." (Luke 15:24, paraphrase)

(DL) Distinguish then, by the help of God, the things which differ. Do not yield to that prejudice which is engendered by the malice of Satan, that foe of our race. Would you have me give up what I have received of this distinguishing grace so great, so glorious that even angels might envy us, much more man, and that grace which the prophets and the holy men of old hoped for, and which their hearts desired? Would you have me accept in its place the offer you have made me? My whole nature revolts from such a course; my understanding rejects it, my reason rebukes it and bids me shun it. If I were to act so, I could no longer reckon myself an honorable man.

(DM) Then you say, "I summon you to the ways of God," by which you mean raiding those who differ from you, smiting the idolaters with the edge of the sword and plundering them, till they accept the true religion and testify that there is no God but one and that Muhammad is His Prophet. I ask you in the name of God, the judge of all, do you not rather mean that you summon me to the ways of Satan, from whom God has taken His mercy, who exhausted his spleen on the race of men, infusing them with his own wrath and filling them with rage and passion? He has made them his weapons; they are his friends moved at his will, by whom he works his pleasures. How am I to reconcile such a summons with your own statements? For the scriptures, which you hold to be inspired, flatly contradict you. You read there: "Given people among you who teach what is good, practice kindness and cease from evil, they shall prosper." (Qur'an 3:100) Then you read: "It is not your business to guide them, God shall guide whom He will." (Qur'an 2:274) "If the Lord had willed it, all men on earth had believed as one man. Will you compel man to believe? What is there to induce them to believe, save the prompting of God?" (Qur'an 10:99,100a) Do you not see how this contradicts the principles you have laid down? Then you read: "Say, O men, the truth is come to you from your Lord; and who led you into it? He that is rightly directed, is rightly directed for himself, and he who strays must bear the consequences. I am not your guardian. Follow what is revealed to you, and wait till God give the decision. He is the best judge." (Qur'an 10:108-109) "If the Lord had willed, He had made all men one people. And they shall not cease to disagree; save those only on whom the Lord had mercy. To this end hath He made them." (Qur'an 11:120a) So it is written, confirming the word of your master that he was sent of God on a mission of mercy to all men,[130] but what mercy is there in killing and plundering? I have often heard the Jews affirm that the Qur'an is self contradictory. I will not use such language of your sacred books, but I must say that three quotations are absolutely at variance with your own statements. First of all you issue this most urgent summons, and then you turn and contradict your own words. Let me put it thus: What are the ways of Satan if they be not slaughter, plunder and thieving? Can you raise any objection to that or dispute it? If you plead that Moses the prophet slew the idolaters of his day,

we reply: Tell us in God's name, what you read in the Law — What of
the many wonders and signs Moses wrought that he might convince us
that the war he proclaimed was divinely decreed? So with Joshua, who
made the sun and moon stand still, that was his sign, a miracle which
no one could perform save one of the saints of God. But what sign
can your master adduce in proof of the claim he makes? What miracle
can you instance wrought by him? How did he undertake to prove the
truth of his doctrine or enforce his claim? He plundered the property
of man and captured their children; he attacked the saints of God, a
people who had no defence except in His name, who kept His laws and
humbled their hearts before Him, believing in Christ and truly rever-
encing Him, men who had been led into the truth so that their faces
shone, as they will shine forever and ever in the light of God. Nothing
will content you but to describe such conduct as the ways of God. God
forbid that such should be His ways, or the ways of His saints. God
loves not the deeds of evildoers. And what shall I say of the glaring
contradictions when you write: "Let there be no compulsion in religion," (Qur'an 2:257a) and assert that God has said: "Say to those to
whom the book has been given, and to the ignorant people: Have ye
yet accepted Islam? If they have accepted Islam, they have been
rightly guided, but if they turn their backs, it is yours still to deliver the
message." (Qur'an 3:19) You say: "If God had willed, those who came
after them had not fought among themselves, after proof had come to
them. But they differed; some believed, and some rejected. If God
had willed it, they had not fought among themselves, but God doth as
He pleases." (Qur'an 2:254b) And then again your master, addressing
the unbelievers, adds this crowning verse: "You have your own religion,
and I have mine." (Qur'an 109:6) Still further he adds: "Do not strive
with the People of the Book save in the kindliest way." (Qur'an 29:45a)
Yet you summon me to smite men with the edge of the sword, to
plunder, steal and slay, till they embrace the true faith, whether they
will or not. Which of these two statements must I accept, the former
or the latter? If I try to compare your utterances, I find that one
cancels the other. You have issued a summons, the real nature of
which you have not grasped. You do not know which view you yourself
hold, and which you repudiate. What you affirm may be what you
really deny, and so the whole argument is turned upside down, and that

which you deny becomes that which you really affirm. You do not know what you mean, and of course you cannot maintain it against those who subject you to a rigorous cross examination.

(DN) But enough of this. We have made it plain that you contradict yourself and refute you own statements. You say that your master was sent with a message of mercy and kindness to all men, and that there is no compulsion in matters of religion; and yet you affirm that you will smite men with the sword till they embrace the true faith, willingly or unwillingly. The result is that we cannot feel sure of either of your statements, nor can we assent to either, because we are divided between them, not knowing which of them is inspired and ought to be received. Indeed the conclusion to which we are forced by the argument is, that both alike must be set aside; inasmuch as what you regard as true, by which therefore we ought to be guided, may perchance be untrue and ought to be discredited, as that which is not meant for guidance. In fine, God neither wills or wishes either.

(DO) Have you ever heard or read in any inspired book of anyone but your master who aspired to draw men to his own beliefs against their will, under compulsion, and at the edge of the sword? You know the story of Moses and the signs he wrought. Even the Magians, that abominable lot, tell some idle stories by which they affirm that Zoroaster, when he came to the mount of Silan was inspired of God and summoned Kashtasaf the King and his people, and that they obeyed him when they saw his sorceries, the magic and the conjuring which they took as evidence of supernatural power. They saw that he raised a horse to life after it was dead. Such are the trifles he brought from his book of charms of which they say that it is circulated in every language and contains all that is most choice in human speech! They say that he wrote it in 12,000 volumes on buffalo hides, and called it Kindavesta, that is, the Book of Religion. But, when asked as to the interpretation of it, they say that they do not understand it. So it was that Buddha in India, showed the wonderful Phoenix with a young girl inside who told the people that he was a god, whose word was truth in all that he said to him. These are some the stories they circulate. As a matter of fact, you will not find one with any pretensions to be a prophet, whether true or false, who has not adduced some argument or evidence of the genuineness of his claims. Where the gold may be mingled with the alloy, we test it in the scales of which alone can sift the true from the false. This is the course followed by every teacher except your master. We do no see him begin his appeal with any argument but the sword. Surely he is the first who, when he thought to win the consent of men, began by proclaiming: "If they will not acknowledge my claims to be the messenger of the Lord of all, I will smite them with the sword, capture and plunder, for this cause and reason alone."[131] How different it was with Christ, the Savior of the world. You recollect the appeal He made, under similar circumstances. You know the whole story well enough. And do you really think that anyone who claims, as you do, to be a man of knowledge and culture, should issue such a summons to me with my experience of men and things? Night and day I read the words of our Lord, which is the robe and raiment I wrap about my soul, and hear Him say: "Be kind to all men, be pitiful, that ye may be the children of your Father which is in heaven." (Matt. 5:44,45a, paraphrase) What must I think, who have been led by Him along such lines as these, who have reared in a kindly and gracious atmosphere, which has subdued and tempered my whole being, and become, so to speak, the blood in my veins and the marrow in my bones. I have grown up in this genial soil till every hair of my head seems somehow rooted in it. God forbid that my heart should grow hard and rebellious: that I should be possessed by the devil and transformed into the image of Iblis[132] that murderer of mankind. So I judge the rather, because God has honored the human race in that His creative Word has taken our flesh and dwelt among us, so sharing with us the glory of His Godhead. Him all the angels worship saying, "Holy is His name." They praise Him as they praise God; indeed there is no distinction between them in this respect. Thus has grace been added to grace. Thus it is given Him to sit on the right hand of the power of God. This honor He shares with the human nature He has assumed. He is like us, as our brother, yet He is our Maker and God, in as much as the creative Word is united to Him. And then, still further to distinguish Him, God has given Him all power in heaven and on earth to rule the world, to quicken the dead, to pronounce the final judgment on men and angels. Ah, my friend, do you suppose that I will reject the counsel of God and smite with the edge of the sword? That were, surely, to defy God, to frustrate His Word, that were to deny His goodness, poor thanks for all His grace. I pray God that I may not thus forsake and anger Him.

(DP) If you say that even He imposes pains and penalties on men, and if you ask why we should not do as He does, our answer is easy; we do not imitate you, who, when asked as to the nature of the soul, replied: "That is God's affair." (Qur'an 17:87)[133] These who heard you thought they had never heard such an answer given. Our reply is this: God does not afflict His servants with a desire to trouble them, or because He hates them. If He did, why should He ever have made them? But He made them of His goodwill and kindness to them. He drew them from the wide womb of an uncreated night, and called them into being that He might translate them from this transient state, this baseless fabric of an empty unsubstantial vision, to an eternal home where joy reigns immortal and undimmed. Now you would not say of one who transferred his friend from a provincial town to the capital of a great empire and from a humble sphere to a place of great honor and influence, that he wronged him in so doing. You would say that he did well by him; aimed from the first to last at his advancement. So when you say that God afflicts man with sore pains and grievous afflictions, we reply that, in so doing He means to fit us for the recompense and reward. If by the continuance of His favor to us, we finally attain to these and are made worthy of them, may we not claim that God, most Great and Glorious, has dealt well with us in both estates? He is like a wise and kindly doctor, who drugs a sick man with medicines which are distasteful to both taste and smell;[134] sometimes he applies the cautery, sometimes he amputates a limb. He forbids what is pleasing in the way of food and drink, and this he does from solicitude, for the welfare of his patient. Do you say that he is animated by a spirit of hate? On the contrary, he aims at the restoration of the patient to health, and to rid him of his infirmities and disorders. He would have him no longer the victim of a loathsome disease, but sound in limb and full of life. If you retort that God, if anxious to show His favor to men, need not have afflicted them with grievous pains; we reply that in the same way He need not have made the world. He might have created (only) the world to come, and transported favored mortals thither without probation or discipline. That was possible as an act of sovereignty, but it would have been an administrative blunder, inasmuch as one might have criticized His action and affirmed that He could not create more than the world. Rather He made the world and designed it, transient as it is, to be a place of probation and commerce, sending us wayfarers hither to use it as travellers use an inn, where they alight to pass the night, and then move onwards to their homes, the final goal of all their wanderings, where they are at rest. So in His providence and great goodness, He, the most High, has dealt with man. He afflicts them with infirmities and pains for their good, for a little while during this short-lived mortal existence. His aim is to make them worthy of what He has in store; that He may perfect His goodness to them in that eternal home where we shall have lasting joy, comfort and contentment that shall never fail.

(DQ) Now, God have mercy on you, who summon us so peremptorily to the obedience of your master. If, when he smote with the sword and scourged men with whips, he had meant well to them in so doing, would he not have admonished them and showed them some courtesy, following the divine methods? But his motives were quite different. He had no care of them in his heart, nor ever thought of them. He had no aim but to profit himself and his friends, and to establish his kingdom. In proof of this I cite his own words: "Let them pay my tribute and accept humiliation." (Qur'an 9:29b) Does not your common sense inform you that he had no desire to reclaim them from the state of idolatry and unbelief in which he found them, to what he considered the true faith? He did not think of that at all; he had no eye save for his own ends, but sought to realize his own purposes, and that was the consolidation of his empire. Yet he says: "Say to those who have the book, and to the ignorant ones also, Do ye accept Islam? If they do, they are well guided, if they turn their back, still you have your message to deliver. God hath regard to His servants." (Qur'an 3:19a) Do we not see that he is bidden to speak out his message articulately, that he is forbidden to kill and capture? Be in earnest, get this matter cleared up, and see how absolutely you contradict yourself.

(DR) But, to my amazement, you describe those of your friends who have fallen in battle, as "martyrs." Well, let me appeal to history, (to see) who best deserve to be described by that name; the Christians slain in the days of the Persian kings and others who suffered for Christ's sake, or your friends, who were slain in the pursuit of worldly ambition and in the wars of conquest. We have heard how patiently the Christians suffered, and even hastened to yield their lives, to shed their blood and that of their children, how they turned their backs on the world with all its comforts and how fixed and imperturbable was their temper, how intense their convictions of the truths they held! They hastened to offer themselves, that they might be tortured, slain and put to death as a sacrifice to God. Where one was slain, 100 more or less, at that very time and place professed the faith for which he died. One of the cruel kings of the Romans persisted in killing a great number of them till one of his own people said: "O king, you think you are diminishing the number of Christians, but you are adding to them every day." When he asked, "How is that?" the reply was given: "You killed so many yesterday, and there are twice their number professing Christianity today." When he asked the reason for this, he was told how the people said that one was sent from heaven to encourage them. On this he sheathed his sword and himself became a Christian.[135] Look at those who were the most thoughtful and intelligent, the most sincere and devoted to their religion; they did not weary of their faith though it meant death by the sword. They were content to suffer what came. Instead of holding back, they showed themselves eager, joyous, full of cheer, convinced that when they suffered most, they were still far short of what was in their hearts to render as a debt of honor for the grace brought to them in the Christian faith. Freely they offered themselves. Some were flayed alive, others were dismembered, others were burnt with fire. Some were thrown to the lions. Some were sawn asunder, remaining strong in the faith they had embraced. There has never been an age when some did not give themselves to death, hating their lives and all that the world could offer them, for the sake of Christ.

(DS) Now we appeal to you: where will you find such a lofty spirit, an inspiration to compare with that of these Christians? The torments they endured were indescribable, yet they went through them with unshrinking faith and overflowing joy. One who was suffering was asked why, while in this state, he kept turning to the right and to the left and then smiling. They said to him: "Is there anything we cannot see, that makes you turn to the right and to the left and smile while you are in such torment?" He answered: "I do not feel any pain, though I am in this torment, and when I turned I saw a young man near me who smiled to me and wiped away the blood from my wounds with a white cloth he held. It seemed to me as if my torments were falling on my tormentors."[136] We have no doubt that he spoke the simple truth, for how else could he have borne his sufferings? All praise to God, you know He has regard to His faithful people and supports them in their time of need. Perhaps you say God might have ordered the angel whom He sent to the martyr's side to wipe the blood from his wounds, rather to avert those were tormenting him. In that case you think the result might have been their conversion, but we reply: God, most High, hallowed be His name, if He had wished to gather all men to the true faith and into the true fold, and to compel them to believe; had the power to do so. Instead of that He chose to implant in them a certain moral sense, leaving them to obey as they choose or not, that He might reward them or punish them, not for what He compelled them to do, but according to their desires. Otherwise it would have not been necessary to supply proof of truths which transcend reason. At the time then, He showed to some man signs and wonders such as He withheld from others, fitted to exercise their faith so as to make it plain whether they were obedient in spirit or not. If they had repented simply because of these signs, no reward would have been due to them, because they repented under constraint and compulsion of the miraculous. But He left them to decide for themselves, meantime supplying more abundant grace to His saints. In this way it was made quite clear that their obedience was free, because it was the result of conviction. Special regard was had to the environment of those primitive Christians, to whom faith was possible only as their response to clear proof and convincing reason. Differing widely in race, temper, and religion, they could never be drawn into a common fold except by the influence of wonders and signs. Still the original force of the supernatural remains an abiding factor in the religious problem of today. The evidence is still within our mental horizon. We have heard and cherish the story of the miracles wrought among them by monks and teachers who cast out evil spirits and healed the sick in their churches and monasteries and in the shrines which were built in honor of the martyrs whose sufferings we have described — true martyrs, worthy of the name. In some of these churches you will find the tombs of the martyrs, in others bits of their bones, precious relics from which East and West through Rome, Syria, Persia, Abyssinia, distant islands and the great cities of Iraq, and such grace radiates as disappoints none who appeal to them or shelter near them in the spirit of humble faith. Perhaps the only exception is your master's country, a country never hallowed by the presence of a martyr or chosen as a home by any Christian save two, known to you by name: Sergius, called Nestorius, and John, famous in Medina. Such virtue you will seek in vain, for no claim is made to it save within the Christian Church. It is the Christian inheritance and will be while the world lasts. Now what proofs could there be more clear and luminous to those who desire the truth?

(DT) Still come on, let us continue our examination with such candor and penetration as we can command. Let us have reason, impartial and incorruptible reason, as the umpire in our friendly strife. I ask you then, and may God guide your reply, which of these two is more worthy to be called a martyr and honored as one slain in the ways of the Lord? One who offers himself on the altar of religion, to whom they said: "Worship the sun and the moon and these gods of gold and silver," but he refused, preferring rather to pour out his heart's blood, to lose property, life and children; or one who goes forth to seek the plunder and booty, to indulge in unnatural and unlawful intercourse with women, to dispatch raiding parties in what he calls "sacred wars in the ways of the Lord," saying that he who is killed or kills is sure of pardon?

(DU) O my friend, be honest. Suppose we should come to you and appoint you our umpire in a matter; what judgment must you give if you honor the truth? Suppose we should inform you that a thief was breaking into the house of a friend when the wall fell on him (the

486

thief), or he fell into a pit, or the master of the house surprised him and dealt him a deadly blow, must indemnity be paid to the thief? I am sure that, as umpire, you would not say so. And why do you say that paradise is due to the man who goes among a quiet people dwelling securely in their homes and of whom he knows as little as they know of him, with intent to plunder and to slay, and then boasts of what he has done? Nor are you content with this. You do not return repenting of your sin, asking pardon and suffering remorse because of your crimes, but, on the contrary, you boast that he who kills or is killed in such wars is sure of paradise, and yet you call him "a martyr in the ways of the Lord." If that is the judgment you give, I ask what worse could we have from the hands of Satan, who from the first has been the arch-enemy of mankind? I am certain that reason and honor forbid such a decision. You dare not make it. You see I have not forgotten how you enjoined patience on us, when it was your turn to plead. It was not we who raised this question; you began the discussion, and we have replied. That is how the matter stands. In what we have written, we have studied brevity. We might have enlarged on these lines, following the examples of others; what we have said is our answer, called forth by your initiative. You will see that our reply is like the fire which is latent in stone or iron; when you strike it with your flint, the flame is kindled. So have I sought to reply to you and to any who may come to glance at what I have written. It is all one.

(DV) But now you summon me to the enjoyment of many blessings which you enumerate, all of which are passing and perishing, like any empty dress or like the lightning brand which flashes out for one brief second and then disappears, leaving those who wait for it in unbroken darkness. Even if they were of substantial and abiding value, you could not expect a man of insight and understanding to hanker after them, how much less when they are only fitted for beasts in whom a conscience never wakes, who feed only to die. The world itself has no worth or value in a wise man's eyes; for he knows how quickly it melts away, and leaves not a wrack behind. Swiftly it fades, in a moment of time it has gone forever. Such arguments as these appeal to those only who are who are already a prey to their lower nature. I say it solemnly; I trust I have not shown any inordinate desire for such things. It

487

surprises me that you should hope to catch me with so gross and earthly a net. He whose nature resembled that of the beast may incline to it and yield to its seductions, but men of discrimination, with anything of the ideal in their composition, are free from such low tastes as these on which you play. Indeed it is their eager desire to rid themselves of all these physical disabilities which existence for the time involves. If it were within their power forcibly to rid themselves of these, how gladly would they do so. Why then do you suppose that they still seek for possessions and scheme for power? Not for such ends did God make two creatures; nor for such ends will He raise them from the dead. Your own scriptures affirm: "I have not made jinn or man save that they may worship," (Qur'an 51:56) I cannot see any consistence in your argument. First you say I have made them to worship, then you contradict yourself and demolish the structure you have reared, saying, "Marry whom you will, two, three or four wives," adding, "and of handmaids what your hands have gotten." (Qur'an 4:3) So you make us eat and drink like beasts which care not for the precepts of reason, and have no law from heaven to guide them.

(DW) As to the section which deals with divorce and the conditions under which your master has made it lawful for a woman to return to her husband, were it not for fear of undue length, I would recall to you how God rebuked His people by the mouth of the prophet Jeremiah (Jeremiah 3:1). But you know that the custom is regarded as a scandal and disgrace by all nations who have any religion in them.[137] They repudiate it. I will spare myself the shame of rehearsing it here. I have too much respect for the paper on which I write, to have more to do with it, hating it as I do and desiring to steer clear of it. That is my answer.

(DX) You are good enough to bid me write you with perfect freedom and entirely at my ease. I am not to be the least afraid. You will not take amiss what I may say. Christ our Lord, when He encouraged me in His holy Gospel said: "Fear not of them that kill the body, but have no power to kill the soul, but rather fear Him who can destroy both soul and body in hell." (Matt. 10:28) And I believe His word. No one hath power over me but He who made soul and body. I am the more assured of this from the large tolerance extended to me, through the goodness of God and the Amir of the Faithful and by the perfect fairness and kindness he has shown to any weakling like myself who may approach his Excellency and find a place under his protecting shade. His is no narrow grudging justice. Wide in his sympathies he has embraced us all. May God most High reward him for it, may He realize all his hopes for himself and for his children in this world, and graciously grant him an answer to his prayers in peace.

(DY) As to what you say about this true faith which you profess: whoever has a lot and portion with you in this matter, even I, if I embrace it and profess as you do, shall be like you and reign with you and shall share your honors in this world and in the next; it is all familiar to me. With regard to your religion, enough has already been said. As for honors in this world and in the next, God has given you the caliphate. He has committed it to the people of your religion, and we pray Him to continue you in this grace. As for honor in the world to come, that is only to be measured by God. "Good works" as your master is reported to have said: "Ye son of Manaf,[138] I am not the richer for you in any respects in the sight of God; you cannot give me pedigree other than you will give me good works, and before God, this alone has value: your fear."[139] If he said this, truly honor in the world to come must be an empty name unless it is based on good works. We find that the people of God were of no consideration or distinction in this world; and for the world to come, their good works alone gave them honor. You know as well as we do that good works are our only honor and dignity. We do not dare to boast of what comes to us of the past, of the rank we have inherited among the Arabs, or the fame of our forefathers. In former times it was universally recognized. Every educated person knows that the Kindi were of royal rank, distinguished among all Arabs. But we endorse that word of St. Paul: "He that glorieth, let him glory in the Lord." (I Cor. 1:31) I have no boast but in the faith of Christ by which we attain to good works. Only thus do we truly know God and approach Him in that way which leads to life and saves from the fires of hell. But, when you tell us that your Prophet said: "On the day of judgment everyone will be absorbed in himself, O my people, my people, my family, my family,"[140] and when you tell us the response given to his intercession, surely you are nodding. In good sooth, such promises are vain, such hopes are deceptive. We do not doubt that our Lord and Savior to whom your own scriptures bear witness that He is the cynosure of every eye in this world and in the next, will reward every man according to his works; if good, then good, and if bad, then bad. There is no partiality with Him nor indulgence for any. Let me give you some good advice; have regard to what I say and do not incline to such vain and foolish hopes. Lay a foundation of good works while you are in this world, supply yourself while you are here with that which shall profit you. There is no profit in that day save in religion. Lay aside this itching after idle pleasures. Soon you must depart. Death is nigh, when you must stand before Christ, the true Judge, and render your account, where no excuse is received, where there is no plea, nor prayer, nor place of repentance. Fear God in your heart, O my friend, and know that the fear of God is the best merchandise, yielding interest even where there is no capital. You have seen the eagerness of the monks and how they offered themselves to God. You too should be reasonable, since God has implanted in your soul the faculty of reason. You have no excuse, for I have given you good advice.

(DZ) As to what you say about concessions and how these are brought about, alas, alas, it cannot be. Christ in His holy Gospel, imposing and confirming the Law of His Kingdom has said: "When ye have done all these things which are commanded of you, say, We are unprofitable servants." (Luke 17:10) He adds: "Enter by the straight gate, for wide is the gate and broad is the way that leadeth to destruction, and many are they who enter by it, for straight is the gate and narrow is the way that leadeth unto life, and few there be that find it." (Matt. 7:13,14) These are not the terms you offer, but they are (more) in keeping with the solemnities of the world to come than your wide doors and wonderful facilities. You speak of a passion for scents and women. You say: "Have free intercourse with women." By God to whom we pray for help, before whom your heart lies open, you must turn your back on much you thought most sure and safe. I cannot understand how you do not see that all this is fictitious. I pray God, who leads the wanderer into truth, that He may cause to shine into your darkened soul such light as may guide you safely through the tangled maze of error in which you are enveloped. It is my duty to announce to you and to all men the existence of the Christian society. Surely our prayers are not perfect unless we summon those who wander to the paths of the truth, that God may open their eyes and remove the blindness of error so that they may see their sin and turn to the obedience of the truth and be established in the grace which is given. May He do this for you and all your brethren in the greatness of His power and might.

(EA) But you bid me to lay aside my unbelief, error and faith I profess in the Father, Son and Holy Ghost, along with the worship of the cross, all of which you consider "harmful and unprofitable, unbelief and error." I have dealt at large with that question, and it is hardly needful to rehearse. I have furnished an argument against any who may still think it is worth his while to issue such a phrase while he himself persists in unbelief. As to what you are pleased to call a medley; apparently anything you cannot understand is a medley, according to the proverb: "Man is the enemy of whatever he does not understand"! I pray God it be not so with you. There is no sense in what you say; and certainly you do not judge wisely, nor in your own interests when you argue in this way. It is not so that educated and cultivated people argue. That against what you inveigh as a medley is a divine mystery into which the angels of the presence with the prophets and the apostles desire to look, (ever) since the world was made by God. At first only a suggestion of it was given, a passing glimpse. Nothing more than a covert hint or parable of it[141] until the advent of our Lord, the beloved Son who came from the bosom of the Father. By Him it was revealed to the whole body of His faithful people. He gave them His Word plainly declared and bade them call men everywhere to a knowledge of that Word, which is the name of the Father, Son and Holy Ghost. As to what you say of the worship of the cross, that it is "harmful and does not profit,"[142] so far as you can judge from what you have seen of the honors paid to it and the esteem in which it is held by us, we answer you that we are moved to this by what we see depicted there of the majesty of Christ and His sufferings in the conduct of our redemption. He saved us from sin by His passion and the death He died upon the cross. No words of ours can describe, nor can our thanks repay Him for the grace there revealed. Of this grace the cross is the symbol set before our eyes to stir our hearts that we may give thanks to Him who ministers it and has bestowed it upon us. It is to Him we direct our worship and praise, not to the wood or anything else of which the cross is made. If, as you suppose, we worship the wood of the cross, why should we make it of any other material as we often do, e.g., of gold, silver and precious stones, carving them with our own hands? That surely is proof that we do not direct our worship to the material of which the cross is made, but to Him who is depicted on it.[143] If it is a universal custom to honor all that pertains to the majesty of a king and is connected with his person, particularly his image, so that we do it in reverence, honoring thereby the king and what of his majesty may be represented by it, surely we ought to honor the cross and worship and adore it, for there we see the majesty of Christ our King and the greatness of His grace toward us. There He was crucified for us. Indeed in our age men carry a good custom so far that they kiss the hands and feet of a king, doing homage to him thus; and in this way they enjoy royal favor. This they do from the heart right lovingly and loyally. How then can you deny us the right to worship and adore the cross as I have described? We read in the holy scriptures that the prophets reverenced the ark which was made by Moses at God's command. They worshipped before it. When it was uplifted Moses said: "Arise O Lord, and let thine enemies be scattered," (Num. 10:35) and when it returned he said: "Return O Lord, to the tribes of Israel." (Num. 10:36) In the book of Joshua we are told how the children of Israel fell before the ark and worshipped it, appealing to it against the calamities which befell them. David, when he transferred the ark to Jerusalem, paid it divine honors and offered burnt offerings and sacrifices with his men of arms, singing a hymn of praise beginning with words which recall those of Moses: "Let God arise." (Ps. 68:1a)[144] Thus in honoring the ark they worshipped God, not the wood or anything else about it, and we also worship the cross, following their example. In God's name I ask you, why must oblivion seize you just at this point? It seems as if your prejudice in favor of Islam and your partiality for the Hashimite[145] had completely mastered you and made you forget the path of truth, so as to believe the testimony you have given and endorsed, as to your own experience of the power inherent in the cross.[146] Did you not invoke that sacred symbol when you fell from your beast and again when you fled and met what you met on the way to Umr Karah, and when the lion met you as you were nearing Sabat'ul-Medina? Did you think that I had forgotten these occurrences? Rather, if you have forgotten them, let me remind you of them. And why then, in God's great name, will you deny the grace that stood you in good stead in your time of trouble? Why thus ignore His goodness? Is this the way of one who has been trained to hold fast to the truth? Why do you say that the worship of the cross is harmful? I should like to know what harm it did to you when you invoked it. Anyway, you know that I am a Christian, and we Christians do not worship the cross, we worship the power that dwells in it, the help that comes from it and the salvation received through it. Did we not argue this matter in the presence of one whose verdict you cannot dispute? You know that judgment went against you in that august presence. Why do you turn from what then seemed so certain to you, so absolutely true? Did you not protest that you had proved it and verified it? Is this according to the judgment passed against you by him who you know so well; or do you wish rather to dismiss that incident entirely from your memory? I hope that this judgment which you have passed upon the cross does not represent your real convictions, that you will not frustrate the grace which you have seen dwells in it.

(EB) You are good enough to say that you have a kindly feeling for me in your heart and wish to save me from the hell fire. No doubt this deserves my grateful acknowledgment. At least judged by the letter, I think, however, that I can turn the table on you. Really it is you who owe me thanks. Pray understand my argument, may God enable you to grasp it, for it is valid from first to last. It is not of the nature of idle talk that has neither profit or advantage in it. How best shall I put it? Five times every day you humble yourself before God in prayer. You pray: "Lead me in the right way, with the guidance granted those against whom Thou art not angry, nor do they go astray." (Qur'an 1:5-7) Now if you are really guided, surely, in God's name, you might dispense with this petition and the accompanying prostrations which preface every prayer you make. If He guided you aright, surely it is a loss of time to pray for guidance already received. If you have not got this guidance even after you have sought it so long, tell me, in God's name, who are the favored few of whom you pray night and day that God may guide you in their steps and associate you with them as the elect people sent forth among the men? This true religion which you desire to adopt as your own, and which alone is recognized by heaven; whose is it? Do you refer to the Magians who worship the sun and practice detestable customs which are abhorrent to reason and nature alike? Everyone who has read history knows that no revelation of higher truth has come to them; they do not even hold the doctrine of the unity of God, but worship the devil along with God, praise be His name. Surely they are not favored people. Then are they the Jews? But your master washed his hands clean of them and your scriptures say that the wrath of heaven rests on them; they are reprobates, scattered among the nations, cursed by the mouth of every apostle and prophet. Surely they are no favored people into whose way you pray God to guide you. If you mean the worshippers of al-Lat, al-Uzza, Yaghut, Ya'uq, Kathriya, Shams, Jihar, Hubbal, Nasr, Suwa, Waad, Asaf, Na'dah, Dhul Khaffayn, Manat, Sad, Dhul Halasah and other idols which the Arabs worship in Mecca,[147] then your own scriptures refute you pointedly, for they say: "We have found you in error and led you into the right way." (Qur'an 93:7) For your master was neither Jew nor Christian nor Magian, but what you call "orthodox," a worshipper of Azaf and Na'd. And when God graciously revealed to him the truth, then as we have seen, he prayed to be delivered from those who worshipped idols. If you claim that this way of truth and life is that of Dahri, Samatiyah[148] and the Brahmans, with others of that lot, who resemble the Manicheans in creed and confession, we reply that as you know, your master (had) never heard of them, nor was he present at those sessions where these heresies were refuted. Who then are left to represent this highly favored race, but the Christians? Here at last is the way of life, right guidance from the Lord of all, enriched by the perfect knowledge of God as Word and Spirit, who alone is Glorious and Great, with wise laws and spiritual precepts. This is nothing new, I merely remind you of what you already know. Or can you contradict

what I affirm of the grace revealed to us, the light and leading which
have come to us through the Gospel? Your own master has set his
seal on this; all creeds and nations acknowledge it. Consider then
carefully what we have written. In all the relations of life we ought to
walk warily, particularly in a matter which so intimately concerns our
welfare. And truth must be sought in the right way; you must not
wrong it of its due. May God guide you into the ways of continuance,
in the greatness of His power and might.

(EC) And now let us begin with the utmost reverence; let us cleanse
ourselves in ear and heart that we can recount the Gospel story from
its beginnings. Let me adduce as witness some of the apostles to
whom God entrusted this mystery. He revealed it to them by His
Spirit and commanded them to teach others how He, to whom the
future is known, purposed to perfect His grace and crown His goodness towards man by sending His beloved Son; incarnate among men.
To Him therefore be praise, worship and obedience given by angels,
men and devils, with due submission to the sovereignty which He has
assumed and the deity inherent in Him. He came to teach men plainly
that there is one God in three persons, one true eternal Godhead, that
the grace and goodness given in earlier ages might be consummated by
the revelation of this great mystery. In (the) presence of such overwhelming testimony, cavilling must cease. No man can any longer
plead his ignorance or protest that the truth of God is veiled from
view. No excuse is left to those who willfully disobey it, as said St.
Paul: "That every mouth should be stopped and the world become
guilty before God." (Rom. 3:19b)

(ED) First of all then, God spake by Moses in the book of Genesis,
when Jacob came near to death, he called his sons, blessed them, told
them what was to happen in the last times and confided to them this
mystery. He continued to bless them one after another until he came
to Judah, of whose seed was born the blessed Mary mother of our
Lord. Then he said: "Judah, thou art he of whom thy brethren praise,
thine hand shall be on the neck of thine enemies; thy father's sons shall
do homage to thee. Judah is a lion's whelp; from the prey, my son,
thou art gone up. He croucheth, ready to spring like a lion who shall

rouse them up. The scepter shall not depart from Judah, nor a lawgiver from between his feet till Shiloh come; to Him shall the people make submission." (Gen. 50:8-10a) Look now at this oracle; interpret it spiritually. For if you do not understand it, you cannot profit by it. This oracle can only refer to Christ, the Savior of the world. He sprang from Judah by earthly descent. The children of Israel made submission to Him when He they came under His preaching. His hand, which was the power of Rome, was on the neck of those who were His enemies and opposed to His Gospel. These were slain or scattered on every side. Three days after His crucifixion He appeared to them alive from the dead; and, when they saw the signs and wonders wrought in His name, the people believed on Him. He is the lion's whelp, because He is the Son of God, mighty and strong. The succession of the prophets did not cease till He came, the hope of mankind. To Him all the prophets bear witness, they foretold His (manifestation); they testified to the advent of Christ our Lord, but since His appearing no prophet has arisen in Israel. For Him the nations waited; their hopes centered on Him, and just as a herald has no more place after the King Himself has come, so the star of prophecy paled before the Light of Christ's rising sun. The prophets hailed Him as King. Zechariah said: "Rejoice greatly O daughter of Zion, behold thy King cometh, He is just and clothed with salvation, lowly and riding on an ass and on a colt, the foal of an ass. He shall destroy the chariots from Ephraim and the horses from Jerusalem and the battle bow shall be broken in two, He shall speak peace to the people." (Zech. 9:9,10a) Now tell us, can this be said of any other than Christ, that He should come with righteousness, lowly and having salvation? Did He not at His coming destroy from the Holy Place, which is Mount Zion, the chariots and horses which were prepared for war? He broke the battle bow, a symbol of war, and rode humbly on an ass' colt. He spoke peace to the people and led them into the promised inheritance. In the same way David, as the mouthpiece of God, said: "The Lord said to my Lord, Sit thou on my right hand till I make Thine enemies Thy footstool. The Lord shall send the rod of His power out of Zion; rule Thou among Thine enemies." (Ps. 110:1,2) Now will you try and understand what is implied in this oracle of the prophet? It contains a mystery which calls for thought on the part of those who study the

Psalter, if it is to become plain to them. I remark, then, that according to the custom of the Hebrews since the days of Moses to whom God spoke face to face, the letters which compose the name of God, most High and ever Blessed, have formed what is known as the sacred tetragram. In no other connection is the same combination of letters allowed. These letters were written on the tablets of stone which were given to Moses. Now in this passage "the Lord said to my Lord," the sacred tetragram occurs twice. This is admitted by Jews and Christians. Though they are two hostile camps, yet on this point there is no difference between them, nor does any doubt exist as to the fact. Yet there has been no collusion.[149] Understand then this mystery which God revealed to His servants; if you think, you will find it clear enough. For so it is written: "The Lord said to my Lord." In another place he says: "The Lord looked from the heights of His holy place, from heaven the Lord beheld the earth, to hear the groaning of the prisoner and to loose them that are appointed to death." (Ps. 102:19-20) By "death" here is meant sin, that is, the worship of idols and the forfeiture of that eternal life brought to us by Christ our Lord against the day of Resurrection. The passage proceeds: "To declare the name of the Lord in Zion and His praise in Jerusalem when the people are gathered together and the kingdoms to serve the Lord." (Ps. 102:21,22) So spake the prophet, and accordingly in Jerusalem we see the people gathered together to seek the name of the Lord, i.e., the name of the Father, Son and Holy Ghost, which is the mystical name of the Lord. If a man dispute this, my friend, he must be regarded by all truth-loving people as a hardened unbeliever, whose heart has been darkened by ignorance and blinded by ill will.

(EE) So the blessed Isaiah cries with a loud voice saying: "Say ye to the fearful of heart, Be strong, fear not, behold your God will come with a recompense, even your God with a reward, He shall come and save you. Then the eyes of the blind shall be opened and the ears of the deaf unstopped. Then shall the lame man leap as a hart and the tongue of the dumb shall sing." (Is. 35:4-6a) May God guide you into the truth, that you might see how our scriptures witness to the fact that Christ did all this. He healed the lame man who was 38 years of age, and said to him: "Arise, take up thy bed and go to thy house," (John

5:8)[150] and he arose straightway. He healed the leper, the deaf, the dumb and the demoniac whose story is published in the Gospel along with the comments made by the Jews when they saw the cure; and our Lord rebuked them and refuted their reasoning. In another passage Isaiah says: "Behold, the Lord Himself shall give you a sign; a virgin shall conceive and bear a son, and ye shall call His name Immanuel, i.e., God with us." (Is. 7:14) What could be more clear than this? Yet this is only one of many passages we might quote as to the coming of our Lord.

(EF) But now I fancy you retort that these passages have been "cooked (up)." You escape the inference on the plea that the text has been corrupted; so you can apply your favorite argument and shelter behind it.[151] Let me speak frankly for once and remember what I say, and lay it to heart. I do not argue in the spirit of pride nor from a love of criticism, but that I might win you. My religion imposes this duty on me toward everyone, but I have a special solicitude for you, because of the depths of darkness in which I find you. I do not know that I have found an argument more difficult to dislodge, more desperate to disarm than this which you advance as to the corruption of the sacred text. I marvel that you should allow it. You know that the Jews, though they are hostile to the truth as proclaimed by Him who is the Light of the world and its glory, yet agree with us on this point.[152] Without any collusion between us, the genuineness of these Old Testament scriptures as inspired is established. They are not corrupt, nor have they been added to or taken from. But, without dwelling on that let me apply one test which is fair to both of us. In God's name I ask you, who accuse us of tampering with the text, can you produce a book which has not been tampered with and which witness(es) to the truth as you hold it; a book which can appeal to such signs and wonders as those which bear witness to the prophets and apostles, from whose hands we have received the writings which we still hold, as the Jews also do? I know that you cannot do this, nor even tell us how it can be done. Your own scriptures bear quite conclusive witness on this point. For they say: "If ever you are in doubt as to what we have revealed, ask those who read the earlier scriptures (i.e., the Jews and Christians)." (Qur'an 10: 94a). "Say, We have sent down the Law, in it is good guidance and light; we have sent in their steps Jesus (the) son of Mary in confirmation of what they know of the Law, and we have given him the Gospel, with good guidance and light, in confirmation of what they already know." (Qur'an 5:50). "And if the People of the Book believe and fear God, He will forgive their sins and bring them to a paradise of happiness. If they establish the Law and the Gospel and what was sent down to them from their Lord, they shall eat of that which is above and beneath their feet.[153] From them shall come a people doing righteously, but the majority of them, how evil are their deeds." (Qur'an 5: 70) "Say, O People of the Book, ye stand on nothing till ye establish the Law and the Gospel which has been sent down to you from your Lord." (Qur'an 5:72). See how your own book bears witness to us that the true reading of any passage is our reading. You are required to ask and receive judgment from us on such points. Now then, can you affirm that we have corrupted the text? What is this but to contradict your own scriptures?[154] The situation is plain enough; you witness to the truth of our text — then again you contradict the witness you bear and allege that we have corrupted it; this is the height of folly. What have you to do with lies? They are not in your kind nor of your nature. You attribute impiety to us and say that we have falsified the Word of God, whereas your master witnesses that the true text is ours. Consider, who is the corrupter?[155] We, who have received the scriptures from those who attest their truth by signs and wonders far beyond human power — scriptures concerning which there is general agreement among the people who differ in other points, or one who receives as the Word of God that which has no proof or witness to support its claim,[156] without records, without miracles,[157] who receives it from the hands of those who have transmitted it merely in their native tongue and contents himself with such a proof as if a production of this point could for a moment be compared with the parting of the waters or the raising of the dead? This he received according to a people among whom hatred and rancor lodge, each of whom adds to or takes away as he pleases. And this course he pursues till he ends by claiming that the book is the Word of God, most High, and must be accepted as proof of his own prophetic office. Not satisfied with this, he protests that if anyone will not receive the book and acknowledge it as inspired and himself as God's prophet, he will kill him, plunder his

goods and sell his children into bondage. Quite naturally moved by the
fear of the dread chastisement he might inflict, men accepted his word
without reason or evidence adduced. May God help you judge fairly.
Reason is the only test of such matters, she can distinguish the true
from the false. See whither you are being led, intend your mind and
grasp the situation. I trust your good sense may be the saving of you
from deadly error. For God has appointed reason as the scales in the
hand of justice. Apply what God has given you in this direction. If
you seek for it, the truth will not fail you. So help you God most
High!

(EG) Let us return to the question raised as to the Holy Gospel. We
affirm that it is generally admitted that the witness borne by the
prophets was summed up and sealed by the birth of the long-expected
Christ. Let us now see what were the signs which accompanied Christ
our Lord in proof of His divine sovereignty and authority. The first
beginning of these was a follows: God the merciful, in His kindness to
His creatures, chose from among men whom He had fashioned with
His own hands and stamped His own image, thus honoring them above
all other creatures, a virgin, chaste, pure and holy, without stain or
blame in soul or body, that His Word might lodge in her, taking from
her perfect body of flesh and uniting it to Himself so that He might
dwell among us. He commissioned Gabriel the archangel to carry
tidings to her, the elect of our race, queen of all earth's daughters, the
blessed Mary, (the) daughter of Joakim[158] the mother of Jesus Christ
our Savior God. He came to her with glad tidings, honoring her and
saluting her with these words: "All hail, thou highly favored of *our*
Lord, blessed art thou among women." (Luke 1:28, Diatessaron)
Observe, he did not say, "my Lord;" he included all the angel host with
himself. Who then is that Lord of men and angels alike, but the
eternal Word of God, by whom heaven and earth were made, as David
said? Try and understand this mystery; lay aside the ignorance and
prejudice that blinds you. Continuing his address, Gabriel said: "Thou
shalt conceive and bear a son, and thou shalt call His name Jesus, that
is, the Savior. He shall be great and shall be called the Son of the
Highest, and the Lord God shall give Him the throne of His father

David." (Luke 1:32) While Gabriel thus spake to her, she wondered greatly and answered: "How shall this be to me, who hath not known a man?" (Luke 1:34) And Gabriel said: "The Holy Ghost shall come on thee, and the power of the Highest shall overshadow thee." (Luke 1:34a) Following up the message, he gave her a sign to confirm her faith, that she might not hesitate or doubt, saying: "And also thy cousin Elizabeth is with child in her old age, and this is the sixth month with her who was called barren." (Luke 1:36) Such was the miracle of the annunciation. And now listen to the witness of one who differs from us and yet confirms our argument. Your master of his own freewill and with all solemnity, asserts the truth of all this (by) saying: "And see, the angels say of Mary, 'God hath chosen thee and sanctified thee. He hath chosen thee among women. O Mary, call on thy God and worship Him and give Him thanks and reverence... God hath sent thee glad tidings with His Word, whose name is Messiah, Jesus (the) son of Mary. He is the cynosure of every eye in this world and in the next, of those who stand about the Throne. He shall speak to men in his cradle and in his prime, and shall be reckoned among the upright.' She answered, 'O my Lord, how shall I have a child when no man hath come near me?' He answered her, 'Nay, but God createth what He pleaseth; when once He hath uttered the words. God hath but to say, Be, and it shall be. He shall teach him the scriptures; the Law and the Gospel, and send him to the children of Israel. He shall say, I have come to you with a sign from your Lord; I will fashion this clay into the shape of a bird and breathe on it, and it shall fly. I will give sight to the blind. I will heal the leper. I will tell you what to eat and what to store up in your house. Surely this shall be a sign to you, if you believe I am come to confirm what is already in the Law. I will permit you what is forbidden, and bring you a sign from your Lord. Trust in God and obey Him.' " (Qur'an 3:37,38,40-44). Do you know, or can you recall from the wide field of literature anyone whose coming was thus foretold? Yet so we have it concerning our Lord, as given by God and confirmed by your master.

(EH) Soon after the pure and blessed virgin came to the mother of John (the) son of Zecharias, she and her husband were both righteous, fearing God, and she was with child. And when Mary knocked at the door of her dwelling and saluted her, the child leapt in her womb for joy. Elizabeth said: "Whence is this to me that the mother of my Lord should come to me, for since the voice of salutation sounded in my ear, the babe hath leaped in my womb for joy." (Luke 1:43,44) You know what your master says about Zecharias: "Then Zecharias prayed to his Lord and said, My Lord, give me good seed from Thy presence. And the angel called to him while he stood praying in the temple. God sendeth thee good tidings, John, who shall confirm the promises of the Word from God, a Lord, a saint (son?), a prophet from among the upright." (Qur'an 3:33,34)[159] Now the meaning of this is that Christ is the Word of God and Lord of men. "Confirming the promise" is a description of John, but "the Word of God" and "a Lord" cannot apply to John. He was never credited with having been the "Word of God," nor was he "a Lord." On the other hand, the phrase "a son" and "a prophet among the upright" is applicable to John, who was all that. And indeed, I say it solemnly, if you do not twist the text and pervert it from its meaning, you cannot help seeing that such is the burden of the words. Soon afterwards a star appeared to the Magians, betokening the birth of a great King whose kingdom should have no end. The wise men, well versed in sacred lore, had foretold His coming, and trusted them to as to the time of His appearing. The sign appointed was a star which should go before them and guide them to His feet. For this sign the Magians waited. Led by its light they came from their distant homes to Jerusalem in Judea, till it stood above Bethlehem. There they fulfilled their quest and paid their homage. They saw what they had dreamed; they had what they had hoped. Then they returned, nothing doubting, but filled with joy because they had been so highly honored. The archangel also appeared to a group of shepherds feeding their flocks, and told them of the Lord's birth: "Behold, I bring you glad tidings of great joy, which shall be to all people. For unto you is born this day a Savior which is Christ the Lord." (Luke 2:10) As he ceased speaking, the angel host appeared, hovering beneath earth and heaven, with psalms and hymns, praising God, and saying: "Glory be to God in the highest and on earth peace, goodwill toward men." (Luke 2:14) These shepherds made haste to the place and found the babe wrapped in swaddling clothes lying in a manger. They told what had happened and how they had seen the heavenly host and heard their wondrous song. They told the tale of their coming, so that all who heard it wondered. This is the story of the annunciation and birth of our Lord.[160]

(EI) Now let me tell you briefly as I can the beginnings of the Gospel. When our Lord was 30 years old, John (the) son of Zecharias appeared baptizing with water unto repentance in the river Jordan. Christ came to him that He might be baptized of him, but when John saw him, he said: "Behold the Lamb of God, which taketh away the sins of the world. I have need to be baptized by Thee, and comest Thou to be baptized of me?" (John 1:29 and Matt. 3:14)[161] And Jesus answered and said: "Suffer it to be so now, for thus it becometh us to fulfil all righteousness." (Matt. 3:15) He urged him till he consented, and as Christ came up out of the water, the gates of heaven were thrown open in (the) sight of all who stood by, and they saw the Holy Ghost descending on Him in the shape of a dove, and heard a voice from heaven saying: "This is My beloved Son in whom I am well pleased." (Matt. 3:17) After this, He began to preach, until the day He went up into heaven, stirring men to repentance, to despise the world, to abstain from its pleasures and to forsake friend, family and property that they might cleave to Him, to take delight in good works, refraining from sin and practicing benevolence toward all men. No more must they hate and envy one another, or grasp at riches or take vengeance on their enemies, or requite wrongs done to them, but rather forgive and conquer by kindness. He taught them to draw near to God, He inclined them to such a life, that they might be accounted worthy of a great and enduring reward, a recompense in the world to come. He preached to them the resurrection of the dead and the judgment to come; he who has done well shall have the Kingdom of Heaven as his reward, but he who has done ill shall be punished in hell fire forever. He confirmed His words by the miracles which He wrought and endorsed His promise by manifest signs and tokens such as no mere man could produce. All this He did with the utmost kindness of heart and an entire absence of that pride and arrogance which are the works of the devil. He gave all that was ever asked of Him, asking nothing in return, neither reward nor thanks, but only that men should give themselves to God and glorify Him and bear witness that He had kept

503

His promise and crowned His goodness toward the children of men by the mission of His Word, incarnate for their salvation.

(EJ) And now we come to the first note of the Evangel: "Repent, for the Kingdom of Heaven is at hand." (Matt. 4:17b) Thus He revealed to men the doctrine of repentance and the resurrection which were unknown in the earlier dispensation. He taught them to seek the Kingdom of Heaven and to do works meet for entrance into it. He taught them to turn from the works of darkness in which they had lived and to cultivate such a temper as might insure the forgiveness of their sins. Forty days and nights He fasted, while angels ministered to Him, and while He fasted, He combatted the power of the Evil One and showed men that God could sustain life without the use of bread or water. In this way, by a sort of analogy, He showed us what may be that life after death when man shall no longer be dependent on food or drink.[162]

(EK) Immediately after this he began to publish the new constitution, precepts and maxims of a spiritual order, teaching men that divine Law which represents the mind of God and is free from all carnal sanctions. Of murder He said: "Ye have heard that it was said by the fathers, He who slays shall be slain, but I say to you, if one is angry with a brother for naught, he is guilty, and he who slanders his brother incurs condemnation, and he who injures his brother deserves hell fire. Let not the sun go down while you are angry with your brother." (Matt. 5:21,22 and Eph. 4:26, slight paraphrase) Again He said: "When ye stand praying and remember that a brother has ought against you, stop praying and go, be reconciled to your brother, then come and finish your prayer." (Matt. 5:23,24 paraphrase) So saying He put an end to those blood feuds which had been the fruitful sources of murder in the past. Then He said: "Ye have heard it said, ye shall not commit adultery, but I say unto you that he who looks on a woman with a lustful eye, he hath committed adultery in his heart." (Matt. 5:27,28) Then He taught us that God knows not the surface only, but (also) the heart of men's lives; nothing is hid from Him; nothing secret, and what is done in secret is openly rewarded by Him. Again He said: "Ye have heard that it was said, If a man put away his wife, let him get her a bill of divorce, but I say to you, He that putteth away his wife, except for fornication, gives her over to adultery, and he who marries a divorced woman is an adulterer." (Matt. 5:31,32) Then He rebukes lying thus: "Ye have heard it said, Thou shalt not swear falsely, but I say unto you, Swear not at all." (Matt. 5:33,34a) Then He rebukes their greed of gain and incites them to forgive wrongs and refrain from retaliation. "Ye have heard it said, An eye for an eye and a tooth for a tooth and a wound for a wound, but I say unto you, Resist not evil, but if one smite thee on the right cheek, turn to him the left, and if he seek to take thy coat, refuse him not thy cloak also, and if he compel thee to go a mile, go with him twain. Give to him who asks of thee, and from him who would borrow of thee, turn not away." (Matt. 5:38-40) So an end is put to vexatious litigation, so the fires of battle are quenched. All that alienates man from man is taken away, and they are drawn together in mutual love. Their boorish manners are softened, their savage tempers refined. The age of universal brotherhood under the law of love begins. Again, of kindness and beneficence He says: "Ye have heard it said, Love your neighbors and hate your enemies, but I say, Love your enemies, bless them that curse you, do good to them that wrong you and pray for them who treat you unjustly and persecute you, that you may be the children of your Father in heaven." (Matt. 5:43,44, Diatessaron) Confirming this law, and inciting them to its observance, He says: "If ye do good to them who do good to you, what reward have you? Do not even the publicans the same? But be ye perfect, doing good and showing favor, that you may be like your Lord." (Luke 6:33 and Matt. 5:48, paraphrase) Of righteousness He says: "Have regard to your alms deeds; give them not before man so as to receive kindness in return. But if ye give alms, let not your right hand know what your left hand doeth, that your alms may be in secret, and your Father who seeth in secret shall openly reward you. When you fast, do not distort your faces or lower your voices that men may take notice of you, lest in the praise of man ye lose your reward. When you fast, wash your faces and anoint your heads, and speak cheerfully, that you seem not to man to fast; your Father who seeth in secret will reward you openly." (Matt. 6:2- 4 and 6: 16,17; paraphrase) Rebuking greed, covetousness and avarice, He says: "Lay not up treasure where thieves and moths can reach them, but lay them up in heaven, so shall ye hold them safely. Where your treasure is, there shall your heart be also." (Matt. 6:19, 20) "A servant cannot serve two masters without honoring the one and despising the other; so ye cannot serve God and the world. Take no thought as to what ye shall eat and drink, care rather for your souls and their salvation. This is more needful than caring for the body; for the soul is better than the body. The body cannot exist without the soul. Be like the birds of the air which neither sow nor reap nor gather into barns. They take their breakfast when they are hungry, and depart with a full crop; for your heavenly Father feedeth them. Verily I say unto you, Ye are better than they. Bear not today the burdens of tomorrow; let each day's burden suffice for itself. Nor take thought of supply for the morrow; it is not yours to provide; it shall be provided for you. He who sends the morrow will make provision for it." (Matt. 6:24a,25,26, 34; extreme paraphrase) "Let no one say, See the winter comes, what shall I eat, what shall I wear; or in summer, where shall I get food and drink? Your Father which is in heaven knows that ye have need of these things." (Matt. 6:31,32; paraphrase)

(EL) As to the habit of evil-speaking, He says: "Judge not nor condemn, lest ye be condemned; for with what judgment ye judge, ye shall be judged, and with what measure ye mete, it shall be meted to you." (Matt. 7:1,2) "Seest thou a mote in thy brother's eye while a splinter is in thy own eye? Say not to thy brother, Let me pluck the mote out of thine eye, while a beam is in thy own eye. Take the beam out of thine own eye, then shalt thou see clearly to take the mote out of thy brother's eye." (Matt. 7:3-5; paraphrase) Of prayer, He said : "Ask and ye shall receive, seek and ye shall find, knock and it shall be opened unto you. Is there any of you who if his son ask bread, will give him a stone? Or if he ask fish, will give him a serpent? If you being evil know how to give good gifts to your children, how much rather shall your heavenly Father, with whom all is good, give good gifts to His faithful people." (Matt. 7:7,9-11) Of doing kindness to men, He says: "What ye would that men should do to you, do ye to them. This is the sum of piety wherewith God is well pleased." (Matt. 7:12; paraphrase)

(EM) Perhaps some captious and hypocritical person may find fault with our Lord when He calls God "our Father." Let me answer him. Christ our Lord had it in His heart to make obedience lovely in the eyes of all men, that they might yield it from love and goodwill rather than by constraint and fear. He sought to naturalize it in their hearts that it might banish enmity and obliterate that pride of birth which is of the Evil One. He would have them recognize one another in a brotherly way, as becomes those whom a bond of nature unites to a common father and mother. He would have it thus, under all circumstances. He was not like your master, who sowed hatred among men, saying: "O ye faithful, ye have enemies among your wives and children, beware of them." (Qur'an 64:14a) Christ our Lord taught them saying: "Thus and thus doeth your Father in heaven, thus and thus it shall be done by you." (Matt. 5:45,48; extreme paraphrase) He did this that He might sow the good seed of love in their hearts, and clean out the tares of anger and malice. And verily God, in His greatness and glory, is a merciful and compassionate Father, dealing tenderly and graciously with us. To begin with, He made us (out) of His mere good pleasure, thus showing us favor before we had any being; so He nourishes and sustains us by His grace, visits us in His goodness, is mindful of us in our sin and pardons our transgressions. In His longsuffering He has borne with our ignorance and deals with us not hastily, but as a compassionate father deals with his child. When He chastens us, He mingles mercy with His chastening. He has not dealt with us as we deserved. Who then is more worthy to be called by us "our Father" than is God, most High, blessed forevermore? Surely they have little reason on their side, who impugn the teaching of our Lord on this head.

(EN) On the discharge of religious duties, He says: "Fast and pray, and discharge the duties God has imposed on you; yet, when you have done all these things, say, We are unprofitable servants." (Luke 17:10; extreme paraphrase) All His words and precepts are confirmed by what was seen of His own life, for He fasted and prayed, without house or home, without anything in the way of stores beyond the clothes He wore. One who begged of Him said: "Master, where dwellest Thou, that I may come to Thee there?" (John 1:38; paraphrase) Jesus answered: "Foxes have holes and the birds of the air have nests, but I have neither house nor home where I set my feet, there I find My pillow, where ye seek Me, ye shall find Me." (Luke 9:58; paraphrase)[163] He never spake an untruthful word; never thought or sought or planned or perpetrated a sin. He did not reproach or refuse those who applied to Him. No one who sought His help or begged alms of Him was ever disappointed. So the prophecies concerning Him were fulfilled.

(EO) This He followed up, confirming His words by wonders and signs which He did, healing the sick in numbers known only to Himself. He cleansed the leper, cast out devils and quickened those who were already dead for many days, like Lazarus, the daughter of Jairus, the widow's son and many others. He divined the secrets of men's hearts and what lay hidden there, buried in their bosoms. By a word He healed the paralytic and commanded the lame man to take up his bed and walk. Devils responded to Him, obeying His command, confessing that He was the Son of the living God, who should yet subvert their kingdom. Sins were forgiven and transgressions blotted out by His lifegiving word, according to the Spirit of glory which rested on Him. He opened the eyes of those who were known to have been blind many days, smearing their eyes with clay which He had kneaded in His spittle. For He had power over nature in all her forms. With five loaves and two fish he fed 5000 and 12 baskets of fragments were taken up. Wherever He went He brought blessing. Water poured into vessels was changed into wine at the marriage feast, babes were blessed by Him and infants babbled His praise.[164] He cursed the fig tree, and immediately it withered away. He rebuked the storm and there was a great calm. He was seen walking on the waters. He showed Himself to His disciples on a mountain, talking with Moses and Elias. He discovered to the Samaritan woman the secrets of her past life, and healed a woman in whom was an issue of blood for 12 years, though she only touched His clothes. She thought He would not know, but He knew by the virtue that had gone out of Him, and said to the crowd: "Who touched me?" Then the woman came and worshipped and confessed what she had done. And He said: "Thy faith hath made thee whole, go in peace." (Luke 8:43-48; paraphrase) He commanded the devils to enter into swine, that they should be drowned in the sea, and they obeyed. He did many wonders; the apostles have not told them all, lest their writings should be too bulky, and we too have left out many, lest we should transgress our limits. But I know that you have read the Gospel, where we read in order what the apostles have written down.

(EP) Here too is the word of your master: "We have sent proofs with Jesus (the) son of Mary, and have helped him with the Holy Ghost." (Qur'an 2:81a or 2:254a) Now, how can you be deceived as to the heavenly origin of the works? No one can doubt them, but one in whom wrath usurps the place of reason, who is blinded by anger or seduced by the love of the world to the ruin of his soul. A man of understanding with any self respect, if he reads what I have written with a fair unprejudiced mind and (who) compares the witness of the Gospel with what we know of your master, will have no difficulty in distinguishing the true from the false. Your master's achievements are well within the reach of the average man, as we see and hear of him among the elders, the worthies of a bygone age. If you remind me that the prophets Moses and the others did wonders far beyond mortal power to achieve; here is my reply: I know that the prophets did these wonders, but only after great humiliation, protracted prayer and fervent supplication. They had no indisputable and irresistible authority behind them to carry them through, such as we see in the case of Christ our Lord. The saints wrought miracles as a servant might, submissively, solicitous to execute the commands he has received. Before he divided the sea that the children of Israel might pass over, Moses "ceased not to cry to the Lord," and God said: "Why criest thou to Me; arise and smite the waters with thy staff, and they shall be divided before thee." (Ex. 14:15a,16a; paraphrase) And so Joshua (the) son of Nun, Elias and Elisha humbled themselves and made constant supplication. Such humble supplication is never absent as a condition of the power they possess. Otherwise it had been as when He, the most High and ever Blessed, said to Moses: "Thou shalt not enter the land of promise, for thou hast not sanctified Me before the children of Israel." (Num. 20:12; paraphrase) So Jeremiah prayed, yet God answered: "I will not hear thy prayers nor receive thy requests." (Jer. 7:16; paraphrase) But Jesus Christ, our Lord, the beloved Son of

the Father, did these wonders by the energy of the all-creating Word
which dwelleth in Him. Can anyone question this? As well might he
say that the sun does not shine, or fire burn, and try to look surprised![165] He ought rather to be ashamed of himself.

*[(EQ) Thus then we have transcribed some of the precepts of our Lord,
and recounted some of His wonderful works. Let me remind you how
He chose His first disciples and sent them into the world to preach the
truth. He chose illiterate men, men with no science or education, they
were fishermen and tax gatherers, yet so were there hearts illuminated
with the heavenly light that they overcame philosophers and learned men
and vanquished those who were skilled in debate. Mighty kings, great
rulers (and) high-handed despots humbled themselves before them. The
great ones of the earth were subject to them, the wealthy surrendered their
wealth, the prosperous bowed down before them, and all the wise and
understanding confessed the truth they taught. Learned orators were
silenced by their reasoning and yielded to their authority. None could
deny or gainsay the gracious words which they uttered, or fail to recognize
the goodness of God to them and the hand of God working with them.
These signs and wonders they wrought according to His Word: "Go,
summon all men everywhere to eternal life; preach to them the resurrection. Their bodies shall be raised from the grave and quickened by the
Spirit; they shall be released from the bonds of death and set free from its
power and presence. In order to confirm the promise I will give you this
power to work miracles; freely you have received, freely give. Take no
gold or silver from any man, in My name lay your hands on the sick, and
they shall be healed, on the dead, and they shall live, that the world may
wonder, and that I may plead against them." So they followed in His
steps, preaching forgiveness to all men and summoning them to the truth.
They did this unweariedly, claiming no earthly reward for themselves. He
sent forth 70 men before His ascension; there were also the 12 who had
been with Him from the beginning. His first disciples who had been
companions of His tribulation. By them a faithful record has been
transmitted and authorized among the nations.*

(ER) While He was with them He made a covenant with them: "He

who knows and does these things shall be called great in the kingdom of heaven. When ye pray, pray for the pardon of your sin; multiply not words and make not vain repetitions. Set your hearts on such provision as is requisite for you; your heavenly Father knows your need and what is good for you. Behold I will send you forth as sheep in the midst of wolves; be wise as serpents and harmless as doves. When they bring you before magistrates, take no thought of what you shall speak, for it shall be given unto you in that hour, for it is not ye that speak, but the Spirit of your Father which speaketh in you. Fear not those who kill the body, but have no power over the soul, but rather fear Him who can destroy both body and soul in hell fire. Be assured that if you oppose My commands and deny My Gospel, I will deny you at the last day, when you shall stand with all creation at My judgment seat; but, if you confess My name and are not ashamed of My Gospel, I will confess you among My saints on that great day. Blessed are the poor in spirit, for theirs is the Kingdom of Heaven. Blessed are ye when men shall persecute you and say all manner of evil against you falsely for My sake. Forgive those who are churlish to you, and act fairly even to your enemies. Forgive those who wrong you with the forgiveness of God; if ye will not have mercy on one another, how shall God have mercy on you? Verily I say unto you, that as ye do, it shall be done to you. The light of the body is the eye, if the eye is single, the whole body is full of light, but if the eye is evil, the whole body is full of darkness. If the light that is in you is darkness, how great must your darkness be. Thus a servant, if he know his master, can see his faults, but if he is ignorant of his master, he is blind to his faults. As the body cannot exist without the soul, so religion cannot exist without a good and honest purpose. Look not at the faults of others, lest you rebuke them when they do well; begin by mending your own faults, and cover them over with good deeds. Cast not what is holy to the dogs, nor cast your pearls before swine, lest they trample them under foot and turn and rend you. Beware of false prophets which shall come after Me, without rhyme or reason and with the sword (!) in their hand. Go and summon all men to eternal life, teaching them what I have taught you of spiritual judgment. Teach them that God quickens the dead and shall judge the world. He who has done well shall inherit life eternal, incomparable felicity, unruffled by fear or pain, fed from springs that never fail. He who has done ill and opposed My Gospel, his reward in the day of judgment shall be hell fire and everlasting torment. For he who rejects My claim makes war against God. Behold, I have given you power to confirm your preaching, so that the appeal you make to men may prove irresistible. Lay hands on those who are sick even to death, and they shall recover; so shall ye make My Gospel shine throughout all lands. In every distant spot shall sound the Gospel call; it is for all men, grace vouchsafed to all the seed of Adam. He who obeys shall have good luck, peace and plenty, prosperous times, victory and great spoil. See, I send you forth without scourge or sword or any weapon, without treasure or troops or any force at your disposal by which to resist or compel your enemies; not as men who are in love with strife, not coveting either the wealth of the world or its lusts, and certainly with no concessions to offer. Call men to repentance; make quite clear what you mean and promise, to wit, the Kingdom of Heaven. Confirm it with signs and wonders such as I have given you power to work. Take no man's silver or gold. Eat the labor of your hands, and what is ever of your stores, give as alms to the poor. Go forth with this Gospel, faint not in it, for the Kingdom of Heaven is at hand, and lo, I am with you always."[166]

(ES) Minded to carry His self abasement to the utmost point, He did not withhold Himself from the hands of sinners. They did to Him as He would; they crucified Him on the tree, while He cried: "Father forgive them, for they know not what they do." (Luke 11:34a) Thus in the flesh He died and hung on the cross till the hour of sunset. After that, He was buried and continued in the grave till the morning of the first day. Then He arose, declaring to be the Son of God with power. He was seen of the women who came to the tomb and afterwards by the disciples, once in Galilee, twice in the Upper Room, once by the way while two of them were going to Emmaus and once on the seashore while they were fishing. Again He renewed His charge and reminded them of the covenant He had made with them. So it was until He ascended into heaven, openly in (the) sight of all who were gathered together while they stood looking through the open doors of heaven and seeing the angel host escort Him to the Throne. Meantime it was said to them: "Ye men of Galilee, why stand ye gazing into the heavens? This same Jesus who is taken from you shall come again in like manner as you have seen Him go into heaven." (Acts 1:11) So

He was taken from them, and the angels departed. The hill from which He ascended is the Mount of Olives in Syria, known to this day.

(ET) Having heard these various witnesses, you shall hear one who differs from us, yet openly proclaims: "See, God said, O Jesus, I will take you and raise you up to Myself, and will rid you of those who are unbelievers and place those who follow you above the unbelievers in the day of Resurrection. Then ye shall return to Me, and I will judge between you when ye differ from one another. But those who are unbelievers I will torment with sore torment in this world and (in) the next; they shall have no helpers. But those who believe and do righteousness, their reward shall be great. God loves not evildoers." (Qur'an 3:48-50) Such is the testimony and witness borne to God by your own master, as you yourself allow. Intend your mind, guard yourself, do not be led astray into error. If you do your duty, clear light will arise and truth shine.

(EU) Finally after 10 days had lapsed, the disciples were gathered together in the Upper Room and heard a rushing mighty noise, and the Holy Ghost, the Paraclete was revealed to them and rested on them in tongues of fire, that they might speak with men in their own tongues and work wonders. Thereafter they were scattered, each man to his appointed sphere. And God gave them the power of tongues and knowledge of men. And they, being filled with the Holy Ghost, wrote the Gospel and all the acts of Christ in every tongue. Then the nations bowed and obeyed the call. They forsook the world and chose the better part, leaving their own religions that they might embrace the Christian faith. Everywhere the light of the truth shone and the Gospel day dawned. Conviction came, faith followed, men confessed without doubt or question, they distinguished the true from the false; good guidance from soul-destroying error. They saw signs and wonders which enabled them to follow in that good way, the way of Christ, in which we also, to this day and hour, seek to follow. this is the faith we have received at their hands; we live by it and hope to die in it, that we may rise and stand approved in the presence of Christ our Lord, the Judge of all. This was not the way of your master or his friends, it was their way to kill, steal and smite with the sword. They do so to this day; they incite men to what is forbidden and hurtful to the race, to such an extent that, as you know, they make a boast of what you dare not do. Recall the words of 'Umar (the) son of Khattab: "If a man's neighbor is a Nabatean and he requires his price, let him sell him."[167] This is how they speak and act, not so St. Peter or St. Paul.

(EV) If you say, why do not the monks in our own day work the miracles like the disciples who were sent out by our Lord; here is our reply: When the disciples where sent out to preach the Gospel, they wrought miracles as a necessary part of their mission, that these to whom they preached might know the truth of what they taught. Now today the monks are not preachers. Many of them no doubt exercise their ministry in a private and unostentatious way, that it may be known that this gift of grace continues among men. Should circumstances arise which require them to exercise the supernatural power they possess, they do so; East and West and wherever they go. But if they took in hand to raise all the dead and heal all the sick, no one would ever die, and where would be our hope of the Resurrection and the end of the world? The purpose of the Most High would be frustrated. An occasional dose of their power is permitted them, that by their efforts they may strengthen public confidence and show that they are honored by that God whom night and day they serve. Those who seek them with a true heart and earnest mind have their prayers answered; they receive the blessings which they crave, in answer to the prayers of these good men. You must remember that if miracles were a matter of daily occurrence, as in the time of the holy elders, men would have no praise for their faith and obedience beyond such as you give to the beast whom you compel to move backwards and forwards by the use of a bridle and stick. But God, Blessed be His name, has distinguished us from the beasts in that He has given us reason and imposed on us the task of guarding these evidences of religion which otherwise might be lost. So that we no longer need to see miracles in confirmation of faith, unless indeed we have lost the use of reason and have degraded ourselves to the level of beasts.

(EW) Thus with the utmost brevity, I have recounted to you the story of Christ. Compare what you will of all this with your own religion.

You have received the good guidance I wished to give; God and His angels be witness to me in this. If you turn your back on the idolaters and come forth into the light of the Evangel, which shines so brightly for you, and into the grace of our Lord Jesus Christ, then you shall be as one of the saints and honored in the Kingdom of Heaven. A felicity such as the unenlightened can never know shall be your portion. Surely the truth of God must appeal to you, whom He has distinguished so highly above others with the gift of reason. Be not slack, nor suffer the world to seduce you. Recall what I have written; compare point with point. Apply the precepts of justice. Flee from every false doctrine which imposes on the ignorant who have neither wit nor wisdom, insight nor principle to direct them. This is not one of those matters which men may safely shirk. It is pregnant with results for both estates, the immediate future and that distant day when no excuse shall avail. Be sure that he who abjures the devil and believes in God has got hold of "the right hand" which will never fail him. For myself, I have done my uttermost to advise you, I have kept back nothing, not the smallest jot of what was in my mind. I pray God that He may perfect us both in well-doing; that He may save us from our sins and unite us in His good time with the saints, on whom He has had favor. Peace be with you and mercy from God. Amen.

*****

The editor (Tien) of these pages affirms that nothing has come into his hands for this work except two manuscripts, one of them said to be transcribed from a manuscript in one of the libraries of Constantinople and the other from a manuscript in one of the libraries of Egypt, without the name of the copyist or of him who caused the copy to be made and without date. Both manuscripts are largely corrupt and differ in a number of passages. He has labored to put them together as best he could; he who has done his best is not to be blamed, even if he fails. At the end of the Egyptian manuscript he found a note, of which the following is a literal transcript:

"We have heard that the result of the above correspondence was as follows: The Caliph Ma'mun ordered both letters to be read to him. He listened in silence to the close, and then said that it was not his business to interfere with other people's affairs till he had rid his own soul of anger. As for the Christian, he had no quarrel with him; he must believe what he said; otherwise why should he adhere to his religion? He added that there were two religions, one of them the religion for this world and the other for the next. The religion of this world was the religion of the Magians, and the religion of the next world was the Christian religion. But he added, the true religion is that of the unity as taught by our master, that is the religion which reconciles this world and the next."

As to the letters, the famous savant Abu Rayhan Muhammad (the) son of Ahmad al-Biruni mentions them in his well-known book entitled "The Chronology of Ancient Nations." He there bears witness to the statement made by the Christian as to the practice of human sacrifice among the Sabeans, when he says: " 'Abd al-Masih al-Kindi the Christian records of them in his answer to the letter of 'Abdullah the Hashimite, that they are accustomed to sacrificing men, but are not able to do this openly." As to this 'Abd al-Masih, I have searched, but find no mention of him in any of the histories of Islam save what I have here recorded from Biruni. It is quite certain that he was not related to Yakub (the) son of Ishaq the Kindi, the famous translator of Greek books and known as the philosopher of Islam.

Notes on the Christian's letter:

[1] The word is "Hanifite." See previous note p. 404, n. 8.

[2] The argument is obscure and inconclusive. It moves on a thin sphere congenial enough to the logician, but alien to that of religion which is reality. So far as I can follow it, our author's line of thought is this: God is affirmed to be one. But unity must be of one of three kinds, generic, specific or numeric. Each in turn is proved to be inapplicable to the divine. His opponent then shifts his ground and introduces a new category affirming the unity of God to be essential. But the writer insists on interpreting this essential unity to be one or (the) other of the logical categories to which he is wedded. He asks —

does specific unity, as applied to the divine essence exclude numerical unity, or are they the same insofar as the one God is all? If the answer given be (that) specific unity excludes numerical unity, he reminds his antagonist that in the language of the schools, the species includes various individuals. Are there then various personalities of the divine? If not, does he really mean that specific and numerical unity are the same? If so, what is the specific unity apart from numerical unity? We are forced back on the latter, pure and simply, with all the objections already raised against it; to wit, that it makes God an individual like His creatures and excludes the idea of perfection. For himself (here the writer becomes didactic) he affirms that God is one in the perfection of His essence, but threefold in His personality. He is one in essence in so far as He is distinct from all His creatures; He is also one in number in as far as He is all-inclusive, i.e., you cannot add or take away from Him. But then (and here comes the threefold personality) number is of two kinds, odd and even, and those two kinds may be predicated of each of the Persons within the divine essence, i.e., each may be regarded simply as God, one and indivisible, or as a distinct aspect of the Godhead. However unsatisfactory all this may be, one cannot help thinking that behind the logical hair-splitting there lies an idea which answers to a religious truth. Pure theism (as Jehovah of the Jews, or Allah of the Muslims) cannot long exist. As thus conceived, the Godhead tends either to receive itself into the pure being of the Pantheist, or to divide and so multiply itself as in all forms of nature worship. It is the fullness of the divine nature, the fellowship of love with the Godhead, as revealed by Jesus Christ, which enables us to hold fast the personality and with it the unity of God. And thus, as our author puts it, whichever way we speak of God, as one or as three, we do not detract either from the reality or the perfection of the divine nature.

[3] By Muslims, the virgin Mary, the mother of our Lord, was represented as playing the part in Christian theology of God's wife.

[4] The word "mursal" is used (a) of a tradition which is not traced back to its sources, or (b) of a word of which the series of transmitters is interrupted. Thus applied, it means "of doubtful authority." Here

the application is logical rather than historical and describes a term which is isolated, i.e., positive as opposed to relative.

[5] An apparent reference to Daniel 4:31, though the Masoretic gives this in passive voice: "to you it is declared." A version of the Septuagint does give the active *third* person plural "to you they say." I have been unable to find a source for the first person plural as al-Kindi claims - ed.

[6] On this passage Canon Cheyne has the following note: "It is debated whether these words are the subject or the object of the verb; whether the Spirit is sender or sent. As there is no analogy in the Old Testament for the Spirit being the sender of a prophet and as the Spirit is elsewhere in Isaiah distinctly subordinated to Jehovah, it seems to me safer to take the words 'and His Spirit' as equivalent to 'with His Spirit.' Possibly the particular construction may have been chosen here to indicate the personality if the Spirit; for I cannot but think with Kleinert that we have both here and in Gen. 1:2 a trace of what is known as the Christian doctrine of the Holy Spirit." These words throw some interesting light on our author's treatment of Old Testament passages generally.

[7] I have read "muwarabath." I cannot make anything of the text.

[8] So far as I can see, there is some misplacement of the text, and possibly some misunderstanding of the facts on the part of our author. The caravan of Abu Jahl was raided by the Prophet at a later period, as we shall presently find. I do not read in any of our authorities that Muhammad began the practice of raiding while in Mecca, nor indeed was he then in a position to make such a course possible.

[9] If our author means to impute that Muhammad took the ground by force from the orphan lads, he is scarcely fair to the Prophet. The Banu Najjar were distantly related to him through Salma (the) mother of 'Abd al-Muttalib, with whom he found refuge when he first arrived in Medina. The plot of ground referred to was a neglected plot used

partly as a burial ground and partly as a yard for tying camels up. The
Prophet called the boys and offered to buy this, on which they replied:
"We will make a free gift of it to thee." The Prophet refused the gift,
and the price fixed was ten golden pieces. (Muir's *Life of
Muhammad*.)

[10] Hamza was an uncle of the Prophet and an early convert to
Islam. Abu Jahl was to the end one of the most bitter opponents of
the new faith. His proper name was Amr b. Hashim, but he was called
Abu Jahl, "father of folly," by the Muslims (Sprenger's *Leben*). He is
supposed to be alluded to in the Qur'an in the passage: "There is a
man who disputeth concerning God without knowledge or direction."
(Qur'an 22:3) - see al-Tabari, *History*, vol. 7, p. 10 for reference to
Hamza's raid - ed.

[11] The alternative is this: either Muhammad *was* a prophet and *yet*
his messengers were defeated, contrary to what history leads us to
expect; or Muhammad was *not* a prophet, and the claim made on his
behalf is refuted. The sentence is somewhat involved.

[12] 'Ubayda was a cousin of the Prophet (and) somewhat older than
he. Abu Sufyan was the good adversary of the Prophet. He
commanded at the battle of Uhud, when the Prophet was heavily
beaten. He led troops again and again against Medina, burning the
vineyards around the city and for a time holding it in siege. Slowly it
was borne in on this strong spirit that the tide was against him; as
Muhammad advanced against Mecca (630 A.D.) he made up his mind
to the inevitable and submitted. As father of Mu'awiya, he is the head
of the Umayyad dynasty. - see, al-Tabari, *History*, vol. 7, p. 10 on this
raid of Ubaydah - ed.

[13] Cf. al-Tabari, *History*, vol. 3, p. 71 - ed.

[14] Sa'd b. Waqqas was a nephew of Amina, the Prophet's mother,
(who) converted in his 16th or 17th year. On one occasion in the
valley of Mecca, where he had retired with some like-minded

companions for prayer, he was set on by the unbelievers. From words they came to blows. Sad struck one of his opponents and wounded him. Even afterwards, Sad boasted that he was the first to draw blood in the cause of Islam. - see, al-Tabari, *History*, vol. 7, p. 11, for an account of this raid - ed.

[15] See, al-Tabari, *History*, vol. 7, p. 12 for an account of this raid - ed.

[16] Ibid., p. 13 gives an account of this raid - ed.

[17] Ibid., pp. 28 ff. gives an account of this - ed.

[18] Atabek (or Babak) - a famous brigand described as the "scourge of the Empire" in the days of Ma'mun. When that great prince died, Babak was still powerful in Azerbayjan, whence he struck terror over all N. Persia, and enjoyed the countenance of Arabia and Greece. Motassen sent against him Afshin, one of the ablest of his Turkish generals. He was taken; thousands of captives were released and vast treasure recovered. On his way to the caliph with his doughty prisoner, Afshin received a royal ovation. Each day the caliph sent him a fresh dress of honor with a splendid gift. Babak meantime was kept under guard. The caliph went in disguise to gaze on the "satan of Khurasan" as he was called. He was paraded through the streets and then brought to the palace, where the caliph ordered his own executioner to fall on him and sever him limb from limb (833 A.D.). (Muir's *Caliphate*). - see also Mingana's introduction to the Patriarch Timothy's discussion with the Caliph Mahdi, note 7, and Muir's essay on the age and authorship of al-Kindi's Apology, note 10 - ed.

[19] In al-Tabari, *History*, vol. 9, p. 118, n. 813, Ismail Poonawala shows Baladhuri (*Ansab*, I, 371-84) as giving approximately 60 as the number of raids commissioned by Muhammad - ed.

[20] Usayr was the chief of the Jews at Khaybar. Ibn Rawaha was sent to persuade him to visit Medina, and murdered him and all his

companions on the way thither. - See, Ibn Ishaq, *Life of Muhammad*, p. 665, for an account of this - ed.

[21] Abu Afak the Jew had professed Islam, but still lived with his tribe in upper Medina. Though above 100 years of age, (he) was still active in his opposition to the new faith. He had composed some stinging verses against the Prophet. "Who will rid me of this pestilent fellow?" said Muhammad to those about him. The sequel is as above. - See, Ibn Ishaq, *Life of Muhammad*, p. 675, for an account of this - ed.

[22] The attack created great scandal because it was during the month of Rajah, in which it was forbidden to fight. In consequence of this and in excuse of the Muslims it was immediately revealed to the Prophet as follows: "They will ask thee concerning the sacred months, whether they may make war therein. Say, Warring therein is grievous, but to be obstinate in the ways of God and to deny Him is still worse." (Qur'an 2:214). This 'Abdullah was first known as the Amr of the Faithful. - See, Ibn Ishaq, *Life of Muhammad*, pp. 286 ff., for an account of this - ed.

[23] Qaynuqa' - One of the three Jewish tribe residing near Medina and the first to feel the brunt of the Prophet's anger against their race. The occasion was trifling. A foolish practical jest played on one of their women was followed by a blow which killed the jester. The revenge taken was complete, as narrated above. 'Abdullah b. Ubayy was the leading man of the Banu Khazraj, the original non-Muslim people of Medina. Being on friendly terms with the Jews, he protested against the order given to massacre them to a man, and laid his hand on the Prophet. "Wretch, let me go!" said the Prophet!" "No, I will not let thee go," replied 'Abdullah, "till thou hast compassion on my friends; wilt thou cut them down in one day? As for me, I am one who fears the vicissitudes of fortune." Muhammad was not yet strong enough to ignore such a protest. "Let them be; the Lord curse them and thee too." - See, Ibn Ishaq, *Life of Muhammad*, p.363, for an account of this - ed.

[24] See, al-Tabari, *History*, vol. 7, p. 124, for an account of this - ed.

[25] The mention of Muhammad's name being on the throne of God has been used as an argument against the 9th century dating of al-Kindi's Apology as al-Tabari countered this notion which was (also) held by al-Barbahari almost a century later. Mingana responds to this argument in his introduction to the Patriarch Timothy's dialogue with the Caliph Mahdi, see his notes 16 and 17 (p. 171) and note 16 (p. 406) to 'Abdullah b. Ismail's letter above - ed.

[26] See Wensinck, *Handbook*, p. 158, for a listing of hadith showing Muhammad's love for women, perfume and horses - ed.

[27] *Sahih Bukhari*, The Book of Ghusl, ch. 13, hadith 268, vol. 1, p. 164 gives "30 men" - ed.

[28] Zayd was a slave boy adopted by the Prophet as his son. Some years after he (Zayd) had married Zaynab, Muhammad, going to his house and not finding him home, cast eyes on Zaynab his (Zayd's) wife, who was then in a dress which discovered her beauty to advantage, and (he was) so smitten at the sight that he could not forbear crying out, "God be praised, who turneth the hearts of man as He pleases." This Zaynab failed not to acquaint her husband with on his return home, whereon he thought that he could do no less than divorce his wife in favor of his benefactor. Apprehending the consequences that might ensue, the Prophet affected to dissuade him, but at length, his love for Zaynab being authorized by a revelation, he (Muhammad) acquiesced, and the marriage was consummated. (Sale, p.317). ◄ The subject of Zaynab's marriage to Muhammad was very popular with Christian polemicists, see, Leo, parag. AX; John of Damascus, parag. G. This event is referred to in the Qur'an (33:37) and al-Tabari, *History*, vol. 8 and vol. 9, p. 134 - ed.

[29] The word comes from the word "sa'a," and indicates the act of running, earning, gaining. (Lane). The verb "qarad" means to cut into

or nibble (*secuit rodendo,* Freytag). "qarad" and "'arad," says our author, equal "kinayet," of which Lane gives the following illustration: "You say of a man he has a long suspensory cord to his sword and has many ashes of the cooking pot; by this statement you imply, without saying it, that he is tall of stature and entertains many guests." One can easily understand 'Ali's game.

[30] In this sura it is directed: "As to those who accuse women of reputation and do not produce four witnesses to the fact, scourge them with four score stripes and do not receive their testimony forever." (Qur'an 24:4) It proceeds: "As to those who have published the falsehood concerning Aisha, think it not to be an evil unto you; on the contrary, it is better." (i.e., God has done you the honor of thus exculpating you.) (Qur'an 24:11, where the word "Aisha" has been added - ed.) The penalty was rigidly enforced.

[31] There is some doubt as to the exact dimensions of the Prophet's harem. Sir W. Muir places it at ten wives and two concubines; our author is more generous. (al-Tabari, *History*, vol. 9, pp. 126 ff. and Ibn Ishaq, *Life of Muhammad*, p. 792 n. 918, give the number as fifteen, with whom only thirteen marriage was consummated - ed.) The following notes may be of use:

a) Kadijah - By her the Prophet had two sons and four daughters. She died 619 A.D., a year before the Hagira. During her lifetime the Prophet had no other wife.

b) Aisha (the) daughter of 'Abdullah (the) son of Kuhafa, better known as Abu Bakr (i.e., "father of the virgin"); betrothed to the Prophet when (she) was six years-old. She brought her toys with her, and the Prophet used to play with his girl-wife of an evening. She died late in life, and was known as the "mother of the faithful."

c) Sawda, whose first husband was one of the earliest adherents to the new faith and fled to Abyssinia. Soon after his return, he died and the Prophet married his widow in 619 A.D., a few months after the death of Khadija. She was divorced by the Prophet at a later date on the plea of her advanced age, but she was permitted to remain in his harem.

d) Hafsa - Owing to her displeasure with her husband (Muhammad) because of his intercourse with the Coptic Mary, he divorced her; but, when he saw the offence it gave to 'Umar, her father, he took her back, affirming that Gabriel had revoked the divorce. The political influence of Hafsa (daughter of 'Umar) and of Aisha (as daughter of Abu Bakr) was pretty equally balanced. There was much rivalry between the two ladies, but the youth and vivacity of Aisha maintained her supremacy. Occasionally they made common cause, as against the Coptic Mary.

e) Umm Salma - Her first husband died of a wound received in the battle of Uhud. Four months later the Prophet married his widow, who received his attention as narrated in the text. Our author accuses the Prophet of unfaithfulness to Umm Salma; Sir W. Muir thinks this without ground.

f) Zaynab (the) daughter of Jahsh, wife of Zayd (the) son of Harith. See note 28 above.

g) Zaynab (the) daughter of Khuzayma. Was three times married before the Prophet took her. Like Khadijah, she pre-deceased him.

h) Umm Habiba (the) daughter of Abu Sufyan - Her previous husband Ubaydullah was said to be one of the four inquirers, i.e., persons who were in a state of expectancy of the Prophet prior to the time that Muhammad announced his mission (see Introduction [deleted]). He embraced the new faith. (He later) retired to Abyssinia in the persecution, embraced the Christian faith and died there. On his death bed Muhammad sent for his widow. She was the sister to the caliph Mu'awiya and survived to his caliphate.

i) Maymuna - Maternal aunt of Ibn Abbas, the Prophet's uncle. Some do not allow that there was any formal marriage in this case.

j) Juweira - After the Banu Mustalik had been plundered (626 A.D. - 5 A.H.), the captives were brought to Medina. Juweira was of special beauty and the ransom fixed for her by her captors was far beyond her powers. She applied to the Prophet for easier terms, but he was so charged by her beauty that he paid the ransom already fixed and took her for himself.

k) Safiya (the) daughter of Hayy - Married by the Prophet on the field of battle where her previous husband (Kinana chief of the Khaybar) had been barbarously tortured and then slain. She was only 17 years-old. On the first night the Prophet spent with her, some of his friends kept guard at the tent door with drawn swords, lest a woman so young and so beautiful should try to avenge herself on her captor. But Safiya easily accommodated herself to the new relationship.

l) Fatima - This is a doubtful marriage.

m) Anna (the) daughter of Zazid of the tribe of Kunda; little is known of her.

n) Muleika (the) daughter of Naaman the Kindi will meet us later in the text.

o) Muleika (the) daughter of Ka'ab; a doubtful marriage.

p) Mary the Coptic maid - Sent as a present from the Abyssinian king. The Prophet had no surviving son, and when Mary gave birth to a boy, Ibrahim, there was great rejoicing, but he died early. The Prophet's grief for the little dead boy is one of the most pathetic passages in his story. The envy felt by Aisha and Hafsa towards this friendless girl has been alluded to.

q) Rihana a Jewess - Not further known. Mary and Rihana did not take rank among the Prophet's wives. Three of these ladies offered their hands to the Prophet (Umm Salma, Zaynab bint Khozeima and

Maymuna). See Bate in the *Indian Antiquary* (April 1878) (for a) fuller account.

[32] See, *Sahih Muslim*, Kitab al-Salat, ch. 324, hadith 1999, vol. 2, p. 435, and Wensinck, *Handbook*, p. 236 - ed.

[33] The reasons given in the hadith for Muhammad not visiting his wives for a month (or 29 days) range from Hafsa revealing a secret that Muhammad had visited Maria on Aisha's day to Muhammad visiting Zaynab (d. Jahsh) or Hafsa and having eaten honey with them. See *Sahih Bukhari*, The Book of Oppressions, ch. 26, hadith 648, vol. 3, pp. 387 ff.; The Book of Divorce, ch. 8, hadith 192 (193), vol. 7 pp. 140-41. I have been unable to find a reference to Zaynab (d. Jahsh) refusing flesh sent from Muhammad in this connection - ed.

[34] This is quite similar to the account in *Sahih Bukhari*, The Book of Divorce, ch. 3, hadith 182, vol. 7, pp. 131-32, where "princess" for "queen" and "ordinary man" for "trader" - ed.

[35] The Aad were an ancient Arab tribe to whom, according to the story, the prophet Hud was sent, but they ignored his warnings and were rendered "like the refuse which is carried down by a stream." (Qur'an 23:43). The Thamud were another tribe to whom Salih was sent. "He said, O my people, worship God, ye have no God but Him." (Qur'an 7:71) In their scorn the people pointed to a rock and bid Saleh cause a she camel, big with young, to come forth from it, but when he did this, the people cut off the camel's feet and still refused to believe. In the morning they were all "prostrate on their breasts," i.e., dead. In 570 A.D., the year in which the Prophet was born, Abraha (the) viceroy of Yemen marched against Mecca. He reached Taif and was then furnished with a guide. He then sent an embassy to Mecca, saying that he had no desire to hurt them, he only wished to destroy the Ka'ba with its idol worship to establish the Christian faith. Unable to resist, the people betook themselves to the hills. Meantime a pestilence attacked the invaders. The retreat began, but abandoned by their guide, they perished among the valleys. In the train of Abraha

was led an elephant, so singular an apparition in Arabia that the army was called "the masters of the elephant" (Qur'an 105).

[36] The paragraph is an interlude. The issue first raised is debated in the following paragraph. - For references on the expectation of signs and miracles as a confirmation of prophethood, see note 156 below - ed.

[37] See Leo, parag. BG, - ed.

[38] See Wensinck, *Handbook*, p. 167 - ed.

[39] *Fatah ul-Bari*, vol. 7, p. 23, as given in *Sahih Bukhari*, Vol 5, p. 10, n. 1 - ed.

[40] I have ventured to read an adjective from the verb "darajah," I cannot find the word printed in the text in any Arabic lexicon, nor do I find mention of this particular miracle in the long list given by Muhammad Inayat Ahmad (Lahore, 1894). - *Sahih Muslim*, Kitab Fada'il al-Sahabah, ch. 993, hadith 5881, vol. 4, p. 1276 - ed.

[41] See Wensinck, *Handbook*, p. 167 - ed.

[42] Ibid., p. 167 - ed.

[43] Ibn Ishaq, *Life of Muhammad*, p. 516 - ed.

[44] *Sahih Bukhari*, The Book of al-Maghazi, ch. 81, hadith 713, vol. 5, p. 510 - ed.

[45] In 628 A.D. (6 A.H.) the Prophet made an attempt to visit Mecca in the sacred month. But the Quraysh opposed his advance. During the march he alighted at Hudaybiya. The wells were choked with sand, but the Prophet took an arrow from his quiver, the only implement at hand, and bade one of his followers descend into the well and scrape away the sand; a simple but successful device, magnified

into the miracle narrated in our text. (See Muir's *Muhammad*).

[46] Whatever the status of such a hadith was in the time of al-Kindi, a similar one, in all probability referring to the same event, can be found in *Sahih Bukhari*, The Virtues and Merits of the Prophet, ch. 24, hadith 774, p. 498 - ed.

[47] There are quite a number of hadith concerning sayings attributed to Muhammad. Though I have not been able to find this particular hadith, the introduction to Abu Da'ud, *Sunan* is said to contain some showing the relationship between the Qur'an and hadith. See Wensinck, *Handbook*, p. 231 - ed.

[48] Though there appear to be no Muslim sources for Muhammad ever saying that he would be resurrected as Jesus was on the third day, al-Kindi's accusation is not entirely without merit. Muhammad died on a Monday, June 7, 632, but according to most major Islamic histories he was buried in the middle of the night Wednesday without even Aisha's knowledge (Ibn Ishaq, *Life of Muhammad*, p. 688, al-Tabari, *History*, vol. 9, p. 209). It appears that the normal procedure, however, was to bury the dead on the day of their death (to precede the rapid decay of the corpse which was increased by the heat of the season), as in the case of Abu Bakr who died in August (*Shorter Encyclopedia of Islam*, p. 9) and was buried within a few hours of his death (*Sahih Bukhari*, Actions While Praying, ch. 92, hadith 469, vol. 2, p. 265). Quite often Western and Eastern scholars of Islam attribute the delay in Muhammad's burial to disagreements in the Muslim community at the time as to who was to be their new leader. The vast majority of Islamic sources show that 'Umar didn't believe that Muhammad was dead at all and that he threatened anyone who should maintain such a thing. 'Umar is reported to have said that Muhammad had just gone to be with Allah as Moses had for forty days and that he would return (Ibn Ishaq, *Life of Muhammad*, p. 682; al-Tabari, *History*, vol. 9, p. 184). Nöldeke and Schwally (*Geschichte des Qorans*, vol. 2, p. 83) show Shahrastani (ed. Cureton I, 11) as maintaining that 'Umar alluded to Jesus the son of Mary instead of Moses in this statement,

and *Sahih Bukhari*, The Virtues and Merits of the Companions of the Prophet, ch. 6, hadith 18, vol. 5, p. 13 shows 'Umar as saying that Muhammad was to be resurrected. One result of these somewhat apparent contradictions is that some Western scholars of Islam have brought the charge that Qur'an 3:138 and other verses (concerning Muhammad's being mortal) were added to the text of the Qur'an by Abu Bakr at a later date. Schwally and Nöldeke (as the major Islamic histories also show) believe 'Umar to have forgotten this verse in the moment of his shock over Muhammad's death and see no reason why 'Umar would have allowed Abu Bakr to add such a verse (*Geschichte des Qorans*, vol. 2, pp. 81-2). However, if Muhammad had said that he was to be resurrected and then was not, this would have been reason enough for a fairly well organized cover-up on the part of Abu Bakr, 'Umar and even the rest of the community. (This could have also been a cause of the apostasy of the Arabs after Muhammad's death.) The accounts of Muhammad's burial being delayed because of the choice of the first caliph seems to be extremely superficial. Furthermore, even if Qur'an 3:138 was originally part of the Qur'an, Abu Bakr still waited a few days to bury Muhammad's corpse. In view of the many inconsistencies concerning the death of Muhammad, it is quite possible that there were Muslim hadith in al-Kindi's day which reported that he was to be resurrected in a manner similar to Jesus. Moreover, it appears that none of the later Muslim apologists even tried to respond to al-Kindi's charge, though they must certainly have known of it at least through al-Biruni. Be that as it may, the matter of Muhammad's resurrection has long been a subject of dispute in Muslim circles, see Fritz Meier, "Eine auferstehung Mohammeds bei Suyuti," *Der Islam*, vol. 62 (1985), pp. 20-58 - ed.

[49] Most major Islamic traditions and histories report that Muhammad died in Aisha's lap, see *Sahih Bukhari*, Actions While Praying, ch. 94, hadith 471, vol. 2, p. 267 - ed.

[50] "Sahuli" is rendered by some (to) be "beaten" or "washed," from "sahul," i.e., one who beats or washes and so whitens cloth. - (three garments, two of Suhar) See Ibn Ishaq, *The Life of Muhammad*,

p. 688, al-Tabari, *History*, vol. 9, p. 203 - ed.

[51] See *Sahih Bukhari*, The Book of Holding Fast to the Qur'an and the Tradition, ch. 2, hadith 388, vol. 9, p. 286, which reports the apostasy of some of the Arabs after the death of Muhammad and how Abu Bakr fought with them to receive the same amount of Zakat they formerly gave Muhammad - ed.

[52] Cf. Ibn Ishaq, *The Life of Muhammad*, p. 239 - ed.

[53] There were several attempts to murder Muhammad during his lifetime, but I have been unable to find a reference to this particular incident in any of the major Islamic sources - ed.

[54] See note 51 above - ed.

[55] This statement of al-Kindi conforms with the majority witness of Islamic tradition and histories - ed.

[56] It is not known exactly to whom al-Kindi is referring here, but it could have been one of the followers of Ibn Ishaq (d. cir. 150 A.H. - 767 A. D.), who was also accused of having Shiite sympathies (Ibn Hisham, *The Life of Muhammad*, ed. Guillaume, p. xii-xvii.).

[57] Hostility towards the Jews was unfortunately predominant during this era of church history. See, Leo, parag. BC - ed.

[58] Cf. Matt 11:13 (paraphrase - "My coming" for "John."). The second notion, namely that Jesus said no prophet was to come after Him, has no Biblical support whatsoever. The Patriarch Timothy I also made this mistake, only to correct it later; see, Timothy, parag. AZ, n. 150. Sadly, the belief that no prophet is to appear after Christ is still predominant among Eastern Christians - ed.

[59] Cf. John 10:8 (Diatessaron gives: "For all, as many as came, are thieves and robbers.") In his zeal to find verses against Muhammad,

either al-Kindi or later copyists appear to have modified this verse to suit their own aims - ed.

[60] On the question whether Muhammad could read and write and how far study influenced his utterances, see a discussion in Sprenger's *Life* (English Version Books). See Nöldeke, "The Qur'an," p. 6, n. 6 - ed.

[61] For the facts behind this legend, see Introduction [deleted]. - See Appendix A - ed.

[62] Since al-Kindi appears himself to have been Nestorian, this passage thus presents good evidence that the text was tampered with by non-Nestorian Christians at some time during its transmission - ed.

[63] Praying: "Effecit ut perseverarat in lite."

[64] 'Ali was so called as (the) father of Hasan and Husayn.

[65] See Jeffery, *Materials*, p. 182, for the Muslim sources for this tradition - ed.

[66] Hajjaj - A famous (or rather infamous) soldier who rose to power in the caliphate of 'Abd al-Malik. Mecca was at that time held by Ibn Zubayr, who represented the 'Alid party against the Umayyad dynasty. After a siege of seven months it fell (691 A.D.) into the hands of Hajjaj, who had the bodies of Ibn Zubayr and two of his officers impaled. Tradition puts the number of lives sacrificed by Hajjaj, apart from the carnage of the battle, at 120,000. He was fond of making copies of the Qur'an with his own hand as a work of merit and distributing the same, but he was bitterly opposed to the text of Ibn Mas'ud, declaring that he would behead anyone who used it. (Muir's *History of the Caliphate*). See also Muir's essay on the authorship and age of al-Kindi's Apology, n. 13; see Appendix A - ed.

[67] A mere figment of our author. Gabriel is rather to be identified

with the Holy Spirit, as the medium of revelation. - See p. 388 and Qur'an 26:193 - ed.

[68] See Jeffery, *Materials*, pp. 182 ff., for more information on 'Ali's Qur'an codex - ed.

[69] See *Sahih Muslim*, Kitab al-Salat, ch. 291, hadith 1799, vol. 2, pp. 393-4; and Jeffery, *Materials*, pp. 20 ff., for more information on Ibn Mas'ud's codex - ed.

[70] This hadith is similar to *Sahih Bukhari*, The Book of the Virtues of the Qur'an, ch. 7, hadith 521, vol. 6, pp. 486-7 - ed.

[71] The word might mean either "one who recites best," or rather "one who is most sound in his knowledge of the Qur'an, retaining most of it in his memory." In those old days "to read" was always "to recite." - *Sahih Bukhari*, Book of Commentary, ch. 9, hadith 8, vol. 6, p. 10 - ed.

[72] A similar hadith is the famous *Sahih Bukhari*, The Book of the Virtues of the Qur'an, ch. 3, hadith 510, vol. 6, p. 478 - ed.

[73] "The disposition is true, but not the case here alleged for it." (Muir, *Apology*, p. 74). See Jeffery, *Materials*, pp. 20-1, p. 14. - ed.

[74] See reference in note 72 above - ed.

[75] A notable adventurer who, beginning as a brigand, soon raised a great following. By his lieutenants, Mecca was besieged and burned in 200 A.H. The event must have been quite recent when al-Kindi wrote. - See Muir's essay on the authorship and age of al-Kindi's Apology, p. 370 - ed.

[76] Mukhtar - Another of the adventurers, of whom there were so many at this time. He assisted Ibn Zubayr to resist the attack of Hajjaj on the city of Mecca. After a heavy defeat, he took refuge in

Kufa, till hunger drove him out with 19 of his followers to meet their fate.

[77] See the reference to note 72 above - ed.

[78] For Sura Nur, which is said to have contained more than 100 verses, see Nöldeke and Schwally in *Geschichte des Qorans*, vol. 2, p. 97. In Suyuti, *el-Itkan*, vol. 2, p. 65-6, Sura Ahzab is said to have once been as long as Sura Baqara - ed.

[79] "Barat" means "declaration of immunity," otherwise known as "repentance." Others attribute the important omission in our text to the nature of the sura and call it the Sura of Punishment. The two final suras are known as the Incantation suras. They were both very brief, and this may have tempted some to add to their length by the introduction of other matter, as has been in the case of the sura Baqara (the Cow) which is composite. - Nöldeke and Schwally were of the opinion that the bismillah between Qur'an 8 and 9 was probably due to an omission in an early copy rather than that the two suras were previously one; see, *Geschichte des Qorans*, vol. 2, pp. 80 and 41 n. 2 - ed.

[80] Though I have not been able to find a reference for this alleged saying of Ibn Mas'ud, it is quite well known that his Qur'an codex did not contain the suras 1, 113 and 114; see, Jeffery, *Materials*, p. 21 - ed.

[81] Sir W. Muir says, "That the comment should have been omitted, if it ever was in the Qur'an, as unaccountable. There must, however, have been some foundation for 'Umar's speech, as stoning is still by Muslim law the punishment for adultery, and the only authority for the practice is the withdrawn verse." - See, Suyuti, *el-Itkan*, vol. 2, p. 68, for 'Umar's statement - ed.

[82] "Al-Mut'a" is a temporary marriage. The contract does not specify for how long it shall be valid (See R.W. Smith's *Kinship and Marriage in Early Arabia*). 'Uthman is said to have claimed that this

particular type of marriage was allowed by the Qur'an and the anathematizes the man who, too fastidious, excised the passage. Mut'a is (actually) the gift given to the divorced wife. - Oddly enough, Sunni traditions typically portray 'Umar as the one who forbade Mut'a; see *Shorter Encyclopedia of Islam*, p. 418 - ed.

[83] See Suyuti, *el-Itḳan*, vol. 2, p. 65 for Ibn 'Umar's remark on no one possessing the whole of the Qur'an - ed.

[84] I have been unable to find this saying of 'Umar's in any major Islamic source - ed.

[85] See Jeffery, *Materials*, p. 115 - ed.

[86] 'Ali appears to have been against the practice of Mut'a (*Sahih Muslim*, Kitab al-Nikah, ch. 541, hadith 3263, vol. 2, p. 708 - ed.

[87] A great battle (656 A.D.) 36 A.H. when 'Ali defeated the forces led by Zubayr and Tatha against him and (which were) accompanied by Aisha who aided them. ('Ali was accused of the murder of the late Caliph 'Uthman.) Aisha rode on a camel which became to the gallant men who fought for the mother of the faithful, the center of the battle. Hence the name given to the whole affair. The origin of the longstanding feud between 'Ali and Aisha has been already noted. - I have been unable to find references for these traditions concerning 'Ali in major Islamic sources - ed.

[88] An-Nadim (d. 995 A.D.) reports having seen several manuscripts recorded which were transcribed as having been Ibn Mas'ud's even in his day; see *Fihrist*, vol. 1, p. 57 - ed.

[89] An-Nadim also records seeing a Qur'an codex written in the handwriting of 'Ali and that the family of Hasan retained it as an inheritance; see *Fihrist*, vol. 1, p. 63 - ed.

[90] Exactly which book is meant is not clear. The Qur'an contains

several similar verses - ed.

[91] The argument that the Qur'an was Muhammad's miracle (as he himself was illiterate) is still prevalent among Muslims - ed.

[92] See Finkel in Jahiz, n. 34 - ed.

[93] "Diodorous tells us that the inhabitants of parts of Arabia towards Syria lived by agriculture and trade; but, with the Nabateans, the land began to be arid and barren, and they led the lives of robbers, plundering their neighbors far and wide. The name is probably connected with Nebaioth though Margoliouth denies this." (*Dictionary of the Bible*). For their rapid advance northwards into Syria and the empire founded there; see Ewald's *History of Israel* (vol. 5). The civilization to which they had attained is used later by our author as an argument against them in contrast to the pure-bred Arab of the desert.

[94] Three pretenders who rose to disturb the closing days of the Prophet's life. One by one they were judged by Abu Bakr. It was the slaughter of the faithful in the battle of Yamma (garden of death) that induced Abu Bakr on the suggestion of 'Umar to collect the Qur'an, lest all who could recite it should die and it be wholly lost. Sir W. Muir protests against the too favorable judgment passed by our author on the utterances of Musaylima, which (in the form they are presented in Muslim tradition) he prefers to describe as "the veriest rubbish." (Muir, *Apology*, p. 81, n. 1 - ed.)

[95] See note 34 above - ed.

[96] For the style of poetry on which so unfavorable a judgment in passed, full of bombast, the reader may be referred to the amusing account of a poetical contest between the chiefs of the Banu Tamim and Hasan b. Thabit, on the issues of which the prophetic claims of Muhammad were staked, as given by Sir W. Muir (p.420). The real judgment to be passed on the value of Arabic poetry and its influence on history, is of course very different from that given here. - See

Nöldeke, "The Qur'an," pp. 10-15, for the poetic merit of the Qur'an - ed.

[97] Al-Kindi is also referring indirectly to the Qur'anic preconception of Paradise - ed.

[98] Muir in *The Caliphate*, p. 52, gives al-Tabari, *Tarikh*, i, 2031 as the reference for this speech of Khalid b. Walid - ed.

[99] In this (and) a few other passages, I have embodied a phrase, the origin of which the reader will have no difficulty in identifying. In each case the phrase borrowed correctly, I think, convey's our author's meaning. I have omitted the inverted commas lest I should be accused of the anachronism of making al-Kindi quote from Tennyson, Milton, Shakespeare, etc.!

[100] Cf. Jahiz, parag. N, n. 64 - ed.

[101] The reference is no doubt to 'Ali. It was affirmed that Gabriel had been charged to communicate the Qur'an to 'Ali; but, by mistake, he went to Muhammad.

[102] Person unknown. - Ibn Rabban in *Religion and Empire*, responds to someone's attack that according to the Bible Ishmael would be "a wild ass of men" (Gen. 16:12a, Peshitta). Mingana is of the opinion that al-Kindi meant Ishmael here - ed.

[103] "As usual the illustrations go in depreciation of Abu Bakr, as was the fashion of the 'Alids at al-Ma'mun's court. A few reigns later, no one would have dared to repeat traditions affecting the character of the first three caliphs." (Muir, *Apology*, p. 87, n. 2) - I have been unable to find this tradition in any major Islamic source - ed.

[104] Though I have not been able to find this exact hadith, there are several dealing with telling lies about Muhammad; see Wensinck, *Handbook*, p. 165 - ed.

[105] The argument is lengthy and involved. a) First of all the history of the Qur'an is reviewed and the conclusion drawn that the present text is quite unreliable. b) Next the argument from style is considered. The Qur'an is found to contain a large number of foreign words. By use of his logical weapons the author tries to force the conclusion that, as (the) Arabic equivalents of these words may be found in writers earlier than Muhammad, they must have been introduced not by him, but by other and alien hands. Thus, from another point of view, the corruption of the text is supposed to be established. c) And again the poetic form into which much of the Qur'an is cast is shown to be no proof either of inspiration or authenticity as all foreign writers mainly affected it. "The passionate is seldom pure" — mingled with this argument are digressions 1) on the author's birth, 2) on the nature of Arabic poetry, 3) a long account of the various converts to Islam, whose conversion is, without exception, attributed to impure motives, and 4) the conduct of the Jews who have done their best to introduce the fictitious and absurd.

[106] On this legal phrase, the following notes from al-Biruni may be given: "At the time of paganism the Arabs used their months in a similar way to the Muslims: their pilgrimage went wandering through the four seasons of the year. But then they desired to perform the pilgrimage at such time as their merchandise (hides, skins, fruits etc.) was ready for the market and to fix it according to an invariable rule, so that it should occur in the most agreeable and abundant season of the year. Therefore they learned a system of intercalation from the Jews about 200 years before the Hagira, and they used intercalation in a similar way to the Jews, adding the difference between their year and the solar-lunar year when it summed up to one complete month, to the months of their year. Then their intercalators themselves, so called Kalamis of the tribe of Kinana, rose after the pilgrimage had been finished to deliver a speech to the people at the fair and intercalated the month by calling it the next following month by the name of that month in which they were. This proceeding they called "nasi," i.e., postponement. One of their poets has said:

'We have no intercalator under whose banner we march; He declared the month sacred or profane as he liked.' "

Muhammad disused this custom and returned to the simple lunar year, with (the) results already noted in connection with the fast of Ramadan.

[107] See above parag. BX, n. 25 - ed.

[108] According to Mingana, this is a Nestorian hymn; see Timothy, p. 171, n. 10 - ed.

[109] Reference is uncertain. - See n. 102 above - ed.

[110] I have been unable to find the origin of this saying - ed.

[111] "Ahli Bayt" generally refers to the direct relatives of Muhammad and occupies a very special place in Shiite theology - ed.

[112] I have been unable to find the origin of this saying - ed.

[113] The close of the passage, while very interesting, is a little obscure; apparently the meaning is this: If there is to be any comparison between Muhammad and the Jews, then on his own testimony the precedence must be given to the latter. This our author must say lest it be thought that he has no answer to give to the claims advanced by the Prophet. On the hand, and for himself, he believes in the equality of all men in point of birth, etc.

[114] An obvious reference to the Islamic ritual washings and prayer - ed.

[115] Al-Kindi's argument here lacks all Biblical support - ed.

[116] Oddly enough, what appears to have survived of early Muslim traditions tells us little or nothing about whether or not Muhammad

was circumcised. One tradition listed by Wensinck, *Handbook*, p. 157, reports that Muhammad was born circumcised and with his navelstring severed. Were this truly the case other major Islamic sources would have no doubt shown the same - ed.

[117] The Muslim use of the example of Christ in circumcision, direction of prayer, not eating pork, etc., was widespread; see, Leo, parags. AJ, AN, AP; Timothy, AB, AC, AD - ed.

[118] Cf. Timothy, parags. AB, AC - ed.

[119] Circumcision is nowhere mentioned in the Qur'an, and I have not been able to find a Qur'an verse fitting al-Kindi's description here - ed.

[120] Here follows in the original passage (that) which good taste forbids us to render in English. It adds nothing to the argument and only illustrates the extraordinary difference in point of taste between East and West.

[121] Al-Kindi's explanation for the Jewish dietary laws is not only un-Biblical, but also extremely incomplete - ed.

[122] The practice (is) peculiar to Arabia - see Canon Cheyne on "Circumcision" (*Encyclopaedia Britannica*). In this connection the word for circumcision equals "degradation" and is so rendered in what follows. - The practice of circumcision is not only peculiar to Arabia, but is also performed in other parts of the Muslim world. This subject also came up in other Christian-Muslim discussions; see Leo, parag. AP, n. 86; John of Damascus, parag. J; Jahiz, parag. T - ed.

[123] See al-Tabari, *History*, vol. 3 - ed.

[124] The author stumbles again. "The only change made by Muhammad in the season of the pilgrimage was to abolish the

intercalary month so that the pilgrimage shifts with the lunar, instead of being stationary, according to the luni-solar year." Muir (*Apology*, p.93). - The effect of this shifting with the lunar year means that the time for the pilgrimage comes about 10 days earlier each year, thus the pilgrimage is performed but once a year, and because of this shift, at different time periods from year to year. Al-Kindi certainly could have explained this better, but I do not think he was all that wrong in his statements on this matter - ed.

[125] The stone on which Abraham is believed to have stood when he built the Ka'ba. It is said to have served as a scaffold, rising or falling as required. Others say that he set foot on this stone when he came to visit the wife of Ishmael. Sarah had made him promise that he would not alight or touch ground (See Sprenger).

[126] *Sahih Bukhari*, Chapters About Sadaqat ul-Fitr, ch. 56, hadith 675, vol. 2, pp. 394-5; *Sahih Muslim*, Kitab al-Hajj, ch. 484, hadith 2912-, vol. 2, pp. 642-3 - ed.

[127] There are several versions of this hadith which differ slightly from one another; their chains of transmitters are various, so it is difficult to tell who al-Kindi meant here - ed.

[128] Cf. Qur'an 2:230. This subject was very popular among early Christian polemicists; see Leo, parag. AY; John of Damascus, parag. G - ed.

[129] The verb "jana" means "to gather," i.e., to bend over the ripe fruit. No doubt it is connected with the verb which occurs two lines above, though they are given separately in the lexicon.

[130] "The words are not quoted literally; but the expression occurs in more than one passage, as Sura 21:107; 28:47." (Muir, *Apology*, p. 97, n. 1)

[131] This appears to be a rhetorical device used by al-Kindi to sum

up the mission of Muhammad - ed.

[132] A pathetic name for the Evil One from Balara (4th century), i.e., "to despair." Compare a previous passage: "The ways of Satan from whom God has taken His mercy."

[133] See Ibn Ishaq, *The Life of Muhammad*, pp. 136-39 for more on the occasion of this verse - ed.

[134] Cf. Religious Dialogue, parag. P - ed.

[135] I have been unable to find a reference to this in other works - ed.

[136] I have been unable to find a reference to this in other works - ed.

[137] See note 127 above - ed.

[138] Manaf (the) son of Qusayy and father of Hashim, was the ancestor not only of the Prophet, but of the Umayyads, 'Alids and Abbasids. The appeal therefore is of the widest. The other, on whose the good works the Prophet relies, is no doubt himself.

[139] I have not been able to find a reference to this in major Islamic sources - ed.

[140] See the letter of al-Hashimi, parag. AU, n. 26 - ed.

[141] Literally "a wink."

[142] Muslim arguments against the worship of the cross as practiced by the Eastern churches were developed early on and became widespread; see Leo, parag. AW; John of Damascus, parag. F; Timothy, parag. BB - ed.

[143] Cf. Leo, parag. AX - ed.

[144] That the Israelites sang this Psalm as they brought the ark to Jerusalem has no direct support in the Bible - ed.

[145] I.e., the Prophet Muhammad.

[146] In the passage which follows reference is made to events of which we know nothing. Apparently on various occasions when in danger of his life, the Muslim had invoked the cross. Apparently too in a previous discussion in the presence of the Amir Ma'mun, that amiable and impartial monarch had been pleased to assign the honors of the day to the Christian, as having made out the better case. Of this incident our author makes a use which is perhaps hardly worthy of the serious discussion in which he is engaged.

[147] In regard to the case of pre-Islamic Arabia some information may be found R. W. Smith's *Kinship and Marriage*. A fuller account may be had in Wellhausen's *Skizzen* and in Krehl's *Religion der Vorislamischen Araber*. The two first mentioned in (the) text may safely be regarded as "merely titles," probably of one and the same supreme deity (See R. W. Smith). Al-Lat is probably the feminine of Allah (mother of the gods), al-Uzza: the mighty one. In Herodotus al-Lat appears as "Alilat." According to the Arab writers, Yaghut, Ya'uq, Nasr, Waad and Sawa were good people who lived in the days of Noah and were worshipped by their descendants after the flood (See Krehl and Wellhausen). Azaf and Na'ila were originally persons of less honorable fame. Azaf (the) son of 'Amr and Na'ila (the) daughter of Sahl committed fornication in the Ka'ba and were changed into stones, which were placed on as-Safa and al-Marwa, hills near Mecca, where they were afterwards worshipped. On the other hand, in most cases the immediate object of worship is a stone. In Sawa's case, e.g., the stone is said to have been buried in the deluge, but (then) exhumed by the Evil One in order to tempt men. It is said to have had the form of a woman. Al-Lat and al-Uzza were also worshipped as stones. Manat was a shapeless stone. The Quraysh swore by al-Lat, al-Uzza and

Manat. Again, several of these deities point back to an original totem (animal) worship. Yaghut, e.g., is the lion-god, Ya'uq is the horse-god and Nasr is the vulture. In the case of Dhul Halash we have a suggestion of primitive tree worship. The name means "the lady of the temple within whose precincts the falash tree was cultivated." Aga in Kathra may be connected (See Krehl) with ath-Thara, the rain-god, the Arabic title for Pleiades (Hebrew "Kimah," i.e., "the cluster") a constellation widely worshipped in Shemite lands and known by the Arabs as an-Najum, i.e., the star *par excellence*. In this case we have the original star worship, so with Shams, the sun and Sad (Sadayn), the name for Mercury and Venus, gods of good luck. Hobal had the figure of a man with an arrow in his hand, i.e., the archer. Dhul Khaffayn is the two-headed god.

[148] Probably both eastern tribes with whom, in the course of their conquests, the Muslims had come into contact. The sessions which our author alludes to were no doubt public discussions in which the Muslim doctors sought to win the conquered races over to the faith. Akbar, the great Muslim ruler in India (1600 A.D.), was in the same way famous for his policy of conciliation and justice. "All religions were put upon a political equality, and Jews, Parsees, Hindees and Christians were invited to his court to discuss with the mullahs about religion." (See *Desire of India*).

[149] The argument which follows seems to be wrecked on the fact that, while the word "Lord" occurs twice, it represents two distinct words in the original; "Jehovah" and "Adonai." The tetragram occurs only once, not twice as our author asserts. Our Lord's argument from the same passage is based, not on the use of any particular word, but on the fact that David imputes to his son a certain Lordship and precedence.

[150] Al-Kindi apparently confuses the occasion of John 5:5-8 with that of Luke 5:24 here - ed.

[151] The Muslim charge that the Jews and Christians had corrupted

the scriptures developed quite early; see Leo, parags. H, N; John of Damascus, parag. D; Timothy, parags. AS, CL - ed.

[152] The argument that the enmity between Jews and Christians is the best guarantee that the Old Testament was not corrupted, also seems to have been widespread; see Leo, parag. K; Timothy, parag. CN - ed.

[153] That is, they should enjoy blessings both in heaven and earth.

[154] This contradiction between Muslim doctrine and the Qur'an is even more evident in that the Torah, Psalms and Gospel are said to be God's Word and several verses in the Qur'an (6:34,115; 18:26) show that no one can change God's Word - ed.

[155] Although al-Kindi himself appears to have quoted some texts rather freely himself, cf. Leo, parag. U - ed.

[156] Christian polemicists charged that Muhammad had no prophetic witness to his mission; see Leo, parag. G; John of Damascus, parag. C - ed.

[157] The expectation that one's prophethood should be confirmed by signs and miracles certainly was not anything new (Matt. 12:38; I Cor. 1:22), and since these were lacking for Muhammad (e.g., see parags. CC, CE above) Christians used this as an argument against his being a prophet; see, John of Damascus, parags. AI-AJ; Timothy, parag. AU - ed.

[158] According to Muslim writers, the virgin's father was Amram, possibly by confusion with the father of Moses and Aaron. Some Christian writers give his name as above (as) "Joakim."

[159] "He (al-Kindi) applies 'lord' (*Syed*) to Jesus, whereas by the construction it clearly refers to *John*." (Muir, *Apology*, p. 116, n. 3) - ed.

[160] Al-Kindi gives the reverse order for coming of the magi and the proclamation to the shepherds. The Diatessaron correctly has the events concerning the shepherds prior to the coming of the magi - ed.

[161] These two scripture references appear to have been taken from the Diatessaron, where they are separated from each other by John 1:30,31 - ed.

[162] The Arabic Diatessaron gives: "...and He fasted forty days and forty nights; and tasted nothing in those days..." (trans. Hill) apparently whence the idea that Jesus did not even drink water. Al-Kindi also shows here the reverse order of Jesus' being tempted in the wilderness and the beginning of His ministry - ed.

[163] Al-Kindi uses both of these passages out of context - ed.

[164] Cf. Religious Dialogue, parag. AQ - ed.

[165] Cf. Leo, parag. C - ed.

[166] The paragraphs EQ and ER appear to be later corruptions to the text. The alleged quotations from the Bible in this section are at times absurd and ridiculous. Even though al-Kindi himself paraphrases some Bible passages, the verses to which he is referring can at least be found; this, however, is not the case with the alleged quotations in these passages, which have obviously been modified to be anti-Islamic - ed.

[167] I have been unable to locate a reference for this saying in major Islamic sources - ed.

EDITOR'S PREFACE

'ALI TABARI'S
"BOOK OF RELIGION
AND EMPIRE"

The *Book of Religion and Empire* was first translated into English from an apparently "unique manuscript" by A. Mingana and published for the John Rylands Library in 1922. This was followed one year later by Mingana's edition of the Arabic text of the book.[1] In 1924 Nöldeke did a review of *Book of Religion and Empire* in which he also corrected some translation errors in the English version and misprints in the Arabic.[2] Later in the same year Bouyges contested the authenticity of 'Ali Tabari's alleged work in a 16-page booklet.[3]

In his review of the dispute between Bouyges and Mingana, Graf lists the objections of Bouyges as follows: This particular work of 'Ali Tabari is not mentioned in any bibliographies, the style of the argumentation and the vocabulary used appear to be modern, Mu'tazilite expressions which are at times used in the text would not have been possible under the Caliph Mutawakkil, that the speech of the decree attributed to Mutawakkil concerning Christians differs substantially from that transmitted by the Muslim historian Tabari, the citation of chapter and verse in the work betray modern methodology, where the Peshitta is not quoted chapter division is in harmony with modern editions of the Bible, mistakes made in relating Bible histories would not have been possible for a former Christian, the work shows a deficiency of psychological unity, etc.[4]

Graf shows that the Director of the John Rylands Library had the manuscript re-investigated by other scholars, Orientalists and Muslims of renown, who all came to the same conclusion of those who had previously examined the manuscript, that is, that it was genuine.[5] Mingana also responded reiterating the unquestionable authenticity of the *Book of Religion and Empire*, but without addressing the majority of Bouyges' objections.[6] Mingana appeals to the use of Bible texts by later Muslim polemicists, which texts must have been originally translated and quoted by 'Ali Tabari,[7] (since none of the later Muslim scholars knew Syriac) as his main line of defence. Graf shows that Bouyges, not at all satisfied with either of these replies, then advanced the theory that the *Book of Religion and Empire* must have been written in the 20th century by an imitator, and gave lack of finances as his excuse for not being able to publish his objections in more detail.[8]

Though complaining that Mingana should have published more information concerning the description of the manuscript, Nöldeke voiced no reservations for considering it authentic in his review of the work. If indeed the styles of argumentation and vocabulary of the *Book of Religion and Empire* imply a more modern authorship, as Bouyges suggested, certainly Nöldeke, who reviewed it, and Margoliouth, who was consulted in its translation, would have made mention of possible inconsistencies in this regard. The problem of the book not being mentioned in any bibliographies should also not be viewed as being too grave, as the author himself is mentioned (under a variety of names). As Mingana shows, the scripture references he employed appear to have been used by later Muslim polemicists. In considering the impossibility of the usage of Mu'tazilite expressions under Mutawakkil, one must also take into account that Jahiz was also hired by this Caliph to work on his anti-Christian literature campaign. The fact that 'Ali Tabari gives chapter references to Bible passages and that these at times correspond with modern chapter division, should also not be seen as a serious objection, since any industrious writer of his day certainly could have done the same, and the various chapter numbering systems of ancient Bible translations vary from manuscript to manuscript.[9] Even practicing Christians such as al-Kindi do not seem to have been infallible in the area of recounting Biblical histories,[10] not to mention intentional errors which those who had left the faith were capable of.

Theologically, it is obvious that the book was written by a former Syrian Christian, whose extensive use of Bible passages (mostly from the Peshitta) far exceeds that of any other Muslim scholar previous to him. In order to facilitate the application of Biblical materials, 'Ali Tabari seems to have dispensed with the Islamic accusation that the Torah, Zabur and Injil had been corrupted. Oddly enough though, Jahiz also states that the Torah was uncorrupted,[11] and it may well have been that Mutawakkil himself had instituted this change in his great literature campaign in order to promote the conversion of more Christians to Islam. Whatever the case may be, this doctrinal reversal not only appears to have been short-lived, but was probably the largest factor adversely affecting the preservation of Tabari's and Jahiz's works in this field.

'Ali Tabari's main argument with respect to many Old Testament passages is at the same time his greatest flaw. As Nöldeke remarked in his review, Tabari, in trying to find prophecies he could attribute to Muhammad, assumes that the Syriac word "marya" ("lord") is "adhonai" in the Hebrew text.[12] In the majority of cases, however, the word is not "adhonai," but "YHWH," and thus Tabari's interpretation, literally taken, leads to heresy for Muslims as well. Due to this deficiency, Nöldeke concludes that the Hebrew and Greek texts of the Bible were unknown to Tabari,[13] and indeed in all the places where he makes reference to the Hebrew, Tabari errs.[14] Although he does not address the majority of the arguments put forward by al-Kindi in his Apology, Tabari does not seem to have been unfamiliar with them.[15] Al-Kindi mentions the tetragram in his somewhat flawed exegesis of Ps. 110:1-2, and Tabari must have had some knowledge of this peculiarity also, for he quotes this same reference in attempting to show that the word "lord" can also be applied to humans.[16]

Indeed, one can hardly presume that 'Ali Tabari made all of his mistakes in good faith. In a number of Old Testament passages he omits the words "Jacob" or "Israel" in order claim that a prophecy applies to Muhammad and none other. Tabari also attempts to show that the wilderness of Paran is near Mecca[17] and as Nöldeke noted, that the daughter of Zion (and Zion itself) is Mecca.[18] Tabari's biased and misleading description of Christianity also indicates that the author regarded his goal as far more important than the means he used in trying to achieve it.[19]

Not all of what Tabari wrote was unjustified. The reasons given by the author for Christians rejecting Muhammad: 1) There is no witness of him in earlier prophecies; 2) There are no miracles of Muhammad mentioned in the Qur'an; and 3) Christ said no prophet would arise after Him;[20] (though perhaps in reality not the main reasons) were, however, accusations which were current in the early Christian polemic.[21] Tabari naturally claims to have proven all of these ideas as false in his book, but since he takes many Bible passages out of context simply to attribute them to Muhammad and since even the Qur'an denies that Muhammad performed miracles,[22] only one of his arguments possesses a measure of merit, i.e., that the New Testament attests to the continuation of prophetic ministry after the ascension of Christ.[23]

Of the alleged Biblical prophecies concerning Muhammad, Tabari received at least three of them, the Prophet of Deut. 18:15[24] the camel rider of Is. 21:7[25] and the Paraclete of John 14, 15 and 16,[26] from his Muslim predecessors. On the other hand though, Tabari evidently rejected the well-known Muslim tradition in which a distorted version of Is. 42:1-7 is said to have foretold Muhammad's ministry.[27] *The Book of Religion and Empire* is definitely apologetic in nature, for aside from his short definition of Christianity, which has already been mentioned above, Tabari advances very few accusations against his "cousins" in the faith. The one charge of the Christians to which Tabari dedicates perhaps an inordinate amount of verbiage (only at length to call the alleged transmitter a "blockhead" and a "dolt"),[28] regards the person of Ishmael and the prophecy of Gen. 16:12. Mingana believes that this subject was implied in an ambiguous statement found in al-Kindi's *Apology* and discusses this topic in his introduction to the text.

Some sections of the *Book of Religion and Empire* have been deleted from this edition as they contributed little information relative to the Christian-Muslim dialogue overall. For those interested in the entire text of 'Ali Tabari's book, we recommend A. Mingana's translation of *The Book of Religion and Empire*, The University Press, Manchester, 1922, in which the following text first appeared.

Notes:

[1] Graf, *Orientalistische Literaturzeitung*, 1927, 7, p. 511.

[2] Nöldeke, *Deutsche Literaturzeitung*, 1924, 1, pp. 22-28.

[3] *Le "Kitab ad-din wa'd-dawlat" récemment édité et traduit par Mr. A. Mingana, est-il authentique?*, Beyrouth, Juillet 1924; as taken from Graf, *OL*, 1927, 7, p. 511.

[4] Graf, *OL*, 1927, 7, p. 512.

[5] Ibid. pp. 512-3.

[6] Ibid. p. 513.

[7] Mingana references Goldziher's article "Über Muhammad, Polemik gegen ahl al-Kitab," (ZDMG, xxxii, 1878, pp. 341-395) in "Remarks on Tabari's Semi-Official Defence of Islam," *Bulletin of John Rylands Library* 9 (1925), pp. 236-9, and adds a brief discussion of Bible passages used by Nisaburi, who seems to have taken them from 'Ali Tabari and who, moreover, appeared earlier than the scholars cited by Goldziher.

[8] Graf, *OL*, 1927, 7, p. 513.

[9] See Bruce M. Metzger, *The Text of the New Testament*, pp. 22-3.

[10] See al-Kindi, notes 150 and 160.

[11] Jahiz, p. 689-690, n. 2.

[12] Nöldeke, *DL*, 1924, 1, p. 24; see Tabari, parag. EB.

[13] Nöldeke, *DL*, 1924, 1, pp. 23-4.

[14] Tabari, parag. EP, n. 202; EV, n. 215; (n. 213).

[15] Tabari, notes 86, 87, 144, 145, 153.

[16] Tabari, parag. EY.

[17] Tabari, parags. EB and GL.

[18] Nöldeke, *DL*, 1924, 1, p. 24; Tabari, parags. ED and GL.

[19] Tabari, parag. GY.

[20] Tabari, parag. AF.

[21] Prophetic witness: Leo, parags. G and AH; John of Damascus, parag. C; Timothy, parag. AM; Religious Dialogue, parags. K and Z. Absence of Miracles: John of Damascus, parags. AH-AK; Timothy, parag. AU; Religious Dialogue, parag. Y; al-Kindi, parags. CA, CC and CE. No Prophet After Jesus: Timothy, parag. AZ; (al-Kindi, parag. EG).

[22] Cf. al-Kindi, parag. CC and Mingana, p. 556.

[23] Tabari, parags. AJ and AK.

[24] Timothy, parag. CA; Tabari, parag. DY.

[25] Leo, parag. BC; Timothy, parag. AV; Tabari, parag. EQ.

[26] Leo, parags. P and Q; Timothy, parags. AN-AP; Tabari, parags. GC-GF.

[27] Tabari, n. 227.

[28] Tabari, parags. DJ and DS.

THE BOOK OF RELIGION
AND EMPIRE
translated and edited
by A. Mingana

ISLAMIC APOLOGY

SYRIAN CONVERT
TO ISLAM
'Ali Tabari
c. 855 A.D.

INTRODUCTION

I.

THE present work may possibly attract the attention of some scholars and students of comparative religion. It is a semi-official defence of Islam written at the command, with the assistance and in the court of the Caliph Mutawakkil (A.D. 847-861); the adversaries more frequently attacked are the Christians, who, thanks to their numerical strength, to the vigilance of the Eastern-Syrian Patriarchs residing in Baghdad, and to the influence of a successive series of court-physicians, were the strongest opponents of the State religion at the time of the 'Abbasid dynasty; in the second rank come Jews, Hindus, Buddhists and Parsees, who, however, are more severely handled. The work is also likely to throw a great light on the religious tendencies of Muhammadanism at the time of its greatest expansion and orthodoxy.

It is not our intention to give here a synopsis of the general plan adopted in the execution of the work, nor to express an opinion on its intrinsic merits and demerits.[1] We leave the reader to draw his own conclusions on the subject; but in order to help him in this task we have ventured to add a few short notes to some statements which, to use a sentence of the author's, not two learned men can regard as irrefragable.

The second half of the eighth and the first half of the ninth centuries were, owing to the somewhat tolerant attitude of the Caliphs of Baghdad, marked by the first serious shock of opinion between Christians and Muslims. It was at this time that, in answer to certain objections advanced by the Christians, the ingenuity of the Muslim writers gathered from scattered materials and purely oral sources the weapons which in the same field of controversy would place them on even terms with their seemingly more favored opponents. We do not believe that the imposing number of Muhammad's miracles and prophecies (with which we should compare Qur'an 29:49; 13:27-30; 17:92-97) would have been so skillfully elaborated at so late a date as the eighth century, if their compilers had not been forced so to act by ready adversaries who had made the subject of thaumaturgy a special point in their polemics against them. We have here and there isolated cases of public discussions before this period. The earliest and most important record seems to be the colloquy which took place in Syria between the Arab generals and the Monophysite Patriarch of Antioch, John I., in the eighteenth year of the Hagira, Sunday, 9th May, A.D. 639).[2] The Syriac text of this document has been published by F. Nau,[3] and we have given a summary of it in the *Journal of the Manchester Egyptian and Oriental Society* (1916, p. 35 sqq.). On the other hand, we know nothing about the discussion between the Umayyad 'Abdul-Malik b. Marwan (A.D. 692-705) and Ibrahim, son of Rahib (monk) Tabarani.[4]

The outcome of the discussion in the second half of the eighth century is known, on the Christian side, by the Syriac writings of Timothy, Patriarch of the East Syrian Church (A.D. 780-823). In one of his letters[5] he records, by way of question and answer, the gist of the public discussion that he had before the Caliph Mahdi about A.D. 783. At the end of the same century Abu Nuh of Anbar, the secretary of the Muslim Governor of Mosul, wrote a refutation of the Qur'an, which Ebed Jesus of Nisibis[6] has registered in his *Catalogue*, compiled in A.D. 1298. Assemani mentions a work entitled *Discussion between the monk Abu Karah and the Commander of the Faithful*,[7] and Steinschneider,[8] who has included it in his book as No. 64, believes that this Commander of the Faithful was the Caliph Ma'mun (A.D. 813-833). This treatise does not seem, however, to be of importance, and it is even possible that it consists of a record by an author of a later date of an event which had taken place several decades earlier; and the same may be said of the above discussion between b. Marwan and Tabarani.

During the reign of Ma'mun, in whose time the edict against the dogma of the eternity of the Qur'an was issued, the better-known *Apology of Christianity* by Kindi saw the light. The exhaustive study of W. Muir[9] renders it unnecessary for us to enter into detail concerning this work, but it would be useful here to remark that the present defence seems to be an attempt to refute lucubrations similar to those of Timothy or Kindi at an interval of some twenty-five to thirty years. The epithet "Garcemite," however, that the author applies to his adversary, points to a man living or born in the region of Mosul or that of the two Zabs, the word used by the author in this connection being *Jurmukani* (cf. p. 618).

Facing the Muslim side, it is worth noticing that the author of the present Defence speaks of some polemical dissertations which in our days seem to be lost (p. 3). It would be interesting also to have more details about the pamphlet entitled *Answer to Christians* by 'Amr b. Bahr al-Jahiz,[10] the celebrated Mu'tazili writer who died A.D. 869; it is recorded by Hajji Khalifa in his Bibliographical Dictionary,[11] and by Steinschneider;[12] and we have no reliable information concerning the controversial dissertation of Abu 'Isa Muhammad al-Warraq, which occasioned an answer by the monophysite Yahya b. 'Adi of Takrit,[13] who died in A.D. 974. Without dilating on the numerous but not very instructive publications of later generations we may, therefore, venture to assert that the present work, apart from its intrinsic value, is in order of date one of the most ancient.

The historical environment which gave birth to the present Defence is not too complex. The period of religious toleration referred to above was briskly changed by Mutawakkil into an era of recrudescence of Islamic tendencies. This Caliph, whom Bar Hebraeus calls "a hater of Christians,"[14] ordered that all churches built since the commencement of Islam should be demolished, and forbade the employment of Christians in government offices and the display of crosses on Palm Sunday; he also gave orders that wooden figures of demons should be fixed on their doors, that they should wear yellow cowls and a zonarion round the waist, that they should ride saddles with wooden stirrups with two globes behind the saddle, that the men's clothes should have inserted a couple of patches of color different from that of the clothes themselves, each patch to be four inches wide, and the two patches were also to be of different color. Any Christian woman who went out of doors was to wear a yellow tunic without band.[15] Under these circumstances, it is highly creditable to the author not to have employed a stringent style in his dealings with the "members of the protected cults" (*dhimmis:* said mostly of Jews and Christians). On the other hand, his propensity to flatter is explicable by the pride of Mutawakkil, who was pleased to be described as "the shadow of God spread between Him and His creation,"[16] or "the rope extended between God and His servants."[17]

The promulgation of the edict of the above persecution is ascribed by Tabari to 235/849. From the general tenor of the present Defence it is clear, however, that either the persecution had not yet begun when the work was written, or that the work was edited some years after the edict of the persecution was issued, i.e., at a time when, owing to the unpopularity of its enactments, or to the changed attitude of the Caliph himself, it had reached the stage of a slow and natural death. The first hypothesis seems to be irreconcilable with the author's statement on p. 138 [deleted] that 867 years had passed since the Messiah. This appears to be a chronological error, as al-Mutawakkil was murdered in 861. The second would require, as events moved in the palaces of the caliphs,[18] a year not far remote from A.D. 855, or six years after the promulgation of the edict of the persecution. This date has the advantage of harmonizing with the author's statement on p. 138.

II.

Since this Defence represents the first published work of 'Ali Tabari, it will be useful to gather all the available information concerning his life and his works. Unfortunately, historical references to him found in writers of later date are scanty and confused. The very same surname of his father, the Syriac vocable *Rabban*, has been read *Zain, Zail, Rain,* etc., by many historians, and this mistake, which can easily be accounted for by the use of early and undotted Arabic letters on the part of Muslim writers, who hardly knew any other Semitic language besides Arabic, has been repeated by some well-known Arabists, in spite of the clear explanation given to it by the author himself in his medical work entitled *Kunnash*. This last Syriac word, or its Arabic equivalent *Jami'*, was adopted by many Christian and Muslim physicians as constituting the best title to be given to their "complete" repertory of Greco-Oriental physiology and therapeutics or general pathology. Such is the title of two works by John b. Serapion, one by George b. Bokhtisho',one by the priest Aaron, one by Isaac b. Hunain, one by Sahir, one by Razi, one by Theodore, etc.[19]

The mention made of Tabari by the Islamic authorities may be summarized as follows:

1. *The General Historians.* The better known compatriot of our Tabari, i.e., the famous historian Muhammad Tabari, mentions the author four times in his *Annales*, under the name: 'Ali b. Rabban, the Christian writer (see 3, 2, 1276-1277; ibid. 1283; ibid. 1293, edit. De Goeje), all in connection with Maziar of Tabaristan; and Mas'udi in his *Muruj* (viii, 326, edit. B. de Meynard) gives a quotation from him describing a bird called *Kikam*.

2. *Fihrist* (Flügel, p. 296).[20] " 'Ali b. Zail,[21] [with a Lam] Abul-Hasan

'Ali b. Sahl at-Tabari. He wrote to Maziar b. Qaran. When he became a Muslim at the hands of Mu'tasim, the latter drew him near to
himself, and his merits became known in the court. Then Mutawakkil
bestowed honor upon him and made him of the number of his table-
guests. He was a literary man and his books are: *Paradise of Medicine;
Gift to the Kings; The Kunnash; Utility of Food, Drink and Medicinal
Herbs.*" The author of the *Fihrist*, who was writing about 120 years
after the death of Tabari. seems to have distinguished him from 'Ali b.
Rain, "the Christian" whom he mentions on p. 316[22] as author of a
book on *Literature and Proverbs According to Persians, Greeks and Arabs.* In reality this 'Ali appears to be identical with the author of this
Defence. Further, is not the *Kunnash* the same work as that entitled
Paradise of Medicine? We shall presently see that this book is preserved in some public libraries as having both titles. The British
Museum MS.[23] expressly states, "This is the index of the chapters of
the *Kunnash* of 'Ali b. Rabban, which is entitled *Paradise of Medicine*."

3. *Ibn al-Kifti* (edit. Lippert, 1913, p. 231). " 'Ali b. Zain[24] at-Tabari,
abul-Hasan the physician. He excelled in the medical science, and was
at the service of the governors of Tabaristan. He studied philosophy
and devoted himself to natural science. After an insurrection which
took place in Tabaristan, he went to Ray, where he became tutor to
Muhammad b. Zakaria' ar-Razi, who learned much from him. Thence
he repaired to Samarra where he settled and wrote his *Kunnash*
entitled *Paradise of Medicine*... He is mentioned by Muhammad Ishaq
an-Nadim in his book, in which he says: " 'Abdul-Hasan 'Ali b. Zain,
who is Sahl at-Tabari. Zain is the name of Sahl, because he was a
Rabbi to the Jews." This last information is erroneous, because the
author of the *Fihrist* clearly states that the father of Tabari was a
Christian (cf. here pp. 19, 50); further, the reading of "Zain" instead of
"Rabban" in this quotation is evidently an error of the copyist, because
it is the word "Rabban" and not "Zain" which means *Rabbi.*

4. *Ibn Abi Usaibi'ah* (edit. of the press of Wahab, 1882, p. 309). "Ibn
Rabban at-Tabari, who is abul-Hasan, 'Ali b. Sahl, b. Rabban at-Tabari." Ibn Nadim of Baghdad says (that his name was) Rabl, with a

Lam, and relates about him as follows: "He was the writer of Maziar b. Qaran; when he became Muslim at the hands of Mu'tasim, the latter drew him near to himself, and his merits became known in the court. Then the Caliph Mutawakkil made him of the number of his table-guests. He was a literary man and he instructed Razi in the medical profession. He was born and brought up in Tabaristan. Among his sayings is the following: 'An ignorant physician is liable to death.' Ibn Rabban at-Tabari has among other books: *Paradise of Medicine...; Gentleness of Life; Gift to the Kings; The Kunnash; Utility of Food, Drink and Medicinal Herbs; Preservation of Health; Enchantment; Scarification; Preparation of Food.*"

5. *Yaqut* reports in his geographical dictionary (edit. Wüstenfeld, ii, 608): "Something like the above narration has been recorded by 'Ali b. Zain at-Tabari, the writer of Maziar. He had acquired medicine and has works on many subjects." We consulted Yaqut's *Dictionary of Learned Men*, recently edited by D. S. Margoliouth, but were unable to find in it any reference to our author; nor is there any mention of him in Sam'ani's *Ansab*, an introduction to which was written in 1912 by the same scholar.

6. *Ibn Khallikan* (life, 717, 8, p. 75 of Wüstenfeld's edit.) writes about Razi the celebrated physician: "He studied medicine under the physician abul-Hasan 'Ali b. Zain at-Tabari, who has well-known works such as the *Paradise of Medicine*. He was first a Christian, then he became a Muslim."

7. Far more important is the following historical notice transmitted by the author himself in his work *Paradise of Medicine*[25] above mentioned: "My father was one of the writers of Marw, and one of the most esteemed and learned men in it. He had a remarkable zeal for the acquisition of piety and the acquaintanceship of those who excelled in it. He was a constant reader of books of medicine and philosophy, and he preferred medicine to the profession of his fathers. His aim in it was not vainglory nor money, but esteem and consideration. He was for that surnamed *Rabban*, which means 'our master' and 'our teach-

er.' "

8. In the MS. containing the present Defence, the first leaf, which has begun to fade, has been transcribed afresh by a sixteenth century hand with the following historical note: "This (MS.) has been transcribed from the autograph of the author. 'Ali b. Zain, the writer of this book — may God have mercy on him — says, 'My father was a writer to Maziar, the master of Tabaristan.' When Mu'tasim took Maziar at the hand of 'Abdullah b. Tahir, ('Ali) asked for safety, and then he became one of the table-guests of the Caliph Mutawakkil 'ala Allah, and beatitude was ascribed to him. He became an eminent scholar, a traditionist and a man of many works. The book has been transcribed from the autograph of its author, which fact will also be mentioned at the end of the work. It is an excellent book, the merit of which is known only by the man who studies it with care."

In addition to all these references it should be noted that the medical works of Tabari are frequently quoted or referred to in books of a later date, under the name "Tabari." See Badr ad-Din Qalanisi's *Qarabadin* (MS. 435 in the John Rylands Library; passim) and Nafis Kirmani's Commentary on Najib ad-Din Samarqandi's *Ashab wa 'Alamat*, where he is sometimes given his full name: 'Ali b. Zain Tabari (see fol. 402a, MS. 221 of the John Rylands Library).

Finally we should record the fact that at the bottom of the first page the titles of the following three chapters of a work by the author are transcribed apparently from an autograph: on the three denominations, the Melkites, the Jacobites and the Nestorians (p. 110); on the sentences differently worded by the Apostles (p. 126); on the ambiguous letters wherewith they have argued in favor of their laws (p. 131). The work alluded to seems to have been the *Book of Replies to Christians* mentioned on pp. 632 and 638, below.

These are the original notices about the author, who at the beginning of his Defence calls himself "freedman" of the Caliph Mutawakkil. This might more appropriately be referred to Mu'tasim (A.D. 833-841), in whose time Maziar b. Qaran b. Wandahormiz of Tabaristan was finally defeated by 'Abdullah b. Tahir,[26] and who, according to Bar Hebraeus, freed at his death-bed eight thousand slaves bought with his money.[27]

That the writer was an eminent physician and moralist is established by the above quotations. He was also the nephew of the Syrian doctor, Abu Zakkar Yahya b. Nu'man, whom he mentions by name, and to whom he attributes a polemical work lost in our days.[28] If abu Zakkar is the same man as Zakariya' mentioned by Bar Bahlul in his Syriac lexicon and identified by some critics with abu Yahya al-Marwazi — an identification which seems to us very doubtful — the year of his death should be ascribed to the second quarter of the first half of the ninth century, because the author of this Defence speaks of him in terms which suggested that he lived shortly before the final edition of this book. Confusion between physicians and moralists of the ninth century is frequent in the works of a later date, and the time has not yet come to speak of them in an irrefragable manner. If we were allowed to add a remark to the identification of Zakariya with abu Yahya al-Marwazi,[29] we would say that an identification with abu Zakariya' Yahya b. Masuwaih,[30] the physician of the Caliphs Ma'mun, Mu'tasim, Wathiq and Mutawakkil, would be in more harmony with the general course of events. On the one hand, the name given to him by the author does not conflict with this surmise, and on the other hand, the year of his death commonly believed to have been A.D. 854-855 would be in consonance with the text of our Defence, written certainly between 847 and 861, and probably in 855.

III.

THE manuscript which contains the text of this Defence is, so far as we are aware, unique. It is numbered 631 in the Crawford collection of the John Rylands Library, measures 210 x 127 mm. and consists of 73 leaves of paper, with 19 lines to the page. The first leaf, which, as stated above, had begun to fade, has been written afresh by a sixteenth-century hand. If the scribe's statement is correct — and we have no reason to question it — the MS. is a transcript from the author's autograph. This appears in the note translated above, which refers us to the colophon at the end of the MS. Unfortunately, this colophon cannot be deciphered in its totality. The sentences which can be read with safety may be translated as follows:

"The book was finished — and glory and praise be to God — on the morning of Friday 4 Muharram of the year six hundred and sixteen — may God make good its beginning! Has copied it out for himself the servant soliciting the mercy and the forgiveness of the Almighty God: 'Abdul-Hamid b. Husain b. Bashik, who thanks the Almighty God for His favors and blesses His Prophet, our Master Muhammad, with his family and companions and gives them peace forever."

The date A.H. 616 (A.D. 1219) is also found on the first page, written by the sixteenth-century hand, while at the bottom of the last page the following words are read in a thirteenth-century hand: "I said This is the last work copied by Jamal ud-Din, who died shortly after he had finished it." Can this Jamal ud-Din be identified with the above 'Abdul-Hamid?

On folios 1a, 19b and 59b, marginal notes dated 1148/1735; 1149/1736 bear the name of a owner, a certain Musa al-Maulawi. It is evidently this man who has added a few philological and historical notes on the narrow margins of the book, and vocalized some difficult words. These stray notes are the only data that we possess as to the provenance of the MS.,[31] which was apparently written in Baghdad forty years before its sack by the hordes of Hulaku. From the footnotes of pp. 97, 106, 131, etc., and from some passages of the text, it would appear that the MS. is a transcript from a first or rough draft made by the author, but it is possible to admit that some of these passages were marginal notes which have been misplaced by the copyist.

The translation given in the present volume preserves the Arabic coloring of the original, but contains a few explanatory words not found in the text and safeguards the interests of a general reader not necessarily an Arabist. We have inserted some footnotes to elucidate difficult points and have compared the historical and traditional sayings reported by the author with the following authorities:

Buk.   The *Sahih* of Bukhari; the edition of Cairo, A.H. 1313, in nine volumes.

Hish.   Ibn Hisham's *Life of the Prophet;* edition of Cairo, A.H. 1332, by Tahtawi in three volumes.

I.S.   The *Tabaqat* of Ibn Sa'd, edited at Leyden under the direction of E. Sachau, in seven volumes.

Musl.   The *Sahih* of Muslim; edition of Cairo, A.H. 1327, in two volumes.

Musn.   *Musnad* of Ahmad b. Hanbal; edition of Cairo, A.H. 1313, in six volumes.

Tab.   The *Annals of Tabari;* edited at Leyden under the direction of De Goeje, in fifteen volumes.

Taj.   *Taj al-'Arus.* The Arabic dictionary, edition of Cairo, in ten volumes.

Had we extended our comparisons to all the traditional books, we should have swollen the footnotes without appreciable advantage.

Other historians and theologians are quoted without abbreviations and with full reference to the edition which we have used.

It must not be inferred that our comparative apparatus implies that the same tradition is registered *verbatim* by the writers referred to in the footnote. It is a well-known fact that an identical tradition is sometimes so confusedly worded by the authors of the ninth century that the readers can scarcely recognize its extent and purpose, and more specially the occasions and circumstances which gave birth to it. As to the meager historical value of this tardy *Hadith*, the reader should consult the recent and well-known publications of Professors Margoliouth, Goldziher, Wensinck, Snouck, Hurgronje and Lammens, in the light of which many lucubrations by ancient critics have become antiquated.

With regard to the Bible quotations found in the book, since the author is mostly dependent only on the Syriac version, we have collated his translation with the Peshitta. This collation is complete so far as the Pentateuch is concerned, but for the rest of the sacred Books a note has been added only in case of a mistranslation or misquotation.[32]

About the author's sources nothing can be stated with any degree of certitude. On the one hand, the historical details in the section dealing with the Prophet and the orthodox caliphs, are often preceded by the formulae "It has come to our knowledge," "It has been related," which may equally point to oral traditions and to written sources. On the other hand, there is no reason for denying the probability that Tabari was in the privileged position of having ready access to the archives and library of the Court in which, it is to be presumed, the few bio-graphical works (most of which are now lost) preceding the present Defence, were to be found. On p. 582 the author is speaking of works written from the time of the appearance of Islam down to his own day, and now and then he endeavors to furnish important details of circum-stantial evidences; so on p. 594 he states, in connection with a miracle of the Prophet, that the descendants of the man to whom the wolf spoke, were in his own time known by the epithet "the children of the man to whom the wolf spoke."

Concerning a Biblical version quoted by the author on pp. 615, 628, and 630 and attributed to him by a certain Marcus the *tarjaman*, we could find no definite traces. From the *Fihrist* (pp. 23-24) we know that the Old and New Testaments were translated into Arabic long before the tenth Christian century, but we have no reason to identify the problematic Marcus Ya'qubi called Badawi, therein mentioned as an author of an Arabic book, with Marcus the *tarjaman* spoken of in the present Defence. On p. 306 the *Fihrist* mentions an earlier but still more problematic Marcus.

On the authority of *Cod. Vat. Arab.*, 13, of the end of the eighth century, we may state that an Arabic Version of the Gospels was in existence about A.D. 750 (cf. Scholz's *Krit. Reis.*, 118 seq., and Guidi's *Ev.*, p. 8). Further, the historian Michael the Syrian (edit. Chabot, ii, p. 431) attributes an Arabic translation of the Gospels to the Christian Arabs assembled at the above public discussion which took place in Syria in A.D. 639.[33] This, if we mistake not, is the oldest date to which any Christian historian has ascribed the existence of an Arabic Version of the Gospels, but great importance should not be attached to a mere historical tradition without subsequent data of a concrete and positive order.[34]

We believe that the problem of "Marcus, the translator," may be satisfactorily solved in the following manner: in the still unpublished repertory of the East Syrian exegesis, entitled *Gannath Bussamé*,[35] a tradition is registered to the effect that the Hebrew text of the Old Testament was translated into the Syriac Peshitta of our days by the disciple Mark, probably Mark the evangelist himself. There is no necessity, therefore, to resort to the hypothesis that the author was dependent in his scriptural quotations upon a pre-existent Arabic Version of the Bible. The Syriac statement of the *Gannath* may be translated as follows:

> Some people report that Mark himself translated the Old Testament from Hebrew into Syriac, and that he presented his translation to James, the brother of our Lord, and to the Apostles, who appended their approbation to it and gave it to the inhabitants of Syria.

The above tradition had evidently gained an unchallenged credit in the Christian and Muslim circles of the middle of the ninth century.

It is a pleasing duty to express here my sincerest thanks to my colleague, Dr. H. Guppy, the chief librarian of the John Rylands Library, for many good suggestions and for his unfailing kindness in providing the necessary research material to which all the merits of the present work are to be attributed; and to my friend, Prof. D. S. Margoliouth ofOxford for help in the deciphering of some Arabic words which had almost completely faded away.

JOHN RYLANDS LIBRARY,
27th June, 1922.

I.

PROLOGUE.

IN THE NAME OF GOD THE COMPASSIONATE AND THE MERCIFUL WHOSE ASSISTANCE WE SOLICIT:

(A) SAYS 'Ali son of Rabban Tabari, the freedman of the Commander of the Faithful: Praise be to God for the religion of Islam which whoso embraces shall be successful, whoso maintains shall be rightly guided, whoso upholds shall be saved, and whoso impugns shall perish. It is by it that the Creator has been made known; it is for it that nations are craving and souls have longed; it is by it that hope is fulfilled sooner or later, because it is the living light and the crossing to the eternal abode of perfect happiness in which there is no grief nor illusion. God, the Most High, has made us of the number of the people of the *Sunnah*, and has caused us to avoid falsehood and the injuries it brings to its adherents; God is indeed to be praised and blessed, and there is no end to His Kingdom, and nobody can change His words. He is the Benefactor and the Wise who has revealed the truth and enlightened it, and has created His servants, sent His Apostle, His Beloved and His Friend, to those who were in doubt about Him, calling them to the eternal victory and the shining light.

(B) When the hour came and was near, God, the Most High, sent our prophet, Muhammad — may God bless and save him — to all creatures, as preacher, warner and illuminating lamp. [36] He proclaimed the order of his Lord, and overawed his enemies into respect and fear by persuasion and dissuasion and by imparting to them the knowledge of a thorough reformation. He exhorted to Heaven and its beatitude and prevented from being unmindful of hell and its fire. He conveyed on the part of God the revelation which the angel Gabriel communicated to him and to which falsehood shall not come from before it nor from behind it. [37] He did not set aside any truth that the prophets had brought forth before him, but confirmed and corroborated it and ordered belief in them and praises in favor of the first and last of them.

(C) God said in His perspicuous book. "Say, We believe in God, and what has been revealed to us and what has been revealed to Abraham and Ishmael and Isaac and Jacob and the Tribes and what was brought to Moses and Jesus and what was brought unto the Prophets from their Lord; we will not distinguish between any one of them, and unto Him are we resigned." (Qur'an 2:130)

(D) And He said: "The Apostle believed in what has been sent down to him from his Lord, and the believers all believed on God and His angels and His Books and His Apostles. We make no difference between any of his Apostles" — and the rest of the verse (Qur'an 2:285). And about those who associate gods with God, or give Him a companion, He said:

(E) "Say, He is God alone, God the Eternal; he begets not, and is not begotten, nor is there like unto Him anyone." (Qur'an 112:1-4) And He said:

(F) "Say, O ye people of the Book, come to a word laid down plainly between us and you, that we will not serve other than God, nor associate aught with Him, nor take each other for lords rather than God. But if they return back, then say, Bear witness that we are resigned." (Qur'an 3:57) And He said:

(G) "Is he who has laid down his foundation upon the fear of God

and His goodwill better, or he who has laid his foundation on a crum-
bling wall of sand, which crumbles away with him into the fire of hell?
But God guides not a people who do wrong." (Qur'an 9:110)

(H) It is to these points that his proclamations were directed, it is on
them that he founded the edifice of his call, and it is with them that he
started the legislation of his religion and the stipulations of his truth
which the polytheists among the Arabs and the holders of the inspired
book have denied. They have hidden his name and changed his portrait found in the Books of their prophets — peace be with them.[38] I
shall demonstrate this, disclose its secret and withdraw the veil from it,
in order that the reader may see it clearly and increase his conviction
and his joy in the religion of Islam. In that I shall tread a path more
direct and advantageous than that opened by some other writers of
books on this subject. Some of them have shortened, curtailed and
contracted their argument and have not explained it satisfactorily; some
of them have argued in poetry against the *People of the Book* and in
ignorance of their Books; and some of them have crammed the two
faces of their books with addresses to Muslims rather than to polytheists, then have put forth their proofs in a most elaborate and difficult
discourse. The adversary would be right if he wished to say that these
writers resembled a collector of firewood by night, who indiscriminately
picks up small and big pieces, or a person carried away in a torment,
who suddenly shouts out unpleasant or refined phrases; and that that
with which they argued was not to demonstrate but to conceal, not to
enlighten but to blind, not to lessen difficulty but to increase it. He
who writes a book on this high, illuminating and enlightening subject
which involves a general utility to adherents to all religions, has to
make it comprehensible and easy; has to discuss and compete with his
adversary and not to bully and offend him; he is to be intelligible and
not obscure; courteous and not abusive; he is to use indulgence, to
embellish the [tenor of his speech][39] by making it lucid, and to bring
forth proofs and replies which, when addressed [to the adversary],[39]
should cause him to abandon his religious claim and his faith. If he
does that to him, he will ride on him, hit him with his arrow and lead
him with his bridle.

(I) I have aimed at this by help of the Most High God and have made the meanings of my sentences easy, in order that the reader may understand them and not be in doubt. I did not leave the members of the protected cults any argument, any difficult question, any contentious point, that I have not mentioned and then refuted and solved by the succor and assistance of God and by the blessing of His Caliph, the Imam Ja'far al-Mutawakkil 'ala-Allah, Commander of the Faithful — may God prolong his life — who guided me and made me profit by words heard from him. He is in earnest and eager that such books should be spread and perpetuated in order to strengthen the motives of credibility of the Faith, to make its proofs triumph and to convince of his merit therein those who ignore it and do not recognize how God has singled out Islam and its followers in His time and renewed for them His benefits; nor how, through the gentleness of His administration, He has made Himself felt by them in multiplying, increasing and honoring them.

(J) I have found that the people who have contradicted Islam have done so for four reasons: *firstly*, because of doubts about the history of the Prophet — may God bless and save him; *secondly*, because of disdain and egregious insolence; *thirdly*, because of tradition and custom; *fourthly*, because of folly and stupidity. By my life, had they discerned and grasped the truth of that history, they would not have rejected it. And since they have sought what is with God, by contradicting the command of God, we must needs to prove this history to them, expel doubt from them and explain to them the origins and the subdivisions of stories, their causes and their courses and the way to discern their veracity from their falsehood and the reasons through which and for which people have accepted their prophets and responded to their missionaries. We shall next compare our story with theirs, the men who transmitted ours to us with those who handed down theirs to them; if the proofs that we have for believing in our Prophet are the same as those they possess for believing in theirs, they will have no excuse before God and before their own conscience for disbelieving in our Prophet, though believing in theirs, because if two opponents bring forth the same evidence to establish certain claim, they have both the same right to it, and what is due to one must necessarily be due to the other.

II.

ON THE DIFFERENT FORMS OF STORIES AND COMMON AGREEMENTS.

(K) EVERY story is of two kinds; it is either true or false. It has, also, three tenses; it is either past, or present, or future. Certain stories may be sometimes true and sometimes false; as if you would say: "Such and such a man came or went"; this may be true and may also be false. Some stories are true at all times, past and future, gone or to come, because they are of the domain of the clear, universal and common fact; as if one would say: "The firmament has finished its diurnal rotations or it will finish it tomorrow"; or if somebody says: "The sun rose yesterday, or will rise next year"; or if he says: "The majority of the quadrupeds give milk in bringing forth"; or "The majority of birds lay after they have been covered and hatch when they have laid." These and similar examples constitute a fact, true in its totality, at all times and are of the category of the first and commonest agreement.

(L) Some stories are wholly false at all times, past or future, as if one would say: "This has more light than the sun and is sweeter than honey; this horse is swifter than lightening or more nimble than a tick"; or if he says: "All people gathered together so that none was left"; or, "Such and such a man is the best of men and is more learned than all of them; has a precious object worth everything; his country is the most fertile of all the countries created by God." This and similar kinds of speech are wholly false, but they are used by the majority of mankind in their figurative style and are not considered as wrong.

(M) After this first and commonest agreement that I have mentioned, there is a second common agreement which involves less universality and generality; such is the story of Adam and Eve, and of their being the parents of mankind. This is true for us in an indubitable manner, because of the credence attributed to it by the majority of mankind and of the testimony borne by the prophets to its truth; but it is considered as lie and falsehood by many people, such as the Indians, Sabeans and the like.

(N) After this second common agreement, there is a third common agreement which involves less generality and universality; such is the story of the Greeks, the Indians and the Chinese; because although most people who narrate it are from the low and common class, yet it is true and indubitable, because of the constant agreement and the numerous testimonies that it possesses.

(O) After this third agreement, there is a fourth one which involves less generality and universality; such is the story of the appearance of Alexander, of the Tababi'ah and of the King Jam and the like; it is accepted as true, because of the great number of people who believe in it; but people who believe in the story of the above-mentioned countries are more numerous than those who believe in the story of the Tababi'ah and Alexander.

(P) A fifth common agreement is transmitted to one another by people who adhere to it from a long period, like the story of the Buddhists, *Zindiks*[40] and Magians; it is true and indubitable to them, but it is an unmistakable falsity to us; it began with juggleries and quibbles; then through tradition and heredity, habit and custom, it became to them a religion.

(Q) That it is a characteristic note of stories to lay easily hold upon mind and imagination is true and undeniable. There are indeed stories which by their queerness please the hearer, whose face in listening to them blushes with blood and whose eyes shed tears and blink fast from immoderate laughter. Some of them expel the tears of the hearer, render his body frigid and cause the radiance of his face to droop; such is the news of unhappy and disastrous events. Some of them excite the hearer to munificence and make him generous to the one who is asking for help and soliciting favor; such is the case of the glorification of generous people and the description of praises and rewards which in exchange for their liberality they receive in this world and in the world to come. Some of them make the hearer avaricious and turn him away from generosity; such is the news of a man whose extravagance has reduced to poverty and constrained to penury and misery. Some of them incite him to anger and irritation and make him stretch his hand to strike and his tongue to disapprove. Some of them kindle his passion, move him and take possession of his eager desires; such is the record of chaste and attractive maidens and the bestowal of encomium on their good qualities, their fragrance, the smoothness of their touch and the beauty of their smile; especially when this record is adorned with gems of melodies which excite to emotion and infatuation.

(R) Some of them incite people to rush into dreadful things and to put their life in danger and that at an interval of more than a thousand years after the death of the first narrator; such is the case of what we are told of the Buddhists of India and of Magians and the like. Some of the Indians consume themselves with different kinds of burning; some of them expose their bodies to birds of prey, that they may eat it; some of them wander about like madmen in a waterless desert in order that they may perish therein; some of them throw themselves from a high mountain and fall upon a tree of iron set up with edged ramifications as sharp as swords and spears — out of zeal for facts handed down to them by some insolent liars who took them from some astute deceivers.

(S) I mentioned these facts in order that the reader may know that he ought to avoid them and to flee from them towards the harbors of wisdom and the ports of thought and consideration. They are indeed most detrimental to the souls, which they affect more swiftly than deadly arrows and vehement passions. They enter the heart from two doors, the deceitfulness and delusiveness of which are great on account of fanciful and unreal conceptions; these are the two senses of hearing and vision, by means of which the insinuations of historical events are grasped. The sense of vision makes sometimes a single object appear as two and a crooked object as straight, like poles in rivers; it makes sometimes a non-existent object as existent, as in illusion and mirage. As to hearing, sometimes one believes a murmuring of the wind to be the thunder and a simple imitation of a dog, a lion and a ring-dove to be the actual whining, or roaring or cooing.

III.

DIRECTIONS FOR THE VERIFICATION OF STORIES:

(T) I HAVE first spoken of the division of stories and of the strange way in which they impress soul and body through the accidents and happenings of the past. Now what nations have agreed to in their argumentation and considered as thorough investigation and caution is that when someone is claiming right, or telling a certain story, if he brings two or three men endowed with sound judgment and discrimination, truth is established and suspicion and doubt are expelled from the judge and the criminal. As to the history of the prophets, its issues being such as to lead to heaven or to hell, we will not be satisfied with two witnesses, nor with an oath, nor with the avowal of a whole community, if account is not taken of the testimonies of truth and the analogical evidences that I shall set forth below.

(U) We have already seen that communities great in number, exalted in rank and renowned in men of high intellectual and mental acumen bear witness to all the claims laid by many astute liars, as in the case of the *Zindiks* and the Magians. This happens either through tradition and habit, as we have shown, or through stupidity and chicanery, or through constraint and compulsion (as) this Zoroaster, the pseudo-prophet of the Magians did. He did not cease to wait repeatedly upon King Bishtasaf until he reached him, and then he threw the seed of his false suggestions into his breast; next, he did not cease to circumvent him by the mention of God and his cult and to turn round him on all

575

sides in order to remove his refractoriness, until he changed his belief and bent him to his opinions. Then he showed him the Dualism which in his mind made good before his eyes the intercourse with mothers and daughters and the eating of filthy and stinking muck; after that it was the monarch who constrained the inhabitants of his kingdom to his belief.

(V) Mani did similarly. He appeared at a time in which there were generally two religions: Christianism and Magianism. He deceived the Christians by telling them that he was the messenger of the Christ — peace be with Him — and circumvented the Magians by agreeing with them to the two principles.

(W) After having seen that there is a common agreement such as this and another one such as that found in Islam, it becomes evident that the acceptance of every common agreement is wrong, and the rejection of every common agreement is an error and that the common agreement is not sufficient by itself to prove the veracity of a prophetic office, which, indeed, needs signs and marks of truth,[41] such as God has accumulated in the case of the Prophet[42] — may God bless and save him. He who intends to verify historical events such as these, or to redress them, has therefore to investigate the story that comes to his knowledge and to examine its purpose and its defects; if he finds in it and with it something which would contradict it and make it a falsity, no other demonstration is wanted; such is the fact of Musailamah, the liar. When he claimed the prophetic office, he was asked about the Prophet — may God bless and save him — and he answered that he held him to be a speaker of the truth and believed in his prophetic office, but the Prophet — may God bless and save him — having been asked about him, denounced him. In the positive answer of Musailamah there was something to negative it; thus he gave the lie to himself and showed signs of contradiction and stupidity. It is for this reason that learned men have said that when a forger and false dogmatizer claims the prophetic office, God does not give him any respite till from his own tongue there flows the contradiction with which one might argue against those who believed in him; as God has done in the case of Zoroaster, Mani and the like, who contradicted, gainsaid themselves and became inconsistent.

(X) Zoroaster said that Hormiz — name of their god — was eternal, compassionate, omniscient and omnipotent; then he ascribed to him the description used by ignorant and stupid people, in saying that Satan was born of his mind and that God was unable to destroy him. Mani too, did similarly in saying first that God was eternal, omnipotent, incomparable, and in saying next that darkness was eternal and God would be overcome and His followers defeated and made captive. He who believes in him who gives the lie to himself is in great error.

(Y) So also are the Christians; having said at the beginning of their profession of faith: "We believe in God, Creator of everything visible and invisible," and then adding that the Christ is Creator and not created, contradiction appears in their utterances. And if we turn to the Books of their faith, we find that they are not in alignment with their belief, because all of them affirm that God is Creator and every-thing else is created. I have demonstrated this point in the part that follows this, where I have explained what concerns all Christian denom-inations, and where I have set forth one hundred and thirty arguments against them from the Books of the prophets, apart from rational demonstrations, illustrative examples and illuminating analogies. In this I have for aim their instruction, their guidance and the fulfillment of the duty of love and compassion that God has imposed upon some creatures towards one another. As to what concerns the Jews and others, I have treated it in the fourth part in a short but significant manner.

(Z) The one interesting point which is treated here and which contains refutations of a restricted dimension and easy, is that of the news reaching an intelligent man of sound judgment, who examines it carefully and turns it upside down thoroughly; if he finds in it and with it something which would impair its genuineness and contradict it, or if he finds it at variance with the religious books of the people, he will have no need of anything else for its refutation, and the manifestation of its falsity and groundlessness. When the truth is quickly found, the mind is relieved. This Mu'awiah did with a man from Basra who had

577

asked him for two thousand palm-tree trunks for the erection of his house. Mu'awiah questioned him: "What are the dimensions of thy house?" The man answered; "Two parasangs by two parasangs." Mu'awiah asked: "Is thy house in Basra, or is Basra in thy house?" The man answered: "My house is in Basra." Mu'awiah then said: "All Basra is less than two parasangs." In the story itself there was something testifying to its falsity.

(AA) Another man said while in Iraq "We were at Qumis,[43] in a garden situated on the western side of the town at a distance of three hundred parasangs." The man to whom this story was told said: "Therefore, we are now in the middle of that garden, since there is less than this distance between Qumis and Iraq."

(AB) Fakhir said also the same in his book where he prefers Qahtan to 'Adnan. After having mentioned that 'Adi, son of Hatim had a son, he added: "Where have you another one like him? His father told him to drive away strangers from his table, but the boy refused, saying: 'Father, command this to other than me.' " And Fakhir said: "The boy is a generous man, son of a generous father; and is a magnanimous man, son of a magnanimous father, who himself was son of a magnanimous father." Now I find that the fact itself contradicts his saying. The father had ordered the boy to drive away people from his table; this the boy disliked and rejected; the boy is, therefore, a generous man, son of an avaricious father, and a magnanimous man, son of an ungenerous father.

(AC) Let the man who wishes to verify the history of the prophets and inquire into it, act likewise; let him examine the testimonies of truth and the analogical evidences which I have found abundantly existent in ten different manners with regard to the Prophet — may God bless and save him — in such a way that they are not due to anyone but Christ — peace be with Him. I will explain this point and set it forth clearly, in order that the onlooker may know that he with whom these prerogatives are found, the prophetic office must necessarily be ascribed to him and a strict accountability to God rests with the man who disbelieves in him:

(AD) *First,* the Prophet — may God bless and save him — called to One, Eternal, Omniscient and Just God, whom no one can overcome and hurt; in that he was in conformity with all the prophets. *Second,* he was pious, upright, sincere and his laws and prescriptions are praiseworthy. *Third,* he — peace be with him — wrought clear miracles which only the prophets and the chosen ones of God can work. *Fourth,* he prophesied about events hidden from him, which took place during his lifetime. *Fifth,* he prophesied about many events concerning this world and its kingdoms, which were realized after his death. *Sixth,* he produced a book which by necessity and by undeniable arguments is a sign of prophetic office. *Seventh,* his victory over the nations is also by necessity and by undeniable arguments a manifest sign of prophetic office. *Eighth,* his missionaries who transmitted his history are most honest and righteous men, to whose like nobody can attribute lie and falsehood. *Ninth,* he — peace be with him — is the last of the prophets, and if he had not been sent, the prophecies of the prophets about him and about Ishmael — peace be with both of them — would have been vain. *Tenth,* the prophets — peace be with them — prophesied about him long before his appearance and described his mission, his country, his time and the submission of nations to him and of kings to his nation.

(AE) These are clear prerogatives and sufficient testimonies which if somebody can show forth as due to him, his arrow will not miss its butt, his truth will triumph and will have the right to be acknowledged; and he who throws them away and rejects them, his efforts would be fruitless and this world and that to come would be lost to him. I shall treat this point succinctly, chapter by chapter, and I shall show forth the testimonies of the prophets about it. I shall not restrict myself to one prophet, but I shall appeal to many of them; nor shall I be satisfied with one prophecy, but I shall bring forth more than sixty prophecies. What I most desire is that God should turn my effort to union and admonition, and to outlet from blindness to anyone who is not insolent and arrogant, nor obstinately set in folly and perverseness.

(AF) If we ask especially the Christians why they disbelieve in the Prophet — peace be with him — they would say because of three reasons: *first,* because we do not see that a prophet has prophesied about him prior to his coming; *second,* because we do not find in the Qur'an the mention of a miracle or a prophecy ascribed to the man who produced it; *third,* because the Christ has told us that no prophet will rise after Him. These are their strongest objections, and I will refute them, by the help of God. If I am able to prove that the contrary of what they assert is true, and that for our belief in prophets there is no such necessary condition as they mention, they will have no more excuse before God and their conscience, and those who adduce such pleas and cling to them are in the path of unbelief and perdition.

(AG) The answer to their saying that no prophet has prophesied about the Prophet and that the prophetic office of the prophets is not true and acceptable except when it is preceded by other prophecies, because he who believes in a prophet who has no previous prophecy about him would be in error and unbelief, is this: let them tell us who prophesied about the prophet Moses himself — may God bless him — or about David, or about Isaiah, or about Jeremiah, who are considered by them as the greatest of the prophets — peace be with them —; and since there is no previous prophecy about them, he who believes in them would, therefore, contradict the truth for falsehood and thus incur the wrath of the Lord of the worlds. The answer to their saying that in the Qur'an there is no mention of a miracle wrought by the Prophet — may God bless and save him — and that he who has no record in his book of a sign or miracle has no reason to be acknowledged, is this: let them show us the miracle wrought by David and recorded in his Psalter; if they do not find it for us, why and for what reason have they called him a prophet, while no prophet has previously prophesied about him and there is no record of a miracle in his Book?

(AH) From what I have explained it has become evident that, in the process of the verification of the history of the prophets, there is no need of a previous prophecy about them, nor of a mention in their books of their miracles or outward signs of their claims. There are

indeed prophets who, as stated above, have in their Books the record
of a miracle and a manifest prophecy, but about whom no previous
prophet has prophesied; and no one has for that denied their claim;
such is the case of Moses, Daniel, Isaiah and the like — peace be with
them. There are also prophets on whom God has bestowed all these
prerogatives; such as the case of the Christ — peace be with Him — who
has wrought wonderful miracles, foretold hidden and unknown things
and has previous prophecies about Him prior to His appearance.
There are prophets who have miracles recorded in their Books, but
who did not prophesy; such is the case of Elisha, who gave life to two
dead men, but has no direct prophecy. Some prophets, such as Ezekiel
and Hosea and others, did not work any miracle, and they prophesied;
but their prophecy having been realized long after their death, people
who saw them and acknowledged them had no reason for their belief
in them, in the absence of a miracle shown by then to their contemporaries. There are some prophets who have in their Books neither
miracle nor prophecy, nor convincing stories and (yet) are counted
among the prophets; such is the case of Malachi, Haggai and Nahum,
whose books of prophecies do not exceed three or four pages, for each
one of them; such is, also, the case of Miriam the prophetess, Moses's
sister, and of Hanna the prophetess, who have neither Book, nor
prophecy, nor miracle, nor sign and (yet) they have counted them
among the prophets. O my cousins, why and for what reason have you
called these prophets?

(AI) This being the condition of the Christians, why do they disbelieve
in the prophetic office of the Prophet — peace be with him — who
actually possesses the above mentioned prerogatives, some of which are
perpetuated in the Qur'an and some in the Tradition, which is of equal
value to the Qur'an with the sole difference that those which are
contained in the Qur'an afford stronger and clearer argument and
more cogent prophecy. How can they reject them with the explanation
that I shall give of the prophecies of the pious prophets about him and
with the allusions of the majority of them to his prophetic office and to
his time — may the peace and blessings of God be with all of them. If
you say that you have rejected and avoided the Prophet — may God
bless and save him — because there is no prophet after the Christ, I

will make it clear from your own Books that the man who whispered this into your ears and made it flow from your tongues was not an adviser but a deceiver to you, not reliable but suspect.

(AJ) To this effect it is written in the eleventh chapter of the Book of Acts, which contains the Epistles of the Apostles, that "In those days, prophets came from Jerusalem, and one of them, called Agabus, stood up and prophesied to them that in those countries there will be famine and great dearth." (Acts 9:28) It is said in this same chapter that "In the church of Antioch, there were prophets and teachers, as Barnabas and Simon and Lucius of the town of Cyrene and Manael and Saul." (Acts 13:1) All these five prophets, according to what is recorded, were in Antioch. Some of the women prophetesses are also mentioned. It is said in the nineteenth chapter of this book that "Philip the interpreter had four daughters prophetesses." (Acts 21:9) Luke said too, in the book of the Acts, that the group going to Antioch "went to the house[44] of Judas and Silas, because they also were prophets." (Acts 15:32)

(AK) The Christians are therefore short of evidence for their claim, and their saying is incoherent, and their arguments have been refuted and overthrown; it has become evident that after the Christ there were people whom they have called Apostles and Prophets; such is the case of Paul himself.

(AL) I shall now, by the help and assistance of God, explain the ten prerogatives which I have set forth. I shall present in each chapter what is perpetuated in the Qur'an as a reproach against those who pretend that there is no mention of a miracle in it. I wish the reader of this book to realize its merit and the excellence of its value and to know that those born in the religion of Islam and firmly attached to it, who have profusely dealt with this subject, did not reach what I have attained;[45] he who has a doubt in his breast, let him compare my book, the prophecies, the convincing and peremptory proofs which it contains, the riddles and the intricacies which I have carefully examined, with all that other writers have written since the appearance of Islam down to our own time. This is due to the help and assistance of God and to the blessings of the Commander of the Faithful — may God strengthen him — and to the obligations which God imposes through him on his friends and freedmen. It is he — may God prolong his life — who called me to this work, guided me in it and convinced me that on account of it I should be entitled to a great reward from God and a good memory from man. Before I became a Muslim I was neglectful, led astray, unaware of right direction and groping my way far from what was later disclosed to me. Thanks and blessings be to God who has lifted up the veil from my sight, opened the locks for me and saved me from the darkness of error!

IV.

CHAPTER I.

THE PROPHET — PEACE BE WITH HIM — CALLED TO THE UNITY OF GOD AND TO THE SAME SUBJECT AS THAT INCLUDED IN THE FAITH OF ABRAHAM AND ALL THE PROPHETS — PEACE BE WITH THEM:

(AM) The most trustworthy witness to this is the Qur'an, which shows that the Prophet — peace be with him — called only to the God of Abraham, Ishmael, Isaac and Jacob, to the unity of God and to what pious prophets had proclaimed and sound minds had demonstrated. Among other things God the Most High said in the Qur'an:

"Say, He is God alone; God the Eternal; He begets not and is not begotten, nor is there like unto Him anyone." (Qur'an 112:1-4) And He said:

"God bears witness that there is no God but He, and the angels and those possessed of knowledge, standing up for justice. There is no God but He, the mighty, the wise." (Qur'an 3:16) And He said:

"Say, O God, Lord of the Kingdom, Thou givest the kingdom to

583

whomsoever Thou pleasest and abasest whom Thou pleasest; in Thy hand is good. Verily Thou art mighty over all." (Qur'an 3:25) And He said:

"How can ye disbelieve in God, when ye were dead and He made you alive, and then He will take your life and then make you alive again and then to Him will ye return." (Qur'an 2:26) About the excellence of God, His mercy and His justice, He said:

"Whoso does right, it is for his soul, and whoso does evil, it is against it, for thy Lord is not unjust towards His servants." (Qur'an 41:46) And He said:

"And he who gains a good action, we will increase good for him thereby; verily, God is forgiving and grateful." (Qur'an 42:22) And He said:

"And he who does the weight of an atom of good shall see it, and he who does the weight of an atom of evil shall see it." (Qur'an 99:7-8) And He said:

"What befalls thee of good, it is from God, and what befalls thee of bad it is from thyself." (Qur'an 4:81) And He said:

"God will not require of the soul save its capacity; it shall have what it has earned, and it shall owe what has been earned from it." (Qur'an 2:286) In exalting the grace of God and His compassion for His servants, He said:

"Verily, God would not wrong by the weight of an atom; and if it is a good work, He will double it and bring from Himself a mighty reward" (Qur'an 4:44) And He said:

"We did not wrong them, but they wronged themselves." (Qur'an 10:103) And He said:

"And when they swerved, God made their hearts to swerve; for God guides not the people who work abomination." (Qur'an 61:5)   And He said:

"That is because they believed and then disbelieved, wherefore is a stamp set on their hearts so that they do not understand." (Qur'an 63:3)   And He said:

"He who brings a good work shall have ten like it; but he who brings a bad work shall be recompensed only with the like thereof, and they shall not be wronged." (Qur'an 6:161)   And He said:

"How will it be when we have gathered them together for a day whereof there is no doubt, when each soul shall be paid what it has earned?" (Qur'an 3:24)

This is the faith of Adam, of Noah, of Abraham and of all the prophets and righteous men — may God's blessings be with them; and the adversaries do not doubt and suspect it.

V.

CHAPTER II.

ON THE MERIT OF HIS PRESCRIPTIONS AND HIS LAWS:

(AN) AS to the dictations and prescriptions of his religion, they are: love of God the Most High; love of parents; strengthening of the ties of relationship; generosity with one's possessions; devotion to gratuitous benefactions; asceticism; fasting; prayer; general alms; legal alms; forgiveness of the culprit; fulfillment of engagements; avoidance of deceit and falsehood; getting rid of wrongs by the kindliest way; prohibition of intoxication, immorality, adultery and usury; ordinances for spreading safety and justice; striking off the head of recalcitrant unbelievers, and other points without which there is no firm religion and world. Among other things is the following saying of the most High God:

"For those who expend in alms, in prosperity and adversity, for those who repress their rage and those who pardon men; God loves the kind." (Qur'an 3:128) And this other saying:

"Those who expend their wealth by night and day, secretly and openly, they shall have their reward with their Lord. No fear shall come on them, nor shall they grieve." (Qur'an 2:275) And He said:

"Take to pardon and order what is kind, and shun the ignorant; and if an incitement from the devil incites you, then seek refuge in God; verily, He both hears and knows." (Qur'an 7:198-199) And He said:

"And twist not thy cheek proudly, nor walk in the land haughtily; verily, God loves not every arrogant boaster; but be moderate in thy walk and lower thy voice; verily, the most disagreeable of voices is the voice of asses." (Qur'an 31:17-18) And He said:

"He will not catch you up for a casual word in your oaths, but He will catch you up for what your hearts have earned." (Qur'an 2:225) And He said:

"Say, I have no power over myself for harm or for profit, save what God will." (Qur'an 10:50) And He said:

"God desires for you what is easy and desires not for you what is difficult." (Qur'an 2:181) And He said:

"Verily, men resigned and women resigned and believing men and believing women and devout men and devout women and truthful men and truthful women and patient men and patient women and humble men and humble women and almsgiving men and almsgiving women and fasting men and fasting women and men who guard their private parts and women who guard their private parts and men who remember God much and women who remember Him, — God has prepared for them forgiveness and a mighty reward." (Qur'an 33:35) And He said:

"Verily, God bids you do justice and good and give to kindred their due, and He forbids you to sin and do wrong and oppress; He admonishes you, haply ye may be mindful." (Qur'an 16:92) And He said:

"And obey not any mean swearer, a back-biter, a walker about with slander, a forbidder of good, a transgressor, a sinner, rude and base-born too." (Qur'an 68:10-13)

(AO) God did not leave a question which would edify and reform His servants, nor a counsel which would tend to please Him without having spoken of it.

What shows the merit of the divine call of the Prophet — peace be with him — is that he extended his proclamation to all mankind, without sending a special and particular invitation to some people to the exclusion of others, as the rest of the prophets had done,[46] except the Christ — peace be with Him. Indeed He generalized His call and promised pardon and Heaven to all. Other prophets struck blindly with the sword those who were round them and squandered their fortune, without calling, forgiving, edifying and warning, as the Prophet — may God bless and save him — was commanded to do.

(AP) As to the asceticism of the Prophet — may God bless and save him — his austerity and his disregard of the allurements and deceitfulness of this world, I will relate some facts from which it will be inferred that from a man of his devotion and temperance no one conceives deceit and falsehood. It has been related of him — peace be with him — that it was only after much pain and anxiety that he ate sufficiently bread or meat.[47] When he — may God bless and save him — gave his daughter Fatima for marriage to 'Ali — may God be pleased with both of them — the only dowry that he gave her was a bed woven with twisted palm-leaves, a pillow of skin stuffed with palm-tree fibers, an earthen pot, a water-skin and a basket containing some raisins and dates.[48] — 'Aisha — may god be pleased with her — said: "We used to stay forty days without firelight." Having been asked on what they lived, she answered: "On water and dates."[49]

(AQ) Fatima would grind herself the grains for flour; her hands became sorely hurt and traces of the handle of the mill were seen in them;[50] she complained of that to the Prophet — may God bless and save him — and asked him for a servant to serve her; and he answered her: "My little daughter, I have not in my house a place to contain all the Muslim women of whom you are one; therefore remember and thank God frequently."[51] — He — peace be with him — would fasten tightly a stone on his stomach out of hunger, eat sitting on the ground, put, when sleeping, his hand under his head as a pillow and wear his mantle and say: "I am a servant, I eat and sleep like a servant."[52] — He too — may God bless and save him — would produce from his weeping, while in prayer, a noise resembling that of the boiling of a cooking-pot.[53]

(AR) Among the traditions referring to the magnanimity of his conduct — peace be with him — and to the gravity of his character, is that the angel Gabriel — peace be with him — came to him and said: "O Muhammad, I brought thee the magnanimity of conduct of this world and of the world to come; thou shouldst join with the man who broke with thee, give to the man who deprived thee and forgive the man who wronged thee." — And he said: "Visit the sick, give food to the hungry and take away the chains from the captives."[54] He — may God bless and save him — forbade tittle-tattle, frequent questions and extravagance.[55] — In commanding moderation and content in one's condition, he — peace be with him — said: "The Holy Spirit has whispered in my mind[56] that a person will not die until he has completely provided for his livelihood." — And he said: "He who visits the sick is upon the palm-trees of Paradise."[57] — And he — peace be with him — said: "I am not for games and pleasures, and games and pleasures are not for me."[58]

(AS) And he said in praise of asceticism: "He who accumulates wealth will come in the day of judgment having over his eyes a scald-headed snake with two black specks."[59] — And he — peace be with him — said: "Fear the Fire by giving alms, although it be but one half of a date."[60] — And he said: "I stood in the door of heaven, and I saw that those who entered through it were generally poor, while the rich were cast in prison."[61]

(AT) He too — peace be with him — would say: "God has mercy on the man who owes his safety to his silence, or speaks when speech is necessary for success." — It is related also of him — peace be with him — that he never compelled anyone to give anything; that he never asked anything from anyone, except for the sake of God; and that no one ever asked him anything without his giving it to him for the sake of God.[62]

(AU) What the Most High God has prescribed and laid down to His people in the matter of prayers, ablutions and preliminary preparations dealing with washing after excretion, cleansing the teeth, rinsing the mouth and other purifications; attendance to public prayer with humble devotion, silence, keeping of ranks, quiet, reiteration of genuflexion and prostration and the utterance of words at each genuflexion and prostration, in order that their knowledge might extend to everybody, little or grown up, male slave or female slave, — all this is as something due to the dignity and the majesty of the Creator, when His servant is present before Him and asking from Him.

(AV) It is related also of him — peace be with him — that one day, on the occasion of a temporary interruption of his revelations, he told some people who were present with him: "How can revelations not be interrupted when you do not trim your nails, nor clip your moustache, nor cleanse your finger-joints."[63] He too — peace be with him — would say: "No human speech fits prayer, which is only for glorification, praise and reading of the Qur'an." This was against the deed of those who came to it when stinking with foul smell or polluted and those who interrupted their prayers with talks, games, spitting and eructation.

(AW) It is related also of the Prophet — may God bless and save him — that, speaking on behalf of the Most High God, he said: "I have prepared for my servants what eye has not seen, ear has not heard and the heart of a man has not conceived; except that with which I have made them acquainted."[64]

(AX) Among the things which make his religion easy and free from restraint is what God has ordered, through him, about the meal at daybreak, the shortening of prayer for the sick and the travellers and his saying that the three days following the Day of Sacrifice should be for eating, drinking and making use of marriage.

(AY) One of the marks of the merit of his religion and of the reasonableness of the prescriptions of the Qur'an is that we find that the Torah which is in the hands of the *People of the Book* says: "Everyone who kills should be killed."[65] Now Moses himself — peace be with him — and David and other prophets as well as kings of the Children of Israel have killed many people, but they have not deserved to be killed. [66] The Qur'an limits and defines that in saying: "And whoso kills a believer purposely, his reward is hell, to dwell therein for aye." (Qur'an 4:95)[67] It has been related of him — peace be with him — that he said: "He who slays a person with whom he is on terms of peace will not perceive the odor of Paradise."[68] This is a restricted, limited, corrected and polished order.

(AZ) Moses and Jesus — peace be with them — said: "Every claim is settled by two or three witnesses;" (Deut. 19:15b; Matt. 18:16) So the Jews and Christians say. But it happens that the two witnesses are wicked and liars; God, therefore, said through the Prophet — may God bless and save him — "And bring as witnesses two men of equity among you." (Qur'an 65:2)[69] In this He limited and enlightened the point at issue with a short, significant, important and clear saying.

(BA) Moses — peace be with him — ordered the Children of Israel to curse openly, by the tongue of the nation, anyone who transgresses or neglects something from the laws and the prescriptions of the Torah;[70] but it happens that the one who had transgressed some of them, or had trespassed and committed shortcomings against them, repents and shows penitence and is no more worthy of curse. Therefore the Qur'an says: "Those who when they do a crime or wrong themselves remember God and ask forgiveness for their sins — and who forgives sins save God? — and do not persevere in what they did, the while they know; these have their reward: pardon from their Lord and gardens beneath which flow, dwelling therein for aye; for pleasant is the reward of those who act like this." (Qur'an 3:129-130).[71] These are messages and points which demonstrate that the man who laid them down was sound, steadfast, pious, devout and was not a plagiarist, an appropriator of others' rights, nor one making light of things and lacking gravity.

IV.

CHAPTER III.

THE MIRACLES OF THE PROPHET — MAY GOD BLESS AND SAVE HIM — WHICH HAVE BEEN DENIED AND REJECTED BY THE *PEOPLE OF THE BOOK.*

(BB) I WILL only relate the miracles of the Prophet — peace be with him — which afford ground for argument with equitable people. I will begin the subject with what is found in the Qur'an, in order that the adversary may not say that if the Prophet — may God bless and save him — had wrought a miracle, it would have been mentioned in it, in the same manner as the miracles of Moses and Jesus — peace be with them — are recorded in the Torah and the Gospel.

(BC) Among his miracles which took place in his time — peace be with him — and to which the Qur'an bears witness, is that he was transferred in a single night from the Sacred Mosque to the Remote Mosque;[72] and this is the saying of the Most High God:

"Celebrated be the praises of Him who took His servant by night from the Sacred Mosque to the Remote Mosque, the precinct of which we have blessed, to show him our signs." (Qur'an 17:1)[73]

(BD) The Arabs rejected this, saying: "When and how could he cover in a single night the distance which takes two months to go and return?" Then Abu Bakr — may God be pleased with him — went to him and asked him about it. And he — peace be with him — said: "Yes; and I encountered the caravan of such and such a tribe in such and such a valley; one of their camels had bolted away, and I directed them to it. I met too with the caravan of such and such a tribe while they were asleep; I drank water from one of their vessels; their caravan is now coming preceded by a dusky camel carrying two sacks, one black and the other black and white." People rushed towards the caravan route, and behold, the caravan was coming preceded by a dusky camel; and they could not find an objection to this miracle.[74] By my life, it is a clear and sufficient miracle, recorded in the Qur'an and accepted by the unanimity of the Muslims.

(BE) Among the Prophet's miracles which God has mentioned in His Book is that when the polytheists harmed him and sneered at him, He said to him: "Therefore publish what thou art bidden, and turn aside from the idolaters; verily, we are enough for thee against the scoffers." (Qur'an 15:94-95) This too is found in the Qur'an, and there are not two men who hold discordant views about it and about its interpretation; it is that five persons of high standing among the polytheists were sneering at him and harming him. Gabriel — peace be with him — came and said to him: "When they make the circuit of the holy house, ask what thou wilt from God, and I will do it against them as punishment." One of them, Lahab (the) son of Abu Lahab, met him in the circuit, and the Prophet — may God bless and save him — said: "Let God's dog eat thee;" and a lion devoured him. Then Walid b. Mughira met him, and the Prophet — may God bless and save him — made a sign to a wound that he had in the sole of his foot, and it became recrudescent and killed him. Then Aswad b. 'Abd Yaghuth met him, and the Prophet made a sign to his belly; and he became dropsical and died. Then Aswad b. Muttalib met him, and he threw a leaf on his face saying: "May God blind him and cause his son to die"; all this happened to him. The 'As b. Wa'il met him, and he made a sign to the hollow of his foot, and a thorn entered into it and killed him. Then Harith b. Talatilah met him, and he made a sign to him, and he burst out with pus and perished.[75] It is in this way that the Prophet — may God bless and save him — was delivered from the *Scoffers,* who were men of high standing and chiefs of the tribe.

(BF) It has been related on the authority of Aminah, the mother of
the Prophet — may God bless and save him — that when he fell from
the womb she saw light coming out of him and that he fell on all fours,
his face and sight being directed towards heaven.[76]

(BG) Among his resplendent miracles noticed by all who saw him in
the *Day of Badr,* is that he threw dust on the face of the polytheists
and said: "Confusion seize their faces!"[77] and they fled and were killed.

(BH) Anas b. Malik — may God be pleased with him — has reported
that he heard the cry of a man saying: "O Apostle of God! The
houses have been destroyed by the violence of rain"; and he — peace
be with him — said: "Let it fall round us and not upon us." And Anas
said: "I saw with my eyes the clouds moving away from the town."[78] —
He too — may God bless and save him — said once to the polytheists
who were present with him: "If any of you can pronounce the name of
his father or of his brother, I am a liar"; and none of them was able to
pronounce it. — Two handfuls of dates were brought to him in the *Day
of the Ditch,* and he ordered that they should be laid before him. His
herald cried to the army, and everybody ate and was satisfied. — In the
Day of Badr, the sword of 'Ukkasha b. Mihsan was broken, and he
said: "O Prophet of God, my sword is broken"; and the Prophet —
peace be with him — took the stem of a plant used as firewood and
gave it to him and said to him: "Shake it"; and 'Ukkashah shook it,
and it became a sword with which he went forth and fought; and later,
it remained with him all the time.[79] — And he too — peace be with him
— took a pebble, which he moved with his hand, and it praised God;
then he put it in the hand of Abu Bakr and it praised; then he put it in
the hand of 'Umar and then in the hand of 'Uthman and it praised in
their hands.

(BI) It is reported on the authority of Ibn 'Abbas — may God have
mercy upon him — that a man on a foray took the nestlings of a bird.
The bird came to the Apostle of God — may God bless and save him —

and flapped its wings near his head, then it fell in his hands. The Prophet — peace be with him — said: "Who took the nestlings of this bird? Fetch them and give them back to it." They found them with a Muslim and gave them back to it.

(BJ) It has been related that a camel knelt on his hands and then bellowed. The Prophet — may God bless and save him — called its owner and said: "This camel has complained and told me that it was with thee since its youth and thou workedst with it; but now that it was old thou wishedst to kill it." The man answered: "It has told the truth, O Prophet of God, because I am not feeding it."[80]

(BK) It has been related too that Banu Ghifar wished to slaughter a calf, which spoke and said: "O Children of Ghifar! A happy event! A crier is crying in Mecca 'There is no God but Allah"; and they left it and went to Mecca, where they found that the Prophet — may God bless and save him — had appeared; and they believed in him.[81]

(BL) It has been related that a wolf made a raid on some sheep; the shepherds said one to another; "Are you not amazed at this wolf?" The wolf spoke and said: "You are more to be amazed than I; a prophet has appeared in Mecca calling to God, and you do not answer him."[82] All these are well-known facts among all Muslims, who do not deny anything from them because they did not take place behind closed doors. What corroborates the miracle of the wolf is that the children of the man to whom the wolf spoke are called down to our own day, "The children of the man to whom the wolf spoke"; they transmit the fact among themselves, and they are traced back to it, in order that it may be not be forgotten, and that no one may have a reason to discredit it.

(BM) And he — peace be with him — invoked curses upon the Arabs, and rain was withheld from them, and the land was affected with drought. It has been told too of him — peace be with him — that he apprised Abu Sufyan of a secret affair which had taken place between him and his wife Hind. Abu Sufyan was amazed at that and said to himself: "She has disclosed my secret; I will surely pound her hand on her foot." But the Prophet — may God bless and save him — said: "Do not commit any injustice against Hind; she has not published any secret." Then Abu Sufyan said: "I had suspected her and was perplexed about her; but since thou hast told me what I was telling to myself, I ascertained that she is innocent of what I suspected her."

(BN) Among the noted miracles of the Prophet — peace be with him — is the fact handed down by Anas b. Malik, who said: "My mother took dates mixed with butter and curd and sent them to the Prophet — may God bless and save him — praying him to eat from them. The Prophet — may God bless and save him — stood up and said to his friends: 'Let us start.' When my mother noticed the crowd, she said 'O Apostle of God, I have only prepared something sufficient for thy food, thine alone.' " And Anas has said: "The Prophet — may God bless and save him — called for divine blessing and said to me, 'Get in the crowd in companies of ten'; and they ate their fill and went out; and we too ate and were satisfied."[83]

(BO) It has been related on the authority of Ya'la b. Umayya[84] that the Prophet — may God bless and save him — being once on a journey, wished to make his ablutions[85] and said to me: "Go to those two trees and tell them that the Apostle of God — may God bless and save him — commands them to draw near each other." And the two trees came furrowing the ground until they reached each other; the Apostle of God — may God bless and save him — made then his ablutions between them and ordered them to go back to their place; and they went.[86] It has been related too that a Jew invited him to dinner and offered him a poisoned sheep; but he, — peace be with him — said: "This sheep tells me that it is poisoned." The Jew avowed that and said: "I wished to test thee and said to myself, 'If he is a prophet, the matter will not be hidden from him, but if he is an impostor, he will eat of it, and I will rid people of him.' "[87]

(BP) It has been related on the authority of Jabir b. 'Abdallah al-Ansari, who said: "We set off on a journey with the Prophet — may God bless and save him — and we were very thirsty. We hurried towards him, and there was with him a drinking vessel in which there was water. He put his hand in it and caused the water to jet out of his fingers, as if there were springs. We drank and quenched our thirst and made our ablutions; and we were four hundred men."[88]

(BQ) This is enough for this work; had we intended to exhaust the subject, the book would have been too bulky; but in what has been written there is remedy for the man whom God wishes to guide and to save. Some of it is taken from the men from whom the Muslims took the Qur'an and who are considered as reliable in all that is handed down to the nation from them. They resemble in that the Apostles of the Christ — peace be with Him — who transmitted to the Christians portions of the Gospel and handed them down to them the history of the Christ. Therefore, if those men are reliable and worthy of confidence in transmitting his history, they are not to be suspected in all that they have related of him; but if they are not reliable in that point, they are to be suspected in all that they have transmitted and are deceivers, first of themselves and then of all men.

VII.

CHAPTER IV.

THE PROPHET — PEACE BE WITH HIM — FORETOLD EVENTS UNKNOWN TO HIM, WHICH WERE REALIZED IN HIS DAYS.

(BR) WE will begin this chapter also with what is found in the Qur'an, in order to strengthen our argument and destroy the excuses of the adversaries. The Most High God said to His Apostle — may God bless and save him — "Ye shall verily enter the Sacred Mosque, if God please, in safety, with shaven heads and cut hair, ye shall not fear." (Qur'an 48:27) And they entered it when he was still alive, as God had said. — And He said: "And when those who misbelieve were crafty with thee to detain thee a prisoner, or kill thee, or drive thee forth; they were crafty, but God was crafty too, for God is the best of the crafty ones." (Qur'an 8:30)[89] And it happened as God had said, and they wished to be crafty with him, but God thwarted their craftiness and foiled their stratagem.

(BT) And God said: "O ye who believe! Remember God's favors to you when hosts came to you and we sent against them a wind and hosts that ye could not see." (Qur'an 33:9)[90] With them God struck the infidels in the face; and it happened as He had said. — And He said: "We will cast dread into the hearts of those who misbelieve; strike off their necks then and strike off from them every finger tip." (Qur'an 8:12) And it happened as God had told him,[91] and He did to them what he was ordered to do. And He said: "Dost thou not look on those who were hypocritical, saying to their brethren who misbelieved amongst the People of the Book, 'If ye be driven forth, we will go forth with you; and we will never obey anyone concerning you; and if ye be fought against we will help you.' But God bears witness that they are surely liars. If they be driven forth, these will not go forth with them; and if they be fought against, these will not help them, or if they do help them, they will turn their backs in flight; then shall they not be helped." (Qur'an 59:11) It happened as God had said to His Prophet — may God bless and save him — because those men have been driven forth, and these their brethren did not go forth with them; and they have been fought against, and they did not help them.

(BU) What can man say against these miracles, while the Qur'an mentions them and the Muslim community bears witness to their veracity, and all its members subscribe to their authority, and men and women converse about them? If, while they are contained in the Qur'an, it is allowed to consider them false and revile them, we will not believe the adversaries who say that the Torah and the Gospel do not contain falsehood to which the eyewitnesses of events had deliberately shut their eyes. If then this cannot be said about the Torah and the Gospel and their contemporaries, it is not allowed with regard to the Qur'an and its holders. — About the breakers of faith from the polytheists of the Quraysh, the Most High God said: "Fight against them! God will torment them by your hands and disgrace them and aid you against them and heal the breasts of a people who believe"; (Qur'an 9:14) and it happened as He said.

(BV) Among authentic stories is the one transmitted by Sa'd b. 'Ubadah as-Sa'idi, who said: "We were on a foray with the Prophet — may God bless and save him — and with us there was a man who would kill every polytheist against whom he came to fight. We mentioned this to the Prophet — may God bless and save him — and he said, 'Is he not from the people of the fire?' " And Sa'd added: I did not cease to follow him, in order to see the end of his story. He was wounded and considering death too slow, he put his sword on his navel and pressed himself against it until he killed himself."[92]

(BW) It is related too of him — peace be with him — that he said to Khalid b. Walid and his friends when he sent them against Ukaidir of Dumat al-Jandal: "You will find him on the roof of his house, directing cows,"[93] and they found him in that state.[94] It has been related too of him — may God bless and save him — that his she-camel went astray, and he began to ask for her. The hypocrites said: "This Muhammad claims to know the secrets of heaven, and he does not know where his she-camel is." He knew upon what they were communing with themselves and said: "I know but what my Lord tells me; and He has told me that my she-camel is in such and such a valley, her head entangled in a tree." They sought for her and found her in such a state.[95]

(BX) It has been related of him — may God bless and save him — that one day he gathered the people and announced to them the death of Najashi, King of the Abyssinians, prayed for him and said four times "God is most great."[96] In that very day there came the news of his death, while the sea was separating him from the land of the Abyssinians and Mecca was not a highway like the highways of East and West.[97]

VIII.

CHAPTER V.

THE PROPHECIES OF THE PROPHET — PEACE BE WITH HIM — WHICH WERE REALIZED AFTER HIS DEATH.

(BY) WE will this chapter also with the prophecies of the Prophet — may God bless and save him — which are mentioned in the Qur'an, in order that no argument may be left to the people of incredulity and obstinacy upon which to lean, nor a hold at which they may clutch. Among other sayings is the following of the Most High God: "Have We not expanded thy breast? and set down from thee thy load which galled thy back? and exalted thee for thy renown?" (Qur'an 94:1-4) That is to say, his name shall be invoked and mentioned after that of God in every sermon, enchantment, discussion, marriage, prayer and the like.

(BZ) Among other sayings is the following of the Most High God: "When there comes God's help and victory, and thou shalt see men enter into God's religion by troops; then celebrate the praises of thy Lord and ask forgiveness of Him, He is relentant." (Qur'an 110:1-3) In this Sura he foretold the nearness of his death to his nation, and what was to take place after him on the subject of people entering by troops and masses into his religion; and this was realized. The adversaries look at it after a long time, and they do not deny it. — And the Most High God said: "A.L.M. The Greeks are overcome in the nighest parts of the land; but after being overcome, they shall overcome in a few years." (Qur'an 30:1-2) And it happened as he said, in a war between Chosrau and Caesar, and it became evident to the Arabs that his revelation was true. This was incessantly spoken of by them, by their children and their women in their houses, and they were expecting it and seeking information concerning it until it was noticed by one and all.

(CA) And He said too; "God promises those of you who believe and do right that He will give them the succession in the earth as He gave the succession to those before them, and He will establish for them their religion which He has chosen for them and give them after their fear, safety in exchange." (Qur'an 24:54) This is also a prophecy which has been fulfilled and realized, and no one can find a way to deny it, because God has given to the Muslims the succession of the earth, established for them their religion and changed their fear into safety. What miracle and what prophecy are truer and clearer than these?

(CB) And He said too: "He it is who sent His Apostle with guidance and the religion of truth to make it prevail over every other religion averse although idolaters may be." (Qur'an 9:33) God and His Apostle — peace be with him — proved right, and his religion has prevailed over every other religion, and the adherents of every religion have submitted to him. — And He said too to the Arabs who had lingered behind: "Ye shall be called out against a people endowed with vehement valor and shall fight them, or they shall become Muslims. And if ye obey, God will give you a good reward; but if ye turn your backs as ye turned your backs before, He will torment you with grievous woe." (Qur'an 48:16)

(CC) These were the men who had fallen away from the Prophet — may God bless and save him — to whom he foretold that they would fight against the Greeks and the Persians unless these become Muslims. This happened as it is in the Qur'an, and the onlookers bear witness to its veracity. What can the adversaries say about these prophecies, and what answers and arguments can they find against them when they are realized, fulfilled and spread manifestly East and West? And if a scoffer holds them in contempt, or is not satisfied with them and is resolved to refute and contradict them, he will not destroy except his own soul, will not irritate except his own Lord, will not change except his own fate and will not be able to find for us in his own Books except what is like them.

(CD) Among indubitable traditions it is related that the Prophet — may God bless and save him — said: "I have five names: I am *Muhammad;* and *Ahmad;* and *Effacing,* by means of which God effaces infidelity; and *Gatherer,* who will gather people; and *Final,* that is to say, the last of the Prophets."[98] His saying — peace be with him — was fulfilled, and by him God has closed prophecies and blotted out infidelity, that is to say, He weakened it and lessened it in effacing it from the middle and the heart of the earth and in leaving a shadow of it in its ends and borders. — It has been related too that he was on a mountain which shook under him; he said to it: "Be quiet, there are only on thee a prophet, a just man and a martyr";[99] there were with him Abu Bakr, for whose sake he named "just man," and 'Umar and 'Uthman, who

were martyred after him. And he — peace be with him — would say to
his friends; "I have the precedence over you to the pool";[100] and God
took him before them.

  (CE) And he — peace be with him — said to Fatimah — may God be
pleased with her — in the illness of which he died: "Thou wilt follow
me more quickly than any other of my relatives."[101] And from his relatives she was the first to die after him. — And he said to 'Ali, son of
Abu Talib — may God be pleased with him — in pointing to his head
and to his beard: "This will be tinged with that."[102] Afterwards 'Ali
was affected with a dangerous illness, and his relatives said to him:
"We are anxious about thee from this illness." And he said: "I do not
fear it, because the Apostle of God — may God bless and save him —
said to me: 'This will be tinged with that.' " And this too was realized,
because 'Ali recovered from that illness and was struck on his head
with a sword and killed. — And he — peace be with him — said to
'Uthman: "God will clothe thee with a shirt; and the people will force
thee to take it off; but do not yield." When 'Uthman was besieged and
the people bade him take off the caliphate, he said to them: "The
Prophet — may God bless and save him — told me so and so, and for
that I shall not do what you are saying"; and he was killed.[103] And he
— may God bless and save him — said to 'Ammar b. Yasir: "A rebellious band will kill thee."[104] And he was killed in a battle between 'Ali
and Mu'awiah. And Mu'awiah did not deny this tradition, but said: "It
was not my troops who killed him; but the man who deceived him and
made him go forth to fight, he killed him."

  (CF) And he too — peace be with him — said to Zubair b. 'Awwam:
"Thou shalt fight against 'Ali and in that thou shalt be unjust towards
him." He did so, and 'Ali reproached him. — And he — may God
bless and save him — said to his wife 'Aisha — may God be pleased
with her — "The dogs of Haw'ab will bark against thee." When she
went to Basra, she heard barking in her night journey; and she asked
about the place, and she was answered: "It is the watering place called
Haw'ab." She remembered his saying — peace be with him — and she
said: "Verily to God we belong and verily unto Him we return,"
(Qur'an 2:151)[105] and repented that she had travelled there.[106] — And he

— peace be with him — used to say about Hasan (the) son of 'Ali — peace be with both of them — "This my son is a *Sayyid* and God will reconcile through him two Muslim parties."[107]

(CG) And he — peace be with him — said: "The earth has been collected together for me, and I saw its Eastern and Western parts, and the empire of my nation will reach the spot from which it has been collected together for me."[108] He also seized a pickaxe in the *Day of the Ditch,* and with it he struck a flint which had defied those who were digging; a spark came out of it, and he — peace be with him — said "In this spark I saw the cities of Chosrau." Then he struck another blow and another spark came out; and he said: "In it I saw the cities of Caesar. Verily God will give them to my nation after me."[109] — It has been told of him — peace be with him — that at the end of a journey he would worship and perform two *rakahs,*[110] and repair to Fatima — may God be pleased with her. He went to her after he had left the *Ditch;* and she began to weep and to kiss his mouth; and he said to her; "O Fatima, why art thou weeping?" And she said: "O Apostle of God, I see thee shabby, weary and clothed in worn out garments." And he said: "O Fatima, God has revealed to thy father that it is He who places dignity or lowliness in every house, be it of clay or of hair; and He has revealed to me that my lowliness will be of short duration."[111]

(CH) It has been related that Anas b. Malik said, "I was in a walled garden with the Prophet — may God bless and save him — and I heard a knock at the door; and he said to me, 'O Anas, rise and open the door to the corner and declare to him that he will go to Heaven, and tell him that he will be set over my community after me.' And I went and lo! I was face to face with Abu Bakr — may God be pleased with him — and I declared to him what I had heard, and I went in. Then another man knocked at the door, and he said, 'Rise and open the door to him, and tell him that he will go to Heaven, and that he will be set over my community after Abu Bakr.' I opened the door, and lo! I was with 'Umar — may God be pleased with him — and I did what I was commanded to do. Then I heard another knock at the door, and he — peace be with him — said to me, 'Rise and open the door to the new-comer, and tell him that he will go to Heaven and that he will govern the community after 'Umar'; and lo! I was with 'Uthman — may God be pleased with him."[112]

(CI) It has been related of him — peace be with him — that he used to say: "The death of this generation shall not take place before you have seen people whose faces are like two-fold shields."[113] He too — may God bless and save him — would say: "Which is the most sterile of your countries?" And they answered: "Khurasan." And he said: "It will be a source of blessings for you after me." None of the sons of this 'Abbasid dynasty and of others ignores that Abu Muslim[114] started without any doubt that victory and Caliphate were due to this 'Abbasid house. When he approached Hirah, he sent a messenger to ask after the members of the family of Abul-'Abbas who were there. When the messenger saw them, he questioned them "Which of you is the son of 'Harithiyah?"[115] and this was Abul-'Abbas,[116] the Commander of the Faithful — may God forgive his sins — because it was told in the Tradition that the first one who would become caliph would be the son of Harithiyah; this they did not suspect.[117] What is more wonderful is that the Umayyads did not doubt that the Caliphate would go to its owners from the members of this house, and for that they were killing them and tracking them under every stone. Meantime the inhabitants of Khurasan were sending messengers to them when they were at Sharat, to strengthen their hope. They did not question the justice of their cause, and when those of them who have been killed were killed, victory dawned in the time decreed by God in traditions handed down to us.

(CJ) It has come to our knowledge that Abul-'Abbas received the news of the conquest of Yemen and of Sind[118] in the very same day; and he showed a great sorrow. His household said to him : "O Commander of the Faithful! It is a day of joy; what does this sorrow mean?" And he said to them: "Have you then forgotten the tradition transmitted from the Prophet — may God bless and save him — that the man who would conquer Yemen and Sind in one day, his death would be near?" He had fever on that very day and died some days later.

(CK) It has been related of the Prophet — may God bless and save him — that he wrote letters begun with the mention of his name, one to Chosrau and the other to Caesar, and called them to Islam.[119] As to Caesar, he put his missive on the pillow and wrote him an answer couched in civil language. As to Chosrau, he tore up his missive and wrote to Phiruz the Dailamite,[120] when still in Yemen, bidding him repair to the Prophet — may God bless and save him — seize him and slay him. And the Prophet said: "O my God! Tear up his kingdom"; and his kingdom was torn up, as you see. And Phiruz went and informed the Prophet — may God bless and save him — of the order he had received about him. The Prophet — may God bless and save him — said to him: "My Lord has informed me that thy lord has been slain. Do not touch me until the news is verified by thee." The news reached him, and Phiruz became Muslim on account of what he had seen and heard; and he called to Islam the Persians who were in Yemen, and they became Muslims. And when 'Ansi, the liar, appeared in Yemen claiming the prophetic office, the Prophet — may God bless and save him — wrote to Phiruz ordering him to kill him. And Phiruz entered his house when he was asleep, bent back his neck, pounded it, and killed him. — He too — peace be with him — said: "The Caliphate will not cease to be in the family of the Quraysh."[121]

(CL) And the Prophet — may God bless and save him — said to 'Abbas, his uncle, who had brought him to his young son 'Abdallah — may the grace of God be with both of them — "This boy will be the most learned of my nation in religion, and the best versed in the interpretation of the Revelation." He prayed over him, spat in his mouth and said: "O my God, make him versed in religion and teach him interpretation." And he became as he was told, and he was for that called the *Habr*.[122]

(CM) Among the evidences of the favors which God confers on the Prophet — peace be with him — and on all who believe in him, is the fact, transmitted by noted and well-known traditions, of 'Umar b. al-Khattab asking water from Heaven in the name of 'Abbas (the) son of 'Abdul-Muttalib — may God be pleased with both of them — in the

Year of Drought.[123] He took him by the hand, went forth, and said: "O my God! We come to Thee asking water from Thee through the intercession of the uncle of Thy Prophet." They did not discontinue until a cloud mounted up, which sent a copious rain.[124]

(CN) And he used to say to his companions; "By the One who has sent me with the truth, although evening finds you humble, you will shine so as to become stars by means of which people will be guided, and so that it will be said: So-and-so has related that he heard the Apostle of God — may God bless and save him — say such and such a thing"; and you see that this happened as he said.

(CO) It has been related too that 'Ikrima, son of Abu Jahl, when still idolater, killed in battle a man from the *Helpers;* and the Prophet — may God bless and save him — smiled. A man from the *Helpers* said to him: "Didst thou smile, O Apostle of God, because one of thy kin killed one of us?" He answered: "No; but I smiled because both of them have the same rank in Heaven." And 'Ikrima became Muslim afterwards and was slain in the action of Ajnadain in the country of the Greeks.[125] — And he — peace be with him — said to 'Adi, son of Hatim: "O 'Adi, become Muslim and thou wilt be safe. O 'Adi, I think that what impedes thee from this is the poverty which thou findest in those who are round me, and the conspiracy through which men have become one band against us. Hast thou seen Hirah?" 'Adi said: "No." And he said: "The time is near when from there a woman will travel on a camel without escort to make the circuit of the holy house; and verily, the treasures of Chosrau, son of Hormiz, will be open to us, three times."[126] And 'Adi added: "I saw myself all that the Prophet — peace be with him — had foretold."

(CP) And Abu Bakr — may God be pleased with him — said when the Arabs turned from Islam[127] and he sent troops against them: "The Apostle of God — may God bless and save him — has promised the Muslims victory and conquest from God, and God will make his religion prevail over every other religion; and God will not fail in His promise." God has, indeed, confirmed and realized the prediction and the saying of the Prophet — may God bless and save him — and every doubt has been expelled.

IX.

CHAPTER VI.

THE PROPHET — MAY GOD BLESS AND SAVE HIM — WAS AN UNLETTERED MAN, AND THE BOOK WHICH GOD BROUGHT DOWN TO HIM AND WHICH HE MADE HIM RECITE IS A SIGN OF PROPHETIC OFFICE.

(CQ) AMONG the miracles of the Prophet — may God bless and save him — is the Qur'an. It has, indeed, become a miracle of meanings, which no writer of books on this subject has tried to explain without recognizing his incompetence and renouncing his discourse and his claim to such an explanation. When I was a Christian, I did not cease to say in accordance with an uncle of mine, who was one of the learned and eloquent men among Christians, that rhetoric was not a sign of prophetic office on account of its being common to all nations. But when I waived tradition and customs and broke with the promptings of habit and education and examined the meanings of the Qur'an, then I found that the question was as it holders believed it to be. I have never met with a book written by an Arab, or a Persian, or an Indian, or a Greek, which contained, like the Qur'an, unity, praise and glorification of the Most High God; belief in His Apostles and Prophets; incitement to good and permanent works; injunction for good things and prohibition of evil things; exhortation to Heaven and restraining from Hell. Who has ever written, since the creation of the world, a book with such prerogatives and qualities, with such influence, sweetness and charm upon the heart and with such attraction, felicity and success, while its producer, the man to whom it was revealed, was unlettered, not even knowing how to write and having no eloquence whatever? This is without doubt and hesitation a mark of prophetic office.

(CR) Moreover, I found that all books worthy of everlasting fame do not fail to deal either with the world and it inhabitants, or with religion. As to the books of literature, philosophy and medicine their aim and purpose are not like ours and are not counted among books of revelations and religion. As to the books dealing with religion, the first one to name, and the first one which came into existence, is the Torah, which is in the hands of the *People of the Book.* Now we find that it deals commonly with the genealogies of the Children of Israel, their exodus from Egypt, their halts and their departures and the name of the places in which they halted; and it contains too, high laws and prescriptions which dazzle the mind and which the intellectual capacity and power of men are unable to comprehend. What the Qur'an contains from these historical events is as a reminiscence of the days of the favors of God as edification, warning and admonition. As to the Gospel, which is in the hands of the Christians, the greater part of it is the history of the Christ, His birth and His life; and with that it contains good maxims of morality, remarkable advice, sublime wisdom and excellent parables, in which, however, there are only short and small portions of laws, prescriptions and history. As to the Book of Psalms, it contains historical events, praises and hymns of high beauty and sublime character, but it does not contain any laws and prescriptions.

(CS) As to the Books of Isaiah, Jeremiah and other prophets, the greater part of them deals with curses to the Children of Israel, with the announcement of the ignominy reserved to them, with withholding favors from them, inflicting punishments and chastisements on them and other kinds of evils.

(CT) The wicked *Zindiks* have used abuses and invectives against these Books saying: "The Wise and Merciful could not have revealed such things, nor have ordered the prescriptions dealing with the sprinkling of blood on the altar and on the garment of the priests and the *imams;* with the burning of bones, with the obscenities and garbage mentioned therein; with persistency in anger and wrath; with the order to desert the houses when their walls shine with white, because this would be a leprosy affecting these houses;[127] with the command to a group of Israelites to march one against another with unsheathed swords and to fight with endurance amongst themselves until they had perished in striking and beating one another.[128] The Jewish people put this into action and did not rebel, and they agreed without flinching to endanger their life and perish. People who do these things with promptitude are obedient and not rebellious, friends and not enemies; and friendly and obedient people do not deserve to be ordered to kill and to destroy one another."

(CU) Then Moses — peace be with him — ordered that they should go to two mountains close to each other and that six tribes from them should ascend one mountain and six tribes another mountain and that some men from them[129] should read, one by one, the prescriptions and the laws of the Torah and say: "He who transgresses these prescriptions, or neglects them, or loses something from them, is cursed." The tribes who were on the other mountain answered with *Amen* to those who were cursing in a loud voice.[130] Moses did not leave any of them without curses and even instigated them to curse their successors after them; and they did it promptly, obediently and without opposition.[131] In that they were led to discomfiture before they were fixed in their homes and to a general curse before they could perceive the odor of victory and happiness.

(CV) Of the same kind is the saying of the Prophet Ezekiel, that God told him to shave his head and his beard with a sharp and keen sword.[132] Similar is the saying of the Prophet Hosea, that God commanded him to marry an adulteress woman, who brought him forth two children; and ordered him to call one of them *I will not have mercy* and the other *They are not my partisans,* "in order that the Children of Israel might know that I will not have mercy on them, and will not consider them as friends and partisans."[133] And Hosea too, said on behalf of God about the Jews that their mother was an adulteress and that they were born of an illegitimate union.[134] One of the prophets also said to the Jews, on behalf of God,[135] that their mother was pleased with the males of Egypt.[136] And after a sermon to the Children of Israel, Isaiah said that he who told this was the Lord whose light is in Zion and furnace in Jerusalem.[137]

(CW) Not a single letter resembling such things is found in the Qur'an, which is interwoven with the Unity of God, hymns, praises, prescriptions, laws, history, promises, threats, persuasion and dissuasion;[138] with prophecies and announcements concerning good things congruous to the majesty of God, His wisdom and His might; with the consolidation of hope in His forgiveness, His mercy and His acceptance of repentance; and with other questions by which souls are encouraged and hopes fearlessly confirmed. God indeed says in it: "Verily God is forgiving and merciful; and who forgives sins except God?" (Qur'an 3:129) And He says too, "O My servants who have been extravagant against their own souls, be not in despair of the mercy of God; verily, God forgives sins, all of them; verily, He is forgiving and merciful." (Qur'an 39:54)[139]

(CX) It is right to state that this book is a sign of prophetic office, because there has not been a book similar to it since the beginning of the world, and since the time wherein people began to write on parchment. Moreover, it possesses other striking prerogatives full of light and mystery; viz., other books, and especially those written by philosophers, have been written by literary and scientific men after meditation and deep thought, and after they had been brought up in towns, heard facts and conversed with learned men. But the Prophet — may God bless and save him — was not like them, but he was an unlettered *Abtahi*[140] who had not learned from an Egyptian, or a Greek, or an Indian, or a Persian and had not frequented the sittings of literary men in search of literature or for reading books; and he produced a book which has astonished the linguists, the eloquent and ready speakers and subjugated to him the necks of the Arab nation. He said on behalf of the Most High God: "Say, 'Bring ten Suras like it devised; and call upon whom ye can beside God, if ye do tell the truth.' " (Qur'an 11:16) There was no one left in the nation to murmur and to speak, but all befriended him, submitted and yielded.

(CY) Then the learned men among the protected cults object that the Prophet — peace be with him — should have been an unlettered man, because God does not spare His prophets the knowledge of writing, this knowledge being the best He could bestow upon them and the least of His secrets and miracles He could reveal to them. The answer to this objection is that the Most High God has qualified each one of them with what He pleased. Some of them were excellent speakers, such as David; and some of them were lispers and stammerers, such as Moses. Some of them gave life to the dead and rent asunder the sea and made springs of water jet out of the rocks to the exclusion of others. Some of them were literary men and writers, such as Solomon; and some were unlettered, such as David, who said in his Psalter; "Because I did not know how to write" (Ps. 71:15, Peshitta Version); this is not a dishonor to him, as it is not a dishonor to Christ not to have been a dexterous spearer,[141] a skilled archer, a surveyor, an architect. And as it was not considered a dishonor for Moses not to have had fluency and eloquence of speech, or not have walked on the air, or not to have healed a blind man and a leper, and as it is not considered a dishonor for David and others — peace be with them — that God did not take them up to Heaven in the way that He did for others. It is not permissible to say that God was grudging towards this and that prophet in what He had granted to this and that prophet. He who says this is insolent and a rebel.

(CZ) Do we not see that Simon Cephas, Matthew and Luke, disciples of Christ — peace be with them — have not been traduced because they did not reach the measure of Paul in eloquence and rhetoric? Likewise it is not a dishonor to the Prophet — may God bless and save him — to have been an unlettered man, like David. On the contrary, God has made of this point a resplendent miracle and an argument against the men of his nation who disbelieved in him; because it became evident to the Muslim communities and to the members of the protected cults that he had not produced the Qur'an as an outcome of literary eloquence or earthly wisdom.

(DA) He was — peace be with him — brief, concise and slow in his speech, and he blamed the loquacious and talkative. It has come to our knowledge that 'Aisha — may God be pleased with her — would say: "The Prophet — may God bless and save him — did not continue his speech uninterruptedly, as you do; his speech was concisely cut short, and you display yours ceaselessly.[142] He went one day to speak, but was embarrassed and became silent; then he said: "This difficulty in speaking fluently affects sometimes the prophets." And he — peace be with him — heard somebody using pompous verbosity of speech and articulating with affectation, and he silenced him;[143] then he went and said to those who were present; "Be natural in your speech, and let Satan fascinate you not; verily, people among you whom I most love and who will be nearest me in the day of Resurrection, are those who have the best work; and people among you whom I most hate, and who will be the remotest from me in the day of Resurrection are those who have the worst work; verily, I do hate the chatterers, the pretentious and those who indulge in grandiloquence."

(DB) Therefore, the question of his being unlettered, for which he has been blamed by the men of the protected cults, is not a dishonor nor a discredit to him; on the contrary, it is a proof of and an enlightening argument in his favor. If a literary and eloquent man had brought forth such a book as that I have described, it would have been a miracle; what would then be the case if its author were a man of the desert and unlettered? This is a clear proof that God has made him pronounce it and that the Holy Spirit has assisted and directed him in it.

X.

CHAPTER VII.

THE VICTORY OF THE PROPHET — MAY GOD BLESS AND SAVE HIM — IS A MARK OF PROPHETIC OFFICE.

(DC) AMONG the miracles of the Prophet — may God bless and save him — is his victory, which all Muslims have used as an argument.[144] I believed formerly, as other Christians believe, that victory was a point common to all nations and that what was common was not a sign of prophetic office. When I awoke from the intoxication of error and arose from the slumber of indecision and got rid of the aberration of tradition, I knew then that the question was not as they believed. Because the Prophet — may God bless and save him — came out an orphan, unique and poor, as the Most High God said: "Did He not find thee an orphan and give thee shelter. And find thee erring and guide thee? And find thee poor with a family and nourish thee?" (Qur'an 93:6-8)[145] And he called all the Arabs and all the nations to the belief in the Most High God while people were shooting at him from one bow, sneering at him and stirred against him; this did not deter him, nor did it discourage him, but he preached his religion without flinching and went forward towards what God had ordered him, without shrinking. When he noticed that they were rejecting his order, thinking evil of him and not entering willfully into the religion and the grace of God, he made them enter into it by force; his claim then triumphed and the Arabs one and all submitted to him; next, miracles and prophecies succeeded one another among them, and the new religion became dear to them and truth resplendent; then, after their hate and their enmity, their love and attachment to him reached what the adversaries see and hear.

(DD) Who has ever claimed such a victory in the name of God since the creation of the world by God? A victory comprising conditions and good qualities such as to call to the Creator of Heaven and earth, abstraction from this world, encouragement for the world to come, prevention from associating other gods and helpers with God and from committing iniquity and impurity? A victory which was realized in such a decisive and unquestionable way, in all the countries and regions of the earth, on sea and land, from the extreme Sus[146] to the deserts of Turkestan and Tibet, by means of devotees and deeply pious leaders and by proclamations in the name of the God of Abraham, Ishmael, Isaac, Jacob and the rest of the prophets? His disciples were distinguished by contempt of the world, abstinence from its possessions and cares and self-denial in every pleasure and passion; and were satisfied with food strictly for the maintenance of the body; and had such orders for equality of asseveration and right in judicial decisions that if a believing Muslim had killed a member of (the) protected cults, an unbeliever, the Muslim would have to be killed as retaliation and justice;[147] we know with certainty that such a victory undoubtedly takes the place of a sign of prophetic office.[148]

(DE) As to the victories of other nations, which they oppose to us, if they had relinquished the passions which blind and deafen, and discerned their motives, they would have known that the victory of Alexander, of Ardashir, son of Babak and of others was not in God, nor for God, nor for His prophets, but its aim was solely fame, power and reputation, while the victors were either Atheists,[149] or Dualists, or Pagans; and this cannot be compared with the dignity and sublimity of the victory of Islam. To this victory there is another sufficient and decisive evidence, viz., it cannot fail to have emanated either from God or from Satan; if they confess that it is from God, Islam is then true and they ought to accept it and embrace it; and if they pretend that is from Satan, Satan would then be in agreement and not in disagreement with God and His prophets, obedient and not rebellious, since he would have helped the man who had called to the One and Eternal God and promoted the religion of the man who had ordered fasting and prayer, prohibited fornication, unbelief, immorality and iniquity and made the exaltation and glorification of God his rallying-cry in fighting, his vanguard in attacking and his armor in charging and thrusting. He who believes that Satan would help to make such a religion prevail and be maintained has indeed a good opinion of him and contradicts what God and His prophets have said about him. How can Satan help a man who calls to such a religion as this in which his roots are pulled up, his chances cut off and his followers and disciples utterly destroyed?

(DF) Some wicked people thought the same of thing of the Messiah — peace be with Him — and the Rabbis of the Jews said of Him: "This one drives out demons by means of the prince of the demons." But the Christ said to them: "Every kingdom which is divided against itself shall perish and shall not stand, and every city in which there is disunion and disagreement shall not last and shall not be firm; if it is Satan who casts out Satan, how then can his kingdom and his might last?" (Matt. 12:24-26) And the Jews were put to shame.

(DG) This is our argument against those who say of the Prophet —

may God bless and save him — what the Jews said of the Messiah — peace be with Him. Among what the Prophet — peace be with him — related on behalf of God about Satan is the following saying: "Ay, the partisans of Satan, they are losers." (Qur'an 58:20) And he said: "Verily the devil is to you a foe, so take him as a foe; he only calls his partisans to be the fellows of the blaze." (Qur'an 35:6) And he said: "Go forth therefrom, for verily, thou art pelted, and verily, upon thee is My curse unto the day of Judgment." (Qur'an 38:78-79) And he said: "I will surely fill hell with thee and with those who follow thee amongst them all together." (Qur'an 38:85) And he said: "O ye who believe, follow not the traces of Satan." (Qur'an 24:21) And he said: "I seek refuge in the Lord of men, the King of men, the God of men, from the evil of the Whisperer who slinks off." (Qur'an 114:1-4) And the Prophet — peace be upon him — ordered us to take refuge in God from him, in every prayer at every opportune moment by saying: "I take refuge in the Hearer and the Knower, from the stoned Satan."[150]

(DH) If Satan helps the man who curses him and unveils his wickedness to the world, we shall not be secure against the fact that all the religions which appeared in the name of a Unique God might have been in agreement with Satan and from him. All the nations agree that Satan enjoins association of other gods with God and worship of idols and fire; that he favors adultery, fornication and treachery, which are the objects of his desire and his suggestions; that he is an enemy of God and an enemy of His prophets who command the contrary of all this. Since Satan cannot be of the followers of God, the victory of the Prophet is then from God and not from someone else.

[Sections XI - XV have been deleted in this edition.]

XVI.

CHAPTER IX.

IF THE PROPHET — MAY GOD BLESS AND SAVE HIM — HAD NOT APPEARED, THE PROPHECIES OF THE PROPHETS ABOUT ISHMAEL — PEACE BE WITH HIM — AND ABOUT

THE PROPHET — PEACE BE WITH HIM — WHO IS THE LAST OF THE PROPHETS, WOULD HAVE NECESSARILY BECOME WITHOUT OBJECT.

(DI) THE Most High God does not contradict His promise, nor does He belie His words and disappoint the man who puts his trust in Him. He had announced to Abraham — peace be with him — and Hagar — God's mercy be with her — clear and joyful messages, which we do not see fulfilled and realized except by the appearance of the Prophet — may God bless and save him. Indeed, to Hagar messages have been announced such as no wife of ancient men can claim the like of them, after the virgin Mary, mother of the Christ — peace be with him. Moreover, to Mary — peace be with her — the Christ was announced once only, while to Hagar Ishmael was announced twice; and to his father — peace be with him — he was announced several times. God willing, I will explain this in its due place.

(DJ) What the Most High God revealed to Abraham — peace be with him — exclusively about Ishmael is His saying through Moses — peace be with him — in the tenth chapter of the first Book of the Torah. God said there to Abraham — peace be with him — "I have heard (thy prayer)[151] about Ishmael; I have blessed him, increased him and magnified him exceedingly: twelve princes shall he beget, and I will make him a great nation." (Gen. 17:20) This is in the version of Marcus, the translator (tarjaman); but in the Torah, translated by seventy-two Jewish priests, it is said: "He will beget twelve nations."[152] No promises and no announcements about anyone could be greater than the saying of the Most High God: "I have blessed him, increased him and multiplied him exceedingly." Less than this coming from the Most High God is great and not so much as this is sublime, because the measure that God considers as considerable and exceeding great, there is no measure greater than it. This is a rebuke and a rebuff to that rude and impudent man who found fault with Ishmael and derided him, because God said about him: "He will be a wild ass of men." I will explain it in this chapter as a rebuke against that blockhead and dolt.[153]

615

(DK) Moses — peace be with him — had already prophesied with a prophecy similar to this in the ninth chapter of the first Book, saying that when Hagar fled from Sarah, the angel of God appeared to her and said: "O Hagar, Sarai's maid, whence comest thou, and where art thou going?" (Hagar answering him) said: "I flee from my mistress Sarai." The angel of the Lord said unto her: "Return to thy mistress and submit to her; because I will multiply (thy posterity and) thy seed, that it shall not be numbered for multitude,[154] and behold thou shalt be with child and shalt bear a son and shalt call his name Ishmael, because God hath heard (thy affliction) and thy humility; and he will be a wild ass of men, and his hand will be over all, and the hand of all (stretched) to him,[155] and his abode shall be on all his brother's frontiers." (Gen. 16:8-13) This is the second announcement uttered face to face by the angel to Hagar — peace be with her — on behalf of the Most High God; and he told her that God would make her son's hand the higher and the hand of all others the lower with regard to him. We have not seen that this point of the prophecy of Moses — peace be with him — was fulfilled and realized except after the appearance of the Prophet Muhammad — may God bless and save him.

(DL) And Moses said in the thirteenth chapter of the first Book, that God said to Abraham: "And also the son of thy bondwoman will I make a great nation, because he is from thy seed." (Gen. 21:13) This is the third prophecy about Ishmael — peace be with him. After this saying, Moses said: "And when Abraham rose up in the morning (he took out of his habitation Hagar and his child in conformity to the wish of Sarah and went to where God had ordered him about her; and he gave her food and provisions and put the child on her shoulder and sent her away on her journey. And Hagar departed)[156] and wandered in the wilderness (called) Beersheba; and her water was spent;[157] and she cast the child under one of the shrubs and went off[158] at a distance of a bowshot[159] in order that she[160] might not see the death of her son. And for that she was weeping and grieved. And God heard the voice of the lad and the angel of God called to Hagar out of heaven and said, 'What aileth thee Hagar? Let thy heart rejoice, for God hath heard the voice of the lad;[161] arise, lift him up and take hold of him, for (God) will make him a great nation.' And God opened her eyes, and behold!¹⁶² a well of water; and she crawled and filled the bottle (from it) and gave the lad drink from it. And God was with her and with the lad¹⁶³ until he grew; and his abode was in the wilderness of Paran, and he applied himself to learn archery." (Gen. 21:14-21)

(DM) This prophecy of Moses¹⁶⁴ — peace be with him — about Ishmael and his mother Hagar is similar to the saying of the angel Gabriel to the virgin Mary: "Our Lord is with thee, O blessed among women." (Lk. 1:28) The Christians have been deluded by this saying and have said that God was dwelling in her, because Gabriel said to her: "Our Lord is with thee"; but Moses — peace be with him — said the same thing about Hagar, that "God was with her and with the lad until he grew."

(DN) These are four messages exclusively about Ishmael — peace be with him. Two of them came down to Abraham and two to Hagar. Let that stupid and feeble-minded man find us messages more numerous, more resplendent and genuine than these from the Most High God, which have followed one another over parents for the sake of their child, since the beginning of the world.¹⁶⁵

(DO) The messages delivered by God to Abraham concerning all his posterity and children are also two; one of them is the saying of the Most High God to Abraham, when he offered his son¹⁶⁶ for sacrifice: "Because thou hast done this deed,¹⁶⁷ and hast not withheld thy son, thine only son, by myself I do swear that I will bless thee, I will multiply thy posterity (and I will make them) as the number of the stars of the heaven, and as the sand of the sea shores; and thy children shall inherit the countries of their enemies; and in them¹⁶⁸ shall all the nations of the earth be blessed." (Gen. 22: 16-18) The Torah says too: "Abraham said, 'Behold I am dying, and I have no child, and no successor; and my heir is my servant,¹⁶⁹ and one born in my house.' Then the Lord said to him, 'This shall not be thine heir. Get out¹⁷⁰ and look toward the stars of heaven; if thou art able to number them, thou shalt number also thy children.' " (Gen. 15:4-5)

(DP) The first four prophecies are exclusively about Ishmael, and

617

Ishmael has, too, a share with Isaac and his other brethren in the last two; these make six peremptory prophecies and messages about him. In spite of this, that rude Garmecite,[171] wicked and ignorant, pretends that Ishmael is not counted among the children of Abraham — peace be with him. The above words were realized and fulfilled by the appearance of the Prophet[172] — may God bless and save him. Prior to that all Christians and Jews knew that the children of Abraham, known by his name and related to him,[173] did not cease to be among the various nations of the earth. A company of them were in Egypt as slaves to Pharaohs and Copts, treated rudely and oppressed; and a company of them were in the direction of the deserts and in the Hidjaz, amidst hardships and wars. Those who dwelt in Egypt went, later, to Syria where war was waged against them morning and evening by those who were around them. Then they were not long in being scattered, banished, stripped of their power, deprived of the kingdom and dispersed in different regions and countries of the earth. Bands of black men[174] and waves of white men molested them until the Prophet — may God bless and save him — appeared; then after a long time all the prophecies were realized and the messages fulfilled, and the children of Ishmael triumphed over those who were around them, pulverized them, scattered them in the air, as the prophets — peace be with them — had foretold, and ground them. They spread in all the regions of the earth like young locusts, and in competing with other nations they became as their life-blood,[175] and excelled them at the measure of the distance of the Pleiades from the earth, in India, Abyssinia, extreme Sus,[176] Turkestan and Khazar;[177] they reigned too, in the East and West, and where the waves of the Mediterranean and the Euxine seas[178] collide. The name of Abraham appeared then in the mouth of all nations, morning and evening, and there is at present no man, no woman, no male slave, no female slave, rich or poor, happy or unhappy, on sea or on land, who does not believe in one God, glorify the God of Abraham and seek His protection.

(DR) As to Judaism, it had appeared only in one section of mankind. As to Christianity, although it appeared in a great and glorious nation, yet in the land of Abraham and his wife Sarah and their forefathers and in the land of Hagar and her forefathers, it had not wielded the scepter and held absolute power and sway such as those vouchsafed by God to their inhabitants through the Prophet — may God bless and save him.

(DS) In favor of what I have claimed, I shall now bring testimonies from the prophets, but I should first begin by refuting that rude Garmecite who belittled Ishmael and blamed him on account of the description given him by God. Were it not for his stupidity and the weakness of his intelligence, he would have known that the words of revelation have meanings and mysteries understood only by people who are far advanced in science. The Torah said that God: "became a lion and devoured the children of Israel"; (Num. 24:9) it is said too in the Torah, that "God is a burning fire"; (Ex. 24:17) and God is neither fire nor a ravenous beast; but these are taken as illustrations for wrath, irritation, punishment and revenge. The Christ called the head of the Apostles, the one whom he ordered to shepherd His community, *Simeon the stone* (Peter); and He called all His nation *Sheep;* and He called Himself *Lamb of God.* If one were tempted to answer that stupid and weak-minded man, one would tell him that a wild ass is stronger and more powerful than a sheep, which is devoured by the wolf and coveted by the dog and the fox. There is indeed no animal among the quadrupeds weaker and less powerful than it. If that ignorant dolt and his followers return to the interpretation of these names, we also will begin to interpret and say:

(DT) The interpretation of the *wild ass* comprises many meanings, one of which is that God — may He be blessed and exalted — indicated by this name that Ishmael — peace be with him — would dwell in dry and arid lands, protect his consort and be warlike and jealous in the same way as the wild ass dwells in the deserts, castrates the male organ from his young ones out of jealousy and attacks vigorously herds pertaining to other males, not ceasing to fight against the male in kicking it and biting it, until it has conquered its female and its herd. When it has got them, it keeps them and protects them and defends their young ones and does not eat them as lions and wolves do; these seek victory only to devour and to gulp, but wild asses seek victory

619

from the love of action and sport.

(DU) Further, God called Ishmael by this name in order that no means may be found for denying him — peace be with him — a dwelling in the deserts, and in order to signify that God had placed him in these deserts for a great and beautiful purpose, viz., that He, the Most High, wished to preserve his genealogy and to keep intact his freedom, in order that he might not have that slavery among the nations that others had, nor be expatriated and torn away as others have been.

(DV) Let that miserable idiot understand these meanings and not vilify the one about whom God — may He be blessed and exalted — said that "He has blessed him and magnified him exceedingly." He who belittles him that God has magnified is like the man who magnifies him that God has belittled: suffice it to say that the one who does this does it to his shame and his confusion!

(DW) The wild ass has also the meaning which the Persians and other peoples have given to it; they called a man warlike, courageous and skilled in the art of fighting *"Gor";* hence Bahram Gor got his surname; and *Gor* means a "wild ass"; through it the inhabitants of Tabaristan have been called *Goriyah,* and for the same reason a bold and courageous man is called *Gor-mardan,* i.e., the wild ass of men; likewise the Arabs call a courageous man *"Ram of the tribe,"* and compare him with the stallion and the male camel kept for breeding and with other animals.

XVII.

CHAPTER X.

THE PROPHECIES OF THE PROPHETS ABOUT THE PROPHET — MAY GOD BLESS HIM AND THEM, AND SAVE HIM AND THEM.

(DX) I HAVE already mentioned four prophecies about Ishmael —

peace be with him — which contain testimonies to the truth of the religion of the Prophet — may God bless and save him — which only the ignorant ignore and the stupid deny. If the Prophet — may God bless and save him — had not been sent, these prophecies would have been vain and inexplicable.[179] I shall mention from other prophecies of the prophets — peace be with them — those which are as clear as something seen with one's own eyes. Some of them have indeed described his time, his country, his mission, his followers, his *Helpers* and have clearly mentioned him by name.

(DY) The fifth prophecy alluding to him and pointing to his prophetic office and to his truth is the saying of Moses — peace be with him — to the children of Israel, found in the eleventh chapter of the fifth and the last Book of the Torah; "The Lord your God will raise up from the midst of you and from your brethren a Prophet like unto me; unto him ye shall hearken." (Deut. 18:15) And the Torah said, in this same chapter, in confirmation and explanation of this saying, that the Lord said to Moses — peace be with him — "I will raise them up a Prophet from among their brethren, like unto thee; and whosoever will not hearken unto my words which that man shall deliver in My name I will avenge Myself on him." (Deut. 18:18-19) And God has not raised up a prophet from among the brethren of the children of Israel, except Muhammad — peace be with him; the phrase "from the midst of them" acts as a corroboration and limitation, viz., that he will be from the children of their father and not from an avuncular relationship of his. As to the Christ — peace be with Him — and the rest of the prophets — may God bless them — they were from the Israelites themselves; and he who believes that the Most High God has not put a distinction between the man who is from the Jews themselves and the man who is from their brethren, believes wrongly.[180]

(DZ) The one who might claim that this prophecy is about the Christ — peace be with Him — would overlook two peculiarities and show ignorance in two aspects; the first is that the Christ — peace be with Him — is from the children of David, and David is from themselves, and not from their brethren; the second is that he who says once that

Christ is the Creator and not created, and then pretends that the Christ is like Moses, his speech is contradictory and his saying is inconsistent.[181] Similarly wrong would he be who would pretend that this prophecy is about Joshua, son of Nun, because Joshua is not counted among the prophets and has delivered nothing on behalf of God to the children of Israel, but what Moses — peace be with him — had already delivered, and also because he is from themselves and not from their brethren.

(EA) Therefore, the prophet that the Most High God "has raised up from among their brethren" is Muhammad — may God bless and save him — and whosoever contradicts him God will wreak vengeance upon him. You see already distinct traces of vengeance upon those who have rejected him, and clear marks of grace upon those who have accepted him.

(EB) And Moses said in the twentieth chapter of this Book: "The Lord came from (Mount) Sinai,[182] and rose up from Seir and appeared from Mount Paran with tens of thousands of saints at His right hand. He gave them (power) and made them to be loved by nations and called blessings on all His saints." (Deut. 23:2-3) Paran is the land which Ishmael — peace be with him — inhabited; for this reason God had previously mentioned it in the Torah, saying: "And he learned archery in the wilderness of Paran." (Gen. 21:20-21) All people knew that Ishmael dwelt in Mecca,[183] and his children and successors who are in it and around it know the abode of their grandfather and do not ignore his land and his country; — and "the Lord" rose up from Paran! If this is not as we have mentioned, let them show us "a lord" who appeared from Mount Paran; and they will never be able to do so. The name *"lord"* refers here to the Prophet — may God bless and save him; it is a word applied by Arabs and non-Arabs to the Most High God, or to men, His servants, as if you would say *"the lord of the house,"* as the Syrians call the man whom they wish to exalt: *Mari* = "my lord," "my master," *mar* meaning in Syriac "lord."[184]

XVIII.

THE PROPHECIES OF DAVID ABOUT THE PROPHET — GOD BLESS AND SAVE BOTH OF THEM.

(EC) AND the prophet David — peace be with him — said in the forty-fifth Psalm:[185] "Therefore God hath blessed thee for ever; gird then thy sword, O giant, because thy majesty and thy *Hamd* are the conquering majesty and *Hamd*.[186] Ride thou on the word of truth and on the course[187] of piety, because thy law and thy prescriptions are associated with the majesty of thy right hand;[188] and thy arrows are sharp, and the people fall under thee." (Ps. 45:2-5) We do not know anyone to whom the features of girding a sword, sharpness of arrows, majesty of the right hand and falling down of people under him are due, except the Prophet — may God bless and save him — who rode on the word of truth, humbled himself before God in devotion and fought the idolaters until the true faith prevailed.

(ED) And David — peace be with him — said in the forty-eighth Psalm: "Great is our Lord and He is greatly *Mahmud*;[189] and in the city of our God and in His mountain, there is a Holy One and a *Muhammad*;[190] and the joy of the whole earth." (Ps. 48:1-2) This prophecy of David — peace be with him — is clearness and explicitness itself which cannot suffer any ambiguity. David has indeed mentioned the Prophet by name.

(EE) And David — peace be with him — said in the fiftieth Psalm: "God hath shown from Zion a *Mahmud* crown. Then God shall come and not be idle; and fires shall devour before Him, and they shall be very tempestuous round about him." (Ps. 50:2-3) Do you not see that the prophet David — peace be with him — does not strip from any of this prophecies the mention of *Muhamad* or *Mahmud*, as you read it yourselves? His saying "a *mahmud* crown means that he is a *Muhammad* and a *mahmud* head and leader. The meaning of "Muhammad," "Mahmud," and "Hamid" is linguistically identical. The example of "crown" is given to mean lordship and leadership.

(EF) And he said too, in the seventy-second Psalm, in confirmation and corroboration of the preceding prophecies: "He shall have dominion from sea to sea and from the rivers unto the end of the earth. They that dwell in the islands shall bow before him on their knees, and his enemies shall lick the dust. The kings of Tarshish and of the isles shall bring him presents, and the kings of Sheba and the kings of Seba shall offer gifts. All kings shall fall down before him, and all nations shall (obey him and) submit to him.[191] For he shall deliver (the persecuted and) the needy from him who is stronger then he, and he shall look after the weak who has no helper. He shall have mercy for the weak and the poor, and shall save their souls from harm and violence; and precious their blood shall be in his sight. And he shall remain, and to him shall be given of the gold and of the countries of Sheba; and prayer shall be made for him continually, and daily shall he be blessed, like a great quantity of corn on the surface of the earth; and he shall make his fruits grow on top of the mountains, like those which grow on the Lebanon; and he shall make something like the grass of the earth to shoot up in his town; and his memory shall endure for ever; his name exists before the sun, and all nations shall be blessed by him, and all of them shall give him *Hamd*" (or: call him *Muhammad*). (Ps. 72:8-12)[192]

(EG) This is an efficient and sufficient prophecy, in which there is no ambiguity and difficulty. We do not know anyone who reigned from sea to sea and from the rivers which God has mentioned in the Torah; Tigris, Euphrates, Pison and Gihon and before whom kings bowed on their knees and whose enemies licked dust and to whom the kings of Yemen brought presents, except the Prophet — may God bless and save him — and his nation, and except Mecca and the traces of Abraham's steps which it contains.[193] And we do not know anyone who is blessed and prayed for continually, except Muhammad — may God bless and save him — in the following saying of the believing nations: "O God, pray over Muhammad and the family of Muhammad, and bless Muhammad and the family of Muhammad."[194] Which sign is more obvious and which prophecy is clearer and more luminous than this, especially when the prophet David — peace be with him — closed his prophecy by saying: "And all nations shall be blessed by him and call him Muhammad"? And the meaning of *Muhammad* and *Mahmud* is one.

(EH) And David — peace be with him — said in the hundred and tenth Psalm: "The Lord is at thy right hand, and He shall strike through kings in the day of His wrath; (He shall weaken the prop of the kingdom) and shall judge among them in justice.[195] He shall multiply the (dead bodies) and the corpses and shall cut off the heads of many people in the earth and shall drink in his journey from (the water of) the valleys; therefore his head shall be lifted up (to the heights)." (Ps. 110:5-7) This is also a description as clear as something seen with the eye.[196] Who is the one at whose right hand the Lord was, who judged in justice, who cut off heads and who multiplied dead bodies and corpses, except him — may God bless and save him — and his nation?

(EI) And he said too, in the hundred and forty-ninth Psalm: "For the Lord hath taken pleasure in His people and hath beautified the poor with salvation; let the saints be strong in glory and sing to him in their beds and praise God with their throats; because in their hands is the two-edged sword to execute vengeance upon the heathen and punishment upon the nations — to bind their kings with chains and their exalted ones (and nobles) with fetters, to bring them to the written (and decided) judgment. *Hamd* to all his saints." (Ps. 149:4-9) Do you not see — may God guide you — that these peculiarities refer exclusively to the Prophet — may God bless and save him — and to his nation? It is he who has the two-edged sword with him, it is he who with his nation has executed vengeance upon the giants of Persia and the tyrants of the Greeks and others, and it is he whose followers have bound the kings with chains and conducted their nobles and their children in chains and fetters and who sing to God in their beds and glorify Him morning and evening and continually in saying: "God is supremely great; and much praise be to God."

(EJ) And he — peace be with him — said in the hundred and fifty-second Psalm — which is attributed to Isaiah — peace be with him — mentioning the Arabs and their country, and not leaving any room for reply and excuse: "Let the wilderness and the cities thereof rejoice, and let (the land of) Kedar become meadows. Let the inhabitants of caves sing and shout forth from the tops of the mountains the *Hamd* of the Lord and declare His praises in the islands. For the Lord shall come forth as a mighty man and as a man of war, stirring up for pride. He shall rebuke, shall be mighty and shall kill His enemies." (Is. 42:11-13)[197] To whom does the wilderness belong, O my cousins — may God guide you — except to this nation? And who is Kedar, except the descendants of Ishmael — peace be with him — who inhabit caves and give *Hamd* to the Lord and declare His praises at daybreak and at midday? And who is he who rebuked, became mighty and killed his enemies, except Muhammad[198] — may God bless and save him —and his nation? As to the meaning of David's saying: "The Lord shall come forth," we have demonstrated above that the name "Lord" refers to men of high standing and noble.[199]

XIX.

THE PROPHECIES OF ISAIAH ABOUT THE PROPHET — MAY GOD BLESS AND SAVE HIM.

(EK) HE said in the second chapter of his book: "The Lord will be mighty in that day and lifted up alone over all the pine trees of Lebanon that are high and elevated and over all the oak trees which are in the land of Bashan and over all the high mountains and over every hill that is lifted up and over every lofty tower and over every inaccessible mountain and over all the ships of Tarshish and over all pleasant and handsome imagery. He will destroy the idols in an open destruction, and (people) will hide in the caves of the rocks and in the holes of the earth from the terror of God the Most High, and from the glory of His *Hamd*" (Is. 2:12-19) Isaiah is in accordance with the prophet David — peace be with both of them — who said: "Thy majesty and Thy *Hamd* are the conquering *Hamd*" (Ps. 45:3, paraphrase)[200] It is as if these two prophecies were two rays coming from a single reflecting center. As to the mountains and trees, they mean men of high and low estate and kings; instances for this are numerous in their Books.

(EL) In the third chapter he said on behalf of the Most High God: "I will lift up an ensign to the nations from a remote country and hiss unto them from the ends of the earth, and they will come swiftly and quickly; they will not be weary, nor will they stumble; they will not slumber neither will they sleep; they will not loose the girdle of their loins and the lachet of their shoes will not be broken. Their arrows are sharp, and their bows are bent; and their horses' hoofs are like flint in solidity, and their wheels are as swift as whirlwinds; and their roaring is like that of lions and like that of a young lion roaring for prey, and no one can escape him. In that day he will overtake them like the roaring and the colliding waves of the sea; and they will look unto the earth, and they will only see distress and darkness; and the light shall be darkened from the dust of their masses." (Is. 5:26-30)

(EM) This is the saying of the Most High God. And the children of Ishmael — peace be with him — the nation of the Prophet — may God bless and save him — are those for whom God hissed; and they came from their country with haste, without weariness and sloth; their arrows were sharp and their bows bent; the hoofs of their horses were like rock and flint, and their roaring was like the roaring of lions; it is they that had prey from East and West, and no one could escape them. The giants became like lambs with them, and dust was stirred by their onslaught, while paths and defiles were too narrow for them.

(EN) And he — peace be with him — said in the fifth chapter, in explanation of his preceding prophecies: "The nation which was in darkness saw a resplendent light, and those that were in deep darkness and under the shadow of death, light hath shined upon them. Thou hast multiplied partisans and followers of whom thou wast proud. As to them, they joy in thy hands like those who joy in the day of harvest and like those who joy at the division of spoils. Because thou hast broken the yoke which had humbled them, and the staff which was on their shoulders; and thou hast bruised the rod which had enslaved them, as thou hast broken those whom thou didst break in the day of Midian." (Is. 9:2-4)

(EO) This resembles the description which the Most High God gave in the Qur'an about the Prophet — may God bless and save him — saying: "And he will ease them of their burden and of the yokes which were upon them." (Qur'an 7: 156) See — may God guide you — and examine who is he who has broken the yoke from the children of Ishmael, destroyed the power of the enemies and bruised the rod of the mighty. Has that light shone on anyone except on the dwellers in that dark desert of the pagan posterity of Ishmael?[201]

(EP) And he said in this chapter: "Unto us a child is born, and unto us a child is given, whose government is on his shoulder." (Is. 9:6) He means by that "his prophecy is on his shoulder." All this is according to the books of the Syrians which Marcus has translated; but in the Hebrew it is said: "The sign of prophecy is on his shoulder."[202] This is what the Muslims call "the seal of prophecy." This is, therefore, a clear allusion to the portraiture of the Prophet[203] — may God bless and save him — and a reference to his face and his moles.[204]

(EQ) And he said in the tenth chapter, enlightening what was obscure and explaining what was difficult in his prophecies: "Thou wilt come from the country of the South,[205] from a remote country, and from the land of the desert, hastening and passing through like tempests and storms from the winds. We have seen a grievous and dreadful vision; the treacherous dealer dealeth treacherously, and the spoiler spoileth. Go up, O mountains of Elam and mountains of Media.[206] All the object of your desire and of your dispute hath ceased. Therefore is my loin filled with pain, and I feel the pangs of a woman in travail. I am pained, so that I cannot hear, and I am dismayed, so that I cannot see. My heart fainteth, and dim-sightedness hath affrighted me. What I loved as agreeable and pleasant has become terrifying and as something dreadful. Prepare ye then the tables; and ye who watch and spy lift up your eyes and eat and drink. Let the princes and the leaders rise up to their shields. Let them anoint them with ointment, for thus hath the Lord said unto me: 'Go, and set the watchman on the watch to declare what he seeth.' And what he hath seen was a pair of horsemen, one riding on an ass and another riding on a camel; and he hath heard great and long speech. And the watchman told me secretly and said in my ear: 'I am the permanent Lord, and I stand continually upon the watch tower and the high place of vision day and night.' While I was in that condition, behold, one of the horsemen approached saying: 'Babylon is fallen, is fallen and all the graven images of her gods are broken unto the ground. That which I have heard from the mighty Lord, God of Israel, have I declared unto you.' " (Is. 21:1-10)[207]

(ER) This too, is a clear and obvious prophecy which only the man who deceives himself and throws away his intelligence can reject. As no reasonable man dares feign ignorance and say that there was in the world a rider on an ass more appropriate to this prophecy than the Christ — peace be with Him — so also no man with sound judgment and intelligence is allowed to say that there was in the world a rider on a camel more appropriate to this prophecy than the Prophet — may God bless and save him — and his nation.[208] Are not the men of intelligence and science amongst the *People of the Book* ashamed to attribute such a clear and sublime prophecy to some rude and barbarous people?[209]

(ES) The prophet Isaiah has explained his saying and has not left them in blindness and has opened their deaf ears in adding: "Thus saith the Lord, thou wilt come from the country of the South (= of Yemen)." Then he explained that by saying: "From a remote country and from the land of the desert," in order that no objection may be left to the adversary. Then he added, saying "The gods of Babylon are fallen, are fallen, and have been destroyed." Now, there were incessantly in the country of Babylon kings who worshipped now idols, now fires, till the appearance of the Prophet — may God bless and save him — who destroyed their might, pullled down the temples of their idols and their fires and brought them into his religion either of free will or by force. Did not the adversaries feel abashed in saying that the rightly guided prophets of the family of Isaac — peace be with them — prophesied about the kings of Babylon, Media, Persia and Khuzistan,[210] and neglected to mention such an eminent Prophet and such a great and Abrahamic nation, and such a victorious Empire, or that God had hidden and concealed such a nation from them?

(ET) As to his saying: "I saw a treacherous dealer dealing treacherously," he designates by it Persia, Khuzistan and the land of Nabatia, which he has mentioned in saying to them: "Go back unsuccessful to your countries and retire like banished and plundered people."[211]

(EU) And he said in this chapter: "In the forest which is on the way to Duranim[212] shall ye lodge in the evening. O inhabitants of the South, welcome with water him that is thirsty and receive with food the scattered and dispersed people; because the sword hath scattered them; and their dispersion was from sharp spear-heads, bent bows and a grievous and fierce war." (Is. 21:13-14)[213] Who are these thirsty people who come forth from the direction of the South, whom the Most High has ordered the inhabitants of the country to meet? Or who are the peoples expatriated and scattered by war? And who are those whom God hath commanded to receive with water and food, except the Arabs, when they rose to fight against the neighboring nations, Persians, Greeks and others, who separated them from water and pasture?

(EV) And he said in the eleventh chapter: "From the ends of the earth have we heard song and hymn to the righteous and the pious saying: 'A secret to me, a secret to me,'[214] and saying 'Woe is me; the treacherous dealers have dealt treacherously. I am surrounding you, O inhabitants of the earth, with fear, pit and snare; and he who fleeth from war shall fall into the pit; and he who cometh up out of the pit shall be taken in the snare, for the doors of heaven are open, and the foundations of the earth shake and tremble." (Is. 24:16-18) This is according to the translation of Marcus, while the Hebrew, which is the original, says: "We have heard from the ends of the earth the voice of *Muhammad*."[215] And Mecca is in the ends of the earth and on the sea-shore. Let them tell us when and in what generation have the polytheists and the unbelievers suffered such terrors, punishments and calamities such as those they have endured under this Arab Empire?

(EW) And he said in the sixteenth chapter, explaining the preceding prophecies and rebuking men of obstinacy and delusion: "Let the inhabitants of the arid desert rejoice, and let the wilderness and the desert be glad; let them blossom like the autumn crocus, and let them rejoice and flourish like a mountain goat, because they will be given by *Ahmad* the glory of Lebanon,[216] and something like the excellency of watery meadows and luxuriant gardens. And they shall see the glory of Allah — may He be exalted and glorified — and the excellency of our God." (Is. 35:1-2) Do you not see — may God guide you — in this prophecy that Isaiah — peace be with him — has given to you and which the Revelation has mentioned the Arabian deserts and wildernesses and the freshness, brightness and honors prepared for them by *Ahmad* — peace be with him? Does any doubt still disturb you after he has mentioned him by name and described the dry desert?

(EX) And he said in the nineteenth chapter, adding more light and clearness: "Someone cried in the wilderness: 'Prepare the way for the Lord, and make straight in the desert the way for our God. All the valleys shall be filled with water, and they will overflow; and the mountains and the hills shall become low; and the hillocks shall be levelled, and the rough ground shall be plain and smooth; and the glory of the Lord shall be revealed, and everyone shall see it, because the Lord hath said it.' " (Is. 40:3-5) Do you know — may God guide you — a nation which God has called from the desert and the wilderness and to which He has made the rough places straight, the sterile lands fertile and the dry land rich with pasture; to which He has made the valleys overflow with water for their thirsty ones; and to which He has subjugated the giants and the kings whom He has represented by the above hills and mountains — except this Arab nation for which the Tigris became like a beaten track?[217] When they reached it, they said unanimously: "He who has protected us on land will also protect us on sea"; then they crossed it, while on the other side were Chosrau and his warriors and the *Marzubans;*[218] they despised him, and they did not recoil from him when they were half naked, barefooted and protecting their heads with nothing but their wrists.

(EY) And he said in this chapter: "The Lord God will appear with might, and His arm with strength and power. His reward is with Him and His work before Him, like the shepherd who shepherds his flock; and He will gather His sheep with His arm and carry them in His bosom, and He will feed Himself those that give suck." (Is. 40:10-11) We have already proved in what has preceded and in our book of *Reply to the Different Denominations of Christians* that the words "God" and "Lord" are applied also to men. This prophecy corroborates this statement since Isaiah declared that the "Lord God" was a man whose reward was before him, and his work before him.[219] He alluded by this to the Prophet — may God bless and save him — because it is he whose reward was before him, and it is he who freely distributes his presents and gifts to the fighters for God's sake, from the spoils of the successors and victories which accompanied him. His saying: "He is like the shepherd who shepherds the flock," is a figure of the tenderness of the Prophet — may God bless and save him — and his gentleness towards his co-religionists; because the Most High God says about him — may God bless and save him — "Now hath an Apostle come unto you from among yourselves; your iniquities press heavily upon him. He is careful over you and towards the faithful, compassionate, merciful." (Qur'an 9:129)[220] And the Most High God said to Moses — peace be with him — "I shall make thee a god to Pharaoh." (Ex. 7:1) And it is said in the Torah: "The sons of the Most High God saw the daughters of men that they were fair and handsome, and they took them as wives." (Gen. 6:2) And the prophet David — may God bless and save him — said: "The Lord said to my Lord." (Ps. 110:1) In all these passages it has been demonstrated that the two words "God" and "Lord" were applied to men.[221]

(EZ) And Isaiah — peace be with him — said in this chapter: "Who hath raised the Pious One[222] from the East and hath called him to his foot, in order to give him the nations and to awe by him the kings and to make his swords as abundant as dust and earth and his bows as numerous as disseminated sheaves? He shall overcome them and strike them in the face; then he shall bring forth peace; and shall not set off for a journey on foot." (Is. 41:2-4) This is similar to what the Most High God has said in the Qur'an. About his saying: "Who hath raised the Pious One from the East," the land of Hidjaz and that of Iraq with their neighborhood are to the inhabitants of Syria, east; and Syria, to the inhabitants of Barqah and of Ifriqiyah is east; and the land of Yemen and that of Hidjaz are called by the learned men, south. The one "called to the foot" of the "friend of God"[223] is the Prophet — may God bless and save him — and it is to him that God has given the nations; and it is by him that He has scolded the kings, and they were awed; and it is he whose archers and sword-bearers are innumerable; and it is by him that God has struck the nations in the face, has defeated and humbled them, and then has brought them to faith, which is Islam, and peace, as the Most High God says through the prophet Isaiah — peace be with him.

(FA) And he said in the twentieth chapter: "O family of Abraham, my friend, whom I have strengthened! I have called thee from the ends of the earth and from its plateaus and elevated places; I have called thee and said to thee: 'Thou art my servant, and I have chosen thee; and I have not made a secret of it. Fear thou not, for I am with thee, and be not dismayed, for behold I am thy God. I have strengthened thee, then I have helped thee, and with my strong and righteous hand I have upheld thee; for that, they that have the advantage over thee shall be ashamed and confounded; and they that fight and oppose thee shall be as nothing and disappear, and the people who resist thee shall perish. Thou shalt seek them and shalt not find any trace of them, because they shall cease and they shall be as something forgotten before thee; for I, the Lord, have strengthened thy right hand. I said unto thee, 'Fear not,' because I am thy help; and thy redeemer is the Holy One of Israel, saith God the Lord. I have made thee a sharp threshing instrument which thresheth all that is under it, and beateth it thoroughly. Thou shalt do likewise; thou shalt make the mountains low and thresh them, and thou shalt make the towns and the hills as chaff that winds shall carry away and whirlwinds shall scatter; and thou shalt rejoice then and rest in the Lord and become *Muhammad*[224] in the Holy One of Israel." (Is. 41:8-16)

(FB) This is a living prophecy, a saying clear and not difficult, distinctly and not ambiguously worded. The man spoken to is from the family of Abraham and from the descendants of Ishmael, who are represented by a pestle which triturates and a threshing instrument which pounds the mountain in the name of the God of Muhammad, whom He has mentioned by name, in saying, "He shall become *Muhammad* in the Most High God." Truth has become manifest, and the veil has been withdrawn. And if a sophist squabbles here, the most he could say would be that the meaning of the Syriac word is "he became *Mahmud*," and not "*Muhammad*"; but he who knows the Arabic language and is versed in its grammar will not contradict us in saying that the meaning of *Mahmud* and of *Muhammad* is identical.[225]

(FC) And he said in this chapter: "The poor and the weak seek water, and there is no water for them; their tongues have withered with thirst; and I, the Lord, will then answer their call, and will not forsake them; but I will open them for rivers on the mountains and will make fountains flow in the desert; I will create pools of water in the wilderness and will make springs of water flow in the dry land; I will grow, in the waste deserts, the pine tree, the myrtle and the olive tree; and I will plant in the arid desert the handsome cypress, that they may all of them see, and know, and consider, and understand that the hand of God hath done this, and the Holy One of Israel hath created it." (Is. 41:17-20) O my cousins, how can you find an escape from this clear and living prophecy? What could you say about it after Isaiah mentioned the countries described in the dry lands, the deserts and the wilderness of Arabia, the springs to which God has given outlet, the rivers which He has caused to flow, and the different kinds of trees He has planted therein? Then Isaiah mentioned the poor and the thirsty people of the desert and the Hidjaz,[226] and declared that it is the hand of the Most High God that has done it. He who rejects and throws away this prophecy has neither religion, nor shame, nor fairness. The name of the Prophet — may God bless and save him — having been mentioned in the preceding prophecy, what have you now left, O ye who doubt? And what would be the reasonable and acceptable excuse for the man who makes himself deaf and blind with regard to it?[227]

(FD) And he said in the twenty-first chapter: "Let the beasts of the desert, from jackals to ostriches, honor Me and exalt Me, because I have given water in the wilderness, and I have made rivers to flow in the country of Ashimun, in order that My chosen people might drink from them; let then My people that I have chosen drink from them." (Is. 43:20-21) He who has doubts about the preceding prophecies will have no excuse in ignoring or feigning to ignore, that the ostriches only live in the wilderness. He has mentioned the foxes and ostriches as an illustration referring to a people dwelling in the desert and the wilderness. He who squabbles about this and tries to make it ambiguous is on the way to perdition.[228]

(FE) And he said in the twenty-second chapter, on behalf of the Most High God: "I am the Lord, and there is no God besides Me; I am He from whom no secret is hidden; I declare to (My) servants what hath not been done, before it is done, and I reveal unto them the events and the unknown things, and I will do all My pleasure: calling a bird from the desert and from the far and remote country." (Is. 46:9-11) This is the Prophet — may god bless and save him — and it is he with whom God was pleased on account of the diligence which he had shown in pleasing and loving Him. If the adversaries shout and quibble, let them tell us where are the deserts and the waste lands which the Most High God has described, and who is the man whom He has called, and who pleased Him.

(FF) And he said in the twenty-third chapter, speaking to mankind of the Prophet — may God bless and save him — "Listen O isles, and understand, ye nations. The Lord hath invested me with majesty from far and from the womb hath He made mention of my name. And He hath made my tongue as sharp as a sword when I was still in the womb. And He hath hidden me in the shadow of His right hand, And He hath put me in His quiver as a chosen shaft; and He hath kept me close for His secret, and said unto me, 'Thou art My servant.' My piety and my justice are therefore before the Lord, truly; and my works are in the hands of my God,[229] and I became *Muhammad*[230] with the Lord, and in my God are my strength and power." (Is. 49:1-5) If somebody denies the name of *Muhammad* in these verses, let it be then *Mahmud;* he will not find any other objection.[231] It is, indeed, he whose tongue has been made by God as a sword, and this tongue is the perspicuous Arabic, which He had hidden in His quiver for His secret and His divine Economy which He has revealed; and it is he who, morning and evening, says through his community "There is no strength and there is no power except by God."

(FG) And he said in the twenty-sixth chapter what would enlighten, corroborate and confirm his preceding prophecies, and spoke to Hagar — peace be with her — "Sing, O woman of few children and desolate, and rejoice in *Hamd*, O barren; because the children of the deserted and ill-treated have become more numerous than those of the fortunate and favorite. And the Lord said to her, 'Enlarge the places of thy tents and stretch forth the curtains of thy habitations. Spare not, and be not weak, but lengthen thy cords and strengthen thy stakes, for thou shalt spread and extend in the earth, on the right hand and on the left, and thy seed shall inherit the nations, and they shall inhabit the desolate and ruined towns." (Is. 54:1-4)[232]

(FH) Would that I knew what they might say about this prophecy in which the Most High God has mentioned both Sarah and Hagar — peace be with them — and in which Isaiah — peace be with him — has described the tents of the descendants of Hagar. To whom do these refer and are suitable, but to the children of Hagar and her posterity? To whom do the tents and tent-cords belong, except to her descendants? You would perhaps say that the Prophet meant by them the Abyssinians and the Turks, because they also have tents and stakes (!) He who makes himself so blind as to reject this prophecy is really blind, having little sight for himself, and rebelling openly against his Lord; so much so that the Most High God has not left any doubt, but has repeated, enlightened and explained His saying.

(FI) And on behalf of the Most High God, he said in the twenty-eighth chapter: "By Myself have I sworn, and from My mouth the word of righteousness have I shown forth, which has no contradiction and change: unto me every knee shall bow and every tongue shall swear, and they shall say one and all that the grace is from the Lord." (Is. 45:23-24)[233] Which is the community which swears by the name of God, and who are those who kneel down to the name of the One God, praise His grace, morning and evening, and exalt Him and pray to Him as One, except the Muslims?[234] As to the Christians, they attribute grace and merits to the Christ, and say at the beginning of their prayers at the altars: "May the grace of Jesus Christ be fulfilled on us."[235]

(FJ) And Isaiah prophesied in this chapter revealing the secrets of the preceding prophecy, and rebuking blind and ignorant people. He did not leave the sophist any excuse nor the obstinate any outlet, for he spoke to Hagar, saying: "O thou plunged and immersed with pains, who hast not possessed happiness nor comfort, behold, I will set thy stones in beryl and consolidate thy foundations in sapphire, and adorn thy walls with rubies and thy gates with carbuncles and embellish the borders of thy house with precious stones. All thy children shall recognize Me there and shall not deny Me, and I shall make peace general to thy sons. In righteousness and justice shalt thou be embellished. Decline then from oppression and aversion, for thou art safe from them; and turn away from humility and lowliness, for they shall not come near thee; and whosoever is sent by Me shall come to thee and shall dwell in thee; and thou shalt be a refuge and a protection for those who dwell and live in thee." (Is. 54:11-15) Examine this prophecy — may God guide you — since you are intelligent and skilled in controversy and see for yourselves, since you are responsible people; do you know another "plunged and immersed in pains" besides Hagar, and does this address suit another one besides her and her children? What honor is greater and higher than the testimony of God to the effect that all of them know Him and do not ignore Him, and that He has made their country a "refuge" and a "protection," that is to say an asylum and place of safety. Mecca has indeed been built in mosaic work and with the best stones, and the diadems of kings have been brought into it. He who has his two ears let him hear my speech and my advice; let him ponder over these testimonies and analogies, let him sit alone with this book and with my other book entitled *Book of Replies to Christians;* let him seek true guidance from God and work for the deliverance of his soul, before its condemnation overtakes him.

(FK) He prophesied too in this chapter, called and cried, saying: "O those who thirst, come ye to the water and the watering-place, and he that hath no money, let him go and take food and drink and have wine and milk without money and without price." (Is. 55:1) This prophecy of Isaiah points to the grants of God to the posterity of Hagar, the nation of the Prophet — may God bless and save him — that they will go, in the world to come, to what the Most High has promised them: "rivers of wine and rivers of milk, the taste whereof changes not, and rivers of wine delicious to those who drink." (Qur'an 47:16) Ponder over the similarity and resemblance which exists between the two prophecies.

(FL) And he said in this chapter: "I have set thee as a witness to the peoples, a leader and a commander to the nations, in order that thou mightest call the nations that thou knewest not; and the nations that knew thee not will come to thee in haste with eagerness, because of the Lord thy God, the Holy One of Israel, who hath made thee *Ahmad.*[236] Seek ye then what is with the Lord, and if ye know Him, listen to Him, and when He is near to you, let the sinner forsake his sin and the unrighteous man his way, and let him return unto me that I may have mercy on him, and let him be converted to our God, whose mercy and goodness are abundant." (Is. 55:4-7) He who ponders over this prophecy and examines it carefully will not be in need of any other, because Isaiah has mentioned the Prophet — may God bless and save him — by name and has said: "God hath made thee *Ahmad.*" If the adversary prefers to say: "It is not *Muhammad,* but *Mahmud,*" we will agree with him, because their meaning is identical. And the nations came to him in haste and eagerness, and God made him a leader to the nations, a caller to God, as Isaiah says, and an illuminating lamp.

(FM) And he said in the twenty-eighth chapter that the Most High "God looked, and there was no justice,[237] and it displeased him; and

He saw that nobody was vindicating the truth; therefore the Lord
wondered at that and sent His intercessor[238] and brought salvation unto
him with His arm and upheld him with His grace. And he put on piety
as a breastplate and laid upon his head the helmet of help and salvation; and clothed himself with the garments of deliverance to take
vengeance upon those who hated and opposed him. To the inhabitants
of the islands he will pay recompense, so that the name of God might
be feared from the western parts of the earth and His glory revered
from its eastern parts." (Is. 59:15-18) The Prophet — may God bless
and save him — has put on righteousness as a breastplate, laid on his
head the helmet of help and salvation, clothed himself with garments of
deliverance and vengeance against the enemies of God, repaid recompense to the inhabitants of the islands and made manifest the name of
God in the Eastern and Western parts of the earth, the inhabitants of
which submitted to him. Where is your escape from this, and what is
your argument against these prophecies realized through him? And
how can a man, who has stubbornly contradicted God and deafened
himself towards His revelation and His call flee from Him?

(FN) And he prophesied in this chapter about what only the weak-
minded people would reject, and the most ignorant and blind would
ignore; because he again mentioned Hagar, and spoke to her and to
Mecca, the country of her children, saying: "Arise, and make thy lamp
shine; for thy time is come and the glory of God is rising upon thee.
For the darkness hath covered the earth, and fog hath overspread the
nations. The Lord shall shine upon thee, and His glory shall be seen
upon thee. And the Gentiles shall come to thy light, and the kings to
the brightness of thy rising. Lift up thy sight round about and contemplate; they shall all gather themselves together to them and they shall
make pilgrimage[239] to thee. Thy sons shall come to thee from a remote
country, and thy daughters shall be nursed in canopies and in couches.
Thy heart shall be enlarged, because the sea shall be converted unto
thee, and the armies of the Gentiles shall make pilgrimage to thee,[239]
and thou shalt throng with numerous camels, and thy land is too small
for the files of animals which shall gather to thee. The rams of Midian
and of Ephah shall be brought to thee, and the inhabitants of Sheba
shall come to thee and shall tell the favors of God and shall praise

Him. All the flocks of Kedar shall come to thee, and the lambs of Nebaioth shall minister unto thee. They shall offer on My altar what pleases Me, and then I will renew a *Hamd* to the house of my *mahmadah*." (Is. 60:1-7)

(FO) This too — may God guide you — is a prophecy which was realized, and a sign which was fulfilled and made true; the Gentiles[240] have come to the light of the faith, and the treasures of the sea have been converted unto this Muslim nation; the droves of the nations have gone to Mecca, and camels of high breed and files of animals have thronged its population, and the inhabitants of Yemen and of Sheba have repaired to it. What is more forceful and to the point for the enlightenment of the opponents is that Kedar and Nebaioth are from the children of Ishmael — peace be with him — who dwelt around Mecca and became its possessors and ministers. God has indeed renewed a *Hamd* to the house of His *mahmadah*: *Muhammad* — may God bless and save him! If this is not so, let them then name other than the Prophet — may God bless and save him — and other than Mecca; let them compare this portrait with this description and model his characteristics upon those of these prophecies, in order that the veil may be rent open and truth made manifest.

(FP) And he said in this chapter: "Thus saith the Lord, the inhabitants of the isles shall wait for Me, with those that are in the ships of Tarshish, as they did before. They shall bring thy sons from a remote country, their silver and their gold with them, unto the name of the Lord thy God, the Holy One of Israel, who hath made thee *Ahmad*[241] and honored thee. And the sons of strangers shall build upon thy rampart, and their kings shall minister unto thee; and thy gates shall be open continually at all times of night and day, and they shall not be shut; and the multitudes of the Gentiles[242] shall enter into thee, and their kings shall be brought captive to thee; for the nation and kingdom that will not serve thee shall perish,[243] yea those nations shall be utterly wasted with sword. Honor shall come unto thee from the fine pine tree of Lebanon and from its fir tree, in order that My house may be made fragrant with it, and the place of My foot glorified with the abode of My honor. The sons also of them that afflicted thee shall come unto thee, and all they that harmed thee and persecuted thee shall kiss the prints of thy feet. I will set thee for a honor for ever, and for beatitude and joy in all generations. And thou shalt suck the milk of the Gentiles, shalt have a share in the spoil of kings and taste from thy raids upon them, Then thou shalt know that I am the Lord thy Savior; because for brass I will give thee gold, and for iron silver, and for wood brass, and for stones iron; and I will make peace to be thy leader and righteousness and justice thy might, and the Lord shall be unto thee a light and a lamp for ever." (Is. 60:9-19)

(FQ) Understand, O my cousins, this prophecy and see who it is whose rampart has been built by strangers, who has been ministered unto by mighty ones, to whom kings have been brought bound and fettered, and who wasted and destroyed with (the) sword every kingdom and nation which did not submit to him. Do you know for the foot of the "Friend of God,"[244] a place mentioned besides Mecca to which people go in the pilgrim's garb of humility, at the door of which they worship and to which they repair from the ends of the earth in answer to the divine call?

(FR) And he said in the twenty-fourth chapter, speaking also to the Prophet — may God bless and save him — "Thus saith the Lord, The holy One of Israel: 'He whose soul was despised and dishonored, whom the nations mocked, whom the followers of the ruler scorned, before him shall kings arise when they see him, and rulers shall bow down, because the promise of God is true. It is the Holy One of Israel who hath elected thee and chosen thee, and it is He who saith: "In an acceptable time have I answered thee, and in difficulties[245] have I helped thee. I have chosen thee and established thee for a covenant to the Gentiles and a light to the nations,[246] in order that (the) earth may be made secure by thee. Thou shalt inherit the waste places and thou shalt say to the prisoners: 'Go forth and be loose,' and to them that are in prison: 'Show yourselves and set off and feed your flocks in the ways, because in that time your pastures shall be found in every direction and in every path.' They shall not hunger nor thirst; neither shall the *simooms* nor suns smite them, because their *Rahman* [247] is with them; even to the springs and the fountains of water he shall guide them. And he shall make all the mountains ways and roads to them, and with them they will dispense with paths and beaten tracks. And people shall come from a far and remote country, these from the South, these from the sea and these from the sea of Sinim. Sing, O Heaven, and be joyful, O earth, and break forth into *Hamd*, O mountains, for the Lord, hath comforted His people and hath pitied the afflicted of His creatures." ' " (Is. 46:7-13)

(FST) This is clearness and not ambiguity, distinctness and not confusion; it is an obvious prophecy corroborating that which precedes it. By my life, it is only the Prophet and his nation whom the prophet Isaiah — peace be with him — has mentioned as being despised and dishonored, who inherited the waste places, released the captives from prisons and bonds[248] and fed their flocks in the highways, after the state of siege and the hardships in which the Arabs lived under Chosrau and Caesar;[249] and it is only to them that the mountains became ways and roads. As to the meaning of his saying: "The Holy One of Israel," since he was speaking to the children of Israel, he called God by the name given Him by the children of Israel.

(FT) And he said in this chapter, a part of which he devoted to an address to Hagar and to Mecca: "I have graven thee upon the palms of my hands, therefore thy walls are continually before me. Thy children shall make haste and come to thee; and they shall drive out from thee them that wish to harm thee and destroy thee. Lift up thine eyes above and behold: they shall come to thee and to the last man they shall gather together to thee. As I live, saith God, swearing by His name, 'Thou shalt surely put them on as a garment, and thou shalt be a adorned with crowns as a bride. And thy desert, thy waste places and the land to which they banished thee and in which they pressed thee shall be too narrow for thee, by reason of the great number of their inhabitants and of them that wish to dwell therein. And they that opposed thee and swallowed thee up shall flee from thee. The children of thy restricted fecundity will say to thee: "O desolate woman of little offspring, the countries have become too straight for us; therefore clear ye a way and remove that we may extend in their desert." Then thou shalt speak to thyself and say: "Who hath begotten me all these, while I am lonely, desolate and a woman of little offspring, and while I am deserted, grieved and enslaved? Who hath then brought up these to me, and who hath taken care of them for me?' ' " (Is. 49:16-21)

(FU) Is there anything more distinct, precise, lucid and luminous than this? God has sworn by Himself and His oath is true, and His engagement unbreakable — that He will make the nations as garments to be worn by them and as an ornament for their decoration; this is true in the case of the Arabs and their Mecca,[250] which is adorned every year with the highest silk brocades and diadems and to which the finest pearls and ex-votos are brought from the house of the Caliphate[251] and from all the countries of the Empire. And whose the owner of the deserts and waste places in which he was too narrowly pressed and to which he was banished, except this nomad and *Hijazic* nation? And whose the woman without protection, lonely, grieved, deserted and enslaved to who God spoke, except Hagar? Is there any intelligent and sensible man among the adversaries who would give good advice to his soul, and pity it?

(FV) And he said in this chapter: "Thus saith the Lord, 'I will lift Mine hand upon the Gentiles, and set up a standard to them; and the people shall bring thy sons in their hands and they shall carry thy daughters upon their shoulders. And kings shall be thy nursing fathers and the highest and noblest among their women thy nursing mothers; and they shall bow down to see with their face toward the earth, and lick up the dust of thy feet; and thou shalt know then that I am the Lord, and they that wait for Me shall not be ashamed.' " (Is. 49:22-23)

(FW) This is also a prophecy which has not been vain and without object. Nations have indeed brought to Mecca[252] — from the extreme of (the) East and West, from Sind and India, from the countries of the Berbers, and from the deserts — the posterity and the descendants of Hagar born in their country, and conducted them with pomp to their home. Their kings too, and the noblest of their women nursed the sons and daughters of Ishmael — peace be with him — and the nations bowed down to them in Mecca, with their face toward the earth in worship[253] and giants licked the prints of the foot of Abraham and of the feet of the feet of the Prophet — may God bless and save them — in humility, as benediction and devotion.

(FX) And he said in this chapter: "Who is this that cometh from Edom with garments more red than ripening dates?[254] I see him glorious in his garment and his attire and mighty on account of his horses and his armies; it is I that speak in righteousness and save the nations. It is to us an opportune day for exemplary punishment. The hour of deliverance hath become near, and the year of my salvation hath come to hand. And I looked and there was none to help me; and I wondered that there was none to yield to my view; therefore my own arm brought salvation unto me, and confirmed my foot with fury; and I have trodden down the people in mine anger, and I have made their frontiers waste with my breath and my fury, and I have buried their strength under the earth." (Is. 63:1-6)

(FY) Examine this also, and be not of the number of those who doubt. And Isaiah prophesied in this chapter in addition to the preceding prophecy and said on behalf of God: "I have made thee a name *Muhammad;* look then from thy habitations and dwellings, O *Muhammad*, O Holy One, for thou art the Lord, our father and our savior, and thy name is from everlasting." (Is. 63:14-16; Peshitta, extreme paraphrase)[255] This is similar to the preceding prophecy of the prophet David — peace be with him — who said: "His name exists before the sun," (Ps. 72:17)[256] and to his saying in the Psalter "In His mountain there is a Holy One and a *Muhammad*." (Ps. 48:1)[257]

(FZ) This mention by name is sufficient for the man not overcome by his stupidity, and the period of whose aberration is not lengthened. As to the meaning of the saying of Isaiah — peace be with him — that he is a "Holy One," the word "Holy" in the Syriac language means "a just and pure man"; likewise the name of "the Lord" refers to "lords," as

we have already demonstrated.[258] He who is not convinced by this
prophecy and does not submit to it will openly contradict the Lord who
has mentioned the Prophet twice by name, so as not to leave the
adversaries in doubt. If a sophist quibbles and says that the saying of
the Most High God: "O Muhammad, O Holy One," refers to the
"dwellings" which He had mentioned, the Syriac text would contradict
him, because if "dwellings" were intended it would have exhibited
"Holy Ones and Muhammads," and it would not have said "Holy One
and Muhammad."[259]

(GA) And he said in this chapter: "Go through, go through the gate,
and retrace the way for the nation. Level the highway, smooth it and
remove the stones from its footpaths, and lift up the standard and the
road-mark for the people. For the Lord hath made His voice heard by
all that are in the ends of the earth. Say thou to the daughter of Zion,
'The coming of thy Savior is near; His reward is with Him and His
work before Him.' And they shall be called a 'Holy People' redeemed
by the Lord,' And thou shalt be called 'City, whose power hath been
transferred to her by God from her enemies,' and 'whom her Lord
hath not forsaken.' " (Is. 62:10-12)

(GB) The Arabs are the holy people that the Lord has redeemed; and
the city from whose enemies power has been transferred to her, and
those who have been avenged are Mecca and its inhabitants.[260] This is
constant in the figurative style of the Arabs who say: "Ask the city,"
(Qur'an 12:82) to mean "Ask the inhabitants of the city."

[The sections XX - XXVII have been deleted in this edition]

XXVIII.

THE PROPHECY OF THE CHRIST ABOUT THE PROPHET — MAY GOD BLESS AND SAVE BOTH OF THEM.

(GC) ON this subject the Christ — peace be with Him — uttered a
sentence recorded and perpetuated in the Book of John, in the fifteenth chapter of his Gospel: "The Paraclete, the Spirit of truth, whom

My Father will send in My name, He shall teach you everything."
(John 14:26)[261] The Paraclete then, whom God would send after the
Christ, and who would testify to the name of the Christ — peace be
with Him — is the One who would teach mankind everything that they
did not know before. Now among the disciples of the Christ there has
not been, down to our time, a single one who taught mankind anything
besides what the Christ had already taught; the Paraclete, therefore, is
the Prophet — may God bless and save him — and the Qur'an is the
knowledge that the Christ has called "everything."[262]

(GD) And John said[263] about Him in the sixteenth chapter: "If I go
away, the Paraclete will not come unto you. And when He is come,
He will reprove the world of sin. He shall not speak anything of
Himself, but will direct you in all truth and will announce to you events
and hidden things." (John 16:7,8, 13) John said too, about Him: "I will
pray My Father to give you another Paraclete who will be with you for
ever." (John 14:16)

(GE) The interpretation of the saying: "He will send in My name," is
this: as the Christ was called Paraclete, and Muhammad also was
called by the same name,[264] it is not strange on the part of Christ to
have said: "He will send in My name," that is to say He will be "my
namesake" (or: "my equal," *sami*). Indeed it seldom happens that the
Christ — peace be with Him — is mentioned in a chapter of the Books
of the prophets — peace be with them — without a simultaneous mention of the Prophet — may God bless and save him — as adhering to
Him and making one pair with Him, because he came after Him.

(GF) When I examined carefully the word "Paraclete," and I searched
deeply for the meaning of the saying of the Christ, I found another
wonderful mystery in it; it is that if somebody counts the total numerical value of its letters, it will be equivalent to same total as that of the
letters of the words: *Muhammad b. 'Abdallah, an-Nabbiyul-Hadi*.[265] If
somebody says that one number is missing, because the word is *Para-
cleta*,[266] we will answer that the letter *Alif* is a paragogical addition to
the Syriac nouns. The words which would be exactly equivalent to the

numerical value of the word, without any addition and diminution, are: *Muhammad Rasulun Habibun Tayyibun.*[267] If someone says that the same number is obtainable from other names, this will not be possible for him until he brings forth, from scriptural evidence, the man who would answer to the description given by the Christ in His saying: "The Paraclete whom He will send, the Spirit of truth whom My Father will send in My name, He shall teach you everything"; and he will not be able to find a way for that.

(GG) And the disciple of John said in his Epistle found in the Book of Acts, which is the history of the Apostles:[268] "My beloved, believe not every spirit, but discern the spirits that are of God. Every spirit that confesseth that Jesus Christ hath come and was in the flesh is of God, and every spirit that confesseth not that the Christ was in flesh, is not of God." (I John 4: 1-3) The Prophet — may God bless and save him — has believed that the Christ has come, that He was in flesh and that He was the Spirit of God and "His Word which He cast into Mary." (Qur'an 4:169) His spirit, therefore, is, on the testimony of John and of others, a true and just spirit, coming from the Most High God, and the spirit of those who pretend that the Christ is neither in flesh nor a man is from somebody outside God.

(GH) And Simon Cephas, the head of the Apostles said in the Book of Acts: "The time hath come that judgment must begin at the house of God." (I Pet. 4: 17) The interpretation of this is that the meaning of the house of God mentioned by the Apostle is Mecca, and it is there and not at another place that the new judgment began.[269] Somebody says that he meant the judgment of the Jews, the answer is that the Christ had already told them that "There shall not be left one stone upon another that shall not be thrown down and remain in destruction till the day of the Resurrection." (Matt. 24:2; etc.)

(GI) It has become evident that the new judgment mentioned by the Apostle is the religion of Islam and its judgment. This is similar to the saying of the prophet Zephaniah — peace be with him — who said on behalf of God: "I will renew to the people a chosen language"; (Zeph.

3:9)[270] Arabic was the new and chosen language for the new judgment and religion. Daniel too — peace be with him — said in this sense what we have already mentioned. There was not in that time a house related to God to which the adversary might cling and say that the judgment began there, except Mecca. If somebody says the Apostle meant the Christian religion, how could he say about a religion and a judgment which had already appeared for some time: "The time hath come that it must begin"? This is an impossible hypothesis.

(GJ) And the evangelist Luke reports in the eleventh chapter of his Gospel that the Christ said to His disciples: " 'When I sent you without purse and scrip and shoes, were ye harmed and lacked ye anything?' And they said: 'No.' Then He said: 'But now, he that hath no purse, let him buy one and likewise scrip: and he that hath no sword, let him sell his garment and buy a sword with it for himself.' " (Luke 22:35-36) The laws and prescriptions that the Christ had promulgated and preached were only submission, resignation and obedience; when then, at the end of His life He ordered His disciples and the standard-bearers of His religion to sell their garments in order to buy swords, men of discernment and intelligence know that He referred to another Dispensation, viz., to that of the Prophet — may God bless and save him — in pointing to his swords and arrows which the prophets had described prior to his coming.[271]

(GK) Simon Cephas unsheathed his sword and drew it out of its scabbard in the night in which the Jews seized the Christ, and struck with it one of the soldiers,[272] and cut off his ear; but the Christ — peace be with Him — took it with His hand and returned it back to its place in the soldier's head, and it became immediately as sound as it was before; and then He said to Simon: "Put up the sword into the sheath. He who draws the sword shall be killed with the sword." (Matt. 24:51-52; John 20:10-11; Luke 22:50-51) In this He referred to the sword-drawers of His nation and His followers, but He referred to the Muslim Dispensation when He ordered His disciples to sell their garments in order to buy swords; and swords are not bought except for the sake of unsheathing them and striking with them.

(GL) And Paul, the foremost among the Christians, whom they call an apostle, said in his Epistle to the Galatians: "Abraham had two sons, the one by a bond-maid, the other by a free-woman. But he who was of the free-woman was by promise from God. Both are an allegory for the two laws and covenants. Hagar is compared with Mount Sinai, which is in Arabia, and answereth to Jerusalem which now is. But Jerusalem, which is in heaven, answereth to his free wife." (Gal. 4:22-26) Paul has settled many points by this saying. The *first* is that Ishmael and Hagar inhabited the country of the Arabs, which he called the countries of Arabia; the *second* is that Mount Sinai, which is in Syria, extends and links up with the desert countries, since he says that Hagar is compared with Mount Sinai, which is in the countries of Arabia[273]; and Sinai is the mountain mentioned in the Torah at the beginning of these prophecies: "The Lord came from Sinai and rose from Seir and appeared from Mount Paran." (Deut. 33:2)[274] In this Paul testified that the Lord, who according to the saying of the Torah, came from Sinai, was the Prophet[275] — may God bless and save him — and that it was he who appeared in the countries of Arabia. We have demonstrated above that the meaning of the word "Lord" refers to "prophets" and to "lords." What would be clearer and more distinct than the mention by the name of the countries of the Arabia? He meant by this vocable the country of the Arabs, but he wrote it in a foreign and unnatural manner, *Arab* instead of *'Arab*.[276]

(GM) The *third* meaning is that Jerusalem answers to Mecca; and the *fourth* is that this second law and this second covenant are, without any doubt, from heaven. Paul called both of them by one name and did not distinguish between them in any way. As to the supremacy that he gave to the free-woman and to his saying that the son of the bond-woman was not born by promise, it is one-sidedness and prejudice on his part, because in the convincing passages of the Torah about Ishmael, which I have quoted above, there is sufficient evidence to show that he also was born, not only by one promise, but by several promises.

(GN) These are clear prophecies and established facts, perpetuated throughout the ages, which, if somebody apart from the Muslims claims, his only gain will be the deadliest arrow and the greatest lie: this will only be done by a wretched Jew or a babbling Christian, excusing with it themselves and deceiving themselves and others. It is indeed evident to the Christians especially and to the Jews generally that God has intensified His wrath against the children of Israel, has cursed them, forsaken them and their religion and told them that He will burn the stem from which they multiplied, destroy the mass of them and plant others in the desert and in the waste and dry land. On this subject, how great is my amazement at the Jews, who avow all these things and do not go beyond contemplating them, and burden themselves with claims through which they become full of illusion and deception. To this the Christians bear witness by their evidence against the Jews, morning and evening that God has completely destroyed them, erased their traces from the register of the earth and annihilated the image of their nation.

(GO) As to the community of the Christ — peace be with Him — they have no right to claim the prophecies that I have succinctly quoted about the Prophet — may God bless and save him. They cannot claim to have made kings captives, to have enslaved princes and conducted them linked together with bonds and fetters, to have inherited desert and waste lands, to have beheaded people, to have multiplied killing and havoc in the earth and other peculiarities which are fitting and due only to Ishmael and Hagar and their descendants and to Mecca and its pilgrims.

(GP) Moreover, many prophets have distinctly mentioned by name the Prophet — may God bless and save him — have described him with his sword-bearers and archers and told that death and rapacious birds shall go before his armies and that his country shall be overcrowded with numerous caravans of camels and files of animals and that he shall destroy the nations and the kings opposing him. All these confirm his religion, enhance his rank and testify to the veracity of what his messengers have told about him. This is especially the case with Daniel who closed all the prophecies with something that expels every doubt, and this is that the God of Heaven will set up an everlasting kingdom which shall not change and perish. He who does not submit to him that God has chosen and raised is to be scorned and despised.

[The sections XXIX - XXXII have been deleted in this edition]

XXXIII.

CONCLUSION.

(GQ) NOW that you know — may God guide you — that our common agreement is in accordance with your common agreement on the point that God is just, that He loves justice and those who practice it and that He has forbidden injustice and iniquity, it is just and fair that you should look back into the motives for which you have accepted your religion and see what they are. If it becomes evident to you that they are only possible and praiseworthy stories transmitted to you by a successor from his predecessor and by a last from a first man, it is also through such stories that we have accepted the Prophet — peace be with him.

(GR) Moreover, among those who handed down to you those stories of yours, there was none who claimed that he had taken from an eyewitness, among his fathers or grandfathers who had seen the Christ or Moses — peace be with them — as the Arabs claim on the authority of their fathers and their grandfathers who had seen the Prophet — peace be with him. Indeed, a man among the Arabs records on the authority of his grandfather or the grandfather of his grandfather, or a man of his relatives, what they have seen and transmitted to their successors. As to your stories, they have been handed down to you by a man Iraq, who took them from a man of Jazirah, who in his turn took them from a man of Syria, who himself took them from a Hebrew; or by a Persian, who took them from a Greek; or by an Eastern, who took them from a Western, through obscure and irregular channels. How then, could you refute or blame the man who says: "I have accepted this religion of Islam and believed in it by means of the evidences and testimonies through which you have accepted your own religion"? Or who says: "When I saw members of a nation great in rank and high in dignity with regard to number, power, pity, wisdom and uprightness, telling me what we have related above, as having heard it from their fathers and grandfathers, and showing a Book they transmit to one another, century after century, which calls to the Unity of God and His glorification and to the belief in His apostles and prophets; which refuses to acknowledge associates and equals with God; which enjoins the best and highest things and that which is in harmony with the rules and the recommendations of the prophets; which warns its adherents against evil and evildoers; and which foretells events, which were realized time after time and year after year; then, when I found that the Books of those of the prophets in whom you believe had testified to our Prophet and prophesied about his empire and his religion as we have already demonstrated, I embraced such a religion, and hoped for what through it I shall have with God."?

(GS) If you pretend that there is no obligation to acknowledge the man of such description, prophetic office, merits and evidences, all that you yourself claim will be abolished, and with all your belief you will be thrown into unbelief. And if you excuse yourself with reference to Dualists and Pagans and the like, that they also transmit stories from their religious leaders and relate wonders of their messengers and deceivers and prove the veracity of their stories from their own religious books and written histories — we have already spoken of that at the beginning of this book, with such evidence that the only men who would close their ears to it would be those who whose only aim is to quibble and to refrain from serious discussion, and whose only religion is obstinacy and arrogance; such false leaders, because they have contradicted themselves and have called men to impurity and aberration, have gone astray, and because they have associated other gods with God, have run into perdition. Such men are not to be compared with a man whose leader was truth, whose aim was true guidance, whose distinctive mark was devotion and asceticism and whose call was to One and Unique God, the God of Abraham and of the rest of the prophets — peace be with them — and about whom the prophets had prophesied in terms which are now quite obvious.

(GT) Waive, therefore, suspicions and excuses, O my cousins — may God guide you — and walk in the safest and most direct way, and avoid the most misleading and crooked path. If you ponder well, it will become evident to you that the motives and reasons for which we have accepted the prophetic office of the Prophet — peace be with him — are similar to the motives and the reasons for which you have accepted Christ and Moses — peace be with both of them; therefore, if we are wrong and exposed to the punishment of God, so also are you. Discuss therefore, with your own souls, summon us to the tribunal of your mind and intelligence, and argue for us and for yourselves, against us and against yourselves, in order that the veil may be withdrawn from you; you will then, by the assistance of God, see the truth for itself.

(GU) If somebody blames the Prophet — peace be with him — and says that he — peace be with him — attributed evil to God, the answer is that he has pronounced clear statements about the justice, mercy and might of God; and these we have mentioned at the beginning of this book. And God — may He be blessed and exalted — said to Moses — peace be with him — "I will harden Pharaoh's heart, that he should not bring you out of the land of Egypt." (Ex. 7:3-4) And the prophet Isaiah — peace be with him — said: "God hath made peace and hath created both good and evil." (Is. 65:7) And Paul, who has the precedence among the Christians and whom they obey, said in his Epistle to Timothy: "In a great house there are not only vessels of silver and gold, but also vessels of wood and of earth; some to honor and some to dishonor." (II Tim. 2:20) He means by that the world and all the happy and wretched people who are in it.

(GV) At the end of this book I will ask you — may God guide you — a general, decisive and convincing question, "What would you say of a man coming to this country from the regions of India and China, with the intention of being rightly guided, of inquiring into the religions found in it and of acquainting himself with the customs of its inhabitants?"

(GW) It will be said to him that some of its inhabitants belong to a religion called *Magianism*. They worship stars and fires and pretend that God is the creator of darkness and evil; that war is never at rest between them and because they do not obtain their desire, they have neither peace nor respite and are powerless and bewildered; that the will of God and His pleasure are that one should have intercourse with one's mother and daughter, purify himself with the rotten fluid excretion of cows and cleave to immoral converse and dance; that the spirits of their dead come back to them once a year, partake of the food and drink put before them, and at their withdrawal provision themselves;[277] and they have some other vicious and occult customs similar to those we have mentioned at the beginning of this book, with filthy habits and clear signs of vengeance from God on them and ancient prophecies against them found in the Books of the prophets, to which we have referred above.

(GX) Some of its inhabitants belong to a religion called *Zindikism*. Their religion is similar to that of the Magians, and it goes even in advance of it in error, perverseness, filth, impurity and stupidity.

(GY) Some of its inhabitants belong to a religion called *Christianism*. A branch of them pretend that when God saw that the power of Satan was becoming supreme and his strength formidable, and that the prophets were unable to resist him, He found for Himself an eternal and everlasting Son, not rivalled by any other creature, who entered into the womb of a woman and was born of her; then He grew up and strove with Satan; but Satan seized Him, killed Him and then crucified Him at the hands of a band of his followers.[278] Another branch of them assume that the One who was killed was only the temple and the habitation of that Son, with whom He had become so united that this eternal Son ate the same food as that of the created, went to the place of easement with Him and was killed with Him.[279]

(GZ) Some of its inhabitants belong to a religion called *Judaism*. They have in their hands Books of some men whom they call prophets and relate how these prophets have cursed them and report that God has completely forsaken them, execrated their religion, scattered them in all regions, extinguished their light and sworn that He will never pity them again.[280]

(HA) Some of its inhabitants belong to this pure and sublime religion called *Islam*. They say that God is One, Eternal, who has no partner with Him, and whom no one can overcome because to Him belong omnipotence and everlastingness. He has no child and no father, and He is the Compassionate, the Merciful, the First and the Last. Their Prophet has prescribed, on behalf of God, piety to parents, fasting, prayer, purity and cleanliness; has made lawful for them the good things and forbidden the evil things, and has promised Heaven and warned against Fire.

(HB) In which of these religions and creeds would that Indian or that Chinese wish to believe, and to which of them would he incline, and of which of them would he approve, if he were a man of broad mind, sound judgment and an enquirer after mere truth and nothing else?

(HC) And what would be the argument of God against any one of His servants who would say to Him, Just and Compassionate as He is, who does not wrong anybody by the weight of an atom:[281]

(HD) "I heard a preacher call to Thy Unity, magnify Thee, praise Thee and glorify Thee; and I responded to him. I heard[282] him order us to believe in Thy prophets and in Thy Chosen Ones, and prescribe prayer, fasting and alms; and I obeyed him, in the hope of the reward which I shall have with Thee, and in obedience to Thy order. I heard him urge us to go on pilgrimage to a far and remote country; and I made this pilgrimage and did not hesitate. I heard him exhort us to wage war against Thy enemies who disbelieve in Thee, and do not pray to Thee; and I prayed to Thee and fought a holy war, with all my might and not half-heartedly, wishing in all things to please Thee. I saw disgraceful and occult religions and creeds — such as those I have mentioned above — and I cast them aside, left them completely, and held to what I thought was the most solid handle and the best way to please Thee. O my God, if I have mistaken what I have chosen, and have erred in what I have selected, Thou hast the strongest reason to pity Thy servant who exerted his utmost in the search of what is with Thee, but mistook the way to come to Thee."

(HE) O my cousins, this is an acceptable saying, and not a despicable excuse, even with the imperfect and exacting servants of God; how much more so then with the Most Compassionate of the merciful and the most equitable judge who does not require of a soul more than its capacity?

(HF) Examine then — may God guide you — these arguments and illustrations, throw away mischievous prejudices and remove the veil from your eyes and the covers and the locks from your hearts; content yourselves in the chapters that I have written, either with the one which deals with the prophetic office, or with the one concerning the stories related of the Prophet — peace be with him — or with the one relating to the resplendent victory won in the name of the God of Abraham; or with the one on the living Book of the Qur'an and its merits, which I have set forth above; or with the one on the successive prophecies of the prophets and the meanings and interpretations that I have given to them. Listen to my advice, because I have sifted for you my admonitions, and know that I have sought in what I have written neither vain glory nor distinction, but only what is with God, who does not disappoint the man who trusts in Him, and in compliance with the wish of His Caliph and servant Ja'far al-Mutawakkil 'ala Allah, the Commander of the Faithful — may God strengthen him.

(HG) I expect gratitude and ask for consideration from pious and magnanimous Muslims, and also from more intelligent and able men among the members of the protected cults, since I have demonstrated to the common people among them what I have thoroughly investigated, and disclosed to them what I know with certitude, and made them understand what I myself understood, intending by that that they should participate in the light brought to me, and in the final success for which I hope. In case I am right in what I have said, my merit and my success should redound on me and on them. And in case I am wrong, the blame should be laid on me to the exclusion of them. I crave the continuation of divine protection and assistance, and I take refuge with God from my want of requisite knowledge, in beseeching Him to remove scandal and to grant me the garment of modesty and righteousness and the attainment of what sooner or later I hoped from Him, in what I have written and said.

(HH) This my book, which I have entitled *Book of Religion and Empire*,[283] has exclusively demonstrated the unsoundness and fallacy of Judaism, the villainy and falseness of Dualism and Atheism,[284] and the onlooker already observes their downfall and their eclipse and sees that resplendent light and true faith are exclusively in Islam.

(HI) I first thank God for His guidance to me, then His servant and Caliph Ja'far al-Mutawakkil 'ala Allah, Commander of the Faithful — may God prolong his life — who invited and attracted me to him, along with other people of the protected cults, by persuasion and dissuasion and by the respect and consideration that he has for all. It is for this reason that I have devoted the first chapter of this book to a description of what my community has experienced from his munificence, from the tokens of his mercy, the gentleness of his administration, the prosperity of his reign and the great number of his conquests; and to show the obligation of Muslims and non-Muslims alike to love him, to obey him and to be grateful to him.

(HJ) Peace be with those who follow true guidance, who befriend piety, who love righteousness and virtue, who seek partisans for them and who exhort to them!

Notes:

[1] A short essay in this direction was published in *J.R.A.S.*, 1920, pp. 481-488. In some respects it is the weightiest of all the works on Islam that we have read for a long time, and during the last seven years we have perused more than seven hundred Arabic MSS. on different subjects. The author has displayed a literary art which has certain

merits of its own, and which, from many sentences such as "if the adversaries shout," appears to have been dictated to him by a series of public discussions held in the court of Mutawakkil.

[2] See the *Dialogue Between John I and the Amir of the Hagarenes*, p. 11 - ed.

[3] *Journal Asiatique*, 1915, 248.

[4] Mentioned by Steinschneider, *Polem. u. apolog. Liter.*, 1877, No. 65, p. 82. - See Preface, pp. v ff., pp. 269-270, above. - ed.

[5] I read it in a MS., cf. *al-Machriq* for May and June, 1921. - See *The Patriarch Timothy I and the Caliph Mahdi*, p. 169 - ed.

[6] Assemani, *B.O.*, iii, i, p. 212.

[7] Ibid., iii, i, p. 609.

[8] *Polem. u. apolog. Liter.*, p. 80.

[9] *Apology of al-Kindy in Defence of Christianity*, London. I read the Arabic text in the edition of the Nile Mission Press, 1912. A recent reviewer in the *Jewish Quarterly Review* has unsuccessfully tried to throw doubts on the authenticity of this book which from internal and external evidence is certainly one of the most genuine compositions that we possess in the literature of the 9th century. Cf. Casanova, *Mahomet et la fin du monde*, ii, *Notes Complémentaires*.

[10] See Jahiz, *A Reply to the Christians*, p. 689 - ed.

[11] iii, 353.

[12] Ibid., No. 61, p. 73.

[13] Ibid., pp. 128 and 146. See the recent work of A. Périer, *Yahia*

b. *Adi, Petits traités apologétiques* (1920).

[14] *Chron. Syr.*, p. 155 (edit. Bedjan).

[15] Tabari, 3, 3, 1387 seq., analysed in J. Zaydan's *Ummayyads and Abbasids* (translated by D. S. Margoliouth), p. 169.

[16] Mas'udi, vii, 278-279 (B. de Meynard).

[17] Tabari, 3, 3, 1387.

[18] The best work on the life in the palaces of the caliphs is Miskawaihi's *Tajarib* (or "Experiences of Nations"), translated by D. S. Margoliouth in 1921 (Oxford, vols. i-iv).

[19] See *Fihrist*, pp. 296-303 (trans. Dodge, vol. 2, pp. 741 ff.).

[20] See an-Nadim, *Fihrist*, trans. Dodge, p. 741 - ed.

[21] Possibly an error for *Rahl*. Cf. the quotation from b. Abi Usaibi'ah and b. al-Kifti given below.

[22] See an-Nadim, *Fihrist*, trans. Dodge, vol. 2, pp. 696 ff. - ed.

[23] Cod. CCCCXLV, p. 218, in Rieu's catalogue.

[24] This word is rightly corrected into Rabban in the edition of Cairo, A. H. 1326. See pp. 128 and 155.

[25] Cod. CCCCXLV of the British Museum, p. 217 (Rieu). The works is also found in Cod. 6257 of Berlin, v, p. 513 (Ahlwardt), and in Cod. 1910 of Gotha iii, p. 456 (Pertsch). Cf. also Cod. DLXVII of Oxford, p. 135 (Uri).

[26] Tabari, 3, 2, 1268 seq.

[27] *Chron. Syr.*, p. 153 (Bedjan).

[28] See p. 147.

[29] Cf. *Fihrist*, p. 263, and Usaibi'ah, i, pp. 234-235.

[30] Cf. *Fihrist*, pp. 295-296, and Steinschneider in ZDMG, 1893, xlvii, pp. 351-354.

[31] The words "In Egypt" are also clearly read at the top of the title-page after a truncated line.

[32] The reader will doubtless notice the difference in the numbers of the chapters of the Bible used by the author. The numbers of the chapters of his Bible are those formerly in use in the East Syrian (Nestorian) Church.

[33] There is some evidence that what was translated in A.D. 639 was Tatian's *Diatessaron*, see John I, p. 7, above - ed.

[34] No account has been taken above of the tradition recorded by some writers that Khadijah's relative, Waraqah, had translated the Gospels into Arabic in the name of the Prophet. We have likewise omitted as valueless some other traditions transmitted in the late *hadith*, the authors of which probably possessed less information than we do on the subject.

[35] Page 260 of Syr. MS. 41 of the John Rylands Library.

[36] Qur'an 33:45.

[37] Qur'an 41:42, etc.

[38] Cf. Qur'an 7:156 and I.S. i, ii, 89, and i, i, 123 and passim in Buk. Musl. Hish.

[39] The words between brackets have completely disappeared from the text and have only been guessed.

[40] Manichaeans, Atheists.

[41] The idea that a prophet's mission should be confirmed by signs and miracles was frequently used by early Christian polemicists against Islam; see Leo, parag. G; John of Damascus, parag. C; al-Kindi, parag. CA-CC, n. 156.

[42] See above p. 500, n. 42 - ed.

[43] In Tabaristan.

[44] The translator has misunderstood the Syriac particle *dibaith*, which means *partisans, companions* and has rendered it literally by the word *house*.

[45] It is rather obvious that the author's rather high opinion of his own work was not shared by later Muslim polemicists, who not only failed to preserve its text but also any mention of it - ed.

[46] The witness of the Qur'an on this subject tends to show that Muhammad viewed himself as a messenger alone to the Arabs; see Qur'an 12:2; 14:4, etc. - ed.

[47] Cf. I.S. i, ii, 114-119. *Musl.* ii, 531 - *Sahih Muslim*, Kitab al-Zuhd wa al-Raqa'iq, ch. 716, hadith 7084, vol. 4, p. 1534 - ed.

[48] *Musn.* i, 84, 93, 104, 108.

[49] I.S. i, ii, 114-119. *Buk.* iii, 167; viii, 107 (*Sahih Bukhari*, The Book of Foods, ch. 24, vol. 7, pp. 241 ff.; The Book of ar-Riqa'iq, ch. 17, hadith 465, vol. 8, p. 311 - ed.). *Musl.* ii, 531 (*Sahih Muslim*, Kitab al-Zuhd wa al-Raqa'iq, ch. 1214, hadith 7089, vol. 4, pp. 1534. - ed.).

[50] *Musn.* i, 96, 106, 123, 136.

[51] The most trusted collections of hadith present Muhammad in a less favorable light than the author would have us believe. The general story is as follows: upon hearing that a new group of captives (slaves) were being brought in, Fatima asked Muhammad (by way of 'Aisha) to send her one; instead of giving her one, he visited 'Ali and Fatima after they had gone to bed, and sitting between them told them that certain prayers were better for them than receiving a slave; see *Sahih Bukhari*, The Book of Provision, ch. 6, hadith 274, vol. 7, p. 210; *Sahih Muslim*, Kitab al-Dhikr, ch. 1133, hadith 6577, vol. 4, p. 1427 - ed.

[52] Cf. *Buk.* v, 120; viii, 105 (*Sahih Bukhari*, The Book of al-Maghazi, ch. 29, hadith 427, vol. 5, pp. 296-7; The Book of ar-Riqa'iq, ch. 17, hadith 459, vol. 8, p. 307 - ed.). *Musl.* ii, 193 (*Sahih Muslim*, Kitab al-Ashriba, ch. 849, hadith 5065, vol. 3, p. 1126 - ed.). (Jahiz, *Avares*, 240,241,424 (edit. Van Vloten). I.S. i, ii, 114,159.

[53] Lane's *Lexicon*, i, 52.

[54] *Buk.* iv, 71; vii, 130 - *Sahih Bukhari*, The Book of Wasaya, ch. 172, hadith 282, vol. 4, p. 180; The Book of Patients, ch. 4, hadith 552, vol. 7, p. 375 - ed.

[55] Cf. *Buk.* passim in Riqaq. - *Sahih Bukhari*, The Book of ar-Riqa'iq, vol. 8, pp. 282 ff. - ed.

[56] See Lane, iii, 1188.

[57] *Musl.* ii, 383 (*Sahih Muslim*, Kitab al-Birr wa 's-Silat-i-wa 'l-Adab, ch. 1063, hadith 6227, vol. 4, p. 1363 - ed.). For this tradition see *Taj*, vi, 81.

[58] See Lane, iii, 862.

[59] Cf. *Taj.* v. 393.

[60] *Musl.* i, 375 (*Sahih Muslim*, Kitab al-Zakat, ch. 373, hadith 2215, vol. 2, p. 486 - ed.). *Hish.* ii, 93 (Ibn Hisham in *Life of Muhammad*, ed. Guillaume, p. 231 - ed.). *Buk.* iv, 207; viii, 122, 126 (*Sahih Bukhari*, The Virtues and Merits of the Prophet, ch. 24, hadith 793, vol. 4, p. 510; The Book of ar-Riqa'iq, ch. 49, hadith 547, vol. 8; ch. 51, hadith 568, vol. 8, p. 369 - ed.). *Musn.* i, 388, 446.

[61] Cf. *Buk.* iv, 122; viii, 105, 124 (*Sahih Bukhari*, The Book of the Beginning of Creation, ch. 7, hadith 464, vol. 4, p. 305; The Book of Riqa'iq, ch. 16, hadith 456, vol. 8, p. 306; ch. 51, hadith 554, vol. 8, p. 362 - ed.). See also *Musn.* i, 224, 355; ii, 175.

[62] Cf. I.S. i, ii, 92. *Musl.* 290.

[63] *Musn.* i, 123.

[64] I Cor. 2:9; Is. 64:4. This well-known tradition of Bukhari (*Sahih Bukhari*, The Book of the Beginning of Creation, ch. 7, hadith 467, vol. 4, p. 306; Book of Commentary, ch. 233, hadith 302, vol. 6, p. 288; The Book of Tauhid, ch. 35, hadith 589, pp. 435-6; *Sahih Muslim*, Kitab al-Janna wa Sifat Na'imiha wa Ahliha, ch. 1171, hadiths 6782, 6783, vol. 4, p. 1473 - ed.) is well catalogued in *Taj* ix, 380.

[65] Cf. Ex. 21:12 - ed.

[66] The instance of Moses occurred before the advent of the Law; in the case of David it is openly shown that he did deserve death (II Sam. 12:5) for his deed - ed.

[67] The author here makes a comparison of dissimilar topics, i.e., the civil punishment for killing vs. the spiritual punishment for the same. The superior counterpart to Qur'an 4:95 is Matt. 5:21,22. The injunction of civil punishment "life for life, eye for eye..." (Ex. 21:23b,24a) is also found in the Qur'an (5:49). During his own life, Muhammad had several people outright murdered and yet felt no need to repent; e.g.,

Ibn Hisham in *Life of Muhammad*, ed. Guillaume, pp. 675-676 - ed.

[68] *Buk.* iv, 103; ix, 14 (*Sahih Bukhari*, The Book of the Obligation of the Khumus, ch. 25, hadith 391, vol. 4, p. 259; The Book of ad-Diyat, ch. 30, hadith 49, vol. 9, p. 37 - ed.) See Lane, iii, 1178.

[69] The author conceals the fact that the same passage in the Law, Deut. 19:15-19, prescribes a thorough investigation and the punishment for false witnesses - ed.

[70] There is no such command in the Torah. The author's negligence to mention the message of the New Testament in this area (e.g., Luke 6:28) could have hardly been unintentional - ed.

[71] The Old Testament is filled with examples on repentance; e.g., Ezek. 33:14-16 - ed.

[72] The commentators believe that these terms refer to the Ka'ba of Mecca and the temple of Jerusalem respectively.

[73] See the commentators.

[74] *Hish.* ii, 7 - Ibn Hisham in *Life of Muhammad*, ed. Guillaume, p. 184 - ed.

[75] See the commentators Zamakhshari and Baydawi on Qur'an 15:94, possibly quoting *Hish.* ii, 13 - Ibn Hisham in *Life of Muhammad*, ed. Guillaume, p. 187 - ed.

[76] Cf. I.S. i, i, 63, 97. *Hish.* i, 155 - Ibn Hisham in *Life of Muhammad*, ed. Guillaume, p. 69 - ed.; *Tab.* 1, 2, 968-9.

[77] See the historians of Badr - Lit. "Faces have become ugly." See also *Musn.* i, 368.

[78] I.S. i, ii, 117. *Hish.* i, 255 (Ibn Hisham in *Life of Muhammad*, ed.

Guillaume, p. 129 - only remotely related - ed.) *Buk*. ii, 34 - *Sahih Bukhari*, Chapters Concerning al-Istisqa, ch. 8, hadith 129, vol. 2, p. 70 - ed.

[79] I.S. i, i, 125. *Hish*. ii, 225 - Ibn Hisham in *Life of Muhammad*, ed. Guillaume, p. 305 - ed.

[80] Cf. I.S. i, i, 124.

[81] Cf. I.S. i, i, 102-103. *Hish*. i, 201 - Ibn Hisham in *Life of Muhammad*, ed. Guillaume, p. 93 (occurs among the Quraysh and not the Banu Ghifar) - ed.

[82] Cf. I.S. i, i, 144. *Buk*. iv, 182 - *Sahih Bukhari*, The Book of the Prophets, ch. 46, hadith 677, vol. 4, pp. 450-1 (this tradition shares less relation to this reference than the following) : The Virtues and the Merits of the Companions of the Prophets, ch. 6, hadith 39, vol. 5, pp. 27-8 (this still does not fit the referenced narration exactly) - See al-Kindi, parag. CE for his remarks on hadith in which animals are alleged to have spoken - ed.

[83] Cf. *Buk*. (passim). *Musl*. ii, 192 (*Sahih Muslim*, Kitab al-Ashriba, ch. 848, hadith 5058, vol. 3, pp. 1124-5 - Umm Sulaim instead of Umm Malik and barley loaves instead of dates, butter and curd - ed.) Cf. also I.S. i, i, 117 and i, ii, 124.

[84] A notable man in the province of Yemen, and according to *Tab*. (1, 3, 1253), the first chronologist - Tabari, *History*, vol. 4, 158 - ed.

[85] Nöldeke in *Deutsche Literaturzeitung*, 1924, p. 27, remarks that the word "ablution" as used here does not mean the ablution for the ritual prayers, but rather is a euphemism for the ablution performed after one relieves himself - ed.

[86] Cf. I.S. i, i, 112; *Musl*. in *Sirah* - See al-Kindi, parag. CE, n. 42 - ed.

[87] I.S. i, i, 113-114; ii, ii, 6-7; iv, 104. *Buk*. iv, 104; vii, 157 (*Sahih Bukhari*, The Book of the Obligation of the Khumus, ch. 27, hadith 394, vol. 4, pp. 261-2; The Book of Medicine, ch. 55, hadith 669, vol. 7, pp. 449-50 - ed.). *Musl*. ii, 246 (*Sahih Muslim*, Kitab as-Salam, ch. 917, hadith 5430, vol. 3, p. 1194 - ed.). Cf. *Musn*. i, 397 - See al-Kindi, parag. CE - ed.

[88] Cf. *Buk*. vii, 129 (*Sahih Bukhari*, The Book of Drinks, ch. 31, hadith 543, vol. 7, p. 370 - ed.). *Musl*. ii, 278-279, and 543 (*Sahih Muslim*, Kitab al-Fada'il, ch. 954, hadiths 565-6, vol. 4, pp. 1230 ff.; Kitab al-Zuhd wa al-Raqa'iq, ch. 1234, hadith 7149, vol. 4, pp. 1545 ff. - ed.). *Musn*. i, 251, 324, 402. I.S. i, i, 117-118, 121. Cf. *Tab*. 1, 4, 1703 - Tabari, *History*, vol. 9, p. 60 - ed.

[89] The use of the phrase "if God please," within this "prophecy" casts doubt on the certainty of its foretelling something in the future - ed.

[89] The use of past tense in this verse precludes its having "foretold" an event - ed.

[90] See note 89 above - ed.

[91] The author has confused the recipient of this message; it was the angels and not Muhammad - ed.

[92] *Buk*. iv, 74; viii, 136. - *Sahih Bukhari*, The Book of Jihad, ch. 182, hadith 297, vol. 4, pp. 189-90; The Book of al-Qadr, ch. 4, hadith 604, vol. 8, pp. 394-5 - ed.

[93] Nöldeke in *Deutsche Literaturzeitung*, 1924, p. 27, shows that this "jasidu 'lbaqara" should be "hunting wild cows" and not "directing cows" - ed.

[94] Ibn Hisham in *Life of Muhammad*, ed. Guillaume, pp. 607-8 - ed.

[95] *Hish.* iii, 335 - Ibn Hisham in *Life of Muhammad*, ed. Guillaume, pp. 605-6 - ed.

[96] Cf. *Buk.* v. 56 - *Sahih Bukhari*, The Merits of the Ansar, ch. 37, hadith 220, vol. 5, p. 139 - ed.

[97] The Prophet having apparently announced the death of Najashi while at Medina and not at Mecca (*Tab.* 1, 4, 1720 - Tabari, *History*, vol. 9, p. 77 - ed.) the author here wishes only to convey the idea that the shortest way from Abyssinia to the former was through the latter.

[98] I.S. i, i, 65. *Buk.* iv, 194 (*Sahih Bukhari*, The Virtues and Merits of the Prophet, ch. 15, hadith 732, vol. 4, pp. 481-2 - ed.). *Musl.* ii, 301 (*Sahih Muslim*, Kitab al-Fada'il, ch. 982, hadith 5810, vol. 4, pp. 1254-5 - ed.) *Tab.* 1, 4, 1788 - Tabari, *History*, vol. 9, p. 156 - ed.

[99] *Musn.* i, 187, 188, 189.

[100] *Buk.* viii, 132 (*Sahih Bukhari*, The Book of ar-Riqa'iq, ch. 53, hadith 589, vol. 8, p. 384 - ed.). *Musl.* ii, 283 (*Sahih Muslim*, Kitab al-Fada'il, ch. 960, hadith 5682, vol. 4, p. 1236 - ed.). "The Pool of the Apostle" is that of which the Prophet's people will be given to drink on the day of Resurrection (*Taj.* v, 23). See also *Musn.* i, 257, 402, 406, 439, 453, 455. Its description is in ii, 162.

[101] *Musl.* ii, 341 (*Sahih Muslim*, Kitab Fada'il al-Sahabah, ch. 1007, hadith 6003, vol. 4, p. 1306 - ed.). I.S. ii, ii, 40.

[102] *Musn.* i, 102.

[103] Cf. I.S. iii, i, 46. *Taj.* iv, 428.

[104] Cf. *Musn.* ii, 164.

[105] A sentence of the Qur'an (2:151) proverbial on the occasion of a misfortune.

[106] *Tab.* 1, 6, 3109.

[107] *Buk.* ix, 62 - *Sahih Bukhari*, The Book of Afflictions, ch. 21, hadith 225, vol. 9, p. 174 - ed.

[108] *Taj al-'Arus (s.v.)*.

[109] Cf. *Tab.* 1, 3, 1467-9; and *Hish.* ii, 73 (reference is incorrect) - Ibn Hisham in *Life of Muhammad*, ed. Guillaume, p. 452 (where Salman al-Farisi, and not Muhammad, was using the pickaxe) - ed.

[110] Genuflexions at prayer.

[111] Lit. "until it reaches where night has reached."

[112] *Buk.* v, 9, 14; ix, 60 (*Sahih Bukhari*, The Virtues and the Merits of the Companions of the Prophet, ch. 6, hadith 23, vol. 5, pp. 17-8; ch. 7, hadith 42, vol. 5, p. 30; The Book of Afflictions, ch. 17, hadith 217, vol. 9, pp. 168-70 [all these traditions give Abu Musa in place of Anas b. Malik and contain other variations] - ed.). *Musl.* ii, 321 (*Sahih Muslim*, Kitab al-Fada'il al-Sahabah, ch. 995, hadith 5909, vol. 4, p. 1282 [with Abu Musa in place of Anas b. Malik and other variations] - ed.). Cf. *Musn.* ii, 165.

[113] *Buk.* iv, 44, 206 (*Sahih Bukhari*, The Book of Jihad, ch. 95, hadith 178, vol. 4, p. 110; The Virtues and Merits of the Prophet, ch. 24, hadith 787, vol. 4, p. 508 - ed.). *Musl.* ii, 505 (*Sahih Muslim*, Kitab al-Fitan wa Ashrat as-Sa'ah, ch. 1205, hadith 6957, vol. 4, p. 1507 - ed.). *Musn.* i, 4, 7.

[114] The Khurasanian ringleader of the revolution which overthrew the Umayyad dynasty in favor of the 'Abbasids.

[115] A femine gentilic from Harith, the tribe of the mother of Abul-'Abbas *Saffah* of the following note. Her father was called 'Ubaydullah

b. 'Abdallah b. 'Abdal-Maddan, b. Dayyan al-Harithi. (See *Tab*. iii, 88 and 2499).

[116] Abul-'Abbas surnamed *Saffah*, the first 'Abbasid Caliph (A.D. 750-754).

[117] Such remarks tend to cast serious doubt as to whether such a hadith ever really existed before Abul-'Abbas' became caliph - ed.

[118] Sind was conquered by the Muslims in the time of Hajjaj (Yaqut, *Geogr. Dict.*, iii, 166). Evidently the author refers here to the conquest of Sind and Yemen to the 'Abbasid cause (cf. *Tab*. iii, i, 80); about the invasions of Sind see Beladhori's *Futuh*, pp. 431-446 (edit. Goeje).

[119] Cf. *Buk*. i, 22; iv, 46; vi, 9 (*Sahih Bukhari*, The Book of Revelation, ch. 1, hadith 6, vol. 1, pp. 7 ff.; The Book of Jihad, ch. 99, hadith 187, vol. 4, p. 115; Book of Commentary, ch. 56, hadith 75, vol. 6, pp. 57 ff. - ed.). *Musn*. i, 243, 263, 305. *Musl*. ii, 81 (*Sahih Muslim*, Kitab al-Jihad wa 'l-Siyar, ch. 729, hadith 4382, vol. 3, p. 971 - ed.). *Tab*. 1, 3, 1571, etc.

[120] A governor established by the Sasanian Kings of Persia (*Tab*. 1, 4, 1763 - Tabari, *History*, vol. 9, p. 123 - ed.; 1857-1867. *Hish*. (i, 67-68 - Ibn Hisham in *Life of Muhammad*, ed. Guillaume, pp. 30 ff. - ed.) ascribes a similar incident to Badhan, about whom see *Tab*. 1, 4, 1851-1853.

[121] *Buk*. iv, 188; ix, 68 (*Sahih Bukhari*, The Virtues and Merits of the Prophet, ch. 2, hadith 705, vol. 4, pp. 463-4; The Book of Ahkam, ch. 2, hadith 254, vol. 9, p. 191 - ed.). *Musl*. ii, 107 *Sahih Muslim*, Kitab al-Imara, ch. 754, hadith 4476, vol. 3, p. 1009 - ed.

[122] *Buk*. v. 29, and in 'Ilm (*Sahih Bukahri*, The Virtues and the Merits of the Companions of the Prophet, ch. 24, hadith 100, vol. 5, p. 69 - ed.). Cf. *Musl*. ii, 351 (*Sahih Muslim*, Kitab Fada'il al-Sahabah,

ch. 1022, hadith 6055, vol. 4, pp. 1320-1 - ed.). "Habr" means *priest, doctor.* See also *Musn.* i, 266, 269, 315, 335, 359.

[123] Or: *of Ashes.* In the 17th or 18th year of the Flight there was no rain for a long time, and men and cattle perished in great number. (*Tab.* 1, 5, 2570 et seq.).

[124] Cf. I.S. iii, i, 232.

[125] This battle is described by *Tab.* 3, 4, 2306-7, etc.

[126] *Buk.* iv, 207 - *Sahih Bukhari*, The Virtues and Merits of the Prophet, ch. 24, hadith 793, vol. 4, pp. 510-1 - ed.

[127] Cf. Lev. 14:33 seq.

[128] Ex. 32:27-28.

[129] The Levites.

[130] Cf. Deut. 27:11 seq.

[131] The author misrepresents the text of the Torah here by exchanging an active construction for a passive one, obviously to suit his own aims - ed.

[132] Ezek. 5:1.

[133] Hos. 1:2 seq.

[134] Cf. ibid.

[135] Though he does not make use of the common Muslim charge that the Bible has been changed, the author attempts to discredit its being God's Word by first mentioning a passage as the saying of a prophet. When citing the Qur'an, however, the author, up until this

point in the text, immediately presents the text as the saying of God and not Muhammad. Christian polemicists also applied this tactic against Muslims - ed.

[136] Cf. Ezek. 16:26.

[137] Is. 31:9.

[138] The author conveniently neglects to mention the curses of the Qur'an (9:30; 111:1; etc.) in his brief comparative synopsis - ed.

[139] The author rather dishonestly means to suggest that such forgiveness is not to be found in the Bible - ed.

[140] Gentilic of *Abtah*, a clan of the tribe of the Quraysh (*Hish*. i, 163); and one of the names of the Prophet.

[141] Lit. "Spear-player," a title of three poets mentioned in *Taj*. (s.v.).

[142] Cf. I.S. i, ii, 97. *Buk*. iv, 200 - *Sahih Bukhari*, The Virtues and Merits of the Prophet, ch. 22, hadith 768, vol. 4, p. 494 - ed.

[143] Cf. *Musn*. ii, 94.

[144] See Leo, parag. BG and al-Kindi, parag. CD - ed.

[145] Cf. al-Kindi, parag. BU, on this passage - ed.

[146] In Morocco (*Yaqut*, iii, 189).

[147] This is against the doctrine of *Musn*. ii, 178, 180. The author's view is shared by Abu Hanifa.

[148] The author here seems to reveal his own reservations concerning the credibility of the previously referenced hadiths which purport to

show the signs of Muhammad's prophethood - ed.

[149] In Arabic *Dahri*, i.e., believing in the eternity of matter.

[150] This sentence is not found in the Qur'an; it is perhaps quoted from a traditional saying.

[151] In the Biblical quotations of the following pages the words between the parentheses are missing in the Syriac Version.

[152] Sept., δώδεκα ἔθνη γεννήσει.

[153] Al-Kindi said to his opponent with reference to an unnamed man: "Including a person whom thou knowest and whose name I should tremble to write," *Apology*, p. 89 (edit. Muir) - al-Kindi, parag. DD, n. 109 - ed. The person alluded to by the Christian apologist seems to have been Ishmael, the wild ass. [deleted]

[154] The Arabic lacks "And the angel of the Lord said to her" found in Syriac.

[155] I.e., soliciting favor from him. These words explain the meaning of "a higher and a lower hand" of the following lines. The higher or upper hand is that which gives, and the lower hand is that which receives. A saying to this effect on the part of the Prophet is reported by Bukhari and Muslim. See also Qastallani's *Irshad*, iii, 30-32, and Ibn Hanbal's *Musn*. ii, 67.

[156] All this is somewhat paraphrastic.

[157] The Syriac adds; "from the water skin."

[158] Syr. adds: "against (him)."

[159] Syr. adds: "because she said."

[160] Syr. "I."

[161] Syr. adds: "where he is."

[162] Syr. "and she saw."

[163] The translator misunderstood the Syriac corroborative which only means "with the lad."

[164] Technically, of course, this was no prophecy of Moses - ed.

[165] Since there are no prophecies concerning Ishmael in the Qur-'an, the author was restricted to using texts from the Torah, which he could not then maintain had been corrupted. On the matter of the prophecies spoken of Ishmael, one could easily make a far better case that the prophecies given Abraham and Sarah regarding Isaac were superior, not to mention the wealth of prophecies concerning Jesus which preceded His incarnation - ed.

[166] In harmony with the Qur'an (37:101 sqq.) the author cleverly sidesteps the issue of whether this was Isaac or Ishmael - ed.

[167] Syr. "Order, message."

[168] Syr. "in thy seed."

[169] All this is somewhat paraphrastic.

[170] The last words are somewhat paraphrastic.

[171] The *Qamus* explains this word as being a relative adjective referring to the *Jaramiqah* about whom see *Tab*. 1, 2, 827. The word seems to me to be the Syriac relative adjective "Gramqaya" from Bayt Garmai, (a) country bordering the ancient Adiabene, on the east bank of the Tigris and the two Zabs.

[172] Technically none of the direct prophecies concerning Ishmael could have been fulfilled by Muhammad, as no mention of a future prophet was made in them - ed.

[173] I.e., were called "Ishmaelites." Syriac writers even before the time of Muhammad called the Arabs by this name. See our *Narsai Homiliae*, i, pp. 115-117; and our *Sources Syriaques*, i, pp. 111, 123, 144, and ii, p. 174.

[174] Lit. "red." The *Taj* says that two epithets "black and white" comprise all mankind, the red type being included in the word "white."

[175] Many ancient philosophers believed the soul to reside in the blood; cf. Aristotle, *De animâ* 1, 2; cf. Lev. 17:18.

[176] In Morocco.

[177] Country corresponding approximately with the ancient Hyrcania; see *Yaqut* (ii, 436).

[178] Lit. "of the two seas": *Bahrain*.

[179] See note 172 above - ed.

[180] Cf. Timothy, parags. CA-CC.

[181] In Acts 3:19-25 this passage from Deut. 18 is shown as having been fulfilled by Jesus Christ. A standard interpretation of v. 15: "The LORD your God will raise up for a Prophet like me *from among you, from among your brethren*..." is that Jesus was physically of the children of Israel and from the tribe of Judah, and not of Levi as Moses. The context of Deut. 18:15,16 shows moreover that the promised Prophet, although "like Moses" and "from among them," would indeed be God Himself - ed.

[182] In Arabic "Sinin," as in the Qur'an 95:2.

[183] Paran is located on the southern end of the Sinai peninsula, not near Mecca as the author would have one believe - ed.

[184] The word which the author refers to rather falsely in Deut. 33:2 is YHWH and not Adhonai; cf. Nöldeke, *Deutsche Literaturzeitung*, 1924, p. 24 - ed.

[185] One of the complaints mentioned by Graf, which Bouyges brought against the authenticity of this work of 'Ali Tabari was that where Bible quotations to not seem to follow the Peshitta, the numbering of chapters fits our present system of chapter division. Since all of the various versions of chapter numberings are not known, it is somewhat presumptuous to use this argument. For mention of this objection: cf. G. Graf, *Deutsche Literaturzeitung*, 1926, p. 512 - ed.

[186] This is more in accordance with the East Syrian version which repeats twice the word "glory."

[187] Syr. "meekness."

[188] Syr. "Thy law is in the fear of thy right hand."

[189] Such a construction rather quickly approaches what for Sunnis is heresy and some Shiite groups dogma: a deification of Muhammad - ed.

[190] A not very natural rendering of a Syriac sentence meaning "In the city of our God and in His holy and glorious mountain." Strictly speaking, however, it can have the meaning given to it by the author. See below p. 131 [deleted]; - Nöldeke shows that the author has exchanged a dative construction for an accusative one to achieve his purpose; see *Deutsche Literaturzeitung*, 1924, p. 24 - ed.

[191] Syr. "Shall fear," or "worship him."

[192] I.e., "shall praise him." - The person described in this Psalm of Solomon (Ps. 72) is either a king or a king's son, neither of which fit Muhammad, who was neither the son of a king, nor did he have a son who survived him.

[193] Allusion to the traditional *Makam Ibrahim* containing the "stone" which, yielding under the weight of Abraham, bears the impression of his foot. It is situated close to the Ka'ba.

[194] Cf. Qur'an 33:56, Religious Dialogue, parags. AJ and AM - ed.

[195] The Syriac is: "He shall judge the Gentiles."

[196] By context, the person described in Ps. 110:5-7 is God Himself - ed.

[197] These verses along with Ex. 15:1-21 and Deut. 32:1-43 are incorporated with the Psalter in the East Syrian or Nestorian breviary (*Breviarium Chaldaicum*, Paris, 1886, vols. i, ii, iii, pp. 332-337).

[198] The person referred to in Is. 42:13 as seen in this passage is God Himself - ed.

[199] The word "Lord" in Is. 42:13 is YHWH and not Adhonai as the author would have us believe; see note 184 above - ed.

[200] Cf. supra, p. 88 - parag. EC - ed.

[201] The "people" described in Is. 9:1-4 are those of Zebulon, Naphtali and Galilee, which prophecy is shown to have been fulfilled by Jesus in Matt. 4:12-17 - ed.

[202] The Hebrew also has "government" משרה.

[203] The Is. 9:6-7 prophecy describes a son who though being born, is called "...Mighty God, Eternal Father..." This prophecy was clearly

fulfilled by Jesus Christ, and not Muhammad as the author attempts to show - ed.

[204] Cf. Ibn Taymiya's *al-Jawah us-Sahih* ii, 211. The seal of the prophecy is well described by I.S. i, ii, 131.

[205] The author is playing here on the Arabic word *tayammana*, meaning to go to Yemen, or in the direction of the right hand, i.e., for the Northern Arabs: *Yemenwards* or *southwards*.

[206] In the text *Mahin* (about which see *Tab.* i, 2627, 2632, etc.); this bears out the generally accepted opinion that *"Mah"* is to be identified with *"Mede."* See also p. 137 [deleted].

[207] Peshitta - ed.

[208] Cf. Ibn Taimiyah's *Jawah* (ibid).

[209] This passage in Is. 21 was often used by early Muslim polemicists as a prophecy concerning Jesus and Muhammad; the Christian replies to this claim in general appear to have resembled each other; cf. Leo, parag. BC; Timothy, parag. AV - ed.

[210] Country extending between Ahwaz, Basra and Ispahan (*Yaqut*, i, 497).

[211] See below about Is. 24:16-18. The sentence is misplaced.

[212] According to the Peshitta reading.

[213] Evidently the author did not consult the Hebrew text where there is very probably a clear mention of Arabia, which is missing in Syriac.

[214] Possibly a literal translation of the Syriac expression *Raz li*, meaning figuratively "woe is me."

[215] There is no such a thing in the Hebrew Massoretic text. The only difference between the Syriac and Hebrew texts is that the former has *"the force of the righteous,"* while the latter exhibits *"glory to the righteous."*

[216] The Syriac is simply: "And in glory it (i.e., the desert) will be given the honor of Lebanon."

[217] The New Testament shows this prophecy of Isaiah to have been fulfilled by John the Baptist; see Matt. 3:3; Mk. 1:2,3; Lk. 3:4-6 and John 1:23 - ed.

[218] High dignitaries. The above saying is (curiously enough) reported by Michael the Syrian (ii, 423 edit. Chabot).

[219] The word for "God" in Is. 40:10 is YHWH and thus not to be identified as a god or, as in this case, Muhammad - ed.

[220] The author's book mentioned above seems to be identical with the one mentioned above (p. 638) under the title: *Book of Reply to Christians*.

[221] In Ex. 7:1 it is YHWH speaking of Moses as "elohim," in Ps. 110:1 it is YHWH who is speaking to the Lord ("Adhon") - ed.

[222] The Syriac version has "piety."

[223] I.e., Abraham. The author alludes here also to the *Makam Ibrahim* found in the Ka'ba of Mecca. (See above, p. 624, n. 192).

[224] Syr. "Thou shalt be glorified."

[225] The author has conveniently left off the first part of Is. 41:8 which reads: "But you, Israel, My servant Jacob, whom I have chosen..." in order to change the context of this passage - ed.

[226] For the linguistic meaning given by Arab writers to the word *Hidjaz*, see Lammen's *Le berceau de l'Islam*, p. 13. It is generally used in the sense of "barrier." - cf. Nöldeke, *Deutsche Literaturzeitung*, 1924, 1, p. 24 - ed.

[227] The author has omitted the words "God of Israel" from Is. 41:17 and seems to have decided not to use the well-known Muslim tradition which claims that a distorted version of Is. 42:1-7 is a prophecy foretelling Muhammad; see *Sahih Bukhari*, The Book of Sales, ch. 51, hadith 335, vol. 3, pp. 189-190; Book of Commentary, ch. 273, hadith 362, vol. 6, pp. 345-6 - ed.

[228] From the context of the verses preceding and following this passage; i.e., Is. 43: 14,15,22-26 (Peshitta); the "chosen people" are Israel - ed.

[229] The author has omitted the words which refer to Jacob and Israel.

[230] Syr. "I was glorified."

[231] The people described in Is. 49:1-5, are Israel, as v. 3 shows: "you are my servant, Israel...." - ed.

[232] The Syriac, "shall make the desolate and ruined towns inhabited." The Arabic sentence may also bear this meaning.

[233] These verses precede the above quotations in the Book of Isaiah, but have been cited after them. The same phenomenon will also occur below, and this would imply that our MS. may be considered as a transcript from the first draft of the author's of the author's autograph.

[234] Cf. Phil. 2:10,11 - ed.

[235] These words are found at the beginning of the Syro-Nestorian liturgy. See *Misale juxta ritum Ecclesiae Syrorum Orientalium*, Mosul, 1901, p. 27.

[236] Syr. "has glorified thee."

[237] Or: judgment.

[238] By context, the subject of this passage is YHWH, who Himself is intercessor. Muhammad is nowhere mentioned as an intercessor in the Qur'an; this doctrine was a later development in Islam - ed.

[239] Syr. "will come."

[240] Since the Muslims themselves are Gentiles, one must question what meaning the author attaches to this word - ed.

[241] Syr. "Glorified thee."

[242] See note 240 above - ed.

[243] Lit. "Its veils shall be scattered."

[244] Allusion to the Ka'ba; cf. pp. 90 and 101.

[245] Syr. and Hebr. "in the day of salvation."

[246] See note 240 above - ed.

[247] Name given to God in the Qur'an; it is the Aramaic adjective — substantive "rahman," meaning "compassionate."

[248] For Muhammad and his nation, it can quite easily be shown that generally the reverse was true, as in the case of the Banu Qurayza, all of whose surviving women and children he took captive as slaves; see Ibn Hisham in *Life of Muhammad*, pp. 461 ff. - ed.

[249] For the hardships of the Arab Christians see pp. 20-21, above - ed.

[250] The one being addressed in Is. 49:14-21 is Zion and neither Mecca, nor Hagar; cf. Nöldeke, *Deutsche Literaturzeitung*, 1924, p. 24 - ed.

[251] I.e., Baghdad.

[252] The object of Is. 49:22,23 is again Zion and not Mecca - ed.

[253] The theology of this statement is somewhat confused; in orthodox Islam the worship of any but God is heresy - ed.

[254] So the author seems to have understood the Syriac word *Busar* (Bozrah). Cf., however, *Taj*, iii, 42.

[255] Along with a substantial amount of text, the words "Abraham" and "Israel" have also been omitted - ed.

[256] Cf. supra p. 624.

[257] Cf. p. 632.

[258] The word for "Lord" in Is. 63:16 quoted above is YHWH, and not Adhonai; thus this passage can only refer to God - ed.

[259] Strictly speaking, the Syriac text yields to the interpretation given to it by the author because the word meaning "dwelling" (*mediara*) is as he says, in singular; but the Hebrew text, by having suffix-pronouns in the second member of the *status contructus*, renders 'Ali's interpretation improbable. See below, p. 130 [deleted].

[260] The author gives no explanation for how he justifies the identification of Mecca for Zion - ed.

[261] Syr. "The Holy Spirit."

[262] The claim that the Paraclete was Muhammad was used quite often by early Muslim polemicists somewhat in an attempt to find a confirmation of Qur'an 7:156; 61:6; etc. See: Leo, parags. P-Q; Timothy, parags. AN-AP; Leo, parag. Y - ed.

[263] The author credits this saying to John and not to Jesus, perhaps again intending to cast doubt on the reliability of the text - ed.

[264] In the *Shifa* of Yahsubi, "Paraclete" is given as a name of Muhammad. (In the chapter of the Prophet's names.) - In more recent times, some Muslims have even ventured to change the word "Parakletos" (παράκλητος) to "Periklutos" (περικλῦτος); cf. *Sahih Bukhari*, Introduction, vol. 1, p.lx and Aziz us-Samad, *Islam and Christianity*, pp. 97-98, who wrongly states that "Periklutos" means "Comforter" and "Parakletos" means "Illustrious" or "Renowned" - ed.

[265] I.e., "Muhammad, the rightly guiding prophet, son of 'Abdallah."

[266] According to the Syriac pronunciation.

[267] I.e., "Muhammad is a beloved and good apostle."

[268] The Bible used by the author incorporated the Acts and the Catholic Epistles under one title *Praxis*, as it is in the Syrian Churches.

[269] The author has taken this verse out of context, for the second part of I Pet. 4:17 (NASB) continues: "and if it begins with us first, what will be the outcome for those who do not obey the gospel of God?" - ed.

[270] Cf. supra, p. 121 [deleted].

[271] The context of Luke 22:35-38 is that an Old Testament passage must be fulfilled, and after one of the disciples produces two swords, Jesus replied that that was sufficient - ed.

[272] According to all of the Gospel reports it was a slave of the high priest, and not a soldier - ed.

[273] The comparison made between Hagar and Sarah, Ishmael and Isaac, Sinai and Jerusalem with "the Jerusalem above" contrasts life under the law with life under grace in Gal. 4:21-31. The author misconstrues the intended meaning of the word Arabia, from the Sinai peninsula to mean Mecca; see parag. EB above - ed.

[274] Cf. supra p. 622.

[275] The word for "Lord" in Deut. 33:2 is YHWH and not Adhonai, and so this verse refers to God Himself, and not a human. The author could hardly have meant that Muhammad was God - ed.

[276] The author refers to the Syriac version here, curiously enough, the word is written in the Greek way without the strong guttural at the beginning.

[277] This information is not without historical interest.

[278] Allusion to the Jacobites. - It can hardly be said that the high priest and his group were followers of Jesus - ed.

[279] Allusion to the Nestorians. - Rather oddly, the author fails to mention the deity of Christ directly in his extremely distorted description of Christianity - ed.

[280] In his apparent zeal for Islam the author goes to no pains to hide his bias against other religions. Logically, however, this approach would probably have had a very negative effect on those he up until this point was trying to reach for his cause - ed.

[281] Cf. Qur'an 4:44; etc.

[282] Lit. "I saw."

[283] *Kitab ud-Din wa'd-Daulah*.

[284] More especially the doctrine of the eternity of matter.

AL-JAHIZ'S
"A REPLY TO
THE CHRISTIANS"

Joshua Finkel's article "A Risala of Al-Jahiz" not only closes our present investigation of the Christian-Muslim dialogue prior to 900 A.D., but this particular essay of Jahiz, of which a partial translation is presented here, also shows that a rather abrupt turning-point had been reached in these discussions.

As we have seen, a general period of religious toleration had eisted during the reign of the 'Abbasid Caliph al-Ma'mun (813-833 A.D.). Ma'mun's court espoused certain 'Alid views and officially catered to the Mu'tazilites by proclaiming that the Qur'an was created and not eternal.[1] It is this last fact which is of special interest here, for Jahiz was himself Mu'tazilite and began his government service under Ma'-mun.[2]

There is good reason to believe that the Mu'tazila was at first a political group which came about as a result of the conflict between 'Uthman and 'Ali. Later though, they became more theological in nature, some of their better known characteristics being that they attempted to be apologetic, polemic and Qur'anic. In the question of the Qur'an being eternal or created, a problem which in itself probably never would have come up were it not for the polemic approaches of the Christians, the Mu'tazilites parted with most Muslims by believing that it was created.[3]

When al-Mutawakkil (847-861 A.D.) came to power both the 'Alids and the Mu'tazilites fell into disfavor with the court. Finkel argues that the reasons for Mutawakkil's persecution of these two groups were that the 'Alids represented a political threat to the throne, while the continued support of the Mu'tazila, which was still a minority, would have only furthered the spiritual disharmony already existent in the empire.[4] In addition to this, Mutawakkil also began persecuting the non-Muslim peoples of his realm, most notably the Christians,[5] against whom he also mounted an extensive literature program.[6] Oddly enough, Mutawakkil also hired the Mu'tazilite Jahiz to take part in this anti-Christian project. Finkel attempts to explain this paradox by showing the high esteem the court had for Jahiz's qualities as a writer,[7] but there is probably yet another issue at hand here. Jahiz was valued more for his scholarship than for his penmanship, as one of Finkel's own sources shows,[8] and thus Mutawakkil's choice of Jahiz seems to point more to a shortage of Muslim scholars in the court than anything else. The illustration of this deficiency is further magnified by Jahiz's apparent inability to read anything but Arabic[9] and his belief that the Greeks were an extinct race.[10]

It is obvious from the internal evidence that "A Reply to the Christians" was written with the Nestorians in mind, and this should come to us as no great surprise. Of all the Christian groups of this time period, it was the Nestorians who were nearest Islam both geographically and theologically, and it was again the Nestorians who were their most successful spiritual opponents. Jahiz's commentary on the polemical methods of the Christians can perhaps best be seen in the *Apology* of al-Kindi, who more than any other antagonist of Islam in this collection, made extensive use of Islamic hadith. In describing the success of Christianity in his day, Jahiz essentially admits not only to the failure of the Islamic polemic in general, but also to that of the Mu'tazilites when they had more influence with the caliphate. What remained to be done to thwart the growth of Christianity was to dictate legal and theological reforms in favor of a more orthodox Muslim society; and that is exactly what Mutawakkil was trying to do.

For an interesting biography of Jahiz and a bibliography of his works, consult an-Nadim's *Fihrist*, trans. Dodge, pp. 397 ff.

Joshua Finkel's article was first published in the *Journal of the American Oriental Society*, vol. 47, pp. 311-34.

[1] al-Tabari, *History*, vol. 32, pp. 199 ff. and al-Kindi, p. 372.

[2] Nyberg, "Al-Mu'tazila," *Shorter Encyclopedia of Islam*, p. 424, and *Encyclopedia of Islam*, New Edition, vol. 2, p. 385.

[3] Ibid., pp. 424-6.

[4] See p. 696, below.

[5] Tabari, p. 558, above.

[6] Finkel notes that 'Ali Tabari's *Book of Religion and Empire* was also contracted by Mutawakkil. See p. 696.

[7] p. 694.

[8] p. 693.

[9] p. 699.

[10] Jahiz, parag. K.

A RISALA OF AL-JAHIZ
Joshua Finkel
Brooklyn

A REPLY TO CHRISTIANS

MU'TAZILITE MUSLIM
'Abu 'Uthman 'Amr ibn
Bahr al-Jahiz
d. 869 A.D.

DURING MY STAY in Cairo in 1925-1926 I chanced to come across an edition of the Kamil lil-Mubarrad (published by al-Tubi, Cairo, 1323-4) which contained on the margin a collection of epistles by Jahiz. Since the greater part of these letters had not appeared in print elsewhere, I immediately became interested in the collection. Upon closer examination of the contents I realized that the text was corrupt to such an extent as to make unintelligible the meaning of many an important passage.

Assuming that the publisher made use of a local manuscript, I set out immediately in search for his sources, and shortly afterwards found that in the library of the 'Azhar Mosque, and in the private collection of Taymur Pasha there were manuscripts which have all the epistles printed on the margin of the Kamil. Perusing both manuscripts I further discovered that the Cairene publisher had printed only part of the epistle "A Reply to the Christians" contained in these manuscripts.

I assume now that al-Tubi must have felt much like Ibn Qutayba with regard to the part of the essay which he tacitly omitted,[1] and that Jahiz's emphatic statement about the text of the Torah as being true and uncorrupted[2] was not at all to the liking of this publisher.[3]

Since this completely published essay engaged most of my interest I decided to edit the whole Risala with the help of the two Cairene manuscripts. Continuing in my search for additional manuscripts I soon learned that several essays of Jahiz were to be found in the private collection of Nur al-Din Bey Mustafa. Of these I chose for editing two unpublished essays not contained in either of the aforementioned local manuscripts. The *Radd 'ala l-Nasara* and the two Risalas of Nur al-Din Bey's library were published by me in Cairo in 1926 under the title *Three Essays of 'Abu 'Uthman 'Amr b. Bahr al-Jahiz*.

The 'Azhar MS. (No. 6836, dated 1313 A.H.), and the Taymur MS. ('Adab division, No. 19, dated 1315 A.H.) were written by the same copyist, whose name is Muhammad al-Zamrani. This copyist adds in the colophon of the Taymur cod. that he made this copy from a MS. dated 403 A.H., whose scribe was a certain Abu l-Qasim 'Ubayd Allah b. 'Ali.

Since the same errors generally occur in both the modern codices it is safe to assume that al-Zamrani availed himself of the same source for each transcript. As for al-Tubi, he may have used either the original or a modern copy—an independent source would be highly improbable. It should be added that there is also found in the British Museum a collection of extracts from various writings of Jahiz. Rieu[4] informs us that the manuscript was transcribed by 'Abd Allah a-Mansuri in 1294 A.H. in Cairo, from a unique copy which belonged to Shaikh 'Ali al-Laythi, which in turn had been transcribed from an old manuscript. The tenth of the Rasa'il in this collection is our *Radd 'ala l-Nasara*.

Hirschfeld gives us further information about this collection in the Volume of Oriental Studies presented to Browne, Cambridge, 1922 (pp. 200-209). The *Radd 'ala l-Nasara* Hirschfeld mentions there only by name, but in a much earlier article of his in the *Jewish Quarterly Review* he had already cited and translated a paragraph of this essay.[5] The variations exhibited in this excerpt are so few and insignificant as to make one inclined to believe that the "old MS." referred to by Rieu may have been no other codex than the one employed by al-Zamrani.

Besides the untoward circumstances of being compelled to rely on such transcripts for the edition of the text, another factor affects much more deeply the status of the present Risala. In both Cairene manuscripts, as well as in the edition of al-Tubi, there appears the name of a certain 'Ubayd Allah b. Hassan as the person responsible for the abridged form of the Rasa'il. However, in perusing the essays one realizes that 'Ubayd Allah has not curtailed them with a regard for the preservation of the symmetry of their original parts, for he has no scruples whatsoever in shocking the reader here and there with a sudden break in the line of the argument; and his crude method, therefore, speaks well for the authenticity of what is left of the original. Moreover, the spells of verbosity which Jahiz is subject to, his stock-phrases and peculiar modes of expression are faithfully reproduced by 'Ubayd Allah, so that these considerations in themselves should exclude all suspicion of paraphrase.

Since al-Zamrani indicates the date of the original manuscript as that of 403 A.H. it follows that our redactor could have made his abridgement not later than the beginning of the 5th century of the Hagira. And this is all I know about him; I could not find in the various books of reference so much as mention of an 'Ubayd Allah b. Hassan whose lifetime would have fit into the interval between the period of the literary activity of Jahiz and the 11th century of the Christian era.

The translation which I offer below is limited to that part of the Risala in which the subject-matter and its treatment may be characterized as unique in the whole range of Muhammadan polemical literature. Here, not Christianity is so much attacked as the high degree of civilization attained by the Oriental Christians at that time.

The portions of the text that precede and follow the part I just referred to, consist of theological disputations concerning Jesus and Muhammad, and of discussions about the genuineness of the texts of the Taurat, 'Injil and Qur'an. Though many points brought out by the author are novel even in this connection, inasmuch as they reflect the opinions entertained by the Mu'tazilite Mutakallimun of the 9th century, for whose general views even we have no contemporary source except Jahiz, I have, nevertheless, not included these portions in the translation, for they would complicate the introduction with lengthy discussions of various Mu'tazilite doctrines for which the present short paper is not intended.

I give no references in the footnotes to such names and events as are generally recorded in the standard works of modern scholars on the life of Muhammad and the history of the Caliphs. The parentheses, which I sometimes place around a word or a sentence in the translation, show that the equivalent does not exist in the original, but that I consider the text to be pregnant with its meaning.

I realize that I have fallen short of my task in more than one point, especially in my failure to include Byzantine and Syriac sources as illustrative of the life of the Christians in Muhammadan countries in the time of Jahiz.

Introduction
I

Abu 'Uthman 'Amr b. Bahr al-Jahiz (died 869) is one of the greatest Arabic authors of all times.[6] His encyclopedic knowledge is amazing. While there were other authors no less versatile than he in the numerous branches of learning, none could make full use of them as he did, and none could focus on a single subject so many rays of erudition.

The present essay "A Reply to the Christians" illustrates this point fully. Jahiz managed to crowd into this short treatise theology, philosophy, psychology, sociology, history, folklore and what not. Behind this multifarious material Jahiz stands supreme. His personality is felt thoughout every page. His method and style are peculiarly his own. Even if knowledge, method and style were not to be considered, there would still remain a paradox—the "Jahizian idea," if I may call it so; there would still remain that paragraph which no one but Jahiz could write.

What is this Jahizian idea? It is Jahiz's ability to write anything about everything and be affected by nothing. He may praise ʻAli in one epistle and attack him in another.[7] He may extol the exploits of non-Arabs in one essay[8] and assail the Shuʻubiyya in another.[9] And he would praise and attack with such vigor and show of sincerity as no real partisan could boast. He could curse and bless like Balaam.

He could write on anything. In his capital work, the *Kitab al-Hayawan*, the introduction of heterogeneous material often resolves itself into queer digressions. These digressions, full of useful information and instructive in themselves, may be said to contribute nothing to the subject under discussion. A pair of shoes, an elephant and a configuration of stars may well be imagined to form the topics of three contiguous paragraphs. In his flight of ideas we may come across the wildest associations. In his short treatises, however, Jahiz is intent upon making the varied data bear upon the single topic.

The epistles which he wrote are numerous.[10] It is to be presumed that he wrote them under the stress of circumstances. He received a salary from the public treasury[11] and, naturally, he would have to cater to the caliph of his day. Undoubtedly, during the reign of Ma'mun, Jahiz had the opportunity to be much more outspoken in his opinions. In the days of Mutawakkil, however, when orthodox reaction set in and freedom of speech was supressed, we would expect to see a turning point in the literary activity of Jahiz.

The present essay seems to have been written at the express wish of the court. Fath b. Kakan,[12] the favorite courtier of Mutawakkil, in a letter to Jahiz, urges him to hasten its completion. Fath assures him that his pension will be paid a year in advance and that he will also be indemnified for all the arrears in his salary. He tells Jahiz that he has commended him to the Caliph and that were it not for our author's great scholarship, Jahiz would receive a compulsory invitation to the palace and would be deprived of his opinions by force.[13] The last clause undoubtedly refers to Jahiz's Muʻtazilite doctrines. It is fair to assume that, if he had been summoned to the court, he would have renounced his Mu'tazilite beliefs—the very confession of the faith of his sect. One could hardly expect Jahiz to become a martyr.

Mutawakkil, in the course of his persecution of the Christians, might have assigned the writing of this epistle to more than one scholar of the ranks of the staunch orthodox Muslims who would have been only too ready to pounce upon the Christians with all the venom and fury of his blind prejudice. Instead Mutawakkil entrusted this task to Jahiz, a man who had been in close association with Christians, and had been suspected of harboring indifferent views toward religion in general,[14] because the court well knew that it could depend upon the pen of Jahiz more than upon the convictions of others. It is amusing to think that the present Risala in which Jahiz appears to release a rancor pent up in his breast for years is merely a propaganda pamphlet written to order, of the completion of which he was urgently reminded. Mutawakkil's expectations were bourne out by the results. While there are other anti-Christian writings extant in Muhammadan literature, no work goes so directly to the vital features of the problem, no work is so potential of deadly effect.

Even eliminating these court influences, Jahiz would still look two ways at once and blow hot and cold in the same breath.[15] If so, what was Jahiz's relation to truth? Was he a man devoid of principles and ideals? It looks very much like it. He was essentially a skeptic. His skepticism, however, he expressed in his own way. Instead of boldly indicating doubt, he merely hinted at the existence of possibilities. To possibilities which happened to be in conflict with the serious conventional beliefs of his day, he would not attach the weight of his consideration, i.e., he would not even comment upon them as being "possibilities." He would merely present them and say: This is the claim of such and such a sect, and that is the assertion of philosopher so and so. Thus he avoided the danger of being accused of suspended judgment, even by implication, and only ran the risk of being suspected of it. To minimize even this suspicion he employs a distinct technique. It consists in not making un-Muhammadan notions stand out in relief, but in rather relegating them to the background. To this end various devices are used, such as brevity, awkwardness of style, misplacement, ambiguity and others. A contemptuous remark may occasionally accompany an heretical utterance or approval may be accorded to the popular doctrine.[16]

Skepticism as a philosophy is quite sincere. A cynic might say that in veiling his skepticism from sight, Jahiz should be given credit for even that slight courage he displays in not cloaking it wholly from view. However, when we see Jahiz weeping for Hecuba, while Hecuba means nothing to him, we cannot regard him as a man who cherishes principles and ideals in life. On the other hand, when we see him outstripping others in championing their cause, we are bewildered by his genius rather than aroused by his hypocrisy. It is true that Jahiz was neither actor nor lawyer, but their arts, strange to say, spoke through his pen. The fusion of the subjective and objective must have been the secret of his soul. Besides, he was a good psychologist. His extensive travels in many countries undoubtedly enriched his knowledge of human nature.[17] Finally, we must bear in mind that Jahiz was a man of a prodigious amount of learning. He is reputed never to have failed to read a book on which he laid his hands, no matter what its contents.[18] His great absorption in this flux of information prevented him from turning fluctuating feelings into loyalties. He simply drowned his sympathies in the wealth of his knowledge. This is essentially the Jahizian idea: to write about everything and be affected by nothing.

II

It is left now for us to inquire into the times of Mutawakkil and disclose the basic causes for the appearance of the present Risala.

During the reign of Ma'mun and Mu'tasim and Wathiq the Muslim empire was a hot-bed of all sorts of heresies. Their successor Mutawakkil, a man of no mean political vision, felt great apprehension lest this spiritual turmoil shatter which embraced in its fold a jumble of ethnic groups that had adopted the new faith either by coercion or for sheer convenience. He therefore set out to make the empire safe for orthodoxy and broadcast a decree forbidding polemics between the members of the various Muslim sects.[19] He immediately directed his attack against two Muslim sects, the Mu'tazilites and the Shiites, notably the latter, which he persecuted mercilessly,[20] because politically they identified themselves as the 'Alid faction that aspired to set up a rival dynasty. Naturally, the problem of the protected cults might also assume now a serious aspect. The edict of 'Umar against the Jews and Christians had to be revived.

Feeling ran especially high against the Christians. While from the outside the country was harassed by the raids of the Byzantine army and fleet, the Christians helped to foment uprisings in some provinces from within. The Christians also formed culturally a very active minority that proved remarkably successful in its educational and economic pursuits. Colloquial Greek and Syriac were either mother-tongues or second languages to a great many Christians. A knowledge of Greek and Syriac they acquired through Bible instruction in the Church. To them the old pagan literature was an open book. They translated the books of the ancients for the caliphs and viziers and so won promotion to high social station. The Christians in the West and East, respectively, were also the heirs to the industrial and commercial methods of the Greeks and the Phoenicians. With Byzantium's formid-ible attacks from without and religious turmoil threatening disintegra-tion from within, it was natural that the prosperous Christians living within the confines of the state should at once become the victims of both fear and jealousy. In a word they became for the state a grave problem.

With a view to solving it, Mutawakkil, besides bringing into operation the obsolete injunction of 'Umar, inaugurated a literary campaign against them. He ordered and assisted 'Ali b. Rabban al-Tabari, a Christian turned Muslim, to write a semi-offcial defence and exposition of Islam.[21] In this book the author attempted to prove, by citing scores of passages from the Bible and the New Testament, that the coming of Muhammad was foretold by the Hebrew prophets and Jesus as well as by the apostles. He reminded the Christians to what conditions they had been reduced by reason of being members of a protected cult, and warmly appealed to them to forsake their false faith and embrace Islam.

The tone of the present essay, however, is singularly inimical, and the argument is diabolically calculated to strike at the heart; for Christianity is not merely assailed as a false faith, but also as a social evil. The work done by the Christian translators is treated disparagingly, and, by critical analysis, a serious effort is made to eradicate from the minds of the Muslims all traditionally cherished notions in favor of Christianity.

The Jews, on the other hand, though spoken of with contempt, are reasonably spared, in comparison with the Christians, and occasionally even defended. At that time the Jews presented no serious problem to the revival of Arab chauvinism. It was centuries later that they played the role which the Christians were playing now. Then the Jews in turn had often for the same cause to suffer at the hands of the European Christians what these Oriental Christians were now suffering at the hands of the Muslims.

Be that as it may, the cultural and economic state of the Jews could by no means be so low as Jahiz would have us to believe. We hear of Jewish translators and physicians even as far back as the 8th and 9th centuries. Masarjawayhi[22] supervised for 'Umar b. 'Abd al-'Aziz the translation of the medical book of the priest of Aaron. 'Isma'il[23] is a name of another Jewish physician, who was a contemporary of the famous poet Ibn al-Rumi.

Ibn al-Jauzi informs us that Mutawakkil issued an order forbidding Jews and Christians the study of Arabic, and that, as a result, a revival of Hebrew ensued.[24] This tends to show that the Jews were considered culturally as an influential element.

Nor was the science of Kalam unknown to the Jews. Ibn al-Rawandi,[25] a younger contemporary of Jahiz, whose father was said to be a Jewish convert to Islam, was the *enfant terrible* of both Mu'tazilites and Sunnites. In the whole range of Muhammadan literature we find only him and Abu 'Ala' l-Ma'arri daring to attack Islam openly.[26] Ibn al-Rawandi wrote several polemical treatises for his father's coreligionists. Commenting upon the latter's activity some contemporary Jews remarked to the Muslims: "He will misrepresent the Qur'an to you just as his father misrepresented the Torah to us." When persecuted for his writings he found refuge in the homes of Ibn Lawi and Abu 'Isa al-Ahwazi, both of whom were Jews. To the latter Ibn al-Rawandi dedicated most of his works, and in his home he died.

Lastly, it must be observed, that the occupations of the Jews were far from being limited to those mentioned by Jahiz. The powerful merchant guild of the Radhaniites made extensive journeys through parts of Europe and Asia, reaching even India and China, and the variety of their wares was such that their enterprise might have been justly called "a travelling department store."[27] In 321 A.H., although somewhat later than the period of Jahiz, the greater part of the merchants of Tustar were Jews.[28]

Our author, in this essay, displays his duplicity as unaffectedly as ever. The liberal and broad-minded Jahiz becomes all of the sudden the exponent of the Shafiite code[29] in order to curry favor with Mutawakkil, who was the first caliph to adopt it.[30] But may we not ask: If Jahiz is a sincere Muslim, why does he intentionally strengthen the arguments of the Christians in their attacks upon the Qur'an?[31] Why does he injure his cause in defeat of his own purpose? It is because Jahiz reverts here to his element, to that corner of his restless soul from which he does not see the oneness of truth but the seven colors of its spectrum. He is not at peace with himself, and he does not seem to crave to be so; for Jahiz expresses himself to this effect somewhat as follows: "True knowledge does not consist in the enjoyment one derives from his soul resting peacefully upon the problem it has solved. Possession by the soul of this state is no criterion of truth, nor is it the disposition of knowledge, for the soul may relish its repose in error if, with the force of conviction, it considers error to be the truth."[32]

There is, however, an undercurrent beneath all the vacillating arguments of Jahiz which does not admit of fluctuations and that is his personal argument, his literary jealousy. Great as his knowledge of Greek culture was,[33] he must have felt that this knowledge was not well founded if he could not derive it from the sources, but had to resort instead to the translators, almost all of whom happened to be Christians. For the cause of traditional Islam he had anything but sympathy. It was through this tragic aspect of his literary ambition that this original thinker was swept into the tide of chauvinism. That this handicap must have deeply hurt him may be gathered from his mental compensation that borders on the ridiculous. Without the knowledge of any other language than Arabic,[34] he argues that no translation can be faithful and that two tongues, if acquired, must needs handicap each other, for inasmuch as man possesses only one natural power, this force will of necessity decrease in half when distributed into two liguistic compartments.[35] Thinking that the Bible he used was translated by Jews, he blames the Jews for being literal translators, failing to convey the true meaning of the text.[36] He is convinced that Arabic poetry cannot be translated into any tongue.[37] Thus we see that among the other factors there was also the scholar's "complex" at work. This was the only genuine motive that he could have in writing this Risala. To the political situation in which the Christians were involved he could not be so sensitive as the officials of the court; as a retiring scholar and individualist he must have been far from developing a keen sense for politics.

A contemporary of Jahiz somehow detecting that Jahiz could paint naked truth in any color, wonders how the man will face the Lord on the Day of Resurrection.[38] I admit that it is difficult for me to answer this question. To 'Abdullah b. Hamud, however, this matter was quite clear. He said: "I shall be satisfied with reading the books of Jahiz in Paradise as a substitute for all its delights."[39] Now that the Paradise is deserving of the books of Jahiz, Jahiz will surely be in Paradise.

Be that as it may, the people of Basra, the Sorbonne of Muhammadan learning, prided themselves on the three greatest men they produced.[40] One of them was Jahiz. I heartily agree with the people of Basra.

Translation
(p. 13, l. 9 - p. 22, l. 14)

(A) I shall begin to enumerate the causes which made the Christians more liked by the masses than the Magians, and made men consider them more sincere than the Jews, more endeared, less treacherous, less unbelieving and less deserving of punishment. For all this there are manifold and evident causes. They are patent to one who searches for them, concealed to one who shuns investigation.

(B) The first cause is as follows: The Jews were the neighbors of the Muslims in Medina and other places, and (as is well known) the enmity of neighbors is as violent and abiding as the hostility that arises among relatives. Man indeed hates the one whom he knows, turns against the one whom he sees, opposes the one whom he resembles and becomes observant of the faults of those with whom he mingles; the greater the love and intimacy, the greater the hatred and estrangement. Therefore feuds among relatives and neighbors, in the case of the Arabs as well as of other people, lasted longer and proved more rancorous. When the Emigrants became the neighbors of the Jews—at that time the Helpers had already been enjoying their proximity—the Jews began to envy the Muslims, the blessings of their new faith[41] and the union which resulted after dissension. They proceeded to undermine the belief of our masses and to lead them astray. They aided our enemies and those envious of us. From mere misleading speech and stinging words they plunged into an open declaration of enmity, so that the Muslims mobilized their forces, exerting themselves morally and materially to banish the Jews and destroy them.[42] Their strife became long-drawn and widespread, so that it worked itself up into a rage and created yet greater animosity and more intensified rancor. The Christians, however, because of their remoteness from Mecca and Medina, did not have to put up with religious controversies and did not have occasion to stir up trouble and be involved in war. That was the first cause of our dislike of the Jews and our partiality toward the Christians.

(C) There were, besides, some Muslims who emigrated to Ethiopia and looked upon that country as their haven.[43] This hospitality accorded to Muslims helped to further the friendship between us and the Christians. And as the hearts of the Muslims softened toward the Christians, in like degree they hardened to the Jews, and the less the

Muslims hated the Christians the more they hated the Jews. It is
indeed the nature of man to love the one who does him good or is
instrumental in doing so—no matter whether he does so intentionally or
unwittingly, whether he does so for the glory of God or not.

(D) Another circumstance, which is the most potent cause, is the
wrong interpretation given by the masses to the Qur'anic verses: "Thou
wilt surely find that the strongest in enmity against those who believe
are the Jews and the idolaters; and thou wilt find the nearest in love to
those who believe to be those who say, 'We are Christians,' that is
because there are amongst them priests and monks and because they
are not proud. And when they hear that which hath been sent down to
the apostle read unto them, thou wilt see their eyes overflow with
tears, because of the truth which they perceive therein, saying, 'O Lord,
we believe; write us down therefore with those who bear witness to the
truth; and what should hinder us from believing in God and the truth
which hath come unto us and from earnestly desiring that our Lord
would introduce us into Paradise with the righteous people?' Therefore hath God rewarded them, for what they said with gardens through
which rivers flow; they shall continue therein forever; and this is the
reward of the righteous."[44]

(E) The wrong interpretation of the above verses supplanted that of
the learned, and the Christians craftily used it to seduce the common
and the vulgar. In the very verses lies the proof that here God is not
referring to the Christians we are acquainted with nor to their associates the Melkites and Jacobites, but rather to the type of Bahira[45] and
the kind of monks whom Salman[46] used to serve. There is a vast
difference when we consider the phrase *"Who say* we are Christians"
(as an insinuation) that these monks misnamed themselves or as a real
term to be taken like the word "Jews" (which refers to the Jews who
plotted against Muhammad in Medina).

(F) When Islam first appeared there were two Arab kings, one of
Ghassan and the other of Lakhm, both of whom were Christians.
Arabs were their subjects and paid them tribute. The respect which
these Arabs accorded to their rulers found its root in the esteem that

they held out for their Christian religion. And Tihama, though a tribe that did not pay tribute and was not subject to royalty, still could not refrain from respecting what others respected and from contemning what others contemned. The fact that Nuʿman and the Kings of Ghassan were Christians is known to the Arabs and is common knowledge to the genealogists. Were this not known, I would prove it by quotations from popular verses of poetry and stories worthy of belief.

(G) The Arabs (the Quraysh) traded with Syria; they sent their merchants to the emperors of Byzantium and conducted two yearly caravans,[47] in the winter to Yemen, and in the summer in the direction of Syria. Their summer resort was in Taʾif. They were people of wealth, as is mentioned in the Qurʾan and by men of learning. They also travelled to Ethiopia and appeared as emissaries before the Ethiopian king, who would present them with considerable gifts and honor them according to their rank. They (the Quraysh) did not, however, come in contact with Chosroes, and he in turn did not have intercourse with them.[48] The Byzantine emperors and the Ethiopian kings were Christians. This too gave the Christians advantage over the Jews. And history, as we know, provides the future generations with their prejudices and predilections.

(H) There is still another reason. Christianity was prevalent and widespread among the Arabs except among the tribe of Mudar.[49] Neither did Judaism or Magianism find acceptance in this tribe. Christianity was only popular with that portion of the tribe that emigrated to Hira and which was styled "servants."[50] They have there been absorbed, together with a small number (of other Christians), by some of the tribes. Thus Mudar knew no other religions than idolatry and Islam. Christianity, however, was in most cases, the faith of the Arab kings and prevailed among the following tribes: Lakhm, Ghassan, Harith b. Kaʿb in Najran, Kudaʿa and Tays, not speak of other numerous and well-known tribes.[51] Besides, Christianity gained a foothold in Rabiʿa, and prevailed among the tribes of Taghlib, Abdu l-Qays and scattered portions of Bakr and notably among the prominent families of Dhu Jaddayn. As for Judaism, at the birth of Islam it prevailed in no tribe. It only had converts in Yemen and a small minority of the tribes of 'Iyad and Rabi'a. The bulk of the Jews, and these were Jews by extraction and were descended from Aaron, lived in Yathrib,[52] Himyar, Tayma'a and Wadi l-Kura. Thus what filled the hearts with affection for the Christians were the ties of blood and our regard for royalty.

(I) Moreover, our masses began to realize that the Christian dynasties were enduring in power and that a great number of Arabs was adhering to their faith; that the daughters of Byzantium bore children to the Muslim rulers and that among the Christians were men versed in speculative theology, medicine and astronomy. Cosequently they became in their estimation philosophers and men of learning, whereas they observed none of these sciences among the Jews.

(J) The cause for the lack of science among the Jews lies in the fact that the Jews consider philosophic speculation to be unbelief and Kalam theology an innovation leading to doubt. They assert that there is no lore other than that revealed in the Torah and the books of the prophets; and that faith in medicine and astrology leads to opposition against the standard views of the authorities of old and is conducive to Manichaeism and atheism. So much are they averse to these sciences that they would allow the blood of their practitioner to be shed with impunity and would prohibit discourse with them.

(K) But if our masses knew that the Christians (Arabs) and Byzantines are not men of science and rhetoric and are not people of deep reflection and possess nothing except the handiworks of iron and wood and the crafts of painting and silk-weaving, they would remove them from the roll of men of culture and would strike their names off the list of philosophers and scientists.[53] For the books of *Logic* and *De Generation et Corruptione* ...,[54] etc., were composed by Aristotle, and he was neither Byzantine nor Christian (Arab). And the book *Almagest* was written by Ptolemaemus, and he was neither Byzantine nor Christian. The book of Euclid is Euclid's, and again he was neither Byzantine nor Christian. And the author of the book of Medicine is Galen, neither Byzantine nor Christian. This holds true also of Democrates, Hippocrates, Plato, etc. All these authors belong to a race that has

perished, but whose intellectual impress has endured, and they were
the Greeks.[55] Their religion was unlike the religion of the Christians,
and their mode of living was totally different.[56] The Greeks were
savants, and these are mechanical manipulators. It was by chance of
geographical proximity that they got hold of the Greek books. Either
the authorship of some of the books they falsely ascribed to themselves
or tampered with their contents so as to make them appear Christian.
And if the work was too popular and too well known, so that they
could not change the name of the book, they would tell us that the
Greeks were a group of Byzantine tribes and would boast of the
superiority of their religion over that of the Jews, Arabs and Hindus.
They even went so far as to assert that our scientists were the followers
of the Byzantine writers and our writers their imitators. Such is the
state of affairs!

(L) And the Christian faith—may God have mercy on you—resembles
Manichaeism, and in some of its aspects it is akin to atheism. It is the
cause of all perplexity and confusion. Indeed no other people has
furnished so many hypocrites and waverers as the Christians. This
results, naturally, when weak minds attempt to fathom deep problems.
Is it not a fact that the majority of those who were executed for parad-
ing as Muslims, while hypocrites at heart, were men whose fathers and
mothers were Christians? Even the people who are under suspicion
today have come mostly from their ranks.

(M) Another cause for the admiration accorded by the masses to the
Christians is the fact that they are secretaries and servants to kings,
physicians to nobles, perfumers and money changers, whereas the Jews
are found to be but dyers, tanners, cuppers, butchers and cobblers.
Our people observing thus the occupations of the Jews and the Christians concluded that the religion of the Jews must compare as unfavor-
ably as do their professions and that their unbelief must be the foulest
of all since they are the filthiest of all nations. Why the Christians,
ugly as they are, are physically less repulsive than the Jews may be
explained by the fact that the Jews, by not intermarrying, have intensified the offensiveness of their features. Exotic elements have not
mingled with them; neither have males of alien races had intercourse

with their women, nor have their men cohabited with females of a foreign stock. The Jewish race therefore has been denied high mental qualities, sound physique and superior lactation. The same results (are) obtain(ed) when horses, camels, donkeys and pigeons are in-bred.[57]

(N) And we—may God be gracious to you—do not deny that the Christians are rich and that they wield the sceptre, that their appearance is cleaner and their professions more refined. We do, however, differ with the majority of the people as to which of the two, the Jew or the Christian, is more controversial in word and deceitful in manner, though both be low-born and impure of blood. As for the manifestations of the high social rank of the Christians, we know that they ride highly bred horses and dromedary camels,[58] play polo ...,[59] wear fashionable silk garments[60] and have attendants to serve them. They call themselves Hasan, Husayn, 'Abbas, Fadl and 'Ali and employ also their forenames. There remains but that they call themselves Muhammad and employ the forename Abu l-Qasim.[61] For this very fact they were liked by the Muslims! Moreover, many of the Christians failed to wear their belts, while others hid their girdles beneath their outer garments.[62] Many of their nobles refrained, out of sheer pride, from paying tribute. They returned to Muslims insult for insult and blow for blow. Why indeed should the Christians not do so and even more, when our judges, or, at least the majority of them, consider the blood of a patriarch or bishop as equivalent to the blood of Ja'far, 'Ali, 'Abbas and Hamza?[63] They also believe that a Christian, when he slanders the mother of the Prophet with the accusation of adultery should incur only a slight punishment or reprimand, defending their decision on the ground that the mother of the Prophet was not Muhammadan.[64] Good Lord, what a queer judgment, and how utterly untenable! Was it not the decree of the Prophet that the Christian should not sit on an equal level with the Muslim? Did he not say: "If they insult you, strike them; and if they strike you, kill them?"[65] But the Christians, calumniating his mother with adultery, suffer at the hands of his believers only a slight punishment, for our judges think that forging a lie against the Prophet does not constitute a breach of covenant. But they forget that it is with regard to the Christians, against whom the Prophet decreed that they deliver the tribute in a spirit of gratitude,[66] considering the very receipt of it on our part as a gracious act, for thus we grant them the privilege of being tolerated and give them a guarantee of personal safety. God verily doomed them to abjectness and destitution.

(O) It is indeed incumbent on the ignorant to know that our righteous 'Imams and the leaders of old did not include a prohibition against such slander as a condition for receiving tribute and granting toleration, for no other reason but that they considered this matter to be so glaringly self-evident as not to feel the necessity for recording it in treaties.[67] Nay, if they did so, they would betray anxiety and weakness, and the protected cults would imagine themselves in power to create conditions of this sort. To be sure, people will bind by conditions and declare unequivocally only that which is pregnant with doubt or error, or may be overlooked by judge or witness, or may serve as a loophole for the adversary. But as for the evident and clear, what need is there to commit it to writing? Indeed whenever the imposition of a condition was deemed imperative, and its explicit mention in the contract was not thought to reflect upon the Muslims (the written procedure was invariably) adhered to, as for example the conditions of abjectness and humility, payment of tribute, requisition of churches and the prohibition against helping one Muslim faction in its struggle against the other, etc. With the lowest of the low, with men begging the acceptance of their own ransom, beseeching that their very lives be spared, can it be stipulated and said: "We will grant you the benefits accruing from this covenant on the condition that you defame not the mother of the man who is the seal of the prophets, who is the apostle of the Lord of all creatures, etc.?" Not even the average man will adopt such measures for his rule, much less so the leaders of humanity, the lamps of darkness, the torches of guidance, who are imbued with Arab pride, with the splendor of sovereignty and the victories of Islam.

(P) Moreover, our nation has not been afflicted by Jews, Magians or Sabeans as much as by the Christians; for (in the polemics with us) they choose contradictory statements in Muslim traditions (as the targets for their attacks). (They select for disputations) the equivocal verses in the Qur'an and (hold us responsible for) Hadiths, the chains of guarantors of which are defective.[68] Then they enter into private conversation with our weakminded, and question them concerning the texts which they have chosen to assail. They finally insert into the debate the arguments that they have learned from the Manichaeans. And notwithstanding such malicious discourse they often appear innocent before our men of influence and people of learning; and thus they succeed in throwing dust in the eyes of the staunch believers and in bewildering the minds of those who are weak in faith. And how unfortunate that every Muslim looks upon himself as a theologian and thinks that everyone is fit to lead a discussion with an atheist!

(Q) Moreover, were it not for the Christian theologians, their physicians and astronomers, the books of the Mananiyya, Daysaniyya and Markuniyya ...[69] sects would never reach our young people and the rich. They would be familiar with naught save the book of God and the Sunna of His Prophet, and the heretical writings would remain with their original owners, passing only as heirlooms to the next of kin. Indeed, for all our grief over the seduction of our youth and unintelligent we have primarily the Christians to blame. And when one hears their notions about forgiveness and wanderings in quest of God,[70] their censure for partaking of meats and their predilection for grain products; when one hears them preaching abstinence from marriage and from the begetting of offspring; when one observes them worshipping the Church leaders and praising the bishops for practicing celibacy, one is convinced that there is a resemblance between Christianity and Manichaeism and that the former leans toward the teachings of the latter.

(R) And how marvelous is this! We know that the Christian bishops[71] as well as all inmates of monasteries, whether Jacobites or Nestorians, in fact monks of every description, both male and female, one and all practice celibacy. When we next consider how great is the number of the monks and that most of the clergy adhere to their practices and when we finally take into account the numerous wars of the Christians, their sterile men and women, their prohibition against divorce, polygamy and concubinage—(is it not queer) that, in spite of all this, they have filled the earth and exceeded all others in numbers and fecundity? Alas! This circumstance has increased our misfortunes and made our trials stupendous! Another cause for the growth and expansion of Christianity is the fact that the Christians draw converts from other religions and give none in return (while the reverse should be true), for it is the younger religion that is expected to profit from conversion.

(S) And what points to the lack of compassion on the part of the Christians and to their perversion of heart is the fact that they are singled out from all nations in practicing castration,[72] and castration (as we know) is the greatest mutilation and the gravest sin that a man may commit against himself. They practice it even on innocent and defenceless children. We can accuse no other people of being noted for this practice except those who live in Byzantium and Ethiopia. In other countries castration is extremely rare and, at that, the custom could have been acquired from no others than the Christians.[73] They also castrate their children in order to devote them to the Church.[74] (And this is strange,) for castration is with the Sabeans only a religious rite, and it is not seldom[75] that we hear of worshippers of that sect castrating themselves, though they would not dare castrate their children. Indeed, if all Christians tendencies that I have pointed out were allowed to take their course, progeny would be cut off, religion would become extinct and the world would perish.

(T) And the Christians, though cleaner in dress, though engaged in more refined professions and physically less repulsive, yet inwardly is baser, filthier and fouler; for he does not practice circumcision, does not clean himself from pollution and in addition, eats the flesh of swine. His wife, too, is unclean. She does not purify herself from the defilement of menses and childbirth; her husband cohabits with her in her courses, and, in addition to this, she too is uncircumcized.[76] In spite of their evil natures and overruling lusts, their faith offers no restraints against passion such as eternal hell-fire in the world to come[77] or punishment by religious authority in the world we live in. How indeed can one evade what harms him and pursue what profits him if such be his faith? Can such as we have described set the world aright? Can anyone be more fit to stir up evil and corruption?

(U) Even if one were to exert all his zeal and summon all his intellectual resources with a view to learn the Christians' teachings about
Jesus, he would still fail to comprehend the nature of Christianity,
especially its doctrine concerning the Divinity. How in the world can
one succeed in grasping this doctrine, for were you to question concerning it two Nestorians, individually, sons of the same father and
mother, the answer of one brother would be the reverse of that of the
other. This holds true also for Melkites and Jacobites. As a result, we
cannot comprehend the essence of Christianity to the extent that we
know the other faiths.[78] Moreover, they contend that the method of
analogy should not be applied to religion, nor should the validity of
faith be maintained by overcoming objections, nor should the verity of
a dogma be made subject to the test of intellectual scrutiny. Faith
must be based on the unqualified submission to the authority of the
book and on following blindly the traditions of old. And, by my life,
any man who would profess a faith like Christianity would of necessity
have to offer blind submission as an excuse! The Christians also believe
that the Magians, Sabeans and Manichaeans, who oppose Christianity,
are to be pardoned as long as they do not aim at falsehood and do not
contend stubbornly against the true belief, but when they come to
speak of the Jews, they brand them as obstinate rebels, not merely as
people walking in error and confusion.[79]

Notes:

[1] See note 31.

[2] *Three Essays of Jahiz*, p. 28.

[3] According to Kirkisani the early theologians considered the text of
the Torah to be genuine (Hirschfeld, *Arabic Chrestomathy*, p. 119).
Jahiz introduces a paraphrase of a Biblical verse with the formula *q'l
'llh 'zz w jll* (*al- Hayawan*, vol. 5, p. 41). Raghib al-Isbahani (*Muhad-
arat al'Udaba'*, Cairo, 1326, vol. 2, p. 278) who draws the verse from *al-
Hayawan*, without mentioning Jahiz, omits the formula and substitutes
for it: "The people of the Book believe that God commanded them."

Cf. also Kirkisani's *Radd 'ala l-Muslimin* (*Zeit. für Assyr.*, vol. 26, 1912, p. 102).

[4] Supplement to the Catalogue of the Arabic Manuscripts in the British Museum (No. 1129).

[5] *JQR.*, old series, vol. 13, (1910), pp. 239-40. I am indebted to Professor Alexander Marx for calling my attention to the article. The exerpt corresponds to pp. 28-29 of the text published by me.

[6] Tha'alibi (Yatimat al-Dahr, vol. 3, p. 238) regards him as the master of prose. Thabit b. Qurra considers 'Umar b. al-Khattab, Hasan al-Basri and Jahiz as the three greatest men that Islam produced (Yaqut, *Dictionary of Learned Men*, vol. 6, pp. 69-70). Al-Hamadhani dedicated to Jahiz the fifteenth Makama.

[7] *Lisan al-Mizan* by Ibn Hajar al-'Askalani, vol. 4, p. 356.

[8] al-Baghdadi, *al-Fark bayna l-Firak*, p. 162.

[9] Goldziher, *Muhamm. Studien*, vol. 1, pp. 172-175.

[10] Jahiz enumerates many of his epistles in his introduction to the *Kitab al-Hayawan*. The fullest extant list of the works of Jahiz is to be found in Yaqut's *Dictionary*, vol. 6, 6, pp. 75-78.

[11] Yaqut, *Dictionary*, vol. 6, 6, pp. 75-78.

[12] *Fihrist*, vol. 1, p. 116.

[13] Yaqut, *Dictionary*, vol. 6, 6, pp. 71-72.

[14] See *Lisan al-Mizan*, vol. 4, pp. 355-356 were Jahiz is said not to have performed his prayers and Abu l-Faraj al-Ishbahani is quoted as saying that Jahiz was accused of unbelief. Interesting in this connection is the following veiled self-defence of Jahiz: "No theologian is as

tainted and blameworthy as the one who accuses his opponent of unbelief." (*al-Hayawan*, vol. 1, p. 80).

[15] Mas'udi (*Les Prairies d'Or*, vol. 6, p. 56) has bitterly criticized this duplicity of Jahiz in which he can perceive nothing but "wantonness and jest" and "an attempt to stifle truth and be willfully athwart to those who uphold it." He accordingly makes Jahiz the target of the Qur'anic phrase: "But God will perfect His light, averse although the misbeliever be" (Qur'an 61: 8). Cf. also *Lisan al-Mizan*, vol. 4, p.356 where Jahiz is accused of making the weaker argument appear triumphant.

[16] These devices were later employed in a remarkable degree by the author or authors of the *Ikhwan al-Safa*. Jahiz's influence in this respect is quite a possibility. "He was a 'cautious bird' (A literal translation of *b'q'h*) with little religion" is al-Dhahabi's remark on Jahiz (*Ta'rikh al-Jahmiyya wal-Mu'tazila* by Jamal al-Din al-Kasimi, Cairo, 1331, p. 24).

[17] *al-Hayawan*, vol. 7, p. 15; *Manakib Baghdad* by Ibn al-Jauzi, Cairo, 1342, p. 31.

[18] *Fihrist*, vol. 1, p. 116.

[19] *al-Yakubi*, ed. by Houtsma, vol. 2, p. 592.

[20] See *Rasa'il al-Khuwarizmi* (Constant., 1312, p. 80) where the Shiite author brands Mutawakkil as *'lmtwkl 'ly 'lthyt'n l' 'ly 'lrhmn*.

[21] *The Book of Religion and Empire*, by 'Ali Tabari, translated by A. Mingana, Manchester, 1922.

[22] *Fihrist*, vol. 1, p. 297; *Tabakat al-'Umam* by Ibn Sa'id, Beirut, 1912, p. 88.

[23] *Diwan b. al-Rumi*, ed. by Kamil Kilani, Cairo, n.d., p. 480.

[24] *Talkih Fuhum 'Ahl al-'Athar* by Ibn al-Jauzi ed. by Brockelmann, p. 33.

[25] *Ma'ahid al-Tansis*, Cairo, 1316, pp. 56-57; for other sources see *Le Livre du Triomphe et de la Refutation d'Ibn er-Rawendi l'hérétique par* ... el-Khayyat, published by Nyberg, Cairo, 1925.

[26] Cf. D. S. Margoliouth's article in the *JRAS.*, 1905, p. 80.

[27] Ibn Khurdhadhbeh, pp. 153-154, *Bibl. Geogr. Arab.*, vol. 6, ed. by de Goeje.

[28] The concluding portion of the experiences of the nations by Miskawayhi edited by Amedroz, Arabic text, p. 357.

[29] See note 53.

[30] Suyuti, *Ta'rikh al-Khulafa'*, Cairo, 1305, p. 140.

[31] *Three Essays of Jahiz*, p. 37; Ibn Qutayba bitterly complains of this fact in *Mukhtalif al-Hadith*, Cairo, 1326, p. 72.

[32] Horten, *Die philosophischen Systeme*, Bonn, 1912, p.324.

[33] See note 55 below - ed.

[34] That Jahiz gives here and there a name of an animal in Persian is hardly a proof that he knew the language; see *al-Hayawan*, vol. 1, p. 65 and 69, vol. 5, p. 136.

[35] *al-Hayawan*, vol. 1, pp. 38-40.

[36] *Three Essays of Jahiz*, p. 28.

[37] *al-Hayawan*, vol. 1, p. 37.

[38] *Mukhtalif al-Hadith*, pp. 72-73.

[39] Suyuti, *Bughyat al-Wuat*, Cairo, 1326, p. 282.

[40] Flügel, *Die Classen der hanefitischen Rechtsgelehrten*, p. 126.

[41] Qur'an 2:103.

[42] In the text *wbdhlw' 'dhfshm w'mw'lhm fy qt'lhm w'khr'jhm mn dy'rhm*. The hysteron-proteron employed by Jahiz is in keeping with Qur'an 2:79 and 178 etc.

[43] Ibn Ishaq, *The Life of Muhammad*, trans. Guillaume, pp. 146 ff. - ed.

[44] Qur'an 5:85-88.

[45] Ibn Ishaq, *The Life of Muhammad*, trans. Guillaume, pp. 79-81 - ed.

[46] Ibid., pp. 95-6 - ed.

[47] Qur'an 106.

[48] Abu Sufyan visited the Persian King (*'Ikd al-Farid*, vol. 1, pp. 174-5, Cairo, 1331), but not as a member of an official *wafd* of the Quraysh.

[49] As in a few other instances in the text, this appears to be a distortion by Jahiz. After having mentioned that the Christians were not near either Mecca or Medina, a statement which agrees with the majority of early Islamic sources, Jahiz contradicts himself by saying that Christianity was "prevalent and widespread among the Arabs" with the exception of but one tribe - ed.

[50] *'b'd* the plural of *'bd*, not *'b'd* plural of *''bd*. See *Mukhtasar al-Duwal* by Bar-Hebraeus, p. 250, Beirut, 1890.

[51] For the Jewish and Christian centers in Jahiliyya see *Le Christianisme et la littérature chrétienne en Arabie avant l'Islam* par P. Louis Cheikho, vol. 1, Beirut, 1912. The author has exhausted almost all available material. His inferences and conclusions, however, should be used with caution.

[52] I.e., Medina - ed.

[53] Cf., however, *al-Bayan*, vol. 1, p. 76 and p. 204 (Cairo, 1332) where Jahiz asserts that only Arabs, Persians, Hindus and Byzantines are possessed of a culture and that the rest of mankind are a rabble.

[54] The three dots = *kt'b 'l'lwy* in the text. For a work of Aristotle entitled *'l'th'r 'l'lwy* see *Tabakat al'-Umam* by Ibn Sa'id, Beirut, 1912, p. 25. Professor D. S. Margoliouth thinks that *'l'lwy* stands for the *Meteorologica*.

[55] To Jahiz the Greeks were a race as extinct as Canaan and Thamud (*al-Bayan*, vol. 1, p. 106, Cairo, 1332).

[56] For obvious reasons, Jahiz conveniently avoids mentioning that the ancient Greeks were a pagan society - ed.

[57] Cf. *al-Hayawan*, vol. 1, pp. 63-64 and pp. 71-72, where Jahiz expounds his views on the advantages of cross-breeding and intermarriage.

[58] In the text is the unintelligible *ljug't* for which I propose the emendation *'ljm'z't* = dromedary camels; cf. *al-Hayawan*, *'tkh'dh 'ljm'z't*, vol. 1, p. 41.

[59] In the text here the difficult *thdqr' 'lmdyny*. Professor D. S. Margoliouth has kindly suggested the following interpretation: In

Fagnan's *Additions aux Dictionnaires Arabes*, *thdhq* is said to mean "to learn the Qur'an by heart"; *'lmdyny* may mean "the jurist of Medina," this form being permissible, though *mdny* is more common. The whole phrase would then mean "they acquire by heart the works of Malik."

[60] The wearing of silk garments by Muslim men is strongly condemned in the hadith. Cf. *Sahih Bukhari*, The Book of Gifts, chap. 27, hadith 782, vol. 3, p. 473, and *Sahih Muslim*, Kitab al-Libas wa'l-Zinah, chap. 864, hadith 5141, vol. 3, p. 1141 - ed.

[61] Muhammad forbade the use of the name Abu l-Qasim for any other than himself. Cf. *Sahih Muslim*, Kitab al-Adab, chap. 891, hadith 5314, vol. 3, p. 1168 - ed.

[62] For more information on the dress code for Christians under Mutawakkil, see: Mingana in *The Book of Religion and Empire*, p. ix - ed.

[63] According to the code of Abu Hanifa a Muslim is to be executed for the murder of a Jew or Christian. Al-Shafi'i, however emphasizes the maxim than a believer is not to be slain for an unbeliever. Cf. *Kitab al-'Umm*, vol. 6, p. 33 and vol. 7, p. 292. (Drawn from the quotations of D. S. Margoliouth in *The Early Development of Mohammedanism*, London, 1914, p. 65 and p. 113.) Cf. also Juynboll, *Handbuch des islamischen Gesetzes*, p. 295.

[64] The punishment for a false accusation of adultery (Hadd = 80 stripes) has no legal effect in the absence of any of the following conditions in the persons accused: maturity, sanity, freedom (i.e., the person not being a slave), chastity and profession of Islam. Marwardi, *al-Ahkam al-Sultaniyya*, p. 200, Ch. 19, parag. 4, Cairo, 1327.

[65] These traditions are not considered by Muslims as authentic. - In that the use of the hadith contradicts Mu'tazilite theology generally, this is another example of compromise on the part of Jahiz for his sponsors - ed.

[66] *hty y'tw' 'ljzya 'n yd*, Qur'an 9:29; but evidently Jahiz dies not mean to paraphrase the Qur'anic statement. The phrase in the text, which bears the earmarks of a tradition, refers in all probability to a hadith whose guarantor is Salman. See Ibn al-'Athir Nihaya, vol. 4, p. 264, Cairo 1311. Jahiz's interpretation of *'n yd* = in gratitude is the last of the several quoted by Zamakhshari and Baydawi. The logical sequence is weakly expressed by Jahiz. Jahiz probably meant to say: granted that you cannot punish a Christian with Hadd (80 stripes) when he calumniates as unbelieving woman with adultery, even though that woman may have been the mother of the Prophet; but the act certainly constitutes a breach of covenant, for the Prophet had decreed that the Christians deliver tribute in a spirit of gratitude. If their insult does not constitute legal slander, it is at any rate an act of ingratitude. Having thus broken the covenant we may shed their blood with impunity.

[67] One of the conditions imposed on the tolerated cults at the signing of an act of toleration was the prohibition against falsely accusing a Muslim woman of adultery. See *al-Ahkam al-Sultaniyya*, p. 129, Ch. 13, Cairo, 1327.

[68] That the Christians used the Qur'an itself against the Muslims can be seen in almost all of the dialogues presented in this work. *The Apology of al-Kindi* represents perhaps the best use of hadith against the Muslim position, and oddly enough, many of the traditions al-Kindi did use later found their way into the "genuine" collections of al-Bukhari and Muslim. - ed.

[69] For these sects see *Fihrist*, vol. 1, pp. 338-9. After the Markuniyya there follows in the text *'lfl'nya*, which I cannot identify. It may perhaps be the *'lhyl'nya* mentioned on p. 342 of vol. 1 of the *Fihrist*.

[70] Wandering in quest of God = *sy'ha*; cf. *Talbis 'Iblis* by Ibn al-Jauzi, pp. 317-318 (Cairo, 1340) where the author explains the term as roaming about without a definite object in view such as a place of

worship or a teacher from whom to receive religious instruction. Such practice was prohibited by the Prophet who is quoted there as saying *wl' sy'ha fy 'l'sl'm...*

[71] Translated by me summarily for *j'th'lyq mtr'n* and *'sqf* mentioned in the text. For a Muhammadan source defining these ranks see *Mafatih al'Ulum* by al-Khuwarizmi, p. 78, Cairo, 1342.

[72] Castration is discussed by Jahiz at length in *al-Hayawan*, vol. 1, pp. 48-83. On p. 56 Jahiz states that the Christians perform the operation in such wise as to increase the *voluptas sexualis*.

[73] Ibid., p. 56.

[74] Ibid., p. 56.

[75] That *rbm'* means here "not seldom" follows from p. 58 (*al-Hayawan*, vol. 1): "Some Sabeans whose pedigrees and biographies we know have practiced castration."

[76] Though it is not well attested to in either the Qur'an or "geniune" hadith, the circumcision of women has been practiced in many Islamic countries for centuries. Cf. al-Tabari, *History*, vol. 2, p. 72 - ed.

[77] Sic!

[78] It is at this point that Jahiz essentially admits the cardinal inferiority and failure of the Muslim (and Mu'tazilite) polemic to confront that of the Christians.

[79] For examples of Christian prejudice and bias against the Jews at the time, see: Leo III, parag. BC; Timothy, BG; al-Kindi, CJ, etc.

CONCLUSIONS

THE FIRST three centuries of the Christian-Muslim dialogue to a great degree molded the form of the relationship which was to prevail between the two faiths afterward. During this period, Islam proved itself to be less a wayward sect of the "Hagarenes," from a Christian perspective, and more a separate and antagonistic religion which had sprung up from idolatry. The Muslim perception of Christianity also changed in this time, from the Qur'anic idea of being the group of the *People of the Book* nearest Islam, to the greatest theological and political opponent of the Muslim Empire. The one factor which perhaps most contributed to this gradual (rather than rapid) understanding of each other's beliefs, i.e., the language barrier, was naturally the same factor which most affected the development of the Christian-Muslim dialogue.

After having willingly submitted themselves to Muslim Arab domination without so much as considering the long-term results of their decisions,[1] the Arab Christians of Syria, Palestine and Egypt began with at least one distinct advantage over their Muslim counterparts in the area of multi-lingual capabilities. Both the Bible and the Qur'an could be read by them, and it appears that it was they who finally translated the Gospels into Arabic[2] and possibly even the Qur'an, or parts of it, into Greek[3] or even Syriac.[4] With the exception of the converts to Islam, Muslim scholars in general seem to have known no language other than Arabic,[5] and this in turn hindered their ability to obtain a firsthand knowledge of the Bible and Christian doctrines. In the works of Leo III and John of Damascus we see that Christians had acquired a fairly accurate knowledge of the Qur'an, major Islamic doctrines and their various groups rather early on, whereas even up until the time of the Muslim historian al-Tabari (d. 923), knowledge of the Bible (and even pre-Islamic world history) among Muslim scholars was relatively poor.

Another inhibition for Muslims to read the Bible was self-imposed.
As Muslim Arabs came into continual contact with institutionalized
Christianity, one of the first questions to be solved dealt with how the
Torah and the Gospel were to be accepted by them. It certainly must
not have taken long to see that the Qur'an was in cardinal contradiction to the Bible, and that as they stood, both could not be true repre-
sentations of God's Word. Since the Qur'an already mentioned the
Torah, Psalms and Gospel as being "sent down" by God (Qur'an 3:2;
4:161; 5:48,50), and related how some of the *People of the Book* had
hidden the message of the scriptures and changed the meanings of the
words (Qur'an 2:70,154,169; 4:48; 5:16,45; etc.), the Muslims, in less
obvious contradiction to the Qur'an (6:34,115; 18:26), forged the
doctrine that the Jews and Christians had corrupted the texts of the
Torah and Gospel, and thus, that these should not be read.[6] The
rather adverse effects of this teaching are manifest in the Muslim
polemic of this collection, which aside from the passages corrupted by
'Umar II and the numerous texts quoted by the convert 'Ali Tabari,
rarely exceed five verse references from the Bible. Strangely enough,
only during the "revival of the orthodoxy" under Mutawakkil does this
doctrine, that the Bible had been corrupted, seem to have been re-
versed for a time.[7]

Perhaps the best gauge for measuring the results of the early Christian-Muslim dialogue can be found in evaluating how various doctrines
of these faiths changed with respect to the subjects which had been
discussed in this dialogue. For the Christian churches of the East, the
major doctrinal development of the period between 632 and 900 A.D.
was the iconoclastic controversy. Although some have attempted to
discount the role of Islam in this regard, it is rather hard to believe
that the evolution of the iconoclast movement was totally independent
of, yet coincident with the expansion of Islam. Indeed, Leo III, the
Byzantine Emperor who officially began the controversy with his edict
in 726, was raised in an area in which the ideas and influence of
Muslims were not unknown.[8] One of the earliest and most common
Muslim accusations brought against Christians was that they wor-

shipped the cross, and even though Leo III defends this practice in his reply to 'Umar II, the best that he can offer is the counter accusation that the Muslims worship the Ka'ba.[9]

On the other hand, the changes made to Islamic doctrine during this same period were quite numerous. In the Muslim creed *Fikh Akbar I* of the middle of the 8th century, we see that article eight (which condemns those who reject Moses and Jesus) and article nine (which condemns those who do not know if God is in Heaven or on earth),[10] may well have been drawn up as a result of the early Christian polemic. The very mention of Moses and Jesus, who according to the Qur'an were the recipients of the Torah and Gospel respectively, implies that some Muslim groups were wanting to reject these Books and that this was most probably as a reaction to having been confronted with their texts by Christians. The question whether God is in Heaven or on the earth may perhaps have referred to the limitations Muslims perceived Christians placed on God via the earthly ministry of Jesus.[11]

The first article of *The Wasiyat of Abu Hanifa*, which is estimated to date from the middle of the ninth century, not only defines faith as confession, belief and knowledge in a style generally reminiscent of Rom. 10: 9,10, but also concludes that all the *People of the Book* would possess faith if knowledge were the only criterion.[12] Article nine of the same creed proclaims the Qur'an to be uncreated and condemns those who say that God's speech is created.[13] The issue of whether or not God's Word was created, though not even mentioned in the Qur'an, very definitely had its origins in the polemic of the Christians.[14] What appears to have begun as a Biblical defence for the deity of the Father, the Son (God's Word) and the Holy Spirit,[15] also turned out to be an effective argument for the deity of Christ when based on Qur'an 4:169.[16] This device appears to have come into widespread use early in the Christian polemic and can be found in practically all of the dialogues and correspondences of this collection. The formation of the Mu'tazilites, who believed the Qur'an (i.e., for them God's Word) to have been created, was thus at least partially related to the success of the early Christian polemic. Indeed, the possible reasoning of the

Mu'tazilites on this issue was not devoid of some logic: by rejecting the eternality of God's Word, they could more easily deny the deity of Christ[17] and more readily account for the inconsistencies in the various Qur'an codices in early Islam.[18] In the end though, this belief caused more problems than it solved, as the Christians could then show that the "revelation" of the Qur'an was vastly inferior to that of the Bible,[19] and that the Mu'tazilite idea of God was heretical, which is in fact the essence of this ninth article of the creed.[20]

The 25th article of *The Wasiyat of Abu Hanifa* proclaims Muhammad to be an intercessor before God and can be seen as perhaps the first formal attempt to elevate the position of Muhammad.[21] Though the Qur'an mentions intercession in several passages,[22] it never states that Muhammad is to perform this ministry. In at least two of the dialogues of this collection, however, this topic was discussed,[23] and in that the Bible clearly describes Jesus as the universal intercessor, Muslims seem to have claimed this office for Muhammad in order that he not be outdone by Christ. The development of this doctrine can also be traced in later tradition, where Muhammad is reported to go from saying he is not to be esteemed as better than Jonah,[24] to being equal with Moses[25] and finally to being "the most pre-eminent amongst the descendants of Adam... the first whose intercession will be accepted *by Allah*."[26] In the discussions and treatises of this collection it is obvious that the Christian comparisons of the person of Muhammad to that of Christ[27] provided the impetus for Muslims to elevate Muhammad from the position of a mere prophet to the "lord of mankind"[28] and "lord of the prophets."[29] This doctrine later reaches its terminus in the work of 'Ali Tabari, who in his zeal to attribute Old Testament prophecies to Muhammad as a "lord," inadvertently equates him with God.[30]

The *Fikh Akbar II*, which seems to date from the middle of the tenth century, presents in article three a more developed version of the belief that the Qur'an was uncreated.[31] In something of a reversal of the sixth article of *The Wasiyat of Abu Hanifa*, which seems to promote predestination, the sixth article of the *Fikh Akbar II* proclaims the free-will of man.[32] Although this reversal could have arisen independent of

Christian influence, as C.H. Becker suggests,[33] on the basis of some of the later non-Byzantine discussions on this subject, it appears that Christian apology served as the catalyst, if not the main innovator, of this change.[34]

The eighth article of the *Fikh Akbar II* proclaims the sinlessness of all the prophets.[35] Aside from not being mentioned in the Qur'an, this doctrine is not even found in the earliest collections of the hadith by Bukhari and Muslim. To the contrary, both the Qur'an (40:57; 47:21; 48:2; 110) and numerous traditions show that Muhammad had sins and that he prayed for forgiveness.[36] Since the New Testament teaching of the sinlessness of Jesus was unique in the environment of the time period, this very late development in Islamic doctrine can be viewed as a direct result of the Christian polemic, and tactically one which Muslims obviously felt had to be instituted in order to maintain the superiority of Muhammad to Christ. (The title of the "seal of the prophets" loses a great deal of worth without this change.) One must add that for all their efforts, it also took Christian polemicists quite some time to discover this cardinal difference between Christianity and Islam. Of the works in this collection only one, the fictitious *Religious Dialogue of Jerusalem*, presents this argument.[37]

The ninth article of the *Fikh Akbar II*, which states that Muhammad was never a polytheist (or idolater) and which reiterates his sinlessness as a prophet, is a further modification of article eight. The Qur'an and hadith contradict this doctrine by showing that Muhammad was commanded to "abandon the idols" (Qur'an 74:1-5) and that because of his idolatry there was an intermission in the revelations given him.[38] Somewhat related to this deficiency are the reports that after 'Umar accepted Islam, Muhammad and his followers prayed in the idol-filled Ka'ba[39] and that this same object became the qibla several years *before* its purification from polytheism. Aside from its connection with the question of Muhammad's sinlessness, the desire to free Muhammad from the charge of idolatry may also have been an attempt to raise his status in relation to Jesus. In contrast to the Bible, the Qur'an presents Christ's ministry as having begun shortly after His birth, whereas the earliest versions of the hadith provide information relative to Muhammad's being polytheistic up until shortly after his call at the approximate age of forty. Quite a few of the discussions in this collection mention the pagan origins of Islamic practices, and in particular those with respect to the Ka'ba.[40] It is al-Kindi, though, who directly accuses Muhammad of previously having been an idolater.[41]

In the 16th article of the *Fikh Akbar II* the doctrine of the reality of the prophets' signs and the saints' miracles is expressed.[42] As Mingana pointed out earlier in this collection, according to the Qur'an, Muhammad was not able to produce the evidence of miracles in confirmation of his prophethood.[43] Practically all of the works of the Christian polemicists contained in this book make mention of this deficiency in the case of Muhammad; it is al-Kindi, however, who having had a good knowledge the Islamic hadith of his day, accuses the Muslims of having fabricated the "miracle" traditions in order to improve Muhammad's image.[44] Indeed, the number of signs and wonders attributed to him in the hadith and later histories of Islam is quite astounding and range from miracles surrounding his birth to signs which were made manifest a short time prior to his death.[45] Although this doctrine (that signs are to confirm the ministry of a prophet) may have the Old Testament as its ultimate source (Deut. 18:21,22), it appears that Christian polemicists introduced this teaching to Muslims. In his defence of Islam, 'Ali Tabari cites the alleged lack of miracles for Muhammad as one of the main reasons for why *Christians* did not accept his prophethood.[46] Tabari later presents several traditions to counter this view,[47] many of which, however, had already been commented upon by al-Kindi years earlier.[48]

The 20th article of this creed again declares Muhammad to be an intercessor, which we have already addressed above.

In considering the various dialogues, correspondences and treatises of this collection, it is obvious that the quality of the polemic, be it Islamic or Christian, was directly dependent upon one's knowledge of the other's faith. Al-Kindi, for example, appears to have made ample use of his common language and culture in his research of not only the Qur'an, but Islamic hadith and history as well. 'Ali Tabari also drew from his Christian background and education in quoting numerous Bible references. Both of these works, though by no means perfect, tend to illustrate this point better than any of the others in this collection.

Naturally, one notices differences in approach and subject matter in some of the works. As presented, the Patriarch Timothy I could hardly have been too aggressive in his attack of Islam before the Caliph Mahdi, whereas the Emperor Leo III had little reason for being overly cordial in his correspondence with the distant Caliph 'Umar II. Al-Kindi could afford to be a little more antagonistic after receiving a guarantee of safety from the Caliph Ma'mun, and this is also the alleged arrangement between the monk Ibrahim and the Amir of Jerusalem. John of Damascus was addressing a Christian audience in teaching others how to deal with the polemic of Muslim rivals in Greek, and 'Ali Tabari and Jahiz attacked Christianity in Arabic under the safe sponsorship of the Caliph Mutawakkil.

In the first centuries of Islamic rule there were radical changes in the policies and even dynasties of the caliphate, new religious groups arose, and old religious groups died out, but the main-frame of the Muslim polemic hardly varied. (It is interesting to note that none of the early Christian-Muslim dialogues were preserved by Muslims, and that the alleged correspondence of 'Umar II to Leo III was only found recently.)

Primarily owing to the attention accorded them in *Patrologia Graece*, ed. Migne, the Byzantine polemicists have been the subject of several investigations,[49] and even the polemical works of Muslim writers have been examined as a group.[50] However, the general polemic of the Syrians, whose success Jahiz openly complained of and Tabari despised,[51] probably merits more respect than it has received in the West.

Without question, the Christian polemic as a whole was more effective than its Muslim counterpart, but one must ask what this superiority really achieved in the end. Muslim scholars obviously felt moved to (and did) change numerous traditions and doctrines in order to provide for a more healthy survival of Islam. However, in making Islam more Christianity-resistant, these later modifications also succeeded in making it more anti-Qur'anic. If the acquisition of truth remains our highest goal, it is this last development which the first three centuries of the Christian-Mulsim dialogue have bequeathed to us, and it is incumbent upon all of us not to squander it.

Notes:

[1] John, pp. 20-22.

[2] John, p. 17.

[3] Generally it has been speculated as to whether or not Leo III or John of Damascus knew Arabic based on their references to Qur'anic passages.

[4] Mingana shows that the Nestorians appear to have had a Syriac translation of the Qur'an, or parts of it, as early as the Patriarchate of Timothy I; see Timothy, pp. 172-173.

[5] Jahiz, p. 686.

[6] Cf. *Sahih Bukahri*, The Book of Monotheism, ch. 42, hadith 614, vol. 9, p. 461.

[7] Tabari, p. 549.

[8] Leo III, p. 60.

[9] Leo III, parags. AW and AX; cf. John of Damascus, parag. F.

[10] Wensinck, *Muslim Creed*, p. 104.

[11] In his discussion with the Patriarch John I, 'Amr al-'As asked who ruled Heaven and earth while Jesus was in the womb; see John I, parag. E. The Caliph 'Umar II also seems to have addressed this issue in his letter to Leo III by asking "who was holding the heavens and the earth" while Jesus was on the earth?; see Gaudeul, "Leo and 'Umar," *Islamochristiana*, 10 (1984), p. 145, BNM 4944, l. 48.

[12] Wensinck, *Muslim Creed*, p. 125.

[13] Ibid., p. 127.

[14] Nöldeke, *The Qur'an*, ed. Newman, p. 29.

[15] Leo, parag. V.

[16] John of Damascus, parags. B and E.

[17] Ibid., parag. L.

[18] Nöldeke, *The Qur'an*, ed. Newman, p. 29.

[19] Cf. Ps. 119:89; Is. 40:8; John 1:1; etc.

[20] Cf. John of Damascus, parag. K.

[21] See Becker, *Islamstudien*, vol. 1, p. 387.

[22] See the article on "Shafa'a," *Shorter Encyclopedia of Islam*, pp. 511-2.

[23] Religious Dialogue, parags. I and AJ (see n. 101); al-Kindi, parags. AU and DY.

[24] *Sahih Bukhari*, The Book of the Prophets, ch. 31, hadith 624, vol.

4, p. 413.

[25] Ibid., The Book of Loans...etc., ch. 21, hadiths 594-5, vol. 3, pp. 350-1; The Book of the Prophets, ch. 31, hadith 626, vol. 4, pp. 413-4.

[26] *Sahih Muslim*, Kitab al-Fada'il, hadith 5655, vol. 4, p. 1230.

[27] Cf. Leo, parag. AJ.

[28] Religious Dialogue, parag. AJ; al-Kindi, parags. E and J.

[29] al-Kindi, parag. D.

[30] Tabari, notes 184, 199, 219, 238, etc. Though this doctrine is heretical for Sunnis, some Shiite groups later developed the belief in the deity of Muhammad.

[31] Wensinck, *Muslim Creed*, p. 189.

[32] Ibid., p. 190.

[33] Beck, *Islamstudien*, vol. 1, p. 432.

[34] Timothy, parags. BH, BI, BK; Religious Dialogue, parags. R and S. It is interesting to note that the approach of the Syrians, by using the examples of Satan and Adam, were more Qur'anic, and thus probably much more effective among Muslims, than the somewhat abstract approaches of the Byzantines, cf. John of Damascus, parags. Q-Y.

[35] Wensinck, *Muslim Creed*, p. 192.

[36] *Sahih Bukhari*, The Chapters of the Shortened Prayers (at-Taqsir), ch. 21, hadith 221, vol. 2, pp. 123-4; The Book of al-Maghazi, ch. 81, hadith 715, vol. 5, p. 511; The Book of Commentary, ch. 178, hadith 236, vol. 6, pp. 198 ff.; The Book of Invocations, ch. 10, hadith 329, vol.

8, pp. 221-2; ch. 40, hadith 379, vol. 8, p. 252; ch. 62, hadith 407, vol. 8, p. 271. *Sahih Muslim*, Kitab al-Salat, ch. 186, hadith 965, vol. 1, p. 252; ch. 187, hadith 980, vol. 1, p. 254; ch. 268, hadith 1695, vol. 1, p. 373.

[37] Religious Dialogue, parag. AR.

[38] *Sahih Bukhari*, The Book of Commentary, ch. 345, hadith 478, vol. 6, pp. 452-3.

[39] Ibn Ishaq, *Life of Muhammad*, trans. Guillaume, p. 155.

[40] Leo, parag. AX; John of Damascus, parag. F; al-Kindi, parag. DI; etc.

[41] al-Kindi, parag. BU.

[42] Wensinck, *Muslim Creed*, p. 193.

[43] Tabari, p. 556.

[44] al-Kindi, parags. CC and CE.

[45] Cf. Wensinck, *Handbook*, pp. 166-8, for a general listing of signs directly or indirectly related to Muhammad's ministry.

[46] Tabari, parag. AF.

[47] Tabari, parags. BB sqq.

[48] al-Kindi, parag. CE.

[49] Carl Güterbock, *Der Islam im Lichte der byzantinischen Polemik*, J. Guttentag Verlagsbuchhandlung, Berlin, 1912; Wolfgang Eichner, "Die Nachrichten über den Islam bei den Byzantinern," *Der Islam*, 23 (1936), pp. 132-162, 197-244; Daniel Sahas, *John of Damascus on Islam*, E.J. Brill, Leiden, 1972; etc.

[50] Erdmann Fritsch, *Islam und Christentum im Mittelalter; Beiträge zur Geschichte der muslimischen Polemik gegen das Christentum in arabischer Sprache*, Verlag Müller und Seiffert, Breslau, 1930.

[51] Jahiz, parag. P. See Tabari, parags. DJ and DS, for his heated and reactionary reply to the Syrian accusation against Ishmael; Tabari, p. 550.

The following is an incomplete index of major polemical subjects used
by both Christians and Muslims in this collection. When consulted
together with the General, Bible Reference and Qur'an Refence
indices, practically all of the major topics of the dialogues, treatises and
correspondence of this collection should be readily accessible.

CHRISTIAN THEMES:

Allah prays for Muhammad: Religious Dialogue, AJ, AM.

Confusion of Mary for Miriam (Qur'an): Leo III, AH; John of Damascus, B.

Female circumcision: Leo III, AP; John of Damascus, J; al-Kindi, DH.

Defense of the Trinity (Old Testament): John I, F-H; Leo III, AA-AC;
Religious Dialogue, N, AP; al-Kindi, BN sqq.

Defense of the Trinity (based on Qur'an 4:169): John of Damascus, K,
AJ; Religious Dialogue, L; al-Kindi, BR.

Defense of the Trinity (example of man): Leo III, Y; Timothy, P, V, Z,
DI, DQ; al-Kindi, BO.

Defense of the Trinity (example of the sun): Leo III, W, X; Timothy,
D, F, M, N, P, U, V, AC, DO, DQ, ED, EE; Religious Dialogue,
M, AK.

Defense of the Trinity (misc. examples): Timothy, W, X; al-Kindi, BH sqq.

Divorce and remarriage (Qur'an 2:230): Leo III, AY; John of Damascus, G; al-Kindi, DJ.

Free-will vs. predestination: John of Damascus, R sqq.; Timothy, BJ-BM; Religious Dialogue, S.

On the Ka'ba: Leo III, AJ, AX; John of Damascus, F; Religious Dialogue, I, AU; al-Kindi, DI.

The Law was abolished by Christ: Timothy, AB, AC.

The Law was fulfilled by Christ (Matt. 5:17): al-Kindi, DG.

Mention of the mysterious letters in the Qur'an: Timothy, DL.

Alleged signs of Muhammad: al-Kindi, CC, CE sqq.

Muhammad, Bishr and the poisoned meat: al-Kindi, CE.

Muhammad's claim to be resurrected (as Jesus): al-Kindi, CF.

Muhammad's sinfulness: Religious Dialogue, AR.

Muhammad uncircumcised: al-Kindi, DG.

The monk (Bahira, Sergius, etc.) and Muhammad: John of Damascus, A; al-Kindi, CN.

Muslims distort the text of the Bible: Leo III, U.

Muslims should produce the geniune Gospel: Leo III, AI; Timothy, AS; Religious Dialogue, V.

Parable of the physician and medicine: Religious Dialogue, P sqq.

Parable of the pearl: Timothy, FI sqq.

Prayer toward the East: Timothy, D; Religious Dialogue, AA.

No prophetic witness for Muhammad: Leo, G; John of Damascus, C.

No prophet after Jesus: John of Damascus, AJ (implied); Timothy, AZ; al-Kindi, ED.

Qur'an corrupted: Leo III, S; Religious Dialogue, I; al-Kindi, CN sqq.

Signs and miracles confirm prophethood: John of Damascus, AI-AJ; Timothy, AU; Religious Dialogue, P, T; al-Kindi, BO, BU, CA, CB, CD.

Succession of Revelation: Timothy, AU.

The use of the plural "we" in the Qur'an: Timothy, DG; al-Kindi BO.

Women described as "fields" in Qur'an (2:223): Leo III, AX; John of Damascus, G.

Zayd and Zaynab: Leo III, AX; John of Damascus, G; al-Kindi, BY.

MUSLIM THEMES:

The Bible was changed (distorted): Leo III, F, H, AK; John of Damascus, D; Timothy, AS, CL; Religious Dialogue, B, V; Tabari, H.

Integrity of the Bible: al-Kindi, Q; Tabari, A, FI.

If the Bible were not corrupted Muhammad would be found in them: Timothy, CL.

Jesus prayed: Leo III, AK, n. 75; Timothy, AH; Religious Dialogue, AJ.

Who ruled Heaven and earth when Jesus in womb?: John I, E and n. 69.

The Jews did God's will by killing Jesus: John of Damascus, Y; Timothy, BH; Religious Dialogue, R.

Predestination: John of Damascus, Q sqq.; Timothy, BI sqq.; Religious Dialogue, S sqq.

Prophets after Christ: Tabari, AI-AK.

Prophets who showed miracles, had prophecy and were foretold (the Christ): Tabari, AH.

Prophets showing miracles but not foretold: Tabari, AH.

Prophets showing miracles but having no prophecy: Tabari, AH.

Prophets who prophesied without miracles: Tabari, AH.

No miracles were wrought by David as recorded in the Psalms: Tabari, AG.

No previous prophecy about David, Isaiah or Jeremiah: Tabari, AG.

Prophets without (Book) prophecy or miracle: Tabari, AH.

Sacrifice changed: Leo III, AN.

Satan must be stronger than God if Jesus was killed: Timothy, (BJ); Tabari, GY.

Worship of the cross: Leo III, AW; John of Damascus, F; Timothy, BB; Religious Dialogue, AT; al-Kindi, AW, (EA).

APPENDIX B

BIBLICAL REFERENCE INDEX

Key: (D) = Diatessaron; (P) = Peshitta; (S) = Septuagint

20:25   471
33:14-16   664
36:25   89
43:7   90
44:2 (PS)   346

Daniel

2:31 sqq   255
4:31   518
5:25-28   437
6:10   121
7:5   255
7:6   255
7:13   253, 267
7:14   253, 267
9:24 sqq   256
9:26   257

Hosea

1:2   670
12:4   119
12:10   265

Joel

2:28   258
2:29   258
2:30   258

Micah

5:2   81

Habakkuk

1:5   89

Zephaniah

3:9   647, 648

Zechariah

9:9   255, 496
9:10   496
11:12   82
13:7   257

Malachi

4:4-6   260

Matthew

1:1 sqq   ix
1:23   266
2:5   351
2:6   351
3:3   678
3:11   260
3:14   503
3:15   503
3:17   ix, 342, 503
4:12-17   676
4:16   153
4:17   504
5:17   168, 251, 471
5:21   504, 663
5:22   504, 663
5:23   504
5:24   504
5:27   504

John

APPENDIX C

QUR'ANIC REFERENCE INDEX

6:100 35
6:109 253, 254
6:115 544, 720
6:161 584
7:11 122
7:35 403
7:52 345
7:71 526
7:156 35, 55, 106, 135, 252,
      254, 346, 628, 660, 682
7:168 35
7:169 35
7:138 42
7:188 253
7:198 586
7:199 586
8:30 596
8:12 597
9:5 362
9:14 597
9:29 483, 716
9:30 671
9:33 600
9:110 570
9:129 632
10 263
10:50 586
10:94 108, 346
10:99 478
10:100 478
10:103 584
10:108 478
10:109 478
11 263
11:16 609
11:33 253
11:120 478

12 263
12:2 460, 661
12:82 645
13:27-30 556
14 263
14:4 128, 159, 661
15 263
15:94 592
15:95 592
16 455
16:38 128
16:92 587
16:104 121
17:1 591
17:14 128
17:17 262
17:61 142, 439
17:63 118
17:87 349, 482
17:90 389, 452, 460
17:92-97 556
18:26 544, 720
18:48 118
18:85-86 xv
19:7 125
19:16 139, 252
19:17 172, 173, 349
19:28 sqq 2
19:29 2, 119, 139
19:30-35 106
19:34 172, 257
19:35 349
19:59 108
19:91-93 35
20:9-35 125
20:115 118
20:133 253

GENERAL INDEX

Aad, 438, 526.

Aaron (brother of Moses), x, 2, 3, 25, 83, 119, 138, 294, 434, 472, 544.

Abel, 435.

Aban b. Aus, 441.

Abraha (Viceroy of Yemen), 526.

Abraham, 8, 25, 35, 37, 38, 42, 52, 67, 70, 75, 84, 88, 92, 93, 105, 138, 141, 188, 208, 219, 309, 327, 329, 357, 384, 388, 399, 400, 404, 408, 412-415, 423, 438, 469-471, 473, 540, 583, 585, 615-618, 633, 649, 652, 673, 681.

Abu Afak, 430, 521.

Abu Ahmad al-'Askari, 116.

Abu Bakr (Caliph), 31, 293, 367, 376, 433, 444, 454, 455, 459, 467, 530, 535, 536, 591, 600-602, 605.

Abu Hanifa, 671, 715, 721.

Abu Hatim as-Sijistani, 116.

Abu Jahl, 427, 428, 518, 519.

Abu 'Isa b. Muhammad al-Warraq, 557.

Abu Musa, 456, 668.

Abu Nuh, 557.

Abu Rabi'a, 2.

Abu Saraya, 370, 457.

Abu Sufyan, 293, 428, 434, 519, 594, 595, 713.

Abu Talib, 426.

Abu 'Ubayda, 33.

Abu Zakkar Yahya b. Nu'man, 563.

Abul 'Abbas, 603, 669.

Abul Faraj, 368, 710.

Abul Qasim, 705.

Abyssinia, 2, 486, 525.

Acts, 582.

Adam, 3, 77, 85, 118, 122, 148, 149, 176, 188, 192, 212, 270, 284, 298, 305, 309, 310, 325, 326, 328, 345, 413, 435, 572, 585, 722, 728.

Adhonai (Adhon), 543, 675, 676, 678, 681, 683.

Adroh, 13.

Agag, 80.

Agapius, 23, 58.

Ahab (King), 432.

Ahlwardt, W., 659.

Ahmad b. Hanbal, 124.

Ahmad. M., 527.

Alexander the Great, 31.

Alexandria, 14, 16, 21, 35.

Alkosh, 173.

Amina, 311, 519.

Ammonites, 208, 428, 439.

Amorium, 60.

70, 78, 79-83, 91, 94, 95, 120,
128, 145, 182, 198, 213, 223,
224, 233, 236, 238, 245, 259,
261, 297, 298, 309, 327, 330,
331, 385, 423, 436, 492, 496,
500, 580, 590, 610, 621, 623-
626, 632, 663.
  de Boor, 100.
  de Goeje, 101, 351, 712.
  de Meynard, B., 659.
  de Sacy, 367, 369, 378, 379.
  Democrates, 703.
  Desvergers, N., 35, 37, 44.
  Diatessaron, 7, 345, 356, 544,
545, 660.
  di Matteo, I., viii, xiv, 107.
  Dodge, B., xvii, 659.
  Duval, R., 39.

  Ebed Jesu, 368, 557.
  Eden, 187, 251, 270.
  Edessa (Haran, Urfa), 19, 29,
278, 318, 342, 343, 412, 413,
460.
  Edomites, 208.
  Egypt, v, 12, 15, 19, 20-22, 35,
87, 204, 206, 245, 246, 275, 279,
337, 361, 365, 382, 413, 414,
428, 447, 458, 471, 472, 515,
607, 608, 618, 653, 660, 719.
  Ehrhart, 102.
  Eichner, W., ix-xi, xv-xvii, 102,
729.
  Elam, 195, 628.
  Elihu, 345.
  Elijah, 66, 166, 203, 211, 212,
245, 260, 306, 432, 442, 508,

509.
  Elisha, 66, 245, 442, 509, 581.
  Elizabeth, 211, 330, 331.
  Emmaus, 512.
  Enoch, 203.
  Esau, 208.
  Esdras, 69, 109, 111.
  Ethiopia, 700, 702, 708.
  Euclid, 703.
  Euphemianus, 276.
  Euphrates, 19, 33, 41, 279,
624.
  Eve, 176, 408, 435, 572.
  Ewald, 535.
  Ezekiel, 66, 68, 69, 88, 306,
385, 581, 608.
  Ezra, 109, 110, 111.

  Fadal b. 'Abbas, 444.
  Fagnan, 715.
  Fath b. Kakan, 693.
  Fatima bt. Abu Dahak, 434,
525.
  Fatima bt. Muhammad, 587,
601, 602, 662.
  Filler, E., 103.
  Finck, 103.
  Finkel, J., 56, 535, 685, 686,
689.
  Fischer, A., 113.
  Flügel, G., 378, 559, 713.
  Freytag, 523.
  Fritsch, E., viii-ix, xiv, 113,
730.
  Furqan (Qur'an), 206.

  Gabriel (angel), 1, 211, 242,

556, 725.
Ibrahim b. Muhammad, 525.
Iconoclast, 53, 133.
'Imran (see Amram).
'Ikrima b. Abu Jahl, 605.
India, 405, 474, 480, 543, 574, 643, 653, 698.
Iraq, 114, 578, 633, 651.
Irene (Empress), 266.
Isaac, 25, 75, 141, 188, 374, 413-415, 435, 583, 618, 673, 683.
Isaiah, 51, 66, 68, 82, 97, 182, 198, 213, 233, 255, 257, 298, 330, 385, 424, 435, 436, 498, 518, 580, 581, 607, 608, 625, 629, 631, 632, 636-638, 644, 679.
Ishmael, 19, 21, 37, 208, 256, 327, 374, 473, 536, 540, 583, 615-617, 619, 620, 622, 626, 628, 634, 640, 644, 683.
Ishmaelites, 37, 138, 259, 374, 674.
Isho'yabb, 113.
Ismail Poonawala, 520
Israel (-ites), 3, 68, 69, 79, 81, 82, 96, 118, 124, 197, 206, 208, 212, 218, 225, 293, 312, 331, 400, 413, 414, 428, 429, 435, 437, 447, 469, 471, 472, 496, 509, 541, 549, 590, 607, 608, 629, 674, 679, 681.
Iziants, K., 102.

Ja'far, 705.
Ja'far b. Abu Talib, 2, 4.

Jabarites, 114.
Jabir b. 'Abdullah, 595.
Jacob, 25, 66, 75, 79, 80, 87, 188, 208, 242, 405, 413, 414, 549, 583, 679.
Jacob Baradaeus, 385, 405.
Jacob of Edessa, 31.
Jacobites, v-vi, 13-20, 23, 38, 40, 44, 163, 164, 171, 172, 243, 244, 262, 269-271, 368, 369, 377, 385, 562, 683, 701, 707, 709.
Jahiliyya, 714.
al-Jahiz, Abu 'Amr, 62, 114, 115, 357, 549, 557, 685, 686, 689-695, 698, 699, 709-713, 715-717, 725.
Jahiziyya (Jahizites), 49, 62, 114.
Jahwidan, 115.
Jambres (magician in Egypt), 246.
Jannes (magician in Egypt), 246.
Jeffery, A., xiii, xvi-xvii, 47, 49, 53, 54, 57, 531-534.
Jehovah (see YHWH), 517, 518, 543.
Jehuda Hannasi, 109.
Jeremiah, 66, 68, 79, 87, 149, 161, 199, 257, 385, 436, 488, 509, 580, 607.
Jerusalem, 13, 18, 29, 69, 121, 126, 130, 137, 187, 269, 275, 279, 282, 312, 407, 434, 437, 439, 440, 460, 496, 497, 502, 542, 582, 608, 649, 664, 723.

Jesus Christ, vii-x, 1, 2, 3, 8, 15-17, 24-26, 35, 42, 50, 51, 63-65, 67-69, 71, 72, 76, 78, 79-85, 86, 87, 89, 91-93, 96-98, 105, 106, 112, 117, 119, 120, 121, 122, 123, 125, 126, 130, 138, 140, 144, 151, 152, 158, 159, 165, 175-180, 182, 183, 187-206, 209, 210, 212, 215, 216, 238-243, 245, 251, 252, 256, 257, 259, 260, 270, 282, 285, 288-290, 297, 300, 302-313, 315, 319-323, 325, 327-331, 337, 338, 344, 347-354, 371, 376, 377, 484, 488, 489-492, 496-498, 500, 501, 503, 509, 513, 519, 528, 529, 539, 544, 545, 580, 587, 590, 591, 596, 613, 615, 621, 629, 637, 645-648, 650, 651, 653, 673, 674, 676, 677, 696, 709, 721-723.

Jews, 1, 13, 15, 19, 42, 45, 51, 60, 66, 68, 69, 89, 94, 95, 107, 109, 110, 120, 122, 125, 126, 164, 165, 193, 199, 200-202, 213-216, 241, 252, 258, 270, 282, 285, 304, 307, 312, 319, 331, 345, 348, 357, 372-374, 376, 384, 415, 419, 438, 442, 447, 448, 454, 455, 460, 465, 468-470, 478, 497, 520, 537, 543, 544, 555, 590, 595, 608, 613, 648, 650, 696, 697, 699, 700-702, 704-706, 720.

Joakim, 500, 544.

Job, 50, 64, 66, 225, 298, 341, 345, 385.

Joel, 207.

John (the Baptist), 1, 3, 66, 152, 161, 187, 211, 212, 276, 313, 331, 501-503, 544, 678.

John (the Apostle), 71, 112, 385, 645, 647.

John I (Patriarch), v, 3, 7, 8, 11-13, 15-17, 22, 24, 28, 32, 33, 43, 45.

John IV (Patriarch), 368.

John VII (Patriarch), 40.

John Chrysostom, 376.

John of Damascus, v, vii, x, xv, 37, 51, 52, 53, 60, 120, 127, 128, 129, 130, 133-138, 156, 164, 270, 345, 357, 719, 726.

John of Nikiou, 20-22, 39.

John of Phenek, 104.

Joseph (administrator of Egypt), 203, 204, 413.

Joseph (husband of Mary), 3.

Joseph, I., 54, 115.

Josephus, 126.

Joshua, 67, 245, 358, 385, 428, 446, 447, 453, 479, 492, 509.

Jubba'ites, 114.

Judaism, 1, 654, 702.

Judah, 66, 68, 69, 81, 83, 109, 119, 206, 331, 495, 496, 502, 674.

Judas Iscariot, 36.

Judas Maccabee, 23.

Jurayji, 3.

Justin Martyr, 105.

Juwayriya, 525.

Juynboll, T., 715.

Mercury, 543.

Mesopotamia, 12, 13, 29.

Metzger, B., 551.

Micah (prophet), 331.

Michael the Syrian, 7, 15, 19, 23, 29, 32-34, 36, 40-42, 44, 45, 100, 105, 567, 678.

Midianites, 96.

Migne, P., ix, xv, 61, 138, 144, 161, 725.

Milton, J., 536.

Mina, 127, 391, 408.

Mingana, A., viii, xiv, xvii, 109, 163, 165, 166, 169, 260, 356, 406, 520, 522, 538, 547, 548, 550, 551, 555, 711, 715, 724, 726.

Miriam (sister of Moses), x, 83, 119, 581.

Moab (-ites), 80, 119, 208.

Mongolian, 19.

Monophysites, 164, 405, 556.

Montanists, 60.

Moriah (Mount), 413.

Morocco, 671.

Moses, 8, 24, 26, 35, 52, 70, 75, 78, 80, 83, 85, 90, 92, 120, 124, 138, 140, 150-152, 188, 206-209, 217, 218, 223, 225, 246, 259, 293, 294, 297, 298, 301, 310, 311, 329, 337, 358, 384, 412, 414, 421, 422, 434, 435, 438, 446, 447, 450-453, 460, 472, 478, 479, 492, 495-497, 508, 528, 544, 581, 590, 591, 608, 610, 616, 617, 621, 622, 651, 663, 674, 678, 721,

722

Mosul, 557.

Mu'awiya (Caliph), 60, 519, 577.

Mu'tasim (Caliph), 562, 563, 695.

Muhammad (prophet), vi, ix-xi, 1, 2, 3, 13, 19, 31, 35, 38, 42, 43, 50-52, 63, 66, 70, 72, 83, 84, 91, 93, 99, 104-107, 111-113, 117, 120, 121, 125, 128-130, 134, 138, 142, 143, 151, 156, 157, 164, 165, 171, 190-194, 196, 206, 208, 209, 211, 215, 217-219, 223, 252, 253, 255, 256, 258, 259, 261, 265, 270, 271, 286, 288, 336, 341, 346, 348, 349, 356-358, 362, 370, 371, 378, 382-385, 388, 389, 425, 428, 434, 452, 454, 458, 468, 469, 478, 518, 519, 522, 526, 529-531, 536-540, 542, 544, 549, 550, 564, 568, 587, 598, 600, 621-626, 633-636, 638, 644-647, 653, 661, 662, 664, 671, 672, 674, 676-680, 682, 683, 691, 692, 696, 701, 705, 722, 724.

Muhammad b. Marwan, 125.

Muir, W., 355, 356, 360, 361, 365, 378, 406, 409, 519, 523, 528, 531-533, 535, 536, 539, 544, 557, 672.

Mukhtar, 457, 532.

Mulayka bt. Ka'b, 434, 525.

Mulayka bt. Naaman, 463, 525.

Munkar (angel), 403.
Muqaddasi, 266, 343, 351.
Murji'ites, 114.
Musaylima, 462, 535, 576.
Musa (Caliph), 237, 238, 246, 265.
Musta b. Ataba, 433.
al-Mutawakkil (Caliph), 170, 547, 549, 555, 558, 561-563, 574, 656, 657, 685-687, 693-695, 697, 711, 715, 720, 725.
Mu'tazilites, vi, 49, 114, 134, 158, 376, 547, 685, 686, 692-694, 696, 715, 721, 722.
Muylderman, 101, 103, 114.
Muzdalifa, 127.

Na'ila bt. Sahl, 542.
Nabateans, 331, 462, 465, 514, 535.
an-Nadim, xvii, 358, 534, 659, 686.
Nahum (prophet), 581.
Najashi (Negus), 598, 667.
Najran, 2, 18, 19, 120, 702.
Nakhla, 431.
Nakir (angel), 403.
Naphtali, 676.
Nasr, 118.
Nau, F., xii, 7, 8, 36, 39, 44, 556.
Nebuchadnezzar (King), 3, 69, 195, 422, 432, 439.
Negus (Najashi), 2.
Nestorians, v-vi, 18-20, 28, 49, 163, 166, 170-172, 249, 251, 256, 269-271, 277, 283, 342,

356, 368, 369, 374, 377, 405, 454, 531, 538, 562, 660, 676, 680, 683, 686, 707, 709, 726.
Neumann, 62.
Newman, N., 727.
Nicephorus Phocas (Emperor), 40.
Nicetas (military leader), 266.
Nicetas of Byzantium, ix-xii, xv-xvi.
Night of Doom (Qadr), 390.
Nihavend, 131.
Nineveh, 405, 436.
Nishapur, 277.
Nisaburi, 551.
Nisibus, 405.
Noah, 19, 70, 188, 329, 413, 414, 421, 438, 471, 542, 585.
Nöldeke, T., 528, 529, 531, 533, 535, 547, 548, 550-552, 665, 666, 679, 681, 727.
Nyberg, 687, 712.

Padua, 119.
Paraclete, 51, 56, 71, 112, 113, 165, 192, 205, 207, 253, 311, 312, 324, 550, 645, 646, 682.
Patkanian, K., 102, 104.
Paul (apostle), 276, 385, 434, 489, 495, 514, 582, 610, 649.
Pentapolis, 14, 22, 33, 35.
Pérez, J., 43.
Périer, A., 659.
Périer, J., 34.
Perizzites, 439.
Perlmann, M., 107, 110.
Persia, 19, 23, 115, 669.

BIBLIOGRAPHY

Aziz-us-Samad, Ulfat. *Islam and Christianity*. Karachi: Ashraf Publications, 1970.

Becker, C. H. *Islamstudien*. 2 vols. Hildesheim: Georg Olms Verlagsbuchhandlung, 1967.

Browne, L. E. "The Patriarch Timothy and the Caliph Al-Mahdi," *The Moslem World*, vol. 21 (1931), pp. 38-45.

Charfi, Abdelmajid. "Christianity in the Qur'an Commentary of Tabari," *Islamochristiana*, vol. 6 (1980), pp. 105-148.

The Chronography of Gregory Abû'l-Faraj (Bar Hebraeus). Trans. Ernest A. Wallis Budge. Oxford: 1932, repr. 1976.

The Earliest Life of Christ, etc. The Diatessaron of Tatian. Ed. and trans. J. Hamlyn Hill. Edinburgh: T. & T. Clark, 1894.

Eichner, Wolfgang. "Die Nachrichten über den Islam bei den Byzantinern," *Der Islam*, vol. 23 (1936), pp. 133-162, 197-244.

Finkel, Joshua. "A Risala of Al-Jahiz," *Journal of American Oriental Society* (1927), pp. 311-334.

Fritsch, Erdmann. "Islam und Christentum im Mittelalter," *Inaugural Dissertation*. Schlesischen Friedrich-Wilhelm-Universität zu Breslau, 1930.

Gaudeul, Jean-Marie. "The Correspondence between Leo 'Umar," *Islamochristiana*, No. 10, (1984), pp. 109-157.

771

Gibb, H. A. R., and Kramers, J. H., eds. *Shorter Encyclopedia of Islam*. Leiden: E. J. Brill, 1974.

Goldziher, Ignaz. "Ueber die Eulogien der Muhammedaner," *ZDMG*, vol. 50 (1896), pp. 97-128.

_____. "Ueber muhammedanische Polemik gegen Ahl al-kitab," *ZDMG*, vol. 32 (1878), pp. 341-387.

Graf, G. "On Objections to Mingana's book by Ali Tabari," *Deutsche Literaturzeitung* (1924), pp. 511-513.

_____. *Geschichte der christlichen arabischen Literatur*. 5 vols. Città del Vaticano: Bibliotheca Apostolica Vaticana, 1944-1953.

The Greek New Testament. Ed. Kurt Aland, et al. Stuttgart: Württemberg Bible Society, 1975.

Griffith, Sidney H. "The Monks of Palestine and the Growth of Christian Literature in Arabic," *The Muslim World*, vol. 78 (1978), pp. 1-28.

Guillanne, Alfred. "A Debate between Christian and Moslem Doctors," *Journal of the Royal Asiatic Society*, Cent. Supplement (1924), pp. 233-244.

Guillanne, Alfred. "Theodore Abu Qurra as Apologist," *The Moslem World*, vol. 15 (1925), pp. 42-51.

Güterbock, Carl. *Der Islam im Lichte der Byzantinischen Polemik*. Berlin: Guttentag Verlagsbuchhandlung, 1912.

Holy Bible. Trans. George M. Lamsa. San Francisco: Harper, repr. n. d.

Ibn Ishaq, Muhammad. *The Life of Muhammad*. Trans. A. Guillaume. Karachi: Oxford University Press, 1955.

Jeffery, A. "Ghevond's Text of the Correspondence Between 'Umar II and Leo III," *Harvard Theological Review*, no. 37 (1944), pp. 269-322.

_____. *Materials for the History of the Text of the Qur'an*. Leiden: E. J. Brill, 1937, repr. AMS Press, 1975.

Joseph, Isya. *Devil Worship*. Boston: The Gorham Press, 1919.

Kassis, Hanna E. *A Concordance of the Qur'an*. Baroda: Oriental Institute, 1938.

al-Kindi, Abd al-Masih ibn Ishaq. *The Apology of Al-Kindy*. Trans. and ed. William Muir. London: Society for Promoting Christian Knowledge, 1887.

_____. *The Apology of Al-Kindy*. Ed. Anton Tien. London: Society for Promoting Christian Knowledge, 1885.

_____. *The Apology of Al-Kindy*. Trans. Anton Tien, previously unpublished manuscript MS 25190 of the School of Oriental and African Studies, London, n.d.

Der Koran. Trans. Max Henning, et al. Wiesbaden: VMA Verlag, n.d.

The Holy Koran. Trans. Abdullah Yusuf Ali. New York: Hafner Publishing Co., 1946.

The Koran Interpreted. Trans. A. J. Arberry. New York: Macmillan, repr. 1986.

Meier, Fritz. "Eine auferstehung Mohammeds bei Suyuti," *Der Islam*, vol. 62 (1985), pp. 20-58.

Mingana, A. "An Ancient Syriac Translation of the Kur'an Exhibiting new Verses and Variants," repr. from *Bulletin of the John Rylands Library*, vol. 9 (1925).

_____. "The Apology of Timothy the Patriarch before Caliph Mahdi," *Bulletin of the John Rylands Library*, vol. 12 (1928), pp. 137-226.

_____. *The Book of Religion and Empire*. New York: Longmans, Green & Co., 1922.

_____. *Catalogue of the Mingana Collection of Manuscripts*. Vol. 1. Cambridge, England: W. Heffer and Sons Ltd., 1933.

_____. "Remarks on Tabari's Semi-Official Defence of Islam," *Bulletin of John Ryland's Library*, vol. 9 (1925), pp. 236-240.

an-Nadim, Muhammad ibn Ishaq. *The Fihrist of al-Nadim*. Trans. and ed. Bayard Dodge. New York: Columbia University Press, 1970.

Nau, F. "Un Colloque du Patriarche Jean-Faits Divers," *Journal Asiatique* (1915), pp. 225-279.

New American Standard Bible. Chicago: Moody Press, 1975.

Nöldeke, Theodor. Review of *The Book of Religion and Empire*, by Ali Tabari, Mingana, 1923, *Deutsche Literaturzeitung* (1926), pp. 21-27.

_____. *The Qur'an: an Introductory Essay, etc.* Ed. N. A. Newman. Hatfield, PA: Interdisiplinary Biblical Research Institute, 1992.

_____ and Schwally, Friedrich. *Geschichte des Qorans*. Hildesheim: Georg Olms Verlagsbuchhandlung, 1961.

The Koran Interpreted. Trans. A. J. Arberry. New York: Macmillan, 1955.

Rahman, H. U. *A Chronology of Islamic History*. London: Mansell Publishing Ltd., 1989.

Sahas, Daniel J. *John of Damascus on Islam*. Leiden: E. J. Brill, 1972.

Sahih Bukhari. Trans. Muhammad Muhsin Khan. 9 vols. Chicago: Kazi Publications, 1976.

Sahih Muslim. Trans. Abdul Hamid Siddiqi. 4 vols. Lahore: Sh. Muhammad Ashraf, 1976.

Septuaginta. Ed. Alfred Rahlfs. Stuttgart: Deutsche Bibelgesellschaft, repr. 1979.

The Septuagint with Apocrypha: Greek and English. Trans. Lancelot C. L. Brenton. Peabody, MA: Hendrickson Publishers, repr. 1986.

Steinschneider, Moritz. *Polemische und apologetische Literatur in arabischer Sprache*. Hildesheim, repr. 1966.

Suyuti, Jalaladdin. *El-Itkan fi Ulumi'l Kur'an*. Trans. Sakip Yildiz and Hüseyin Avni Chelik. 2 vols. Istanbul: Hikmet Neshriyat, 1987.

al-Tabari, Abu Ja'far Muhammad ibn Jarir. *The History of al-Tabari*. Ed. Ehsan Yar-Shater. New York: State University of New York, 1988.

Voorhis, J. W. "John of Damascus on the Moslem Heresy," *The Moslem World*, XXIV (1934), pp. 391-398.

_____. "The Discussion of a Christian and Saracen," *The Moslem World*, XXV (1935), 266-273.

Vollers, K. "Das Religionsgespräch von Jerusalem," *Zeitschrift für Kirchengeschichte*, vol. 29 (1908), pp. 29-71, 197-221.

Watt, W. Montgomery. "Ash-Shahrastani's Account of Christian Doctrine," *Islamochristiana*, vol. 9, pp. 249-259.

Wensinck, A. J. *The Muslim Creed*. Frank Cass and Co. Ltd., 1965.

_____. *A Handbook of Early Muhammadan Tradition*. Leiden: E. J. Brill, 1927.